Seventh Edition
Global Edition

SUPPLY CHAIN MANAGEMENT

STRATEGY, PLANNING, AND OPERATION

Sunil Chopra

Kellogg School of Management

Pearson

Harlow, England • London • New York • Boston • San Francisco • Toronto • Sydney • Dubai • Singapore • Hong Kong
Tokyo • Seoul • Taipei • New Delhi • Cape Town • Sao Paulo • Mexico City • Madrid • Amsterdam • Munich • Paris • Milan

Vice President, Business, Economics, and UK Courseware: Donna Battista
Director of Portfolio Management: Stephanie Wall
Director, Courseware Portfolio Management: Ashley Dodge
Senior Sponsoring Editor: Neeraj Bhalla
Editorial Assistant: Linda Albelli
Associate Acquisitions Editor, Global Edition: Ananya Srivastava
Project Editor, Global Edition: Paromita Banerjee
Product Marketer: Kaylee Claymore
Product Marketing Assistant: Marianela Silvestri
Manager of Field Marketing, Business Publishing: Adam Goldstein
Executive Field Marketing Manager: Thomas Hayward
Vice President, Production and Digital Studio, Arts and Business: Etain O'Dea
Director of Production, Business: Jeff Holcomb
Managing Producer, Business: Melissa Feimer
Content Producer: Sugandh Juneja
Content Producer, Global Edition: Vamanan Namboodiri
Senior Manufacturing Controller, Global Edition: Angela Hawksbee

Operations Specialist: Carol Melville
Design Lead: Kathryn Foot
Manager, Learning Tools: Brian Surette
Content Developer, Learning Tools: Lindsey Sloan
Managing Producer, Digital Studio and GLP, Media Production and Development:
 Ashley Santora
Managing Producer, Digital Studio: Diane Lombardo
Digital Studio Producer: Regina DaSilva
Digital Studio Producer: Alana Coles
Digital Content Project Lead: Courtney Kamauf
Manager, Media Production, Global Edition: Vikram Kumar
Project Managers: Ronel Mirano and Raja Natesan, Pearson CSC
Interior Design: Pearson CSC
Cover Design: Lumina Datamatics
Cover Art: Cosmo Condina North America/Alamy Stock Photo; Geoffrey
 Robinson/Alamy Stock Photo; and PhotoAlto/Alamy Stock Photo

Acknowledgments of third-party content appear on the appropriate page within the text.

PEARSON and ALWAYS LEARNING are exclusive trademarks owned by Pearson Education, Inc. or its affiliates in the U.S. and/or other countries.

Pearson Education Limited
KAO Two
KAO Park
Harlow
CM17 9NA
United Kingdom

and Associated Companies throughout the world

Visit us on the World Wide Web at: www.pearsonglobaleditions.com

© Pearson Education Limited 2019

ISBN 10: 1-292-25789-X
ISBN 13: 978-1-292-25789-1

British Library Cataloguing-in-Publication Data
A catalogue record for this book is available from the British Library.

10 9 8 7 6 5 4 3 2

Typeset in Times NR MT Pro by Cenveo® Publisher Services
Printed and bound by CPI Group (UK) Ltd, Croydon CR0 4YY

Dedication

I would like to thank my colleagues at Kellogg for all I have learned from them about logistics and supply chain management. I thank Peter Meindl for his collaboration during earlier editions of this book. I am grateful for the love and encouragement that my parents, Krishan and Pushpa, and sisters, Sudha and Swati, have always provided during every endeavor in my life. I thank my children, Ravi and Rajiv, for the joy they have brought me. Finally, none of this would have been possible without the constant love, caring, and support of my wife, Maria Cristina.

—Sunil Chopra

ABOUT THE AUTHOR

SUNIL CHOPRA

Sunil Chopra is the IBM Distinguished Professor of Operations Management and Information Systems at the Kellogg School of Management. He has served as the interim dean and senior associate dean for curriculum and teaching, and the codirector of the MMM program, a joint dual-degree program between the Kellogg School of Management and the McCormick School of Engineering at Northwestern University. He has a PhD in operations research from SUNY at Stony Brook. Prior to joining Kellogg, he taught at New York University and spent a year at IBM Research.

Professor Chopra's research and teaching interests are in supply chain and logistics management, operations management, combinatorial optimization, and the design of telecommunication networks. He has won several teaching awards at the MBA and Executive programs of Kellogg. He has authored more than 50 papers and two books.

He has been a department editor for *Management Science* and an associate editor for *Manufacturing & Service Operations Management, Operations Research,* and *Decision Sciences Journal.* He has also consulted for several firms in the area of supply chain and operations management.

CONTENTS

PREFACE

This book is targeted toward an academic as well as a practitioner audience. On the academic side, it is appropriate for MBA students, engineering master's students, and senior undergraduate students interested in supply chain management and logistics. It can also serve as a suitable reference for both concepts as well as providing a methodology for practitioners in consulting and industry.

NEW TO THIS EDITION

The seventh edition has focused on changes that enhance students' ability to sharpen their critical thinking and data analytics skills as they study with the book. All concepts discussed in the book are linked to strategic decision making in a supply chain, and all quantitative ideas are illustrated using spreadsheets that can be implemented in practice. Some specific changes in the seventh edition include:

- The link between supply chain decisions and the financial performance of a firm is developed in detail in Chapter 3.
- The concepts underlying the design of distribution networks are illustrated in the context of omni-channel retailing in Chapter 4. The evolution of retailing is used throughout the book to illustrate the link between supply chain concepts and strategic decision making in a supply chain.
- Each section of each chapter in the book is associated with a clearly identified learning objective that is summarized at the end of the section.
- We have added new mini-cases in Chapters 5, 8, and 15. Information in other cases has been updated to be current.
- New exercises have been added in several chapters.
- For all numerical examples discussed in the book, we have developed spreadsheets that students can use to understand the concept at a deeper level. These spreadsheets are referred to in the book and allow the student to try different "what-if" analyses. These spreadsheets are available at *http://www.pearsonglobaleditions.com* along with basic guidance on how they may be created and used.
- We have continued to add current examples throughout the book, with a particular focus on bringing in more global examples.

SOLVING TEACHING AND LEARNING CHALLENGES

To be successful, supply chain practitioners must be able to formulate effective supply chain strategy and be able to solve any resulting supply chain problems using the available analytical tools. In a supply chain class this creates the challenge of teaching students to think strategically while supporting their decisions with robust quantitative analysis. This book is designed to help faculty and students overcome this challenge through its conceptual and pedagogical structure. Conceptually, the book aims to develop an understanding of the following key areas and their interrelationships:

- The strategic role of a supply chain
- The key strategic drivers of supply chain performance
- Analytic methodologies for supply chain analysis

To illustrate the strategic importance of good supply chain management, we provide many current examples to show how companies have succeeded through effective supply chain management or failed because of weak supply chain management. Our strategic framework, the use of Excel-based models to explain analytic methodologies, and several mini-cases to help students internalize the link between the analytic methodologies and strategic decision making provide pedagogical support for faculty using the book.

A Consistent Strategic Framework

Within the strategic framework, we identify facilities, inventory, transportation, information, sourcing, and pricing as the key drivers of supply chain performance. The book is structured to dig deeper into each driver to understand its role in the success of a supply chain, its interaction with other drivers, analytic methodologies to support decisions related to the driver, and managerial levers related to the driver that help improve supply chain performance.

Every analytic methodology is illustrated with its application in Excel. Students have access to the associated Excel file along with instructions to construct and use the file. The Excel files help students deepen their understanding of the link between the analytic models and the strategic decisions they support.

Mini Cases

Most chapters have mini cases that can be used by faculty to ensure that students can apply the concepts and methodologies in the context of strategic decision making for a business.

DEVELOPING CAREER SKILLS

Skills learned in this book will be of great use no matter what path students choose to follow. The book is developed with the premise that good strategic decisions cannot be made without access to relevant analytics, and all analytics should be designed to support decision making. As a result, students will develop critical thinking, the ability to formulate and analyze problems, and support their recommendations with analytics that uses data literacy and computing skills.

- Every chapter in the book pushes students to think critically in order to define and solve supply chain problems. For example, Chapter 4 develops a framework for distribution networks and then pushes students to think about how retailing may evolve in the future as consumer preferences and technology change. The first part of the chapter teaches frameworks and concepts related to the design of distribution networks. The last part of the chapter then pushes the students to analyze retailing by applying the knowledge they have gained in order to decide how retailers need to change in order to succeed in the 21st century.

- All the analytics in the book are developed through the use of Microsoft Excel. This helps students develop data literacy, computing skills, and the knowledge of how to apply information technology to support decision making. The analytics that are developed in these chapters in turn support the framework laid out in Chapter 4. Whereas Chapter 4 helps students to think conceptually about why certain retailing models have succeeded for selling jewelry while others have failed, the succeeding chapters help students quantify financial metrics for different retail networks. As a result, students learn how to use data and models to improve strategic decision making.

Excel Based Models

TABLE OF CONTENTS OVERVIEW

INSTRUCTOR TEACHING RESOURCES

At the Instructor Resource Center, *http://www.pearsonglobaleditions.com*, instructors can easily register to gain access to a variety of instructor resources available with this text in downloadable format. If assistance is needed, our dedicated technical support team is ready to help with the media supplements that accompany this text. Visit *https://support.pearson.com/getsupport* for answers to frequently asked questions and toll-free user support phone numbers.

This program comes with the following teaching resources.

Supplements available to instructors at *www.pearsonglobaleditions.com*	Features of the Supplement
Instructor's Solution Manual developed by the author	• Case Teaching Notes and Worksheets • Spreadsheets for all quantitative examples • Discussion questions • Example figures • Additional exercises • Solutions to all questions and problems in the book
Test Bank authored by Geoff Willis of the University of Central Oklahoma	2000 multiple-choice, true/false, short-answer, and graphing questions with these annotations: • Correct answer • Difficulty level (1 for straight recall, 2 for some analysis, 3 for complex analysis) • Learning outcome reference • Topic covered • AACSB learning standard (Analytical Thinking; Information Technology; Application of Knowledge)
TestGen® Computerized Test Bank	TestGen allows instructors to: • Customize, save, and generate classroom tests • Edit, add, or delete questions from the Test Item Files • Analyze test results • Organize a database of tests and student results.
PowerPoint Presentations authored by Jeff Heyl of the Lincoln University	Slides include all the graphs, tables, and equations in the textbook.

For Students

The following material is available to students at *http://www.pearsonglobaleditions.com*:

- Spreadsheets for numerical examples discussed in the book. These provide the details of the example discussed, but are live and allow the student to try different what-if analyses.
- Spreadsheets that allow students to build every table shown in Chapters 5 through 16.
- Online chapter: Chapter A: Information Technology in a Supply Chain.
- Technical Note: Routing and Scheduling in Transportation. This note is also bundled with the Instructor's Manual available on *www.pearsonglobaleditions.com*.

ACKNOWLEDGMENTS

I would like to thank the many people who helped throughout this process. I thank the reviewers whose suggestions significantly improved the book, including: Steven Brown, Arizona State University; Ming Chen, California State University, Long Beach; Sameer Kumar, University of Saint Thomas; Frank Montabon, Iowa State University; Brian Sauser, University of North Texas; and Paul Venderspek, Colorado State University, and Michael Godfrey, University of Wisconsin Oshkosh.

I would also like to thank my editor, Neeraj Bhalla, content producer, Sugandh Juneja, editorial assistant, Linda Albelli, and the people at Pearson CSC, including Nicole Suddeth, Ronel Mirano, and Raja Natesan, for their efforts with the book. Finally, I would like to thank you, the readers, for reading and using this book. I hope it contributes to all your efforts to improve the performance of companies and supply chains throughout the world. I would be pleased to hear your comments and suggestions for future editions of this text.

Sunil Chopra
Kellogg School of Management, Northwestern University

GLOBAL EDITION ACKNOWLEDGMENTS

Pearson would like to thank and acknowledge the following people for their contribution to the Global Edition.

Contributors

Kate Dunne, *Galway-Mayo Institute of Technology*

Reviewers

Merwyn Strate, *Hult International Business School*
Hauck Zsuzsanna, *University of Pecs*

1

Understanding the Supply Chain

LEARNING OBJECTIVES

After reading this chapter, you will be able to

1.1 Discuss the goal of a supply chain and explain the impact of supply chain decisions on the success of a firm.

1.2 Define the three key supply chain decision phases and explain the significance of each one.

1.3 Describe the cycle and push/pull views along with the macro processes of a supply chain.

1.4 Identify important issues and decisions to be addressed in a supply chain.

1.5 Develop skills that employers have identified as critical to success in the workplace.

In this chapter, we provide a conceptual understanding of what a supply chain is and the various issues that must be considered when designing, planning, or operating a supply chain. We identify the goal of a supply chain and discuss the significance of supply chain decisions for the success of a firm. We also provide several examples from different industries to emphasize the variety of supply chain issues and decisions that companies need to consider at the strategic, planning, and operational levels.

WHAT IS A SUPPLY CHAIN?

1.1 Discuss the goal of a supply chain and explain the impact of supply chain decisions on the success of a firm.

A *supply chain* consists of all parties involved, directly or indirectly, in fulfilling a customer request. The supply chain includes not only the manufacturer and suppliers, but also transporters, warehouses, retailers, and even customers themselves. Within each organization, such as a manufacturer, the supply chain includes all functions involved in receiving and filling a customer request. These functions include, but are not limited to, new product development, marketing, operations, distribution, finance, and customer service.

Consider a customer walking into a Toyota dealership to purchase a new car. The supply chain begins with the customer and his or her need for a car. The next stage of this supply chain is the dealer that the customer visits. The dealer has several cars in inventory that may have been supplied from the assembly plant using trucks from a third party. The assembly plant, in turn,

gets various modules such as electronics and powertrain from a variety of Tier 1 suppliers. Each Tier 1 supplier receives material from several Tier 2 suppliers. For example, the electronics supplier receives cameras from the camera supplier and the dashboard display from another supplier. Each of these suppliers receives raw materials from lower tier suppliers. This supply chain is illustrated in Figure 1-1, with the arrows corresponding to the direction of physical product flow.

A supply chain is dynamic and involves the constant flow of information, product, and funds among different stages. In our example, the dealer provides the product, as well as pricing and availability information, to the customer. The customer transfers funds to the dealer. The dealer conveys sales data and replenishment orders to the assembly plant, which sends cars back to the dealer on a truck. The dealer transfers funds to the auto manufacturer after the replenishment. The manufacturer also provides pricing information and sends delivery schedules to each dealer. Similar information, material, and fund flows take place across the entire supply chain.

In another example, when a customer makes a purchase online from Amazon, the supply chain includes, among others, the customer, Amazon's website, the Amazon warehouse, the carrier who delivers packages to customers, and all of Amazon's suppliers and their suppliers. The website provides the customer with information regarding pricing, product variety, and product availability. After making a product choice, the customer enters the order information and pays for the product. The product is then picked and shipped from an Amazon warehouse. As its inventory diminishes, the warehouse places replenishment orders with suppliers.

A typical supply chain may involve a variety of stages including customers, retailers, wholesalers, distributors, manufacturers, and suppliers. Even though the term supply chain may imply that only one player is involved at each stage, most supply chains are actually networks where each stage receives product from several suppliers and sends output to several customers. It may be more accurate to use the term supply network or supply web to describe the structure of most supply chains.

A critical point to keep in mind is that the customer is an integral part of any supply chain. In fact, the primary purpose of any supply chain is to satisfy customer needs and, in the process, generate profit for itself. The functioning of a supply chain involves three key flows – information, product, and funds - as illustrated in Figure 1-2. The goal when designing a supply chain is to structure the three flows in a way that meets customer needs in a cost effective manner. For example, Apple serves its customers in a variety of ways depending upon their needs. Customers

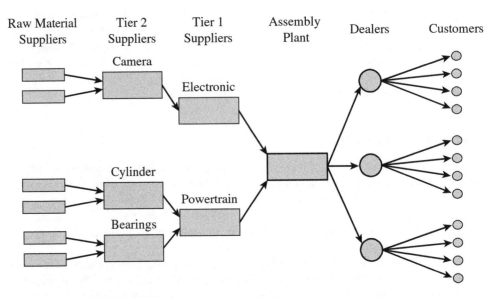

Figure 1-1 Stages of an Automotive Supply Chain

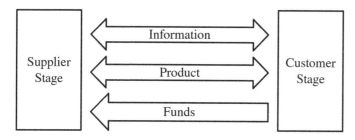

Figure 1-2 The Three Flows in a Supply Chain

can walk into an Apple store (or a third party store) or go online to purchase a product. Standard products are stocked at the stores and customers can leave the store with their phone or computer after paying the appropriate funds. Orders placed online can either be delivered at home or be picked up at an Apple store. The time taken for home delivery depends on whether the product is stocked by Apple at its warehouse or not. Personalized and custom-configured items take longer because they are not stocked at the warehouse but produced after the customer order arrives. Observe that Apple changes the flow of information, product, and funds based on the customer needs and product characteristics. The goal of this book is to develop concepts and methodologies that can be used to design supply chains that effectively meet customer needs while generating supply chain profits.

THE OBJECTIVE OF A SUPPLY CHAIN

The objective of every supply chain should be to maximize the net value generated. The net value a supply chain generates is the difference between what the value of the final product is to the customer and the costs the entire supply chain incurs in filling the customer's request. We will refer to this difference as the *supply chain surplus*.

Supply Chain Surplus = Customer Value − Supply Chain Cost

The value of the final product may vary for each customer and can be estimated by the maximum amount the customer is willing to pay for it. The difference between the value of the product and its price remains with the customer as consumer surplus. The rest of the supply chain surplus becomes supply chain profitability, the difference between the revenue generated from the customer and the overall cost across the supply chain. For example, the $60 that a customer pays Best Buy for a wireless router represents the revenue the supply chain receives. Customers who purchase the router clearly value it at or above $60. Thus, part of the supply chain surplus is left with the customer as consumer surplus. The rest stays with the supply chain as profit. Best Buy and other stages of the supply chain incur costs to convey information, produce components, store them, transport them, transfer funds, and so on. The difference between the $60 that the customer paid and the sum of costs incurred across all stages by the supply chain to produce and distribute the router represents the supply chain profitability: the total profit to be shared across all supply chain stages and intermediaries. The higher the supply chain profitability, the more successful the supply chain. For most profit-making supply chains, the supply chain surplus will be strongly correlated with profits. Supply chain success should be measured in terms of supply chain surplus and not in terms of the profits at an individual stage. (In subsequent chapters, we see that a focus on profitability at individual stages may lead to a reduction in overall supply chain surplus.) A focus on growing the supply chain surplus pushes all members of the supply chain toward growing the size of the overall pie.

Having defined the success of a supply chain in terms of supply chain surplus, the next logical step is to look for sources of value, revenue, and cost. For any supply chain, there is only

one source of revenue: the customer. The value obtained by a customer purchasing a car at a Toyota dealership depends on several factors, including the functionality and features of the car, the variety of options available, and the service offered by the dealer. The customer is the only one providing positive cash flow for the Toyota supply chain. All other cash flows are simply fund exchanges that occur within the supply chain, given that different stages have different owners. When the dealer pays Toyota, it is taking a portion of the funds the customer provides and passing that money on to Toyota. All flows of information, product, or funds generate costs within the supply chain. Thus, the appropriate management of these flows is a key to supply chain success. Effective *supply chain management* involves the management of supply chain assets and product, information, and fund flows to grow the total supply chain surplus. A growth in supply chain surplus increases the size of the total pie, allowing contributing members of the supply chain to benefit.

In this book, we have a strong focus on analyzing all supply chain decisions in terms of their impact on the supply chain surplus. These decisions and their impact can vary for a wide variety of reasons. For instance, consider the difference in the supply chain structure for fast-moving consumer goods that is observed in the United States and India. U.S. distributors play a much smaller role in this supply chain compared with their Indian counterparts. We argue that the difference in supply chain structure can be explained by the impact a distributor has on the supply chain surplus in the two countries.

Retailing in the United States is largely consolidated, with large chains buying consumer goods from manufacturers. This consolidation gives retailers sufficient scale that the introduction of an intermediary such as a distributor does little to reduce costs—and may actually increase costs because of an additional transaction. In contrast, India has millions of small retail outlets. The small size of Indian retail outlets limits the amount of inventory they can hold, thus requiring frequent replenishment—a retail order can be compared with the weekly grocery shopping for a family in the United States. The only way for a manufacturer to keep transportation costs low is to bring full truckloads of product close to the market and then distribute locally using "milk runs" with smaller vehicles. The presence of an intermediary that can receive a full truckload shipment, break bulk, and then make smaller deliveries to the retailers is crucial if transportation costs are to be kept low. Most Indian distributors are one-stop shops, stocking everything from cooking oil to soaps and detergents made by a variety of manufacturers. Besides the convenience provided by one-stop shopping, distributors in India are also able to reduce transportation costs for outbound delivery to the retailer by aggregating products across multiple manufacturers during the delivery runs. Distributors in India also handle collections, because their cost of collection is significantly lower than what it would cost each manufacturer to collect from retailers. Thus, the important role of distributors in India can be explained by the growth in supply chain surplus that results from their presence. The supply chain surplus argument implies that as retailing in India begins to consolidate, the role of distributors will diminish.

The Importance of Supply Chain Decisions

There is a close connection between the design and management of supply chain flows (product, information, and funds) and the success of a supply chain. Amazon, Seven-Eleven Japan, and Walmart are examples of companies that have built their success on superior design, planning, and operation of their supply chain. In contrast, the failure of many online businesses, such as Webvan, can be attributed to weaknesses in their supply chain design and planning. The rise and subsequent fall of the bookstore chain Borders illustrates how a failure to adapt its supply chain to a changing environment and customer expectations hurt its performance. Dell Computer is another example of a company that had to revise its supply chain design in response to changing technology and customer needs. We discuss these examples later in this section.

Seven-Eleven Japan is an example of a company that has used excellent supply chain design, planning, and operation to drive growth and profitability. It has used a very responsive

replenishment system along with an outstanding information system to ensure that products are available when and where customers need them. Its responsiveness allows the company to change the merchandise mix at each store by time of day to precisely match customer demand. As a result, the company has grown total store sales from 1 billion yen in 1974 to almost 2.7 trillion yen in 2016, with profits in 2016 totaling 304 billion yen.

Walmart has been a leader at using supply chain design, planning, and operation to achieve success with its brick-and-mortar stores. From its beginning, the company invested heavily in transportation and information infrastructure to facilitate the effective flow of goods and information. Walmart designed its supply chain with clusters of stores around distribution centers to facilitate frequent replenishment at its retail stores in a cost-effective manner. Frequent replenishment allows stores to match supply and demand more effectively than the competition. Walmart has been a leader in sharing information and collaborating with suppliers to bring down costs and improve product availability. The results are impressive. In its 2016 annual report, the company reported a net income of about $14.7 billion on revenues of about $482 billion. Despite its success with large Walmart stores, the company has had some difficulty being successful with small format stores as well as the online channel where they offer an expanded assortment. Over the years the company has realized that the supply chain structure that is effective for the brick-and-mortar channel requires modification to be effective for the online channel. Similarly, the supply chain that is very effective for large format stores is not so effective for small format stores.

The failure of many online businesses, such as Webvan and Kozmo, can be attributed to their inability to design appropriate supply chains or manage information, product, and fund flows effectively. In the late 1990s, Webvan designed a supply chain with large warehouses in several major cities in the United States, from which groceries were delivered to customers' homes. This supply chain design could not compete with traditional supermarket supply chains in terms of cost. Traditional supermarket chains bring product to a store close to the consumer using full truckloads, resulting in very low transportation costs. They turn their inventory relatively quickly and let the customer perform most of the picking activity in the store. In contrast, Webvan turned its inventory marginally faster than supermarkets but incurred much higher transportation costs for home delivery, as well as high labor costs to pick customer orders. As a result, Webvan failed in its efforts to compete with supermarkets on price. The company folded in 2001, within two years of a very successful initial public offering.

As the experience of Borders illustrates, a failure to adapt supply chains to a changing environment can significantly hurt performance. Borders, along with Barnes & Noble, dominated the selling of books and music in the 1990s by implementing the superstore concept. Compared with small local bookstores that dominated the industry prior to that, Borders was able to offer greater variety (about 100,000 titles at superstores, relative to fewer than 10,000 titles at a local bookstore) to customers at a lower cost by aggregating operations in large stores. This allowed the company to achieve higher inventory turns than local bookstores and with lower operating costs per dollar of sales. In 2004, Borders achieved sales of almost $4 billion, with profits of $132 million. Its model, however, was already under attack with the growth of Amazon, which offered much greater variety than Borders at lower cost by selling online and stocking its inventories in a few distribution centers. Borders' inability to adapt its supply chain to compete with Amazon led to a rapid decline. The company declared bankruptcy in 2010.

Dell is another example of a company that enjoyed tremendous success based on its supply chain design, planning, and operation but then had to adapt its supply chain in response to shifts in technology and customer expectations. Between 1993 and 2006, Dell experienced unprecedented growth of both revenue and profits by structuring a supply chain that provided customers with customized PCs quickly and at reasonable cost. By 2006, Dell had a net income of more than $3.5 billion on revenues of just over $56 billion. This success was based on two key supply chain features that supported rapid, low-cost customization. The first was Dell's decision to sell directly to the end customer, bypassing distributors and retailers. The second key

aspect of Dell's supply chain was the centralization of manufacturing and inventories in a few locations where final assembly was postponed until the customer order arrived. As a result, Dell was able to provide a large variety of PC configurations while keeping low levels of component inventories.

In spite of this tremendous success, the changing marketplace presented some new challenges for Dell. Whereas Dell's supply chain was well suited for highly customized PCs, the market shifted to lower levels of customization. Given the growing power of hardware, customers were satisfied with a few model types. Dell reacted by adjusting its supply chain with regard to both direct selling and building to order. The company started selling its PCs through retail chains such as Walmart in the United States and GOME in China. It also outsourced a large fraction of its assembly to low-cost locations, effectively building to stock rather than to customer order. Unlike Borders, Dell is making a significant effort to adapt its supply chain to changing times. It remains to be seen whether these changes will improve Dell's performance.

SUMMARY OF LEARNING OBJECTIVE 1

The goal of a supply chain should be to grow overall supply chain surplus. Supply chain surplus is the difference between the value generated for the customer and the total cost incurred across all stages of the supply chain. A focus on the supply chain surplus increases the size of the overall pie for all members of the supply chain. Supply chain decisions have a large impact on the success or failure of each firm because they significantly influence both the revenue generated and the cost incurred. Successful supply chains manage flows of product, information, and funds to provide a high level of product availability to the customer while keeping costs low.

1.2 Define the three key supply chain decision phases and explain the significance of each one.

DECISION PHASES IN A SUPPLY CHAIN

Successful supply chain management requires many decisions relating to the flow of information, product, and funds. Each decision should be made to raise the supply chain surplus. These decisions fall into three categories or phases, depending on the frequency of each decision and the time frame during which a decision phase has an impact. As a result, each category of decisions must consider uncertainty over the decision horizon.

1. *Supply chain strategy or design:* During this phase, a company decides on the structure of the supply chain for the next several years. It decides what the chain's configuration will be, how resources will be allocated, and what processes each stage will perform. Strategic decisions made by companies include whether to outsource or perform a supply chain function in-house, the location and capacities of production and warehousing facilities, the products to be manufactured or stored at various locations, the modes of transportation to be made available along different shipping legs, and the type of information system to be used. Hyundai Motor's decision to build a second manufacturing plant in India in 2008 is a supply chain design or strategic decision. A firm must ensure that the supply chain configuration supports its strategic objectives and increases the supply chain surplus during this phase. The two Hyundai plants have allowed the firm to cost effectively serve the growing Indian market and also use its Indian plants to serve global demand for small cars. In 2015, Hyundai was the second largest automobile manufacturer and the largest automobile exporter in India. Supply chain design decisions are typically made for the long term (a matter of years) and are expensive to alter on short notice. Consequently, when companies make these decisions, they must take into account uncertainty in anticipated market conditions over the following few years.

2. *Supply chain planning:* For decisions made during this phase, the time frame considered is a quarter to a year. Therefore, the supply chain's configuration determined in the strategic phase is fixed. This configuration establishes constraints within which planning must be done. The goal of planning is to maximize the supply chain surplus that can be generated over the planning horizon given the constraints established during the strategic or design phase. Companies start the planning phase with a forecast for the coming year (or a comparable time frame) of demand and other factors, such as costs and prices in different markets. Planning includes making decisions regarding which markets will be supplied from which locations, the subcontracting of manufacturing, the inventory policies to be followed, and the timing and size of marketing and price promotions. For example, Hyundai's decisions regarding markets supplied by its two Indian plants and target production quantities at each plant are classified as planning decisions. In the planning phase, companies must include uncertainty in demand, exchange rates, and competition over this time horizon in their decisions. Given a shorter time frame and better forecasts than in the design phase, companies in the planning phase try to incorporate any flexibility built into the supply chain in the design phase and exploit it to optimize performance. As a result of the planning phase, companies define a set of operating policies that govern short-term operations.

3. *Supply chain operation:* The time horizon here is weekly or daily. During this phase, companies make decisions regarding individual customer orders. At the operational level, supply chain configuration is considered fixed and planning policies are already defined. The goal of supply chain operations is to handle incoming customer orders in the best possible manner. During this phase, firms allocate inventory or production to individual orders, set a date by which an order is to be filled, generate pick lists at a warehouse, allocate an order to a particular shipping mode and shipment, set delivery schedules of trucks, and place replenishment orders. Because operational decisions are being made in the short term (minutes, hours, or days), there is less uncertainty about demand information. Given the constraints established by the configuration and planning policies, the goal during the operation phase is to exploit the reduction of uncertainty and optimize performance.

The design, planning, and operation of a supply chain have a strong impact on overall profitability and success. It is fair to state that a large part of the success of firms such as Seven-Eleven Japan and Walmart can be attributed to their effective supply chain design, planning, and operation.

In later chapters, we develop concepts and present methodologies that can be used at each of the three decision phases described earlier. Most of our discussion addresses the supply chain design and planning phases.

SUMMARY OF LEARNING OBJECTIVE 2

Supply chain decisions may be characterized as strategic (design), planning, or operational, depending on the time horizon over which they apply. Strategic decisions relate to supply chain configuration. These decisions have a long-term impact that lasts for several years. Strategic decisions define the constraints for planning decisions, and planning decisions define the constraints for operational decisions. Planning decisions cover a period of a few months to a year and include decisions regarding production plans, subcontracting, and promotions over that period. Operational decisions span from minutes to days and include sequencing production and filling specific orders.

1.3 *Describe the cycle and push/pull views along with the macro processes of a supply chain.*

PROCESS VIEWS OF A SUPPLY CHAIN

A supply chain is a sequence of processes and flows that take place within and between different stages and combine to fill a customer need for a product. There are two ways to view the processes performed in a supply chain.

1. *Cycle view:* The processes in a supply chain are divided into a series of cycles, each performed at the interface between two successive stages of the supply chain.
2. *Push/pull view:* The processes in a supply chain are divided into two categories, depending on whether they are executed in response to a customer order or in anticipation of customer orders. *Pull* processes are initiated by a customer order, whereas *push* processes are initiated and performed in anticipation of customer orders.

Cycle View of Supply Chain Processes

Given the five stages of a supply chain as shown in Figure 1-3, all supply chain processes can be broken down into the following four process cycles:

- Customer order cycle
- Replenishment cycle
- Manufacturing cycle
- Procurement cycle

Each cycle occurs at the interface between two successive stages of the supply chain. Not every supply chain will have all four cycles clearly separated. For example, a grocery supply chain in which a retailer stocks finished-goods, inventories, and places replenishment orders with a distributor is likely to have all four cycles separated. Dell, in contrast, bypasses the retailer and distributor when it sells servers directly to customers.

Each cycle consists of six subprocesses, as shown in Figure 1-4. Each cycle starts with the supplier marketing the product to customers. A buyer then places an order that is received by

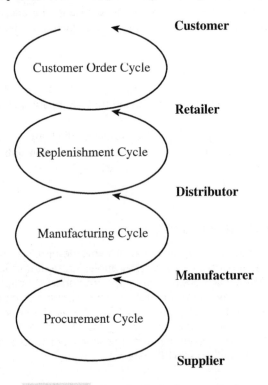

Figure 1-3 Supply Chain Process Cycles

the supplier. The supplier supplies the order, which is received by the buyer. The buyer may return some of the product or other recycled material to the supplier or a third party. The cycle of activities then begins again. The subprocesses in Figure 1-4 can be linked to the source, make, deliver, and return processes in the supply chain operations reference (SCOR) model. The SCOR model provides a description of supply chain processes, a framework for relationships between these processes, and a set of metrics to measure process performance. The description of the supply chain in the SCOR model is similar to the cycle view of supply chains discussed in this section.

Depending on the transaction in question, the subprocesses in Figure 1-4 can be applied to the appropriate cycle. When customers shop online at Amazon, they are part of the customer order cycle—with the customer as the buyer and Amazon as the supplier. In contrast, when Amazon orders books from a publisher to replenish its inventory, it is part of the replenishment cycle—with Amazon as the buyer and the publisher as the supplier.

Within each cycle, the goal of the buyer is to ensure product availability for its customers and to achieve economies of scale in ordering. The supplier attempts to forecast buyer orders and reduce the cost of receiving the order. The supplier then works to fill the order on time and improve efficiency and accuracy of the order fulfillment process. The buyer then works to reduce the cost of the receiving process. Reverse flows are managed to reduce cost and meet environmental objectives.

Even though each cycle has the same basic subprocesses, there are a few important differences among the cycles. In the customer order cycle, demand is external to the supply chain and thus is uncertain. In all other cycles, order placement is uncertain but can be projected based on policies followed by the particular supply chain stage. For example, in the procurement cycle, a tire supplier to an automotive manufacturer can predict tire demand precisely once the production schedule at the manufacturer is known. The second difference across cycles relates to the scale of an order. A customer buys a single car, but the dealer orders multiple cars at a time from the manufacturer, and the manufacturer, in turn, orders an even larger quantity of tires from the supplier. As we move from the customer to the supplier, the number of individual orders declines and the size of each order increases. Thus, sharing of information and operating policies across supply chain stages becomes more important as we move further from the end customer.

The detailed process description of a supply chain in the cycle view is useful when considering operational decisions because it clearly specifies the roles of each member of the supply chain. The cycle view is used by enterprise resource planning (ERP) systems to support supply chain operations.

Figure 1-4 Subprocesses in Each Supply Chain Process Cycle

Push/Pull View of Supply Chain Processes

All processes in a supply chain fall into one of two categories, depending on the timing of their execution relative to end customer demand. With pull processes, execution is initiated in response to a customer order. With push processes, execution is initiated in anticipation of customer orders based on a forecast. Pull processes may also be referred to as *reactive processes* because they react to customer demand. Push processes may also be referred to as *speculative processes* because they respond to speculated (or forecasted), rather than actual, demand. The *push/pull boundary* in a supply chain separates push processes from pull processes, as shown in Figure 1-5. Push processes operate in an uncertain environment because customer demand is not yet known. Pull processes operate in a predictable environment where customer demand is known. They are, however, often constrained by inventory and capacity decisions that were made in the push phase.

Let us compare a make-to-stock environment like that of L. L. Bean and a build-to-order environment like that of Ethan Allen to compare the push/pull view and the cycle view.

L. L. Bean executes all processes in the customer order cycle *after* the customer order arrives. All processes that are part of the customer order cycle are thus pull processes. Order fulfillment takes place from product in inventory that is built up in anticipation of customer orders. The goal of the replenishment cycle is to ensure product availability when a customer order arrives. All processes in the replenishment cycle are performed in anticipation of demand and are thus push processes. The same holds true for processes in the manufacturing and procurement cycles. In fact, raw material such as fabric is often purchased six to nine months before customer demand is expected. Manufacturing itself begins three to six months before the point of sale. The processes in the L. L. Bean supply chain break up into pull and push processes, as shown in Figure 1-6.

Ethan Allen makes customized furniture, such as sofas and chairs, for which customers select the fabric and finish. In this case, the arrival of a customer order triggers production of the product. The manufacturing cycle is thus part of the customer order fulfillment process in the customer order cycle. There are effectively only two cycles in the Ethan Allen supply chain for customized furniture: (1) a customer order and manufacturing cycle and (2) a procurement cycle, as shown in Figure 1-7.

All processes in the customer order and manufacturing cycle at Ethan Allen are classified as pull processes because they are initiated by customer order arrival. The company, however, does not place raw material orders in response to a customer order. Raw material inventory is

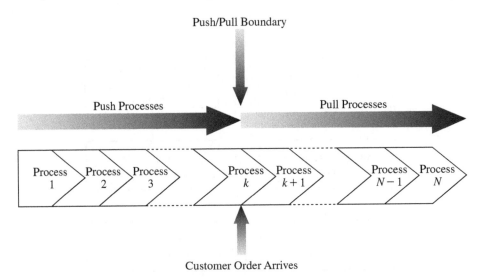

Figure 1-5 Push/Pull View of the Supply Chain

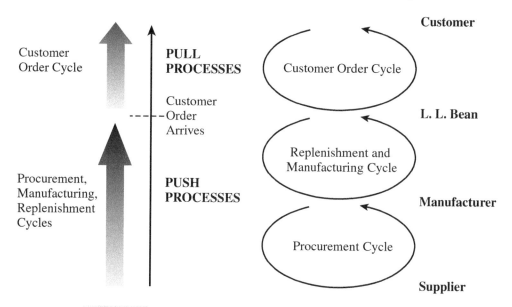

Figure 1-6 Push/Pull Processes for the L. L. Bean Supply Chain

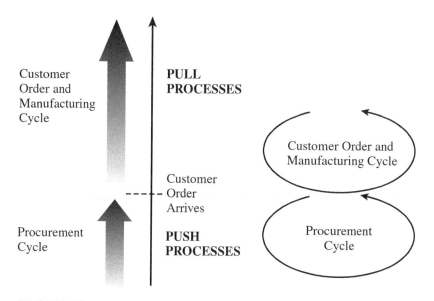

Figure 1-7 Push/Pull Processes for Ethan Allen Supply Chain for Customized Furniture

replenished in anticipation of customer demand. All processes in the procurement cycle for Ethan Allen are thus classified as push processes, because they are in response to a forecast.

A push/pull view of the supply chain is very useful when considering strategic decisions relating to supply chain design. The goal is to identify an appropriate push/pull boundary such that the supply chain can match supply and demand effectively.

The paint industry provides an excellent example of the gains from suitably adjusting the push/pull boundary. The manufacture of paint requires production of the base, mixing of suitable colors, and packing. Until the 1980s, all these processes were performed in large factories, and paint cans were shipped to stores. These qualified as push processes, as they were performed to a forecast in anticipation of customer demand. Given the uncertainty of demand, though, the paint

supply chain had great difficulty matching supply and demand. In the 1990s, paint supply chains were restructured so mixing of colors was done at retail stores after customers placed their orders. In other words, color mixing was shifted from the push to the pull phase of the supply chain even though base preparation and packing of cans were still performed in the push phase. The result is that customers are always able to get the color of their choice, whereas total paint inventories across the supply chain have declined.

Supply Chain Macro Processes in a Firm

All supply chain processes discussed in the two process views and throughout this book can be classified into the following three macro processes, as shown in Figure 1-8:

1. *Customer relationship management (CRM):* all processes at the interface between the firm and its customers
2. *Internal supply chain management (ISCM):* all processes that are internal to the firm
3. *Supplier relationship management (SRM):* all processes at the interface between the firm and its suppliers

These three macro processes manage the flow of information, product, and funds required to generate, receive, and fulfill a customer request. The CRM macro process aims to generate customer demand and facilitate the placement and tracking of orders. It includes processes such as marketing, pricing, sales, order management, and call center management. At an industrial distributor such as W.W. Grainger, CRM processes include the preparation of catalogs and other marketing materials, management of the website, and management of the call center that takes orders and provides service. The ISCM macro process aims to fulfill demand generated by the CRM process in a timely manner and at the lowest possible cost. ISCM processes include the planning of internal production and storage capacity, preparation of demand and supply plans, and fulfillment of actual orders. At W.W. Grainger, ISCM processes include planning for the location and size of warehouses; deciding which products to carry at each warehouse; preparing inventory management policies; and picking, packing, and shipping actual orders. The SRM macro process aims to arrange for and manage supply sources for various goods and services. SRM processes include the evaluation and selection of suppliers, negotiation of supply terms, and communication regarding new products and orders with suppliers. At W.W. Grainger, SRM processes include the selection of suppliers for various products, negotiation of pricing and delivery terms with suppliers, sharing of demand and supply plans with suppliers, and the placement and receipt of replenishment orders.

Observe that all three macro processes are aimed at serving the same customer. For a supply chain to be successful, it is crucial that the three macro processes are well integrated. The importance of this integration is discussed in Chapters 9 and 10. The organizational structure of the firm has a strong influence on the success or failure of the integration effort. In many firms, marketing is in charge of the CRM macro process, manufacturing handles the ISCM macro

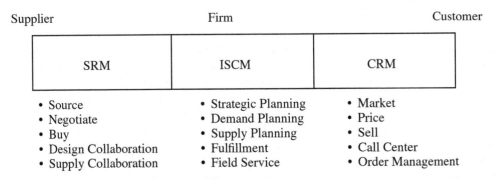

Figure 1-8 Supply Chain Macro Processes

process, and purchasing oversees the SRM macro process—with little communication among them. It is not unusual for marketing and manufacturing to have different forecasts when making their plans. This lack of integration hurts the supply chain's ability to match supply and demand effectively, leading to dissatisfied customers and high costs. Thus, firms should structure a supply chain organization that mirrors the macro processes and ensures good communication and coordination among the owners of processes that interact with one another.

SUMMARY OF LEARNING OBJECTIVE 3

The cycle view divides processes into cycles, each performed at the interface between two successive stages of a supply chain. Each cycle starts with an order placed by one stage of the supply chain and ends when the order is received from the supplier stage. A push/pull view of a supply chain characterizes processes based on their timing relative to that of a customer order. Pull processes are performed in response to a customer order, whereas push processes are performed in anticipation of customer orders. All supply chain processes within a firm can be classified into three macro processes: CRM, ISCM, and SRM. The CRM macro process consists of all processes at the interface between the firm and the customer that work to generate, receive, and track customer orders. The ISCM macro process consists of all supply chain processes that are internal to the firm and work to plan for and fulfill customer orders. The SRM macro process consists of all supply chain processes at the interface between the firm and its suppliers that work to evaluate and select suppliers and then source goods and services from them. Integration among the three macro processes is crucial for successful supply chain management.

EXAMPLES OF SUPPLY CHAINS

In this section, we consider several supply chains and raise questions that must be answered during their design, planning, and operation phases. In later chapters, we discuss concepts and present methodologies that can be used to answer these questions.

1.4 *Identify important issues and decisions to be addressed in a supply chain.*

Gateway and Apple: Two Different Journeys into Retailing

Gateway was founded in 1985 as a direct sales manufacturer of PCs with no retail footprint. In 1996, Gateway was one of the first PC manufacturers to start selling PCs online. After many years of selling its PCs without a retail infrastructure, however, Gateway introduced an aggressive strategy of opening Gateway retail stores throughout the United States in the late 1990s. Its stores carried no finished-goods inventory and were showrooms focused on helping customers select the right configuration to purchase. All PCs were manufactured to order and shipped to the customer from one of the assembly plants.

Initially, investors rewarded Gateway for this strategy and raised the stock price to more than $80 per share in late 1999. However, this success did not last. By November 2002, Gateway shares had dropped to less than $4, and Gateway was losing a significant amount of money. By April 2004, Gateway had closed all its retail outlets and reduced the number of configurations offered to customers. In August 2007, Gateway was purchased by Taiwan's Acer for $710 million. By 2010, Gateway computers were sold through more than 20 different retail outlets, including Best Buy and Costco. As one can imagine, this was quite a transition for the company to experience.

In contrast, Apple has enjoyed tremendous success since it opened its first retail store in 2001. By 2016, Apple had more than 460 stores worldwide, with sales of over $20 billion. Unlike Gateway, Apple has always carried product inventory at its stores. Given its product designs, Apple carries relatively little variety in its stores. In 2014, Apple retail stores had an average revenue per square foot of $4,799, the highest among all retailers.

The following questions highlight supply chain decisions that have a bearing on the difference between Apple's and Gateway's performance:

1. Why did Gateway choose not to carry any finished-product inventory at its retail stores? Why did Apple choose to carry inventory at its stores?
2. What are the characteristics of products that are most suitable to be carried in finished-goods inventory at a retail store? What characterizes products that are best manufactured to order?
3. How does product variety affect the level of inventory a retail store must carry?
4. Is a direct selling supply chain without retail stores always less expensive than a supply chain with retail stores?
5. What factors explain the success of Apple retail and the failure of Gateway Country stores?

Zara: Apparel Manufacturing and Retail

Zara is a chain of fashion stores owned by Inditex, Spain's largest apparel manufacturer and retailer. In 2015, Inditex reported sales of about 21 billion euros from more than 7,000 retail outlets in about 88 countries. In an industry where customer demand is fickle, Zara has grown rapidly with a strategy to be highly responsive to changing trends with affordable prices. Whereas design-to-sales cycle times in the apparel industry have traditionally averaged more than six months, Zara has achieved cycle times of four to six weeks. This speed allows Zara to introduce new designs every week and to change 75 percent of its merchandise display every three to four weeks. Thus, Zara's products on display match customer preferences much more closely than do those of the competition. The result is that Zara sells most of its products at full price and has about half the markdowns in its stores compared with the competition.

Zara manufactures its apparel using a combination of flexible and quick sources in Europe (mostly Portugal and Spain) and low-cost sources in Asia. This contrasts with most apparel manufacturers, who have moved most of their manufacturing to Asia. About 40 percent of the manufacturing capacity is owned by Inditex, with the rest outsourced. Products with highly uncertain demand are sourced out of Europe, whereas products that are more predictable are sourced from its Asian locations. More than 40 percent of its finished-goods purchases and most of its in-house production occur after the sales season starts. This compares with less than 20 percent production after the start of a sales season for a typical retailer. This responsiveness, along with the postponement of decisions until after trends are known, allow Zara to reduce inventories and forecast error. Zara has also invested heavily in information technology to ensure that the latest sales data are available to drive replenishment and production decisions.

In 2012, Inditex distributed to stores all over the world from eight distribution centers located in Spain. The group claimed an average delivery time of 24 to 36 hours for European stores and up to a maximum of 48 hours for stores in America or Asia from the time the order was received in the distribution center (DC) to the time it was delivered to the stores. Shipments from the DCs to stores were made several times a week. This allowed store inventory to closely match customer demand.

The following questions raise supply chain issues that are central to Zara's strategy and success:

1. What advantage does Zara gain against the competition by having a very responsive supply chain?
2. Why has Inditex chosen to have both in-house manufacturing and outsourced manufacturing? Why has Inditex maintained manufacturing capacity in Europe even though manufacturing in Asia is much cheaper?
3. Why does Zara source products with uncertain demand from local manufacturers and products with predictable demand from Asian manufacturers?

4. What advantage does Zara gain from replenishing its stores multiple times a week compared with a less frequent schedule?

5. Do you think Zara's responsive replenishment infrastructure is better suited for online sales or retail sales?

W.W. Grainger and McMaster-Carr: MRO Suppliers

W.W. Grainger and McMaster-Carr sell maintenance, repair, and operations (MRO) products. Both companies have catalogs and web pages through which orders can be placed. W.W. Grainger also has several hundred stores throughout the United States. Customers can walk into a store, call in an order, or place it via the website. W.W. Grainger orders are either shipped to the customer or picked up by the customer at one of its stores. McMaster-Carr, on the other hand, ships almost all its orders (although a few customers near its DCs do pick up their own orders). W.W. Grainger has nine DCs that both replenish stores and fill customer orders. McMaster has five DCs from which all orders are filled. Neither McMaster nor W.W. Grainger manufactures any product. They both primarily serve the role of a distributor or retailer. Their success is largely linked to their supply chain management ability.

Both firms offer several hundred thousand products to their customers from inventory along with many other products that are drop shipped from suppliers. Both firms face the following strategic and operational issues:

1. How many DCs should be built, and where should they be located?

2. How should product stocking be managed at the DCs? Should all DCs carry all products?

3. What products should be carried in inventory and what products should be left with the supplier to be shipped directly in response to a customer order?

4. What products should W.W. Grainger carry at a store?

5. How should markets be allocated to DCs in terms of order fulfillment? What should be done if an order cannot be completely filled from a DC? Should there be specified backup locations? How should they be selected?

Toyota: A Global Auto Manufacturer

Toyota Motor Corporation is Japan's top auto manufacturer and has experienced significant growth in global sales over the past two decades. A key issue facing Toyota is the design of its global production and distribution network. Part of Toyota's global strategy is to open factories in every market it serves. Toyota must decide what the production capability of each of the factories will be, as this has a significant impact on the desired distribution system. At one extreme, each plant can be equipped only for local production. At the other extreme, each plant is capable of supplying every market. Before 1996, Toyota used specialized local factories for each market. After the Asian financial crisis in 1996–97, Toyota redesigned its plants so it could also export to markets that remain strong when the local market weakens. Toyota calls this strategy "global complementation."

Whether to be global or local is also an issue for Toyota's parts plants and product design. Should parts plants be built for local production or should there be a few parts plants globally that supply multiple assembly plants? Toyota has worked hard to increase commonality in parts used around the globe. Although this has helped the company lower costs and improve parts availability, common parts caused significant difficulty when one of the parts had to be recalled. In 2009, Toyota had to recall about 12 million cars using common parts across North America, Europe, and Asia, causing significant damage to the brand as well as to the finances.

Any global manufacturer like Toyota must address the following questions regarding the configuration and capability of the supply chain:

1. Where should the plants be located, and what degree of flexibility should be built into each? What capacity should each plant have?

2. Should plants be able to produce for all markets or only for specific contingency markets?

3. How should markets be allocated to plants and how frequently should this allocation be revised?
4. How should the investment in flexibility be valued?

Amazon: Online Sales

Amazon sells books, music, and many other items over the Internet and is one of the pioneers of online consumer sales. Amazon, based in Seattle, started by filling all orders using books purchased from a distributor in response to customer orders. As it grew, the company added warehouses, allowing it to react more quickly to customer orders. By 2015, Amazon had over 100 locations in the United States and another 100 in the rest of the world. It used the U.S. Postal Service and other package carriers, such as UPS and FedEx, to send products to customers. Outbound shipping-related costs at Amazon in 2015 were over $10 billion.

Amazon has continued to expand the set of products that it sells online. Besides books and music, Amazon has added many product categories such as toys, apparel, electronics, jewelry, industrial supplies, grocery items, and shoes. In 2009, one of its largest acquisitions was Zappos, a leader in online shoe sales. This acquisition added a great deal of product variety: According to the Amazon annual report, this required creating 121,000 product descriptions and uploading more than 2.2 million images to the website. In 2010, another interesting acquisition by Amazon was diapers.com. Unlike Zappos, this acquisition added little variety but considerable shipping volumes.

In 2016, Amazon opened its first physical bookstore with plans to open more. By the end of 2016 there were reports that Amazon planned to open small brick-and-mortar stores that would sell produce, milk, meats and other perishable items. Several questions arise concerning how Amazon is structured and the product categories it continues to add:

1. Why is Amazon building more warehouses as it grows? How many warehouses should it have, and where should they be located?
2. Should Amazon stock every product it sells?
3. What advantage can online players derive from setting up a brick-and-mortar location? How should they use the two channels to gain maximum advantage?
4. What advantages and disadvantages does the online channel enjoy in the sale of shoes and diapers relative to a retail store?
5. For what products does the online channel offer the greater advantage relative to retail stores? What characterizes these products?

Macy's and W.W. Grainger: Omni-Channel Retailing

After selling for decades from its department stores, Macy's made a big push into omni-channel retailing, allowing customers to have a seamless experience between shopping online or at a store. Customers could browse online and then experience the product at a store or order online after seeing a product at the store. Omni-channel is not just about ordering, however; it is also about fulfillment. Orders placed on any channel could access Macy's entire assortment. By 2012, Macy's had equipped 292 Macy's stores to fulfill online orders or orders from other stores that were sold out of a particular item. If customers desired, orders placed online could be picked up at select stores and items purchased online could be returned to stores. By 2015, this approach was presenting some challenges.

Macy's approach of using stores to fulfill online orders is similar to what W. W. Grainger practiced until about 2001. At that time, about 50 percent of the units and 30 percent of sales dollars were shipped to customers from Grainger stores. In 2001, Grainger embarked on a network redesign where the fulfillment of online orders was shifted from stores to DCs. The goal was to take advantage of picking and transportation efficiencies by aggregating online order fulfillment from DCs.

Any omni-channel retailer must address the following questions:

1. Should online orders be filled from stores or fulfillment centers? What role(s) should each facility play?
2. How should store inventories be managed in an omni-channel setting?
3. Should returns be kept at a store or sent to a fulfillment center?

SUMMARY OF LEARNING OBJECTIVE 4

At a strategic level, a supply chain designer must decide whether to build a responsive supply chain like Zara or focus on lower costs. A decision must be made on the location and capacity of each facility and whether it will be dedicated or flexible in terms of the products it produces and markets it serves. The designer must decide whether products will be sold directly to customers, through distributors like Grainger, or through brick-and-mortar retailers like Macy's. If opting for omni-channel retail, the designer must decide which facilities will fulfill different customer orders. The planner must then decide on the production levels at each production site and inventory levels at each DC and retail store. As customer orders arrive, the operations manager must decide how each order will be fulfilled given the available inventory and production schedule. The goal when making all these decisions is to maximize the supply chain surplus.

DEVELOPING SKILLS FOR YOUR CAREER

1.5 Develop skills that employers have identified as critical to success in the workplace.

If you are not an operations or supply chain major, you may think that this book is not relevant to you. Let me assure you it is. Whether or not you plan on a career in operations or supply chain management, the lessons you will learn in this book will help you develop career skills that are useful no matter what path you take. Employers have identified communication, critical thinking, collaboration, knowledge application and analysis, business ethics and social responsibility, data literacy, and information technology application and computing skills as being important for success in the 21st century. This book helps you develop several of these skills.

A key theme that permeates this book is the link between strategic decision making and analytics. Good strategic decisions cannot be made without access to relevant analytics, and all analytics should be designed to support decision making. Thus, every chapter in the book pushes students to think critically in order to define and solve supply chain problems. For example, Chapter 4 develops a framework for distribution networks and then pushes students to think about how retailing may evolve in the future as consumer preferences and technology change. The first part of the chapter teaches frameworks and concepts related to the design of distribution networks. The last part of the chapter then pushes the students to analyze retailing by applying the knowledge they have gained in order to decide how retailers need to change in order to succeed in the 21st century.

Analytics that supports these frameworks is then discussed in detail in the following chapters. For example, Chapter 11, 12, and 13 help students learn the analytics related to inventory management in a supply chain. All the analytics in the book are developed through the use of Microsoft Excel. This helps students develop data literacy, computing skills, and the knowledge of how to apply information technology to support decision making. The analytics that are developed in these chapters in turn support the framework laid out in Chapter 4. Whereas Chapter 4 helps students to think conceptually about why certain retailing models have succeeded for selling jewelry while others have failed, the succeeding chapters help students quantify financial metrics for different retail networks. As a result, students learn how to use data and models to improve strategic decision making. This is a skill that will be of great importance in the 21st century where decision makers will face rapidly changing environments and a surplus of data that must be reconciled when making decisions.

SUMMARY OF LEARNING OBJECTIVE 5

Skills learned in this book will be of great use no matter what path students choose to follow. The book is developed with the premise that good strategic decisions cannot be made without access to relevant analytics, and all analytics should be designed to support decision making. As a result, students will develop critical thinking, the ability to formulate and analyze problems, and support their recommendations with analytics that uses data literacy and computing skills.

DISCUSSION QUESTIONS

1. What is supply chain management? Will a supply chain always look like a 'chain'?
2. Should the members of a supply chain maximize individual profits in order to increase the overall supply chain surplus? Explain.
3. What are some strategic, planning, and operational decisions that must be made by H&M, a Swedish apparel retailer?
4. Consider the supply chain involved when a customer purchases a cup of coffee at a local café. Identify the cycles in this supply chain and the location of the push/pull boundary.

5. Consider the supply chain involved when a customer buys a garment from apparel retailer Benetton, which is similar to the L.L. Bean example discussed in the chapter. Identify the push/pull boundary and two processes each in the push and pull phases.
6. In what way do supply chain flows affect the success or failure of a firm such as Benetton? List two supply chain decisions that have a significant impact on supply chain profitability.
7. List some of the strategic, planning, and operational decisions that an automotive manufacturer must make with regards to its supply chain.

BIBLIOGRAPHY

Aronow, Stan, Mike Burkett, Jim Romano, and Kimberly Nilles. "The 2016 Supply Chain Top 25: Lessons from Leaders." *Supply Chain Management Review* (September–October 2016): 10–21.

Cavinato, Joseph L. "What's Your Supply Chain Type?" *Supply Chain Management Review* (May–June 2002): 60–66.

Fisher, Marshall L. "What Is the Right Supply Chain for Your Product?" *Harvard Business Review* (March–April 1997): 83–93.

Fuller, Joseph B., James O'Conner, and Richard Rawlinson. "Tailored Logistics: The Next Advantage." *Harvard Business Review* (May–June 1993): 87–98.

Kopczak, Laura R., and M. Eric Johnson. "The Supply Chain Management Effect." *Sloan Management Review* (Spring 2003): 27–34.

Lambert, Douglas M. "The Eight Essential Supply Chain Management Processes." *Supply Chain Management Review* (September 2004): 18–26.

Lee, Hau L. "Aligning Supply Chain Strategies with Product Uncertainties." *California Management Review* (Spring 2002): 105–119.

Poirier, Charles C., Francis J. Quinn, and Morgan L. Swink. *Diagnosing Greatness: Ten Traits of the Best Supply Chains.* Ft. Lauderdale, FL: J. Ross Publishing, 2009.

Robeson, James F., and William C. Copacino, eds. *The Logistics Handbook.* New York: Free Press, 1994.

Shapiro, Roy D. "Get Leverage from Logistics." *Harvard Business Review* (May–June 1984): 119–127.

Slone, Reuben E. "Leading a Supply Chain Turnaround." *Harvard Business Review* (October 2004): 114–121.

2

Achieving Strategic Fit in a Supply Chain

LEARNING OBJECTIVES

After reading this chapter, you will be able to

2.1 Explain why achieving strategic fit is critical to a company's overall success.

2.2 Describe how a company achieves strategic fit between its supply chain strategy and its competitive strategy.

2.3 Identify the main levers to deal with uncertainty in a supply chain.

2.4 Discuss the importance of expanding the scope of strategic fit across the supply chain.

In Chapter 1, we discussed the importance of supply chain design, planning, and operation to a firm's success. In this chapter, we define supply chain strategy and explain how creating a strategic fit between a company's competitive strategy and its supply chain strategy affects performance. We identify key levers that can be used to deal with uncertainty in a supply chain. We also discuss the importance of expanding the scope of strategic fit from one operation within a company to all stages of the supply chain.

COMPETITIVE AND SUPPLY CHAIN STRATEGIES

A company's *competitive strategy* defines, relative to its competitors, the set of customer needs that it seeks to satisfy through its products and services. For example, Walmart aims to provide high availability of a variety of products of reasonable quality at low prices. Most products sold at Walmart are commonplace (everything from home appliances to clothing) and can be purchased elsewhere. What Walmart provides is a low price and product availability. McMaster-Carr sells maintenance, repair, and operations (MRO) products. It offers more than 500,000 products through both a catalog and a website. Its competitive strategy is built around providing the customer with convenience, variety, and responsiveness. With this focus on responsiveness, McMaster does not compete based on low price. Clearly, the competitive strategy at Walmart is different from that at McMaster.

We can also contrast Blue Nile, with its online retailing model for diamonds, with Zales, which sells diamond jewelry through retail outlets. Blue Nile has emphasized the variety of

2.1 Explain why achieving strategic fit is critical to a company's overall success.

diamonds available from its website and the fact that its prices are significantly lower than its bricks-and-mortar competition. Customers, however, have to wait to get their jewelry and do not have any opportunity to touch and see it before purchase (Blue Nile does provide a 30-day return period, though). At Zales, in contrast, a customer can walk into the retail store, be helped by a salesperson, and leave immediately with a diamond ring. The variety available at a Zales store, however, is limited. Whereas Blue Nile offers more than 190,000 stones on its site, a typical Zales store carries fewer than a thousand.

In each case, the competitive strategy is defined based on how the customer prioritizes product cost, delivery time, variety, and quality. A McMaster-Carr customer places greater emphasis on product variety and response time than on cost. A Walmart customer, in contrast, places greater emphasis on cost. A Blue Nile customer, purchasing online, places great emphasis on product variety and cost. A customer purchasing jewelry at Zales is most concerned with fast response time and help in product selection. Thus, a firm's competitive strategy will be defined based on its customers' priorities. Competitive strategy targets one or more customer segments and aims to provide products and services that satisfy these customers' needs.

To see the relationship between competitive and supply chain strategies, we start with the value chain for a typical organization, as shown in Figure 2-1.

The value chain begins with new product development, which creates specifications for the product. Marketing and sales generate demand by publicizing the customer priorities that the products and services will satisfy. Marketing also brings customer input back to new product development. Operations transforms inputs to outputs according to specifications to create the product. Distribution either takes the product to the customer or brings the customer to the product. Service responds to customer requests during or after the sale. These are core processes or functions that must be performed for a successful sale. Finance, accounting, information technology, and human resources support and facilitate the functioning of the value chain.

To execute a company's competitive strategy, all these functions play a role, and each must develop its own strategy. Here, *strategy* refers to what each process or function will try to do particularly well.

A *product development* strategy specifies the portfolio of new products that a company will try to develop. It also dictates whether the development effort will be made internally or outsourced. A *marketing and sales* strategy specifies how the market will be segmented and how the product will be positioned, priced, and promoted. A *supply chain strategy* determines the nature of procurement of raw materials, transportation of materials to and from the company, manufacture of the product or operation to provide the service, and distribution of the product to the customer, along with any follow-up service and a specification of whether these processes will be performed in-house or outsourced. Supply chain strategy specifies what the operations, distribution, and service functions, whether performed in-house or outsourced, should do particularly well. Because our focus here is on supply chain strategy, we define it in more detail. Supply chain strategy includes a specification of the broad structure of the supply chain and what many traditionally call "supplier strategy," "operations strategy," and "logistics

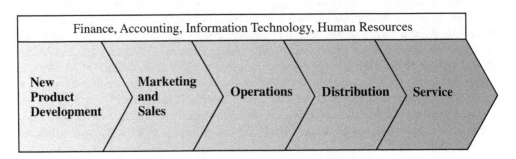

Figure 2-1 The Value Chain in a Company

strategy." For example, Dell's initial decision to sell direct, its 2007 decision to start selling PCs through resellers, and Cisco's decision to use contract manufacturers define the broad structure of their supply chains and are all part of their supply chain strategies. Amazon's decision in 2016 to open bookstores and announce the opening of "convenience" stores is a part of its supply chain strategy. Supply chain strategy also includes design decisions regarding inventory, transportation, operating facilities, and information flows. For example, Amazon's decisions to build warehouses to stock some products and to continue using distributors as a source of other products are part of its supply chain strategy. Similarly, Toyota's decision to have production facilities in each of its major markets is part of its supply chain strategy.

For a firm to succeed, all functional strategies must support one another and the competitive strategy. For example, Seven-Eleven Japan's success can be related to the excellent fit among its functional strategies. Marketing at Seven-Eleven has emphasized convenience in the form of easy access to stores and availability of a wide range of products and services. New product development at Seven-Eleven is constantly adding products and services, such as bill payment services that draw customers in and exploit the excellent information infrastructure and the fact that customers frequently visit Seven-Eleven. Operations and distribution at Seven-Eleven have focused on having a high density of stores, being very responsive, and providing an excellent information infrastructure. The result is a virtuous cycle in which supply chain infrastructure is exploited to offer new products and services that increase demand, and the increased demand in turn makes it easier for operations to improve the density of stores, responsiveness in replenishment, and the information infrastructure. What Seven-Eleven has achieved is something we refer to as strategic fit.

Strategic fit requires that both the competitive and supply chain strategies of a company have aligned goals. It refers to consistency between the customer priorities that the competitive strategy hopes to satisfy and the capabilities that the supply chain strategy aims to build. For a company to achieve strategic fit, it must accomplish the following:

1. The competitive strategy and all functional strategies must fit together to form a coordinated overall strategy. Each functional strategy must support other functional strategies and help a firm reach its competitive strategy goal.
2. The different functions in a company must appropriately structure their processes and resources to be able to execute these strategies successfully.
3. The design of the overall supply chain and the role of each stage must be aligned to support the supply chain strategy.

A company may fail either because of a lack of strategic fit or because its overall supply chain design, processes, and resources do not provide the capabilities to support the desired strategic fit. Consider, for example, a situation in which marketing is publicizing a company's ability to provide a large variety of products quickly; simultaneously, distribution is targeting the lowest-cost means of transportation. In this situation, it is likely that distribution will delay orders so it can get better transportation economies by grouping orders together or using inexpensive but slow modes of transportation. This action conflicts with marketing's stated goal of providing variety quickly. Similarly, consider a scenario in which a retailer has decided to provide a high level of variety while carrying low levels of inventory but has selected suppliers and carriers based on their low price and not their responsiveness. In this case, the retailer is likely to end up with unhappy customers because of poor product availability.

To elaborate on strategic fit, let us consider the evolution of Dell and its supply chain between 1993 and the present. Between 1993 and 2006, Dell's competitive strategy was to provide a large variety of customizable products at a reasonable price. Given the focus on customization, Dell's supply chain was designed to be very responsive. Assembly facilities owned by Dell were designed to be flexible and to easily handle the wide variety of configurations requested by customers. A facility that focused on low cost and efficiency by producing large volumes of the same configuration would not have been appropriate in this setting.

The notion of strategic fit also extended to other functions within Dell. Dell PCs were designed to use common components and to allow rapid assembly. This design strategy clearly aligned well with the supply chain's goal of assembling customized PCs in response to customer orders. Dell worked hard to carry this alignment to its suppliers. Given that Dell produced customized products with low levels of inventory, it was crucial that suppliers and carriers be highly responsive. For example, the ability of carriers to merge a PC from Dell with a monitor from Sony allowed Dell not to carry any Sony monitors in inventory.

Starting in 2007, however, Dell altered its competitive strategy and had to change its supply chain accordingly. With a reduced customer focus on hardware customization, Dell branched out into selling PCs through retail stores such as Walmart. Through Walmart, Dell offers a limited variety of desktops and laptops. It is also essential that monitors and other peripherals be available in inventory because a customer buying a PC at Walmart is not willing to wait for the monitor to show up later. Clearly, the flexible and responsive supply chain that aligns well with a customer need for customization does not necessarily align well when customers no longer want customization but prefer low prices. Given the change in customer priorities, Dell has shifted a greater fraction of its production to a build-to-stock model to maintain strategic fit. Contract manufacturers like Foxconn that are focused on low cost now produce many of Dell's products well in advance of sale. To maintain strategic fit, Dell's supply chain has moved from a relentless focus on responsiveness to a greater focus on low cost.

SUMMARY OF LEARNING OBJECTIVE 1

Strategic fit requires that all functions within a firm and stages in the supply chain target the same goal—one that is consistent with customer needs. A lack of strategic fit between the competitive and supply chain strategies can result in the supply chain taking actions that are not consistent with customer needs, leading to a reduction in supply chain surplus and a decrease in supply chain profitability.

2.2 *Describe how a company achieves strategic fit between its supply chain strategy and its competitive strategy.*

HOW IS STRATEGIC FIT ACHIEVED?

What does a company need to do to achieve that all-important strategic fit between the supply chain and competitive strategies? A competitive strategy will specify, either explicitly or implicitly, one or more customer segments that a company hopes to satisfy. To achieve strategic fit, a company must ensure that its supply chain capabilities support its ability to satisfy the needs of the targeted customer segments.

There are three basic steps to achieving strategic fit, which we outline here and then discuss in more detail:

1. *Understanding the customer and supply chain uncertainty:* First, a company must understand the customer needs for each targeted segment and the uncertainty these needs impose on the supply chain. These needs help the company define the desired cost and service requirements. The supply chain uncertainty helps the company identify the extent of unpredictability of demand and supply that the supply chain must be prepared for.
2. *Understanding the supply chain capabilities:* Each of the many types of supply chains is designed to perform different tasks well. A company must understand what its supply chain is designed to do well.
3. *Achieving strategic fit:* If a mismatch exists between what the supply chain does particularly well and the desired customer needs, the company will either need to restructure the supply chain to support the competitive strategy or alter its competitive strategy.

Understanding the Customer and Supply Chain Uncertainty

To understand the customer, a company must identify the needs of the customer segment being served. Each customer in a particular segment will tend to have similar needs, whereas customers

in a different segment can have very different needs. Let us compare Seven-Eleven Japan and a discounter such as Sam's Club (a part of Walmart). When customers go to Seven-Eleven to purchase detergent, they go there for the convenience of a nearby store and are not necessarily looking for the lowest price. In contrast, low price is very important to a Sam's Club customer. This customer may be willing to tolerate less variety and even purchase large package sizes as long as the price is low. Even though customers purchase detergent at both places, the demand varies along certain attributes. In the case of Seven-Eleven, customers are in a hurry and want convenience. In the case of Sam's Club, they want a low price and are willing to spend time getting it. In general, customer demand from different segments varies along several attributes, as follows:

- ***Quantity of the product needed in each lot:*** An emergency order for material needed to repair a production line is likely to be small. An order for material to construct a new production line is likely to be large.
- ***Response time that customers are willing to tolerate:*** The tolerable response time for the emergency order is likely to be short, whereas the allowable response time for the construction order is apt to be long.
- ***Variety of products needed:*** A customer may place a high premium on the availability of all parts of an emergency repair order from a single supplier. This may not be the case for the construction order.
- ***Service level required:*** A customer placing an emergency order expects a high level of product availability. This customer may go elsewhere if all parts of the order are not immediately available. This is not apt to happen in the case of the construction order, for which the customer is likely place the order well in advance of delivery.
- ***Price of the product:*** The customer placing the emergency order is apt to be much less sensitive to price than the customer placing the construction order.
- ***Desired rate of innovation in the product:*** Customers at a high-end department store expect a lot of innovation and new designs in the store's apparel. Customers at Walmart may be less sensitive to new product innovation.

Although we have described several attributes along which customer demand varies, our goal is to identify one key measure for combining all of these attributes. This single measure then helps define what the supply chain should do particularly well.

IMPLIED DEMAND UNCERTAINTY At first glance, it may appear that each of the customer need categories should be viewed differently, but in a fundamental sense, each customer need can be translated into the metric of *implied demand uncertainty,* which is demand uncertainty imposed on the supply chain because of the customer needs it seeks to satisfy.

We make a distinction between demand uncertainty and implied demand uncertainty. *Demand uncertainty* reflects the uncertainty of customer demand for a product. *Implied demand uncertainty*, in contrast, is the resulting uncertainty for only the portion of the demand that the supply chain plans to satisfy based on the attributes the customer desires. For example, a firm supplying only emergency orders for a product will face a higher implied demand uncertainty than a firm that supplies the same product with a long lead time, as the second firm has an opportunity to fulfill the orders evenly over the long lead time.

Another illustration of the need for this distinction is the impact of service level. As a supply chain raises its level of service, it must be able to meet a higher and higher percentage of actual demand, forcing it to prepare for rare surges in demand. Thus, raising the service level increases the implied demand uncertainty even though the product's underlying demand uncertainty does not change.

Both the product demand uncertainty and various customer needs that the supply chain tries to fill affect implied demand uncertainty. Table 2-1 illustrates how various customer needs affect implied demand uncertainty.

TABLE 2-1 Impact of Customer Needs on Implied Demand Uncertainty

Customer Need	Causes Implied Demand Uncertainty to . . .
Range of quantity required increases	Increase because a wider range of the quantity required implies greater variance in demand
Lead time decreases	Increase because there is less time in which to react to orders
Variety of products required increases	Increase because demand per product becomes less predictable
Required service level increases	Increase because the firm now has to handle unusual surges in demand
Rate of innovation increases	Increase because new products tend to have more uncertain demand
Number of channels through which product may be acquired increases	Increase because customer demand per channel becomes less predictable

As each individual customer need contributes to the implied demand uncertainty, we can use implied demand uncertainty as a common metric with which to distinguish different types of demand.

Fisher (1997) pointed out that implied demand uncertainty is often correlated with other characteristics of demand, as shown in Table 2-2. An explanation follows:

1. Products with uncertain demand are often less mature and have less direct competition. As a result, margins tend to be high.
2. Forecasting is more accurate when demand has less uncertainty.
3. Increased implied demand uncertainty leads to increased difficulty in matching supply with demand. For a given product, this dynamic can lead to either a stockout or an oversupply situation. Increased implied demand uncertainty thus leads to both higher oversupply and a higher stockout rate.
4. Markdowns are high for products with greater implied demand uncertainty because oversupply often results.

First, let us take an example of a product with low implied demand uncertainty—such as table salt. Salt has a low margin, accurate demand forecasts, low stockout rates, and virtually no markdowns. These characteristics match well with Fisher's chart of characteristics for products with highly certain demand.

On the other end of the spectrum, a new smartphone has high implied demand uncertainty. It will likely have a high margin, inaccurate demand forecasts, high stockout rates (if it is successful), and large markdowns (if it is a failure). This, too, matches well with Table 2-2.

TABLE 2-2 Correlation Between Implied Demand Uncertainty and Other Attributes

	Low Implied Uncertainty	High Implied Uncertainty
Product margin	Low	High
Average forecast error	10%	40% to 100%
Average stockout rate	1% to 2%	10% to 40%
Average forced season-end markdown	0%	10% to 25%

Source: Based on Marshall L. Fisher, "What Is the Right Supply Chain for Your Product?" Harvard Business.

TABLE 2-3 Impact of Supply Source Capability on Supply Uncertainty

Supply Source Capability	Causes Supply Uncertainty to . . .
Frequent breakdowns	Increase
Unpredictable and low yields	Increase
Poor quality	Increase
Limited supply capacity	Increase
Inflexible supply capacity	Increase
Evolving production process	Increase

Source: Based on Hau L. Lee, "Aligning Supply Chain Strategies with Product Uncertainties." California.

Lee (2002) pointed out that along with demand uncertainty, it is important to consider uncertainty resulting from the capability of the supply chain. For example, when a new component is introduced in the consumer electronics industry, the quality yields of the production process tend to be low and breakdowns are frequent. As a result, companies have difficulty delivering according to a well-defined schedule, resulting in high supply uncertainty for electronics manufacturers. As the production technology matures and yields improve, companies are able to follow a fixed delivery schedule, resulting in low supply uncertainty. Table 2-3 illustrates how various characteristics of supply sources affect the supply uncertainty.

Supply uncertainty is also strongly affected by the life-cycle position of the product. New products being introduced have higher supply uncertainty because designs and production processes are still evolving. In contrast, mature products have less supply uncertainty.

We can create a spectrum of uncertainty by combining the demand and supply uncertainty. This implied uncertainty spectrum is shown in Figure 2-2.

A company introducing a brand-new smartphone based on entirely new components and technology faces high implied demand uncertainty and high supply uncertainty. As a result, the implied uncertainty faced by the supply chain is extremely high. In contrast, a supermarket selling salt faces low implied demand uncertainty and low levels of supply uncertainty, resulting in a low implied uncertainty. Many agricultural products, such as coffee, are examples of supply chains facing low levels of implied demand uncertainty but significant supply uncertainty based on weather. The supply chain thus faces an intermediate level of implied uncertainty.

Understanding the Supply Chain Capabilities

After understanding the uncertainty that the company faces, the next question is: How does the firm best meet demand in that uncertain environment? Creating strategic fit is all about designing a supply chain whose responsiveness aligns with the implied uncertainty it faces.

Figure 2-2 The Implied Uncertainty (Demand and Supply) Spectrum

We now categorize supply chains based on different characteristics that influence their responsiveness and efficiency.

First, we provide some definitions. *Supply chain responsiveness* includes a supply chain's ability to do the following:

- Respond to wide ranges of quantities demanded
- Meet short lead times
- Handle a large variety of products
- Build highly innovative products
- Meet a high service level
- Handle supply uncertainty

These abilities are similar to many of the characteristics of demand and supply that led to high implied uncertainty. The more of these abilities a supply chain has, the more responsive it is.

Responsiveness, however, comes at a cost. For instance, to respond to a wider range of quantities demanded, capacity must be increased, which increases costs. This increase in cost leads to the second definition: *Supply chain efficiency* is the inverse of the cost of making and delivering a product to the customer. Increases in cost lower efficiency. For every strategic choice to increase responsiveness, there are additional costs that lower efficiency.

The *cost-responsiveness efficient frontier* is the curve in Figure 2-3 showing the lowest possible cost for a given level of responsiveness. Lowest cost is defined based on existing technology; not every firm is able to operate on the efficient frontier, which represents the cost-responsiveness performance of the best supply chains. A firm that is not on the efficient frontier can improve both its responsiveness and its cost performance by moving toward the efficient frontier. In contrast, a firm on the efficient frontier can improve its responsiveness only by increasing cost and becoming less efficient. Such a firm must then make a trade-off between efficiency and responsiveness. Of course, firms on the efficient frontier are also continuously improving their processes and changing technology to shift the efficient frontier itself. Given the trade-off between cost and responsiveness, a key strategic choice for any supply chain is the level of responsiveness it seeks to provide.

Supply chains range from those that focus solely on being responsive to those that focus on a goal of producing and supplying at the lowest possible cost. Figure 2-4 shows the responsiveness spectrum and where some supply chains fall on this spectrum.

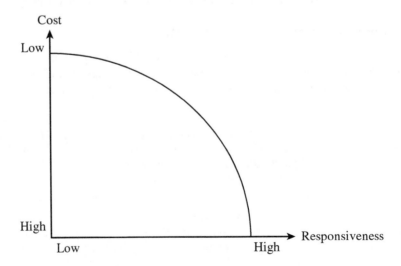

Figure 2-3 Cost-Responsiveness Efficient Frontier

Figure 2-4 The Responsiveness Spectrum

The more capabilities constituting responsiveness a supply chain has, the more responsive it is. Seven-Eleven Japan replenishes its stores with breakfast items in the morning, lunch items in the afternoon, and dinner items at night. As a result, the available product variety changes by time of day. Seven-Eleven responds quickly to orders, with store managers placing replenishment orders less than 12 hours before they are supplied. This practice makes the Seven-Eleven supply chain very responsive. Another example of a responsive supply chain is W.W. Grainger. The company faces both demand and supply uncertainty; therefore, the supply chain has been designed to deal effectively with both to provide customers with a wide variety of MRO products within 24 hours. An efficient supply chain, in contrast, lowers cost by eliminating some of its responsive capabilities. For example, Sam's Club sells a limited variety of products in large package sizes. The supply chain is capable of low costs, and the focus of this supply chain is clearly on efficiency.

Achieving Strategic Fit

After mapping the level of implied uncertainty and understanding the supply chain position on the responsiveness spectrum, the third and final step is to ensure that the degree of supply chain responsiveness is consistent with the implied uncertainty. The goal is to target high responsiveness for a supply chain facing high implied uncertainty, and efficiency for a supply chain facing low implied uncertainty.

For example, the competitive strategy of McMaster-Carr targets customers that value having a large variety of MRO products delivered to them within 24 hours. Given the large variety of products and rapid desired delivery, demand from McMaster-Carr customers can be characterized as having high implied demand uncertainty. If McMaster-Carr designed an efficient supply chain, it may carry less inventory and maintain a level load on the warehouse to lower picking and packing costs. These choices, however, would make it difficult for the company to support the customer's desire for a wide variety of products that are delivered within 24 hours. To serve its customers effectively, McMaster-Carr carries a high level of inventory and picking and packing capacity. Clearly, a responsive supply chain is better suited to meet the needs of customers targeted by McMaster-Carr even if it results in higher costs.

Now, consider a dry pasta manufacturer such as Barilla. Dry pasta is a product with relatively stable customer demand, giving it a low implied demand uncertainty. Supply is also quite predictable. Barilla could design a highly responsive supply chain in which pasta is custom made in small batches in response to customer orders and shipped via a rapid transportation mode such as FedEx. This choice would obviously make the pasta prohibitively expensive, resulting in a loss of customers. Barilla, therefore, is in a much better position if it designs a more efficient supply chain with a focus on cost reduction.

From the preceding discussion, it follows that increasing implied uncertainty from customers and supply sources is best served by increasing responsiveness from the supply chain. This

relationship is represented by the "zone of strategic fit" illustrated in Figure 2-5. For a high level of performance, companies should move their competitive strategy (and resulting implied uncertainty) and supply chain strategy (and resulting responsiveness) toward the zone of strategic fit.

The next step in achieving strategic fit is to assign roles to different stages of the supply chain that ensure the appropriate level of responsiveness. It is important to understand that the desired level of responsiveness required across the supply chain may be attained by assigning different levels of responsiveness and efficiency to each stage of the supply chain as illustrated by the following examples.

IKEA is a Swedish furniture retailer with large stores in about fifty countries. IKEA has targeted customers who want stylish furniture at a reasonable cost. The company limits the variety it needs to stock by selling unassembled furniture and designing modular components that are used in multiple finished products. The large scale of each store and the limited variety of components sold decrease the implied uncertainty faced by the supply chain. IKEA stocks all components in inventory and serves customers from stock. Thus, it uses store inventory to absorb all the uncertainty faced by the supply chain. The presence of inventory at large IKEA stores allows replenishment orders to its manufacturers to be more stable and predictable. As a result, IKEA passes along little uncertainty to its manufacturers, who tend to be located in low-cost countries and focus on efficiency. IKEA provides responsiveness (in the form of immediate availability) in the supply chain, with the stores absorbing most of the uncertainty and being responsive, and the suppliers absorbing little uncertainty and being efficient.

In contrast, another approach for responsiveness may involve the retailer holding little inventory. In this case, the retailer does not contribute significantly to supply chain responsiveness, and most of the implied demand uncertainty is passed on to the manufacturer. For the supply chain to be responsive, the manufacturer now needs to be flexible and have low response times. An example of this approach is England, Inc., a furniture manufacturer located in Tennessee. Every week, the company makes several thousand sofas and chairs to order, delivering them to furniture stores across the country within three weeks. England, Inc.'s retailers allow customers to select from a wide variety of styles and promise relatively quick delivery. This imposes a high level of implied uncertainty on the supply chain. The retailers, however, do not carry much inventory and pass most of the implied uncertainty on to England, Inc. The retailers can thus be efficient because most of the implied uncertainty for the supply chain is absorbed by England, Inc., with its flexible manufacturing process. England, Inc., itself has a choice of how much

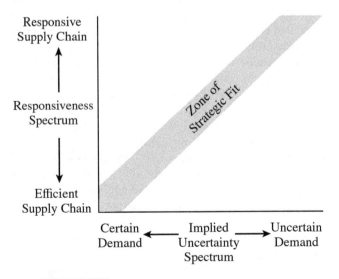

Figure 2-5 Finding the Zone of Strategic Fit

uncertainty it passes along to its suppliers. By holding more raw material inventories, the company allows its suppliers to focus on efficiency. If it decreases its raw material inventories, its suppliers must become more responsive.

The preceding discussion illustrates that the supply chain can achieve a given level of responsiveness by adjusting the role of each of its stages. Making one stage more responsive allows other stages to focus on becoming more efficient. The best combination of roles depends on the efficiency and flexibility available at each stage. The notion of achieving a given level of responsiveness by assigning different roles and levels of uncertainty to different stages of the supply chain is illustrated in Figure 2-6. The figure shows two supply chains that face the same implied uncertainty but achieve the desired level of responsiveness with different allocations of uncertainty and responsiveness across the supply chain. Supply Chain I has a very responsive retailer that absorbs most of the uncertainty (e.g., by holding inventory), allowing (actually requiring) the manufacturer and supplier to be efficient. Supply Chain II, in contrast, has a very responsive manufacturer that absorbs most of the uncertainty (e.g., through flexible operations), thus allowing the other stages to focus on efficiency.

To achieve complete strategic fit, a firm must also ensure that all its functions maintain consistent strategies that support the competitive strategy. All functional strategies must support the goals of the competitive strategy. All substrategies within the supply chain—such as manufacturing, inventory, and purchasing—must also be consistent with the supply chain's level of responsiveness. Table 2-4 lists some of the major differences in functional strategy between supply chains that are efficient and those that are responsive.

Tailoring the Supply Chain for Strategic Fit

Our previous discussion focused on achieving strategic fit when a firm serves a single market segment and the result is a well-defined and narrow strategic position. Although such a scenario holds for firms like IKEA, many firms are required to achieve strategic fit while serving many customer segments with a variety of products across multiple channels. In such a scenario, a

Figure 2-6 Different Roles and Allocations of Implied Uncertainty for a Given Level of Supply Chain Responsiveness

TABLE 2-4　Comparison of Efficient and Responsive Supply Chains

	Efficient Supply Chains	**Responsive Supply Chains**
Primary goal	Supply demand at the lowest cost	Respond quickly to demand
Product design strategy	Maximize performance at a minimum product cost	Create *modularity* to allow postponement of product differentiation
Pricing strategy	Lower margins because price is prime customer driver	Higher margins because price not a prime customer driver
Manufacturing strategy	Lower costs through high utilization	Maintain capacity flexibility to buffer against demand/supply uncertainty
Inventory strategy	Minimize inventory to lower cost	Maintain *buffer inventory* to deal with demand/supply uncertainty
Lead-time strategy	Reduce, but not at the expense of costs	Reduce aggressively, even if the costs are significant
Supplier strategy	Select based on cost and quality	Select based on speed, flexibility, reliability, and quality

Source: Based on Marshall L. Fisher, "What Is the Right Supply Chain for Your Product?" Harvard Business.

"one size fits all" supply chain cannot provide strategic fit, and a tailored supply chain strategy is required. For example, Zara sells trendy items with unpredictable demand along with basics, such as white T-shirts, with a more predictable demand. Whereas Zara uses a responsive supply chain with production in Europe for trendy items, it uses a more efficient supply chain with production in Asia for the basics. This tailored supply chain strategy provides a better strategic fit for Zara compared with using a single supply chain. Another example is Levi Strauss, which sells both customized and standard-sized jeans. Demand for standard-sized jeans has a much lower demand uncertainty than demand for customized jeans. As a result, Levi Strauss must tailor its supply chain to meet both sets of needs.

In each of the previous examples, the products sold and the customer segments served have different implied demand uncertainty. When devising supply chain strategy in these cases, the key issue for a company is to design a tailored supply chain that is able to be efficient when implied uncertainty is low and responsive when it is high. By tailoring its supply chain, a company can provide responsiveness to fast-growing products, customer segments, and channels while maintaining low cost for mature, stable products and customer segments.

Tailoring the supply chain requires sharing operations for some links in the supply chain, while having separate operations for other links. The links are shared to achieve maximum possible efficiency while providing the appropriate level of responsiveness to each segment. For instance, all products may be made on the same line in a plant, but products requiring a high level of responsiveness may be shipped using a fast mode of transportation, such as FedEx. Products that do not have high responsiveness needs may be sent by slower and less expensive means such as truck, rail, or even ship. In other instances, products requiring high responsiveness may be manufactured using a flexible process, whereas products requiring less responsiveness may be manufactured using a less responsive but more efficient process. The mode of transportation used in both cases, however, may be the same. In other cases, some products may be held at regional warehouses close to the customer, whereas others may be held in a centralized warehouse far from the customer. W.W. Grainger holds fast-moving items with low implied uncertainty in its decentralized locations close to the customer. It holds slow-moving items with higher implied demand uncertainty in a centralized warehouse. Appropriate tailoring of the supply chain

helps a firm achieve varying levels of responsiveness for a low overall cost. The level of responsiveness is tailored to each product, channel, or customer segment. Tailoring of the supply chain is an important concept that we develop further in subsequent chapters.

The concept of tailoring to achieve strategic fit is important in industries such as high-tech and pharmaceuticals, in which innovation is critical and products move through a life cycle. Let us consider changes in demand and supply characteristics over the life cycle of a product. Toward the beginning stages of a product's life cycle:

1. Demand is very uncertain, and supply may be unpredictable.
2. Margins are often high, and time is crucial to gaining sales.
3. Product availability is crucial to capturing the market.
4. Cost is often a secondary consideration.

Consider a pharmaceutical firm introducing a new drug. Initial demand for the drug is highly uncertain, margins are typically high, and product availability is the key to capturing market share. The introductory phase of a product's life cycle corresponds to high implied uncertainty, given the high demand uncertainty and the need for a high level of product availability. In such a situation, responsiveness is the most important characteristic of the supply chain.

As the product becomes a commodity product later in its life cycle, the demand and supply characteristics change. At this stage, it is typically the case that:

1. Demand has become more certain, and supply is predictable.
2. Margins are lower as a result of an increase in competitive pressure.
3. Price becomes a significant factor in customer choice.

In the case of a pharmaceutical company, these changes occur when demand for the drug stabilizes, production technologies are well developed, and supply is predictable. This stage corresponds to a low level of implied uncertainty. As a result, the supply chain must change. In such a situation, efficiency becomes the most important characteristic of the supply chain. The pharmaceutical industry has reacted by building a mix of flexible and efficient capacity for which use is tailored to the product life cycle. New products are typically introduced using flexible capacity that is more expensive but responsive enough to deal with the high level of uncertainty during the early stages of the life cycle. Mature products with high demand are shifted to dedicated capacity that is highly efficient because it handles low levels of uncertainty and enjoys the advantage of high scale. The tailored capacity strategy has allowed pharmaceutical firms to maintain strategic fit for a wide range of products at different stages of their life cycle.

SUMMARY OF LEARNING OBJECTIVE 2

To achieve strategic fit, a company must first understand the needs of the customers being served and the capabilities of all supply sources. Both the needs and the capabilities should be used to identify the implied uncertainty that the supply chain must absorb. The second step is to understand the supply chain's capabilities in terms of efficiency and responsiveness. The key to strategic fit is ensuring that supply chain responsiveness is consistent with customer needs, supply capabilities, and the resulting implied uncertainty. Tailoring the supply chain is essential to achieving strategic fit when supplying a wide variety of customers with many products through different channels.

SUPPLY CHAIN LEVERS TO DEAL WITH UNCERTAINTY

2.3 Identify the main levers to deal with uncertainty in a supply chain.

There are five basic levers that can be used to deal with uncertainty in a supply chain – capacity, inventory, time, information, and price. Let us start with an example where all five levers are commonly used. Consider a fashion retailer preparing for the fall season. The retailer starts by looking at historical sales and any other information available relating to consumer preferences.

The better the available information, the less uncertainty the retailer faces with regards to anticipated customer demand. Given the uncertainty of demand and the level of service planned for its customers, the retailer must decide on the level of inventory to start the season with. This will depend on the available supply capacity and the time taken by the supplier to fulfill a replenishment order. The more the available supply capacity and the quicker that a replenishment order arrives, the less the starting inventory required by the retailer. As the season progresses, the retailer may decrease prices to spur demand if the available inventory seems to be too high. Finding the right combination of actions in each of the five levers is critical for the retailer's success. As shown in Figure 2-7, a supply chain achieves strategic fit by finding the right balance between these levers to respond to the implied uncertainty it faces.

We now discuss each of the levers and the role they play in dealing with uncertainty.

CAPACITY A combination of excess capacity and flexible capacity can help a supply chain deal with uncertainty. An example of both is the paint mixer found in paint stores in most parts of the world. The mixers are flexible and can mix paint in a large variety of colors. This allows the paint store to deal with the uncertainty of which color a particular customer may want to buy. The capacity of a mixer is large enough that it helps the paint store deal with the uncertainty of the number of customers who will arrive at any time looking for paint. A supply chain must consider the cost of excess capacity and flexibility when using capacity as a lever to deal with uncertainty.

INVENTORY Holding inventory is one of the most common levers used in practice to deal with uncertainty. Most of the inventory sitting at a Chanel store is held because there is uncertainty about the product that customers walking into the store may purchase. A dealer holds a variety of cars in inventory because demand is uncertain. A supply chain must consider the cost of holding inventory when using this lever to deal with uncertainty.

TIME A combination of speedy supply and the willingness of customers to wait can help a supply chain deal with uncertainty. Zara uses its ability to replenish its stores quickly to reduce the underlying uncertainty of demand. Its ability to replenish its stores within 48 hours leaves it vulnerable to uncertainty of demand only over that 48-hour period. In contrast, customers at an integrated steel mill often wait weeks for their product to be delivered. The long promised lead times allow the steel mill to aggregate demand over a long period of time, thus reducing its uncertainty. A supply chain must consider the cost of speedy supply and the potential loss of customers by making them wait when using time as a lever to deal with uncertainty.

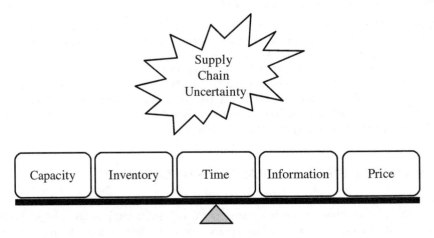

Figure 2-7 Five Key Levers to Deal with Supply Chain Uncertainty

INFORMATION Uncertainty is nothing but an absence of the right information. Thus, investing in the appropriate information can help a supply chain reduce the uncertainty it faces. A well-publicized example is that of Target trying to identify pregnant women so they could send them specially designed ads in their second trimester, which is when expectant mothers start buying new things for themselves and the baby[1]. Statisticians at Target identified about 25 products whose purchasing patterns for shoppers allowed Target to assign each shopper a "pregnancy prediction" score. This information was used by the company to send coupons to each shopper that were timed to match with her needs during specific stages of the pregnancy. Investment in the appropriate information (as opposed to data) allowed Target to significantly reduce its uncertainty when targeting shoppers.

PRICE Prices of products and services that vary over time can help a supply chain deal with uncertainty. Prices of baseball games and even Disney theme parks are higher on busy days. This is similar to what airlines and hotels have done for years by dynamically changing the price they charge based on unused seats or hotel rooms. Close to the scheduled time, prices of seats and rooms go up or down based on whether demand has been high or low up to that point. Apparel retailers constantly vary the discount they offer based on unsold inventory. In each instance, lower prices are used to spur demand if unsold inventory is high relative to demand or higher prices are charged if unsold inventory is low relative to demand. A supply chain needs a lot of real time information about inventory, demand, and customer response to effectively implement dynamic pricing.

As shown in Figure 2-7, a supply chain must find the right balance of these levers to deal with uncertainty. When capacity is cheap, a supply chain may over invest in capacity to save on the other levers. Department stores in India stock almost all men's pants based only on waist size and not length. Tailors on site customize the length in a short period of time as customers finish shopping. The investment in low cost capacity at each store significantly reduces the inventory held at the store. In contrast, a retailer like The Gap in the United States stocks pants based on both waist size and length. While this solution increases the amount of inventory held, it decreases the investment in centralized production capacity. In any supply chain, finding the right balance among the levers is the key to strategic fit.

SUMMARY OF LEARNING OBJECTIVE 3

The implied uncertainty that a supply chain needs to absorb depends on the needs of the customer segment(s) targeted. Capacity, inventory, time, information, and price are the five levers that a supply chain can use to deal with this uncertainty. Investing more in one lever generally allows the supply chain to invest less in one or more of the other levers. To achieve strategic fit, a supply chain must find the right balance between investments in the five levers to effectively serve the target customer segment(s).

EXPANDING STRATEGIC SCOPE

2.4 Discuss the importance of expanding the scope of strategic fit across the supply chain.

A key issue relating to strategic fit is the scope, in terms of supply chain stages, across which the strategic fit applies. *Scope of strategic fit* refers to the functions within the firm and stages across the supply chain that devise an integrated strategy with an aligned objective. At one extreme, every operation within each functional area devises its own independent strategy, with the objective of optimizing its local performance. In this case, the scope of strategic fit is restricted to an operation in a functional area within a stage of the supply chain. At the opposite extreme,

[1] Charles Duhigg. "How Companies Learn Your Secrets," *New York Times*, February 16, 2012, http://www.nytimes.com/2012/02/19/magazine/shopping-habits.html.

all functional areas across all stages of the supply chain devise aligned strategies that maximize supply chain surplus. In this case, the scope of strategic fit extends to the entire supply chain.

In this section, we discuss how expanding the scope of strategic fit improves supply chain performance. For example, IKEA has achieved great success by expanding its scope of strategic fit to include all functions and stages within the supply chain. Its competitive strategy is to offer a reasonable variety of furniture and home furnishings at low prices. Its products are designed to be easy to assemble using modular components. Its stores are large and carry all components in inventory. The large stores and modular design allow IKEA to move final assembly and last-mile delivery (two high-cost operations) to the customer. As a result, all functions within the IKEA supply chain focus on efficiency. Its suppliers concentrate on producing large volumes of a few modules at low cost. Its transportation function focuses on shipping large quantities of high-density unassembled modules at low cost to the large stores. The strategy at every stage and function of the IKEA supply chain is aligned to increase the supply chain surplus.

Intraoperation Scope: Minimizing Local Cost

The *intraoperation scope* has each stage of the supply chain devising its strategy independently. In such a setting, the resulting collection of strategies typically does not align, resulting in conflict and a loss of supply chain surplus. This limited scope was the dominant practice during the 1950s and 1960s, when each operation within each stage of the supply chain attempted to minimize its own costs. As a result of this narrow scope, the transportation function at many firms may have shipped full truckloads without any regard for the resulting impact on inventories or responsiveness, or the sales function may have offered trade promotions to enhance revenue without any consideration for how those promotions affected production, warehousing, and transportation costs. The resulting lack of alignment diminished the supply chain surplus.

Intrafunctional Scope: Minimizing Functional Cost

Over time, managers recognized the weakness of the intraoperation scope and attempted to align all operations within a function. For example, the use of air freight could be justified only if the resulting savings in inventories and improved responsiveness justified the increased transportation cost. With the *intrafunctional* view, firms attempted to align all operations within a function. All supply chain functions, including sourcing, manufacturing, warehousing, and transportation, had to align their strategies to minimize total functional cost. As a result, product could be sourced from a higher-cost local supplier if the resulting decrease in inventory and transportation costs more than compensated for the higher unit cost.

Interfunctional Scope: Maximizing Company Profit

The key weakness of the intrafunctional view is that different functions within a firm may have conflicting objectives. For example, marketing and sales may focus on revenue generation, whereas manufacturing and distribution focus on cost reduction. In this case, the actions taken by the two functions are often in conflict and hurt the firm's overall performance. Over time, companies have realized the importance of expanding the scope of strategic fit and aligning strategy across all functions within the firm. With the interfunctional scope, the goal is to maximize company profit. To achieve this goal, all functional strategies are developed to align with one another and with the competitive strategy.

The goal of aligning strategies across functions results in warehouse operations within McMaster-Carr carrying high inventory and excess capacity to ensure that marketing's promise of next-day delivery is always met. The company's profits grow because the increased margin that customers are willing to pay for high reliability more than compensates for the higher

inventory and warehouse expense. The company enjoys high profits because all functions align their strategy around the common objective of reliable next-day delivery of a wide variety of MRO products.

Intercompany Scope: Maximizing Supply Chain Surplus

The goal of only maximizing company profits can sometimes lead to conflict between stages of a supply chain. For example, both the supplier and the manufacturer in a supply chain may prefer to have the other side hold most of the inventory, with the goal of improving their own profits. If the two parties cannot look beyond their own profits, the more powerful party will simply force the other to hold inventories without any regard for where inventories are best held. The result is a decrease in the supply chain surplus—the total pie that both parties get to share.

The intercompany scope proposes a different approach. Instead of just forcing the inventory onto the weaker party, the two parties work together to reduce the amount of inventory required. By working together and sharing information, they can reduce inventories and total cost, thus increasing the supply chain surplus. The higher the supply chain surplus, the more competitive the supply chain is.

A good example of the intercompany approach is how Walmart and P&G plan promotions jointly. The two companies have a team (with employees from both parties) that works to ensure that the promotion is timed and executed to benefit both sides. Before the initiation of this collaborative effort, promotions at Walmart sometimes required P&G to run its facilities with overtime at high cost. The result was a decrease in the supply chain surplus because the product was sold at a discount at a time when it was being produced at high marginal cost. The collaborative teams now try to increase the supply chain surplus by timing the promotion to have high sales impact while minimizing the marginal cost increase. They work to ensure that the product is produced in such a manner that all promotion demand is met without generating excess unsold inventories.

Agile Intercompany Scope

Up to this point, we have discussed strategic fit in a static context; that is, the players in a supply chain and the customers' needs do not change over time. In reality, the situation is much more dynamic. Product life cycles are getting shorter, and companies must satisfy the changing needs of individual customers. A company may have to partner with many firms, depending on the product being produced and the customer being served. Firms' strategies and operations must be agile enough to maintain strategic fit in a changing environment.

Agile intercompany scope refers to a firm's ability to achieve strategic fit when partnering with supply chain stages that change over time. For example, a company may select both a responsive as well as an efficient supplier for a product. An agile intercompany scope would allow the firm to use the low cost supplier to supply the predictable portion of demand for the product with the responsive supplier being the backup who comes through when demand exceeds supply available from the low cost supplier. The agility to shift demand between the efficient and responsive supplier increases the overall supply chain surplus in an unpredictable environment.

SUMMARY OF LEARNING OBJECTIVE 4

The scope of strategic fit refers to the functions and stages within a supply chain that coordinate strategy and target a common goal. When the scope is narrow, individual functions try to optimize their performance based on their own goals. This practice often results in conflicting actions that reduce the supply chain surplus. As the scope of strategic fit is enlarged to include the entire supply chain, actions are evaluated based on their impact on overall supply chain performance, which helps increase supply chain surplus.

DISCUSSION QUESTIONS

1. How would you characterize the competitive strategy of the Swedish furniture retailer IKEA? What are the key customer needs that IKEA aims to satisfy?
2. How would demand uncertainty and implied demand uncertainty differ for a product like the iPhone 6s Plus?
3. What would be the impact of increasing product variety on implied demand uncertainty faced by a supermarket chain like 7-Eleven?
4. Does implied demand uncertainty correlate with the characteristics of demand, particularly for high markdown products? Why?
5. Reconsider the previous four questions for other companies—an online book seller like the U.K.-based Book Depository, a retailer like the French multinational Carrefour, an automotive manufacturer like the Japanese multinational Toyota, and a discount retailer like the British supermarket retailer ASDA.
6. It is important to have strategic fit between a supply chain and its competitive strategy. What is the supply chain design that would fulfil this purpose? List the capabilities it should have.
7. What do you expect the level of implied demand uncertainty to be for jasmine rice produced by Thailand sold at a supermarket? Explain your answer with reference to Fisher's model.
8. Assume a new drug has been developed for the Ebola virus (EVD). Briefly describe the new drug's demand and supply characteristics at the beginning of its product life cycle.
9. What are some problems that can arise if the same roles are assigned to different stages of a supply chain in order to achieve a strategic fit? Describe how roles should be assigned to help a retailer and a manufacturer work together to expand the scope of strategic fit.
10. With the help of examples, identify the five basic levers that can be used to deal with uncertainty in a supply chain. Describe the role of each lever in enabling a supply chain to achieve strategic fit and effectively serve the target customer segment.

BIBLIOGRAPHY

Blackwell, Roger D., and Kristina Blackwell. "The Century of the Consumer: Converting Supply Chains into Demand Chains." *Supply Chain Management Review* (Fall 1999): 22–32.

Bovet, David M., and David G. Frentzel. "The Value Net: Connecting for Profitable Growth." *Supply Chain Management Review* (Fall 1999): 96–104.

Fine, Charles H. Clock Speed, Winning Industry Control in the Age of Temporary Advantage. Reading, MA: Perseus Books, 1999.

Fisher, Marshall L. "What Is the Right Supply Chain for Your Product?" *Harvard Business Review* (March–April 1997): 83–93.

Fuller, Joseph B., James O'Conner, and Richard Rawlinson. "Tailored Logistics: The Next Advantage." *Harvard Business Review* (May–June 1993): 87–98.

. Gattorna, John. "Supply Chains Are the Business." *Supply Chain Management Review* (September 2006): 42–49.

Gilmore, James H., and B. Joseph Pine II. Markets of One: Creating Customer Unique Value Through Mass Customization. Boston: Harvard Business School Press, 2000.

Lee, Hau L. "Aligning Supply Chain Strategies with Product Uncertainties." *California Management Review* (Spring 2002): 105–119.

Lee, Hau L. "The Triple-A Supply Chain." *Harvard Business Review* (October 2004): 102–112.

Lee, Hau L. "Don't Tweak Your Supply Chain—Rethink It End to End." *Harvard Business Review* (October 2010): 62–69.

Magretta, Joan. "Fast, Global, and Entrepreneurial: Supply Chain Management, Hong Kong Style." *Harvard Business Review* (September–October 1998): 102–114.

Magretta, Joan. "The Power of Virtual Integration: An Interview with Dell Computer's Michael Dell." *Harvard Business Review* (March–April 1998): 72–84.

Nardone, Robert, and Sean Monahan. "How Unilever Aligned Its Supply Chain and Business Strategies." *Supply Chain Management Review* (November 2007): 44–50.

Olavson, Thomas, Hau Lee, and Gavin DeNyse. "A Portfolio Approach to Supply Chain Design." *Supply Chain Management Review* (July–August 2010): 20–27.

Pine, B. Joseph, II. Mass Customization. Boston: Harvard Business School Press, 1999.

Ross, David F. "The Intimate Supply Chain." *Supply Chain Management Review* (July–August 2006): 50–57.

Shapiro, Roy D. "Get Leverage from Logistics." *Harvard Business Review* (May–June 1984): 119–127.

Shapiro, Roy D., and James L. Heskett. Logistics Strategy: Cases and Concepts. St. Paul, MN: West Publishing Company, 1985.

Stalk, George, Jr., and Thomas M. Hout. Competing Against Time. New York: Free Press, 1990.

Swan, Daniel, Sanjay Pal, and Matt Lippert. "Finding the Perfect Fit." *Supply Chain Quarterly* (Quarter 04, 2009): 24–33.

CASE STUDY

The Demise of Blockbuster

After struggling with debt and strong competition from Netflix and Redbox, Blockbuster, Inc. filed for bankruptcy in September 2010. This was a sad end for a company that had dominated the movie rental business in the 1990s. Blockbuster Inc. was founded by David Cook in 1985 with its first rental outlet in Dallas. Cook planned to take advantage of a highly fragmented video rental market, in which most of the stores were relatively modest family operations that carried a small selection of former big hit movies mainly due to the high cost distributors typically charged (about $65 per tape). With 8,000 tapes covering 6,500 titles, Blockbuster had a much broader and deeper inventory compared with that of its nearest competitor. The store operations were also greatly streamlined by a computerized system for inventory control and checkout. The store was a huge success, which prompted the addition of three more locations by mid-1986.

In 1986, because of liquidity problems, Cook was forced to turn over the whole company to a group of investors led by Wayne Huizenga. Between 1987 and 1993, Huizenga grew Blockbuster into an enormous success. During this period, Blockbuster opened stores around the globe at the rate of about one every 24 hours. By 1993, Blockbuster was the leading global provider of in-home movie and game entertainment, with more than 3,400 stores throughout the Americas, Europe, Asia, and Australia. Blockbuster stores were a ubiquitous neighborhood feature that stayed open 365 days a year, generally from 10 a.m. to midnight. Merchandise selection, quantity, and formats were customized at the store level to meet the needs and preferences of local customers.

In the early 2000s, though, Blockbuster began to see real competition from the burgeoning online rental market as DVDs started to replace tapes. Its major competitor was Netflix, launched in 1997. In addition to being cheaper to purchase than tapes, DVDs were well suited for shipping by mail because they were less expensive to ship and less fragile than tapes.

Netflix challenged Blockbuster on two key dimensions—variety and late fees. Whereas Blockbuster stores generally carried about 3,000 titles, Netflix initially offered more than ten times that amount. In addition, Netflix did not charge Blockbuster's greatly disliked "late fees," instead allowing customers to keep titles as long as they wanted. Netflix's monthly subscription plan offered unlimited mail-order rentals for $9, the cost of two rentals at a Blockbuster store.

Meanwhile, Redbox, a unit of Coinstar Inc., operated vending machines that rented DVDs for as little as $1 a night. Despite its best efforts, Blockbuster's brick-and-mortar stores could not match the low-cost operating models of Netflix and Redbox, leading to its bankruptcy (see financial results in Table 2-5).

Netflix

Netflix was founded in 1997 by Reed Hastings as a pay-per-rental mail-order video rental company. After experimenting with both pay-per-rental and subscription, the company settled on a subscription-based strategy by the end of 1999. By 2010, Netflix had 13 million members and was the world's largest subscription service, sending DVDs by mail and streaming movies and television episodes over the Internet. For $8.99 a month, Netflix members could have any of more than 100,000 DVD titles delivered to their homes and could instantly watch a smaller set of television episodes and movies streamed to their televisions and computers. Netflix shipped some 2 million discs daily in the United States.

Netflix focused its strategy around offering a large variety of titles, helping customers navigate titles with a sophisticated recommendation engine, and ensuring that titles reached customers quickly. Whereas a bricks-and-mortar rental store typically carried about 3,000 titles, in 2010 Netflix offered its customers a selection of more than 100,000 DVD titles, most of which were old releases. In 2009, about 70 percent of the DVDs shipped by Netflix were titles with release dates older than thirteen weeks.

In 2010, Netflix had about 60 regional distribution centers across the United States, with sophisticated systems to track customers' DVD queues. As the distribution center processes were linked to the recommendation software, movies that were likely to be in stock were recommended to customers. When the distribution center received a watched DVD back from a customer, a new one from the customer's rental queue was shipped out. These distribution centers were highly automated for rapid processing and were located within driving distance of several U.S. Postal Service processing facilities. Netflix estimated that it would spend about $600 million in 2010 on shipping expenses.

TABLE 2-5 Financial Results for Blockbuster, Netflix, and Coinstar in 2009 (in millions of dollars)

	Blockbuster	Netflix	Coinstar
Revenue	4,062	1,670	1,145
Cost of revenue	1,884	1,079	793
Gross profit	2,178	591	352
Operating expenses			
Sales, general, and administrative	2,020	289	150
Total operating expenses	2,533	399	267
Operating income	(355)	192	85
Net income from continuing operations	(518)	116	29
Net income	(558)	116	54
ASSETS			
Receivables	79	—	61
Inventories	639	37	104
Total current assets	1,060	411	391
Property and equipment at cost	2,374	266	759
Accumulated depreciation	(2,125)	(134)	(358)
Net property, plant, and equipment	249	132	400
Total assets	1,538	680	1,223

Netflix's ability to rent older titles was very appealing to studios that had historically seen little revenue from this content. Netflix bought older DVDs from studios at cost and, in turn, provided them a percentage of the subscription revenue based on utilization for rentals over a specified period (typically 6–12 months). For newer content, Netflix did not attempt to serve the entire initial rush of rental demand. Given the higher initial cost of purchase, the company purchased only a limited number of new release DVDs, preferring instead to wait a few weeks and buy the bulk of its supply at lower cost. Customers could put new titles into their queues and receive them when the DVDs became available in stock.

Between 2005 and 2009, Netflix delivered excellent financial results and grew revenues by 150 percent and profits by about 175 percent. Despite the strong performance of its DVD rental business, however, the company was focused on increasing the fraction of digital content it delivered. Its streaming service, launched in 2007, allowed customers to watch select movies and content on the Netflix website via their PCs. By 2009,

the Netflix service offered more than 17,000 titles (although most new releases were not included in the selection) streamed through a variety of devices. By 2013, the streaming service contributed majority of Netflix's revenue, although most of the profits still came from the DVD mailing business.

Redbox

The concept of Redbox originated in 2002 within McDonald's Ventures, LLC, which was working to identify new ways to drive traffic to its restaurants and provide added convenience and relevance to customers. Redbox's first kiosk was launched in 2004 in Denver. Coinstar, Inc. purchased Redbox in early 2009.

Redbox's strategy was based on targeting the budget-conscious movie renter who wanted to quickly rent a DVD for immediate use. Redbox met this need by placing its automated red kiosks at easily accessible locations, where customers could rent movies for $1 per night. Movies could be returned to any Redbox machine and no membership was required.

By early 2010, Redbox had approximately 23,000 kiosks nationwide, including in select McDonald's restaurants, leading grocery stores, and Walmart, Walgreens, and 7-Eleven stores. Redbox had expanded to over 40,000 kiosks by 2012. Retailers, who were struggling to keep people shopping, realized that having a DVD kiosk in a store created foot traffic. In some cases, retailers even offered discounts that essentially made it free for Redbox to install a kiosk.

Each Redbox kiosk carried about 630 discs, comprising 200 of the newest movie titles. A Redbox kiosk rented its average DVD 15 times at an average of $2 per transaction. After that, the used DVDs were made available for sale to customers for $7.

By mid-2010, Redbox accounted for 25 percent of DVD rental volume, more than Blockbuster. The company was on course to generate more than $1 billion in annual sales, faster than Netflix was able to achieve that milestone.

Study Questions

1. In what ways did Blockbuster achieve better strategic fit than local stores?
2. How much implied uncertainty do Netflix and Redbox face? What levers do they use to deal with this uncertainty?
3. How did Netflix and Redbox achieve better strategic fit than Blockbuster?

CHAPTER

3

Supply Chain Drivers and Metrics

LEARNING OBJECTIVES

After reading this chapter, you will be able to

3.1 Describe key financial measures of firm performance.

3.2 Identify the major drivers of supply chain performance.

3.3 Define the key performance metrics for facilities and discuss their role in creating strategic fit between the supply chain strategy and the competitive strategy.

3.4 Define the key performance metrics for inventory and discuss its role in creating strategic fit between the supply chain strategy and the competitive strategy.

3.5 Define the key performance metrics for transportation and discuss its role in creating strategic fit between the supply chain strategy and the competitive strategy.

3.6 Define the key performance metrics for information and discuss its role in creating strategic fit between the supply chain strategy and the competitive strategy.

3.7 Define the key performance metrics for sourcing and discuss its role in creating strategic fit between the supply chain strategy and the competitive strategy.

3.8 Define the key performance metrics for pricing and discuss its role in creating strategic fit between the supply chain strategy and the competitive strategy.

In this chapter, our goal is to link key financial measures of firm performance to supply chain performance. We introduce the three logistical drivers—facilities, inventory, and transportation—and the three cross-functional drivers—information, sourcing, and pricing—that determine the performance of any supply chain. We discuss how these drivers are used in the design, planning, and operation of the supply chain. We define several metrics that can be used to gauge the performance of each driver and its impact on strategic fit and financial performance.

3.1 Describe key financial measures of firm performance.

FINANCIAL MEASURES OF PERFORMANCE

In Chapter 1, we discussed how growing the supply chain surplus is the ultimate goal of a supply chain. Our premise was that increasing the surplus allows for a growth of supply chain profitability, which facilitates an improvement in the financial performance of each member of the

supply chain. In this section, we define important financial measures that are reported by a firm and affected by supply chain performance. In later sections, we link supply chain drivers and associated metrics to the various financial measures. The definitions of financial measures in this section are taken from Dyckman, Magee, and Pfeiffer (2011). To illustrate the various financial measures, we use the financial results reported in 2013 by Amazon.com and Nordstrom Inc. in Table 3-1 and assume a tax rate of 0.35.

From a shareholder perspective, return on equity (ROE) is the main summary measure of a firm's performance.

$$ROE = \frac{Net\ Income}{Average\ Shareholder\ Equity}$$

Whereas ROE measures the return on investment made by a firm's shareholders, return on assets (ROA) measures the return earned on each dollar invested by the firm in assets. ROA captures the return generated by a firm's operating and investing activities, without regard for how these activities are financed.

$$ROA = \frac{Earnings\ before\ Interest}{Average\ Total\ Assets} = \frac{Net\ Income\ +\ [Interest\ Expense \times (1 - Tax\ Rate)]}{Average\ Total\ Assets}$$

For the financial results reported in Table 3-1, Table 3-2 contains the evaluation of various financial metrics for Amazon.com and Nordstrom Inc. In Table 3-2, we have used 2013 numbers in place of averages, when calculating the various financial metrics. In 2013, Nordstrom had a higher ROE of 38.42 percent compared to Amazon's 2.81 percent. A portion of the difference in ROE can be explained by Nordstrom's much higher ROA of 10.37 percent compared to Amazon's ROA of 0.91 percent. The remaining difference is explained by the amplification of returns provided by the financing used by the two firms. The difference between ROE and ROA is referred to as *return on financial leverage* (ROFL). In 2013, Amazon {Nordstrom} had ROFL = 1.90 percent {28.05 percent}. ROFL captures the amount of ROE that can be attributed to financial leverage (such as accounts payable and debt). In Amazon's case, a significant portion of the financial leverage in 2013 came from accounts payable rather than debt. Thus, an important ratio that defines financial leverage is accounts payable turnover (APT).

$$APT = \frac{Cost\ of\ Goods\ Sold}{Accounts\ Payable}$$

In 2013, Amazon's APT of 2.48 was much lower than Nordstrom's APT of 7.35. The small APT indicates that Amazon was able to use the money it owed suppliers to finance a considerable fraction of its operations. In 2013, Amazon effectively financed its own operations for about 52/2.48 = 20.97 weeks with its suppliers' money.

ROA can be written as the product of two ratios—profit margin and asset turnover—as shown below:

$$ROA = \frac{Earnings\ before\ Interest}{Sales\ Revenue} \times \frac{Sales\ Revenue}{Total\ Assets} = Profit\ Margin \times Asset\ Turnover$$

Thus, a firm can increase ROA by growing the profit margin and/or increasing the asset turnover. In 2013, Nordstrom achieved a much higher profit margin of 6.91 percent compared to Amazon (0.49 percent) while achieving an asset turnover of 1.50 that was only a little bit lower than Amazon's asset turnover of 1.85. The higher profit margin allowed Nordstrom to achieve a higher ROA than Amazon. Profit margin can be improved by receiving better prices from customers or by reducing the various expenses incurred in the supply chain. Although Nordstrom's higher profit margin can be explained partly by its customers' willingness to pay for the greater responsiveness that Nordstrom provides, good supply chain management also allows a firm to decrease the expenses incurred to serve customer demand. An important component of expense

TABLE 3-1 Selected Financial Data for Amazon.com and Nordstrom Inc.

Period Ending	Amazon.com 31-Dec-13	Nordstrom Inc. 2-Feb-13
Total Revenue	74,452,000	12,148,000
Cost of Goods Sold	54,181,000	7,432,000
Gross Profit	20,271,000	4,716,000
Selling, General, and Administrative	19,526,000	3,371,000
Operating Income or Loss	745,000	1,345,000
Total Other Income/Expenses Net	−98,000	–
Earnings Before Interest and Taxes	647,000	1,345,000
Interest Expense	141,000	160,000
Income Before Tax	506,000	1,185,000
Income Tax Expense	161,000	450,000
Minority Interest	−71,000	–
Net Income	274,000	735,000
Assets		
Cash and Cash Equivalents	8,658,000	1,285,000
Short-Term Investments	3,789,000	–
Net Receivables	4,767,000	2,129,000
Inventory	7,411,000	1,360,000
Current Deferred Tax Assets, Net		227,000
Other Current Assets	–	80,000
Total Current Assets	24,625,000	5,081,000
Property, Plant, and Equipment (PP&E)	10,949,000	2,579,000
Goodwill	2,655,000	175,000
Other Assets	1,930,000	254,000
Total Assets	40,159,000	8,089,000
Liabilities and Stockholder Equity		
Accounts Payable	21,821,000	1,011,000
Short-/Current Long-Term Debt	–	7,000
Accrued Salaries, Wages, and Related Benefits		404,000
Other Current Liabilities	1,159,000	804,000
Long-Term Debt	3,191,000	3,124,000
Other Liabilities	4,242,000	341,000
Deferred Long-Term Liability Charges	–	485,000
Total Liabilities	30,413,000	6,176,000
Total Stockholder Equity	9,746,000	1,913,000

is selling, general, and administrative (SG&A), where both Amazon and Nordstrom had comparable spending on SG&A for each dollar of revenue. In Amazon's case, a significant expense is outbound shipping cost. In its 2015 annual report, the company reported outbound shipping costs of $11.54 billion. After accounting for shipping revenue, the net loss on outbound shipping was

TABLE 3-2 A Comparison of Financial Metrics for Amazon.com and Nordstrom Inc.

Metric	Amazon.com	Nordstrom Inc.
ROE	$\dfrac{274}{9{,}746} = 2.81\%$	$\dfrac{735}{1913} = 38.42\%$
ROA	$\dfrac{274 + 141 \times (1 - 0.35)}{40{,}159} = 0.91\%$	$\dfrac{735 + 160 \times (1 - 0.35)}{8{,}089} = 10.37\%$
ROFL	1.90%	28.05%
Profit Margin	$\dfrac{274 + 141 \times (1 - 0.35)}{74{,}452} = 0.49\%$	$\dfrac{735 + 160 \times (1 - 0.35)}{12{,}148} = 6.91\%$
Asset Turnover	$\dfrac{74{,}452}{40{,}159} = 1.85$	$\dfrac{12{,}148}{8{,}089} = 1.50$
APT	$\dfrac{54{,}181}{21{,}821} = 2.48$	$\dfrac{7{,}432}{1{,}011} = 7.35$
ART	$\dfrac{74{,}452}{4{,}767} = 15.62$	$\dfrac{12{,}148}{2{,}129} = 5.71$
INVT	$\dfrac{54{,}181}{7{,}411} = 7.31$	$\dfrac{7{,}432}{1{,}360} = 5.46$
PPET	$\dfrac{74{,}452}{10{,}949} = 6.80$	$\dfrac{12{,}148}{2{,}579} = 4.71$
C2C	$-\dfrac{1}{2.48} + \dfrac{1}{15.62} + \dfrac{1}{7.31}$ $= -0.20 \text{ years} = -10.53 \text{ weeks}$	$-\dfrac{1}{7.35} + \dfrac{1}{5.71} + \dfrac{1}{5.46}$ $= 0.22 \text{ years} = 11.56 \text{ weeks}$
SG&A / Revenue	$\dfrac{19{,}526}{74{,}452} = 26.23\%$	$\dfrac{3{,}371}{12{,}148} = 27.75\%$

reported to be $5.02 billion, about 19 times its net income that year. Clearly, a reduction in outbound shipping costs can have a significant impact on Amazon's profit margin.

The key components of asset turnover are accounts receivable turnover (ART); inventory turnover (INVT); and property, plant, and equipment turnover (PPET). These are defined as follows:

$$ART = \frac{Sales\ Revenue}{Accounts\ Receivable}; INVT = \frac{Cost\ of\ Good\ Sold}{Inventory}; PPET = \frac{Sales\ Revenue}{PP\ \&\ E}$$

Amazon collected its money from sales relatively quickly with an ART of 15.62, whereas Nordstrom took almost 3 times longer with an ART of 5.71. It is impressive that Nordstrom turned its inventory almost as fast as Amazon (5.46 vs. 7.31 turns) despite being a brick-and-mortar retailer with several hundred stores. PPET is a measure of the revenue generated by a firm for each dollar invested in PP&E. Amazon generated $6.80 of revenue for each dollar invested in PP&E compared to $4.71 for Nordstrom. Amazon achieved a higher asset turnover than Nordstrom by turning its inventory faster and generating higher revenue per dollar invested in PP&E. A company can improve its asset turnover by turning its inventory more quickly or using its existing warehousing and technology infrastructure to support a higher level of sales (or decreasing the warehousing and technology infrastructure needed to support the existing level of sales). Nordstrom achieved a higher ROA than Amazon because it had a much higher profit margin. A company can improve its profit margin by increasing a customer's willingness to pay or decreasing operating expense.

Another useful metric is the cash-to-cash (C2C) cycle, which roughly measures the average amount of time from when cash enters the process as cost to when it returns as collected revenue.

TABLE 3-3 Selected Financial Metrics Across Industries, 2000–2012

Industry	Average Operating Margin	Average C2C Cycle (days)	Average Inventory Turns	Average SG&A Cost/ Revenue
Pharmaceutical	0.25	190.3	2.0	0.31
Medical device manufacturers	0.18	211.6	2.2	0.36
Consumer packaged goods	0.17	28.3	5.6	0.31
Food	0.16	37.4	6.2	0.23
Consumer electronics	0.12	9.3	43.8	0.14
Apparel	0.10	127.7	3.2	0.35
Chemical	0.09	78.1	5.3	0.09
Automotive	0.04	75.9	9.9	0.13

Source: Based on Abby Mayer, "Supply Chain Metrics That Matter: A Closer Look at the Cash-to-Cash Cycle (2000–2012)." Supply Chain Insights LLC report, November 11, 2013.

$$C2C = -Weeks\ Payable\ (1/APT) + Weeks\ in\ Inventory(1/INVT)$$
$$+Weeks\ Receivable\ (1/ART)$$

With a C2C of -10.53 weeks in 2013, Amazon collected its money from the sale of products more than 10 weeks before it had to pay its suppliers. Table 3-3 shows selected financial metrics across industries. It is interesting to observe that the consumer electronics industry has an average C2C cycle of only 9.3 days, whereas medical device manufacturers average more than 200 days.

It is worth pointing out that PPET has been coming down for Amazon as it has increased its investment in infrastructure. In 2010, Amazon achieved a PPET of 14.17 compared to 6.80 in 2013. It is important to understand which metrics Amazon hopes to improve with its increased investment in infrastructure.

There are two important measures, however, that are not explicitly part of a firm's financial statements: markdowns and lost sales. *Markdowns* represent the discounts required to convince customers to buy excess inventory. Financial statements show only the revenue received from sales, not the revenue that "could" have been received. For General Motors (GM), one of the biggest problems in the early part of the twenty-first century was the discounts required to move excess inventory from dealer lots. These discounts significantly hurt financial performance. In 2010, one of the biggest improvements in financial performance for GM was its ability to sell its cars with much smaller discounts because the supply chain had far less excess inventory. *Lost sales* represent customer sales that did not materialize because of the absence of products the customer wanted to buy. Every lost sale corresponds to product margin that is lost. Both markdowns and lost sales reduce net income and arguably represent the biggest impact of supply chain performance on the financial performance of a firm. Firms such as Seven Eleven Japan and Zara have achieved strong financial performance in large part because their supply chains allow a better matching of supply and demand, thereby reducing markdowns and lost sales.

In the next section, we identify key drivers of supply chain performance that influence the financial performance of a firm. Our goal is to understand how these drivers may explain the difference in financial performance between firms such as Amazon and Nordstrom.

SUMMARY OF LEARNING OBJECTIVE 1

The key financial metrics of firm performance include return on equity; return on assets; accounts payable turnover; profit margin; asset turnover; accounts receivable turnover; inventory turns; property, plant, and equipment turns; cash-to-cash cycle; and SG&A/revenue. Markdowns and lost sales are two important financial measures of supply chain performance that are not recorded in financial statements.

A FRAMEWORK FOR SUPPLY CHAIN DECISIONS

3.2 *Identify the major drivers of supply chain performance.*

The strategic fit discussed in Chapter 2 requires that a company's supply chain achieve the balance between responsiveness and efficiency that best supports the company's competitive strategy. This requires a supply chain structure that suitably deals with the uncertainty implied by the strategy. Related to the five levers to deal with uncertainty that were discussed in Chapter 2, we identify six supply chain drivers whose interaction defines the performance of a supply chain as shown in Figure 3-1. Facilities, inventory, and transportation together form the logistical drivers responsible for the effective production, storage, and movement of goods. Information, sourcing, and pricing form the set of cross-functional drivers that play a role in every supply chain activity. Observe that the five drivers – facilities, inventory, transportation, information, and pricing – correspond directly to the five levers – capacity, inventory, time, information, and price – for dealing with uncertainty. Sourcing is added as a sixth driver because this is a decision that must be made for each supply chain activity. It is important to realize that these drivers do not act independently but interact to determine the overall supply chain performance. Good supply chain design and operation recognize this interaction and structure the drivers to achieve the desired level of responsiveness at the lowest possible cost, thus improving the supply chain surplus and the firm's financial performance.

Having more facilities generally makes a chain more responsive but increases the amount of inventory required, whereas having fewer, central facilities creates higher efficiency. Holding higher levels of inventory increases the responsiveness of a supply chain, whereas keeping inventory low increases the chain's efficiency. Using faster modes of transportation increases a chain's responsiveness and may lower the inventory required, whereas using slower modes generally increases efficiency but may require more inventory. Investing in information can vastly improve

Figure 3-1 Supply Chain Decision-Making Frame work

the supply chain performance on both responsiveness and efficiency. This investment, however, must be made based on the strategic position supported by the other drivers. Appropriate sourcing decisions raise supply chain profits by assigning supply chain functions to the right party, which brings higher economies of scale or a higher level of aggregation of uncertainty. Pricing can be used to attract the right target customer segment. Differential pricing can be used to attract customers who value responsiveness as well as customers who want efficiency. The supply chain can then be structured to provide responsiveness to some customers while improving overall efficiency.

We illustrate this framework using Walmart as an example. Walmart's competitive strategy is to be a reliable, low-cost retailer for a wide variety of mass-consumption goods. This strategy dictates that the ideal supply chain will emphasize efficiency but also maintain an adequate level of responsiveness in terms of product availability. Walmart uses the three logistical and three cross-functional drivers effectively to achieve this type of supply chain performance. With the inventory driver, Walmart maintains an efficient supply chain by keeping low levels of inventory. For instance, Walmart pioneered cross-docking, a system in which inventory is not stocked in a warehouse but rather is shipped to stores from the manufacturer with a brief stop at a distribution center (DC), where product is transferred from inbound trucks from the supplier to outbound trucks to the retail store. This lowers inventory significantly because products are stocked only at stores, not at both stores and warehouses. With respect to inventory, Walmart favors efficiency over responsiveness. On the transportation front, Walmart runs its own fleet, to keep responsiveness high. This increases transportation cost, but the benefits in terms of reduced inventory and improved product availability justify this cost in Walmart's case. In the case of facilities, Walmart uses centrally located DCs within its network of stores to decrease the number of facilities and increase efficiency at each DC. Walmart builds retail stores only where the demand is sufficient to justify having several of them supported by a DC, thereby increasing efficiency of its transportation assets. Walmart has invested significantly more than its competitors in information technology, allowing the company to share information across the supply chain with suppliers that manufacture only what is being demanded. As a result, Walmart is a leader in its use of the information driver to improve responsiveness and decrease inventory investment. With regard to the sourcing driver, Walmart identifies efficient sources for each product it sells. Walmart feeds them large orders, allowing them to be efficient by exploiting economies of scale. Finally, for the pricing driver, Walmart practices "everyday low pricing" (EDLP) for its products. This ensures that customer demand stays steady and does not fluctuate with price variations. The entire supply chain then focuses on meeting this demand in an efficient manner. Walmart uses all the supply chain drivers to achieve the right balance between responsiveness and efficiency so its competitive strategy and supply chain strategy are aligned.

Another example is the sale of furniture at IKEA. The primary goal of this supply chain is to deliver a low price and acceptable quality. Modular design and unassembled furniture allow IKEA to carry components rather than finished products in inventory at its stores. The large stores and low component variety allows IKEA to keep inventories low while ensuring a high level of availability. Relatively large and stable replenishment orders for components allow IKEA's suppliers to focus on efficiency. Low-cost modes of transportation are used to ship densely packed components from suppliers to stores. In this instance, holding relatively low-cost component inventory at IKEA stores allows the supply chain to become efficient by lowering transportation and production costs. In contrast, some U.S. furniture makers have chosen to focus on providing variety without relying on the customer to assemble modular components at home. Given the high variety and high prices of the furniture, keeping inventory of all finished products at a retailer would be very expensive. In this case, the supply chain has been designed so the retailer carries little inventory. Customers place their orders with the retailer after seeing one variant of the furniture and selecting among the various options. The supply chain is made responsive by using information technology to convey order information effectively, structuring

flexible manufacturing facilities to be able to produce quickly in small lots, and using responsive transportation to deliver the furniture to the customer. In this instance, responsive facilities, transportation, and information are used to lower inventory costs. As the rest of this chapter will illustrate, the key to achieving strategic fit and strong financial performance across the supply chain is to structure the supply chain drivers appropriately to provide the desired level of responsiveness at the lowest possible cost.

Doheny et al. (2010) point out that supply chain performance affects nearly 35 percent of the financial performance of apparel retailers. As a percentage of sales, they state that markdowns, representing 10 to 30 percent of sales, and lost sales, representing 5 to 10 percent of sales, are the dominant drivers of retailers' financial performance. They further state that transportation represents 2 to 5 percent, warehousing 1 to 3 percent, store product handling 3 to 5 percent, and inventory costs 2 to 5 percent of sales. Although the precise fraction will vary for different supply chains, it is evident that supply chain performance along the six drivers has a significant influence on a firm's financial performance.

We devote the next six sections to a detailed discussion of each of the three logistical and three cross-functional drivers, their roles in the supply chain, and their impact on strategic fit and financial performance.

SUMMARY OF LEARNING OBJECTIVE 2

The major drivers of supply chain performance are facilities, inventory, transportation, information, sourcing, and pricing. Each driver affects the balance between responsiveness and efficiency and the resulting strategic fit. Thus, it is important for supply chain designers to structure the six drivers appropriately to achieve strategic fit.

FACILITIES

3.3 Define the key performance metrics for facilities and discuss their role in creating strategic fit between the supply chain strategy and the competitive strategy.

Facilities are the actual physical locations in the supply chain network where product is stored, fabricated, or assembled. The two major types of facilities are production sites and storage sites. Decisions regarding the role, location, capacity, and flexibility of facilities have a significant impact on the supply chain's performance. For example, in 2015, Amazon increased the number of warehousing facilities (and, as a result, experienced an increase in PP&E) located close to customers to improve its responsiveness. In contrast, Best Buy tried to improve its efficiency in 2013 by shutting down retail facilities even though it reduced responsiveness. Facility costs show up under PP&E if facilities are owned by the firm or under SG&A if they are leased. In this section, we discuss the role that facilities play in the supply chain and critical facility-related decisions that supply chain managers need to make.

Role in the Supply Chain

Firms can increase responsiveness by increasing the number of facilities, making them more flexible, or increasing capacity. Each of these actions, however, comes at a cost. Increasing the number of facilities increases facility and inventory costs but decreases outbound transportation costs and reduces response time. Increasing the flexibility or capacity of a facility increases facility costs but decreases inventory costs and response time. Thus, each supply chain must find the appropriate trade off when designing its facilities network. Whereas IKEA has become profitable by opening a few hundred large stores (no more than one or two per city) to grow efficiency, Seven-Eleven Japan has grown profitability by opening a highly dense network of stores (often hundreds per city) to provide responsiveness. Both companies are successful because the facility decisions are aligned with the supply chain strategy.

EXAMPLE 3-1	Toyota and Honda

Both Toyota and Honda use facilities decisions to be more responsive to their customers. These companies have an end goal of opening manufacturing facilities in every major market that they enter. Although there are other benefits to opening local facilities, such as protection from currency fluctuation and trade barriers, the increase in responsiveness plays a large role in Toyota's and Honda's decision to place facilities in their local markets. Toyota maintains about 20 percent excess capacity at each plant to meet demand effectively despite any fluctuations in demand or production delays. The flexibility of Honda facilities to assemble both SUVs and cars in the same plant allowed the company to stay profitable in the downturn of 2008. While competitors' SUV production facilities were idle, Honda facilities maintained a high level of utilization.

Components of Facilities Decisions

Decisions regarding facilities are a crucial part of supply chain design. We now identify components of facilities decisions that companies must analyze.

CAPABILITY Firms must decide whether production facilities will be flexible, dedicated, or a combination of the two. Flexible capacity can be used for many types of products but is often less efficient, whereas dedicated capacity can be used for only a limited number of products but is more efficient. Firms must also decide whether to design a facility with a product focus or a functional focus. A product-focused facility performs all functions (e.g., fabrication *and* assembly) needed for producing a single type of product. A functional-focused facility performs a given set of functions (e.g., fabrication *or* assembly) on many types of products. A product focus tends to result in more expertise about a particular type of product at the expense of the functional expertise that comes from a functional methodology.

For warehouses and DCs, firms must decide whether they will be primarily cross-docking facilities or storage facilities. At cross-docking facilities, inbound trucks from suppliers are unloaded; the product is broken into smaller lots and is quickly loaded on to store-bound trucks. Each store-bound truck carries a variety of products, some from each inbound truck. For storage facilities, firms must decide on the products to be stored at each facility.

LOCATION Deciding where a company will locate its facilities constitutes a large part of the design of a supply chain. A basic trade-off here is whether to centralize to gain economies of scale or to decentralize to become more responsive by being closer to the customer. Companies must also consider a host of issues related to the various characteristics of the local area in which the facility is situated. These include taxes and tariffs, quality of workers, cost of workers, cost of facility, availability of infrastructure, proximity to customers, the location of that firm's other facilities, and other strategic factors.

CAPACITY Companies must also determine a facility's capacity to perform its intended function. A large amount of excess capacity allows the facility to respond to wide swings in the demands placed on it. Excess capacity, however, costs money and therefore can decrease efficiency. A facility with little excess capacity will likely be more efficient per unit it produces than one with a lot of unused capacity. The high-utilization facility, however, will have difficulty responding to demand fluctuations. A firm must also determine how flexible the capacity will be. Whereas flexible capacity is expensive, it is better able to deal with fluctuations in demand across products. Therefore, a company must make a trade-off to determine the right amount of capacity and flexibility to have at each of its facilities.

DEMAND ALLOCATION Companies must determine the markets (in terms of both geography and products) that each facility will serve. Given the location, capacity, and flexibility of facilities, the allocation of geographic markets and products to facilities should be revisited at least annually as market conditions change.

FACILITY-RELATED METRICS Facility-related decisions affect both the financial performance of the firm and the supply chain's responsiveness to customers. On the financial side, facility decisions have an impact on the cost of goods sold, assets in PP&E (if facilities are owned), and SG&A expense (if facilities are leased). A manager should track the following facility-related metrics that influence supply chain performance:

- *Capacity* measures the maximum amount a facility can process.
- *Utilization* measures the fraction of capacity that is currently being used in the facility. Utilization affects both the unit cost of processing and the associated delays. Unit costs tend to decline (PPET increases) and delays increase with increasing utilization.
- *Processing/setup/down/idle time* measures the fraction of time that the facility was processing units, being setup to process units, unavailable because it was down, or idle. Ideally, utilization should be limited by demand and not setup or down time.
- *Quality losses* measure the fraction of production lost as a result of defects. Quality losses hurt both financial performance and responsiveness.
- *Production cost per unit* measures the average cost to produce a unit of output. These costs may be measured per unit, per case, or per pound, depending on the product.
- *Theoretical flow/cycle time of production* measures the time required to process a unit if there are absolutely no delays at any stage.
- *Actual average flow/cycle time* measures the average actual time taken for all units processed over a specified duration, such as a week or a month. The actual flow/cycle time includes the theoretical time and any delays. This metric should be used when setting due dates for orders.
- *Product variety* measures the number of products or product families processed in a facility. Processing costs and flow times are likely to increase with product variety.
- *Volume contribution of top 20 percent SKUs and customers* measures the fraction of total volume processed by a facility that comes from the top 20 percent of SKUs or customers. An 80/20 outcome, in which the top 20 percent contribute 80 percent of volume, indicates likely benefits from focusing the facility so separate processes are used to process the top 20 percent and the remaining 80 percent.
- *Average production batch size* measures the average amount produced in each production batch. Large batch sizes will decrease production cost but increase inventories.
- *Production service level* measures the fraction of production orders completed on time and in full.

SUMMARY OF LEARNING OBJECTIVE 3

The major facility related decisions include identifying the number of facilities, the extent of flexibility, the level of capacity, and the markets served by each facility. Increasing the number of facilities, their flexibility, or their excess capacity increases responsiveness but hurts efficiency. Key facility-related metrics are capacity, utilization, processing/setup/down/idle time, quality, theoretical flow/cycle time of production, actual flow/cycle time, product variety, volume contribution of top 20 percent SKUs/customers, average production batch size, and service level.

3.4 *Define the key performance metrics for inventory and discuss its role in creating strategic fit between the supply chain strategy and the competitive strategy.*

INVENTORY

Inventory encompasses all raw materials, work in process, and finished goods within a supply chain. The inventory belonging to a firm is reported under assets. Changing inventory policies can dramatically alter the supply chain's efficiency and responsiveness. For example, W.W. Grainger makes itself responsive by stocking large amounts of inventory and satisfying customer demand from stock even though the high inventory levels reduce efficiency. Such a practice makes sense for Grainger because its products hold their value for a long time. A strategy using high inventory levels, though, can be dangerous in the fashion apparel business where inventory loses value relatively quickly with changing seasons and trends. Rather than hold high levels of inventory, Spanish apparel retailer Zara has worked hard to shorten new product and replenishment lead times. As a result, the company is very responsive but carries low levels of inventory. In this section, we discuss the role that inventory plays in the supply chain and how managers use inventory to drive supply chain performance.

Role in the Supply Chain

Inventory exists in the supply chain because of a mismatch between supply and demand. This mismatch is intentional at a steel manufacturer, where it is economical to manufacture in large lots that are then stored for future sales. The mismatch is also intentional at a retail store where inventory is held in anticipation of unknown future demand. In these instances, inventory is held to reduce cost or increase the level of product availability.

Inventory affects the assets held, the costs incurred, and responsiveness provided in the supply chain. High levels of inventory in an apparel supply chain improve responsiveness but also leave the supply chain vulnerable to the need for markdowns, lowering profit margins. A higher level of inventory also facilitates a reduction in production and transportation costs because of improved economies of scale in both functions. This choice, however, increases inventory holding cost. Low levels of inventory improve inventory turns but may result in lost sales if customers are unable to find products they are ready to buy. In general, managers should aim to reduce inventory in ways that do not increase cost or reduce responsiveness.

Inventory also has a significant impact on the material flow time in a supply chain. *Material flow time* is the time that elapses between when material enters the supply chain to when it exits. For a supply chain, *throughput* is the rate at which sales occur. If inventory is represented by I, flow time by T, and throughput by D, the three can be related using Little's law as follows:

$$I = DT \tag{3.1}$$

For example, if an Amazon warehouse holds 100,000 units in inventory on average, and sells 1,000 units daily, Little's law tells us that the average unit spends $100,000/1,000 = 100$ days in inventory. If Amazon were able to reduce flow time to 50 days while holding throughput constant, it would reduce inventory to 50,000 units. Note that in this relationship, inventory and throughput must have consistent units.

EXAMPLE 3-2	**Amazon.com**

Amazon attempts to provide a wide variety of books (among other products) to its customers. Best-selling books are stocked in many regional warehouses close to customers for high responsiveness. Slower-moving books are stocked at fewer warehouses to lower the cost of inventory at the expense of some responsiveness. Some of the slowest-moving books are not held in inventory but are obtained from the publisher/distributor or printed on demand when requested by a customer. Amazon changes the form, location, and quantity of inventory it holds by the level of sales of a book to provide the right balance of responsiveness and efficiency.

Components of Inventory Decisions

We now identify major inventory-related decisions that supply chain managers must make to find the right balance between efficiency and responsiveness.

CYCLE INVENTORY *Cycle inventory* is the average amount of inventory used to satisfy demand between receipts of supplier shipments. The size of the cycle inventory is a result of the production, transportation, or purchase of material in large batches. Companies produce or purchase in large batches to exploit economies of scale and lower cost in the production, transportation, or purchasing process. With the increase in batch size, however, comes an increase in inventory and associated carrying costs. As an example of a cycle inventory decision, consider an online book retailer. This retailer's sales average around 10 truckloads of books a month. The cycle inventory decisions the retailer must make are how much to order for replenishment and how often to place these orders. The retailer could order 10 truckloads once each month or it could order one truckload every three days. The basic tradeoff supply chain managers face is between ordering in large batches and holding high levels of cycle inventory or ordering more frequently and incurring a higher replenishment cost.

SAFETY INVENTORY *Safety inventory* is inventory held in case demand exceeds expectation; it is held to counter uncertainty. If the world were perfectly predictable, only cycle inventory would be needed. Because demand is uncertain and may exceed expectations, however, companies hold safety inventory to satisfy an unexpectedly high demand. Managers face a key decision when determining how much safety inventory to hold. For example, a toy retailer such as Toys "R" Us must calculate its safety inventory for the holiday buying season. If it has too much safety inventory, toys will go unsold and may have to be discounted after the holidays. If the company has too little safety inventory, however, then Toys "R" Us will lose sales, along with the margin those sales would have brought. Therefore, choosing safety inventory involves making a trade-off between the costs of having too much inventory and the costs of losing sales owing to not having enough inventories.

SEASONAL INVENTORY *Seasonal inventory* is built up to counter predictable seasonal variability in demand. Companies using seasonal inventory buildup inventory in periods of low demand and store it for periods of high demand, when they will not have the capacity to produce all that is demanded. Managers face key decisions in determining whether to build seasonal inventory and, if they do build it, in deciding how much to build. If a company has volume flexibility and can rapidly change the rate of its production system at very low cost, then it may not need seasonal inventory. However, if changing the rate of production is expensive (e.g., when workers must be hired or fired), then a company would be wise to establish a smooth production rate and build up its inventory during periods of low demand. Therefore, the basic tradeoff supply chain managers face in determining how much seasonal inventory to build is the cost of carrying the additional seasonal inventory versus the cost of having a more flexible production rate.

LEVEL OF PRODUCT AVAILABILITY *Level of product availability* is the fraction of demand that is served on time from product held in inventory. A high level of product availability provides a high level of responsiveness but increases cost because much inventory is held but rarely used. In contrast, a low level of product availability lowers inventory holding cost but results in a higher fraction of customers who are not served on time. The basic trade-off when determining the level of product availability is between the cost of inventory to increase product availability and the loss from not serving customers on time.

INVENTORY-RELATED METRICS Inventory-related decisions affect the cost of goods sold, the C2C cycle, the assets held by the supply chain, and its responsiveness to customers.

A manager should track the following inventory-related metrics that influence supply chain performance:

- *C2C cycle time* is a high-level metric that includes inventories, accounts payable, and receivables.
- *Average inventory* measures the average amount of inventory carried. Average inventory should be measured in units, days of demand, and financial value.
- *Inventory turns* measure the number of times inventory turns over in a year. It is the ratio of average inventory to either the cost of goods sold or sales.
- *Products with more than a specified number of days of inventory* identify the products for which the firm is carrying a high level of inventory. This metric can be used to identify products that are in oversupply or to identify reasons that justify the high inventory, such as price discounts or a product being a very slow mover.
- *Average replenishment batch size* measures the average amount in each replenishment order. The batch size should be measured by SKU in terms of both units and days of demand. It can be estimated by averaging over time the difference between the maximum and the minimum inventory (measured in each replenishment cycle) on hand.
- *Average safety inventory* measures the average amount of inventory on hand when a replenishment order arrives. Average safety inventory should be measured by SKU in both units and days of demand. It can be estimated by averaging over time the minimum inventory on hand in each replenishment cycle.
- *Seasonal inventory* measures the amount by which the inflow of product exceeds its sales (beyond cycle and safety inventory). Seasonal inventory is built up solely to deal with anticipated spikes in demand.
- *Fill rate* measures the fraction of orders/demand that is met on time from inventory. Fill rate should be averaged not over time but over a specified number of units of demand (say, every thousand or million).
- *Fraction of time out of stock* measures the fraction of time that a particular SKU had zero inventory. This fraction can be used to estimate the lost sales during the stockout period.
- *Obsolete inventory* measures the fraction of inventory older than a specified obsolescence date.

SUMMARY OF LEARNING OBJECTIVE 4

The major inventory related decisions include identifying the batch size, the safety inventory, the seasonal inventory, and the level of product availability. Increasing the safety inventory and level of product availability increases responsiveness but hurts efficiency. Increasing the batch size and seasonal inventory increases holding costs but may decrease production, transportation, and purchasing costs. Key inventory-related metrics are average inventory, turns, products with more than a specified number of days of inventory, average replenishment batch size, average safety inventory, seasonal inventory, fill rate, and fraction of time out of stock.

3.5 *Define the key performance metrics for transportation and discuss its role in creating strategic fit between the supply chain strategy and the competitive strategy.*

TRANSPORTATION

Transportation entails moving inventory from point to point in the supply chain. Transportation can take the form of many combinations of modes and routes, each with its own performance characteristics. Transportation choices have a large impact on supply chain responsiveness and efficiency. For example, a mail-order catalog company can use a faster mode of transportation such as FedEx to ship products, thus making its supply chain more responsive—but also less efficient, given the high costs associated with using FedEx. This choice may allow the company to reduce inventories by holding them in a single warehouse in Memphis. In contrast, McMaster-Carr and W.W. Grainger have structured their supply chains to provide next-day service to most of

their customers using ground transportation. To facilitate this level of responsiveness both companies have multiple warehouses across the United States resulting in higher inventory and facility costs than would be incurred in a single warehouse. Outbound transportation costs of shipping to the customer are typically included in SG&A, whereas inbound transportation costs are typically included in the cost of goods sold. In this section, we discuss the role that transportation plays in the supply chain and key transportation-related decisions that supply chain managers must make.

Role in the Supply Chain

Transportation moves product between different stages in a supply chain and affects both responsiveness and efficiency. Faster transportation is more expensive but allows a supply chain to be more responsive. A supply chain using faster transportation may carry lower inventories and have fewer facilities.

The appropriate choice of transportation allows a firm to adjust the location of its facilities and inventory to find the right balance between responsiveness and efficiency. A firm selling high-value items such as pacemakers may use rapid transportation to be responsive while centralizing its facilities and inventory to lower cost. In contrast, a firm selling low-value, high-demand items like light bulbs may carry a fair amount of inventory close to the customer but then use low-cost transportation such as sea, rail, and full trucks to replenish this inventory from plants located in low-cost countries.

EXAMPLE 3-3 **Blue Nile**

Blue Nile is an online retailer of diamonds that has used responsive transportation with FedEx to ship diamonds to customers in the United States, Canada, and several countries in Europe and Asia. Given the high value of diamonds, Blue Nile offers free shipping for overnight delivery. Responsive shipping, however, allows Blue Nile to centralize its inventory of diamonds and eliminate the need for expensive storefronts. In spite of the high transportation costs, Blue Nile has very low costs compared with those of bricks-and-mortar retailers because of the low facility and inventory expenses. Blue Nile is thus able to offer significantly lower prices than its bricks-and-mortar competition.

Components of Transportation Decisions

We now identify key components of transportation that companies must analyze when designing and operating a supply chain.

DESIGN OF TRANSPORTATION NETWORK The transportation network is the collection of transportation modes, locations, and routes along which product can be shipped. A company must decide whether transportation from a supply source will be direct to the demand point or will go through intermediate consolidation points. Design decisions also include whether or not multiple supply or demand points will be included in a single run.

CHOICE OF TRANSPORTATION MODE The mode of transportation is the manner in which a product is moved from one location in the supply chain network to another. Companies can choose among air, truck, rail, sea, and pipeline as modes of transport for products. Information goods can also be sent via the Internet. Each mode has different characteristics with respect to the speed, size of shipments (individual parcels to pallets to full trucks to entire ships), cost of shipping, and flexibility that lead companies to choose one particular mode over the others.

TRANSPORTATION-RELATED METRICS Inbound transportation decisions affect the cost of goods sold (COGS), whereas outbound transportation costs are part of the SG&A. Thus,

transportation costs affect the profit margin. A manager should track the following transportation-related metrics that influence supply chain performance:

- *Average inbound transportation cost* typically measures the cost of bringing product in to a facility. Ideally, this cost should be measured per unit brought in, but it is often measured as a percentage of sales or COGS. The inbound transportation cost is generally included in COGS. It is useful to measure this cost separately for each supplier.
- *Average incoming shipment size* measures the average number of units or dollars in each incoming shipment at a facility.
- *Average inbound transportation cost per shipment* measures the average transportation cost of each incoming delivery. Along with the incoming shipment size, this metric identifies opportunities for greater economics of scale in inbound transportation.
- *Average outbound transportation cost* measures the cost of sending product out of a facility to the customer. Ideally, this cost should be measured per unit shipped, but it is often measured as a percentage of sales. It is useful to separate this metric by customer.
- *Average outbound shipment size* measures the average number of units or dollars on each outbound shipment at a facility.
- *Average outbound transportation cost per shipment* measures the average transportation cost of each outgoing delivery. Along with the outgoing shipment size, this metric identifies opportunities for greater economies of scale in outbound transportation.
- *Fraction transported by mode* measures the fraction of transportation (in units or dollars) using each mode of transportation. This metric can be used to estimate whether certain modes are over used or under used.

SUMMARY OF LEARNING OBJECTIVE 5

The major transportation related decisions include designing the transportation network and selecting the transportation mode. Faster modes of transport are more expensive but can improve responsiveness while helping decrease inventory and facility costs. Key transportation-related metrics are average inbound transportation cost, average incoming shipment size, average inbound transportation cost per shipment, average outbound transportation cost, average outbound shipment size, average outbound transportation cost per shipment, and fraction transported by mode.

3.6 Define the key performance metrics for information and discuss its role in creating strategic fit between the supply chain strategy and the competitive strategy.

INFORMATION

Information consists of data and analysis concerning facilities, inventory, transportation, costs, prices, and customers throughout the supply chain. Information is potentially the biggest driver of performance in the supply chain because it directly affects each of the other drivers. Information presents management with the opportunity to make supply chains more responsive *and* more efficient. For example, Seven-Eleven Japan has used information to better match supply and demand while achieving production and distribution economies. The result is a high level of responsiveness to customer demand while production and replenishment costs are lowered. Information technology related expenses are typically included under either operating expense (typically under SG&A) or assets. For example, in 2012, Amazon included $4.54 billion in technology expense under operating expense and another $454 million under fixed assets to be depreciated. In this section, we discuss the role that information plays in the supply chain, as well as key information-related decisions that supply chain managers must make.

Role in the Supply Chain

Good information can help improve the utilization of supply chain assets and the coordination of supply chain flows to increase responsiveness and reduce costs. Seven-Eleven Japan uses information to improve product availability while decreasing inventories. Wal-Mart uses information

on shipments from suppliers to facilitate cross-docking and lower inventory and transportation expense. Li & Fung, a global trading group supplying time-sensitive consumer goods such as apparel, uses information on its third-party manufacturers to source each order from the most appropriate supplier. Airlines routinely use information to offer the right number of seats at a discount price, leaving sufficient seats for business customers who make reservations at the last minute and are willing to pay a higher price. Each of these examples illustrates the importance of information as a key driver that can be used to provide higher responsiveness while simultaneously improving efficiency.

Even though the sharing of information can help a supply chain better meet customer needs at lower cost, there is a danger in the assumption that more information is always better. As more information is shared across a supply chain, the complexity and cost of both the required infrastructure and the follow-up analysis grow exponentially. As more information becomes available, however, the marginal value provided by additional information diminishes. It is thus important to evaluate the minimum information required to accomplish the desired objectives. For example, it may often be enough if aggregate sales, rather than detailed point-of-sale data, are shared between a retailer and a manufacturer. Aggregate information is cheaper to share and provides most of the value with regard to better production planning. The trade-off between complexity and value is important to consider when setting up the information infrastructure. The following example illustrates how information can be used to improve supply chain performance.

EXAMPLE 3-4	**DHL**

DHL is a logistics and parcel delivery company that operates in more than 140,000 destinations with a presence in more than 220 countries, which involves working in diverse local environments with different languages, cultures, and local knowledge. For DHL, working locally means that its employees and customers have access to accurate tracking information on their packages in their local language. DHL moved from a decentralized information system involving 50 systems to a centralized integrated system to reduce risk and decrease costs and, at the same time, improve customer service. This resulted in a 40 percent reduction in infrastructure costs, coupled with more reliable communications throughout DHL's worldwide operation.[*]

Components of Information Decisions

We now consider key components of information that a company must analyze to improve efficiency and responsiveness within its supply chain.

DEMAND PLANNING *Demand planning* is the process of generating the best estimate of future demand based on historical sales, planned marketing and promotion efforts, and other factors such as the economy and the competition. Besides accounting for all factors that influence demand, a critical element of a good demand plan is the recognition that all forecasts are wrong. Thus, a good demand plan must include an estimation of forecast error. Given a demand plan and an estimate of forecast error, it is then possible to design a supply plan that appropriately balances responsiveness and efficiency.

COORDINATION AND INFORMATION SHARING *Supply chain coordination* occurs when all stages of a supply chain work toward the objective of maximizing total supply chain profitability based on shared information. Lack of coordination often results in different stages of the supply chain having plans that do not align. As a result, responsiveness suffers because the right product is not available at the right time or place, and efficiency suffers because each stage of the supply chain must constantly react to unexpected demand or lack of supply. Coordination among

[*]*Source:* Sullivan, L. "DHL Taps Several Vendors for RFID Project," *TechWeb News*, March 8, 2006; Bloch, M., and Schaper, M. "Building a Global IT Organization: An Interview with DPWN's Managing Director of IT," *The McKinsley Quarterly*, May 2006.

different stages in a supply chain is thus critical for success and requires each stage to share appropriate information with other stages.

SALES AND OPERATIONS PLANNING *Sales and operations planning* (S&OP) is the process of creating an overall supply plan (production and inventories) to meet the anticipated level of demand (sales). The S&OP process starts with sales and marketing communicating their needs to the supply chain, which, in turn, communicates to sales and marketing whether the needs can be met, and at what cost. The goal of S&OP is to come up with an agreed-upon sales, production, and inventory plan that can be used to plan supply chain needs and project revenues and profits. The sales and operations plan becomes a critical piece of information to be shared across the supply chain because it affects both the demand on a firm's suppliers and the supply to its customers.

INFORMATION-RELATED METRICS A manager should track the following information-related metrics that influence supply chain performance:

- *Forecast horizon* identifies how far in advance of the actual event a forecast is made. The forecast horizon must be greater than or equal to the lead time of the decision that is driven by the forecast.
- *Frequency of update* identifies how frequently each forecast is updated. The forecast should be updated somewhat more frequently than a decision will be revisited, so large changes can be flagged and corrective action taken.
- *Forecast error* measures the difference between the forecast and actual demand. The forecast error is a measure of uncertainty and drives all responses to uncertainty, such as safety inventory or excess capacity.
- *Variance from plan* identifies the difference between the planned production/inventories and the actual values. These variances can be used to raise flags that identify shortages and surpluses.
- *Ratio of demand variability to order variability* measures the standard deviation of incoming demand and supply orders placed. A ratio less than 1 potentially indicates the existence of the bullwhip effect, which is discussed in Chapter 10.

SUMMARY OF LEARNING OBJECTIVE 6

The major information related decisions include coming up with a demand plan as well as a sales & operations plan that optimally matches supply and demand. It is important that information is shared across the supply chain to ensure that plans at different stages are coordinated. Key information-related metrics are forecast horizon, forecast error, variance from plan, and ratio of demand variability to order variability.

SOURCING

3.7 Define the key performance metrics for sourcing and discuss its role in creating strategic fit between the supply chain strategy and the competitive strategy.

Sourcing is the choice of who will perform a particular supply chain activity, such as production, storage, transportation, or the management of information. At the strategic level, these decisions determine what functions a firm performs and what functions the firm outsources. Sourcing decisions affect both the responsiveness and efficiency of a supply chain. After Motorola outsourced much of its production to contract manufacturers in China, for instance, it saw its efficiency improve but its responsiveness suffer because of the long lead times. To make up for the drop in responsiveness, Motorola started flying in some of its products from China even though this choice increased transportation cost. Flextronics, an electronics contract manufacturer, is hoping to offer both responsive and efficient sourcing options to its customers. It is trying to make its production facilities in high-cost locations very responsive while keeping its facilities in low-cost countries efficient. Flextronics hopes to become an effective source for all customers using this

combination of facilities. Sourcing costs show up in the cost of goods sold, and monies owed to suppliers are recorded under accounts payable. In this section, we discuss the role that sourcing plays in the supply chain and key sourcing-related decisions that managers need to make.

Role in the Supply Chain

Sourcing is the set of business processes required to purchase goods and services. Managers must first decide whether each task will be performed by a responsive or efficient source and then whether the source will be internal to the company or a third party. Sourcing decisions should be made to increase the size of the total surplus to be shared across the supply chain. Outsourcing to a third party is meaningful if the third party raises the supply chain surplus more than the firm can on its own. In contrast, a firm should keep a supply chain function in-house if the third party cannot increase the supply chain surplus or if the risk associated with outsourcing is significant. For example, W.W. Grainger outsources package delivery to a third party because it is very expensive to build this capability in-house. In contrast, Grainger owns and operates its warehouses because there is sufficient scale to justify this choice. Sourcing decisions should aim to provide the appropriate level of responsiveness at the lowest cost.

The following example illustrates how Zara has sourced appropriately to be efficient for basic products and responsive for trendy products.

EXAMPLE 3-5	Zara

Zara has a sourcing strategy that varies by product type. For basic products such as white T-shirts, Zara aims for efficiency because demand is predictable. These products are sourced from suppliers in low cost countries. For trendy products for which demand is unpredictable, in contrast, Zara sources from company-owned factories in Europe. These factories are not low cost, but they are flexible and responsive to the rapidly evolving needs of the trendy market.

Components of Sourcing Decisions

We now consider key sourcing decisions that are made with in a firm.

IN-HOUSE OR OUTSOURCE The most significant sourcing decision for a firm is whether to perform a task in-house or outsource it to a third party. Within a task such as transportation, managers must decide whether to outsource all of it, outsource only the responsive component, or outsource only the efficient component. This decision should be driven in part by its impact on the total supply chain surplus. It is best to outsource if the growth in total supply chain surplus is significant with little additional risk.

SUPPLIER SELECTION Managers must decide on the number of suppliers they will have for a particular activity. They must then identify the criteria along which suppliers will be evaluated and how they will be selected. A portfolio of suppliers with complementary capabilities is generally superior to having multiple suppliers that are similar. Rather than having two similar suppliers who are reasonably efficient and responsive, it is better to have a low cost supplier who focuses on efficiency and a responsive supplier who absorbs the requests that cannot be handled by the low cost supplier on time.

PROCUREMENT *Procurement* is the process of obtaining goods and services within a supply chain. Managers must structure procurement with a goal of decreasing the total cost of ownership and increasing supply chain surplus. This leads to different objectives when procuring

different types of products. For example, a firm should set up procurement for direct materials to ensure good coordination between the supplier and buyer. In contrast, the procurement of MRO products should be structured to ensure that transaction costs are low.

SOURCING-RELATED METRICS Sourcing decisions have a direct impact on the cost of goods sold and accounts payable. The performance of the source also affects quality, inventories, and inbound transportation costs. A manager should track the following sourcing-related metrics that influence supply chain performance:

- *Days payable outstanding* measures the number of days between when a supplier performed a supply chain task and when it was paid for that task.
- *Average purchase price* measures the average price at which a good or service was purchased during the year. The average should be obtained by weighting each price by the quantity purchased at that price.
- *Range of purchase price* measures the fluctuation in purchase price during a specified period. The goal is to identify if the quantity purchased correlated with the price.
- *Average purchase quantity* measures the average amount purchased per order. The goal is to identify whether a sufficient level of aggregation is occurring across locations when placing an order.
- *Supply quality* measures the quality of product supplied.
- *Supply lead time* measures the average time between when an order is placed and when the product arrives. Long lead times reduce responsiveness and add to the inventory the supply chain must carry.
- *Percentage of on-time deliveries* measures the fraction of deliveries from the supplier that were on time.
- *Supplier reliability* measures the variability of the supplier's lead time as well as the delivered quantity relative to plan. Poor supplier reliability hurts responsiveness and adds to the amount of inventory the supply chain must carry.

SUMMARY OF LEARNING OBJECTIVE 7

The major sourcing related decisions include deciding whether an activity will be insourced or outsourced, identifying key factors in supplier selection, and selecting the supplier portfolio. Key sourcing-related metrics are days payable outstanding, average purchase price, range of purchase price, average purchase quantity, percentage on-time deliveries, supply quality, and supply lead time.

3.8 *Define the key performance metrics for pricing and discuss its role in creating strategic fit between the supply chain strategy and the competitive strategy.*

PRICING

Pricing determines how much a firm will charge for the goods and services that it makes available in the supply chain. Pricing affects the behavior of the buyer of the good or service, thus affecting demand and supply chain performance. For example, if a transportation company varies its charges based on the lead time provided by the customers, it is likely that customers who value efficiency will order early to get a lower price and customers who value responsiveness will wait until the last moment even though it costs more. Differential pricing provides responsiveness to customers that value it and low cost to customers that do not value responsiveness as much. Any change in pricing affects revenues directly but could also affect costs based on the impact of this change on the other drivers. In this section, we discuss the role that pricing plays in the supply chain.

Role in the Supply Chain

Pricing affects the customer segments that choose to buy a product, thus influencing the customer needs that the supply chain must fulfill. This directly affects the supply chain in terms of the level of responsiveness required as well as the demand profile that the supply chain attempts to serve. Pricing is also a lever that can be used to match supply and demand, especially when the supply chain is not very flexible. Short-term discounts can be used to eliminate supply surpluses or decrease seasonal demand spikes by moving some of the demand forward. All pricing decisions should be made with the objective of increasing firm profits. This requires an understanding of the cost structure of performing a supply chain activity and the value this activity brings to the supply chain. Strategies such as EDLP may foster stable demand that allows for efficiency in the supply chain. For example, Costco, a membership-based wholesaler in the United States, has a policy that prices are kept steady but low. The steady prices ensure that demand stays relatively stable. The Costco supply chain exploits the relative stability of demand to be efficient. In contrast, some manufacturing and transportation firms use pricing that varies with the response time desired by the customer. Through their pricing, these firms are targeting a broader set of customers, some of whom need responsiveness while others need efficiency. In this case, it becomes important for these firms to structure a supply chain that can meet the two divergent needs. Amazon uses a menu of shipping options and prices to identify customers who value responsiveness and those who value low cost. This identification allows the company to serve both effectively, as shown in the following example.

EXAMPLE 3-6	**Amazon.com**

Amazon offers its customers a large menu of prices for products that are purchased from the company. For example, in January 2014, a person purchasing two books worth $40 could use standard shipping (3 to 5 business days) at a cost of $4.98, two-day shipping at a cost of $14.97, one-day shipping at a cost of $24.97, or free shipping (5 to 8 business days). The pricing menu allows Amazon to attract customers with varying levels of desired responsiveness. Whereas customers paying for one-day shipping impose a high degree of uncertainty on Amazon, customers opting for free shipping can be used to level out the work load at the warehouse over time. Amazon can thus use its pricing to provide responsiveness to those who value it while using customers who want a low price to help it improve its efficiency.

Components of Pricing Decisions

We now describe key components of pricing decisions that affect supply chain performance.

PRICING AND ECONOMIES OF SCALE Most supply chain activities display economies of scale. Changeovers make small production runs more expensive per unit than large production runs. Loading and unloading costs make it cheaper to deliver a truckload to one location than to four. In each case, the provider of the supply chain activity must decide how to price it appropriately to reflect these economies of scale. A commonly used approach is to offer quantity discounts. Care must be taken to ensure that quantity discounts offered are consistent with the economies of scale in the underlying process. Otherwise, there is a danger of customer orders being driven primarily by the quantity discounts, even though the underlying process does not have significant economies of scale.

EVERY DAY LOW PRICING VERSUS HIGH–LOW PRICING A firm such as Costco practices EDLP at its warehouse stores, keeping prices steady over time. Costco will go to the extent of not offering any discount on damaged books to ensure its EDLP strategy. In contrast, most supermarkets practice high–low pricing and offer steep discounts on a subset of their product every week. The Costco pricing strategy results in relatively stable demand. The high–low pricing strategy results in a peak during the discount week, often followed by a steep drop in demand during the following weeks. The two pricing strategies lead to different demand profiles that the supply chain must serve.

FIXED PRICE VERSUS MENU PRICING A firm must decide whether it will charge a fixed price for its supply chain activities or have a menu with prices that vary with some attribute, such as the response time or location of delivery. If marginal supply chain costs or the value to the customer vary significantly along some attribute, it is often effective to have a pricing menu. The online retailer Jet.com varies the price charged for a product based on the basket of goods a customer has already purchased. The company changes the price of a product to reflect any pick, pack, and ship economies the purchase provides given the current basket. In the United Kingdom, Tesco charges its customers a lower price for coming to a pickup location compared to getting home delivery of their order. In the two examples, the pricing menu tries to reflect the true cost of fulfillment and use this information to influence customer buying behavior.

PRICING-RELATED METRICS Pricing directly affects revenues but can also affect production costs and inventories, depending on its impact on consumer demand. A manager should track the following pricing-related metrics. With menu pricing, each metric should be tracked separately for each segment in the menu:

- *Profit margin* measures profit as a percentage of revenue. A firm needs to examine a wide variety of profit margin metrics to optimize its pricing, including dimensions such as type of margin (gross, net), scope (SKU, product line, division, firm), and customer type.
- *Days sales outstanding* measures the average time between when a sale is made and when the cash is collected.
- *Incremental fixed cost per order* measures the incremental costs that are independent of the size of the order. These include changeover costs at a manufacturing plant or order processing or transportation costs that are incurred independent of shipment size at a mail-order firm.
- *Incremental variable cost per unit* measures the incremental costs that vary with the size of the order. These include picking costs at a mail-order firm or variable production costs at a manufacturing plant.
- *Average sale price* measures the average price at which a supply chain activity was performed in a given period. The average should be obtained by weighting the price with the quantity sold at that price.
- *Average order size* measures the average quantity per order. The average sale price, order size, incremental fixed cost per order, and incremental variable cost per unit help estimate the contribution from performing the supply chain activity.
- *Range of sale price* measures the maximum and the minimum of sale price per unit over a specified time horizon.
- *Range of periodic sales* measures the maximum and minimum of the quantity sold per period (day/week/month) during a specified time horizon. The goal is to understand any correlation between sales and price and any potential opportunity to shift sales by changing price over time.

SUMMARY OF LEARNING OBJECTIVE 8

The major pricing related decisions include deciding whether the firm will offer quantity discounts, whether it will offer everyday low pricing or prices that vary over time, and whether it will offer a fixed price or a menu of prices that vary along some dimension such as response time. Pricing-related metrics are profit margin, days sales outstanding, incremental fixed cost per order, incremental variable cost per unit, average sale price, average order size, range of sale price, and range of periodic sales.

DISCUSSION QUESTIONS

1. Are there any exceptions to the claim that sourcing decisions are always an important factor affecting the supply chain performance for all industries?
2. The flow of information is becoming increasingly important in supply chain management. Describe the key effects of information on supply chain performance in terms of responsiveness and efficiency with reference to the logistics industry.
3. Discuss the following proposition with reference to an automobile garage that handles maintenance and repair: "Modal choice decisions could improve the responsiveness of the supply chain performance."
4. "Price decisions only affect buyers' behavior and not the responsiveness of the supply chain." Comment on this statement with reference to shipping logistics.
5. Consider a retailer like Marks & Spencer (M&S), which is outsourcing parts of its delivery services to a logistics provider. When should such a company choose to operate its own account operation to provide delivery services?
6. What would be the effects of high-low pricing adopted by a supermarket chain on supply chain performance?
7. Identify examples of industries in which product customization by the end customer has proliferated while still maintaining short lead times and competitive pricing. How have the supply chains in these industries adapted to deliver such products?
8. How can the full set of logistical and cross-functional drivers be used to create strategic fit for a furniture manufacturer, specializing in kitchen cabinetry, that targets both time-sensitive and price-conscious customers?
9. Which supply chain drivers should a firm focus on to improve its profit margins?
10. What is the role of supply chain drivers in improving a firm's asset turnover? Refer to the key components of asset turnover to support your answer.

BIBLIOGRAPHY

Davis, Thomas S., and Robert A. Novack. "Why Metrics Matter." Supply Chain Management Review (July/August 2012): 10–17.

Doheny, Mike, Karl-Hendrik Magnus, Paulo Marchesan, Brian Ruwadi, Chris Turner, and Nursen Ulker. "Driving Productivity in the Apparel Supply Chain." December 17, 2010. Available at https://operations-extranet.mckinsey.com/html/knowledge/article/20101213_apparel_supply_chain.asp

Dyckman, Thomas R., Robert P. Magee, and Glenn M. Pfeiffer. Financial Accounting. Westmont, IL: Cambridge Business Publishers, 2011.

Hofman, Debra. "The Hierarchy of Supply Chain Metrics." Supply Chain Management Review (September 2004): 28–37.

Johnson, John. "Metrics that Count." Supply Chain Management Review (March/April 2016): 36–41.

Marien, Edward J. "The Four Supply Chain Enablers." Supply Chain Management Review (March-April 2000): 60–68.

Mayer, Abby. "Supply Chain Metrics That Matter: A Closer Look at the Cash-to-Cash Cycle (2000-2012)." Supply Chain Insights LLC report (November 11, 2013).

Presutti, William D., Jr., and John R. Mawhinney. "The Supply Chain-Finance Link." Supply Chain Management Review (September 2007): 32–38.

CASE STUDY

Seven-Eleven Japan Co.

Established by Ito Yokado in 1973, Seven-Eleven Japan set up its first store in Koto-ku, Tokyo, in May 1974. The company was first listed on the Tokyo Stock Exchange in October 1979. On September 1, 2005, Seven & i Holdings Co. Ltd., was established as the holding company for Seven-Eleven Japan, Ito-Yokado, and Denny's Japan.

As a result, detailed financial results for Seven-Eleven Japan have not been available since then and are reported only as the convenience store portion of Seven & i Holdings. Seven-Eleven Japan realized a phenomenal growth between 1985 and 2016. During that period, the number of stores in Japan increased from 2,299 to more than

19,000. Globally, the firm had more than 60,000 convenience stores by September 2016 and was the world's largest chain in terms of retail outlets. Global revenues for Seven & i from convenience store operations were 2,675 billion yen in 2016 with an operating income of 352 billion yen. The firm opened over 1,600 new stores in Japan in 2016. Customer visits to Seven-Eleven outlets averaged more than 1,000 per store per day in 2013.

Company History and Profile

Both Ito-Yokado and Seven-Eleven Japan were founded by Masatoshi Ito. He started his retail empire after World War II, when he joined his mother and elder brother and began to work in a small clothing store in Tokyo. By 1960, he was in sole control, and the single store had grown into a $3 million company. After a trip to the United States in 1961, Ito became convinced that superstores were the wave of the future. At that time, Japan was still dominated by mom-and-pop stores. Ito's chain of superstores in the Tokyo area was instantly popular and soon constituted the core of Ito-Yokado's retail operations.

In 1972, Ito first approached the Southland Corporation about the possibility of opening Seven-Eleven convenience stores in Japan. After rejecting his initial request, Southland agreed in 1973 to a licensing agreement. In exchange for 0.6 percent of total sales, Southland gave Ito exclusive rights throughout Japan. In May 1974, the first Seven-Eleven convenience store opened in Tokyo. This new concept was an immediate hit in Japan, and Seven-Eleven Japan experienced tremendous growth. By 1979, there were already 591 Seven-Eleven stores in Japan; by 1984, there were 2,001. Rapid growth continued (Table 3-4), resulting in 19,166 stores by 2016.

On October 24, 1990, the Southland Corporation entered into bankruptcy protection. Southland asked for Ito-Yokado's help, and on March 5, 1991, IYG Holding was formed by Seven-Eleven Japan (48 percent) and Ito-Yokado (52 percent). IYG acquired 70 percent of

TABLE 3-4 Stores and Annual Sales for Seven-Eleven Japan

Year	Number of Stores	Annual Sales (billion yen)
1974	15	0.7
1979	801	109.8
1984	2,299	386.7
1989	3,954	780.3
1994	5,905	1,392.3
1999	8,153	1,963.9
2004	10,826	2,440.8
2009	12,753	2,784.9
2010	13,232	2,947.6
2011	14,005	3,280.5
2012	15,072	3,508.4
2013	16,086	3,781.2
2014	16,319	4,008.2
2015	17,491	4,291.0

Source: "Based on Seven Eleven Japan website http://www.sej.co.jp/company/en/s.growth.html."

Southland's common stock for a total price of $430 million.

In 2005, Seven & i Holdings was established through a stock transfer combining Seven-Eleven Japan, Ito-Yokado, and Denny's Japan. In 2015, convenience store operations from Seven-Eleven Japan and other subsidiaries in North America and China contributed 44.3 percent of total revenues from operations and 88.6 percent of operating income for the Seven & i Holdings Company (see Table 3-5 for details). The relative performance of convenience stores within Japanese operations was even more dominant. The discrepancy between

TABLE 3-5 Financial Figures for Seven & i (2013–2015)

For Fiscal Years Ending February 28/29	2013	2014	2015
Total revenues (billion yen)	4,991.6	5,631.8	6,038.9
Total operating income (billion yen)	295.7	339.6	343.3
Convenience store revenues (billion yen)	1,899.5	2,727.8	2,675.9
Convenience store operating income (billion yen)	221.7	276.7	304.1

Source: Based on Seven & i Annual Report 2016.

Tables 3-4 and 3-5 results because Table 3-4 reports sales at both company-owned and franchised stores, whereas Table 3-5 reports revenues for only Seven & i.

The Convenience Store Industry and Seven-Eleven in Japan

The convenience store sector was one of the few business areas that continued to grow during the prolonged slowdown in Japan toward the end of the twentieth century and the start of the twenty-first century. From 1991 to 2013, annual sales at convenience stores more than tripled, from just over 3 trillion to almost 10 trillion yen. As a point of comparison over this period, supermarket sales stayed stable, at about 13 trillion yen.

Japan's convenience store sector gradually consolidated, with larger players growing and smaller operators shutting down. In 2004, the top ten convenience store chains accounted for approximately 90 percent of Japan's convenience stores. By 2015, consolidation had resulted in the top five chains accounting for more than 90 percent and the top three accounting for more than 80 percent of convenience store sales in Japan.

Seven-Eleven Japan had increased its share of the convenience store market since it opened. In 2015, Seven-Eleven was Japan's leading convenience store operator, accounting for a 41.0 percent market share by total store sales in the convenience store segment. This share had increased relative to the 34.3 market share in 2008. Seven-Eleven was very effective in terms of same-store sales. In 2004, average daily sales at the four major convenience store chains excluding Seven-Eleven Japan totaled 484,000 yen. Seven-Eleven stores, in contrast, had daily sales of 647,000 yen—more than 30 percent higher than the combined competition. By 2013, average daily sales per store at Seven-Eleven Japan stores had increased to 668,000 yen. In 2016, Seven-Eleven's operating income of 352 billion yen positioned it as a leader not only of the convenience store sector but also of Japan's retail industry as a whole. Seven-Eleven intended to continue its growth by opening 1,800 new stores in the year ending February 2017. This growth was carefully planned, exploiting the core strengths that Seven-Eleven Japan had developed in the areas of information systems and distribution systems.

The Seven-Eleven Japan Franchise System

Seven-Eleven Japan developed an extensive franchise network and played an important part in the daily operations of this network. The Seven-Eleven Japan network included both company-owned stores and third-party-owned franchises. To ensure efficiency, Seven-Eleven Japan based its fundamental network expansion policy on a market-concentration strategy. Entry into any new market was built around a cluster of 50 to 60 stores supported by a distribution center. Such clustering gave Seven-Eleven Japan a high-density market presence and allowed it to operate an efficient distribution system. Seven-Eleven Japan felt that its market-concentration strategy improved distribution efficiency, brand awareness, efficiency of franchise support services, and advertising effectiveness. It also served as an effective deterrent to competition.

Adhering to its dominant strategy, Seven-Eleven Japan opened the majority of its new stores in areas with existing clusters of stores. For example, the Aichi prefecture, where Seven-Eleven began opening stores in 2002, saw a large increase in 2004, with 108 new store openings. This represented more than 15 percent of the new Seven-Eleven stores opened in Japan that year.

By 2016, Seven-Eleven had stores in 46 of 47 of the prefectures within Japan. With an increased demand for "close-by, convenient stores," Seven-Eleven felt that besides bringing stores to new areas, it could also continue to open stores in densely populated urban areas such as Tokyo, Nagoya, and Osaka.

With Seven-Eleven franchises being highly sought after, less than one of 100 applicants was awarded a franchise (a testament to store profitability). The franchise owner was required to put a significant amount of money up front. Half this amount was used to prepare the store and train the owner. The rest was used for purchasing the initial stock for the store. In 1994, 45 percent of total gross profits at a store went to Seven-Eleven Japan, and the rest went to the store owner. The responsibilities of the two parties were as follows.

Seven-Eleven Japan responsibilities:

- Develop supply and merchandise
- Provide the ordering system
- Pay for the system operation
- Supply accounting services
- Provide advertising
- Install and remodel facilities
- Pay 80 percent of utility costs

Franchise owner responsibilities:

- Operate and manage store
- Hire and pay staff
- Order supplies

- Maintain store appearance
- Provide customer service

Store Information and Contents

Seven-Eleven had more than 19,000 stores in Japan by September 2016 (see Table 3-7). In 2004, Seven-Eleven Japan changed the standard size of new stores from 125 square meters to 150 square meters, still significantly smaller than the size of most U.S. 7-Eleven stores. In 2016, daily sales at a store averaged 655,000 yen (about $5,691 in December 2016 at an exchange rate of about 115 yen to a U.S. dollar), which was almost twice the average at a U.S. store.

Seven-Eleven Japan offered its stores a choice from a set of 5,000 SKUs. Each store carried about 3,000 SKUs on average, depending on local customer demand. Seven-Eleven Japan emphasized regional merchandising to cater precisely to local preferences. Each store carried food items, beverages, magazines, and consumer items such as soaps and detergents. The relative sales across product categories in 2015 for Seven-Eleven Japan are given in Table 3-6.

The food items were classified into four broad categories: (1) chilled-temperature items, including sandwiches, delicatessen products, and milk; (2) warm-temperature items, including box lunches, rice balls, and fresh bread; (3) frozen items, including ice cream, frozen foods, and ice cubes; (4) and room-temperature items, including canned food, instant noodles, and seasonings. Processed food and fast-food items were big sellers for the stores. In 2015, processed and fast foods contributed about 56 percent of the total sales at each store. The top-selling products in the fast-food category were lunch boxes, rice balls, bread-based products, and pasta. By 2013, Seven-Eleven Japan had 171 daily production facilities and 158 distribution centers across Japan.

TABLE 3-6 Sales by Product Category in 2015

	Percentage of Total Sales
Processed foods	26.0
Fast foods	29.8
Fresh/daily foods	13.5
Nonfoods	30.7

Source: Based on Seven & i Annual Report 2016.

Other products sold at Seven-Eleven stores included soft drinks, nutritional drinks, alcoholic beverages such as beer and wine, game software, music CDs, and magazines.

Seven-Eleven was focused on increasing the number of original items that were available only at their stores. The sale of original items at Seven-Eleven was expected to hit 1.4 trillion yen in 2016. In 2007, Seven & i launched Seven Premium private brand products for sale at its stores. By 2016, the sale of Seven Premium products contributed about one trillion yen at a growth rate of about 20 percent. Private brand products were sold across all store formats and were viewed by the company as an important part of the expansion of synergies across its various retail formats.

Store Services

Besides products, Seven-Eleven Japan gradually added a variety of services that customers could obtain at its stores. The first service, added in October 1987, was the in-store payment of Tokyo Electric Power bills. The company later expanded the set of utilities for which customers could pay their bills in the stores to include gas, insurance, and telephone. With more convenient operating hours and locations than banks or other financial institutions, the bill payment service attracted millions of additional customers every year. In April 1994, Seven-Eleven Japan began accepting installment payments on behalf of credit companies. It started selling ski-lift pass vouchers in November 1994. In 1995, it began to accept payment for mail-order purchases. This was expanded to include payment for Internet shopping in November 1999. In August 2000, a meal delivery service company, Seven-Meal Service Co. Ltd., was established to serve the aging Japanese population. Seven Bank was set up as the core operating company for Seven & i in financial services. By 2013, virtually every Seven-Eleven Japan store had an ATM installed, with Seven Bank having almost 18,000 ATMs. The company averaged 111 transactions per ATM per day.

Other services offered at stores include photo-copying, ticket sales (including baseball games, express buses, and music concerts), using multifunctional copiers, and being a pick-up location for parcel delivery companies that typically did not leave the parcel outside if the customer was not at home. In 2010, the convenience stores also started offering some government services, such as providing certificates of residence. The

major thrust for offering these services was to take advantage of the convenient locations of Seven-Eleven stores in Japan. Besides providing additional revenue, the services also got customers to visit the stores more frequently. Several of these services exploited the existing Total Information System (described later) in the store.

In February 2000, Seven-Eleven Japan established 7dream.com, an e-commerce company. The goal was to exploit the existing distribution system and the fact that stores were easily accessible to most Japanese. Stores served as drop-off and collection points for Japanese customers. A survey by Book (a joint venture among Softbank, Seven-Eleven Japan, Yahoo! Japan, and Tohan, a publisher) discovered that 92 percent of its customers preferred to pick up their online purchases at the local convenience store, rather than have them delivered to their homes. This was understandable, given the frequency with which Japanese customers visit their local convenience store; 7dream hoped to build on this preference along with the synergies from the existing distribution system.

The company built Seven Net Shopping, its Internet site that sold about 3 million products in 2015, aimed at combining the group's stores and Internet services. The service enabled customers to buy products that were typically not available at the retail stores. Customers were allowed to order on the Internet with both pick-up and payment at Seven-Eleven stores. No shipping fee was charged for this service. In April 2007, "nanaco" electronic money was offered in Seven-Eleven stores. The service allowed customers to prepay and use a card or cell phone to make payments. The service was offered as a convenience to customers making small purchases and was also a reward system offering one yen's worth of points for every 100 yen spent by the customer. By 2015, 37.17 million nanaco accounts had been issued.

Given Japan's aging population (In 2014, Seven-Eleven estimated that about 47 percent of consumption was by people 60 or older) and an increase in the number of women working outside the home (In 2009, Seven-Eleven estimated that more than 70 percent of women in their 40s worked outside the home), Seven-Eleven wanted to exploit its "close-by convenient stores" to better serve its customers. The company attempted to do this by increasing the number of high daily consumption rate products from 500 to 900 and by bolstering its Seven-Meal service for home delivery.

Seven-Eleven Japan's Integrated Store Information System

From its start, Seven-Eleven Japan sought to simplify its operations by using advanced information technology. Seven-Eleven Japan attributed a significant part of its success to the Total Information System installed in every outlet and linked to headquarters, suppliers, and the Seven-Eleven distribution centers. The first online network linking the head office, stores, and vendors was established in 1979, though the company did not collect point-of-sales (POS) information at that time. In 1982, Seven-Eleven became the first company in Japan to introduce a POS system comprising POS cash registers and terminal control equipment. In 1985, the company, jointly with NEC, developed personal computers using color graphics that were installed at each store and linked to the POS cash registers. These computers were also on the network linking the store to the head office, as well as the vendors. In July 1991, an integrated services digital network (ISDN) was installed. Linking more than 5,000 stores, it became one of the world's largest ISDN systems at that time. Sales data gathered in each store by 11:00 p.m. were processed and ready for analysis the next morning.

The hardware system at a 2012 Seven-Eleven store included the following:

- **_Graphic order terminal:_** This was a handheld device with a wide-screen graphic display, used by the store owner or manager to place orders. When placing an order, the store manager had access (from the store computer) to detailed analysis of POS data related to the particular item. This included sales analysis of product categories and SKUs over time, analysis of waste, 10-week sales trends by SKU, 10-day sales trends by SKU, sales trends for new products, sales analysis by day and time, list of slow-moving items, analysis of sales and number of customers over time, contribution of product to sections in store display, and sales growth by product categories. The store manager used this information when entering an order into the terminal. Once all the orders were placed, the terminal was returned to its slot, at which point the orders were relayed by the store computer to both the appropriate vendor and the Seven-Eleven distribution center.
- **_Scanner terminal:_** These scanners read bar codes and recorded inventory. They were used to receive

products coming in from a distribution center. The delivery was automatically checked against a previously placed order, and the two were reconciled. Before the scanner terminals were introduced, truck drivers waited in the store until the delivery was checked. Once they were introduced, the driver simply dropped the delivery in the store, and a store clerk received it at a suitable time when there were few customers.

- *Store computer:* This linked to the Seven-Eleven network, the POS register, the graphic order terminal, and the scanner terminal. It communicated among the various input sources, tracked store inventory and sales, placed orders, provided detailed analysis of POS data, and maintained and regulated store equipment.

- *POS register:* As soon as a customer purchased an item and paid at the POS register, sales and other data (such as the age and sex of the customer) were stored and transmitted to headquarters through the store computer.

The analyzed and updated data were then sent back to the Seven-Eleven Japan stores via the network each morning. All this information was available on the graphic order terminal with the objective of improving order placement.

The information system allowed Seven-Eleven stores to better match supply with demand. Store staff could adjust the merchandising mix on the shelves according to consumption patterns throughout the day. For example, popular breakfast items were stocked earlier during the day, and popular dinner items were stocked later in the evening. The identification of slow and nonmoving items allowed a store to convert shelf space to introduce new items. About 70 percent of the items sold at a Seven-Eleven store changed in the course of a year. About 100 new products were introduced each week. When a new product was introduced, the decision whether to continue stocking it was made within the first three weeks to ensure that each item contributed to sales and margin and did not waste valuable shelf space.

Seven-Eleven's Distribution System

The Seven-Eleven distribution system tightly linked the entire supply chain for all product categories. All stores were given cutoff times for breakfast, lunch, and dinner ordering. When a store placed an order, it was immediately transmitted to the supplier as well as the DC. The supplier packed each store order and sent all the orders by truck to the DC where they were cross docked onto the appropriate store truck.

The key to store delivery was what Seven-Eleven called the *combined delivery system*. At the DC, deliveries of like products from different suppliers (e.g., milk and sandwiches) were directed into a single temperature-controlled truck. There were four categories of temperature-controlled trucks: frozen foods, chilled foods, room-temperature processed foods, and warm foods. Warm and chilled foods were delivered three times daily, whereas room-temperature products were delivered once a day. Frozen products were delivered three to seven times a week, depending on the weather. Each truck made deliveries to multiple retail stores. The number of stores per truck depended on the sales volume. All deliveries were made during off-peak hours and were received using the scanner terminals. The system worked on trust and did not require the delivery person to be present when the store personnel scanned in the delivery. That reduced the delivery time spent at each store.

This distribution system enabled Seven-Eleven to reduce the number of vehicles required for daily delivery service to each store, even though the delivery frequency of each item was quite high. In 1974, seventy vehicles visited each store every day. By 2006, only nine were necessary. This dramatically reduced delivery costs and enabled rapid delivery of a variety of fresh foods.

As of May 2013, Seven-Eleven Japan had a total of 171 daily production facilities throughout the country that produced items distributed through 158 DCs. None of these DCs carried any inventory; they merely transferred inventory from supplier trucks to Seven-Eleven distribution trucks. The transportation was provided by Transfleet Ltd., a company set up by Mitsui and Co. for the exclusive use of Seven-Eleven Japan.

7-Eleven in the United States

Seven-Eleven had expanded rapidly around the world (Table 3-7). The major growth was in Asia, although the United States continued to be a major market for Seven-Eleven. Once Seven-Eleven Japan acquired Southland Corporation, it set about improving operations in the United States. In the initial years, several 7-Eleven stores in the United States were shut down. The number of stores started to grow beginning in 1998. Historically, the distribution structure in the United States was completely different from that in Japan. Stores in the United States were replenished using direct store delivery (DSD) by some manufacturers, with the remaining

TABLE 3-7 Global Store Distribution for Seven-Eleven in December 2016

Country	Stores
Japan	19,045
Thailand	9,411
United States	8,428
South Korea	7,085
Taiwan	5,087
China	2,270
Malaysia	2,057
Mexico	1,880
Philippines	1,840
Australia	636
Canada	507
Singapore	431
Denmark	187
Sweden	184
Indonesia	166
Norway	155
United Arab Emirates	6
Total	60,695

Source: Based on Seven Eleven Japan website http://www.sej.co.jp/company/en/g_stores.html.

products delivered by wholesalers. DSD accounted for about half the total volume, with the rest coming from wholesalers.

With the goal of introducing "fresh" products in the United States, 7-Eleven started to use combined distribution centers (CDCs) around 2000. By 2003, 7-Eleven had 23 CDCs located throughout North America, supporting about 80 percent of the store network. Following the Japanese approach, CDCs delivered fresh items such as sandwiches, bakery products, bread, produce, and other perishables once a day. A variety of fresh-food suppliers sent product to the CDC throughout the day, where they were sorted for delivery to stores at night. Requests from store managers were sent to the nearest CDC, and by 10:00 p.m., the products were en route to the stores. Relative to Japan, a greater fraction of the food sold, especially hot food such as wings and pizza, was prepared in the store. During this period,

DSD by manufacturers and wholesaler delivery to stores also continued.

This was a period when 7-Eleven worked very hard to introduce new fresh-food items, with a goal of competing more directly with the likes of Starbucks than with traditional gas station food marts. 7-Eleven in the United States had more than 63 percent of its sales from non-gasoline products, which was much higher than the rest of the industry. The goal for 7-Eleven was to continue to increase sales in the fresh-food and fast-food categories with a special focus on hot foods.

In 2009, revenue in the United States and Canada totaled $16.0 billion, with about 63 percent coming from merchandise and the rest from the sale of gasoline. The North American inventory turnover rate in 2004 was about 19, compared to more than 50 in Japan. This, however represented a significant improvement in North American performance, where inventory turns in 1992 were around 12.

Study Questions

1. A convenience store chain attempts to be responsive and provide customers with what they need, when they need it, where they need it. What are some different ways that a convenience store supply chain can be responsive? What are some risks in each case?

2. Seven-Eleven's supply chain strategy in Japan can be described as attempting to micro-match supply and demand using rapid replenishment. What are some risks associated with this choice?

3. What has Seven-Eleven done in its choice of facility location, inventory management, transportation, and information infrastructure to develop capabilities that support its supply chain strategy in Japan?

4. Seven-Eleven does not allow direct store delivery in Japan but has all products flow through its distribution center. What benefit does Seven-Eleven derive from this policy? When is direct store delivery more appropriate?

5. What do you think about the 7 dream concept for Seven-Eleven Japan? From a supply chain perspective, is it likely to be more successful in Japan or the United States? Why?

6. Seven-Eleven is attempting to duplicate the supply chain structure that has succeeded in Japan into the United States with the introduction of CDCs. What are the pros and cons of this approach? Keep in mind that stores are also replenished by wholesalers and DSD by manufacturers.

7. The United States has food service distributors that also replenish convenience stores. What are the pros and cons to having a distributor replenish convenience stores versus a company like Seven-Eleven managing its own distribution function?

CASE STUDY

Financial Statements for Walmart Stores Inc. and Macy's Inc.

Table 3-8 contains the financial results for Walmart and Macy's for 2012. Evaluate the financial performance of each company based on the various metrics discussed in Section 3.1, such as ROE, ROA, profit margin, asset turns, APT, C2C, ART, INVT, and PPET. Can you explain the differences you see in their performance based on their supply chain strategy and structure? Compare the metrics for each company with similar metrics for Amazon and Nordstrom from Table 3-1. Which metrics does each company perform better on? What supply chain drivers and metrics might explain this difference in performance?

TABLE 3-8 Selected Financial Data for Walmart Stores Inc. and Macy's Inc.

Year ended January 31, 2013 ($ millions)	Walmart	Macy's
Net operating revenues	469,162	27,931
Cost of goods sold	352,488	16,725
Gross profit	116,674	11,206
Selling, general, and administrative expense	88,873	8,440
Other Costs		88
Operating income	27,801	2,678
Interest expense	2,251	388
Other income(loss)—net	187	134
Income before income taxes	25,737	2,290
Income taxes	7,981	804
Net income	17,756	1,486
Assets		
Cash and cash equivalents	7,781	1,836
Net receivables	6,768	371
Inventory	43,803	5,308
Prepaid expenses and other	1,588	361
Total current assets	59,940	7,876
Property, plant, and equipment	116,681	8,196
Goodwill	20,497	3,743
Other intangible assets		561
Other assets	5,987	615
Total assets	203,105	20,991
Liabilities and Stockholder Equity		
Accounts payable	59,099	4,951
Short-term debt	12,719	124
Total current liability	71,818	5,075
Long-term debt	41,417	6,806
Other liabilities		3,059
Total liabilities	121,367	14,940
Stockholder equity	81,738	6,051

CHAPTER

4

Designing Distribution Networks and Applications to Omni-Channel Retailing

LEARNING OBJECTIVES

After reading this chapter, you will be able to

4.1 Identify the key factors to be considered when designing a distribution network.

4.2 Discuss the strengths and weaknesses of various distribution options.

4.3 Describe how omni-channel retail may be structured to be both cost effective and responsive to customer needs.

In this chapter, we provide an understanding of the role of distribution within a supply chain and identify factors that should be considered when designing a distribution network. We identify several potential designs for distribution networks and evaluate the strengths and weaknesses of each option. We apply these ideas to discuss the evolution of omni-channel retailing. Our goal is to provide managers with a logical framework for designing an omni-channel portfolio based on product characteristics and customer needs.

FACTORS AFFECTING DISTRIBUTION NETWORK DESIGN IN THE SUPPLY CHAIN

Distribution refers to the steps taken to move and store a product from the supplier stage to a customer stage in the supply chain. Distribution occurs between every pair of stages in the supply chain. Raw materials and components are moved from suppliers to manufacturers, whereas finished products are moved from the manufacturer to the end consumer. Distribution is a key driver of the overall profitability of a firm because it directly affects both the supply chain cost and the customer value. In the apparel retail industry, for example, distribution

4.1 Identify the key factors to be considered when designing a distribution network.

affects about 35 percent of the revenue (including its influence on markdowns and lost sales). In India, the outbound distribution cost of cement is about 30 percent of the cost of producing and selling it.

It would be no exaggeration to state that two of the world's most profitable companies, Seven-Eleven Japan and Walmart, have built the success of their entire business around outstanding distribution design and operation. In the case of Seven-Eleven Japan, effective distribution provides a very high level of customer responsiveness at a reasonable cost. In the case of Walmart, distribution allows the company to provide high availability levels of relatively common products at a very low cost.

The process of designing a distribution network has two phases. In the first phase, the broad structure of the supply chain network is visualized. This phase decides the number of stages in the supply chain and the role of each stage. The second phase then takes the broad structure and converts it into specific locations and their capability, capacity, and demand allocation. This chapter focuses on issues that affect the design of the broad distribution network. Chapters 5 and 6 focus on the second phase, which starts with the broad network and results in a specific supply chain network.

The appropriate distribution network can be used to achieve a variety of supply chain objectives ranging from low cost to high responsiveness. As a result, companies in the same industry often select different distribution networks. Next, we discuss industry examples that highlight the variety of distribution network choices and the issues that arise when selecting among these options.

Until 2007, Dell distributed its PCs directly to end consumers, whereas companies such as HP distributed through resellers. Dell customers waited several days to get a PC, whereas customers could walk away with an HP computer from a reseller. Starting in June 2007, Dell also started selling its PCs through retailers such as Walmart. In the late 1990s, Gateway opened Gateway Country stores, wherein customers could examine the products and have salespeople help them configure a PC that suited their needs. Gateway, however, chose to sell no products at the stores; all PCs were shipped directly from the factory to the customer. By April 2004, Gateway had closed all its stores because of their poor financial performance. Apple Computer, in contrast, has successfully opened many retail stores that sell computers. These companies have chosen different distribution models. How can we evaluate this wide range of distribution choices? Which ones serve the companies and their customers better?

P&G has chosen to distribute directly to large supermarket chains while obligating smaller players to buy P&G products from distributors. Products move directly from P&G to the larger chains but move through an additional stage when going to smaller supermarkets. Texas Instruments, which once used only direct sales, now sells about 30 percent of its volume to 98 percent of its customers through distributors, while serving the remaining 2 percent of customers with 70 percent of the volume directly (Raman and Rao, 1997). What value do these distributors provide? When should a distribution network include an additional stage, such as a distributor? Distributors play a much more significant role for consumer goods distribution in a country such as India compared with the United States. Why might this be the case?

W.W. Grainger stocks about 400,000 SKUs that can be sent to customers within a day of order placement. The remaining slower-moving products are not stocked but instead are shipped directly from the manufacturer when a customer places an order. It takes several days for the customer to receive the product in such cases. Are these distribution choices appropriate? How can they be justified?

As the preceding examples illustrate, firms have many options when designing their distribution networks. An inappropriate network can have a significant negative effect on the profitability of the firm, as is evident in the failure of companies such as Blockbuster and Webvan. The appropriate choice of distribution network grows the supply chain surplus by satisfying customer needs at the lowest possible cost. Next, we identify key factors that influence the performance of a distribution network.

At the highest level, performance of a distribution network should be evaluated along two dimensions:

1. Value provided to the customer
2. Cost of meeting customer needs

Thus, as it compares different distribution network options, a firm must evaluate the impact on customer service and cost. The customer needs that are met influence the company's revenues, which, along with cost, decide the profitability of the delivery network.

Although customer value is affected by many factors, we focus on measures that are influenced by the structure of the distribution network:

- Response time
- Product variety
- Product availability
- Customer experience
- Time to market
- Order visibility
- Returnability

Response time is the amount of time it takes for a customer to receive an order. *Product variety* is the number of different products or configurations that are offered by the distribution network. *Product availability* is the probability of fulfilling a customer order from inventory. *Customer experience* includes the ease with which customers can place and receive orders and the extent to which this experience is customized. It also includes purely experiential aspects, such as the possibility of getting a cup of coffee and the value that the sales staff provides. *Time to market* is the time it takes to bring a new product to the market. *Order visibility* is the ability of customers to track their orders from placement to delivery. *Returnability* is the ease with which a customer can return unsatisfactory merchandise and the ability of the network to handle such returns.

It may seem that a customer always wants the highest level of performance along all these dimensions. In practice, however, this is not the case. Customers ordering a book at Amazon are willing to wait longer than those who drive to a nearby Barnes & Noble store to get the same book. In contrast, customers can find a much larger variety of books at Amazon compared with the selection at the Barnes & Noble store. Thus, Amazon customers trade off fast response times for high levels of variety.

Firms that target customers who can tolerate a long response time require only a few locations that may be far from the customer. These companies can focus on increasing the capacity of each location. In contrast, firms that target customers who value short response times need to locate facilities close to them. These firms must have many facilities, each with a low capacity. Thus, a decrease in the desired response time increases the number of facilities required in the network, as shown in Figure 4-1. For example, Barnes & Noble provides its customers with books on the same day but requires hundreds of stores to achieve this goal for most of the United States. Amazon, in contrast, takes a few days to deliver a book to its U.S. customers, but it uses fewer locations to store its books.

Changing the distribution network design affects the following supply chain costs (notice that these are four of the six supply chain drivers we discussed earlier):

- Inventory
- Transportation
- Facilities
- Information

The other two drivers, sourcing and pricing, also affect the choice of the distribution system; these links will be discussed when relevant.

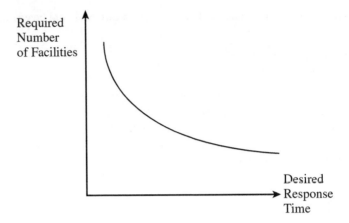

Figure 4-1 Relationship Between Desired Response Time and Number of Facilities

As the number of facilities in a supply chain increases, the required inventory increases (see Chapter 12), as shown in Figure 4-2. To decrease inventory costs, firms try to consolidate and limit the number of facilities in their supply chain network. For example, Amazon is able to turn its inventory about twice as frequently as Barnes & Noble because it has far fewer facilities.

Inbound transportation costs are the costs incurred to bring material into a facility. *Outbound transportation costs* are the costs of sending material out of a facility. Outbound transportation costs per unit tend to be higher than inbound costs because inbound lot sizes are typically larger. For example, an Amazon warehouse receives full truckload shipments of books on the inbound side, but ships out small packages with only a few books per customer on the outbound side. Increasing the number of warehouse locations decreases the average outbound distance to the customer and makes outbound transportation distance a smaller fraction of the total distance traveled by the product. Thus, as long as inbound transportation economies of scale are maintained, increasing the number of facilities decreases total transportation cost, as shown in Figure 4-3. If the number of facilities is increased to a point at which inbound lot sizes are also very small and result in a significant loss of economies of scale in inbound transportation, increasing the number of facilities increases total transportation cost, as shown in Figure 4-3.

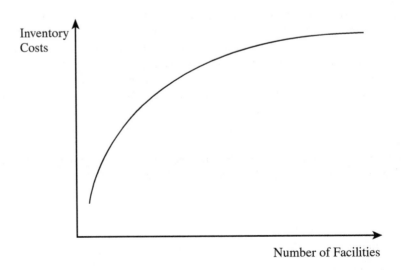

Figure 4-2 Relationship Between Number of Facilities and Inventory Costs

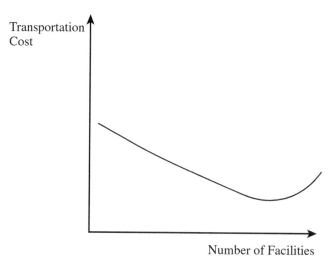

Figure 4-3 Relationship Between Number of Facilities and Transportation Cost

Facility costs decrease as the number of facilities is reduced, as shown in Figure 4-4, because a consolidation of facilities allows a firm to exploit economies of scale.

Total logistics costs are the sum of inventory, transportation, and facility costs for a supply chain network. As the number of facilities increases, total logistics costs first decrease and then increase, as shown in Figure 4-5. Each firm should have *at least* the number of facilities that minimizes total logistics costs. If a firm wants to reduce the response time to its customers further, it may have to increase the number of facilities beyond the point that minimizes logistics costs. A firm should add facilities beyond the cost-minimizing point only if managers are confident that the increase in revenues because of better responsiveness will be greater than the increase in costs because of the additional facilities. Amazon has increased its number of facilities to provide greater responsiveness to its customers. The success of this strategy will depend on how much customers are willing to pay for the improved responsiveness.

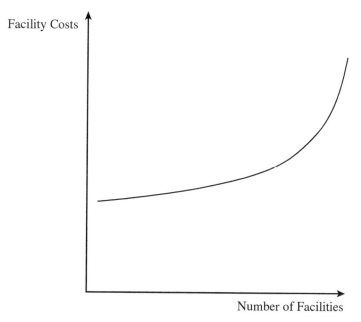

Figure 4-4 Relationship Between Number of Facilities and Facility Costs

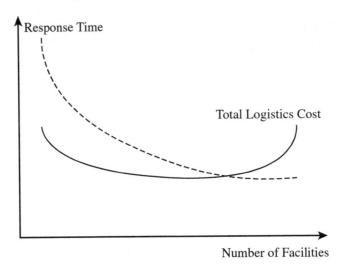

Figure 4-5 Variation in Logistics Cost and Response Time with Number of Facilities

The customer service and cost components listed earlier are the primary measures used to evaluate different delivery network designs. In general, no distribution network will outperform others along all dimensions. Thus, it is important to ensure that the strengths of the distribution network fit with the strategic position of the firm.

SUMMARY OF LEARNING OBJECTIVE 1

A manager must consider the customer needs to be met and the cost of meeting these needs when designing the distribution network. Some key customer needs to be considered include response time, product variety/availability, convenience, order visibility, and returnability. Important costs that managers must consider include inventory, transportation, facilities and handling, and information. Increasing the number of facilities decreases the response time and transportation cost but increases inventory and facility cost.

4.2 *Discuss the strengths and weaknesses of various distribution options.*

DESIGN OPTIONS FOR A DISTRIBUTION NETWORK

In this section, we discuss various distribution network choices from the manufacturer to the end consumer and their relative strengths and weaknesses. When considering distribution between any other pair of stages, such as supplier to manufacturer or even a service company serving its customers through a distribution network, many of the same options still apply. Managers must make two key decisions when designing a distribution network:

1. Will product be delivered to the customer location or picked up from a prearranged site?
2. Will product flow through an intermediary (or intermediate location)?

Based on the firm's industry and the answers to these two questions, one of six distinct distribution network designs may be used to move products from factory to customer. These designs are classified as follows:

1. Manufacturer storage with direct shipping
2. Manufacturer storage with direct shipping and in-transit merge
3. Distributor storage with carrier delivery
4. Distributor storage with last-mile delivery
5. Manufacturer/distributor storage with customer pickup
6. Retail storage with customer pickup

Manufacturer Storage with Direct Shipping

In this option, the retailer takes the order and initiates the delivery request. The product, however, is shipped directly from the manufacturer to the end customer, bypassing the retailer. This option is also referred to as *drop-shipping*. Order information flows from the customer, via the retailer, to the manufacturer, and product is shipped directly from the manufacturer to customers, as shown in Figure 4-6. Many companies such as eBags, Nordstrom.com, and W.W. Grainger, use drop-shipping to deliver goods to the end consumer. In most cases, drop-shipping is used to deliver slow moving items to customers.

The biggest advantage of drop-shipping is the ability to centralize inventories at the manufacturer, which can aggregate demand across all retailers that it supplies. As a result, the supply chain is able to provide a high level of product availability with lower levels of inventory. A key issue with regard to drop-shipping is the ownership structure of the inventory at the manufacturer. If specified portions of inventory at the manufacturer are allocated to individual retailers, there is little benefit of aggregation even though the inventory is physically aggregated. Benefit of aggregation is achieved only if the manufacturer can allocate at least a portion of the available inventory across retailers on an as-needed basis. The benefits from centralization are highest for high-value, low-demand items with unpredictable demand. The decision of Nordstrom to drop-ship low-demand shoes satisfies these criteria. Similarly, bags sold by eBags tend to have high value and relatively low demand per SKU. The inventory benefits of aggregation are small for items with predictable demand and low value. Thus, drop-shipping does not offer a significant inventory advantage to an online grocer selling detergent. For slow-moving items, inventory turns can increase by a factor of six or higher if drop-shipping is used instead of storage at retail stores.

Drop-shipping also offers the manufacturer the opportunity to postpone customization until after a customer has placed an order. Postponement, if implemented, further lowers inventories by aggregating to the component level. For example, a publisher may drop-ship books that have been printed on demand, thus reducing the value of inventory held.

Although inventory costs are typically low with drop-shipping, transportation costs are high because manufacturers are farther from the end consumer. With drop-shipping, a customer order including items from several manufacturers will involve multiple shipments to the customer. This loss in aggregation of outbound transportation also increases cost.

Supply chains save on the fixed cost of facilities when using drop-shipping because all inventories are centralized at the manufacturer. This eliminates the need for other warehousing space in the supply chain. There can be some savings of handling costs as well, because the transfer from manufacturer to retailer no longer occurs. Handling cost savings must be evaluated carefully, however, because the manufacturer is now required to transfer items to the factory warehouse in full cases and then ship out from the warehouse in single units. The inability of a

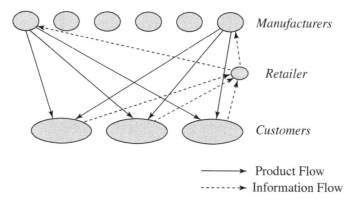

Figure 4-6 Manufacturer Storage with Direct Shipping

manufacturer to develop single-unit delivery capabilities can have a significant negative effect on handling cost and response time. Handling costs can be reduced significantly if the manufacturer has the capability to ship orders directly from the production line.

A good information infrastructure is needed between the retailers and the manufacturer so the retailer can provide product availability information to the customer, even though the inventory is located at the manufacturer. The customer should also have visibility into order processing at the manufacturer, even though the order is placed with the retailer. Drop-shipping generally requires significant investment in information infrastructure.

Response times tend to be long when drop-shipping is used because the order must be transmitted from the retailer to the manufacturer and shipping distances are generally longer from the manufacturer's centralized site. eBags, for example, states that order processing may take from 1 to 5 days and ground transportation after that may take from 3 to 11 business days. This implies that customer response time at eBags will be 4 to 16 days using ground transportation and drop-shipping.

Another issue is that the response time need not be identical for every manufacturer that is part of a customer order. Given an order containing products from several sources, the customer will receive multiple partial shipments over time, making receiving more complicated for the customer.

Manufacturer storage allows a high level of product variety to be available to the customer. With a drop-shipping model, every product at the manufacturer can be made available to the customer without any limits imposed by shelf space. W.W. Grainger is able to offer hundreds of thousands of slow-moving items from thousands of manufacturers using drop-shipping. This would be impossible if each product had to be stored by W.W. Grainger. Drop-shipping allows a new product to be available to the market on the day the first unit is produced.

Drop-shipping provides a good customer experience in the form of delivery to the customer location. The experience, however, suffers when a single order containing products from several manufacturers is delivered in partial shipments.

Order visibility is important in the context of manufacturer storage, because two stages in the supply chain are involved in every customer order. Failure to provide this capability is likely to have a significant negative effect on customer satisfaction. Order tracking, however, becomes harder to implement in a drop-ship system because it requires complete integration of information systems at both the retailer and the manufacturer.

A manufacturer storage network is likely to have difficulty handling returns, hurting customer satisfaction. The handling of returns is more expensive under drop-shipping because each order may involve shipments from more than one manufacturer. Returns can be handled in two ways. One is for the customer to return the product directly to the manufacturer. The second approach is for the retailer to set up a separate facility (across all manufacturers) to handle returns. The first approach incurs high transportation and coordination costs, whereas the second approach requires investment in a facility to handle returns.

The performance characteristics of drop-shipping along various dimensions are summarized in Table 4-1.

Given its performance characteristics, manufacturer storage with direct shipping is best suited for a large variety of low-demand, high-value items for which customers are willing to wait for delivery and accept several partial shipments. Manufacturer storage is also suitable if it allows the manufacturer to postpone customization, thus reducing inventories. It is thus ideal for direct sellers that are able to build to order. For drop-shipping to be effective, there should be few sourcing locations per order.

Manufacturer Storage with Direct Shipping and In-Transit Merge

Unlike pure drop-shipping, under which each product in the order is sent directly from its manufacturer to the end customer, in-transit merge combines pieces of the order coming from different locations so the customer gets a single delivery. Information and product flows for the in-transit

TABLE 4-1 Performance Characteristics of Manufacturer Storage with Direct Shipping Network

Cost Factor	Performance
Inventory	Lower costs because of aggregation. Benefits of aggregation are highest for low-demand, high-value items. Benefits are large if product customization can be postponed at the manufacturer.
Transportation	Higher transportation costs because of increased distance and disaggregate shipping.
Facilities and handling	Lower facility costs because of aggregation. Some saving on handling costs if manufacturer can manage small shipments or ship from production line.
Information	Significant investment in information infrastructure to integrate manufacturer and retailer.

Service Factor	Performance
Response time	Long response time of one to two weeks because of increased distance and two stages for order processing. Response time may vary by product, thus complicating receiving.
Product variety	Easy to provide a high level of variety.
Product availability	Easy to provide a high level of product availability because of aggregation at manufacturer.
Customer experience	Good in terms of home delivery but can suffer if order from several manufacturers is sent as partial shipments.
Time to market	Fast, with the product available as soon as the first unit is produced.
Order visibility	More difficult but also more important from a customer service perspective.
Returnability	Expensive and difficult to implement.

merge network are shown in Figure 4-7. In-transit merge has been used by Apple to serve European customers that purchase a configure-to-order computer along with accessories. The computer is usually configured and shipped from China while the accessories come from a separate location. The two parts of the order are typically merged at an Apple DC and sent as a single delivery to the customer.

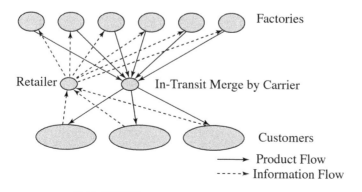

Figure 4-7 In-Transit Merge Network

As with drop-shipping, the ability to aggregate inventories and postpone product customization is a significant advantage of in-transit merge. In-transit merge allows Apple to hold component inventories at the factory in China and accessory inventories locally. This approach has the greatest benefits for products with high value whose demand is difficult to forecast, particularly if product customization can be postponed.

Although an increase in coordination is required, in-transit merge decreases transportation costs relative to drop-shipping by aggregating the final delivery.

Facility and processing costs for the manufacturer and the retailer are similar to those for drop-shipping. The party performing the in-transit merge has higher facility costs because of the merge capability required. Receiving costs at the customer are lower because a single delivery is received. Overall supply chain facility and handling costs are somewhat higher than with drop-shipping.

A sophisticated information infrastructure is needed to allow in-transit merge. In addition to information, operations at the retailer, manufacturers, and the carrier must be coordinated. The investment in information infrastructure is higher than that for drop-shipping.

Response times, product variety, availability, and time to market are similar to those for drop-shipping. Response times may be higher if the shipments from the various sources are not coordinated. Customer experience is likely to be better than with drop-shipping, because the customer receives only one delivery for an order instead of many partial shipments. Order visibility is an important requirement. Implementing visibility is harder before the merge but becomes easier after the merge.

Returnability is similar to that with drop-shipping. As with drop-shipping, problems in handling returns are likely, and the reverse supply chain will continue to be expensive and difficult to implement.

The performance of factory storage with in-transit merge is compared with that of drop-shipping in Table 4-2. The main advantages of in-transit merge over drop-shipping are lower transportation cost and improved customer experience. The major disadvantage is the additional effort during the merge itself. Given its performance characteristics, manufacturer storage with in-transit merge is best suited for low- to medium-demand, high-value items the retailer is sourcing from a limited number of manufacturers. Compared with drop-shipping, in-transit merge

TABLE 4-2 Performance Characteristics of In-Transit Merge

Cost Factor	Performance
Inventory	Similar to drop-shipping.
Transportation	Somewhat lower transportation costs than drop-shipping.
Facilities and handling	Handling costs higher than drop-shipping at merge location; receiving costs lower at customer.
Information	Investment is somewhat higher than for drop-shipping.
Service Factor	**Performance**
Response time	Similar to drop-shipping; may be marginally higher.
Product variety	Similar to drop-shipping.
Product availability	Similar to drop-shipping.
Customer experience	Better than drop-shipping because only a single delivery is received.
Time to market	Similar to drop-shipping.
Order visibility	Similar to drop-shipping.
Returnability	Similar to drop-shipping.

requires a higher demand from each manufacturer (not necessarily each product) to be effective. When there are too many sources, in-transit merge can be difficult to coordinate and implement. In-transit merge is best implemented if there are no more than four or five sourcing locations. The in-transit merge implemented by Apple for customized products is appropriate because product variety is high, but all customized products come on pallets from the same location. In-transit merge thus allows Apple to provide customized products in a single shipment while incurring lower inventory and transportation costs.

Distributor Storage with Carrier Delivery

Under this option, inventory is held not by manufacturers at the factories, but by distributors/ retailers in intermediate warehouses, and package carriers are used to transport products from the intermediate location to the final customer. Amazon and industrial distributors such as W.W. Grainger and McMaster-Carr have used this approach combined with drop-shipping from a manufacturer (or distributor). Information and product flows when using distributor storage with delivery by a package carrier are shown in Figure 4-8.

Relative to manufacturer storage, distributor storage requires a higher level of inventory because of a loss of aggregation. From an inventory perspective, distributor storage makes sense for products with somewhat higher demand. This is seen in the operations of both Amazon and W.W. Grainger. They stock only the slow- to fast-moving items at their warehouses, with very-slow-moving items stocked farther upstream. In some instances, postponement of product differentiation can be implemented with distributor storage, but it does require that the warehouse develop some assembly capability. Distributor storage, however, requires much less inventory than a retail network. In 2013, Amazon used warehouse storage to turn its inventory about twice as fast as the retail network of Barnes & Noble.

Transportation costs are somewhat lower for distributor storage compared with those for manufacturer storage because an economic mode of transportation (e.g., truckloads) can be employed for inbound shipments to the warehouse, which is closer to the customer. Unlike manufacturer storage, under which multiple shipments may need to go out for a single customer order with multiple items, distributor storage allows outbound orders to the customer to be bundled into a single shipment, further reducing transportation cost. Distributor storage provides savings relative to manufacturer storage on the transportation of faster-moving items.

Compared with those for manufacturer storage, facility costs (of warehousing) are somewhat higher with distributor storage because of a loss of aggregation. Processing and handling costs are comparable to those of manufacturer storage unless the factory is able to ship to the end customer directly from the production line. In that case, distributor storage has higher processing costs. From a facility cost perspective, distributor storage is not appropriate for extremely slow-moving items.

Figure 4-8 Distributor Storage with Carrier Delivery

The information infrastructure needed with distributor storage is significantly less complex than that needed with manufacturer storage. The distributor warehouse serves as a buffer between the customer and the manufacturer, decreasing the need to coordinate the two completely. Real-time visibility between customers and the warehouse is needed, whereas real-time visibility between the customer and the manufacturer is not. Visibility between the distributor warehouse and manufacturer can be achieved at a much lower cost than real-time visibility between the customer and manufacturer.

Response time under distributor storage is better than under manufacturer storage because distributor warehouses are, on average, closer to customers, and the entire order is aggregated at the warehouse before being shipped. Amazon, for example, processes most warehouse-stored items within a day and then it takes one to three business days using ground transportation for the order to reach the customer. W.W. Grainger processes customer orders on the same day and has enough warehouses to deliver most orders the next day using ground transport. Warehouse storage limits to some extent the variety of products that can be offered. W.W. Grainger does not store very-low-demand items at its warehouse, relying on manufacturers to drop-ship those products to the customer. Customer convenience is high with distributor storage because a single shipment reaches the customer in response to an order. Time to market under distributor storage is somewhat higher than that under manufacturer storage because of the need to stock another stage in the supply chain. Order visibility becomes easier than with manufacturer storage because there is a single shipment from the warehouse to the customer and only one stage of the supply chain is directly involved in filling the customer order. Returnability is better than it is with manufacturer storage because all returns can be processed at the warehouse itself. The customer also has to return only one package, even if the items are from several manufacturers.

The performance of distributor storage with carrier delivery is summarized in Table 4-3. Distributor storage with carrier delivery is well suited for slow- to fast-moving items. Distributor storage also makes sense when customers want delivery faster than is offered by manufacturer

TABLE 4-3 Performance Characteristics of Distributor Storage with Carrier Delivery

Cost Factor	Performance
Inventory	Higher than manufacturer storage. Difference is not large for faster-moving items but can be large for very-slow-moving items.
Transportation	Lower than manufacturer storage. Reduction is highest for faster-moving items.
Facilities and handling	Somewhat higher than manufacturer storage. The difference can be large for very-slow-moving items.
Information	Simpler infrastructure compared with manufacturer storage.
Service Factor	**Performance**
Response time	Faster than manufacturer storage.
Product variety	Lower than manufacturer storage.
Product availability	Higher cost to provide the same level of availability as manufacturer storage.
Customer experience	Better than manufacturer storage with drop-shipping.
Time to market	Longer than manufacturer storage.
Order visibility	Easier than manufacturer storage.
Returnability	Easier than manufacturer storage.

storage but do not need delivery immediately. Distributor storage can handle somewhat lower variety than manufacturer storage but can handle a much higher level of variety than a chain of retail stores.

Distributor Storage with Last-Mile Delivery

Last-mile delivery refers to the distributor/retailer delivering the product to the customer's home instead of using a package carrier. AmazonFresh, Peapod, Tesco, Instacart, and Google Express provide last-mile delivery in the grocery industry. In the late 1990s, companies such as Kozmo and Urbanfetch tried to set up home-delivery networks for a variety of products, but they failed to survive. The automotive spare parts industry is one in which distributor storage with last-mile delivery is the dominant model. It is too expensive for dealers to carry all spare parts in inventory. Thus, original equipment manufacturers (OEMs) tend to carry most spare parts at a local distribution center typically located no more than a couple of hours' drive from their dealers and often managed by a third party. The local distribution center is responsible for delivering needed parts to a set of dealers and makes multiple deliveries per day. Unlike package carrier delivery, last-mile delivery requires the distributor warehouse to be much closer to the customer. Given the limited radius that can be served with last-mile delivery, more warehouses are required compared to when package delivery is used. The warehouse storage with last-mile delivery network is as shown in Figure 4-9.

Distributor storage with last-mile delivery requires higher levels of inventory than the other options (except for retail stores) because it has a lower level of aggregation. From an inventory perspective, warehouse storage with last-mile delivery is suitable for relatively fast-moving items that are needed quickly and for which some level of aggregation is beneficial. Auto parts required by car dealers fit this description.

Among all the distribution networks, transportation costs are highest for last-mile delivery, especially when delivering to individuals. This is because package carriers aggregate delivery across many retailers and are able to obtain better economies of scale than are available to a distributor/retailer attempting last-mile delivery. Delivery costs (including transportation and processing) can be more than $20 per home delivery in the grocery industry. Last-mile delivery may be somewhat less expensive in large, dense cities, especially if the distributor has very large sales and carries a wide range of products. Amazon, with high sales across a wide variety of product categories, seems better equipped for last-mile delivery than Peapod, which carries only grocery items. A third party serving a wide variety of retailers (such as Google Express) may also be able to provide last-mile delivery effectively, given its ability to amortize its distribution costs across a large stream of deliveries. Transportation costs may also be justifiable for bulky products for which the customer is willing to pay for home delivery. Home delivery of water and large bags of rice has proved quite successful in China, where the high population density has helped decrease

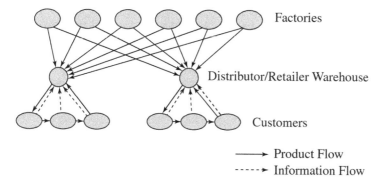

Figure 4-9 Distributor Storage with Last-Mile Delivery

delivery costs. Transportation costs of last-mile delivery are best justified in settings where the customer is purchasing in large quantities. This is rare for individual customers, but businesses such as auto dealerships purchase large quantities of spare parts on a daily basis and can thus justify daily delivery. Home delivery to individual customers can be justified for bulky items such as five-gallon jugs of water in the United States and large bags of rice in China. In each instance, last-mile delivery is cheaper and more convenient than customers picking up their own bottles or bags.

Using this option, facility costs are somewhat lower than those for a network with retail stores but much higher than for either manufacturer storage or distributor storage with package carrier delivery. Processing costs, however, are much higher than those for a network of retail stores because all customer participation is eliminated. A grocery store using last-mile delivery performs all the processing until the product is delivered to the customer's home, unlike a super-market, where the customer does much more work.

The information infrastructure with last-mile delivery is similar to that for distributor storage with package carrier delivery. However, it requires the additional capability of scheduling deliveries.

Response times for last-mile delivery are faster than those for package carriers. Kozmo and Urbanfetch tried to provide same-day delivery, whereas online grocers typically provide next-day delivery. Product variety is generally lower than for distributor storage with carrier delivery. The cost of providing product availability is higher than for every option other than retail stores. The customer experience can be good using this option, particularly for bulky, hard-to-carry items. Time to market is longer than for distributor storage with package carrier delivery because the new product has to penetrate deeper before it is available to the customer. Order visibility is less of an issue, given that deliveries are made within 24 hours. The order-tracking feature does become important to handle exceptions in case of incomplete or undelivered orders. Of all the options discussed, returnability is best with last-mile delivery, because trucks making deliveries can also pick up returns from customers. Returns are still more expensive to handle in this manner than at a retail store, where a customer can bring the product back.

The performance characteristics of distributor storage with last-mile delivery are summarized in Table 4-4. In areas with high labor costs, it is hard to justify last-mile delivery to individual consumers on the basis of efficiency or improved margin. Last-mile delivery may be justifiable if customer orders are predictable and large enough to provide some economies of scale or customers are willing to pay for this convenience. Demand from auto dealers is predictable and large enough (in the sense that every dealer will need deliveries daily) that last mile delivery can be justified based on cost. In the case of groceries, however, last mile delivery requires a customer willingness to pay. Peapod has changed its pricing policies to reflect this idea. Its minimum order size is $60 (with a delivery charge of $9.95), and delivery charges drop to $6.95 for orders totaling more than $100. Peapod offers discounts for deliveries during slower periods based on what its schedule looks like.

Manufacturer or Distributor Storage with Customer Pickup

In this approach, inventory is stored at the manufacturer or distributor warehouse, but customers place their orders online or on the phone and then travel to designated pickup points to collect their merchandise. Orders are shipped from the storage site to the pickup points as needed. Examples include 7dream.com and Otoriyose-bin, operated by Seven-Eleven Japan, which allow customers to pick up online orders at a designated store. Tesco has implemented a "click-and-collect" service in the United Kingdom, where customers can pick up orders they have placed online. Similarly, both Walmart and Home Depot allow customers to place orders online for pickup at a store. In India, Amazon has partnered with local retail stores, which take orders from customers without Internet access and also serve as pick up locations. A business-to-business (B2B) example is W.W. Grainger, whose customers can pick up their orders at one of the W.W. Grainger retail outlets.

TABLE 4-4 Performance Characteristics of Distributor Storage with Last-Mile Delivery

Cost Factor	Performance
Inventory	Higher than distributor storage with package carrier delivery.
Transportation	Very high cost, given minimal scale economies. Higher than any other distribution option.
Facilities and handling	Facility costs higher than manufacturer storage or distributor storage with package carrier delivery, but lower than a chain of retail stores.
Information	Similar to distributor storage with package carrier delivery.
Service Factor	**Performance**
Response time	Very quick. Same-day to next-day delivery.
Product variety	Somewhat less than distributor storage with package carrier delivery but larger than retail stores.
Product availability	More expensive to provide availability than any other option except retail stores.
Customer experience	Very good, particularly for bulky items.
Time to market	Slightly longer than distributor storage with package carrier delivery.
Order visibility	Less of an issue and easier to implement than manufacturer storage or distributor storage with package carrier delivery.
Returnability	Easier to implement than other previous options. Harder and more expensive than a retail network.

The information and product flows shown in Figure 4-10 are similar to those in the Seven-Eleven Japan network. Seven-Eleven has distribution centers where product from manufacturers is cross-docked and sent to retail outlets on a daily basis. An online retailer delivering an order through Seven-Eleven can be treated as one of the manufacturers, with deliveries cross-docked and sent to the appropriate Seven-Eleven outlet. Serving as an outlet for online orders allows Seven-Eleven to improve utilization of its existing logistical assets. In other instances, product may be stored at a DC and shipped to the pickup location in response to a customer order.

Inventory costs using this approach can be kept low, with either manufacturer or distributor storage to exploit aggregation. W.W. Grainger keeps its inventory of fast-moving items at pickup

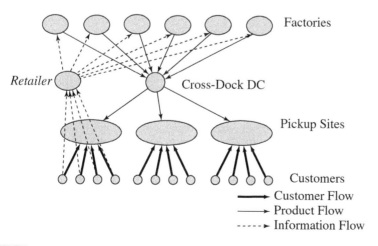

Figure 4-10 Manufacturer or Distributor Warehouse Storage with Consumer Pickup

locations, whereas slow-moving items are stocked at a central warehouse or in some cases at the manufacturer.

Transportation cost is lower than for any solution using package carriers because significant aggregation is possible when delivering orders to a pickup site. This allows the use of truckload or less-than-truckload carriers to transport orders to the pickup site. For a company such as Seven-Eleven Japan or Walmart, the marginal increase in transportation cost is small because trucks are already making deliveries to the stores, and their utilization can be improved by including online orders. As a result, Seven-Eleven Japan and Walmart allow customers to pick up orders without a shipping fee.

Facility costs are high if new pickup sites have to be built. A solution using existing sites can lower the additional facility costs. This, for example, is the case with 7dream.com, Walmart, and W.W. Grainger, for which the stores already exist. Processing costs at the manufacturer or the warehouse are comparable to those of other solutions. Processing costs at the pickup site are high because each order must be matched with a specific customer when he or she arrives. Creating this capability can increase processing costs significantly if appropriate storage and information systems are not provided. Increased processing cost and potential errors at the pickup site are the biggest hurdle to the success of this approach.

A significant information infrastructure is needed to provide visibility of the order until the customer picks it up. Good coordination is needed among the retailer, the storage location, and the pickup location.

In this case, a response time comparable to, or even faster than, package carriers can be achieved. Variety and availability comparable to any manufacturer or distributor storage option can be provided. There is some loss of customer experience, because unlike the other options discussed, customers must pick up their own orders. On the other hand, customers who do not want to pay online can pay by cash using this option. In countries like Japan, where Seven-Eleven has more than 19,000 outlets, it can be argued that the loss of customer convenience is small, because most customers are close to a pickup site and can collect an order at their convenience. In some cases, this option is considered more convenient because it does not require the customer to be at home at the time of delivery. Time to market for new products can be as short as with manufacturer storage.

Order visibility is extremely important for customer pickups. The customer must be informed when the order has arrived, and the order should be easily identified once the customer arrives to pick it up. Such a system is hard to implement because it requires integration of several stages in the supply chain. Returns can potentially be handled at the pickup site, making it easier for customers. From a transportation perspective, return flows can be handled using the delivery trucks.

The performance characteristics of manufacturer or distributor storage with consumer pickup sites are summarized in Table 4-5. The main advantages of a network with consumer pickup sites are that it can lower the delivery cost and expand the set of products sold and customers served online. The major hurdle is the increased handling cost and complexity at the pickup site. Such a network is likely to be most effective if existing retail locations are used as pickup sites, because this type of network improves the economies from existing infrastructure. In particular, such a network can be effective for firms like Seven-Eleven Japan, Walmart, and W.W. Grainger, which have both a network of stores and an online business. Unfortunately, such retail sites are typically designed to allow the customer to do the picking and need to develop the capability of picking a customer-specific order. Such a network can also be very effective in emerging economies like India where there are many local retailers who can potentially serve as pickup locations.

Retail Storage with Customer Pickup

In this option, often viewed as the most traditional type of supply chain, inventory is stored locally at retail stores. Customers walk into the retail store or place an order online or by phone and pick it up at the retail store. Information, product, and customer flows are as shown in Figure 4-11.

TABLE 4-5 Performance Characteristics of Network with Customer Pickup Sites

Cost Factor	Performance
Inventory	Can match any other option, depending on the location of inventory.
Transportation	Lower than the use of package carriers, especially if using an existing delivery network.
Facilities and handling	Facility costs can be high if new facilities have to be built. Costs are lower if existing facilities are used. The increase in handling cost at the pickup site can be significant.
Information	Significant investment in infrastructure is required.
Service Factor	**Performance**
Response time	Similar to package carrier delivery with manufacturer or distributor storage. Same-day pickup is possible for items stored at regional DC.
Product variety	Similar to other manufacturer or distributor storage options.
Product availability	Similar to other manufacturer or distributor storage options.
Customer experience	Lower than other options because of the lack of home delivery. Experience is sensitive to capability of pickup location.
Time to market	Similar to other manufacturer or distributor storage options.
Order visibility	Difficult but essential.
Returnability	Somewhat easier, given that pickup location can handle returns.

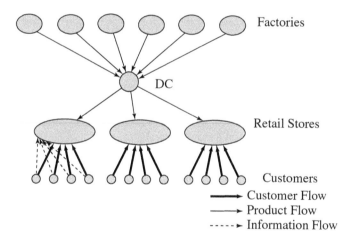

Figure 4-11 Retail Storage with Customer Pickup

Examples of companies that offer multiple options of order placement include Home Depot and Tesco. In either case, customers can walk into the store or order online. A B2B example is W.W. Grainger: Customers can order online, by phone, or in person and pick up their order at one of W.W. Grainger's retail outlets.

Local storage increases inventory costs because of the lack of aggregation. For fast- to very-fast-moving items, however, there is little increase in inventory, even with local storage. Home Depot uses local storage for its fast-moving products while delivering a wider variety of products from a regional location for pickup at the store. Similarly, W.W. Grainger keeps its inventory of fast-moving items at pickup locations, whereas slow-moving items are stocked at a central warehouse.

Transportation cost is much lower than with other solutions because inexpensive modes of transport can be used to replenish product at the retail store. Facility costs are high because many local facilities are required. A minimal information infrastructure is needed if customers walk into the store and place orders. For online orders, however, a significant information infrastructure is needed to provide visibility of the order until the customer picks it up.

Good response times can be achieved with this system because of local storage. For example, both Tesco and W.W. Grainger offer same-day pickup from their retail locations. Product variety stored locally is lower than that under other options. It is more expensive than with all other options to provide a high level of product availability. Customer experience depends on whether or not the customer likes to shop. Time to market is the longest with this option because the new product must penetrate through the entire supply chain before it is available to customers. Order visibility is extremely important for customer pickups when orders are placed online or by phone. Returns can be handled at the pickup site. Overall, returnability is fairly good using this option.

The performance characteristics of a network with customer pickup sites and local retail storage are summarized in Table 4-6. The main advantage of a network with retail storage is that it can lower delivery costs and provide a faster response than other networks. The major disadvantage is the increased inventory and facility costs. Such a network is best suited for fast-moving items or items for which customers value rapid response or the ability to touch and see the product.

Selecting a Distribution Network Design

A network designer needs to consider product characteristics as well as network requirements when deciding on the appropriate delivery network. The various networks considered earlier have different strengths and weaknesses. In Table 4-7, the various delivery networks are ranked

TABLE 4-6 Performance Characteristics of Retail Storage with Customer Pickup Sites

Cost Factor	Performance
Inventory	Higher than all other options.
Transportation	Lower than all other options.
Facilities and handling	Higher than other options. The increase in handling cost at the pickup site can be significant for online and phone orders.
Information	Some investment in infrastructure required for online and phone orders.
Service Factor	**Performance**
Response time	Same-day (immediate) pickup possible for items stored locally at pickup site.
Product variety	Lower than all other options.
Product availability	More expensive to provide than all other options.
Customer experience	Related to whether shopping is viewed as a positive or negative experience by customer.
Time to market	Longest among distribution options.
Order visibility	Trivial for in-store orders. Difficult, but essential, for online and phone orders.
Returnability	Easier than other options because retail store can provide a substitute.

TABLE 4-7 Comparative Performance Rank of Delivery Network Designs

	Retail Storage with Customer Pickup	Manufacturer Storage with Direct Shipping	Manufacturer Storage with In-Transit Merge	Distributor Storage with Package Carrier Delivery	Distributor Storage with Last-Mile Delivery	Manufacturer/ Distributor Storage with Customer Pickup
Response time	1	4	4	3	2	4
Product variety	4	1	1	2	3	1
Product availability	4	1	1	2	3	1
Customer experience	Varies From 1 to 5	4	3	2	1	5
Time to market	4	1	1	2	3	1
Order visibility	1	5	4	3	2	6
Returnability	1	5	5	4	3	2
Inventory	4	1	1	2	3	1
Transportation	1	4	3	2	5	1
Facility and handling	6	1	2	3	4	5
Information	1	4	4	3	2	5

Key: 1 corresponds to the best performance and 6 the worst performance.

relative to one another along different performance dimensions. A ranking of 1 indicates the best performance along a given dimension; as the relative performance worsens, the ranking number increases.

Only niche companies end up using a single distribution network. Most companies are best served by a combination of delivery networks. The combination used depends on product characteristics and the strategic position that the firm is targeting. The suitability of different delivery designs (from a supply chain perspective) in various situations is shown in Table 4-8.

An excellent example of a hybrid network is that of W.W. Grainger, which combines all the aforementioned options in its distribution network. The network, however, is tailored to match the characteristics of the product and the needs of the customer. Fast-moving and emergency items are stocked locally, and customers can either pick them up or have them shipped, depending on the urgency. Slower-moving items are stocked at a national DC and shipped to the customer within a day or two. Very-slow-moving items are typically drop-shipped from the manufacturer and carry a longer lead time. Another hybrid network is used by Amazon, which stocks fast-moving items at most of its warehouses and slower-moving items at fewer warehouses; very-slow-moving items may be drop-shipped from suppliers.

We can now revisit the examples from the computer industry discussed at the beginning of the chapter. Gateway's decision to create a network of retail stores without exploiting any of the supply chain advantages such a network offers was flawed. To fully exploit the benefits of the retail network, Gateway should have stocked its standard configurations (likely to have high demand) at the retail stores, with all other configurations drop-shipped from the factory (perhaps with local pickup at the retail stores if that was economical). Instead, the company drop-shipped all configurations from the factory. Apple has opened several retail stores and actually carries products for sale at these stores. This makes sense, given the low variety and high demand for standard Apple products. For customized products, however, Apple uses drop shipping to serve the customer.

TABLE 4-8 Performance of Delivery Networks for Different Product/Customer Characteristics

	Retail Storage with Customer Pickup	Manufacturer Storage with Direct Shipping	Manufacturer Storage with In-Transit Merge	Distributor Storage with Package Carrier Delivery	Distributor Storage with Last-Mile Delivery	Manufacturer/ Distributor Storage with Customer Pickup
High-demand product	+2	−2	−1	0	+1	−1
Medium-demand product	+1	−1	0	+1	0	0
Low-demand product	−1	+1	0	+1	−1	+1
Very-low-demand product	−2	+2	+1	0	−2	+1
High product value	−1	+2	+1	+1	0	+2
Quick desired response	+2	−2	−2	−1	+1	−2
High product variety	−1	+2	0	+1	0	+2
Low customer effort	−2	+1	+2	+2	+2	−1

Key: +2 = very suitable; +1 = somewhat suitable; 0 = neutral; −1 = somewhat unsuitable; −2 = very unsuitable.

SUMMARY OF LEARNING OBJECTIVE 2

Distribution networks that ship directly to the customer are better suited for a large variety of high-value products that have low and uncertain demand. These networks incur lower facility costs and carry low levels of inventory but incur high transportation cost and provide a slow response time. Distribution networks that carry local inventory are suitable for products with high demand, especially if transportation is a large fraction of total cost. These networks incur higher facility and inventory cost but lower transportation cost and provide a faster response time.

ONLINE SALES AND OMNI-CHANNEL RETAILING

4.3 Describe how omni-channel retail may be structured to be both cost effective and responsive to customer needs.

The twenty first century has seen a major transformation in retail in developed economies such as the United States. Successful models from the late twentieth century such as Borders for selling books, Blockbuster for renting videos, and Circuit City for selling consumer electronics have gone out of business. While it may seem that changing technology and the growth in online retail is responsible for this transformation, a more careful analysis shows that each of the companies cited above was squeezed by a combination of an online and a physical channel. Whereas a decade ago, customers primarily visited stores like Blockbuster to rent movies, today they are likely to segment the channel they use based on the type of movie they watch. Most customers visit Redbox kiosks to rent recent releases while watching a variety of other movies from Netflix. Whereas a decade ago, customers primarily went to an electronics mega store like Circuit City to fulfill all their electronics needs, today they are likely to segment the channel they use based on their electronics needs. They are likely to purchase their basic needs from a brick-and-mortar retailer such as Costco while also shopping online for a wide variety of consumer electronics. In each of these examples, a hybrid combination of a physical channel and an online channel serves customer needs more effectively than using a single channel.

Omni-channel retailing refers to the use of multiple channels to interact with customers and fulfill their orders. The interaction between a customer and a retailer is primarily in terms of three flows – information, product, and funds. The retailer provides product and pricing information to the customer who then places an order. The order information is used by the retailer to move the product to the customer. Finally, payment is transferred from the customer to the retailer. The use of different channels for each flow helps us categorize the components of omni-channel retailing.

We argue that a well-structured omni-channel supply chain can be both cost effective and responsive to customer needs by exploiting the complementary strengths that online and brick-and-mortar channels bring to the supply chain. A combination of multiple channels is often more effective than any single channel at serving a variety of customer needs. Whereas Blockbuster found it quite challenging to provide a wide variety of movies to its customers from its stores, Netflix has no difficulty supplying customers with a wide variety of movies. Between shipping DVDs and streaming, the company offers over a hundred thousand titles. Whereas Netflix is very good at providing a wide variety of movies at low cost, Redbox is much better at making a few new releases available close to customers at low cost. The combination of two companies Redbox and Netflix provides customers with an omni-channel experience that is simultaneously cheaper and more responsive to customer needs than the Blockbuster supply chain. The important observation is that the combination of channels is more effective because the decentralized Redbox channel focuses on providing only the new releases whereas the centralized Netflix channel focuses on providing a wide variety of other movies. It is important for each channel to focus on its strengths for an omni-channel supply chain to be effective.

Our goal in this section is to build a framework for omni-channel retail based on the ideas discussed earlier in this chapter. We first define the alternative channels that can be formed using different combinations of the online and brick-and-mortar channel. Then we discuss the relative strengths of each channel in terms of their ability to meet customer needs and the cost of doing so. This leads to a framework for how omni-channel retail can be either responsive or efficient based on customer needs.

The Alternatives in Omni-Channel Retail

A retail channel must exchange information, product, and funds with customers. Information such as product description and price may be exchanged face-to-face as in a retail store or remotely as when a customer shops online. Product exchange may occur through a customer pickup as when a customer goes to a supermarket to purchase milk and then leaves after having "picked up" the milk. Product exchange may also occur through home delivery as when an online retailer has a package carrier deliver a customer order to her home. We characterize four alternative channels as shown in Figure 4-12 that may result based on the combinations of information and product exchange. We ignore fund transfer in the characterization because funds are usually exchanged through the same channel where information is exchanged. We describe each of the four channels in greater detail.

TRADITIONAL RETAIL Supermarkets, jewelry stores, department stores, and book stores are all examples of traditional retail where a customer has a face-to-face interaction with the product and sales people and leaves the store with the product once a purchase has been made. Traditional retail tends to have many facilities to be close enough to customers to support the face-to-face information exchange and product pick up. These facilities tend to carry a high level of overall inventory because product must be stocked at each retail store. As a result, investment in facilities and inventory tends to be high for the traditional retail channel. Transportation costs incurred by the retailer, however, are the lowest among all channels.

SHOWROOMS An excellent example of this channel structure is Bonobos, an apparel retailer, whose stores (Bonobos Guideshop) "basically don't sell anything." These stores serve as showrooms where customers can try different styles, get advice from sales people, and also get fitted.

Figure 4-12 Alternatives in Omni-Channel Retail

These showrooms facilitate a face-to-face information exchange but do not carry inventory for customers to purchase. If a customer decides to make a purchase, the product is ordered online from the Bonobos website (or at the store). When using a showroom, product can either be picked up at the store or delivered at home. The showrooms carry no inventory for sale, thus significantly reducing inventory and the size of the store required. Relative to traditional retail, this channel saves on inventory and facilities infrastructure but requires a greater investment in transportation and information infrastructure, especially with home delivery.

ONLINE INFORMATION + HOME DELIVERY Amazon is an excellent example of this channel where customers browse for products and order online to have the purchases then delivered at home. Aggregation of inventories in a few locations allows the online channel to have a much lower investment in facilities and inventory compared to traditional retail. Transportation cost, however, tends to be high for home delivery.

ONLINE INFORMATION + PICKUP The high cost of home delivery for the online channel has led several players to offer the option of a pickup location at a lower price. The presence of a pickup location significantly reduces the outbound transportation cost incurred by the online retailer. It does require the customer to travel to the pickup location. A suitable choice of pickup location can lower this travel cost if customers can combine order pickup with other activities they naturally perform at the location. For example, Walmart allows a "free instore pickup" option where people can shop online and pick up the order at the store. This option clearly reduces Walmart's transportation cost because online orders can be shipped to the store along with other products being shipped there. Such an option may also not add much to the transportation cost for a customer if he or she is planning to shop at the Walmart store in any case. In the grocery industry in U.K., pickup locations now dominate as the channel for online grocery shopping. Grocery retailers such as Tesco and ASDA offer a low cost "click & collect" service where customers place their orders online and collect them at a pickup location.

Performance of Channels in Terms of Customer Service

As with distribution networks considered earlier, we start by studying how the various channels perform in terms of customer service elements such as response time, product variety, availability, customer experience, time to market, visibility, and returnability.

RESPONSE TIME TO CUSTOMERS Customers can pick up physical products at a retail store quicker than they can obtain them through other channels. The online channel, however, may be the fastest for information goods that can be downloaded. There is a major effort by companies like Amazon, Instacart, and Google to provide home delivery of physical products within an hour or two. Even when charging customers a premium for this service, none of the providers have yet managed to be profitable doing so.

PRODUCT VARIETY A company can offer a much wider selection of products if customers are willing to remotely access product information. For example, Seven-Eleven Japan offers almost three million products online while its stores carry about three thousand. Offering the same selection at a store would require a huge location with a correspondingly large amount of inventory. The showroom channel can sometimes offer even greater variety than the online channel for products with a significant amount of customization. For example, Indochino, a provider of men's suits has small showrooms that only carry enough inventories so that customers can select fabrics and styles. Customers are fitted in the showrooms and the made-to-measure suits are produced offsite at a low cost location. Through the showroom, Indochino is able to provide a unique product for each customer.

PRODUCT AVAILABILITY By aggregating its inventory, a company selling online or using showrooms improves product availability. Building the product to order allows further improvement in product availability. For example, Indochino carries its inventory at production locations in the form of fabric and components. These inputs are assembled-to-measure for each customer only after an order is placed. The presence of inventory in the form of common components and assembly to order allows Indochino to ensure the availability of each customer's specific style, size, and fit.

CUSTOMER EXPERIENCE Each channel has complementary strengths in terms of customer experience. A customer's ability to touch, feel and see a product and be helped by a sales person, may add a lot of value for customers shopping for an engagement ring at Tiffany. Similarly, the ability to try on a few suits and be measured for an exact fit, may add a lot of value to men seeking a custom tailored suit at an Indochino showroom. In contrast, customers shopping online for groceries at Peapod may value the experience of never having to leave home to shop for their groceries. In developed markets, retailers have worked hard to provide customers with a relatively seamless shopping experience across multiple devices and browsers. For example, Tesco's South Korean affiliate Homeplus allows customers to shop at Seoul subway stations using their smartphone and then continue shopping with an app if their train arrives before the order is complete. In emerging countries like India, however, there is a large segment of the population without Internet access. In those settings, retail stores and showrooms have a significant advantage in allowing customers to touch, feel, and see the product before making a purchase.

FASTER TIME TO MARKET A firm can introduce a new product much more quickly online or through showrooms as compared to retail stores. A firm that sells electronics through retail stores must produce enough units to stock the shelves at its distributors and retailers before it starts to see revenue from the new product. A firm selling online, in contrast, makes a new product available online as soon as the first unit is ready to be produced.

ORDER VISIBILITY Order visibility is critical for customers using the showroom or online channel. It is automatic for customers shopping at a retail store.

RETURNABILITY Returnability is easier when the customer has access to a physical location such as a retail store or showroom. The proportion of returns is likely to be much higher for channels where information exchange is remote.

DIRECT SALES TO CUSTOMERS Manufacturers and other members of the supply chain that do not traditionally have direct contact with customers can use remote information exchange for direct access to customers. For example, in 2015 Nike sold products worth more than a billion dollars directly to customers using the online channel.

EFFICIENT FUNDS TRANSFER The Internet and smart phones can enhance the convenience and lower the cost of revenue collection, especially in small amounts. This capability is particularly effective in emerging markets as shown by the success of M-Pesa in Kenya. M-Pesa was first launched by the Kenyan mobile network operator Safaricom in 2007 to allow users to deposit, withdraw, transfer money and pay for goods and services. By 2015, the service had about 20 million subscribers in Kenya. The large network operator Vodafone has tried to take this service to other emerging markets in Africa, Asia, and Europe.

Performance of Channels in Terms of Cost

We now consider the performance of different channels in terms of the cost of inventory, facilities, transportation, and information.

INVENTORY The online and the showroom channels can lower inventory levels by aggregating inventories in a few locations if customers are willing to wait for delivery. For example, Blue Nile is able to aggregate its inventory of diamonds at two warehouses worldwide. Tiffany, in contrast, needs more inventory because it must carry a significant portion of its stock at hundreds of retail stores. A key point to note is that the relative benefit of aggregation is small for high-demand items with low variability but large for low-demand items with high variability.

The online and showroom channels can operate with very low levels of inventory if they can postpone the introduction of variety until after the customer order is received. Indochino carries very low levels of inventory because it starts production of a customized suit only after an order has been placed. Keeping all inventories in the form of fabric and components results in significantly less inventory compared to keeping it as finished goods. Amazon uses print on demand technology for books that sell in very low volumes, allowing it to reduce inventories.

FACILITIES Two basic types of facility costs must be included in the analysis: (1) costs related to the physical facilities in a network and (2) costs associated with the operations that take place in these facilities. The online channel with home delivery is likely to have the lowest facility costs because it can centralize its operations. The retail channel is likely to have the highest facility costs because it needs many facilities to allow face-to-face information exchange and product pickup. The showroom channel is likely to have facility costs between the two extremes because it needs smaller facilities than a retail store. The online channel with pickup is likely to have low facility costs if using an existing location for pickup but medium facility costs if building new pickup locations.

For example, whereas Blockbuster had about 3,500 stores to rent movies to its customers, Netflix was able to ship DVDs to its customers from less than 60 facilities. Not only did Netflix have much lower costs related to the physical facilities, it also had much better labor utilization and lower operating costs because of the centralization.

When online orders are filled from stores, however, the costs associated with operations can be higher than usual because employees must pick a customer order instead of customers doing so on their own. This increase in costs is often hard to justify if customers are unwilling to pay a premium.

TRANSPORTATION The Internet has significantly lowered the cost of "transporting" information goods in digital form, such as movies, music, and books. For nondigital products, aggregating inventories increases outbound transportation relative to inbound transportation. Compared

to a business with many retail outlets, an online seller with aggregated inventories tends to have higher transportation costs per unit because of the increased outbound costs. Whereas the traditional retail channel incurs the lowest transportation costs, the showroom and online channel with home delivery incur the highest transportation costs. Customer pickup can lower the transportation cost for the showroom and online channel to almost the same as traditional retail if volumes are large enough.

INFORMATION All companies incur costs to build and maintain their information infrastructure. For example, when Amazon purchased Zappos, it had to add about 120,000 product descriptions and more than 2 million photographs to its website. In general, the investment in information infrastructure is higher for channels that provide information remotely and have to track customer orders. The traditional retail channel uses the customer's ability to experience the product physically and then pick it up on her own to reduce the amount they need to invest in information infrastructure.

The relative costs for the various channels are summarized in Table 4-9.

A Framework for Omni-Channel Retailing

As highlighted in Table 4-8, both product characteristics and customer needs will influence the choice of channel best suited to serve the customer. Dell's transition from the online channel to traditional retail, Gateway's failure with the showroom channel, and Apple's success with traditional retail, highlight the importance of understanding product characteristics and customer needs that are best served by each channel.

For our framework, we characterize products along three dimensions–demand uncertainty, value, and information complexity. Value refers to the cost of a unit of product. A box of detergent is a relatively low value product, whereas a diamond is a high value product. Demand for detergent is relatively predictable and has low uncertainty. In contrast, each diamond is unique and it is impossible to predict when a customer will want that particular stone. In general, demand uncertainty grows as product variety increases. A box of detergent can be described with a limited amount of information about the manufacturer and quantity. There are aspects of a diamond ring, however, that are hard to describe and many people will want to see the ring before a purchase. For these people a diamond has a high level of information complexity that can only be resolved once they see the stone. While these three dimensions do not completely characterize a product, we focus on them for our framework.

We characterize customers by their willingness to pay for a variety of service elements such as help with product selection, responsiveness, home delivery, or the ability to shop in an

TABLE 4-9 Relative Costs for Omni-Channel Alternatives

	Traditional Retail	Showrooms + Home Delivery	Online Information + Home Delivery	Online Information + Pickup
Inventory	High	Low - Medium	Low	Low - Medium
Facilities	High	Medium	Low	Low - Medium
Transportation by retailer	Low	High	High	Medium
Transportation by customer	High	High	Low	Medium
Information	Low	High	High	High

upscale environment. *Price conscious* customers will make the effort to select the channel that offers the lowest price. In contrast, *service conscious* customers are willing to pay a premium if a channel provides them service elements that they value. A family with young children may be willing to pay extra to have groceries delivered at home. A bride-to-be may value the experience of shopping at an upscale bridal shop where staff helps her try on and select her wedding dress.

We now characterize the strengths of each channel in terms of product characteristics and customer preferences that they are ideally suited to target.

TRADITIONAL RETAIL This channel is ideally suited to provide predictable demand products (such as detergent) at a low price. The channel is even more price competitive if the shipping cost of the product is high relative to its value (such as for diapers). The channel is also well suited for high information complexity products such as apparel. Given the unpredictable demand of fashion apparel, however, traditional retail can best compete if customers are willing to pay a premium for the in-store service and the ability to try the product. Traditional retail can be price competitive for uncertain demand products if the rate of product return for the online channel is high.

SHOWROOMS This channel is ideally suited to compete on price for products with high information complexity, unpredictable demand, and high value. Fashion goods, men's suits, and expensive cars with lots of options are examples of products that fit this category. The presence of the showroom allows customers to experience the product in person. The absence of inventory at the showroom allows the supply chain to operate with low levels of inventory, thus lowering cost. In many instances, the absence of local inventory allows the supply chain to produce the product to order at lower cost facilities. High fashion products in general seem to be well suited for the showroom channel.

ONLINE INFORMATION + HOME DELIVERY This channel is ideally suited to compete on price for products with unpredictable demand and low information complexity (such as books that are not best sellers). This channel becomes even more price competitive if shipping cost for the product is low relative to its value (which is often the case for high value products). For predictable demand products such as diapers and detergent, this channel can compete for customers who are willing to pay a premium for the convenience of home delivery.

ONLINE INFORMATION + PICKUP This channel is an ideal complement to the home delivery channel because it has a lower delivery cost. It becomes more price competitive than the home delivery channel for products with unpredictable demand and low information complexity. The pickup option can also allow the online channel to become more price competitive for predictable demand products such as groceries and common consumer packaged goods.

Tables 4-10, 4-11, and 4-12 summarize key aspects of our framework for omni-channel retailing. A lot of the rationale supporting this framework is detailed and developed in later chapters in the book.

Let us return to the decisions of Dell, Gateway, and Apple in the context of our framework. In the 1990s, Dell succeeded in selling customized PCs online because the large number of customizable configurations made it very difficult to predict demand for any specific configuration. Dell reduced the information complexity of customization by identifying about ten dimensions (such as memory and processor) where customers could make a choice using drop down menus. The unpredictable demand and low information complexity made customized PCs ideally suited for the online channel in the 1990s. As hardware became more powerful, customization became less important and people were happy with a few standard choices. As variety decreased, demand became more predictable. Thus, Dell's decision to sell lower cost, standard configurations through retail is consistent with our framework. Gateway, in contrast, did not use all the available strengths of its retail network according to our framework. For niche

TABLE 4-10 Product Demand Uncertainty and Omni-Channel Retailing

	Predictable Demand Product	**Unpredictable Demand Product**
Traditional Retail	Compete on price	Compete on service for high information complexity products
Showrooms	Not suitable	Compete on price and variety for high information complexity products
Online Information + Home Delivery	Compete on service	Compete on price and variety
Online Information + Pickup	Compete on ability to provide service at a lower price	More competitive on price than home delivery option

TABLE 4-11 Product Value and Omni-Channel Retailing

	Low Value Product	**High Value Product**
Traditional Retail	Compete on price for predictable demand products	Compete on service for products with uncertain demand and high information complexity
Showrooms	Compete on high variety at reasonable price for high information complexity products	Compete on price for customizable, high information complexity products
Online Information + Home Delivery	Compete on service	Compete on price and variety
Online Information + Pickup	Compete on ability to provide service at a lower price	More competitive on price than home delivery option

TABLE 4-12 Product Information Complexity and Omni-Channel Retailing

	Low Information Complexity Product	**High Information Complexity Product**
Traditional Retail	Compete on price for predictable demand products	Compete on service for uncertain demand products
Showrooms	Not suitable	Compete on price for uncertain demand products
Online Information + Home Delivery	Compete on price for uncertain demand products	Compete on service in terms of variety and availability for uncertain demand products
Online Information + Pickup	Compete on price for uncertain demand products	A slightly cheaper option to compete on service in terms of variety and availability for uncertain demand products

configurations whose demand is unpredictable, it made sense for Gateway to use its stores as showrooms. For standard configurations with predictable demand, however, Gateway would have been better served by carrying such products in inventory at its stores. As per our framework, Gateway would have been more successful if its stores had played a dual role, serving as traditional retail for standard configurations and showrooms for niche configurations. In contrast to Gateway, Apple has fully used all the strengths of its retail network. Its stores serve as

showrooms that let first time buyers experience their products before purchase. The products themselves are standard and have very low variety. The resulting predictability of demand makes them ideally suited for traditional retail. An Apple store serves as both a showroom and traditional retail, something that Gateway failed to do with its stores. Apple carries standard products at its stores while delivering customized products from the assembly plant where they are built to order.

The failure of firms to build a suitably tailored omni-channel portfolio can leave them squeezed in terms of both responsiveness and cost. A classic example of this outcome was the fate of big-box consumer electronics stores like Circuit City. The company got squeezed by the online channel and warehouse clubs like Costco, with each serving different customer needs. Costco only provides a limited variety of popular items. By choosing to focus primarily on predictable demand items, Costco is able to provide them at a low price. The online channel, in contrast, is cost effective in providing customers a wide variety of consumer electronics. The tailored combination of the online channel providing variety at low cost and players like Costco providing the standard products at low cost is much more effective at meeting customer needs in a cost effective manner than a big box retailer like Circuit City. Firms must understand their strengths and weaknesses in each sector of retailing. They can then either choose to only focus on their strengths or add channels to their portfolio that address their weaknesses.

It is important to understand that each of the four channels have complementary strengths that should be tailored to work together effectively. It is not necessary for every firm to operate every channel. Each firm should consider the products it sells and the customers it wants to target when deciding on its omni-channel portfolio. For example, a chain of retail stores may choose to carry inventory for products with predictable demand while serving as a showroom for products with unpredictable demand. The chain of retail stores can also serve as an effective pickup location for online orders. The ability to use its store network as traditional retail, showrooms, and pickup locations creates an effective omni-channel portfolio for the retailer. In the case of consumer electronics, Best Buy has had some success by using its chain of retail stores in this manner. Similarly, Seven-Eleven Japan has had great success using its retail stores as traditional retail for the three thousand most popular items and as a pickup location for another 3 million items. An online channel providing home delivery may choose to add pickup locations if it wants to attract and profitably keep more price sensitive customers. For example, Amazon has added pickup locations on many university campuses to lower its cost of delivery to students. Amazon's partnership in India with local retailers allows it to use their stores as both showrooms and pickup locations. Customers without Internet access are able to obtain product information at the local retail store and then pay with cash when they come to pick up the delivery from Amazon. Amazon and local retailers together create an effective omni-channel portfolio in India.

SUMMARY OF LEARNING OBJECTIVE 3

Omni-channel retailing has the potential to combine the complementary strengths of physical stores and the online channel. Physical stores are good at letting customers experience high information complexity products in person. They are also cost effective at selling products with predictable demand. The online channel, in contrast, is cost effective at selling products with unpredictable demand but cannot let customers experience high information complexity products. An effective portfolio results if brick-and-mortar stores sell predictable demand items, serve as showrooms for high information complexity items with unpredictable demand, and serve as pickup locations for the online channel, while the online channel delivers unpredictable demand items to the customer.

DISCUSSION QUESTIONS

1. What effect does the geographic disparity of customers in a large country, like India or China, have on selecting the number of distributors needed to supply, for example, electrical white goods such as fridges to retailers? Refer to the supply chain costs that such a decision might lead to in your answer.

2. A large, European white goods manufacturer is considering expanding its operations to China using a range of products, localizing some to suit the specific needs of the Chinese market. All localization work is carried out in China. Note that localization generally relates to elements of a product rather than the entire product. What sort of distribution network should this company use?

3. A distributor has heard that one of the major manufacturers from which it buys is considering going direct to the consumer. What can the distributor do about this? What advantages can it offer the manufacturer that the manufacturer is unlikely to be able to reproduce?

4. What type of distribution network is typically best suited for the sale of "click-and-collect" apparel items?

5. What are the advantages of using the drop-shipping distribution network?

6. Consider an online shopping website like Amazon, which implements the drop-shipping arrangement to reduce inventory costs. What are some of the disadvantages such online retailers would face with this system?

7. Using the purchase of an engagement ring as an example, identify whether a brick-and-mortar retailer or an online shop is the most appropriate retail channel(s) for this type of product. How should the selected channel perform in terms of customer service elements?

8. Consider an auto parts retailer implementing distributor storage with last-mile delivery. List some advantages and disadvantages that the retailer would experience with this method.

9. Consider the sale of home improvement products at Home Depot or a chain of hardware stores such as True Value. Which can extract the greater benefit from adding the online channel? Why?

10. Amazon sells books, music, electronics, software, toys, and home improvement products online. In which product category does going online offer the greatest advantage compared with a retail store chain? In which product category does the online channel offer the smallest advantage (or a potential cost disadvantage) compared with a retail store chain? Why?

11. Why should an online seller such as Amazon build more warehouses as its sales volume grows?

12. Amazon has opened bookstores and announced the opening of convenience stores. How can these traditional retail channels allow Amazon to complement its online channel effectively?

BIBLIOGRAPHY

Bell, David R., Santiago Gallino, and Antonio Moreno."How to Win in an Omnichannel World." *MIT Sloan Management Review* (Fall 2014): 56, 45–53.

Brynjolfsson, Erik, Yu Jeffrey Hu, and Mahammad S. Rahman."Competing in the Age of Omnichannel Retailing." *MIT Sloan Management Review* (Summer 2013): 54, 23–29.

Chopra, Sunil. "Designing the Delivery Network for a Supply Chain."*Transportation Research, Part E* (2003): 39, 123–140.

Chopra, Sunil. "How Omni-Channel Can be the Future of Retailing." *Decision* (June 2016): 43(2), 135–144.

Chopra, Sunil. "Movie Rental Business: Blockbuster, Netflix, and Redbox." Kellogg School of Management Case # 5-310-507, 2010.

Chopra, Sunil, and Jan Van Mieghem. "Which e-Business Is Right for Your Supply Chain?" *Supply Chain Management Review* (July–August 2000): 32–40.

Evans, Philip, and Thomas S. Wurster."Getting Real about Virtual Commerce." *Harvard Business Review* (November–December 1999): 84–94.

Hobkirk, Ian."Key Distribution Strategies of Top Omni-Channel Retailers."*Supply Chain Management Review* (December 2015): 16–21.

Lee, Hau L., and Seungjin Whang."Winning the Last Mile of e-Commerce." *Sloan Management Review* (Summer 2001): 54–62.

Olavson, Thomas, Hau Lee, and Gavin DeNyse."A Portfolio Approach to Supply Chain Design." *Supply Chain Management Review* (July–August 2010): 20–27.

Raman, Ananth, and Bharat P. Rao. *A Tale of Two Electronic Component Suppliers.* Harvard Business School Case 9–697–064, 1997.

Ricker, Fred R., and Ravi Kalakota. "Order Fulfillment: The Hidden Key to e-Commerce Success." *Supply Chain Management Review* (Fall 1999): 60–70.

Salcedo, Simon, and Ann Grackin."The e-Value Chain." *Supply Chain Management Review* (Winter 2000): 63–70.

Willcocks, Leslie P., and Robert Plant. "Pathways to e-Business Leadership: Getting from Bricks to Clicks." *Sloan Management Review* (Spring 2001): 50–59.

Shapiro, Carl, and Hal R. Varian. *Information Rules: A Strategic Guide to the Network Economy.* Boston: Harvard Business School Press, 1999.

CASE STUDY

Blue Nile and Diamond Retailing[1]

A customer walks into your jewelry store with printouts of diamond selections from Blue Nile, a company that is the largest online retailer of diamonds. The list price for the customer's desired diamond is only $100 above your total cost for a stone of the same characteristics. Do you let the customer walk, or come down in price to compete?[2]

This dilemma has faced many jewelers. Some argue that jewelers should lower prices on stones to keep the customer. Future sales and add-on sales such as custom designs, mountings, and repairs can then be used to make additional margins. Others argue that cutting prices to compete sends a negative signal to loyal customers from the past who may be upset by the fact that they were not given the best price.

As the economy tightened during the holiday season of 2007, the differences in performance between Blue Nile and bricks-and-mortar retailers were startling. In January 2008, Blue Nile reported a 24 percent jump in sales during its fourth quarter. For the same quarter, Tiffany posted a 2 percent drop in domestic same-store sales, and Zales reported a 9 percent drop. The management at Blue Nile felt that the downturn represented an opportunity to gain market share because of their competitive pricing.

The Diamond Retailing Industry

For both wholesalers and retailers in the diamond industry, 2008 was a very difficult year. It was so bad at the supply end that the dealers' trade association, the World Federation of Diamond Bourses, issued an appeal for the diamond producers to reduce the supply of new gems entering the market in an effort to reduce supply.

However, the world's largest producer, De Beers, appeared unmoved, refusing to give any commitment to curtail production. The company had recently opened the Voorspoed mine in South Africa, which, when fully operational, could add 800,000 carats a year into an already oversupplied market. Historically, De Beers had exerted tremendous control over the supply of diamonds, going so far as to purchase large quantities of rough diamonds from other producers. In 2005, the European Commission forced De Beers to phase out its agreement to buy diamonds from ALROSA, the world's second largest diamond producer, which accounted for most of the diamond production in Russia. Russia was the second largest producer of diamonds in the world after Botswana.

Although discount retailers such as Walmart and Costco continued to thrive, the situation was difficult for traditional jewelry retailers. Friedman's filed for Chapter 11 bankruptcy protection in January 2008, followed by Chicago-based Whitehall in June. When it filed for bankruptcy, Friedman was the third largest jewelry chain in North America, with 455 stores, whereas Whitehall ranked fifth, with 375 stores in April 2008. In February 2008, Zales announced a plan to close more than 100 stores that year. This shakeup offered an opportunity for other players to move in and try to gain market share.

With the weakening economy, the third and fourth quarters of 2008 were particularly hard on diamond retailers. Even historically successful players such as Blue Nile, Tiffany, and Zales saw a decline in sales and a significant drop in their share price. As customers tightened their belts and cut back on discretionary spending, high-cost purchases such as diamond jewelry were often the first to be postponed. The situation worsened as competition for the shrinking number of customers became fiercer. In such a difficult environment, it was hard to judge which factors could best help different jewelry retailers succeed.

Blue Nile

In December 1998, Mark Vadon, a young consultant, was shopping for an engagement ring and stumbled across a company called Internet Diamonds, run by Seattle jeweler Doug Williams. Vadon not only bought a ring but also went into business with Williams in early 1999. The company changed its name to Blue Nile by the end of 1999 because the new name "sounded elegant and upscale," according to Vadon.

On its website, Blue Nile articulated its philosophy as follows: "Offer high-quality diamonds and fine jewelry at outstanding prices. When you visit our website, you'll find extraordinary jewelry, useful guidance,

[1]Sunil Chopra.

[2]Stacey King, "The Internet: Retailers' New Challenge," Professional Jeweller Magazine, August 1999.

and easy-to-understand jewelry education that's perfect for your occasion."[3]

Many customers (especially men) liked the low-pressure selling tactics that focused on education. Besides explaining the four Cs—cut, color, clarity, and carat—Blue Nile allowed customers to "build your own ring." Starting with the cut they preferred, customers could determine ranges along each of the four Cs and price. Blue Nile then displayed all stones in inventory that fit the customer's desired profile. Customers selected the stone of their choice, followed by the setting they liked best. Blue Nile also allowed customers to have their questions resolved on the phone by sales reps who did not work on commission. This low-pressure selling approach had great appeal to a segment of the population. In a *BusinessWeek* article in 2008, Internet entrepreneur Jason Calacanis was quoted as saying that shopping for his engagement ring (for which he spent "tens of thousands of dollars") on Blue Nile "was the best shopping experience he never had."[4]

The company focused on providing good value to its customers. Whereas retail jewelers routinely marked up diamonds by up to 50 percent, Blue Nile kept a lower markup of around 20 percent. Blue Nile believed that it could afford the lower markup because of lower inventory and warehousing expense. Unlike jewelry retailers who maintained stores in high-priced areas, Blue Nile had a single warehouse in the United States in which it stocked its entire inventory.

The company strategy was not without hurdles because some customers did not care as much about underpricing the competition. For example, some customers preferred a piece of fine jewelry from a well-known retailer such as Tiffany to getting a price discount. Also, it was not entirely clear that customers would be willing to spend thousands of dollars on an item they had not seen or touched. To counter this issue, Blue Nile offered a 30-day money back guarantee on items in original condition.

In 2007, the company launched websites in Canada and the United Kingdom and opened an office in Dublin with local customer service and fulfillment operations. The Dublin office offered free shipping to several countries in Western Europe. The U.S. facility handled international shipping to some countries in the Asia–Pacific region. International sales had increased from $17 million in 2007 to more than $81 million in 2015.

By 2007, Blue Nile had sold more than 70,000 rings larger than a carat, with 25 orders totaling more than $100,000. In June 2007, the company sold a single diamond for $1.5 million. *Forbes* called it perhaps "the largest consumer purchase in Web history—and also the most unlikely."[5] The stone, larger than 10 carats, had a diameter roughly the size of a penny. Blue Nile did not have the stone in inventory, but its network of suppliers quickly located one on a plane en route from a dealer in New York to a retailer in Italy. The stone was rerouted to Blue Nile headquarters in Seattle and transported in a Brinks armored carrier to the buyer—and the whole process took only three days.

In February 2014, Blue Nile offered more than 140,000 diamonds on its site. Of these diamonds, more than 50,000 were one carat or larger, with prices up to $2.9 million. Almost 76,000 diamonds on the Blue Nile website were priced higher than $2,500. In 2010, company CEO Diane Irvine said, "We're not positioned as a discounter. We are selling a very high-end product but selling it for much less."[6] The 2012 annual report stated that "we aim to limit our diamond offerings to those possessing characteristics associated with high quality."[7]

In 2012, the company had sales of about $400 million with a net income of $8.4 million. Although sales had risen, income had dropped relative to 2011. The company had also started to offer a broad range of non-engagement products, including rings, wedding bands, necklaces, pendants, bracelets, and gifts and accessories containing precious metals, diamonds, gemstones, or pearls. The company, however, maintained that the engagement category was its core business.

By 2016, Blue Nile had opened five brick-and-mortar "Webrooms" where consultants helped customers who wanted to see, touch and feel an engagement ring before buying. The goal of the Webrooms was to provide the low pressure, online experience in a physical location where customers could directly experience the product before making a purchase. All transactions continued to happen online either through a store tablet or the customer's own device.

[3]Blue Nile Affiliate Program., © 2017, Blue Nile Inc
[4]Jay Greene, "Blue Nile: No Diamond in the Rough," *BusinessWeek e.biz*, May 2000.
[5]Victoria Murphy Barret, "The Digital Diamond District," © 2007, Forbes.com.
[6]Diane Irvine, Creating a Two-Horned Dilemma., © 2010, Fast Company & Inc.
[7]2012 Annual report of Blue Nile, Inc. U.S Securities and Exchange Commission.

In November 2016, Blue Nile entered into an agreement to be acquired by an investor group comprising Bain Capital Private Equity and Bow Street LLC for $500 million in cash.

Zales

The first Zales Jewelers was established by Morris (M. B.) Zale, William Zale, and Ben Lipshy in 1924. Their marketing strategy was to offer a credit plan of "a penny down and a dollar a week." Their success allowed them to grow to twelve stores in Oklahoma and Texas by 1941. Over the next four decades, the company grew to hundreds of stores by buying up other stores and smaller chains.

In 1986, the company was purchased in a leveraged buyout by Peoples Jewelers of Canada and Swarovski International. In 1992, its debt pushed Zales into Chapter 11 bankruptcy for a year. It became a public company again in that decade and operated nearly 2,400 stores by 2005. The company's divisions included Piercing Pagoda, which ran mall-based kiosks selling jewelry to teenagers; Zales Jewelers, which sold diamond jewelry for working-class mall shoppers; and the upscale Gordon's. Bailey Banks & Biddle Fine Jewelers, which offered even pricier products out of fancier malls, was sold by Zale Corporation in November 2007.

Three years of declining market share, lost mostly to discounters such as Walmart and Costco, put pressure on Zales to decide on a makeover by 2005. Zales dumped its lower-value 10-karat gold jewelry and modest-quality diamonds. The goal was to make the jeweler more upscale and fashion conscious, moving away from its promotion-driven, lower-end reputation. Unfortunately, the move was a disaster. There were delays in bringing in new merchandise, and same-store sales dropped. The company lost many of its traditional customers without winning the new ones it desired. It was soon passed by Akron, Ohio-based Sterling (a subsidiary of the Signet Group) as the largest jeweler in the United States. The chief executive officer of Zale Corporation was forced to resign by early 2006.

In August 2006, under a new CEO, Zales started a transition to return to its role as a promotional retailer focused on diamond fashion jewelry and diamond rings. The transition involved selling nearly $50 million in discontinued inventory from its upscale strategy and an expenditure of $120 million on new inventory. As a result of the inventory write-downs, Zales lost $26.4 million in its quarter ending July 31, 2006.

The company had some success with its new strategy but was hurt by the rise in fuel prices and falling home prices in 2007 that made its middle-class customers feel less secure. Its core customers hesitated to buy jewelry as they battled higher prices for food and fuel. Zales reported a profit of $1.5 million in the quarter ending July 31, 2007, but same-store sales fell by 0.5 percent. In February 2008, the company announced a plan to close approximately 105 stores, reduce inventory by $100 million, and reduce staff in company headquarters by about 20 percent. The goal of this plan was to enhance the company's profitability and improve its overall effectiveness. After many years of losses, the company finally reported a profit for 2012 (see Table 4-13).

In May 2014, the Zale Corporation was acquired by Signet Jewelers Limited, the largest specialty retail jeweler in the United States and U.K. Besides Zales, Signet also operated other chains such as Kay Jewelers and Jared. The company's focus on an omni-channel approach allowed it to achieve online sales of almost $360 million in 2015, a significant increase over 2014.

Tiffany

Tiffany opened in 1837 as a stationery and fancy goods emporium in New York City. It published its first catalog in 1845. The company enjoyed tremendous success, with its silver designs in particular becoming popular all over the world. In 1886, Tiffany introduced its now famous "Tiffany setting" for solitaire engagement rings. The Tiffany brand was so strong that it helped set diamond and platinum purity standards used all over the world. In 1950, Truman Capote published his best seller *Breakfast at Tiffany's*, which was released as a successful film in 1961. After more than a century of tremendous success with its jewelry and other products, the company went public in 1987.

Tiffany's high-end products included diamond rings, wedding bands, gemstone jewelry, and gemstone bands with diamonds as the primary gemstone. The company also sold non-gemstone gold, platinum, and sterling silver jewelry. Other products included watches and high-end items for the home, such as crystal and sterling silver serving trays. Besides its own designs, Tiffany also sold jewelry designed by Elsa Peretti, Paloma Picasso, the late Jean Schlumberger, and architect Frank Gehry.

TABLE 4-13 **Select** Financial Data for Blue Nile, Inc., Zale Corporation, and Tiffany & Co. (in millions of dollars) for 2012

	Blue Nile	Zales	Tiffany
Net sales	400.0	1,888.0	3,794.2
Cost of sales	325.0	903.6	1,631.0
Gross profit	75.1	984.4	2,163.2
Selling, general, and administrative expenses	62.8	916.3	1,466.1
Operating income	12.3	35.1	697.2
Net income	8.4	10.0	416.1
Cash and cash equivalents	87.0	17.1	504.8
Net receivables	3.5	—	174.0
Inventories	33.3	767.5	2,234.3
Total current assets	125.9	837.2	3,151.6
Property and equipment	7.9	108.9	818.8
Other assets	12.1	241.2	660.4
Total assets	145.9	1,187.3	4,630.9
Accounts payable	116.2	220.6	295.4
Stockholder equity	14.1	185.3	2,611.3

By 2012, Tiffany had 275 stores and boutiques all over the world, with about 90 of them in the United States. Of its global outlets, Tiffany had more than 50 in Japan and more than 65 in the rest of the Asia-Pacific region. Stores ranged from 1,300 to 18,000 square feet, with an average of 7,100 square feet. Its flagship store in New York contributed about 10 percent of the company's sales in 2007. Besides retail outlets, Tiffany also sold products through a website and catalogs. The company, however, did not offer any engagement jewelry through its website as of 2012. Its high-end products, including jewelry, were sold primarily through the retail stores. The direct channel focused on what Tiffany referred to as "D" items, which consisted primarily of non-gemstone sterling silver jewelry with an average price of $200 in 2007. Category D sales represented about 58 percent of total sales for the direct channel. In contrast, more than half the retail sales came from high-end products such as diamond rings and gemstone jewelry with an average sale price in 2007 higher than $3,000.

Tiffany maintained its own manufacturing facilities in Rhode Island and New York but also continued to source from third parties. In 2007, the company sourced almost 60 percent of its jewelry from internal manufacturing facilities. Tiffany had a retail service center in New Jersey that focused on receiving product from all over the world and replenishing its retail stores. The company had a separate customer fulfillment center for processing direct-to-customer orders.

Until 2003, the company did not purchase any rough diamonds, focusing entirely on the purchase of polished stones. Since then, the company established diamond-processing operations in Canada, South Africa, Botswana, Namibia, Belgium, China, and Vietnam. In 2007, approximately 40 percent of the diamonds used by Tiffany were produced from rough diamonds purchased by the company. Not all rough diamonds could be cut and polished to the quality standards of Tiffany. Diamonds that failed to meet Tiffany's standards were then sold to third parties at market price, sometimes at a loss.

In 2012, 90 percent of Tiffany's net sales came from jewelry, with approximately 48 percent of net sales coming from products containing diamonds of various sizes.[8] Products containing one or more diamonds of one carat or larger accounted for more than 10 percent of net sales in 2007. Select financial details of Tiffany's performance in 2012 are shown in Table 4-13.

The Tiffany brand's association with quality, luxury, and exclusivity was an important part of its success. No other diamond and jewelry retailer enjoyed margins anywhere near those enjoyed by Tiffany. In its annual reports, the company listed the strong brand as a major risk factor because any dilution in its brand image would have a significant negative impact on its margins.

Study Questions

1. What are some key success factors in diamond retailing? How do Blue Nile, Zales, and Tiffany compare on those dimensions?
 How do they compare on various financial measures discussed in Chapter 3?

[8]Tiffany Annual Report, March 2013.

2. What do you think of the fact that Blue Nile carries many stones priced at $2,500 or higher, whereas a large fraction of the products sold from the Tiffany website are priced at around $200? Which of the two product categories is better suited to the strengths of the online channel?

3. What do you think of Tiffany's decision to not sell engagement rings online? What do you think of Blue Nile's growth into the non-engagement category?

4. Given that Tiffany stores have thrived with their focus on selling high-end jewelry, what do you think caused the failure of Zales' upscale strategy in 2006? What products should Zale focus on?

5. Which of the three companies do you think is best structured to deal with weak economic times?

6. What advice would you give to each of the three companies regarding its strategy and structure? How can they best use omni-channel retail?

CHAPTER

5

Network Design
in the Supply Chain

LEARNING OBJECTIVES

After reading this chapter, you will be able to

5.1 Understand the role of network design in a supply chain.

5.2 Identify factors influencing supply chain network design decisions.

5.3 Discuss a framework for making network design decisions.

5.4 Develop an optimization model to design a regional network configuration.

5.5 Develop an optimization model to identify potential sites in a region.

5.6 Develop an optimization model to locate plants and allocate market demand.

I n this chapter, we start with the broad supply chain design discussed in Chapter 4 and focus on the fundamental questions of facility location, capacity allocation, and market allocation when designing a supply chain network. We identify and discuss the various factors that influence the facility location, capacity, and market allocation decisions. We then establish a framework and discuss various solution methodologies for network design decisions in a supply chain.

THE ROLE OF NETWORK DESIGN IN THE SUPPLY CHAIN

5.1 Understand the role of network design in a supply chain.

Supply chain *network design decisions* include how many manufacturing plants, production lines, distribution centers, and cross-dock facilities a firm should have, where they should be located, how much capacity should be allocated to each facility, which products should each facility produce or handle, and which markets should each facility serve.

It is important to make network design decisions in the context of the supply chain strategy because they determine the supply chain configuration and set constraints within which the other supply chain drivers can be used either to decrease supply chain cost or to increase responsiveness. For example, increasing the number of facilities has allowed Amazon to become even more responsive to its customers. Customers in many urban areas in the United States can now get same day delivery and in some instances even one hour delivery. The larger number of facilities, however, has required a high level of investment and increased Amazon's costs.

Facility location decisions have a long-term impact on a supply chain's performance because it is expensive to shut down a facility or move it to a different location. Within most supply chains, production facilities are harder to change than storage facilities. Supply chain network designers must consider that any factories will stay where located for an extended period of a decade or more. Warehouses or storage facilities, though, particularly those that are not owned by the company, can be changed within a year of making the decision. A good location decision can help a supply chain be responsive while keeping its costs low. Toyota, for example, built its first U.S. assembly plant in Lexington, Kentucky, in 1988, and has continued to build new plants in the United States since then. The U.S. plants proved profitable for Toyota when the yen strengthened and cars produced in Japan were too expensive to be cost competitive with cars produced in the United States. Local plants allowed Toyota to be responsive to the U.S. market while keeping costs low.

Managers must consider not only future demand and costs when locating facilities, but also scenarios in which technology may change. Otherwise, facilities may become useless within a few years. For example, an insurance company moved its clerical labor from a metropolitan location to a suburban location to lower costs. With increasing automation, however, the need for clerical labor decreased significantly, and within a few years the facility was no longer needed. The company found it difficult to sell the facility, given its distance from residential areas and airports (Harding, 1988).

The allocation of capacity to facilities can be altered more easily than location, but capacity decisions do tend to stay in place for several years. Allocating too much capacity to a location results in poor utilization and, as a result, higher costs. Allocating too little capacity results in poor responsiveness if demand is not satisfied or high cost if demand is filled from a distant facility. The allocation of supply sources and markets to facilities has a significant impact on performance because it affects total production, inventory, and transportation costs incurred by the supply chain to satisfy customer demand. This decision should be reconsidered on a regular basis so the allocation can be changed as production and transportation costs, market conditions, or plant capacities change. Of course, the allocation of markets and supply sources can be changed only if the facilities are flexible enough to serve different markets and receive supply from different sources.

The allocation of products and flexibility to facilities has a significant impact on both cost and responsiveness. When multiple products are allocated to a facility, costs tend to increase because of the additional flexibility required. A flexible facility, however, can handle fluctuations of demand across its products more effectively than a facility dedicated to a single product. Whereas a dedicated facility would have idle capacity if demand for its product decreased, a flexible facility could use the available capacity to produce more of another product whose demand may have increased. For example, Toyota has plants located worldwide, in each market that it serves. Before 1997, each plant was capable of serving only its local market. This hurt Toyota when the Asian economy went into a recession in the late 1990s. The local plants in Asia had idle capacity that could not be used to serve other markets that were experiencing excess demand. Toyota has added flexibility to each plant to be able to serve markets other than the local one. This additional flexibility helps Toyota deal more effectively with changing global market conditions. Similarly, the flexibility of Honda's U.S. plants to produce both SUVs and cars in the same plant was helpful in 2008 when SUV demand dropped but small-car demand did not.

Network design decisions must be revisited as market conditions change or when two companies merge. For example, as its subscriber base grew by 2010, Netflix mailed DVDs from 58 DCs across the United States to lower transportation cost and improve responsiveness. With the growth in video streaming and the corresponding drop in DVD rentals, Netflix closed almost 20 DCs by the end of 2013. In contrast, Amazon increased the number of DCs in the United States from about 20 in 2009 to about 70 in 2016. Changing the number, location, and demand allocation of DCs with changing demand has been critical to maintaining low cost and responsiveness at both Netflix and Amazon.

Following a merger, consolidating some facilities and changing the location and role of others can often help reduce cost and improve responsiveness because of the redundancies and differences in markets served by either of the two separate firms. Network design decisions may also need to be revisited if factor costs such as transportation have changed significantly. In 2008, P&G announced that it would rethink its distribution network, which was implemented when the "cost of oil was $10 per barrel."

SUMMARY OF LEARNING OBJECTIVE 1

Network design decisions include identifying facility locations, capacities, products handled, and allocating markets to be served by different facilities. These decisions define the physical constraints within which the network must operate as market conditions change. Good network design decisions increase profits by supporting the supply chain strategy.

FACTORS INFLUENCING NETWORK DESIGN DECISIONS

5.2 *Identify factors influencing supply chain network design decisions.*

In this section we examine a wide variety of factors that influence network design decisions in supply chains. Some of these factors are quantifiable and can directly be included in network design models. Other factors, that are often equally important, may not be quantifiable but should be accounted for when designing the supply chain network.

Strategic Factors

A firm's competitive strategy has a significant impact on network design decisions within the supply chain. Firms that focus on cost leadership tend to find the lowest cost location for their manufacturing facilities, even if that means locating far from the markets they serve. Electronic manufacturing service providers such as Foxconn and Flextronics have been successful in providing low-cost electronics assembly by locating their factories in low-cost countries in Asia. In contrast, firms that focus on responsiveness tend to locate facilities closer to the market and may select a high-cost location if this choice allows the firm to react quickly to changing market needs. Zara, the Spanish apparel manufacturer, has a large fraction of its production capacity in Portugal and Spain despite the higher cost there. The local capacity allows the company to respond quickly to changing fashion trends in Europe. This responsiveness has allowed Zara to become one of the largest apparel retailers in the world.

Convenience store chains aim to provide easy access to customers as part of their competitive strategy. Convenience store networks thus include many stores that cover an area, with each store being relatively small. In contrast, discount stores such as Sam's Club or Costco use a competitive strategy that focuses on providing low prices. Thus, their networks have large stores, and customers often have to travel many miles to get to one. The geographic area covered by one Sam's Club store may include a dozen convenience stores.

Global supply chain networks can best support their strategic objectives with facilities in different countries playing different roles. For example, Zara has production facilities in Europe as well as Asia. Its production facilities in Asia focus on low cost and produce primarily standardized, low-value products that sell in large amounts. The European facilities focus on being responsive and primarily produce trendy designs whose demand is unpredictable. This combination of facilities allows Zara to produce a wide variety of products in the most profitable manner.

It is important to consider both strategic fit and cost when allocating products to facilities. For example, when Ford Motor Company introduced the Lincoln Mark VIII model, management was faced with a dilemma. At that time, the Mark VIII shared a platform with the Mercury Cougar. However, the Mark VIII was part of Ford's luxury Lincoln division. Locating the Mark VIII line with the Cougar would have obvious operational advantages because of shared parts and processes. However, Ford decided to locate the Mark VIII line in the Wixom, Michigan,

plant, where other Lincoln cars were produced. The primary reason for doing so was to ensure that the focus on quality for the Mark VIII would be consistent with that of other Ford luxury cars that were produced in Wixom.

Competitive Factors

Companies must consider competitors' strategy, size, and location when designing their supply chain networks. A fundamental decision firms make is whether to locate their facilities close to or far from competitors.

POSITIVE EXTERNALITIES BETWEEN FIRMS *Positive externalities* occur when the collocation of multiple firms benefits all of them. Positive externalities lead to competitors locating close to each other. For example, retail stores tend to locate close to each other because doing so increases overall demand, thus benefiting all parties. By locating together in a mall, competing retail stores make it more convenient for customers, who need drive to only one location to find everything they are looking for. This increases the total number of customers who visit the mall, increasing demand for all stores located there.

Another example of positive externality occurs when the presence of a competitor leads to the development of appropriate infrastructure in a developing area. In India, Suzuki was the first foreign auto manufacturer to set up a manufacturing facility. The company went to considerable effort and built a local supplier network. Given the well-established supplier base in India, Suzuki's competitors have also built assembly plants there, because they now find it more effective to build cars in India rather than import them to the country.

LOCATING TO SPLIT THE MARKET When there are no positive externalities, firms locate to be able to capture the largest possible share of the market. A simple model first proposed by Hoteling explains the issues behind this decision (Tirole, 1997).

When firms do not control price but compete on distance from the customer, they can maximize market share by locating close to each other and splitting the market. Consider a situation in which customers are uniformly located along the line segment between 0 and 1 and two firms compete based on their distance from the customer as shown in Figure 5-1. A customer goes to the closer firm and customers who are equidistant from the two firms are evenly split between them.

If total demand is 1, Firm 1 locates at point a, and Firm 2 locates at point $1 - b$, the demand at the two firms, d_1 and d_2, is given by

$$d_1 = a + \frac{1 - b - a}{2} \quad \text{and} \quad d_2 = \frac{1 + b - a}{2}$$

Both firms maximize their market share if they move closer to each other and locate at $a = b = 1/2$.

Observe that when both firms locate in the middle of the line segment ($a = b = 1/2$), the average distance that customers have to travel is 1/4. If one firm locates at 1/4 and the other at 3/4, the average distance customers have to travel drops to 1/8 (customers between 0 and 1/2 come to Firm 1, located at 1/4, whereas customers between 1/2 and 1 come to Firm 2, located at 3/4). This set of locations, however, is not an equilibrium because it gives both firms an incentive to try to increase market share by moving to the middle (closer to 1/2). The result of competition

Figure 5-1 Two Firms Locating on a Line

is for both firms to locate close together, even though doing so increases the average distance to the customer.

If the firms compete on price and the customer incurs the transportation cost, it may be optimal for the two firms to locate as far apart as possible, with Firm 1 locating at 0 and Firm 2 locating at 1. Locating far from each other minimizes price competition and helps the firms split the market and maximize profits.

Political Factors

The political stability of the region or country under consideration plays a significant role in location choice. Companies prefer to locate facilities in politically stable countries where the rules of commerce and ownership are well defined. While political risk is hard to quantify, there are some indices, such as the Global Political Risk Index (GPRI), that companies can use when investing in emerging markets. The GPRI aims to measure the capacity of a country to withstand shocks or crises along four categories: government, society, security, and economy.

Infrastructure Factors

The availability of good infrastructure is an important prerequisite to locating a facility in a given area. Poor infrastructure adds to the cost of doing business from a given location. In the 1990s, global companies located their factories in China near Shanghai, Tianjin, or Guangzhou—even though these locations did not have the lowest labor or land costs—because these locations had good infrastructure. Key infrastructure elements to be considered during network design include availability of sites and labor, proximity to transportation terminals, rail service, proximity to airports and seaports, highway access, congestion, and local utilities.

The quality of life at selected facility locations can have a significant impact on performance because it influences the available workforce and its morale. In many instances, a firm may be better off selecting a higher-cost location if it provides a much better quality of life. Failure to do so can have dire consequences. For example, an aerospace supplier decided to relocate an entire division to an area with a lower standard of living in order to reduce costs. Most of the marketing team, however, refused to relocate. As a result, customer relations deteriorated, and the company had a very difficult transition. The effort to save costs hurt the company and effectively curtailed the firm's status as a major player in its market (Harding, 1988).

Customer Response Time and Service Level

Firms that target customers who value a short response time must locate close to them. Customers are unlikely to come to a convenience store if they have to travel a long distance to get there. It is thus best for a convenience store chain to have many stores distributed in an area so most people have a convenience store close to them. In contrast, customers shop for larger quantity of goods at supermarkets and are willing to travel longer distances to get to one. Thus, supermarket chains tend to have stores that are larger than convenience stores and not as densely distributed. Most towns have fewer supermarkets than convenience stores. Discounters such as Sam's Club target customers who are even less time sensitive. These stores are even larger than supermarkets and there are fewer of them in an area.

Within the United States, a firm can provide two-day truck delivery to about 85 percent of the country with five or fewer DCs. Increasing the coverage to 95 percent of the country will require more facilities. Similarly, reducing the response time will also require more facilities. For example, McMaster-Carr provides next-day truck delivery to about 85 percent of the United States from five facilities. In contrast, Amazon is able to provide same day delivery to a lower fraction of the population despite having about 70 facilities.

Total Logistics Costs

Total logistics costs are the sum of the inventory, transportation, and facility costs within the supply chain network. Inventory costs include the cost of physical storage, cost of capital, and any obsolescence. Transportation costs include inbound costs to bring supply into the facility and outbound costs to deliver the output of the facility. Facility costs include the cost of the building, equipment, and labor. Inventory and facility costs increase as the number of facilities in a supply chain increases. Transportation costs decrease as the number of facilities increases. If the number of facilities increases to the point at which inbound economies of scale are lost, then transportation costs increase. For example, with fewer facilities, Amazon has lower inventory and facility costs than Barnes & Noble, which has hundreds of stores. Barnes & Noble, however, has lower transportation costs.

The goal of network design is to reduce total logistics costs while ensuring the appropriate level of customer responsiveness. The facilities in a supply chain network should at least equal the number that minimizes total logistics cost. A firm may increase the number of facilities beyond this point to improve the response time to its customers. This decision is justified if the revenue increase from improved response outweighs the increased cost from additional facilities.

Facilities incur both a fixed cost that is independent of utilization and a variable cost that is proportional to the quantity processed. The fixed cost of a facility is dependent upon the production technologies in use and has a significant impact on network design decisions. For example, factories that manufacture semiconductors require a large initial investment and display significant economies of scale. The high fixed cost of the facilities and relatively low transportation cost of the output results in most semiconductor companies building a few high-capacity facilities to serve global demand.

In contrast, bottling plants for Coca-Cola do not have a high fixed cost but transporting the output is relatively expensive. To reduce transportation costs, Coca-Cola sets up many bottling plants all over the world, each serving its local market.

Transportation costs are strongly influenced by fluctuations in freight and fuel costs. For example, in 2010 alone, the Baltic Dry Index, which measures the cost to transport raw materials such as metals, grains, and fossil fuels, peaked at 4,187 in May and hit a low of 1,709 in July. Crude oil prices were as low as about $31 per barrel in February 2009 and increased to about $90 per barrel by December 2010. Network designers must decide whether to deal with these fluctuations with supply chain flexibility or the use of financial instruments.

Macroeconomic Factors

There are several *macroeconomic factors* such as taxes, tariffs, and exchange rates that have a significant influence on the total costs and profits of supply chain networks. Thus, it is imperative that firms take these factors into account when making network design decisions.

TARIFFS AND TAX INCENTIVES *Tariffs* refer to any duties that must be paid when products and/or equipment are moved across international, state, or city boundaries. Tariffs have a strong influence on location decisions within a supply chain. If a country has high tariffs, companies either do not serve the local market or set up manufacturing plants within the country to save on duties that increase total costs. High tariffs lead to more production locations within a supply chain network, with each location having a lower allocated capacity. As tariffs have decreased with the World Trade Organization and regional agreements such as the North American Free Trade Agreement (NAFTA), the European Union, and Mercosur (South America), global firms have consolidated their global production and distribution facilities.

Tax incentives are a reduction in tariffs or taxes that countries, states, and cities often provide to encourage firms to locate their facilities in specific areas. Many countries vary incentives from city to city to encourage investments in areas with lower economic development. Such incentives increase after tax profits for firms and are often a key factor in the final location

decision for many plants. When considering international locations, it is astounding how often tax incentives drive the choice of location, often overcoming all of the other cost factors combined. For instance, Ireland has developed a large high-tech industry by enticing companies with low taxes. Even within nations, local governments may offer generous packages of low to no taxes and free land when firms decide to locate facilities within their jurisdiction. Toyota, BMW, and Mercedes have all chosen their facility locations in the United States due in large part to tax incentives offered by different states.

Developing countries often create *free trade zones* in which duties and tariffs are relaxed as long as production is used primarily for export. This creates a strong incentive for global firms to set up plants in these countries to be able to exploit their low labor costs. In China, for example, the establishment of a free trade zone near Guangzhou led to many global firms locating facilities there in the 1990s.

A large number of developing countries also provide additional tax incentives based on training, meals, transportation, and other services offered to the workforce. Tariffs may also vary based on the product's level of technology. In the 1990s, China waived tariffs entirely for high-tech products in an effort to encourage companies to locate there and bring in state-of-the-art technology. Motorola located a large chip manufacturing plant in China to take advantage of the reduced tariffs and other incentives available to high-tech products.

Many countries also place minimum requirements on local content and limits on imports to help develop local manufacturers. Such policies lead global companies to set up local facilities and source from local suppliers. For example, the Spanish company Gamesa was a dominant supplier of wind turbines to China, owning about a third of the market share in 2005. In that year, China declared that wind farms had to buy equipment in which at least 70 percent of content was local. This forced players such as Gamesa and GE, which wanted a piece of the Chinese market, to train local suppliers and source from them. In 2009, China revoked the local content requirements. By then, Chinese suppliers had sufficiently large scale to achieve some of the lowest costs in the world. These suppliers also sold parts to Gamesa's Chinese competitors, which developed into dominant global players.

EXCHANGE-RATE AND DEMAND RISK Fluctuations in exchange rates are common and have a significant impact on the profits of any supply chain serving global markets. For example, the dollar fluctuated between a high of 124 yen in 2007 and a low of 81 yen in 2010, then back to over 115 yen in 2016. A firm that sells its product in the United States with production in Japan is exposed to the risk of appreciation of the yen. The cost of production is incurred in yen, whereas revenues are obtained in dollars. Thus, an increase in the value of the yen increases the production cost in dollars, decreasing the firm's profits. In the 1980s, many Japanese manufacturers faced this problem when the yen appreciated in value, because most of their production capacity was located in Japan. The appreciation of the yen decreased their revenues (in terms of yen) from large overseas markets, and they saw their profits decline. Most Japanese manufacturers responded by building production facilities all over the world. The dollar fluctuated between 0.63 and 1.15 euros between 2002 and 2008, dropping to 0.63 euro in July 2008. The drop in the dollar was particularly negative for European automakers such as Daimler, BMW, and Porsche, which export many vehicles to the United States. It was reported that every one-cent rise in the euro cost BMW and Mercedes roughly $75 million each per year.

Exchange-rate risks may be handled using financial instruments that limit, or hedge against, the loss due to fluctuations. Suitably designed supply chain networks, however, offer the opportunity to take advantage of exchange-rate fluctuations and increase profits. An effective way to do this is to build some overcapacity into the network and make the capacity flexible so it can be used to supply different markets. This flexibility allows the firm to react to exchange-rate fluctuations by altering production flows within the supply chain to maximize profits.

Companies must also take into account fluctuations in demand caused by changes in the economies of different countries. For example, 2009 was a year in which the economies of the

United States and Western Europe shrank (real GDP in the United States decreased by 2.4 percent), while that in China grew by more than 8 percent and in India by about 7 percent. During this period, global companies with presence in China and India and the flexibility to divert resources from shrinking to growing markets did much better than those that did not have either presence in these markets or the flexibility. As the economies of Brazil, China, and India continue to grow, global supply chains will have to build more local presence in these countries along with the flexibility to serve multiple markets.

Firms must account for fluctuations in exchange rates and demand when designing supply chain networks.

SUMMARY OF LEARNING OBJECTIVE 2

Network design decisions are influenced by non-quantifiable factors including strategic, competitive, political, and infrastructure. These decisions are also influenced by quantifiable factors including desired response time and service levels, total logistics costs, and taxes and tariffs. Network design decisions should be checked for robustness in the face of fluctuations in demand, costs, and exchange rates.

5.3 Discuss a framework for making network design decisions.

FRAMEWORK FOR NETWORK DESIGN DECISIONS

A manager's goal when locating facilities and allocating capacity should be to maximize the overall profitability of the resulting supply chain network while providing customers with the appropriate responsiveness. Revenues come from the sale of product, whereas costs arise from facilities, labor, transportation, material, and inventories. The profits of the firm are also affected by taxes and tariffs. Ideally, profits after tariffs and taxes should be maximized when designing a supply chain network. To design an effective network, a manager must consider all the factors described in Section 5.2 and those discussed in Chapter 4. A manager must consider many trade-offs during network design. For example, building many facilities to serve local markets reduces transportation cost and provides a fast response time, but it increases the facility and inventory costs incurred by the firm.

Managers use network design models in two situations. First, these models are used to decide on locations where facilities will be established and determine the capacity to be assigned to each facility. Managers must make this decision considering a time horizon over which locations and capacities will not be altered (typically in years). Second, these models are used to assign current demand to the available facilities and identify lanes along which product will be transported. Managers must consider this decision at least on an annual basis as demand, prices, exchange rates, and tariffs change. In both cases, the goal is to maximize the profit while satisfying customer needs.

We describe a broad framework for network design that starts at the strategic level discussed in Chapter 4 and ends with specific location, capacity, and market allocation decisions. The four phases of the framework for a global network are as shown in Figure 5-2. We describe each phase in greater detail.

Phase I: Define a Supply Chain Strategy/Design

The objective of the first phase of network design is to define a firm's broad supply chain design as discussed in Chapter 4. This includes determining the stages in the supply chain and whether each supply chain function will be performed in-house or outsourced.

Phase I starts with a clear definition of the firm's competitive strategy as the set of customer needs that the supply chain aims to satisfy. The supply chain strategy then specifies what capabilities the supply chain network must have to support the competitive strategy (see Chapter 2). Next, managers must forecast the likely evolution of global competition and whether competitors in each market will be local or global players. Managers must also identify the existing network,

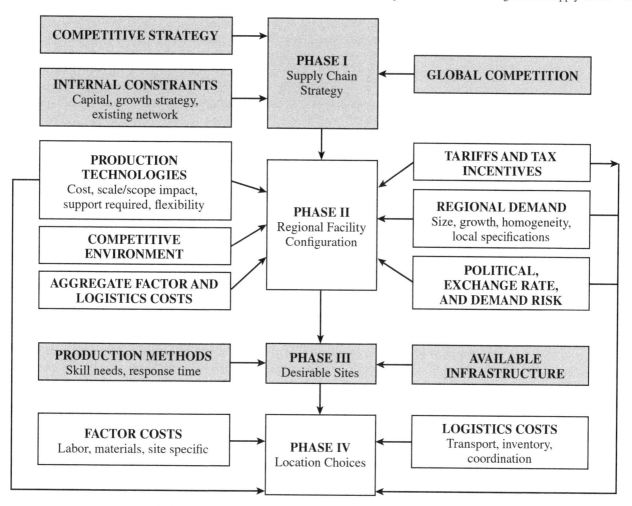

Figure 5-2 Framework for Network Design Decisions

constraints on available capital, and whether growth will be accomplished by acquiring existing facilities, building new facilities, or partnering.

Based on the competitive strategy of the firm, its resulting supply chain strategy, an analysis of the competition, and any constraints, managers must determine the broad supply chain design for the firm.

Phase II: Define the Regional Facility Configuration

The objective of the second phase of network design is to identify regions where facilities will be located, their potential roles, and their approximate capacity.

An analysis of Phase II starts with a forecast of the demand by country or region. Such a forecast must include a measure of the size of the demand and a determination of the homogeneity or variability of customer requirements across different regions. Homogeneous requirements favor large consolidated facilities, whereas requirements that vary across countries favor flexible facilities or smaller, localized, dedicated facilities.

The next step is for managers to identify fixed and variable costs associated with production, storage and transportation activities. At this level of analysis, these costs cannot be location specific and are thus averaged at the regional level. These costs depend upon the extent to which the production technologies display economies of scale or scope. If economies of scale or scope are significant (higher fixed costs), it may be better to have a few facilities serving many markets.

For example, semiconductor manufacturers such as Advanced Micro Devices have few plants for their global markets, given the economies of scale in production. If economies of scale or scope are not significant (lower fixed costs), it may be better for each market to have its own facility.

Next, managers must identify regional tariffs, any requirements for local production, tax incentives, and any export or import restrictions for each market. These inputs help design a network that maximizes after-tax profits. Managers must identify competitors in each region and make a case for whether a facility needs to be located close to or far from a competitor's facility. The desired response time for each market and logistics costs at an aggregate level in each region must also be identified.

Based on all this information, managers identify the regional facility configuration for the supply chain network using network design models discussed in the next section. Models that can be used to obtain a regional configuration are discussed in Section 5.4. The regional configuration defines regions where facilities will be set up, the approximate number of facilities in the network, their capacity, the products produced in each region, and the markets served by each region.

Managers must also identify demand risk, exchange-rate risk, and political risk associated with regional markets. These inputs help test the robustness of the proposed network in the face of these fluctuations. Global network design accounting for risks and uncertainties is discussed in Chapter 6.

Phase III: Select a Set of Desirable Potential Sites

The objective of Phase III is to select a set of desirable potential sites within each region where facilities are to be located. Models that minimize total costs are first used to identify the broad geographic area where potential sites may be located. These models are discussed in Section 5.5. Potential sites should then be selected based on an analysis of infrastructure availability to support the desired production methodologies. *Hard infrastructure requirements* include the availability of suppliers, transportation services, communication, utilities, and warehousing facilities. *Soft infrastructure requirements* include the availability of a skilled workforce, workforce turnover, and the community receptivity to business and industry.

Phase IV: Location Choices and Market Allocation

The objective of Phase IV is to select, from among the potential sites, a precise location and capacity allocation for each facility. Given the potential sites, a more precise estimation of location specific demand, fixed and variable logistics and facility costs, along with tariffs and tax incentives is available. This information is used to design a network that maximizes total profits while accounting for the non-quantifiable factors mentioned in Section 5.2. As demand and costs change over time, the allocation of markets to facilities is revised while accounting for capacity and flexibility that was decided during network design. Models used for final network design and market allocation are discussed in Section 5.6.

SUMMARY OF LEARNING OBJECTIVE 3

The goal of network design is to maximize the supply chain's long-term profitability. The process starts by defining the supply chain strategy, which must be aligned with the competitive strategy of the firm. The supply chain strategy, regional demand, costs, infrastructure, and competitive environment are used to define a regional facility configuration. For regions where facilities are to be located, potentially attractive sites are then selected based on costs and available infrastructure. The optimal configuration is determined from the potential sites using demand, logistics cost, factor costs, taxes, and margins in different markets. The robustness of the network should be checked in the context of various risks and uncertainties faced by the supply chain. The allocation of markets to facilities should be revised as demand and costs change.

MODELS FOR DESIGNING A REGIONAL NETWORK CONFIGURATION

5.4 Develop an optimization model to design a regional network configuration.

The goal of this phase is to obtain a regional network configuration while accounting for demand and costs at a regional level. We discuss the inputs required at this stage and network optimization models that can be used to obtain a regional configuration.

Inputs Required

To obtain the regional network configuration using network optimization models, a manager needs the following information by region: demand, desired response time, fixed cost of opening a facility, variable cost of labor and material, inventory holding cost, transportation cost between every pair of regions, sale price of product, taxes and tariffs, and potential facility capacity. The various costs along with taxes and tariffs are combined to obtain the annualized fixed cost of opening a facility in each region and the variable cost of serving one unit of demand in a region from another region.

We illustrate the design of a regional network in the context of SunOil, a manufacturer of petrochemical products with worldwide sales. The vice president of supply chain is considering several options to meet demand. One possibility is to set up a facility in each region. The advantage of such an approach is that it lowers transportation cost and also helps avoid duties that may be imposed if product is imported from other regions. The disadvantage of this approach is that plants are sized to meet local demand and may not fully exploit economies of scale. An alternative approach is to consolidate plants in just a few regions. This improves economies of scale but increases transportation cost and duties. When designing a regional configuration, the manager must consider these quantifiable trade-offs along with non-quantifiable factors such as the competitive environment and political risk.

The first step is to collect the data in a form that can be used for a quantitative model. For SunOil, the vice president of supply chain decides to view the worldwide demand in terms of five regions—North America, South America, Europe, Africa, and Asia. The data collected are shown in Figure 5-3. Annual demand for each of the five regions is shown in cells B9:F9. Cells B4:F8 contain the variable production, inventory, and transportation cost (including tariffs and duties) of producing in one region to meet demand in each individual region. All costs are in thousands of dollars. For example, as shown in cell C4, it costs $92,000 (including duties) to produce 1 million units in North America and sell them in South America. As shown in cell G4, it costs $6 million in annualized fixed cost to build a low-capacity plant in North America. Observe that the data collected at this stage are at a fairly aggregate level.

There are fixed as well as variable costs associated with facilities, transportation, and inventories at each facility. Fixed costs are those that are incurred no matter how much is produced or shipped from a facility. Variable costs are those that are incurred in proportion to the quantity produced or shipped from a given facility. Facility, transportation, and inventory costs generally display economies of scale, and the marginal cost decreases as the quantity produced at

	A	B	C	D	E	F	G	H	I	J
1	*Inputs - Costs, Capacities, Demands*									
2		Demand Region					Fixed	Low	Fixed	High
		Production and Transportation Cost per 1,000,000 Units								
3	Supply Region	N. America	S. America	Europe	Asia	Africa	Cost ($)	Capacity	Cost ($)	Capacity
4	N. America	81	92	101	130	115	6,000	10	9,000	20
5	S. America	117	77	108	98	100	4,500	10	6,750	20
6	Europe	102	105	95	119	111	6,500	10	9,750	20
7	Asia	115	125	90	59	74	4,100	10	6,150	20
8	Africa	142	100	103	105	71	4,000	10	6,000	20
9	*Demand*	12	8	14	16	7				

Figure 5-3 Cost Data (in Thousands of Dollars) and Demand Data (in Millions of Units) for SunOil

a facility increases. In the models we consider, however, all variable costs grow linearly with the quantity produced or shipped.

SunOil is considering two plant sizes in each location. Low-capacity plants can produce 10 million units a year, whereas high-capacity plants can produce 20 million units a year, as shown in cells H4:H8 and J4:J8, respectively. High-capacity plants exhibit some economies of scale and have fixed costs that are less than twice the fixed costs of a low-capacity plant, as shown in cells I4:I8. All fixed costs are annualized. The vice president wants to know what the lowest-cost network should look like. To answer this question, we next discuss the capacitated plant location model, which can be used in this setting.

Capacitated Plant Location Model

The capacitated plant location network optimization model requires the following inputs:

n = number of potential plant locations/capacity (each level of capacity will count as a separate location)

m = number of markets or demand points

D_j = annual demand from market j

K_i = potential capacity of plant i

f_i = annualized fixed cost of keeping plant i open

c_{ij} = cost of producing and shipping one unit from plant i to market j (cost includes production, inventory, transportation, and tariffs)

In the case of SunOil, $n = 10$ because there are five potential locations and two potential plant capacities. $m = 5$ because there are five markets. The annual demands D_j are in cells B9:F9. Potential plant capacities K_i are in cells H4:H8 and J4:J8. Annualized fixed costs f_i are in cells G4:G8 and J4:J8. The variable costs c_{ij} are in cells B4:F8.

The supply chain team's goal is to decide on a network design that maximizes profits after taxes. For the sake of simplicity, however, we assume that all demand must be met and taxes on earnings are ignored. The model thus focuses on minimizing the cost of meeting global demand. It can be modified, however, to include profits and taxes. Define the following decision variables:

y_i = 1 if plant i is open, 0 otherwise

x_{ij} = quantity shipped from plant i to market j

The problem is then formulated as the following mixed integer program:

$$Min \sum_{i=1}^{n} f_i y_i + \sum_{i=1}^{n} \sum_{j=1}^{m} c_{ij} x_{ij}$$

subject to

$$\sum_{i=1}^{n} x_{ij} = D_j \quad \text{for} \quad j = 1, \ldots, m \tag{5.1}$$

$$\sum_{j=1}^{m} x_{ij} \le K_i y_i \quad \text{for} \quad i = 1, \ldots, n \tag{5.2}$$

$$y_i \in \{0, 1\} \quad \text{for} \quad i = 1, \ldots, n, x_{ij} \ge 0 \tag{5.3}$$

The objective function minimizes the total annual cost (fixed + variable) of setting up and operating the network. The constraint in Equation 5.1 requires that the demand at each regional market be satisfied. The constraint in Equation 5.2 states that no plant can supply more than its capacity. (Clearly, the capacity is 0 if the plant is closed and K_i if it is open. The product of terms, $K_i y_i$, captures this effect.) The constraint in Equation 5.3 enforces that each plant is either open

($y_i = 1$) or closed ($y_i = 0$). The solution identifies the plants that are to be kept open, their capacity, and the allocation of regional demand to these plants.

The model is solved using the Solver tool in Excel (see spreadsheet Figures 5-3 to 7). Given the data, the next step in Excel is to identify cells corresponding to each decision variable, as shown in Figure 5-4. Cells B14:F18 correspond to the decision variables x_{ij} and determine the amount produced in a supply region and shipped to a demand region. Cells G14:G18 contain the decision variables y_i corresponding to the low-capacity plants, and cells H14:H18 contain the decision variables y_i corresponding to the high-capacity plants. Initially, all decision variables are set to be 0.

The next step is to construct cells for the constraints in Equations 5.1 and 5.2 and the objective function. The constraint cells and objective function are shown in Figure 5-5. Cells B22:B26 contain the capacity constraints in Equation 5.2, and cells B28:F28 contain the demand constraints in Equation 5.1. The objective function is shown in cell B31 and measures the total annual fixed cost plus the variable cost of operating the network.

The next step is to use Data to invoke Solver, as shown in Figure 5-6. Within Solver, the goal is to minimize the total cost in cell B31. The variables are in cells B14:H18. The constraints are as follows:

$$B14{:}H18 \geq 0 \quad \{\text{All decision variables are nonnegative}\}$$

$$B22{:}B26 \geq 0 \quad \left\{ K_i y_i - \sum_{j=1}^{m} x_{ij} \geq 0 \quad \text{for} \quad i = 1, \ldots, 5 \right\}$$

$$B28{:}F28 = 0 \quad \left\{ D_j - \sum_{i=1}^{n} x_{ij} = 0 \quad \text{for} \quad j = 1, \ldots, 5 \right\}$$

$$G14{:}H18 \ binary \ \{\text{Location variables } y_i \text{ are binary; that is, 0 or 1}\}$$

Within the Solver Parameters dialog box, select Simplex LP and then click on Solve to obtain the optimal solution, as shown in Figure 5-7. From Figure 5-7, the supply chain team concludes that the lowest-cost network will have high-capacity plants located in South America (cell H15 = 1), Asia (cell H17 = 1), and Africa (cell H18 = 1). The plant in South America meets the North American demand (cell B15), whereas the European demand is met from plants in Asia (cell D17) and Africa (cell D18).

	A	B	C	D	E	F	G	H	I	J
1	Inputs - Costs, Capacities, Demands									
2			Demand Region				Fixed	Low	Fixed	High
			Production and Transportation Cost per 1,000,000 Units							
3	Supply Region	N. America	S. America	Europe	Asia	Africa	Cost ($)	Capacity	Cost ($)	Capacity
4	N. America	81	92	101	130	115	6,000	10	9,000	20
5	S. America	117	77	108	98	100	4,500	10	6,750	20
6	Europe	102	105	95	119	111	6,500	10	9,750	20
7	Asia	115	125	90	59	74	4,100	10	6,150	20
8	Africa	142	100	103	105	71	4,000	10	6,000	20
9	Demand	12	8	14	16	7				
10										
11	Decision Variables									
12			Demand Region - Production Allocation (Million Units)				Plants	Plants		
13	Supply Region	N. America	S. America	Europe	Asia	Africa	(1=open)	(1=open)		
14	N. America	0	0	0	0	0	0	0		
15	S. America	0	0	0	0	0	0	0		
16	Europe	0	0	0	0	0	0	0		
17	Asia	0	0	0	0	0	0	0		
18	Africa	0	0	0	0	0	0	0		

Figure 5-4 Spreadsheet Area for Decision Variables for SunOil

	A	B	C	D	E	F	G	H	I	J
1	**Inputs - Costs, Capacities, Demands**									
2			*Production and Transportation Cost per 1,000,000 Units*	*Demand Region*			**Fixed**	**Low**	**Fixed**	**High**
3	*Supply Region*	N. America	S. America	Europe	Asia	Africa	Cost ($)	Capacity	Cost ($)	Capacity
4	N. America	81	92	101	130	115	6,000	10	9,000	20
5	S. America	117	77	108	98	100	4,500	10	6,750	20
6	Europe	102	105	95	119	111	6,500	10	9,750	20
7	Asia	115	125	90	59	74	4,100	10	6,150	20
8	Africa	142	100	103	105	71	4,000	10	6,000	20
9	*Demand*	12	8	14	16	7				
10										
11	**Decision Variables**									
12			*Demand Region - Production Allocation (Million Units)*				Plants	Plants		
13	*Supply Region*	N. America	S. America	Europe	Asia	Africa	(1=open)	(1=open)		
14	N. America	0	0	0	0	0	0	0		
15	S. America	0	0	0	0	0	0	0		
16	Europe	0	0	0	0	0	0	0		
17	Asia	0	0	0	0	0	0	0		
18	Africa	0	0	0	0	0	0	0		
19										
20	**Constraints**									
21	*Supply Region*	Excess Capacity								
22	N. America	0								
23	S. America	0								
24	Europe	0								
25	Asia	0								
26	Africa	0								
27		N. America	S. America	Europe	Asia	Africa				
28	*Unmet Demand*	12	8	14	16	7				
29										
30	**Objective Function**									
31	Cost =	$ -								

Cell	Cell Formula	Equation	Copied to
B28	=B9 - SUM(B14:B18)	5.1	C28:F28
B22	=G14*H4 + H14*J4 - SUM(B14:F14)	5.2	B23:B26
B31	=SUMPRODUCT(B14:F18,B4:F8) + SUMPRODUCT(G14:G18,G4:G8) + SUMPRODUCT(H14:H18,I4:I8)	Objective Function	—

Figure 5-5 Spreadsheet Area for Constraints and Objective Function for SunOil

The model discussed earlier can be modified to account for strategic imperatives that require locating a plant in some region. For example, if SunOil decides to locate a plant in Europe for strategic reasons, we can modify the model by adding a constraint that requires one plant to be located in Europe. At this stage, the costs associated with a variety of options incorporating different combinations of strategic concerns such as local presence should be evaluated. A suitable regional configuration is then selected.

Accounting for Taxes, Tariffs, and Customer Requirements

All network design models should be structured such that the resulting supply chain network maximizes profits after tariffs and taxes while meeting customer service requirements. We show how the capacitated plant location model can be modified to maximize profits accounting for taxes, even when revenues are in different currencies. The approach outlined, however, can be used to convert any cost minimization network design model to a profit maximization model.

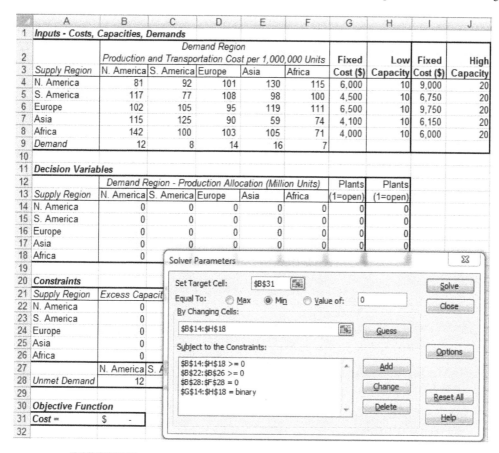

Figure 5-6 Using Solver to Set Regional Configuration for SunOil

If r_j is the revenue from selling one unit in market j, the objective function of the capacitated plant location model can be modified to be

$$Max \sum_{j=1}^{m} r_j \sum_{i=1}^{n} x_{ij} - \sum_{i=1}^{n} F_i y_i - \sum_{i=1}^{n} \sum_{j=1}^{m} c_{ij} x_{ij}$$

This objective function maximizes profits for the firm. When using a profit maximization objective function, a manager should modify the constraint in Equation 5.1 to be

$$\sum_{i=1}^{n} x_{ij} \le D_j \quad \text{for} \quad j = 1, \dots, m \tag{5.4}$$

The constraint in Equation 5.4 is more appropriate than the constraint in Equation 5.1 because it allows the network designer to identify the demand that can be satisfied profitably and the demand that is satisfied at a loss to the firm. The plant location model with Equation 5.4 instead of Equation 5.1 and a profit maximization objective function will serve only that portion of demand that is profitable to serve. This may result in some markets in which a portion of the demand is dropped, unless constrained otherwise, because it cannot be served profitably.

Customer preferences and requirements may be in terms of desired response time and the choice of transportation mode or transportation provider. Consider, for example, two modes of transportation available between plant location i and market j. Mode 1 may be sea and mode 2 may be air. The plant location model is modified by defining two distinct decision variables

	A	B	C	D	E	F	G	H	I	J
1	**Inputs - Costs, Capacities, Demands**									
2			**Demand Region**				**Fixed**	**Low**	**Fixed**	**High**
		Production and Transportation Cost per 1,000,000 Units								
3	Supply Region	N. America	S. America	Europe	Asia	Africa	Cost ($)	Capacity	Cost ($)	Capacity
4	N. America	81	92	101	130	115	6,000	10	9,000	20
5	S. America	117	77	108	98	100	4,500	10	6,750	20
6	Europe	102	105	95	119	111	6,500	10	9,750	20
7	Asia	115	125	90	59	74	4,100	10	6,150	20
8	Africa	142	100	103	105	71	4,000	10	6,000	20
9	Demand	12	8	14	16	7				
10										
11	**Decision Variables**									
12		Demand Region - Production Allocation (Million Units)					Plants	Plants		
13	Supply Region	N. America	S. America	Europe	Asia	Africa	(1=open)	(1=open)		
14	N. America	0	0	0	0	0	0	0		
15	S. America	12	8	0	0	0	0	1		
16	Europe	0	0	0	0	0	0	0		
17	Asia	0	0	4	16	0	0	1		
18	Africa	0	0	10	0	7	0	1		
19										
20	**Constraints**									
21	Supply Region	Excess Capacity								
22	N. America	0								
23	S. America	0								
24	Europe	0								
25	Asia	0								
26	Africa	3								
27		N. America	S. America	Europe	Asia	Africa				
28	Unmet Demand	0	0	0	0	0				
29										
30	**Objective Function**									
31	Cost =	$ 23,751								

Figure 5-7 Optimal Regional Network Configuration for SunOil

x_{ij}^1 and x_{ij}^2 corresponding to the quantity shipped from location i to market j using modes 1 and 2, respectively. The desired response time using each transportation mode is accounted for by allowing shipments only when the time taken is less than the desired response time. For example, if the time from location i to market j using mode 1 (sea) is longer than would be acceptable to the customer, we simply set the decision variable $x_{ij}^1 = 0$ in the plant location model. The option among several transportation providers can be modeled similarly.

SUMMARY OF LEARNING OBJECTIVE 4

The capacitated plant location model can be used to obtain a regional configuration that minimizes total cost or maximizes total profits. The model provides optimal plant locations while ensuring that no plant supplies more than its capacity and each market obtains enough supply to meet demand.

MODELS FOR IDENTIFYING POTENTIAL SITES IN A REGION

5.5 *Develop an optimization model to identify potential sites in a region.*

Having obtained a regional configuration, a manager next identifies potential locations in each region where the company has decided to locate a plant. As a preliminary step, the manager needs to identify the geographic location where potential sites may be considered. In this section we discuss gravity location models that can be useful when identifying suitable geographic

locations within a region. Gravity models are used to find locations that minimize the cost of transporting raw materials from suppliers and finished goods to the markets served.

Inputs Required

This stage uses the results of the regional configuration as inputs for the gravity models, which are run separately for each region and facility. For the region under consideration, a manager needs the following information – demand at the markets served, supply quantity from each supply source, coordinate location of each market served and supply source, transportation cost per unit from each supply source to the facility and from the facility to each market.

We illustrate gravity models in the context of Steel Appliances (SA), a manufacturer of high-quality refrigerators and cooking ranges. SA has one assembly factory located near Denver, from which it has supplied the entire United States. Demand has grown rapidly and the CEO of SA has decided to set up another factory to serve its eastern markets. The supply chain manager is asked to find a suitable location for the new factory. Three parts plants, located in Buffalo, Memphis, and St. Louis, will supply parts to the new factory, which will serve markets in Atlanta, Boston, Jacksonville, Philadelphia, and New York. The coordinate location, the demand in each market, the required supply from each parts plant, and the shipping cost for each supply source or market are shown in Figure 5-8. The coordinate locations are in cells E5:F12. The demand in markets served is in cells D8:D12. The supply quantity from supply sources is in cells D5:D7. The transportation cost per unit is in cells C5:C12.

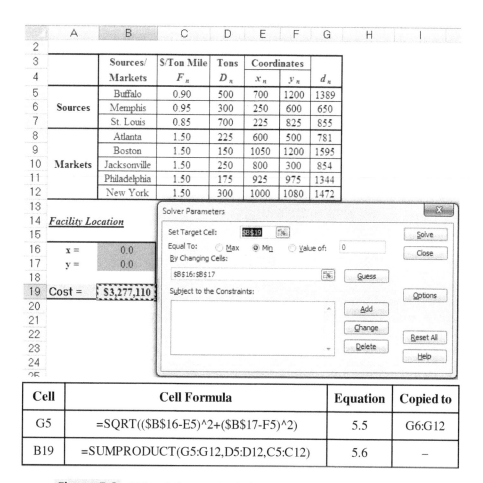

Cell	Cell Formula	Equation	Copied to
G5	=SQRT((B16-E5)^2+(B17-F5)^2)	5.5	G6:G12
B19	=SUMPRODUCT(G5:G12,D5:D12,C5:C12)	5.6	–

Figure 5-8 Using Solver to Optimize Location for Steel Appliances

Gravity Model

Gravity models assume that both the markets and the supply sources can be located as grid points on a plane. All distances are calculated as the geometric distance between two points on the plane. These models also assume that the transportation cost grows linearly with the quantity shipped and the distance traveled. We discuss a gravity model for locating a single facility that receives raw material from supply sources and ships finished product to markets. The basic inputs to the model are as follows:

x_n, y_n: coordinate location of either a market or supply source n

F_n: cost of shipping one unit (a unit could be a piece, pallet, truckload or ton) for one mile between the facility and either market or supply source n

D_n: quantity to be shipped between facility and market or supply source n

In the case of SA, the coordinates x_n are in cells E5:E12, the coordinates y_n are in cells F5:F12, the transportation costs F_n are in Cells C5:C12, and the quantities D_n are in Cells D5:D12.

If (x, y) is the location selected for the facility, the distance d_n between the facility at location (x, y) and the supply source or market n is given by

$$d_n = \sqrt{(x - x_n)^2 + (y - y_n)^2} \tag{5.5}$$

and the total transportation cost (TC) is given by

$$TC = \sum_{n=1}^{k} d_n D_n F_n \tag{5.6}$$

The optimal location is one that minimizes the total TC in Equation 5.6. The optimal solution for SA is obtained using the Solver tool in Excel, as shown in Figure 5-8. The first step is to enter the problem data as shown in cells B5:F12. Next, we set the decision variables (x, y) corresponding to the location of the new facility in cells B16 and B17, respectively. In cells G5:G12, we then calculate the distance d_n from the facility location (x, y) to each source or market, using Equation 5.5. The total TC is then calculated in cell B19 using Equation 5.6.

The next step is to invoke Solver (Data | Solver). Within the Solver Parameters dialog box (see Figure 5-8), the following information is entered to represent the problem:

Set Cell: B19

Equal To: Select *Min*

By Changing Variable Cells: B16:B17

Select GRG Nonlinear as the solving method and click on the Solve button. The optimal solution is returned in cells B16 and B17 to be 681 and 882, respectively.

The manager thus identifies the coordinates $(x, y) = (681, 882)$ as the location of the factory that minimizes total cost TC. From a map, these coordinates are close to the border between North Carolina and Virginia. The precise coordinates provided by the gravity model may not correspond to a feasible location, though. The manager should look for desirable sites close to the optimal coordinates that have the required infrastructure as well as the appropriate worker skills available.

The gravity model can also be solved using the following iterative procedure.

1. For each supply source or market n, evaluate d_n as defined in Equation 5.5.
2. Obtain a new location (x', y') for the facility, where

$$x' = \frac{\sum_{n=1}^{k} \dfrac{D_n F_n x_n}{d_n}}{\sum_{n=1}^{k} \dfrac{D_n F_n}{d_n}} \quad \text{and} \quad y' = \frac{\sum_{n=1}^{k} \dfrac{D_n F_n x_n}{d_n}}{\sum_{n=1}^{k} \dfrac{D_n F_n}{d_n}}$$

3. If the new location (x', y') is almost the same as (x, y) stop. Otherwise, set $(x, y) = (x', y')$ and go back to step 1.

SUMMARY OF LEARNING OBJECTIVE 5

The gravity model can be used to identify potential facility locations in each region. Given the quantity coming from supply sources and market demand, the model identifies the geographic location in a region that minimizes the total transportation cost. This geographic location can be used to identify nearby potential sites that satisfy both hard and soft infrastructure requirements.

MODELS FOR DEMAND ALLOCATION AND PLANT LOCATION

5.6 Develop an optimization model to locate plants and allocate market demand.

Given the potential sites that have been identified, a manager must decide on the location and capacity allocation for each facility. Besides locating the facilities, a manager also decides how demand from each market is to be allocated to facilities. This allocation must account for customer service constraints in terms of response time. The demand allocation decision can be altered on a regular basis as costs change and markets evolve. When designing the network, both location and allocation decisions are made jointly.

Inputs Required

At this stage a manager needs the following information: demand at each market, desired response time, fixed cost of opening a facility, variable cost of labor and material, inventory holding cost, transportation cost between every potential location and market, sale price of product, taxes and tariffs, and potential facility capacity. The various costs along with taxes and tariffs are combined to obtain the annualized fixed cost of opening a facility in each location and the variable cost of serving one unit of demand in each market from each potential location.

We illustrate the relevant network optimization models using the example of TelecomOne and HighOptic, two manufacturers of telecommunication equipment. TelecomOne has focused on the eastern half of the United States. It has manufacturing plants located in Baltimore, Memphis, and Wichita and serves markets in Atlanta, Boston, and Chicago. HighOptic has targeted the western half of the United States and serves markets in Denver, Omaha, and Portland from plants located in Cheyenne and Salt Lake City.

Plant capacities, market demand, variable production and transportation cost per thousand units shipped, and fixed costs per year at each plant are shown in Table 5-1.

TABLE 5-1 Capacity, Demand, and Cost Data for TelecomOne and HighOptic

	Demand City Production and Transportation Cost per Thousand Units (Thousand $)						Annual Capacity (Thousand Units), K	Annual Fixed Cost (Thousand $), f
Supply City	**Atlanta**	**Boston**	**Chicago**	**Denver**	**Omaha**	**Portland**		
Baltimore	1,675	400	685	1,630	1,160	2,800	18	7,650
Cheyenne	1,460	1,940	970	100	495	1,200	24	3,500
Salt Lake City	1,925	2,400	1,425	500	950	800	27	5,000
Memphis	380	1,355	543	1,045	665	2,321	22	4,100
Wichita	922	1,646	700	508	311	1,797	31	2,200
Annual demand (thousand units), D_j	10	8	14	6	7	11		

Models for Allocating Demand to Existing Production Facilities

This model is used by managers to allocate demand among existing production facilities. Whereas the location and capacity of production facilities changes infrequently, the demand allocated to each facility can be altered more frequently as demand and costs change. The demand allocation model requires the following inputs:

n = number of factory locations

m = number of markets or demand points

D_j = annual demand from market j

K_i = capacity of factory i

c_{ij} = cost of producing and shipping one unit from factory i to market j (cost includes production, inventory, and transportation)

The inputs for TelecomOne and HighOptic are provided in Table 5-1. This model assumes that all plants are open and thus their fixed cost is incurred independent of the quantity produced. The goal is to allocate the demand from different markets to the various plants to minimize the total cost of production and distribution. Define the decision variables:

x_{ij} = quantity shipped from factory i to market j

The problem is formulated as the following linear program:

$$\text{Min} \sum_{i=1}^{n} \sum_{j=1}^{m} c_{ij} x_{ij}$$

subject to

$$\sum_{i=1}^{n} x_{ij} = D_j \quad \text{for} \quad j = 1, \dots, m \qquad (5.7)$$

$$\sum_{j=1}^{m} x_{ij} \leq K_i \quad \text{for} \quad i = 1, \dots, n \qquad (5.8)$$

The constraints in Equation 5.7 ensure that all market demand is satisfied, and the constraints in Equation 5.8 ensure that no factory produces more than its capacity.

For both TelecomOne and HighOptic, the demand allocation problem can be solved using the Solver tool in Excel. The optimal demand allocation is presented in Table 5-2 (see spreadsheet *Figures 5-9 to 12*). Observe that it is optimal for TelecomOne not to produce anything in the Wichita facility because of high costs of production and shipping even though the facility is open and the fixed cost is incurred. With the demand allocation as shown in Table 5-2, TelecomOne incurs an annual variable cost of $14,886,000 and an annual fixed cost of $13,950,000, for a total annual cost of $28,836,000. HighOptic incurs an annual variable cost of $12,865,000 and an annual fixed cost of $8,500,000, for a total annual cost of $21,365,000.

TABLE 5-2 Optimal Demand Allocation for TelecomOne and HighOptic

		Atlanta	Boston	Chicago	Denver	Omaha	Portland
TelecomOne	Baltimore	0	8	2			
	Memphis	10	0	12			
	Wichita	0	0	0			
HighOptic	Cheyenne				0	0	11
	Salt Lake				6	7	0

	A	B	C	D	E	F	G	H	I
1	**Inputs - Costs, Capacities, Demands (for TelecomOptic)**								
2			Demand City					Fixed	
			Production and Transportation Cost per 1000 Units						
3	Supply City	Atlanta	Boston	Chicago	Denver	Omaha	Portland	Cost ($)	Capacity
4	Baltimore	1,675	400	685	1,630	1,160	2,800	7,650	18
5	Cheyenne	1,460	1,940	970	100	495	1,200	3,500	24
6	Salt Lake	1,925	2,400	1,425	500	950	800	5,000	27
7	Memphis	380	1,355	543	1,045	665	2,321	4,100	22
8	Wichita	922	1,646	700	508	311	1,797	2,200	31
9	Demand	10	8	14	6	7	11		
11	**Decision Variables**								
12			Demand City - Production Allocation (1000 Units)					Plants	
13	Supply City	Atlanta	Boston	Chicago	Denver	Omaha	Portland	(1=open)	
14	Baltimore	0	0	0	0	0	0	0	
15	Cheyenne	0	0	0	0	0	0	0	
16	Salt Lake	0	0	0	0	0	0	0	
17	Memphis	0	0	0	0	0	0	0	
18	Wichita	0	0	0	0	0	0	0	

Figure 5-9 Spreadsheet Area for Decision Variables for TelecomOptic

	A	B	C	D	E	F	G	H	I
1	**Inputs - Costs, Capacities, Demands (for TelecomOptic)**								
2			Demand City					Fixed	
			Production and Transportation Cost per 1000 Units						
3	Supply City	Atlanta	Boston	Chicago	Denver	Omaha	Portland	Cost ($)	Capacity
4	Baltimore	1,675	400	685	1,630	1,160	2,800	7,650	18
5	Cheyenne	1,460	1,940	970	100	495	1,200	3,500	24
6	Salt Lake	1,925	2,400	1,425	500	950	800	5,000	27
7	Memphis	380	1,355	543	1,045	665	2,321	4,100	22
8	Wichita	922	1,646	700	508	311	1,797	2,200	31
9	Demand	10	8	14	6	7	11		
11	**Decision Variables**								
12			Demand City - Production Allocation (1000 Units)					Plants	
13	Supply City	Atlanta	Boston	Chicago	Denver	Omaha	Portland	(1=open)	
14	Baltimore	0	0	0	0	0	0	0	
15	Cheyenne	0	0	0	0	0	0	0	
16	Salt Lake	0	0	0	0	0	0	0	
17	Memphis	0	0	0	0	0	0	0	
18	Wichita	0	0	0	0	0	0	0	
20	**Constraints**								
21	Supply City	Excess Capacity							
22	Baltimore	0							
23	Cheyenne	0							
24	Salt Lake	0							
25	Memphis	0							
26	Wichita	0							
28		Atlanta	Boston	Chicago	Denver	Omaha	Portland		
29	Unmet Demand	10	8	14	6	7	11		
31	**Objective Function**								
32	Cost =	$ -							

Cell	Formula	Equation	Copied to
B22	= I4*H14 - SUM(B14:G14)	5.1	B23:B26
B29	= B9 - SUM(B14:B18)	5.2	C29:G29
B32	= SUMPRODUCT(B4:G8, B14:G18) + SUMPRODUCT(H4:H8, H14:H18)	Objective function	—

Figure 5-10 Spreadsheet Area for Constraints for TelecomOptic

Figure 5-11 Solver Dialog Box for TelecomOptic

Supply City	Demand City Production and Transportation Cost per 1000 Units						Fixed Cost ($)	Capacity
	Atlanta	Boston	Chicago	Denver	Omaha	Portland		
Baltimore	1,675	400	685	1,630	1,160	2,800	7,650	18
Cheyenne	1,460	1,940	970	100	495	1,200	3,500	24
Salt Lake	1,925	2,400	1,425	500	950	800	5,000	27
Memphis	380	1,355	543	1,045	665	2,321	4,100	22
Wichita	922	1,646	700	508	311	1,797	2,200	31
Demand	10	8	14	6	7	11		

Inputs - Costs, Capacities, Demands (for TelecomOptic)

Decision Variables

Supply City	Demand City - Production Allocation (1000 Units)						Plants (1=open)
	Atlanta	Boston	Chicago	Denver	Omaha	Portland	
Baltimore	0	8	2	0	0	0	1
Cheyenne	0	0	0	6	7	11	1
Salt Lake	0	0	0	0	0	0	0
Memphis	10	0	12	0	0	0	1
Wichita	0	0	0	0	0	0	0

Constraints

Supply City	Excess Capacity
Baltimore	8
Cheyenne	0
Salt Lake	0
Memphis	0
Wichita	0

	Atlanta	Boston	Chicago	Denver	Omaha	Portland
Unmet Demand	0	0	0	0	0	0

Objective Function

Cost =	$ 47,401

Figure 5-12 Optimal Network Design for TelecomOptic

Models for Locating Production Facilities

This model is used by managers to locate new production facilities or to decide which production facilities to shut or keep open. The problem of selecting the optimal location and capacity allocation is very similar to the regional configuration problem discussed earlier. The only difference is that instead of using costs and duties that apply over a region, we now use location-specific costs and duties. As a result, the model used at this stage is the same as the capacitated plant location model discussed when designing the regional network.

We illustrate the model in the context of the merger of TelecomOne and HighOptic into a single entity to be called TelecomOptic. Management believes that significant benefits will result if the two networks are merged appropriately. TelecomOptic will have five factories from which to serve six markets. Management is debating whether all five factories are needed. It has assigned a supply chain team to study the network for the combined company and identify the plants that could be shut down.

Ideally, the problem should be formulated to maximize total profits, taking into account costs, taxes, and duties by location. Given that taxes and duties do not vary among locations, the supply chain team decides to locate factories and then allocate demand to the open factories to minimize the total cost of facilities, transportation, and inventory. Define the following decision variables:

$y_i = 1$ if factory i is open, 0 otherwise

$x_{ij} =$ quantity shipped from factory i to market j

Recall that the problem is then formulated as the following mixed integer program:

$$Min \sum_{i=1}^{n} f_i y_i + \sum_{i=1}^{n} \sum_{j=1}^{m} c_{ij} x_{ij}$$

subject to x and y satisfying the constraints in Equations 5.1, 5.2, and 5.3.

The capacity and demand data, along with production, transportation, and inventory costs at different factories for the merged firm TelecomOptic, are given in Table 5-1. The supply chain team decides to solve the plant location model using the Solver tool in Excel.

The first step in setting up the Solver model is to enter the cost, demand, and capacity information as shown in Figure 5-9 (see sheet *Figure 5-12* in spreadsheet *Figures 5-9 to 12*). The fixed costs f_i for the five plants are entered in cells H4:H8. The capacities K_i of the five plants are entered in cells I4:I8. The variable costs from each plant to each demand city, c_{ij}, are entered in cells B4:G8. The demands D_j of the six markets are entered in cells B9:G9. Next, corresponding to decision variables x_{ij} and y_i, cells B14:G18 and H14:H18, respectively, are assigned as shown in Figure 5-9. Initially, all variables are set to be 0.

The next step is to construct cells for each of the constraints in Equations 5.1 and 5.2. The constraint cells are as shown in Figure 5-10. Cells B22:B26 contain the capacity constraints in Equation 5.1, whereas cells B29:G29 contain the demand constraints in Equation 5.2. The cell B29 corresponds to the demand constraint for the market in Atlanta. The constraint in cell B22 corresponds to the capacity constraint for the factory in Baltimore. The capacity constraints require that the cell value be greater than or equal to ($\geq$) 0, whereas the demand constraints require the cell value be equal to 0.

The objective function measures the total fixed and variable cost of the supply chain network and is evaluated in cell B32. The next step is to invoke Solver, as shown in Figure 5-11.

Within Solver, the goal is to minimize the total cost in cell B32. The variables are in cells B14:H18. The constraints are as follows:

$$B14:G18 \geq 0 \quad \{\text{All decision variables are nonnegative}\}$$

$$B22:B26 \geq 0 \quad \left\{ K_i y_i - \sum_{j=1}^{m} x_{ij} \geq 0 \quad \text{for} \quad i = 1, \ldots, 5 \right\}$$

$$B29{:}G29 = 0 \quad \left\{ D_j - \sum_{i=1}^{n} x_{ij} = 0 \quad \text{for} \quad j = 1, \dots, 6 \right\}$$

H14:H18 *binary* { Location variables y_i are binary; that is, 0 or 1 }

Within the Solver Parameters dialog box, select Simplex LP and click on Solve to obtain the optimal solution, as shown in Figure 5-12. From Figure 5-12, the supply chain team concludes that it is optimal for TelecomOptic to close the plants in Salt Lake City and Wichita, while keeping the plants in Baltimore, Cheyenne, and Memphis open. The total annual cost of this network and operation is $47,401,000. This cost represents savings of about $3 million per year compared with the situation in which TelecomOne and HighOptic operate separate supply chain networks.

More Complex Capacitated Plant Location Models

We now describe two more complex capacitated plant location models. The first model focuses on the case where all supply to a market must come from a single plant. The second model generalizes the problem to the case where the supply chain has an additional stage of warehouses between plants and markets and both plants and warehouses are to be located to minimize the overall production and distribution cost.

THE CAPACITATED PLANT LOCATION MODEL WITH SINGLE SOURCING
In some cases, companies want to design supply chain networks in which a market is supplied from only one factory, referred to as a *single source*. Companies may impose this constraint because it lowers the complexity of coordinating the network and requires less flexibility from each facility. The plant location model discussed earlier needs some modification to accommodate this constraint. The decision variables are redefined as follows:

y_i = 1 if factory is located at site i, 0 otherwise

x_{ij} = 1 if market j is supplied by factory i, 0 otherwise

The problem is formulated as the following integer program:

$$Min \sum_{i=1}^{n} f_i y_i + \sum_{i=1}^{n} \sum_{j=1}^{m} D_j c_{ij} x_{ij}$$

subject to

$$\sum_{i=1}^{n} x_{ij} = 1 \quad \text{for} \quad j = 1, \dots, m \tag{5.9}$$

$$\sum_{j=1}^{m} D_j x_{ij} \le K_i y_i \quad \text{for} \quad i = 1, \dots, n \tag{5.10}$$

$$x_{ij}, y_i \in \{0, 1\} \tag{5.11}$$

The constraints in Equations 5.9 and 5.11 enforce that each market is supplied by exactly one factory.

We do not describe the solution of the model in Excel because it is very similar to the model discussed earlier. The optimal network with single sourcing for TelecomOptic is shown in Table 5-3 (see sheet *Table 5-3 Single Sourcing* in spreadsheet *Figures 5-9 to 12*).

If single sourcing is required, it is optimal for TelecomOptic to close the factories in Baltimore and Cheyenne. This is different from the result in Figure 5-12, in which factories in Salt Lake City and Wichita were closed. The annual cost of operating the network in Table 5-3 is $49,717,000. This cost is about $2.3 million higher than the cost of the network in Figure 5-12, in which single sourcing was not required. The supply chain team thus concludes that single sourcing adds about $2.3 million per year to the cost of the supply chain network, although it makes coordination easier and requires less flexibility from the plants.

TABLE 5-3 Optimal Network Configuration for TelecomOptic with Single Sourcing

	Open/Closed	Atlanta	Boston	Chicago	Denver	Omaha	Portland
Baltimore	Closed	0	0	0	0	0	0
Cheyenne	Closed	0	0	0	0	0	0
Salt Lake	Open	0	0	0	6	0	11
Memphis	Open	10	8	0	0	0	0
Wichita	Open	0	0	14	0	7	0

LOCATING PLANTS AND WAREHOUSES SIMULTANEOUSLY A much more general form of the plant location model needs to be considered if the entire supply chain network from the supplier to the customer is to be designed. We consider a supply chain in which suppliers send material to factories that supply warehouses that supply markets, as shown in Figure 5-13. Location and capacity allocation decisions must be made simultaneously for both factories and warehouses. Multiple warehouses may be used to satisfy demand at a market, and multiple factories may be used to replenish warehouses. It is also assumed that units have been appropriately adjusted such that one unit of input from a supply source produces one unit of the finished product. The model requires the following inputs:

m = number of markets or demand points

n = number of potential factory locations

l = number of suppliers

t = number of potential warehouse locations

D_j = annual demand from market j

K_i = potential capacity of factory at location i

S_h = supply capacity at supplier h

W_e = potential warehouse capacity at location e

F_i = fixed cost of locating a plant at location i

f_e = fixed cost of locating a warehouse at location e

c_{hi} = cost of shipping one unit from supply source h to factory i

c_{ie} = cost of producing and shipping one unit from factory i to warehouse e

c_{ej} = cost of shipping one unit from warehouse e to market j

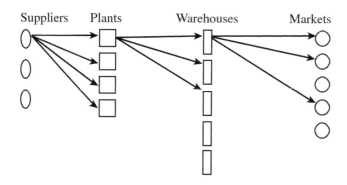

Figure 5-13 Stages in a Supply Network

The goal is to identify plant and warehouse locations, as well as quantities shipped between various points, that minimize the total fixed and variable costs. Define the following decision variables:

y_i = 1 if factory is located at location i, 0 otherwise

y_e = 1 if warehouse is located at location e, 0 otherwise

x_{ej} = quantity shipped from warehouse e to market j

x_{ie} = quantity shipped from factory at location i to warehouse e

x_{hi} = quantity shipped from supplier h to factory at location i

The problem is formulated as the following integer program:

$$Min \sum_{i=1}^{n} F_i y_i + \sum_{e=1}^{t} f_e y_e + \sum_{h=1}^{l}\sum_{i=1}^{n} c_{hi} x_{hi} + \sum_{i=1}^{n}\sum_{e=1}^{t} c_{ie} x_{ie} + \sum_{e=1}^{t}\sum_{j=1}^{m} c_{ej} x_{ej}$$

The objective function minimizes the total fixed and variable costs of the supply chain network subject to the following constraints:

$$\sum_{i=1}^{n} x_{hi} \leq S_h \quad \text{for} \quad h = 1, \ldots, l \tag{5.12}$$

The constraint in Equation 5.12 specifies that the total amount shipped from a supplier cannot exceed the supplier's capacity.

$$\sum_{h=1}^{l} x_{hi} - \sum_{e=1}^{t} x_{ie} \geq 0 \quad \text{for} \quad i = 1, \ldots, n \tag{5.13}$$

The constraint in Equation 5.13 states that the amount shipped out of a factory cannot exceed the quantity of raw material received.

$$\sum_{e=1}^{t} x_{ie} \leq K_i y_i \quad \text{for} \quad i = 1, \ldots, n \tag{5.14}$$

The constraint in Equation 5.14 enforces that the amount produced in the factory cannot exceed its capacity.

$$\sum_{i=1}^{n} x_{ie} - \sum_{j=1}^{m} x_{ej} \geq 0 \quad \text{for} \quad e = 1, \ldots, t \tag{5.15}$$

The constraint in Equation 5.15 specifies that the amount shipped out of a warehouse cannot exceed the quantity received from the factories.

$$\sum_{j=1}^{m} x_{ej} \leq W_e y_e \quad \text{for} \quad e = 1, \ldots, t \tag{5.16}$$

The constraint in Equation 5.16 specifies that the amount shipped through a warehouse cannot exceed its capacity.

$$\sum_{e=1}^{t} x_{ej} = D_j \quad \text{for} \quad j = 1, \ldots, m \tag{5.17}$$

The constraint in Equation 5.17 specifies that the amount shipped to a customer must cover the demand.

$$y_i, y_e \in \{0, 1\}, x_{ej}, x_{ie}, x_{hi} \geq 0 \tag{5.18}$$

The constraint in Equation 5.18 enforces that each factory or warehouse is either open or closed.

This model can be modified to maximize profits instead of minimizing costs by changing the objective function and the constraint in Equation 5.17 as discussed in Section 5.4.

The model can also be modified to allow direct shipments between factories and markets. All the models discussed previously can also be modified to accommodate economies of scale in production, transportation, and inventory costs. However, these requirements make the models more difficult to solve.

SUMMARY OF LEARNING OBJECTIVE 6

The capacitated plant location model can be used to locate production facilities and warehouses to minimize total network costs or maximize network profits. A similar model can also be used to allocate market demand across an existing set of facilities in a supply chain network. Both models optimize the objective function while ensuring that capacity constraints are satisfied and market demand is served.

DISCUSSION QUESTIONS

1. How do the location and size of warehouses affect the performance of a firm such as IKEA? What factors should IKEA consider when deciding where and how big its warehouses should be?

2. How do import duties and exchange rates affect the location decision in a supply chain?

3. How is a significant reduction in fuel costs likely to affect global supply chain networks?

4. As IKEA expands its market, it has built new warehouses. How does this change affect various costs and response times in the IKEA supply chain?

5. ASOS, a British online-only fashion and beauty retailer, sells its products from four main warehouses located in the United Kingdom, the United States, central Europe, and China.

Marks & Spencer (M&S) sells apparel, home products, and luxury food items from more than 1,400 retail locations worldwide, and is supported by 19 distribution warehouses[1]. In both cases, customers may place orders using the Internet or on the phone. Discuss the pros and cons of the two strategies.

6. Consider a firm such as Apple or Dell, with few production facilities worldwide. List the pros and cons of this approach and why it may or may not be suitable for the computer industry.

7. Consider a firm such as Whirlpool, which has more than 30 facilities worldwide. List the pros and cons of having many facilities. Would it be suitable for the white goods industry? Why?

EXERCISES

1. SC Consulting, a supply chain consulting firm, must decide on the location of its home offices. Its clients are located primarily in the 16 states listed in Table 5-4. There are four potential sites for home offices: Los Angeles, Tulsa, Denver, and Seattle. The annual fixed cost of locating an office in Los Angeles is $165,428, Tulsa is $131,230, Denver is $140,000, and Seattle is $145,000. The expected number of trips to each state and the travel costs from each potential site are shown in Table 5-4. Each consultant is expected to take at most 25 trips each year.
 a. If there are no restrictions on the number of consultants at a site and the goal is to minimize costs, where should the home offices be located and how many consultants should be assigned to each office? What is the annual cost in terms of the facility and travel?
 b. If at most 10 consultants are to be assigned to a home office, where should the offices be set up? How many consultants should be assigned to each office? What is the annual cost of this network?

 c. What do you think of a rule by which all consulting projects out of a given state are assigned to one home office? How much is this policy likely to add to cost compared to allowing multiple offices to handle a single state?

2. DryIce, Inc., is a manufacturer of air conditioners that has seen its demand grow significantly. The company anticipates nationwide demand for the next year to be 180,000 units in the South, 120,000 units in the Midwest, 110,000 units in the East, and 100,000 units in the West. Managers at DryIce are designing the manufacturing network and have selected four potential sites—New York, Atlanta, Chicago, and San Diego. Plants could have a capacity of either 200,000 or 400,000 units. The annual fixed costs at the four locations are shown in Table 5-5, along with the cost of producing and shipping an air conditioner to each of the four markets. Where should DryIce build its factories and how large should they be?

3. Sunchem, a manufacturer of printing inks, has five manufacturing plants worldwide. Their locations and capacities are

[1]Marks & Spencer, 2018, Marks & Spencer announces changes to its logistics network [online], Available from https://corporate.marksandspencer.com/media/press-releases/2018/marks-and-spencer-announces-changes-to-its-logistics-network, Accessed February 5, 2018.

TABLE 5-4 Travel Costs and Number of Trips for SC Consulting

State	Travel Costs ($)				Number of Trips
	Los Angeles	Tulsa	Denver	Seattle	
Washington	150	250	200	25	40
Oregon	150	250	200	75	35
California	75	200	150	125	100
Idaho	150	200	125	125	25
Nevada	100	200	125	150	40
Montana	175	175	125	125	25
Wyoming	150	175	100	150	50
Utah	150	150	100	200	30
Arizona	75	200	100	250	50
Colorado	150	125	25	250	65
New Mexico	125	125	75	300	40
North Dakota	300	200	150	200	30
South Dakota	300	175	125	200	20
Nebraska	250	100	125	250	30
Kansas	250	75	75	300	40
Oklahoma	250	25	125	300	55

TABLE 5-5 Production and Transport Costs for DryIce, Inc.

	New York	Atlanta	Chicago	San Diego
Annual fixed cost of 200,000 plant	$6 million	$5.5 million	$5.6 million	$6.1 million
Annual fixed cost of 400,000 plant	$10 million	$9.2 million	$9.3 million	$10.2 million
East	$211	$232	$238	$299
South	$232	$212	$230	$280
Midwest	$240	$230	$215	$270
West	$300	$280	$270	$225

shown in Table 5-6 along with the cost of producing 1 ton of ink at each facility. The production costs are in the local currency of the country where the plant is located. The major markets for the inks are North America, Europe, Japan, South America, and the rest of Asia. Demand at each market is shown in Table 5-6. Transportation costs from each plant to each market in U.S. dollars are shown in Table 5-6. Management must come up with a production plan for the next year.

a. If exchange rates are expected as in Table 5-7, and no plant can run below 50 percent of capacity, how much

should each plant produce and which markets should each plant supply?

b. If there are no limits on the amount produced in a plant, how much should each plant produce?

c. Can adding 10 tons of capacity in any plant reduce costs?

d. How should Sunchem account for the fact that exchange rates fluctuate over time?

4. Sleekfon and Sturdyfon are two major cell phone manufacturers that have recently merged. Their current market sizes are as shown in Table 5-8. All demand is in millions of units.

TABLE 5-6 Capacity, Demand, Production, and Transportation Costs for Sunchem

	North America	Europe	Japan	South America	Rest of Asia	Capacity Tons/Year	Production Cost/Ton
United States	$600	$1,300	$2,000	$1,200	$1,700	185	$10,000
Germany	$1,300	$600	$1,400	$1,400	$1,300	475	15,000 euro
Japan	$2,000	$1,400	$300	$2,100	$900	50	1,800,000 yen
Brazil	$1,200	$1,400	$2,100	$800	$2,100	200	13,000 real
India	$2,200	$1,300	$1,000	$2,300	$800	80	400,000 rupees
Demand (tons/year)	270	200	120	190	100		

TABLE 5-7 Anticipated Exchange Rates for the Next Year

	US$	Euro	Yen	Real	Rupee
US$	1.000	1.993	107.7	1.78	43.55
Euro	0.502	1	54.07	0.89	21.83
Yen	0.0093	0.0185	1	0.016	0.405
Real	0.562	1.124	60.65	1	24.52
Rupee	0.023	0.046	2.47	0.041	1

Sleekfon has three production facilities in Europe (EU), North America, and South America. Sturdyfon also has three production facilities in Europe (EU), North America, and the rest of Asia. The capacity (in millions of units), annual fixed cost (in millions of $), and variable production costs ($ per unit) for each plant are as shown in Table 5-9.

Transportation costs between regions are as shown in Table 5-10. All transportation costs are shown in dollars per unit.

Duties are applied on each unit based on the fixed cost per unit capacity, variable cost per unit, and transportation cost. Thus, a unit currently shipped from North America to

TABLE 5-8 Global Demand and Duties for Sleekfon and Sturdyfon

Market	N. America	S. America	Europe (EU)	Europe (Non-EU)	Japan	Rest of Asia	Africa
Sleekfon demand	10	4	20	3	2	2	1
Sturdyfon demand	12	1	4	8	7	3	1
Import duties (%)	3	20	4	15	4	22	25

TABLE 5-9 Plant Capacities and Costs for Sleekfon and Sturdyfon

		Capacity	Fixed Cost/Year	Variable Cost/Unit
Sleekfon	Europe (EU)	20	100	6.0
	N. America	20	100	5.5
	S. America	10	60	5.3
Sturdyfon	Europe (EU)	20	100	6.0
	N. America	20	100	5.5
	Rest of Asia	10	50	5.0

TABLE 5-10 Transportation Costs Between Regions ($ per Unit)

	N. America	S. America	Europe (EU)	Europe (Non-EU)	Japan	Rest of Asia	Africa
N. America	1.00	1.50	1.50	1.80	1.70	2.00	2.20
S. America	1.50	1.00	1.70	2.00	1.90	2.20	2.20
Europe (EU)	1.50	1.70	1.00	1.20	1.80	1.70	1.40
Europe (Non-EU)	1.80	2.00	1.20	1.00	1.80	1.60	1.50
Japan	1.70	1.90	1.80	1.80	1.00	1.20	1.90
Rest of Asia	2.00	2.20	1.70	1.60	1.20	1.00	1.80
Africa	2.20	2.20	1.40	1.50	1.90	1.80	1.00

Africa has a fixed cost per unit of capacity of $5.00 (=100/20 from Table 5-9), a variable production cost of $5.50, and a transportation cost of $2.20. The 25 percent import duty is thus applied on $12.70 (5.00 + 5.50 + 2.20) to give a total cost on import of $15.88. For the questions that follow, assume that market demand is as in Table 5-8.

The merged company has estimated that scaling back a 20-million-unit plant to 10 million units saves 30 percent in fixed costs. Variable costs at a scaled-back plant are unaffected. Shutting a plant down (either 10 million or 20 million units) saves 80 percent in fixed costs. Fixed costs are only partially recovered because of severance and other costs associated with a shutdown.

a. What is the lowest cost achievable for the production and distribution network prior to the merger? Which plants serve which markets?

b. What is the lowest cost achievable for the production and distribution network after the merger if none of the plants is shut down? Which plants serve which markets?

c. What is the lowest cost achievable for the production and distribution network after the merger if plants can be scaled back or shut down in batches of 10 million units of capacity? Which plants serve which markets?

d. How is the optimal network configuration affected if all duties are reduced to 0?

e. How should the merged network be configured?

5. Return to the Sleekfon and Sturdyfon data in Exercise 4. Management has estimated that demand in global markets is likely to grow. North America, Japan, and Europe (EU) are relatively saturated and expect no growth. South America, Africa, and Europe (Non-EU) markets expect a growth of 20 percent. The rest of Asia/Australia anticipates a growth of 200 percent.

a. How should the merged company configure its network to accommodate the anticipated growth? What is the annual cost of operating the network?

b. There is an option of adding capacity at the plant in the rest of Asia/Australia. Adding 10 million units of capacity incurs an additional fixed cost of $40 million per year. Adding 20 million units of additional capacity incurs an additional fixed cost of $70 million per year. If shutdown

costs and duties are as in Exercise 4, how should the merged company configure its network to accommodate anticipated growth? What is the annual cost of operating the new network?

c. If all duties are reduced to 0, how does your answer to Exercise 5(b) change?

d. How should the merged network be configured given the option of adding to the plant in the rest of Asia/ Australia?

6. StayFresh, a manufacturer of refrigerators in India, has two plants—one in Mumbai and the other in Chennai. Each plant has an annual capacity of 300,000 units. The two plants serve the entire country, which is divided into four regional markets: the north, with a demand of 100,000 units; the west, with a demand of 150,000 units; the south, with a demand of 150,000 units; and the east, with a demand of 50,000 units. Two other potential sites for plants include Delhi and Kolkata. The variable production and transport costs (in thousands of rupees; 1 U.S. dollar is worth about 65 rupees) per refrigerator from each potential production site to each market are as shown in Table 5-11.

StayFresh is anticipating a compounded growth in demand of 20 percent per year for the next five years and must plan its network investment decisions. Demand is anticipated to stabilize after five years of growth. Capacity can be added in increments of either 150,000 or 300,000 units. Adding 150,000 units of capacity incurs a one-time cost of 2 billion rupees, whereas adding 300,000 units of capacity incurs a one-time cost of 3.4 billion rupees. Assume that StayFresh plans to meet all demand (prices are sufficiently high) and

TABLE 5-11 Production and Transport Cost (Thousands of Rupees) per Refrigerator

	North	East	West	South
Chennai	20	19	17	15
Delhi	15	18	17	20
Kolkata	18	15	20	19
Mumbai	17	20	15	17

that capacity for each year must be in place by the beginning of the year. Also assume that the cost for the fifth year will continue for the next 10 years—that is, years 6 to 15. The problem can now be solved for different discount factors. To begin with, assume a discount factor of 0.2—that is, 1 rupee spent next year is worth $1 - 0.2 = 0.8$ rupee this year.

a. How should the production network for the company evolve over the next five years?

b. How does your answer change if the anticipated growth is 15 percent? 25 percent?

c. How does your decision change for a discount factor of 0.25? 0.15?

d. What investment strategy do you recommend for the company?

7. Blue Computers, a major server manufacturer in the United States, currently has plants in Kentucky and Pennsylvania. The Kentucky plant has a capacity of 1 million units a year, and the Pennsylvania plant has a capacity of 1.5 million units a year. The firm divides the United States into five markets: northeast, southeast, midwest, south, and west. Each server sells for $1,000. The firm anticipates a 50 percent growth in demand (in each region) this year (after which demand will stabilize) and wants to build a plant with a capacity of 1.5 million units per year to accommodate the growth. Potential sites being considered are in North Carolina and California. Currently the firm pays federal, state, and local taxes on the income from each plant. Federal taxes are 20 percent of income, and all state and local taxes are 7 percent of income in each state. North Carolina has offered to reduce taxes for the next 10 years from 7 percent to 2 percent. Blue Computers would like to take the tax break into consideration when planning its network. Consider income over the next 10 years in your analysis. Assume that all costs remain unchanged over the 10 years. Use a discount factor of 0.1 for your analysis. Annual fixed costs, production and shipping costs per unit, and current regional demand (before the 50 percent growth) are shown in Table 5-12.

a. If Blue Computers sets an objective of minimizing total fixed and variable costs, where should it build the new plant? How should the network be structured?

b. If Blue Computers sets an objective of maximizing after-tax profits, where should it build the new plant? How should the network be structured?

8. Hot&Cold and CaldoFreddo are two European manufacturers of home appliances that have merged. Hot&Cold has plants in France, Germany, and Finland, whereas CaldoFreddo has plants in the United Kingdom and Italy. The European market is divided into four regions: north, east, west, and south. Plant capacities (millions of units per year), annual fixed costs (millions of euros per year), regional demand (millions of units), and variable production and shipping costs (euros per unit) are as shown in Table 5-13.

TABLE 5-12 Variable Production and Shipping Costs for Blue Computers

	Variable Production and Shipping Cost ($/Unit)					Annual Fixed Cost (Million $)
	Northeast	Southeast	Midwest	South	West	
Kentucky	185	180	175	175	200	150
Pennsylvania	170	190	180	200	220	200
N. Carolina	180	180	185	185	215	150
California	220	220	195	195	175	150
Demand (thousands of units/year)	700	400	400	300	600	

TABLE 5-13 Capacity, Cost, and Demand Data for Hot&Cold and CaldoFreddo

		Variable Production and Shipping Costs					Annual Fixed Cost
		North	East	South	West	Capacity	
Hot&Cold	France	100	110	105	100	50	1,000
	Germany	95	105	110	105	50	1,000
	Finland	90	100	115	110	40	850
Demand		30	20	20	35		
CaldoFreddo	U.K.	105	120	110	90	50	1,000
	Italy	110	105	90	115	60	1,150
Demand		15	20	30	20		

Each appliance sells for an average price of 300 euros. All plants are currently treated as profit centers, and the company pays taxes separately for each plant. Tax rates in the various countries are as follows: France, 0.25; Germany, 0.25; Finland, 0.3; UK, 0.2; and Italy, 0.35.

a. Before the merger, what is the optimal network for each of the two firms if their goal is to minimize costs? What is the optimal network if the goal is to maximize after-tax profits?

b. After the merger, what is the minimum cost configuration if none of the plants is shut down? What is the configuration that maximizes after-tax profits if none of the plants is shut down?

c. After the merger, what is the minimum cost configuration if plants can be shut down (assume that a shutdown saves 100 percent of the annual fixed cost of the plant)? What is the configuration that maximizes after-tax profits?

BIBLIOGRAPHY

Anderson, Kenneth E., Daniel P. Murphy, and James M. Reeve. "Smart Tax Planning for Supply Chain Facilities." *Supply Chain Management Review* (November–December 2002): 46–52.

Ballou, Ronald H. *Business Logistics Management.* Upper Saddle River, NJ: Prentice Hall, 1999.

Bovet, David. "Good Time to Rethink European Distribution." *Supply Chain Management Review* (July–August 2010): 6–7.

Daskin, Mark S. *Network and Discrete Location.* New York: Wiley, 1995.

Drezner, Z., and H. Hamacher. *Facility Location: Applications and Theory.* Berlin: Springer Verlag, 2004.

Harding, Charles F. "Quantifying Abstract Factors in Facility-Location Decisions." *Industrial Development* (May–June 1988): 24.

Jones, Mike. "The Many Flavors of Network Optimization." *Supply Chain Management Review* (November 2015): 42–48.

Korpela, Jukka, AnttiLehmusvaara, and MarkkuTuominen. "Customer Service Based Design of the Supply Chain." *International Journal of Production Economics* (2001) 69: 193–204.

MacCormack, Alan D., Lawrence J. Newman III, and Donald B. Rosenfield. "The New Dynamics of Global Manufacturing Site Location." *Sloan Management Review* (Summer 1994): 69–79.

Mentzer, Joseph. "Seven Keys to Facility Location." *Supply Chain Management Review* (May–June 2008): 25–31.

Tayur, Sridhar, Ram Ganeshan, and Michael Magazine, eds. *Quantitative Models for Supply Chain Management.* Boston: Kluwer Academic Publishers, 1999.

Tirole, Jean. *The Theory of Industrial Organization.* Cambridge, MA: MIT Press, 1997.

CASE STUDY

Designing the Production Network at CoolWipes

Matt O'Grady, vice president of supply chain at CoolWipes, thought that his current production and distribution network was not appropriate, given the significant increase in transportation costs over the past few years. Compared to when the company had set up its production facility in Chicago, transportation costs had increased by a factor of more than four and were expected to continue growing in the next few years. A quick decision on building one or more new plants could save the company significant amounts in transportation expense in the future.

CoolWipes

CoolWipes was founded in the late 1980s and produced baby wipes and diaper ointment. Annual demand for the two products was as shown in Table 5-14. At that time, the company had one factory in Chicago that produced

TABLE 5-14 Regional Annual Demand at CoolWipes (in thousands)

Zone	Wipes Demand	Ointment Demand	Zone	Wipes Demand	Ointment Demand
Northwest	500	50	Lower Midwest	800	65
Southwest	700	90	Northeast	1,000	120
Upper Midwest	900	120	Southeast	600	70

TABLE 5-15 Transportation Costs per Unit

	Northwest	Southwest	Upper Midwest	Lower Midwest	Northeast	Southeast
Chicago	$6.32	$6.32	$3.68	$4.04	$5.76	$5.96
Princeton	$6.60	$6.60	$5.76	$5.92	$3.68	$4.08
Atlanta	$6.72	$6.48	$5.92	$4.08	$4.04	$3.64
Los Angeles	$4.36	$3.68	$6.32	$6.32	$6.72	$6.60

both products for the entire country. The wipes line in the Chicago facility had an annual capacity of 5 million units, an annualized fixed cost of $5 million a year, and a variable cost of $10 per unit. The ointment line in the Chicago facility had an annual capacity of 1 million units, an annualized fixed cost of $1.5 million a year, and a variable cost of $20 per unit. The transportation costs per unit (for both wipes and ointment) are shown in Table 5-15.

New Network Options

Matt had identified Princeton, New Jersey; Atlanta; and Los Angeles as potential sites for new plants. Each new plant could have a wipes line, an ointment line, or both. A new wipes line had an annual capacity of 2 million units, an annual fixed cost of $2.2 million, and a variable production cost of $10 per unit. A new ointment line had an annual capacity of 1 million units, an annual fixed cost of $1.5 million, and a variable cost of $20 per unit. The current transportation costs per unit are shown in Table 5-15.

Matt had to decide whether to build a new plant and if so, which production lines to put into the new plant.

Study Questions

1. What is the annual cost of serving the entire nation from Chicago?
2. Do you recommend adding any plant(s)? If so, where should the plant(s) be built and what lines should be included? Assume that the Chicago plant will be maintained at its current capacity but could be run at lower utilization. Would your decision be different if transportation costs are half of their current value? What if they were double their current value?
3. If Matt could design a new network from scratch (assume he did not have the Chicago plant but could build it at the cost and capacity specified in the case), what production network would you recommend? Assume that any new plants built besides Chicago would be at the cost and capacity specified under the new network options. Would your decision be different if transportation costs were half of their current value? What if they were double their current value?

CASE STUDY

Managing a Merger at Lightning Networks

After receiving regulatory approval from the European Union, Lightning Networks, a major wireless carrier, and SatTV, the largest satellite TV provider in Europe, completed their 50 billion euro merger in 2016. After initial skepticism when the deal was first announced, analysts had warmed to the idea of synergies in the merger. Lightning expected to benefit from the large customer base of SatTV and the company announced that it expected significant annual cost savings within three years of the merger. Simone Durand, senior VP of supply chain at Lightning, was charged with identifying some cost reduction opportunities. She decided to focus her initial attention on the distribution networks the two companies used to fulfill demand for installation and repair products. The merger offered an opportunity to combine the two distribution networks.

The Current Distribution Network

Any new installation or repair by Lightning or SatTV required a set of products for the technician to complete the job. Rather than carrying these products with technicians, both companies had decided to centralize product inventories in a few locations. Annual product demand

TABLE 5-16 Annual Demand in Europe for Lightning Networks (wireless) and SatTV (satellite)

Zone	Wireless Demand	Satellite Demand	Zone	Wireless Demand	Satellite Demand
Northwest	200,000	120,000	Middle South	120,000	120,000
Southwest	100,000	100,000	Northeast	150,000	110,000
Middle North	220,000	100,000	Southeast	90,000	100,000

for the two companies across six regions in Europe was as shown in Table 5-16.

Lightning had served its product needs from three warehouses located in Madrid, Spain; Rotterdam, Netherlands; and Krakow, Poland. SatTV had served its product needs from three warehouses located in Toulouse, France; Munich, Germany; and Budapest, Hungary. Each facility was specialized to handle either wireless or satellite products because of the historical focus of the company it belonged to. The specialization, capacity, and annual fixed cost for each facility were as shown in Table 5-17. The capacity of each warehouse is given in terms of how

much annual demand it can handle. From Table 5-17, observe that the Madrid warehouse can serve demand of up to 370,000 units. The variable cost of shipping one unit (either wireless or satellite) from each warehouse location to each market is shown in Table 5-18.

The Network Options

Simone had a short term and a long term decision to make. In the short term, she had to decide whether to make all the warehouses flexible or not. Making all warehouses flexible required an investment equivalent

TABLE 5-17 Warehouse Specialization, Capacities, and Fixed Costs

Location	Specialization	Capacity	Fixed Cost (euro/year)
Madrid	Wireless	370,000	600,000
Rotterdam	Wireless	420,000	650,000
Krakow	Wireless	310,000	520,000
Toulouse	Satellite	280,000	475,000
Munich	Satellite	290,000	488,000
Budapest	Satellite	250,000	425,000

TABLE 5-18 Variable Distribution Cost per Unit in Euro

	Northwest	Southwest	Middle North	Middle South	Northeast	Southeast
Madrid	2.50	1.50	3.00	2.75	4.00	4.50
Rotterdam	1.75	3.00	1.50	3.00	2.50	3.50
Krakow	3.25	4.00	2.50	3.00	2.00	2.50
Toulouse	2.00	2.00	2.75	2.50	3.75	4.00
Munich	2.25	3.00	2.25	2.50	2.75	3.00
Budapest	3.50	3.75	2.50	2.50	2.50	2.00

to an additional annual cost of 200,000 euro. Flexible warehouses, however, could be used to serve demand for both wireless and satellite products.

In the longer term, Simone had to decide whether to restructure the distribution network. She could choose to close some warehouses, leave others open as they were, or double the capacity of some warehouses. Doubling the capacity of a warehouse would increase its annual fixed cost by 80 percent. Thus, if the capacity of the Madrid warehouse was doubled, its annual fixed cost would be 900,000 euro.

Closing a warehouse would also incur some cost, thus reducing the annual fixed cost that could be saved. Simone's team estimated that closing a warehouse would save 80 percent of the annual fixed cost. Thus, closing the Madrid warehouse would still result in an annual cost of 100,000 euro because only 80 percent of the fixed cost is saved.

Study Questions

1. What is the annual cost if Lightning uses the current network (with warehouses specialized as in Table 5-17) optimally to meet European demand?
2. Should Simone make all warehouses flexible given the additional cost of 200,000 euro per year?
3. What supply chain network configuration do you recommend for the long term if demand is as in Table 5-16? Should any warehouses be closed? Should any warehouses see their capacity doubled?
4. What supply chain network configuration do you recommend for the long term if the Northeast and Southeast demand is expected to increase by 30 percent while all other demands remain as in Table 5-16? Should any warehouses be closed? Should any warehouses see their capacity doubled?

6

Designing Global Supply Chain Networks

LEARNING OBJECTIVES

After reading this chapter, you will be able to

6.1 Identify factors that need to be included in total cost when making global sourcing decisions.

6.2 Define relevant risks and explain different strategies that may be used to mitigate risk in global supply chains.

6.3 Understand decision tree methodologies used to evaluate supply chain design decisions under uncertainty.

6.4 Use decision tree methodologies to value flexibility and make onshoring / offshoring decisions under uncertainty.

Globalization has offered tremendous opportunity, as well as increased risk, in the development of supply chains. High-performance supply chains such as Samsung and Zara have taken full advantage of globalization. In contrast, several supply chains have found themselves unprepared for the increased risk that has accompanied globalization. As a result, managers must account for both opportunities and uncertainties over the long term when designing a global supply chain network. In this chapter, we identify sources of risk for global supply chains, discuss risk mitigation strategies, detail the methodologies used to evaluate network design decisions under uncertainty, and show how they improve global supply chain decisions.

THE IMPACT OF GLOBALIZATION ON SUPPLY CHAIN NETWORKS

6.1 Identify factors that need to be included in total cost when making global sourcing decisions.

Globalization offers companies opportunities to simultaneously increase revenues and decrease costs. In its 2008 annual report, P&G reported that more than a third of the company's sales growth was from developing markets with a profit margin that was comparable to developed market margins. By 2010, sales for the company in developing markets represented almost 34 percent of global sales. Most of Samsung's sales are from outside its home country of Korea. In 2012, overseas revenue represented 86 percent of sales for Samsung. While maintaining a dominant position in developed markets like the United States, it had also penetrated into emerging markets such as China and India. By 2012, Samsung was the leading vendor of smartphones in

both markets. Clearly, globalization has offered both P&G and Samsung a significant revenue enhancement opportunity.

Apparel and consumer electronics are two industries for which globalization has offered significant cost reduction opportunities. Consumer electronics focuses on small, lightweight, high-value items that are relatively easy and inexpensive to ship. Companies have exploited large economies of scale by consolidating production of standardized electronics components in a single location for use in multiple products across the globe. Contract manufacturers such as Foxconn and Flextronics have become giants with facilities in low-cost countries. Apparel manufacture has high labor content, and the product is relatively lightweight and cost effective to transport. Companies have exploited globalization by shifting much apparel manufacturing to low-labor-cost countries, especially in Asia. In 2015, about 36 percent of U.S. apparel imports were from China with another 29 percent coming from Vietnam, Bangladesh, Indonesia, and India. The net result is that both industries have benefited tremendously from cost reduction as a result of globalization.

One must keep in mind, however, that the opportunities from globalization are often accompanied by significant additional risk and uncertainty. In a survey conducted by the consulting company Accenture in 2006, more than 50 percent of the executives surveyed believed that supply chain risk had increased as a result of their global operations strategy. For example, the Japanese earthquake and Tsunami in 2011 disrupted the supply of made-in-Japan car models like the Toyota Prius. As a result, American automakers gained market share at the expense of Toyota. Similarly, flooding in Thailand in 2011 had a significant impact on both the electronics and automotive industries. For example, Honda suspended operations at a Thai assembly plant that could produce 240,000 vehicles a year. As a result, the company reported a sharp fall in quarterly profits. The ability to incorporate suitable risk mitigation into supply chain design has often been the difference between global supply chains that have succeeded and those that have not.

The Accenture survey categorized risk in global supply chains, as shown in Table 6-1, and asked respondents to indicate the factors that affected them. More than a third of the respondents were affected by natural disasters, volatility of fuel prices, and the performance of supply chain partners.

TABLE 6-1 Results of Accenture Survey on Sources of Risk That Affect Global Supply Chain Performance

Risk Factors	Percentage of Supply Chains Affected
Natural disasters	35
Shortage of skilled resources	24
Geopolitical uncertainty	20
Terrorist infiltration of cargo	13
Volatility of fuel prices	37
Currency fluctuation	29
Port operations/custom delays	23
Customer/consumer preference shifts	23
Performance of supply chain partners	38
Logistics capacity/complexity	33
Forecasting/planning accuracy	30
Supplier planning/communication issues	27
Inflexible supply chain technology	21

Source: Data from Jaume Ferre, Johann Karlberg, and Jamie Hintlian, "Integration: The Key to Global Success." Supply Chain Management Review (March 2007): 24–30.

Crude oil spot price and exchange rate fluctuations in 2008 illustrate the extreme volatility that global supply chains must deal with. Crude started 2008 at about $90 per barrel, peaked in July at more than $140 per barrel, and plummeted to below $40 per barrel in December. The euro started 2008 at about $1.47, peaked in July at almost $1.60, dropped to about $1.25 at the end of October, and then rose back to $1.46 toward the end of December. One can only imagine the havoc such fluctuation played on supply chain performance in 2008! Similar fluctuations in exchange rates and crude prices have continued since then.

The only constant in global supply chain management seems to be uncertainty. Over the life of a supply chain network, a company experiences fluctuations in demand, prices, exchange rates, and the competitive environment. A decision that looks good under the current environment may be quite poor if the situation changes. Between 2000 and 2008, the euro fluctuated from a low of $0.84 to a high of almost $1.60. Clearly, supply chains optimized to $0.84 per euro would have difficulty performing well when the euro reached $1.60.

Uncertainty of demand and price drives the value of building flexible production capacity at a plant. If price and demand do vary over time in a global network, flexible production capacity can be reconfigured to maximize profits in the new environment. Between 2007 and 2008, auto sales in the United States dropped by more than 30 percent. Whereas all vehicle categories were affected, the drop in SUV sales was much more significant than the drop in sales of small cars and hybrids. While SUV sales dropped by almost 35 percent, small car sales actually increased by about 1 percent. Honda dealt with this fluctuation more effectively than its competitors because its plants were flexible enough to produce both vehicle types. This flexibility to produce both SUVs and cars in the same facility kept Honda plants operating at reasonably high levels of utilization. In contrast, companies with plants dedicated to SUV production had no option but to leave a lot of idle capacity. In the late 1990s, Toyota made its global assembly plants more flexible so each plant could supply multiple markets. One of the main benefits of this flexibility is that it allows Toyota to react to fluctuations in demand, exchange rates, and local prices by altering production to maximize profits. Thus, supply, demand, and financial uncertainty must be considered when making global network design decisions.

THE IMPORTANCE OF TOTAL COST IN GLOBAL NETWORKS

The importance of comparative advantage in global supply chains was recognized by Adam Smith in *The Wealth of Nations* when he stated, "If a foreign country can supply us with a commodity cheaper than we ourselves can make it, better buy it of them with some part of the produce of our own industry, employed in a way in which we have some advantage."[1] Cost reduction by moving production to low-cost countries is typically mentioned among the top reasons for a supply chain to become global. The challenge, however, is to quantify the benefits (or comparative advantage) of offshore production along with the reasons for this comparative advantage. Whereas many companies have taken advantage of cost reduction through offshoring, others have found the benefits of offshoring to low-cost countries to be far less than anticipated—and, in some cases, nonexistent. The increases in transportation costs since 2000 have had a significant negative impact on the perceived benefits of offshoring. Companies have failed to gain from offshoring for two primary reasons: (1) focusing exclusively on unit cost rather than total cost when making the offshoring decision and (2) ignoring critical risk factors. In this section, we focus on dimensions along which total landed cost needs to be evaluated when making an offshoring decision.

The significant dimensions of total cost can be identified by focusing on the complete sourcing process when offshoring. It is important to keep in mind that a global supply chain with offshoring increases the length and duration of information, product, and cash flows. As a result, the complexity and cost of managing the supply chain can be significantly higher than anticipated. Table 6-2 identifies dimensions along which each of the three flows should be analyzed for the impact on cost and product availability.

[1] W. Strahan and T. Cadell, The Wealth of Nations by Adam Smith, 1776. , as published by Adam Smith.

TABLE 6-2 Dimensions to Consider When Evaluating Total Cost from Offshoring

Performance Dimension	Activity Affecting Performance	Impact of Offshoring
Order communication	Order placement	More difficult communication
Supply chain visibility	Scheduling and expediting	Poorer visibility
Raw material costs	Sourcing of raw material	Could go either way depending on raw material sourcing
Unit cost	Production, quality (production and transportation)	Labor/fixed costs decrease; quality may suffer
Freight costs	Transportation modes and quantity	Higher freight costs
Taxes and tariffs	Border crossing	Could go either way
Supply lead time	Order communication, supplier production scheduling, production time, customs, transportation, receiving	Lead time increase results in poorer forecasts and higher inventories
On-time delivery/lead time uncertainty	Production, quality, customs, transportation, receiving	Poorer on-time delivery and increased uncertainty resulting in higher inventory and lower product availability
Minimum order quantity	Production, transportation	Larger minimum quantities increase inventory
Product returns	Quality	Increased returns likely
Inventories	Lead times, inventory in transit and production	Increase
Working capital	Inventories and financial reconciliation	Increase
Hidden costs	Order communication, invoicing errors, managing exchange rate risk	Higher hidden costs
Stockouts	Ordering, production, transportation with poorer visibility	Increase

Ferreira and Prokopets (2009) suggest that companies should evaluate the impact of off-shoring on the following key elements of total cost:

1. **Supplier price:** should link to costs from direct materials, direct labor, indirect labor, management, overhead, capital amortization, local taxes, manufacturing costs, and local regulatory compliance costs.
2. **Terms:** costs are affected by net payment terms and any volume discounts.
3. **Delivery costs:** include in-country transportation, ocean/air freight, destination transport, and packaging.
4. **Inventory and warehousing:** include in-plant inventories, in-plant handling, plant warehouse costs, supply chain inventories, and supply chain warehousing costs.
5. **Cost of quality:** includes cost of validation, cost of performance drop due to poorer quality, and cost of incremental remedies to combat quality drop.

6. Customs duties, value-added taxes, local tax incentives.
7. Cost of risk, procurement staff, broker fees, infrastructure (IT and facilities), and tooling and mold costs.
8. Exchange rate trends and their impact on cost.

It is important to both quantify these factors carefully when making the offshoring decision and track them over time. As Table 6-2 indicates, unit cost reduction from low labor and fixed costs, along with possible tax advantages, are likely to be the major benefit from offshoring, with almost every other factor being negative. In some instances, the substitution of labor for capital can provide a benefit when offshoring. For example, auto and auto parts plants in India are designed with much greater labor content than similar manufacturing in developed countries to lower fixed costs. The benefit of lower labor cost, however, is unlikely to be significant for a manufactured product if labor cost is a small fraction of total cost. It is also the case that in several low-cost countries, such as China and India, labor costs have escalated significantly. As mentioned by Goel et al. (2008), wage inflation in China averaged 19 percent in dollar terms between 2003 and 2008 compared to around 3 percent in the United States. During the same period, transportation costs increased by a significant amount (ocean freight costs increased 135 percent between 2005 and 2008) and the Chinese yuan strengthened relative to the dollar (by about 18 percent between 2005 and 2008). The net result was that offshoring manufactured products from the United States to China looked much less attractive in 2008 than in 2003.

In general, offshoring to low-cost countries is likely to be most attractive for products with high labor content, large production volumes, relatively low variety, and low transportation costs relative to product value. For example, a company producing a large variety of pumps is likely to find that offshoring the production of castings for a common part across many pumps is much more attractive than the offshoring of highly specialized engineered parts.

Given that global sourcing tends to increase transportation costs, it is important to focus on reducing transportation content for successful global sourcing. Suitably designed components can facilitate much greater density when transporting products. IKEA has designed modular products that are assembled by the customer. This allows the modules to be shipped flat in high density, lowering transportation costs. Similarly, Nissan redesigned its globally sourced components so that they can be packed more tightly for shipping. The use of supplier hubs can be effective if several components are being sourced globally from different locations. Many manufacturers have created supplier hubs in Asia that are fed by each of their Asian suppliers. This allows for a consolidated shipment to be sent from the hub rather than several smaller shipments being sent from each supplier. More sophisticated flexible policies that allow for direct shipping from the supplier when volumes are high, coupled with consolidated shipping through a hub when volumes are low, can be effective in lowering transportation cost.

It is also important to perform a careful review of the production process to decide which parts are to be offshored. For example, a small American jewelry manufacturer wanted to offshore manufacturing to Hong Kong for a piece of jewelry. Raw material in the form of gold sheet was sourced in the United States. The first step in the manufacturing process was the stamping of the gold sheet into a suitable-sized blank. This process generated about 40 percent waste, which could be recycled to produce more gold sheet. The manufacturer faced the choice of stamping in the United States or Hong Kong. Stamping in Hong Kong would incur lower labor cost but higher transportation cost and would require more working capital because of the delay before the waste gold could be recycled. A careful analysis indicated that it was cheaper for the stamping tools to be installed at the gold sheet supplier in the United States. Stamping at the gold sheet supplier reduced transportation cost because only usable material was shipped to Hong Kong. More importantly, this decision reduced working capital requirement because the waste gold from stamping was recycled within two days.

One of the biggest challenges with offshoring is the increased risk and its potential impact on cost. This challenge is exacerbated if a company uses an offshore location that is primarily targeting low costs to absorb all the uncertainties in its supply chain. In such a context, it is often

much more effective to use a combination of an offshore facility that is given predictable, high-volume work along with an onshore or near-shore facility that is designed specifically to handle most of the fluctuation. Companies using only an offshore facility often find themselves carrying extra inventory and resorting to air freight because of the long and variable lead times. The presence of a flexible onshore facility that absorbs all the variation can often lower total landed cost by eliminating expensive freight and significantly reducing the amount of inventory carried in the supply chain.

SUMMARY OF LEARNING OBJECTIVE 1

It is critical that global sourcing decisions be made while accounting for total cost. Besides unit cost, total cost should include the impact of global sourcing on freight, inventories, lead time, quality, on-time delivery, minimum order quantity, working capital, and stockouts. Other factors to be considered include the impact on supply chain visibility, order communication, invoicing errors, and the need for currency hedging. Offshoring typically lowers labor and fixed costs but increases risk, freight costs, and working capital.

RISK MANAGEMENT IN GLOBAL SUPPLY CHAINS

6.2 Define relevant risks and explain different strategies that may be used to mitigate risk in global supply chains.

Global supply chains today are subject to more risk factors than localized supply chains of the past. These risks include supply disruption, supply delays, demand fluctuations, price fluctuations, and exchange rate fluctuations. Similar to in the financial crisis of 2008, underestimating risks in global supply chains and not having suitable mitigation strategies in place can result in painful outcomes. For example, contamination at one of the two suppliers of flu vaccine to the United States led to a severe shortage at the beginning of the 2004 flu season. This shortage led to rationing in most states and severe price gouging in some cases. Similarly, the significant strengthening of the euro in 2008 hurt firms that had most of their supply sources located in Western Europe. In another instance, failure to buffer supply uncertainty with sufficient inventory resulted in high costs rather than savings. An automotive component manufacturer had hoped to save $4 million to $5 million a year by sourcing from Asia instead of Mexico. As a result of port congestion in Los Angeles–Long Beach, the company had to charter aircraft to fly the parts in from Asia because it did not have sufficient inventory to cover the delays. A charter that would have cost $20,000 per aircraft from Mexico ended up costing the company $750,000. The anticipated savings turned into a $20 million loss.

It is thus critical for global supply chains to be aware of the relevant risk factors and build in suitable mitigation strategies. Table 6-3 contains a categorization of supply chain risks and their drivers that must be considered during network design.

Good network design can play a significant role in mitigating supply chain risk. For instance, having multiple suppliers mitigates the risk of disruption from any one supply source. An excellent example is the difference in impact on Nokia and Ericsson when a plant owned by Royal Philips Electronics, located in Albuquerque, New Mexico, caught fire in March 2000. Nokia adjusted to the disruption quickly, using several other supply plants in its network. In contrast, Ericsson had no backup source in its network and was unable to react. Ericsson estimated that it lost revenues of $400 million as a result. Similarly, having flexible capacity mitigates the risks of global demand, price, and exchange rate fluctuations. For example, Hino Trucks uses flexible capacity at its plants to change production levels for different products by shifting workforce among lines. As a result, the company keeps a constant workforce in the plant even though the production at each line varies to best match supply and demand. As illustrated by these examples, designing mitigation strategies into the network significantly improves a supply chain's ability to deal with risk.

Every mitigation strategy comes at a price, however, and may increase other risks. For example, increasing inventory mitigates the risk of delays but increases the risk of obsolescence.

TABLE 6-3 Supply Chain Risks to Be Considered During Network Design

Category	Risk Drivers
Disruptions	Natural disaster, war, terrorism
	Labor disputes
	Supplier bankruptcy
Delays	High capacity utilization at supply source
	Inflexibility of supply source
	Poor quality or yield at supply source
Systems risk	Information infrastructure breakdown
	System integration or extent of systems being networked
Forecast risk	Inaccurate forecasts due to long lead times, seasonality, product variety, short life cycles, small customer base
	Information distortion
Intellectual property risk	Vertical integration of supply chain
	Global outsourcing and markets
Procurement risk	Exchange rate risk
	Price of inputs
	Fraction purchased from a single source
	Industry wide capacity utilization
Receivables risk	Number of customers
	Financial strength of customers
Inventory risk	Rate of product obsolescence
	Inventory holding cost
	Product value
	Demand and supply uncertainty
Capacity risk	Cost of capacity
	Capacity flexibility

Source: Based on Sunil Chopra and Manmohan S. Sodhi, "Managing Risk to Avoid Supply Chain Breakdown." *Sloan Management Review* (Fall 2004): 53–61.

Acquiring multiple suppliers mitigates the risk of disruption but increases costs because each supplier may have difficulty achieving economies of scale. Thus, it is important to develop tailored mitigation strategies during network design that achieve a good balance between the amount of risk mitigated and the increase in cost. Some tailored mitigation strategies are outlined in Table 6-4. Most of these strategies are discussed in greater detail later in the book.

Global supply chains should generally use a combination of mitigation strategies designed into the supply chain along with financial strategies to hedge uncovered risks. A global supply chain strategy focused on efficiency and low cost may concentrate production in a few low-cost countries. Such a supply chain design, however, is vulnerable to the risk of supply disruption along with fluctuations in transportation prices and exchange rates. In such a setting, it is crucial that the firm hedge fuel costs and exchange rates because the supply chain design itself has no built-in mechanisms to deal with these fluctuations. In contrast, a global supply chain designed with excess, flexible capacity allows production to be shifted to whatever location is most effective in a given set of macroeconomic conditions. The ability of such a flexible design to react to fluctuations decreases

TABLE 6-4 Tailored Risk Mitigation Strategies During Network Design

Risk Mitigation Strategy	Tailored Strategies
Increase capacity	Focus on low-cost, decentralized capacity for predictable demand. Build centralized capacity for unpredictable demand. Increase decentralization as cost of capacity drops.
Get redundant suppliers	More redundant supply for high-volume products, less redundancy for low-volume products. Centralize redundancy for low-volume products in a few flexible suppliers.
Increase responsiveness	Favor cost over responsiveness for commodity products. Favor responsiveness over cost for short–life cycle products.
Increase inventory	Decentralize inventory of predictable, lower-value products. Centralize inventory of less predictable, higher-value products.
Increase flexibility	Favor cost over flexibility for predictable, high-volume products. Favor flexibility for unpredictable, low-volume products. Centralize flexibility in a few locations if it is expensive.
Pool or aggregate demand	Increase aggregation as unpredictability grows.
Increase source capability	Prefer capability over cost for high-value, high-risk products. Favor cost over capability for low-value commodity products. Centralize high capability in flexible source if possible.

Source: Based on Sunil Chopra and Manmohan S. Sodhi, "Managing Risk to Avoid Supply Chain Breakdown." *Sloan Management Review* (Fall 2004): 53–61.

the need for financial hedges. Operational hedges such as flexibility are more complex to execute than financial hedges, but they have the advantage of being reactive because the supply chain can be reconfigured to best react to the macroeconomic state of the world.

It is important to keep in mind that any risk mitigation strategy is not always "in the money." For example, flexibility built into Honda plants proved effective only when demand for vehicles shifted in an unpredictable manner in 2008. If there had been no fluctuation in demand, the flexibility would have gone unutilized. Flexibility in the form of the intelligent body assembly system (IBAS) built by Nissan in the early 1990s almost bankrupted the company because the state of the automotive markets was relatively stable at that time. Similarly, the use of fuel hedges that made billions for Southwest Airlines cost it money toward the end of 2008 when crude oil prices dropped significantly.

It is thus critical that risk mitigation strategies be evaluated rigorously as real options in terms of their expected long-term value before they are implemented. In the following sections, we discuss methodologies that allow for the financial evaluation of risk mitigation strategies designed into a global supply chain.

Flexibility, Chaining, and Containment

Flexibility plays an important role in mitigating different risks and uncertainties faced by a global supply chain. Flexibility can be divided into three broad categories—new product flexibility, mix flexibility, and volume flexibility. *New product flexibility* refers to a firm's ability to introduce new products into the market at a rapid rate. New product flexibility is critical in a competitive environment wherein technology is evolving and customer demand is fickle. New product flexibility may result from the use of common architectures and product platforms with the goal of providing a large number of distinct models using as few unique platforms as possible.

The consumer electronics industry has historically followed this approach to introduce a continuous stream of new products. New product flexibility may also result if a fraction of the production capacity is flexible enough to be able to produce any product. This approach has been used in the pharmaceutical industry, in which a fraction of the capacity is very flexible with all new products first manufactured there. Only once the product takes off is it moved to a dedicated capacity with lower variable costs.

Mix flexibility refers to the ability to produce a variety of products within a short period of time. Mix flexibility is critical in an environment in which demand for individual products is small or highly unpredictable, supply of raw materials is uncertain, and technology is evolving rapidly. The fashion and consumer electronics industries are good examples for which mix flexibility is essential in production environments. Modular design and common components facilitate mix flexibility in the electronics industry. Zara's European facilities have significant mix flexibility, allowing the company to provide trendy apparel with highly unpredictable demand.

Volume flexibility refers to a firm's ability to operate profitably at different levels of output. Volume flexibility is critical in cyclical industries. Firms in the automotive industry that lacked volume flexibility were badly hurt in 2008 when demand for automobiles in the United States shrank significantly. The steel industry is an example in which some volume flexibility and consolidation have helped performance. Prior to 2000, firms had limited volume flexibility and did not adjust production volumes when demand started to fall. The result was a buildup of inventories and a significant drop in the price of steel during a downturn. In the early 2000s, a few large firms consolidated and developed some volume flexibility. As a result, they were able to cut production as demand fell. The result has been less buildup of inventory and smaller drops in price during downturns, followed by a quicker recovery for the steel industry.

Given that some form of flexibility is often used to mitigate risks in global supply chains, it is important to understand the benefits and limitations of this approach. When dealing with demand uncertainty, Jordan and Graves (1995) make the important observation that as flexibility is increased, the marginal benefit derived from the increased flexibility decreases. They suggest operationalizing this idea in the concept of *chaining*, which is illustrated as follows. Consider a firm that sells four distinct products. A dedicated supply network with no flexibility would have four plants, each dedicated to producing a single product, as shown in Figure 6-1. A fully flexible network configuration would have each plant capable of producing all four products. The production flexibility of plants is beneficial when demand for each of the four products is unpredictable. With dedicated plants, the firm is not able to meet demand in excess of plant capacity. With flexible plants, the firm is able to shift excess demand for a product to a plant with excess capacity. Jordan and Graves define a chained network with one long chain (limited flexibility), configured as shown in Figure 6-1. In a chained configuration, each plant is capable of producing two products with the flexibility organized so that the plants and their products form a chain. Jordan and Graves show that a chained network mitigates the risk of demand fluctuation almost as effectively as a fully flexible network. Given the higher cost of full flexibility, the results of Jordan and Graves indicate that chaining is an excellent strategy to lower cost while gaining most of the benefits of flexibility.

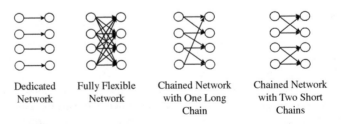

Dedicated Network Fully Flexible Network Chained Network with One Long Chain Chained Network with Two Short Chains

Figure 6-1 Different Flexibility Configurations in Network

The desired length of chains is an important question to be addressed when designing chained networks. When dealing with demand uncertainty, longer chains have the advantage of effectively pooling available capacity to a greater extent. Long chains, however, do have a few disadvantages. The fixed cost of building a single long chain can be higher than the cost of multiple smaller chains. With a single long chain, the effect of any fluctuation ripples to all facilities in the chain, making coordination more difficult across the network. It has also been observed by several researchers that flexibility and chaining are effective when dealing with demand fluctuation but less effective when dealing with supply disruption. In the presence of supply disruption, Lim et al., (2008) have observed that designing smaller chains that contain or limit the impact of a disruption can be more effective than designing a network with one long chain. An example of containment is shown in the last example in Figure 6-1, which shows four plants with the flexibility to produce the four products in the form of two short chains. In this design, any disruption in one of the chains does not affect the other chain. A simple example of containment is hog farming: The farms are large to gain economies of scale, but the hogs are kept separated in small groups to ensure that the risk of disease is contained within a group and does not spread to the entire farm.

SUMMARY OF LEARNING OBJECTIVE 2

The performance of a global supply chain is affected by risk and uncertainty in a number of input factors such as supply, demand, price, exchange rates, and other economic factors. These risks can be mitigated by building suitable flexibility in the supply chain network. Operational strategies that help mitigate risk in global supply chains include carrying excess capacity and inventory, flexible capacity, redundant suppliers, improved responsiveness, and aggregation of demand. Hedging fuel costs and currencies are financial strategies that can help mitigate risk. It is important to keep in mind that no risk mitigation strategy will always pay off. These mitigation strategies are designed to guard against certain extreme states of the world that may arise in an uncertain global environment.

EVALUATING NETWORK DESIGN DECISIONS USING DECISION TREES

6.3 Understand decision tree methodologies used to evaluate supply chain design decisions under uncertainty.

Decision makers should design global supply chain networks considering a portfolio of strategic options—the option to wait, build excess capacity, build flexible capacity, sign long-term contracts, purchase from the spot market, and so forth. In any global supply chain, demand, prices, exchange rates, and several other factors are uncertain and are likely to fluctuate during the life of any supply chain decision. Thus, the various options should be evaluated in the context of future uncertainty. A design methodology that does not account for uncertainty typically undervalues flexible options. The result is often a supply chain that performs well if everything goes according to plan but becomes terribly expensive if something unexpected happens. A manager makes several different decisions when designing a supply chain network. For instance:

- Should the firm sign a long-term contract for warehousing space or get space from the spot market as needed?
- What should the firm's mix of long-term and spot market be in the portfolio of transportation capacity?
- How much capacity should various facilities have? What fraction of this capacity should be flexible?

If uncertainty is ignored, a manager will always sign long-term contracts (because they are typically cheaper) and avoid all flexible or backup capacity (because it is more expensive). Such decisions can hurt the firm, however, if future demand or prices are not as forecast at the time of the decision. Executives participating in the Accenture 2013 Global Manufacturing Study "cited

a variety of volatility-related factors as potential impediments to their ability to grow—including global currency instability, unpredictable commodities costs, uncertainty about customer demand, political or social unrest in key markets, and potential changes in government regulations." It is thus important to provide a methodology that allows managers to incorporate this uncertainty into their network design process. In this section, we describe such a methodology and show that accounting for uncertainty can have a significant impact on the value of network design decisions.

Discounted Cash Flows

Global supply chain design decisions should be evaluated as a sequence of cash flows over the duration of time the decisions will be in place. This requires the evaluation of future cash flows accounting for risks and uncertainties likely to arise in the global supply chain. We first discuss the basics of analysis to evaluate future cash flows before introducing uncertainty.

The present value of a stream of cash flows is what that stream is worth in today's dollars. *Discounted cash flow* (DCF) analysis evaluates the present value of any stream of future cash flows and allows management to compare two streams of cash flows in terms of their financial value. DCF analysis is based on the fundamental premise that "a dollar today is worth more than a dollar tomorrow" because a dollar today may be invested and earn a return in addition to the dollar invested. This premise provides the basic tool for comparing the relative value of future cash flows that will arrive during different time periods.

The present value of future cash flow is found by using a discount factor. If a dollar today can be invested and earn a rate of return k over the next period, an investment of $1 today will result in $1 + k$ dollars in the next period. An investor would therefore be indifferent between obtaining $1 in the next period or $\$1/(1 + k)$ in the current period. Thus, $1 in the next period is discounted by the

$$\text{Discount factor} = \frac{1}{1 + k} \tag{6.1}$$

to obtain its present value.

The rate of return k is also referred to as the *discount rate*, *hurdle rate*, or *opportunity cost of capital*. Given a stream of cash flows $C_0, C_1, \ldots, C_T$ over the next T periods, and a rate of return k, the net present value (NPV) of this cash flow stream is given by

$$\text{NPV} = C_o + \sum_{t=1}^{T} \left(\frac{1}{1 + k} \right)^t C_t \tag{6.2}$$

The NPV of different options should be compared when making supply chain decisions. A negative NPV for an option indicates that the option will lose money for the supply chain. The decision with the highest NPV will provide a supply chain with the highest financial return.

EXAMPLE 6-1

Trips Logistics, a third-party logistics firm that provides warehousing and other logistics services, is facing a decision regarding the amount of space to lease for the upcoming three-year period. The general manager has forecast that Trips Logistics will need to handle a demand of 100,000 units for each of the next three years. Historically, Trips Logistics has required 1,000 square feet of warehouse space for every 1,000 units of demand. For the purposes of this discussion, the only cost Trips Logistics faces is the cost for the warehouse.

Trips Logistics receives revenue of $1.22 for each unit of demand. The general manager must decide whether to sign a three-year lease or obtain warehousing space on the spot market each year. The three-year lease will cost $1 per square foot per year, and the spot market rate is expected to be $1.20 per square foot per year for each of the three years. Trips Logistics has a discount rate of $k = 0.1$. Should the general manager sign a lease?

Analysis

The general manager decides to compare the NPV of signing a three-year lease for 100,000 square feet of warehouse space with obtaining the space from the spot market each year. If the general manager obtains warehousing space from the spot market each year, Trips Logistics will earn $1.22 for each unit and pay $1.20 for one square foot of warehouse space required. The expected annual profit for Trips Logistics in this case is given by the following:

$$\text{Expected annual profit if warehousing} = (100{,}000 \times \$1.22)$$
$$\text{space is obtained from spot market} \quad - (100{,}000 \times \$1.20) = \$2{,}000$$

Obtaining warehouse space from the spot market provides Trips Logistics with an expected positive cash flow of $2,000 in each of the three years. The NPV may be evaluated as follows:

$$\text{NPV(No lease)} = C_o + \frac{C_1}{(1 + k)} + \frac{C_2}{(1 + k)^2} = 2{,}000 + \frac{2{,}000}{1.1} + \frac{2{,}000}{1.1^2} = \$5{,}471$$

If the general manager leases 100,000 sq. ft. of warehouse space for the next three years, Trips Logistics pays $1 per square foot of space leased each year. The expected annual profit for Trips Logistics in this case is given by the following:

$$\text{Expected annual profit with three-year lease} = (100{,}000 \times \$1.22) - (100{,}000 \times \$1.00)$$
$$= \$22{,}000$$

Signing a lease for three years provides Trips Logistics with a positive cash flow of $22,000 in each of the three years. The NPV may be evaluated as

$$\text{NPV(Lease)} = C_o + \frac{C_1}{(1 + k)} + \frac{C_2}{(1 + k)^2} = 22{,}000 + \frac{22{,}000}{1.1} + \frac{22{,}000}{1.1^2} = \$60{,}182$$

The NPV of signing the lease is $60,182 − $5,471 = $54,711 higher than obtaining warehousing space on the spot market.

Based on this simple analysis, a manager may opt to sign the lease. However, this does not tell the whole story because we have not yet included the uncertainty in spot prices and valued the greater flexibility to adjust to uncertainty that the spot market provides the manager. We introduce decision tree analysis that allows for uncertainty and discuss how the inclusion of uncertainty of future demand and costs may cause the manager to rethink the decision.

The Basics of Decision Tree Analysis

A *decision tree* is a graphic device used to evaluate decisions under uncertainty. Decision trees with DCFs can be used to evaluate supply chain design decisions given uncertainty in prices, demand, exchange rates, and inflation.

The first step in setting up a decision tree is to identify the number of time periods into the future that will be considered when making the decision. The decision maker should also identify the duration of a period—a day, a month, a quarter, or any other time period. The duration of a period should be the minimum period of time over which factors affecting supply chain decisions may change by a *significant* amount. "Significant" is hard to define, but in

most cases it is appropriate to use as a period the duration over which an aggregate plan holds. If planning is done monthly, for example, we set the duration of a period at a month. In the following discussion, T will represent the number of time periods over which the supply chain decision is to be evaluated.

The next step is to identify factors that affect the value of the decision and are likely to fluctuate over the next T periods. These factors include demand, price, exchange rate, and inflation, among others. Having identified the key factors, the next step is to identify probability distributions that define the fluctuation of each factor from one period to the next. If, for instance, demand and price are identified as the two key factors that affect the decision, the probability of moving from a given value of demand and price in one period to any other value of demand and price in the next period must be identified.

The next step is to identify a periodic discount rate k to be applied to future cash flows. It is not essential that the same discount rate apply to each period or even at every node in a period. The discount rate should take into account the inherent risk associated with the investment. In general, a higher discount rate should apply to investments with higher risk.

The decision is now evaluated using a decision tree, which contains the present and T future periods. Within each period, a node must be defined for every possible combination of factor values (say, demand and price) that can be achieved. Arrows are drawn from origin nodes in Period i to end nodes in Period $i + 1$. The probability on an arrow is referred to as the *transition probability* and is the probability of transitioning from the origin node in Period i to the end node in Period $i + 1$.

The decision tree is evaluated starting from nodes in Period T and working back to Period 0. For each node, the decision is optimized, taking into account current and future values of various factors. The analysis is based on *Bellman's principle*, which states that for any choice of strategy in a given state, the optimal strategy in the next period is the one that is selected if the entire analysis is assumed to begin in the next period. This principle allows the optimal strategy to be solved in a backward fashion starting at the last period. Expected future cash flows are discounted back and included in the decision currently under consideration. The value of the node in Period 0 gives the value of the investment, as well as the decisions made during each time period. (Tools such as Treeplan are available that help solve decision trees on spreadsheets.)

The decision tree analysis methodology is summarized as follows:

1. Identify the duration of each period (month, quarter, etc.) and the number of periods T over which the decision is to be evaluated.
2. Identify factors such as demand, price, and exchange rate whose fluctuation will be considered over the next T periods.
3. Identify representations of uncertainty for each factor; that is, determine what distribution to use to model the uncertainty.
4. Identify the periodic discount rate k for each period.
5. Represent the decision tree with defined states in each period, as well as the transition probabilities between states in successive periods.
6. Starting at period T, work back to Period 0, identifying the optimal decision and the expected cash flows at each step. Expected cash flows at each state in a given period should be discounted back when included in the previous period.

Evaluating Flexibility at Trips Logistics

We illustrate the decision tree analysis methodology by using the lease decision facing the general manager at Trips Logistics. The manager must decide whether to lease warehouse space for the coming three years and the quantity to lease. The manager anticipates uncertainty in demand and spot prices for warehouse space over the coming three years. The long-term lease is cheaper but the space could go unused if demand is lower than anticipated. The long-term lease may also

end up being more expensive if future spot market prices come down. The manager is considering three options:

1. Get all warehousing space from the spot market as needed.
2. Sign a three-year lease for a fixed amount of warehouse space and get additional requirements from the spot market.
3. Sign a flexible lease with a minimum charge that allows variable usage of warehouse space up to a limit, with additional requirements from the spot market.

We now discuss how the manager can evaluate each decision, taking uncertainty into account.

One thousand square feet of warehouse space is required for every 1,000 units of demand, and the current demand at Trips Logistics is for 100,000 units per year. The manager forecasts that from one year to the next, demand may go up by 20 percent, with a probability of 0.5, or go down by 20 percent, with a probability of 0.5. The probabilities of the two outcomes are independent and unchanged from one year to the next.

The general manager can sign a three-year lease at a price of $1 per square foot per year. Warehouse space is currently available on the spot market for $1.20 per square foot per year. From one year to the next, spot prices for warehouse space may go up by 10 percent, with probability 0.5, or go down by 10 percent, with probability 0.5. The probabilities of the two outcomes are independent and unchanged from one year to the next.

The general manager believes that prices of warehouse space and demand for the product fluctuate independently. Each unit Trips Logistics handles results in revenue of $1.22, and Trips Logistics is committed to handling all demand that arises. Trips Logistics uses a discount rate of $k = 0.1$ for each of the three years.

The general manager assumes that all costs are incurred at the beginning of each year and thus constructs a decision tree with $T = 2$. The decision tree is shown in Figure 6-2, with each node representing demand (D) in thousands of units and price (p) in dollars. The probability of each transition is $0.5 \times 0.5 = 0.25$ because price and demand fluctuate independently.

Evaluating the Spot Market Option

Using the decision tree in Figure 6-2, the manager first analyzes the option of not signing a lease and obtaining all warehouse space from the spot market. He starts with Period 2 and evaluates the profit for Trips Logistics at each node. At the node $D = 144, p = \$1.45$, Trips Logistics must satisfy a demand of 144,000 and faces a spot price of $1.45 per square foot for warehouse space in Period 2. The cost incurred by Trips Logistics in Period 2 at the node $D = 144, p = \$1.45$ is represented by $C (D = 144, p = 1.45, 2)$ and is given by

$$C(D = 144, p = 1.45, 2) = 144{,}000 \times 1.45 = \$208{,}800$$

The profit at Trips Logistics in Period 2 at the node $D = 144, p = \$1.45$ is represented by $P (D = 144, p = 1.45, 2)$ and is given by

$$
\begin{aligned}
P(D = 144, p = 1.45, 2) &= 144{,}000 \times 1.22 - C(D = 144, p = 1.45, 2) \\
&= 175{,}680 - 208{,}800 = -\$33{,}120
\end{aligned}
$$

The profit for Trips Logistics at each of the other nodes in Period 2 is evaluated similarly, as shown in Table 6-5.

The manager next evaluates the expected profit at each node in Period 1 to be the profit during Period 1 plus the present value (in Period 1) of the expected profit in Period 2. The expected profit $EP (D =, p =, 1)$ at a node is the expected profit over all four nodes in Period 2 that may result from this node. $PVEP (D =, p =, 1)$ represents the present value of this expected profit; $P (D =, p =, 1)$, the total expected profit, is the sum of the profit in Period 1 and the present value of the expected profit in Period 2. From the node $D = 120, p = \$1.32$ in Period 1,

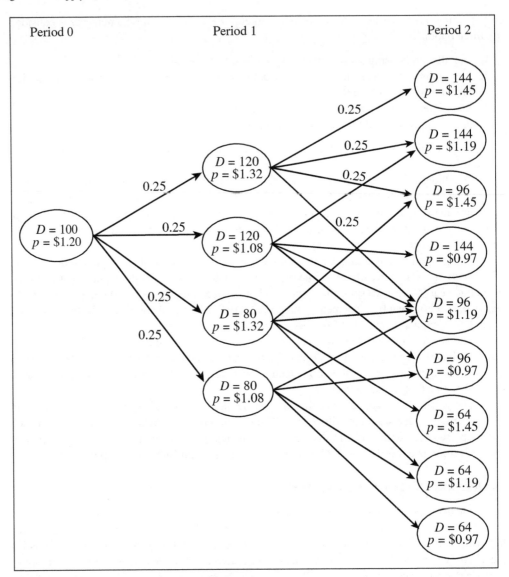

Figure 6-2 Decision Tree for Trips Logistics, Considering Demand and Price Fluctuation

there are four possible states in Period 2. The manager thus evaluates the expected profit in Period 2 over all four states possible from the node $D = 120$, $p = \$1.32$ in Period 1 to be $EP(D = 120, p = \$1.32, 1)$, where

$$
\begin{aligned}
EP(D = 120, p = 1.32, 1) &= 0.25 \times [P(D = 144, p = 1.45, 2) + P(D = 144, p = 1.19, 2) \\
&\quad + P(D = 96, p = 1.45, 2) + P(D = 96, p = 1.19, 2)] = 0.25 \\
&\quad \times [-33{,}120 + 4{,}320 - 22{,}080 + 2{,}880] = -\$12{,}000
\end{aligned}
$$

The present value of this expected value in Period 1 is given by

$$
\begin{aligned}
PVEP(D = 120, p = 1.32, 1) &= EP(D = 120, p = 1.32, 1)/(1 + k) \\
&= -12{,}000/1.1 = -\$10{,}909
\end{aligned}
$$

The manager obtains the total expected profit $P(D = 120, p = 1.32, 1)$ at node $D = 120$, $p = 1.32$ in Period 1 to be the sum of the profit in Period 1 at this node and the present value of future expected profits.

TABLE 6-5 Period 2 Calculations for Spot Market Option

	Revenue	Cost $C(D=,p=,2)$	Profit $P(D=,p=,2)$
$D = 144$, p = 1.45	144,000 × 1.22	144,000 × 1.45	−$33,120
$D = 144$, p = 1.19	144,000 × 1.22	144,000 × 1.19	$4,320
$D = 144$, p = 0.97	144,000 × 1.22	144,000 × 0.97	$36,000
$D = 96$, p = 1.45	96,000 × 1.22	96,000 × 1.45	−$22,080
$D = 96$, p = 1.19	96,000 × 1.22	96,000 × 1.19	$2,880
$D = 96$, p = 0.97	96,000 × 1.22	96,000 × 0.97	$24,000
$D = 64$, p = 1.45	64,000 × 1.22	64,000 × 1.45	−$14,720
$D = 64$, p = 1.19	64,000 × 1.22	64,000 × 1.19	$1,920
$D = 64$, p = 0.97	64,000 × 1.22	64,000 × 0.97	$16,000

$$P(D = 120, p = 1.32, 1) = (120{,}000 \times 1.22) - (120{,}000 \times 1.32) + PVEP(D = 120,$$
$$p = 1.32, 1) = -\$12{,}000 - \$10{,}909 = -\$22{,}909$$

The total expected profit for all other nodes in Period 1 is evaluated as shown in Table 6-6.

For Period 0, the total profit $P(D = 100, p = 1.20, 0)$ is the sum of the profit at Period 0 and the present value of the expected profit over the four nodes in Period 1.

$$EP(D = 100, p = 1.20, 0) = 0.25 \times \left[P(D = 120, p = 1.32, 1) + P(D = 120, p = 1.08, 1) \right.$$
$$+ P(D = 80, p = 1.32, 1) + P(D = 80, p = 1.08, 1) \left. \right] = 0.25$$
$$\times \left[-22{,}909 + 32{,}073 - 15{,}273 + 21{,}382 \right] = \$3{,}818$$

$$PVEP(D = 100, p = 1.20, 0) = EP(D = 100, p = 1.20, 0)/(l + k)$$
$$= 3{,}818/1.1 = \$3{,}471$$

$$P(D = 100, p = 1.20, 0) = (100{,}000 \times 1.22) - (100{,}000 \times 1.20) + PVEP(D = 100,$$
$$p = 1.20, 0) = \$2{,}000 + \$3{,}471 = \$5{,}471$$

Thus, the expected NPV of not signing the lease and obtaining all warehousing space from the spot market is

$$\text{NPV (Spot Market)} = \$5{,}471$$

Evaluating the Fixed Lease Option

The manager next evaluates the alternative whereby the lease for 100,000 sq. ft. of warehouse space is signed. The evaluation procedure is very similar to that for the previous case, but the

TABLE 6-6 Period 1 Calculations for Spot Market Option

Node	$EP(D=,p=,1)$	$p(D=,p=,1) = D \times 1.22 - D \times p$ $+ EP(D=,p=,1)/(1 + k)$
$D = 120, p = 1.32$	−$12,000	−$22,909
$D = 120, p = 1.08$	$16,800	$32,073
$D = 80, p = 1.32$	−$8,000	−$15,273
$D = 80, p = 1.08$	$11,200	$21,382

TABLE 6-7 Period 2 Profit Calculations at Trips Logistics for Fixed Lease Option

Node	Leased Space	Warehouse Space at Spot Price (S)	Profit $P(D = p =, 2) = D \times 1.22 - (100{,}000 \times 1 + S \times p)$
$D = 144, p = 1.45$	100,000 sq. ft.	44,000 sq. ft.	$11,880
$D = 144, p = 1.19$	100,000 sq. ft.	44,000 sq. ft.	$23,320
$D = 144, p = 0.97$	100,000 sq. ft.	44,000 sq. ft.	$33,000
$D = 96, p = 1.45$	100,000 sq. ft.	0 sq. ft.	$17,120
$D = 96, p = 1.19$	100,000 sq. ft.	0 sq. ft.	$17,120
$D = 96, p = 0.97$	100,000 sq. ft.	0 sq. ft.	$17,120
$D = 64, p = 1.45$	100,000 sq. ft.	0 sq. ft.	−$21,920
$D = 64, p = 1.19$	100,000 sq. ft.	0 sq. ft.	−$21,920
$D = 64, p = 0.97$	100,000 sq. ft.	0 sq. ft.	−$21,920

outcome changes in terms of profit. For example, at the node $D = 144, p = 1.45$, the manager will require 44,000 square feet of warehouse space from the spot market at $1.45 per square foot because only 100,000 square feet have been leased at $1 per square foot. If demand happens to be less than 100,000 units, Trips Logistics still has to pay for the entire 100,000 square feet of leased space. For Period 2, the manager obtains the profit at each of the nine nodes, as shown in Table 6-7.

The manager next evaluates the total expected profit for each node in Period 1. Again, the expected profit $EP(D =, p =, 1)$ at a node is the expected profit of all four nodes in Period 2 that may result from this node (see Figure 6-2), and $P(D =, p =, 1)$ is the total expected profit from both Periods 1 and 2. The manager thus obtains the results in Table 6-8.

For Period 0, the expected profit $EP (D = 100, p = 1.20, 0)$ over the four nodes in Period 1 is given by

$$EP(D = 100, p = 1.20, 0) = 0.25 \times [P(D = 120, p = 1.32, 1) + P(D = 120, p = 1.08, 1)$$
$$+ P(D = 80, p = 1.32, 1) + P(D = 80, p = 1.08, 1)]$$
$$= 0.25 \times [35{,}782 + 45{,}382 - 4{,}582 - 4{,}582] = \$18{,}000$$

The present value of the expected profit in Period 0 is given by

$$PVEP(D = 100, p = 1.20, 0) = EP(D = 100, p = 1.20, 0)/(1 + k)$$
$$= 18{,}000/1.1 = \$16{,}364$$

The total expected profit is obtained as the sum of the profit in Period 0 and the present value of the expected profit over all four nodes in Period 1. It is

$$P(D = 100, p = 1.20, 0) = (100{,}000 \times 1.22) - (100{,}000 \times 1) + PVEP(D = 100,$$
$$p = 1.20, 0) = \$22{,}000 + \$16{,}364 = \$38{,}364$$

The NPV of signing a three-year lease for 100,000 sq. ft. of warehouse space is thus

$$NPV(\text{Lease}) = \$38{,}364$$

Observe that the NPV of the lease option under uncertainty is considerably less compared to when uncertainty is ignored ($60,182 from Example 6-1). This is because the lease is a fixed decision, and Trips Logistics is unable to react to market conditions by leasing less space if demand is lower. Rigid contracts are less attractive in the presence of uncertainty.

TABLE 6-8 Period 1 Profit Calculations at Trips Logistics for Fixed Lease Option

Node	$EP(D=, p=, 1)$	Warehouse Space at Spot Price (S)	$P(D=, p=, 1)$ $= D \times 1.22 - (100,000 \times 1 + S \times p) + EP(D =, p =, 1)/(1 + k)$
$D = 120, p = 1.32$	$0.25 \times [P(D = 144, p = 1.45, 2)$ $+ P(D = 144, p = 1.19, 2)$ $+ P(D = 96, p = 1.45, 2)$ $+ P(D = 96, p = 1.19, 2)]$ $= 0.25 \times (11,880 + 23,320$ $+ 17,120 + 17,120) = \$17,360$	20,000	\$35,782
$D = 120, p = 1.08$	$0.25 \times [23,320 + 33,000$ $+ 17,120 + 17,120] = \$22,640$	20,000	\$45,382
$D = 80, p = 1.32$	$0.25 \times [17,120 + 17,120$ $- 21,920 - 21,920] = -\$2,400$	0	$-\$4,582$
$D = 80, p = 1.08$	$0.25 \times [17,120 + 17,120$ $- 21,920 - 21,920] = -\$2,400$	0	$-\$4,582$

Evaluating the Flexible Lease Option

The general manager at Trips Logistics has been offered a contract in which, for an upfront payment of \$10,000, Trips Logistics will have the flexibility of using between 60,000 square feet and 100,000 square feet of warehouse space at \$1 per square foot per year. Trips Logistics must pay \$60,000 per year for the first 60,000 square feet and can then use up to another 40,000 square feet on demand at \$1 per square foot. The general manager decides to use decision trees to evaluate whether this flexible contract is preferable to a fixed contract for 100,000 square feet.

The underlying decision tree for evaluating the flexible contract is exactly as in Figure 6-2. The profit at each node, however, changes because of the flexibility in space used as shown in Table 6-9. If demand is larger than 100,000 units, Trips Logistics uses all 100,000 square feet of warehouse space at \$1 and gets the rest at the spot price. If demand is between 60,000 and 100,000 units, Trips Logistics uses and pays \$1 only for the exact amount of warehouse space

TABLE 6-9 Period 2 Profit Calculations at Trips Logistics with Flexible Lease Contract

Node	Warehouse Space at \$1 ($W$)	Warehouse Space at Spot Price (S)	Profit $P(D=, p=, 2) = D \times$ $1.22 - (W \times 1 + S \times p)$
$D = 144, p = 1.45$	100,000 sq. ft.	44,000 sq. ft.	\$11,880
$D = 144, p = 1.19$	100,000 sq. ft.	44,000 sq. ft.	\$23,320
$D = 144, p = 0.97$	100,000 sq. ft.	44,000 sq. ft.	\$33,000
$D = 96, p = 1.45$	96,000 sq. ft.	0 sq. ft.	\$21,120
$D = 96, p = 1.19$	96,000 sq. ft.	0 sq. ft.	\$21,120
$D = 96, p = 0.97$	96,000 sq. ft.	0 sq. ft.	\$21,120
$D = 64, p = 1.45$	64,000 sq. ft.	0 sq. ft.	\$14,080
$D = 64, p = 1.19$	64,000 sq. ft.	0 sq. ft.	\$14,080
$D = 64, p = 0.97$	64,000 sq. ft.	0 sq. ft.	\$14,080

TABLE 6-10 Period 1 Profit Calculations at Trips Logistics with Flexible Lease Contract

Node	$EP(D=, p=, 1)$	Warehouse Space at $1 ($W$)	Warehouse Space at Spot Price (S)	$P(D=, p=, 1) = D \times$ 1.22 $- (W \times 1 + S \times p)$ $+ EP(D=, p=, 1)/(1 + k)$
$D = 120, p = 1.32$	$0.25 \times [11,880 + 23,320$ $+ 21,120 + 21,120] = \$19,360$	100,000	20,000	\$37,600
$D = 120, p = 1.08$	$0.25 \times [23,320 + 33,000$ $+ 21,120 + 21,120] = \$24,640$	100,000	20,000	\$47,200
$D = 80, p = 1.32$	$0.25 \times [21,120 + 21,120$ $+ 14,080 + 14,080] = \$17,600$	80,000	0	\$33,600
$D = 80, p = 1.08$	$0.25 \times [21,120 + 21,120$ $+ 14,080 + 14,080] = \$17,600$	80,000	0	\$33,600

required. The profit at all nodes where demand is 100,000 or higher remains the same as in Table 6-7. The profit in Period 2 at all nodes where demand is less than 100,000 units increases as shown in Table 6-9.

The general manager evaluates the expected profit EP $(D=, p=, 1)$ from Period 2 and the total expected profit for each node in Period 1, as discussed earlier. The results are shown in Table 6-10.

The total expected profit in Period 0 is the sum of the profit in Period 0 and the present value of the expected profit in Period 1. The manager thus obtains

$$EP(D = 100, p = 1.20, 0) = 0.25 \times [P(D = 120, p = 1.32, 1) + P(D = 120, p = 1.08, 1)$$
$$+ P(D = 80, p = 1.32, 1) + P(D = 80, p = 1.08, 1)] = 0.25$$
$$\times [37,600 + 47,200 + 33,600 + 33,600] = \$38,000$$

$$PVEP(D = 100, p = 1.20, 1) = EP(D = 100, p = 1.20, 0)/(1 + k)$$
$$= 38,000/1.1 = \$34,545$$

$$P(D = 100, p = 1.20, 0) = (100,000 \times 1.22) - (100,000 \times 1) + PVEP(D = 100,$$
$$p = 1.20, 0) = \$22,000 + \$34,545 = \$56,545$$

With an upfront payment of $10,000, the net expected profit under the flexible lease is $46,545. Accounting for uncertainty, the manager at Trips Logistics values the three options as shown in Table 6-11.

The flexible contract is thus beneficial for Trips Logistics because it is $8,181 more valuable than the rigid contract for three years.

TABLE 6-11 Comparison of Different Lease Options for Trips Logistics

Option	Value
All warehouse space from the spot market	\$5,471
Lease 100,000 sq. ft. for three years	\$38,364
Flexible lease to use between 60,000 and 100,000 sq. ft.	\$46,545

SUMMARY OF LEARNING OBJECTIVE 3

Uncertainty in demand and economic factors should be included in the financial evaluation of supply chain design decisions. Decision trees can be used to evaluate supply chain decisions under uncertainty. Uncertainty along different dimensions over the evaluation period is represented as a tree with each node corresponding to a possible scenario. Starting at the last period of the evaluation interval, the decision tree analysis works back to Period 0, identifying the optimal decision and the expected cash flows at each step. The inclusion of uncertainty typically decreases the value of rigidity and increases the value of flexibility.

TO ONSHORE OR TO OFFSHORE: THE VALUE OF FLEXIBILITY IN A SUPPLY CHAIN UNDER UNCERTAINTY

6.4 Use decision tree methodologies to value flexibility and make onshoring / offshoring decisions under uncertainty.

In this section, we discuss a supply chain design decision at D-Solar, a German manufacturer of solar panels, to illustrate the power of the decision tree analysis methodology for designing global supply chain networks while accounting for uncertainty. D-Solar faces a plant location decision in a global network with fluctuating exchange rates and demand uncertainty.

D-Solar sells its products primarily in Europe. Demand in the Europe market is currently 100,000 panels per year, and each panel sells for €70. Although panel demand is expected to grow, there are some downside risks if the economy slides. From one year to the next, demand may increase by 20 percent, with probability 0.8, or decrease by 20 percent, with probability 0.2.

D-Solar has to decide whether to build a plant in Europe or China. In either case, D-Solar plans to build a plant with a rated capacity of 120,000 panels. The fixed and variable costs of the two plants are shown in Table 6-12. Observe that the fixed costs are given per year rather than as a one-time investment. The European plant is more expensive but has greater volume flexibility. The plant is able to increase or decrease production anywhere in the range of 60,000 to 150,000 panels while maintaining its variable cost. In contrast, the Chinese plant is cheaper (at the current exchange rate of 9 yuan/euro) but has limited volume flexibility and can produce only between 100,000 and 130,000 panels. If the Chinese plant is built, D-Solar will incur variable cost for 100,000 panels even if demand drops below that level and will lose sales if demand increases above 130,000 panels. Exchange rates are volatile; each year, the yuan is expected to rise 10 percent, with a probability of 0.7, or drop 10 percent, with a probability of 0.3. We assume that the sourcing decision will be in place over the next three years and the discount rate used by D-Solar is $k = 0.1$. All costs and revenues are assumed to accrue at the beginning of the year, allowing us to consider the first year as period 0 and the following two years as periods 1 and 2.

Evaluating the Options Using Expected Demand and Exchange Rate

A simplistic approach often taken is to consider the expected movement of demand and exchange rates in future periods when evaluating discounted cash flows. The weakness of such an approach is that it averages the trends while ignoring the uncertainty. We start by considering such a simplistic approach for the onshoring and offshoring options. On average, demand is expected to

TABLE 6-12 Fixed and Variable Production Costs for D-Solar

European Plant		Chinese Plant	
Fixed Cost (euro)	**Variable Cost (euro)**	**Fixed Cost (yuan)**	**Variable Cost (yuan)**
1 million/year	40/panel	8 million/year	340/panel

TABLE 6-13 Expected Future Demand and Exchange Rate

Period 1		Period 2	
Demand	Exchange Rate	Demand	Exchange Rate
112,000	8.64 yuan/ euro	125,440	8.2944 yuan /euro

increase by 12 percent $[(20 \times 0.8) + (-20 \times 0.2) = 12]$, whereas the yuan is expected to strengthen by 4 percent $[(10 \times 0.7) + (-10 \times 0.3) = 4]$ each year. The expected demand and exchange rates in the two future periods are shown in Table 6-13.

We now evaluate the discounted cash flows for both options assuming the average expected change in demand and exchange rates over the next two periods.

For the onshoring option, we have the following:

Period 0 profits $= (100,000 \times 70) - 1,000,000 - (100,000 \times 40) = €2,000,000$

Period 1 profits $= (112,000 \times 70) - 1,000,000 - (112,000 \times 40) = €2,360,000$

Period 2 profits $= (125,440 \times 70) - 1,000,000 - (125,440 \times 40) = €2,763,200$

Thus, the DCF for the onshoring option is obtained as follows:

Expected profit from onshoring $= 2,000,000 + 2,360,000/1.1$
$$+ 2,763,200/1.21 = €6,429,091$$

For the offshoring option, we have the following:

Period 0 profits $= (100,000 \times 70) - (8,000,000/9) - (100,000 \times 340/9) = €2,333,333$

Period 1 profits $= (112,000 \times 70) - (8,000,000/8.64) - (112,000 \times 340/8.64) = €2,506,667$

Period 2 profits $= (125,440 \times 70) - (8,000,000/8.2944) - (125,440 \times 340/8.2944) = €2,674,319$

Thus, the DCF for the offshoring option is obtained as follows:

Expected profit from onshoring $= 2,333,333 + 2,506,667/1.1$
$$+ 2,674,319/1.21 = €6,822,302$$

Based on performing a simple DCF analysis and assuming the expected trend of demand and exchange rates over the next two periods, it seems that offshoring should be preferred to onshoring because it is expected to provide additional profits of almost €393,000.

The problem with the preceding analysis is that it has ignored uncertainty. For example, even though the demand is expected to grow, there is some probability that it will decrease. If demand drops below 100,000 panels, the offshore option could end up costing more because of the lack of flexibility. Similarly, if demand increases more than expected (for example, if it grows by 20 percent in each of the two years), the offshore facility will not be able to keep up with the increase. An accurate analysis must reflect these uncertainties and should ideally be performed using a decision tree.

Evaluating the Options Using Decision Trees

For this analysis we construct a decision tree, as shown in Figure 6-3. Each node in a given period leads to four possible nodes in the next period because demand and the exchange rate may go up or down. The detailed links and transition probabilities are shown in Figure 6-3. Demand is in thousands and is represented by D. The exchange rate is represented by E, where E is the number of yuan to a euro. For example, starting with the node $D = 100, E = 9.00$ in Period 0, one can transition to any of four nodes in Period 1. The transition to the node $D = 120, E = 9.90$ in Period 1 occurs if demand increases (probability of 0.8) and the yuan weakens (probability of 0.3).

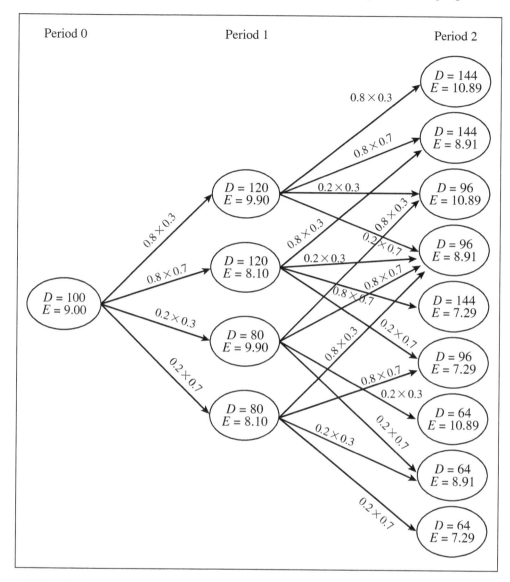

FIGURE 6-3 Decision Tree for D-Solar

Thus, the transition from node $D = 100$, $E = 9.00$ in Period 0 to node $D = 120$, $E = 9.90$ in Period 1 occurs with probability $0.8 \times 0.3 = 0.24$. All other transition probabilities in Figure 6-3 are calculated in a similar manner. The main advantage of using a decision tree is that it allows for the true evaluation of profits in each scenario that D-Solar may find itself.

Evaluating the Onshore Option

Recall that the onshore option is flexible and can change production levels (and thus variable costs) to match demand levels between 60,000 and 150,000. In the following analysis, we calculate the expected profits at each node in the decision tree (represented by the corresponding values of D and E) starting in Period 2 and working back to the present (Period 0). With the onshore option, exchange rates do not affect profits in euro because both revenue and costs are in euro.

PERIOD 2 EVALUATION We provide a detailed analysis for the node $D = 144$ (solar panel demand of 144,000), $E = 10.89$ (exchange rate of 10.89 yuan per euro). Given its flexibility, the

onshore facility is able to produce the entire demand of 144,000 panels at a variable cost of €40 and sell each panel for revenue of €70. Revenues and costs are evaluated as follows:

$$\text{Revenue from the manufacture and sale of 144,000 panels}$$
$$= 144{,}000 \times 70 = \text{€}10{,}080{,}000$$

$$\text{Fixed} + \text{variable cost of onshore plant} = 1{,}000{,}000 + (144{,}000 \times 40)$$
$$= \text{€}6{,}760{,}000$$

In Period 2, the total profit for D-Solar at the node $D = 144, E = 10.89$ for the onshore option is thus given by

$$P(D = 144, E = 10.89, 2) = 10{,}080{,}000 - 6{,}760{,}000 = \text{€}3{,}320{,}000$$

Using the same approach, we can evaluate the profit in each of the nine states (represented by the corresponding value of D and E) in Period 2, as shown in Table 6-14.

PERIOD 1 EVALUATION Period 1 contains four outcome nodes to be analyzed. A detailed analysis for one of the nodes, $D = 120, E = 9.90$, is presented here. In addition to the revenue and cost at this node, we also need to consider the present value of the expected profit in Period 2 from the four nodes that may result. The transition probability into each of the four nodes is as shown in Figure 6-3. The expected profit in Period 2 for the four potential outcomes resulting from the node $D = 120, E = 9.90$ is thus given by

$$EP(D = 120, E = 9.90, 1) = 0.24 \times P(D = 144, E = 10.89, 2) + 0.56 \times P(D = 144, E = 8.91, 2)$$
$$+ 0.06 \times P(D = 96, E = 10.89, 2) + 0.14 \times P(D = 96, E = 8.91, 2)$$
$$= (0.24 \times 3{,}320{,}000) + (0.56 \times 3{,}320{,}000)$$
$$+ (0.06 \times 1{,}880{,}000) + (0.14 \times 1{,}880{,}000) = \text{€}3{,}032{,}000$$

The present value of the expected profit in Period 2 discounted to Period 1 is given by

$$PVEP(D = 120, E = 9.90, 1) = EP(D = 120, E = 9.90, 1)/(1 + K)$$
$$= 3{,}032{,}000/1.1 = \text{€}2{,}756{,}364$$

Next we evaluate the profits for the onshore plant at the node $D = 120, E = 9.90$ from its operations in Period 1, in which the onshore plant produces 120,000 panels at a variable cost of €40 and obtains revenue of €70 per panel. Revenues and costs are evaluated as follows:

TABLE 6-14 Period 2 Profits for Onshore Option

D	E	Sales	Production Cost Quantity	Revenue (euro)	Cost (euro)	Profit (euro)
144	10.89	144,000	144,000	10,080,000	6,760,000	3,320,000
144	8.91	144,000	144,000	10,080,000	6,760,000	3,320,000
96	10.89	96,000	96,000	6,720,000	4,840,000	1,880,000
96	8.91	96,000	96,000	6,720,000	4,840,000	1,880,000
144	7.29	144,000	144,000	10,080,000	6,760,000	3,320,000
96	7.29	96,000	96,000	6,720,000	4,840,000	1,880,000
64	10.89	64,000	64,000	4,480,000	3,560,000	920,000
64	8.91	64,000	64,000	4,480,000	3,560,000	920,000
64	7.29	64,000	64,000	4,480,000	3,560,000	920,000

Revenue from the manufacture and sale of 120,000 panels

$$= 120{,}000 \times 70 = €8{,}400{,}000$$

Fixed + variable cost of onshore plant $= 1{,}000{,}000 + (120{,}000 \times 40)$

$$= €5{,}800{,}000$$

The expected profit for D-Solar at the node $D = 120$, $E = 9.90$ is obtained by adding the operational profits at this node in Period 1 and the discounted expected profits from the four nodes that may result in Period 2. The expected profit at this node in Period 1 is given by

$$P(D = 120, E = 9.90, 1) = 8{,}400{,}000 - 5{,}800{,}000 + PVEP(D = 120, E = 9.90, 1)$$
$$= 2{,}600{,}000 + 2{,}756{,}364 = €5{,}356{,}364$$

The expected profits for all nodes in Period 1 are calculated similarly and shown in Table 6-15.

PERIOD 0 EVALUATION In Period 0, the demand and exchange rate are given by $D = 100$, $E = 9$. In addition to the revenue and cost at this node, we also need to consider the discounted expected profit from the four nodes in Period 1. The expected profit is given by

$$EP(D = 100, E = 9.00, 0) = 0.24 \times P(D = 120, E = 9.90, 1) + 0.56 \times P(D = 120, E = 8.10, 1)$$
$$+ 0.06 \times P(D = 80, E = 9.90, 1) + 0.14 \times P(D = 80, E = 8.10, 1)$$
$$= (0.24 \times 5{,}356{,}364) + (0.56 \times 5{,}356{,}364)$$
$$+ (0.06 \times 2{,}934{,}545) + (0.14 \times 2{,}934{,}545) = €4{,}872{,}000$$

The present value of the expected profit in Period 1 discounted to Period 0 is given by

$$PVEP(D = 100, E = 9.00, 0) = EP(D = 100, E = 9.00, 0)/(1 + k)$$
$$= 4{,}872{,}000/1.1 = €4{,}429{,}091$$

Next, we evaluate the profits from the onshore plant's operations in Period 0 from the manufacture and sale of 100,000 panels.

Revenue from the manufacture and sale of 100,000 panels

$$= 100{,}000 \times 70 = €7{,}000{,}000$$

Fixed + variable cost of onshore plant $= 1{,}000{,}000 + (100{,}000 \times 40)$

$$= €5{,}000{,}000$$

The expected profit for D-Solar at the node $D = 100$, $E = 9.00$ in Period 0 is given by

$$P(D = 100, E = 9.00, 0) = 7{,}000{,}000 - 5{,}000{,}000 + PVEP(D = 100, E = 9.00, 0)$$
$$= 2{,}000{,}000 + 4{,}429{,}091 = €6{,}429{,}091$$

Thus, building the onshore plant has an expected payoff of €6,429,091 over the evaluation period. This number accounts for uncertainties in demand and exchange rates and the ability of the flexible onshore facility to react to these fluctuations.

TABLE 6-15 Period 1 Profits for Onshore Option

D	E	Sales	Production Cost Quantity	Revenue (euro)	Cost (euro)	Expected Profit (euro)
120	9.90	120,000	120,000	8,400,000	5,800,000	5,356,364
120	8.10	120,000	120,000	8,400,000	5,800,000	5,356,364
80	9.90	80,000	80,000	5,600,000	4,200,000	2,934,545
80	8.10	80,000	80,000	5,600,000	4,200,000	2,934,545

Evaluating the Offshore Option

As with the onshore option, we start by evaluating profits at each node in Period 2 and then back our evaluation up to Periods 1 and 0. Recall that the offshore option has limited flexibility and can change production levels (and thus variable costs) only between 100,000 and 130,000 panels. Thus, if demand falls below 100,000 panels, D-Solar still incurs the variable production cost of 100,000 panels. If demand increases above 130,000 panels, the offshore facility can meet demand only up to 130,000 panels. At each node, given the demand, we calculate the expected profits accounting for the exchange rate that influences offshore costs evaluated in euro.

PERIOD 2 EVALUATION The detailed analysis for the node $D = 144$ (solar panel demand of 144,000), $E = 10.89$ (exchange rate of 10.89 yuan per euro) is as follows. Even though demand is for 144,000 panels, given its lack of volume flexibility, the offshore facility is able to produce only 130,000 panels at a variable cost of 340 yuan each and sell each panel for a revenue of €70. Revenues and costs are evaluated as follows:

$$\text{Revenue from the manufacture and sale of 130,000 panels}$$
$$= 130,000 \times 70 = €9,100,000$$

$$\text{Fixed + variable cost of offshore plant} = 8,000,000 + (130,000 \times 340)$$
$$= 52,200,000 \text{ yuan}$$

The total profit for D-Solar at the node $D = 144$, $E = 10.89$ for the offshore option (evaluated in euro), is thus given by

$$P(D = 144, E = 10.89, 2) = 9,100,000 - (52,200,00/10.89) = €4,306,612$$

Using the same approach, we can evaluate the profit in each of the nine states (represented by the corresponding values of D and E) in Period 2 as shown in Table 6-16. Observe that the lack of flexibility at the offshore facility hurts D-Solar profits whenever demand is above 130,000 (lost margin) or below 100,000 (higher costs). For example, when the demand drops to 64,000 panels, the offshore facility continues to incur variable production costs for 100,000 panels. Profits are also hurt when the yuan is stronger than expected.

PERIOD 1 EVALUATION In Period 1, there are four outcome nodes to be analyzed. As with the onshore option, a detailed analysis for the node $D = 120$, $E = 9.90$ is presented here. In addition

TABLE 6-16 Period 2 Profits for Offshore Option

D	E	Sales	Production Cost Quantity	Revenue (euro)	Cost (yuan)	Profit (euro)
144	10.89	130,000	130,000	9,100,000	52,200,000	4,306,612
144	8.91	130,000	130,000	9,100,000	52,200,000	3,241,414
96	10.89	96,000	100,000	6,720,000	42,000,000	2,863,251
96	8.91	96,000	100,000	6,720,000	42,000,000	2,006,195
144	7.29	130,000	130,000	9,100,000	52,200,000	1,939,506
96	7.29	96,000	100,000	6,720,000	42,000,000	958,683
64	10.89	64,000	100,000	4,480,000	42,000,000	623,251
64	8.91	64,000	100,000	4,480,000	42,000,000	−233,805
64	7.29	64,000	100,000	4,480,000	42,000,000	−1,281,317

to the revenue and cost from operations at this node, we also need to consider the present value of the expected profit in Period 2 from the four nodes that may result. The transition probability into each of the four nodes is as shown in Figure 6-3. The expected profit in Period 2 from the node $D = 120$, $E = 9.90$ is thus given by

$$EP(D = 120, E = 9.90, 1) = 0.24 \times P(D = 144, E = 10.89, 2) + 0.56 \times P(D = 144, E = 8.91, 2)$$
$$+ 0.06 \times P(D = 96, E = 10.89, 2) + 0.14 \times P(D = 96, E = 8.91, 2)$$
$$= (0.24 \times 4{,}306{,}612) + (0.56 \times 3{,}241{,}414)$$
$$+ (0.06 \times 2{,}863{,}251) + (0.14 \times 2{,}006{,}195) = €3{,}301{,}441$$

The present value of the expected profit in Period 2 discounted to Period 1 is given by

$$PVEP(D = 120, E = 9.90, 1) = EP(D = 120, E = 9.90, 1)/(1 + k)$$
$$= 3{,}301{,}441/1.1 = €3{,}001{,}310$$

Next, we evaluate the profits at the offshore plant at the node $D = 120$, $E = 9.90$ from its operations in Period 1. The offshore plant produces 120,000 panels at a variable cost of 340 yuan and obtains revenue of €70 per panel. Revenues and costs are evaluated as follows:

$$\text{Revenue from manufacture and sale of 120,000 panels} = 120{,}000 \times 70 = €8{,}400{,}000$$

$$\text{Fixed} + \text{variable cost of onshore plant} = 8{,}000{,}000 + (120{,}000 \times 340)$$
$$= 48{,}800{,}000 \text{ yuan}$$

The expected profit for D-Solar at the node $D = 120$, $E = 9.90$ in Period 1 is given by

$$P(D = 120, E = 9.90, 1) = 8{,}400{,}000 - (48{,}800{,}000/9.90) + PVEP(D = 120, E = 9.90, 1)$$
$$= 3{,}470{,}707 + 3{,}001{,}310 = 6{,}472{,}017$$

For the offshore option, the expected profits for all nodes in Period 1 are shown in Table 6-17.

Observe that for the node $D = 80$, $E = 8.10$, D-Solar has a lower expected profit from the offshore option (Table 6-17) relative to the onshore option (see Table 6-15) because the offshore plant incurs high variable cost, given its lack of flexibility (cost is incurred for 100,000 units even though only 80,000 are sold), and all offshore costs become expensive, given the strong yuan.

PERIOD 0 EVALUATION In Period 0, the demand and exchange rate are given by $D = 100$, $E = 9$. In addition to the revenue and cost at this node, we also need to consider the present value of expected profit from the four nodes in Period 1. The expected profit from Period 1 is given by

$$EP(D = 100, E = 9.00, 0) = 0.24 \times P(D = 120, E = 9.90, 1) + 0.56 \times P(D = 120, E = 8.10, 1)$$
$$+ 0.06 \times P(D = 80, E = 9.90, 1) + 0.14 \times P(D = 80, E = 8.10, 1)$$
$$= (0.24 \times 6{,}472{,}017) + (0.56 \times 4{,}301{,}354)$$
$$+ (0.06 \times 3{,}007{,}859) + (0.14 \times 1{,}164{,}757) = €4{,}305{,}580$$

TABLE 6-17 Period 1 Profits for Offshore Option

D	E	Sales	Production Cost Quantity	Revenue (euro)	Cost (yuan)	Expected Profit (euro)
120	9.90	120,000	120,000	8,400,000	48,800,000	6,472,017
120	8.10	120,000	120,000	8,400,000	48,800,000	4,301,354
80	9.90	80,000	100,000	5,600,000	42,000,000	3,007,859
80	8.10	80,000	100,000	5,600,000	42,000,000	1,164,757

The present value of the expected profit in Period 1 discounted to Period 0 is given by

$$PVEP(D = 100, E = 9.00, 0) = EP(D = 100, E = 9.00, 0)/(1 + k)$$
$$= 4,305,580/1.1 = €3,914,164$$

Next we evaluate the profits from the offshore plant's operations in Period 0 from the manufacture and sale of 100,000 panels.

$$\text{Revenue from manufacture and sale of 100,000 panels} = 100,000 \times 70 = €7,000,000$$

$$\text{Fixed} + \text{variable cost of offshore plant} = 8,000,000 + (100,000 \times 340)$$
$$= 42,000,000 \text{ yuan}$$

The expected profit for D-Solar at the node $D = 100$, $E = 9.00$ in Period 0 is given by

$$P(D = 100, E = 9.00, 0) = 7,000,000 - (42,000,00/9.00) + PVEP(D = 100, E = 9.00, 0)$$
$$= 2,333,333 + 3,914,164 = €6,247,497$$

Thus, building the offshore plant has an expected payoff of €6,247,497 over the evaluation period.

Observe that the use of a decision tree that accounts for both demand and exchange rate fluctuation shows that the onshore option, with its flexibility, is in fact more valuable (worth €6,429,091) than the offshore facility (worth €6,247,497), which is less flexible. This is in direct contrast to the decision that would have resulted if we had simply used the expected demand and exchange rate for each year. When using the expected demand and exchange rate, the onshore option provided expected profits of €6,429,091, whereas the offshore option provided expected profits of €6,822,302. The offshore option is overvalued in this case because the potential fluctuations in demand and exchange rates are wider than the expected change. Using the expected change thus does not fully account for the lack of flexibility in the offshore facility and the big increase in costs that may result if the yuan strengthens more than the expected value.

De Treville and Trigeorgis (2010) discuss the importance of evaluating all global supply chain design decisions using the decision tree or real options methodology. They give the example of Flexcell, a Swiss company that offered lightweight solar panels. In 2006, the company was looking to expand its operations by building a new plant. The three locations under discussion were China, eastern Germany, and near the company headquarters in Switzerland. Even though the Chinese and eastern German plants were cheaper than the Swiss plant, Flexcell management justified building the high-cost Swiss plant because of its higher flexibility and ability to react to changing market conditions. If only the expected values of future scenarios had been used, the more expensive Swiss plant could not be justified. This decision paid off for the company because the Swiss plant was flexible enough to handle the considerable variability in demand that resulted during the downturn in 2008.

When underlying decision trees are complex and explicit solutions for the underlying decision tree are difficult to obtain, firms should use simulation for evaluating decisions (see Chapter 13). In a complex decision tree, thousands or even millions of possible paths may arise from the first period to the last. Transition probabilities are used to generate probability-weighted random paths within the decision tree. For each path, the stage-by-stage decision and the present value of the payoff are evaluated. The paths are generated in such a way that the probability of a path being generated during the simulation is the same as the probability of the path in the decision tree. After generating many paths and evaluating the payoffs in each case, the payoffs obtained during the simulation are used as a representation of the payoffs that would result from the decision tree. The expected payoff is then found by averaging the payoffs obtained in the simulation.

A typical challenge for this type of analysis in practice is specifying the inputs. When finding an accurate input would take an inordinate amount of time, it is often much quicker to use estimates of inputs. Using estimates is fine when they are backed up by sensitivity analysis. By performing sensitivity analysis on the input's range, managers can often show that no matter

where the true input lies within the range, the decision remains the same. When this is not the case, they have highlighted a key variable to making the decision and it likely deserves more attention to arrive at a more accurate answer.

SUMMARY OF LEARNING OBJECTIVE 4

Relying solely on expected trends can lead to flawed decisions when designing global supply chains under uncertainty. It is important to use an approach such as decision trees that accounts for future uncertainty. In the presence of uncertainty, flexibility can be valued as a real option using decision trees. Decision trees allow the valuation of different flexibility alternatives for each potential outcome of an uncertain future. This provides an accurate value of flexibility and other real options such as onshoring. In general, the value of real options such as flexibility and onshoring increases with an increase in uncertainty, while the value of inflexible choices decreases with an increase in uncertainty.

DISCUSSION QUESTIONS

1. According to Ferreira and Prokopets, what should a company like Dell consider when evaluating the impact of an offshoring decision?
2. Should uncertainty be considered when planning supply chain networks? Why or why not?
3. Discuss whether risk mitigation strategies can always keep a company's operating costs to a minimum.
4. Using an example, explain the concept of a cost trade-off when making a supply chain design decision.

5. What strategic options are considered by decision makers when designing a global supply chain network in the context of overcoming future uncertainties? Identify possible uncertainties that must be overcome as part of your answer.
6. What are the main uncertainties faced by a manufacturer when deciding whether to build a plant in Africa or in Europe?
7. Why is the length of a chain important when considering demand uncertainty in designing a supply chain network?

EXERCISES

1. EMS is a small manufacturer of drones that currently builds its entire product in northern Italy. As the market for drones has grown significantly, the Italian plant has reached capacity of 9,500 drones per year. To increase its capacity, EMS is considering two options. The first option is to add 9,500 units of capacity to the Italian plant at an annualized fixed cost of €6 million plus €200 labor per drone. The second option is to have Vitacon, an electronics producer, manufacture the drones at a cost of €400 for each drone (excluding raw materials cost). Raw materials cost €500 per drone, and EMS sells each drone for €2,000.

 EMS must make this decision for a two-year time horizon. During each year, the demand for EMS drones has an 85 percent chance of increasing 60 percent from the previous year and a 15 percent chance of remaining the same as the previous year. Vitacon's prices may change as well. They are fixed for the first year but have a 50 percent chance of increasing 15 percent in the second year and a 50 percent chance of remaining where they are.

 Use a decision tree to determine whether EMS should add capacity to its Italian plant or if it should outsource to Vitacon. What are some other factors that have not been discussed that would affect this decision?

2. Unipart, a manufacturer of auto parts, is considering two B2B marketplaces to purchase its MRO supplies. Both marketplaces offer a full line of supplies at very similar prices for products and shipping. Both provide similar service levels and lead times.

 However, their fee structures are quite different. The first marketplace, Parts4u.com, sells all of its products with a 5 percent commission tacked on top of the price of the product (not including shipping). AllMRO.com's pricing is based on a subscription fee of $10 million that must be paid up front for a two-year period and a commission of 1 percent on each transaction's product price.

 Unipart spends about $150 million on MRO supplies each year, although this varies with their utilization. Next year will likely be a strong year, in which high utilization will keep MRO spending at $150 million. However, there is a 25 percent chance that spending will drop by 10 percent. The second year, there is a 50 percent chance that the spending level will stay where it was in the first year and a 50 percent chance that it will drop by another 10 percent. Unipart uses a discount rate of 20 percent. Assume all costs are incurred at the beginning of each year (so Year 1 costs are incurred now and Year 2 costs are incurred in a year).

From which B2B marketplace should Unipart buy its parts?

3. Alphacap, a manufacturer of electronic components, is trying to select a single supplier for the raw materials that go into its main product, the doublecap. This is a new capacitor that is used by cellular phone manufacturers to protect microprocessors from power spikes. Two companies can provide the necessary materials—MultiChem and Mixemat.

 MultiChem has a solid reputation for its products and charges a higher price on account of its reliability of supply and delivery. MultiChem dedicates plant capacity to each customer, and therefore supply is ensured. This allows MultiChem to charge $1.20 for the raw materials used in each doublecap.

 Mixemat is a small raw materials supplier that has limited capacity but charges only $0.90 for a unit's worth of raw materials. Its reliability of supply, however, is in question. Mixemat does not have enough capacity to supply all its customers all the time. This means that orders to Mixemat are not guaranteed. In a year of high demand for raw materials, Mixemat will have 90,000 units available for Alphacap. In low-demand years, all product will be delivered.

 If Alphacap does not get raw materials from suppliers, it needs to buy them on the spot market to supply its customers. Alphacap relies on one major cell phone manufacturer for the majority of its business. Failing to deliver could lead to losing this contract, essentially putting the firm at risk. Therefore, Alphacap will buy raw material on the spot market to make up for any shortfall. Spot prices for single-lot purchases (such as Alphacap would need) are $2.00 when raw materials demand is low and $4.00 when demand is high.

 Demand in the raw materials market has a 75 percent chance of being high each of the next two years. Alphacap sold 100,000 doublecaps last year and expects to sell 110,000 this year. However, there is a 25 percent chance it will sell only 100,000. Next year, the demand has a 75 percent chance of rising 20 percent over this year and a 25 percent chance of falling 10 percent. Alphacap uses a discount rate of 20 percent. Assume all costs are incurred at the beginning of each year (Year 1 costs are incurred now and Year 2 costs are incurred in a year) and that Alphacap must make a decision with a two-year horizon. Only one supplier can be chosen, as these two suppliers refuse to supply someone who works with their competitor.

 Which supplier should Alphacap choose? What other information would you like to have to make this decision?

4. Bell Computer is reaching a crossroads. This PC manufacturer has been growing at a rapid rate, causing problems for its operations as it tries to keep up with the surging demand. Bell executives can plainly see that within the next half year, the systems used to coordinate its supply chain are going to fall apart because they will not be able to handle the volume of Bell projects they will have.

 To solve this problem, Bell has brought in two supply chain software companies that have made proposals on systems that could cover the volume and the complexity of tasks Bell needs to have handled. These two software companies are offering different types of products, however.

 The first company, SCSoftware, proposes a system for which Bell will purchase a license. This will allow Bell to use the software as long as it wants. However, Bell will be responsible for maintaining this software, which will require significant resources.

 The second company, SC–ASP, proposes that Bell pay a subscription fee on a monthly basis for SC–ASP to host Bell's supply chain applications on SC–ASP's machines. Bell employees will access information and analysis via a web browser. Information will be fed automatically from the ASP servers to the Bell servers whenever necessary. Bell will continue to pay the monthly fee for the software, but all maintenance will be performed by SC–ASP.

 How should Bell go about making a decision regarding which software company to choose? What specific pieces of information does Bell need to know (both about the software and about the future conditions Bell will experience) to make a decision? What are some of the qualitative issues Bell must think about when making this decision?

5. NorthPole Refrigerators is a white goods manufacturer that serves the European market and has recently entered the Chinese market. Current annual demand of its products in China is 4 million, whereas the demand in Europe is 8 million. Over the next two years, the demand in China is expected to go up either by 75 percent, with a probability of 0.6, or by 40 percent, with a probability of 0.4. Over the same period, the demand in Europe is expected to go up by 15 percent, with a probability of 0.5, or go down 15 percent, with a probability of 0.5. NorthPole currently has a production facility in China with a capacity of 4.5 million units per year and a facility in Europe with a capacity of 8.5 million per year. The variable production cost per unit in China is €50, and the variable cost per unit in Europe is €60. It costs €25 to ship a unit between the two markets. Each unit sells for €200 in both markets.

 NorthPole is in the process of deciding whether to add 3 million units or 2 million units of capacity to the China plant. The larger plant increase will cost €25 million, while the smaller addition will cost €20 million. Assume that NorthPole uses a discount factor of 15 percent. What would you recommend?

6. A European apparel manufacturer has production facilities in Italy and China to serve its European market, where annual demand is for 1.9 million units. Demand is expected to stay at the same level over the foreseeable future. Each facility has a capacity of 1 million units per year. With the current exchange rates, the production and distribution cost from Italy is 10 euro per unit, whereas the production and distribution cost from China is 7 euro. Over each of the

next three years, the Chinese currency could rise relative to the euro by 15 percent with a probability of 0.5 or drop by 5 percent with a probability of 0.5. An option being considered is to shut down 0.5 million units of capacity in Italy and move it to China at a one-time cost of 2 million euro. Assume a discount factor of 10 percent over the three years. Do you recommend this option?

7. A clothing manufacturer is setting up capacity in Spain and Poland for the next three years. Annual demand in each market is 1.5 million units and is likely to remain at that level. The two choices being considered by the company are to build 1.5 million units of capacity in each of the two locations. Building two plants will require a one-off cost of €3 million. The variable cost of production in Spain (for either a large or small plant) is currently €10/unit, whereas the cost in Poland is 8 Zolty/unit. The current exchange rate is 1 euro for 4.15 Polish Zloty. Over each of the next three years, the Zloty is expected to strength by 15 percent with a probability of 0.7 or weaken by 10 percent with a probability of 0.3. Assume a discount factor of 8 percent. What should the clothing manufacturer do? At what initial cost differential from building the two plants will the clothing manufacturer be indifferent between the two options?

BIBLIOGRAPHY

Amram, Martha, and Nalin Kulatilaka. *Real Options*. Cambridge, MA: Harvard Business School Press, 1999.

Brealey, Richard A., and Stewart C. Myers. *Principles of Corporate Finance*. New York: McGraw-Hill, 1996.

Chang, Shih-Chia, Neng-Pai Lin, and Chwen Sheu. "Aligning Manufacturing Flexibility with Environmental Uncertainty: Evidence from High-Technology Component Manufacturers in Taiwan." *International Journal of Production Research* (2002): 40(18), 4765–4780.

Chopra, Sunil, and ManMohan S. Sodhi. "Managing Risk to Avoid Supply Chain Breakdown" *Sloan Management Review* (2004): 46(1), 53–61.

Chopra, Sunil, and ManMohan S. Sodhi. "Reducing the Risk of Supply Chain Disruptions" *Sloan Management Review* (2014): 55(3), 73–80.

De Treville, Suzanne, and Lenos Trigeorgis. "It May Be Cheaper to Manufacture at Home." *Harvard Business Review* (October 2010): 84–87.

Farrell, Diana. "Beyond Offshoring: Assess Your Company's Global Potential." *Harvard Business Review* (December 2004): 82–90.

Favre, Donavon, and John McCreery. "Coming to Grips with Rising Supplier Risk" *Supply Chain Management Review* (September 2008): 26–32.

Ferreira, John, and Len Prokopets. "Does Offshoring Still Make Sense?" *Supply Chain Management Review* (January/February 2009): 20–27.

Garber, Randy, and Suman Sarkar. "Want a More Flexible Supply Chain?" *Supply Chain Management Review* (January/February 2007): 28–34.

Goel, Ajay, Nazgol Moussavi, and Vats N. Srivatsan. "Time to Rethink Offshoring?" *McKinsey on Business Technology 14* (Winter 2008): 32–35.

Harding, Mary Lu. "Gauging Total Cost, Supplier by Supplier." *CSCMP's Supply Chain Quarterly* (Q4 2007): 64–68.

Hoberg, Kai, and Knut Alicke. "Lessons for Supply Chains from the Financial Crisis." *Supply Chain Management Review* (September/October 2013): 48–55.

Jordan, W. C., and S. C. Graves. "Principles on the Benefits of Manufacturing Process Flexibility." *Management Science* 41 (April 1995): 577–594.

Lim, Michael, Achal Bassamboo, Sunil Chopra, and Mark S. Daskin. "Flexibility and Fragility: Supply Chain Network Design with Disruption Risks." Working paper, Northwestern University, Evanston, IL, 2008.

Luehrman, Timothy A. "Capital Projects as Real Options: An Introduction." Harvard Business School Case 9–295–074, 1995.

Luehrman, Timothy A. "Investment Opportunities as Real Options: Getting Started on the Numbers." *Harvard Business Review* (July–August 1998): 51–67.

Luehrman, Timothy A. "Strategy as a Portfolio of Real Options." *Harvard Business Review* (September–October 1998): 89–99.

Melnyk, Steven A., David J. Closs, Stanley E. Griffis, Christopher W. Zobel, and John R. Macdonald. "Understanding Supply Chain Resilience." *Supply Chain Management Review* (January/February 2014): 34–41.

Sheffi, Y. *The Resilient Enterprise*. Cambridge, MA: MIT Press, 2005.

Smith, Adam. *An Inquiry into the Nature and Causes of the Wealth of Nations*, 5th ed. London: Methuen & Co., Ltd., 1904.

Swaminathan, Jayashankar M., and Brian Tomlin. "How to Avoid the Six Risk Management Pitfalls." *Supply Chain Management Review* (July/August 2007): 34–42.

Tanowitz, Marc, and David Rutchik. "Squeezing Opportunity Out of Higher Fuel Costs." *Supply Chain Management Review* (October 2008): 34–40.

Trent, Rovbert J. "Managing Risk Through Supply Chain Flexibility." *Supply Chain Management Review* (May/June 2015): 20–25.

Trigeorgis, Lenos. *Real Options*. Cambridge, MA: MIT Press, 1996.

CASE STUDY

BioPharma, Inc.[2]

In 2013, Phillip (Phil) Landgraf faced several glaring problems in the financial performance of his company, BioPharma, Inc. The firm had experienced a steep decline in profits and high costs at its plants in Germany and Japan. Landgraf, the company's president for worldwide operations, knew that demand for the company's products was stable across the globe. As a result, the surplus capacity in his global production network looked like a luxury he could no longer afford.

Any improvement in financial performance was dependent on having the most efficient network in place, because revenues were unlikely to grow. Cutting costs was thus a top priority for the coming year. To help design a more cost-effective network, Landgraf assigned a task force to recommend a course of action.

Background

BioPharma, Inc. is a global manufacturer of bulk chemicals used in the pharmaceutical industry. The company holds patents on two chemicals that are called Highcal and Relax internally. These bulk chemicals are used by the company's pharmaceutical division and are also sold to other drug manufacturers. There are distinctions in the precise chemical specifications to be met in different parts of the world. All plants, however, are currently set up to be able to produce both chemicals for any part of the world.

For 2013, sales of each product by region and the production and capacity at each plant are shown in Table 6-18. The plant capacity, measured in millions of kilograms of production, can be assigned to either chemical, as long as the plant is capable of producing both. BioPharma has forecast that its sales for the two chemicals are likely to be stable for all parts of the world, except for Asia without Japan, where sales are expected to grow by 10 percent annually for each of the next five years before stabilizing.

The Japanese plant is a technology leader within the BioPharma network in terms of its ability to handle regulatory and environmental issues. Some developments in the Japanese plant had been transferred to other plants in the network. The German plant is a leader in terms of its production ability. The plant has routinely had the highest yields within the global network. The Brazilian, Indian, and Mexican plants have somewhat outdated technology and are in need of an update.

Current Plant Costs at BioPharma

After considerable debate, the task force identified the cost structure at each plant in 2013 U.S.$ are as shown in Table 6-19. Each plant incurs an annual fixed cost that is independent of the level of production in the plant. The fixed cost includes depreciation, utilities, and the salaries and fringe benefits of employees involved in general

TABLE 6-18 Sales by Region and Production/Capacity by Plant of Highcal and Relax (in Millions of Kilograms)

Region	Plant	Capacity	Highcal		Relax	
			2013 Sales	2013 Production	2013 Sales	2013 Production
Latin America	Brazil	18.0	7.0	11.0	7.0	7.0
Europe	Germany	45.0	15.0	15.0	12.0	0.0
Asia w/o Japan	India	18.0	5.0	10.0	3.0	8.0
Japan	Japan	10.0	7.0	2.0	8.0	0.0
Mexico	Mexico	30.0	3.0	12.0	3.0	18.0
U.S.	U.S.	22.0	18.0	5.0	17.0	17.0

[2] This case was inspired by *Applichem (A)*, Harvard Business School Case 9-685-051, 1985.

TABLE 6-19 Fixed and Variable Production Costs at Each BioPharma Plant in 2013 (U.S. $)

Plant	Plant Fixed Cost (million $)	Highcal Fixed Cost (million $)	Relax Fixed Cost (million $)	Highcal		Relax	
				Raw Material ($/kg)	Production cost ($/kg)	Raw Material ($/kg)	Production cost ($/kg)
Brazil	20.0	5.0	5.0	3.6	5.1	4.6	6.6
Germany	45.0	13.0	13.0	3.9	6.0	5.0	7.0
India	14.0	3.0	3.0	3.6	4.5	4.5	6.0
Japan	13.0	4.0	4.0	3.9	6.0	5.1	7.0
Mexico	30.0	6.0	6.0	3.6	5.0	4.6	6.5
U.S.	23.0	5.0	5.0	3.6	5.0	4.5	6.5

management, scheduling, expediting, accounting, maintenance, and so forth. Each plant that is capable of producing either Highcal or Relax also incurs a product-related fixed cost that is independent of the quantity of each chemical produced. The product-related fixed cost includes depreciation of equipment specific and other fixed costs that are specific to a chemical. If a plant maintains the capability to produce a particular chemical, it incurs the corresponding product-related fixed cost even if the chemical is not produced at the plant.

The variable production cost of each chemical consists of two components: raw materials and production costs. The variable production cost is incurred in proportion to the quantity of chemical produced and includes direct labor and scrap. The plants themselves can handle varying levels of production. In fact, they can also be idled for the year, in which case they incur only the fixed cost and none of the variable cost.

BioPharma transports the chemicals in specialized containers by sea and in specialized trucks on land. The transportation costs between plants and markets are as shown in Table 6-20. Historical exchange rates are shown in Table 6-21 and the regional import duties in Table 6-22. Given regional trade alliances, import duties in reality vary based on the origin of the chemical. For simplicity's sake, however, the task force has assumed that the duties are driven only by the destination. Local production within each region is assumed to result in no import duty. Thus, production from Brazil, Germany, and India can be sent to Latin America, Europe, and the rest of Asia excluding Japan, respectively, without incurring any import duties. Duties apply only to the raw material, production, and transportation cost component and not to the fixed cost component. Thus, a product entering Latin America with a raw material, production, and transportation cost of $10 incurs import duties of $3.

TABLE 6-20 Transportation Costs from Plants to Markets (U.S.$/kg)

From/To	Latin America	Europe	Asia w/o Japan	Japan	Mexico	U.S.
Brazil	0.20	0.45	0.50	0.50	0.40	0.45
Germany	0.45	0.20	0.35	0.40	0.30	0.30
India	0.50	0.35	0.20	0.30	0.50	0.45
Japan	0.50	0.40	0.30	0.10	0.45	0.45
Mexico	0.40	0.30	0.50	0.45	0.20	0.25
U.S.	0.45	0.30	0.45	0.45	0.25	0.20

TABLE 6-21 History of Exchange Rates in Currency/U.S.$1 (at the Beginning of Each Year)

	Brazilian Real	Euro	Indian Rupee	Japanese Yen	Mexican Peso	U.S. Dollar
2013	2.15	0.75	58.44	97.58	12.75	1.00
2012	1.95	0.78	53.46	79.79	13.15	1.00
2011	1.67	0.72	46.85	79.70	12.42	1.00
2010	1.75	0.75	45.72	87.78	12.63	1.00
2009	1.99	0.72	48.42	93.58	13.48	1.00
2008	1.83	0.68	43.62	103.42	11.13	1.00
2007	1.94	0.73	41.34	117.77	10.92	1.00
2006	2.17	0.80	45.18	116.29	10.89	1.00

TABLE 6-22 Import Tariffs (Percentage of Value of Product Imported, Including Transportation)

Latin America	Europe	Asia w/o Japan	Japan	Mexico	U.S.
30%	3%	27%	6%	35%	4%

Network Options Under Consideration

The task force is considering a variety of options for its analysis. One option is to keep the global network with its current structure and capabilities. Other options include shutting down some plants or limiting the capability of some plants to producing only one chemical. Closing down a plant eliminates all variable costs and saves 80 percent of the annual fixed costs (the remaining 20 percent accounts for costs that are incurred related to the plant shutdown). Similarly, if a plant is limited to producing only one chemical, the plant saves 80 percent of the fixed cost associated with the chemical that is no longer produced. The two options being seriously considered are shutting the Japanese plant and limiting the German plant to a single chemical.

Study Questions

1. How should BioPharma have used its production network in 2013? Should any of the plants have been idled? What is the annual cost of your proposal, including import duties?
2. How should Landgraf structure his global production network? Assume that the past is a reasonable indicator of the future in terms of exchange rates.
3. Is there any plant for which it may be worth adding a million kilograms of additional capacity at a fixed cost of $3 million per year?
4. How are your recommendations affected by the reduction of duties?
5. The analysis has assumed that each plant has a 100 percent yield (percentage output of acceptable quality). How would you modify your analysis to account for yield differences across plants?
6. What other factors should be accounted for when making your recommendations?

CASE STUDY

Global Supply Design for the Future: Nokia

In 2011, there were more than 4.6 billion telephone users worldwide. Until 2010, Nokia was the market leader with 29 percent of total market share but now Apple and Samsung compete for first place in terms of revenue. In 2010, 1.6 billion cell phones were sold, a net increase of 37 percent from 2009, and 250 million handsets were

delivered in the first quarter of 2011. Nokia, a Finish company, originated in the mid-19th century as a paper manufacturer. The conglomerate expanded into the electronics sector in the 1960s and finally into the mobile manufacturing business in the 1980s. Over the past 30 years, the industrial outsourcing trend has stretched manufacturing facilities from in-house production of almost all components to global sourcing, keeping in house only the design and the assembling of final products.

With customers all over the world and suppliers from the United States to China, Nokia faces challenges in the operation of its supply chain and sometimes has some difficult choices to make.

Global Supply Chain Challenges

In 2000, in the facility of a New Mexico subcontractor of integrated circuits, a fire started but was rapidly managed. Integrated components plants require highly sterilized environments, and the fire plus the intervention compromised several months of integrated circuits supply to Nokia. Researchers at the Massachusetts Institute of Technology calculated that when publicly listed companies announce disruption in their supply chains, share prices drop on average 8 percent and take a long time to recover. In addition to the financial element, the rest of the supply chain has to support the strain from replacing a supplier in a minimum amount of time. Furthermore, with wide product ranges and multiplicity of parts, the challenges are growing every year. The lean concept, when pushed to the extreme, could also be a cause of supply chain rupture when an issue arises. Academics and consultants agree that these issues can be overcome, if not avoided, thanks to early and constant communication.

Nokia has to decide to either stay with this integrated circuit supplier or source an alternative plant in China. The expected cost of sourcing a new supplier and implementing the necessary quality assurance procedures is estimated at $2 million. Once in place, for the three following years, this partnership has a 50 percent chance of yielding $100,000 in savings and a 50 percent chance that it will yield $150,000. For this scenario, the discount rate is 3 percent.

The other alternative is to stay with its supplier in New Mexico. The cost of the damage to Nokia's supply chain is estimated at $1.5 million. Supply chain risk assessors have estimated that there is a 60 percent chance the New Mexico's supplier will not yield any additional savings for the three following years and a 40 percent chance that it will result in a yearly $50,000 loss (additional cost) for each of the three following years. For this scenario, the discount rate is 9 percent.

Global Supply Chains Environment

Various suppliers are involved with Nokia globally. The supply chain environment is by nature complex and uncertain. Supply chain designers have started to implement robust communication systems coupled with geo-localization devices and RFID technologies. These technologies enable Nokia to track and monitor shipments' progress around the world, thereby accurately managing its inventory levels. IT is the answer to efficiently managing complex global supply chains; however, IT systems require high levels of standardization from the suppliers' perspective, forcing them to adapt to systems with which they are not necessarily familiar. Thus, this view of standardizing techniques is recognized as a problem that prevents the implementation of true flexibility. The new view of the supply chain is taking into account the old parameters and adding a new one. A flexible supply chain should include systems technology, infrastructures, and human behavior.

The Global Supply Chains of the Future: Dynamic Alignment

The concept of dynamic alignment is often illustrated with cyclists in a team or flocks of geese in V formation. Both examples have the same purpose: a team dynamic to reduce drag and efforts. The alignments are made by each individual rather than by a command center. This innovative view on supply chain dynamics relies on human behavior. Dynamic alignment is the ultimate view of supply chains driven by people power. It has started by aligning the company to the customers' view, and the idea is simply being rolled out now to a new level.

Study Questions

1. Draw a decision tree illustrating Nokia's alternatives between the two suppliers (the existing one and the perspective one in China) and the related sequences.
2. Calculate the NPV for both suppliers. Compare them and select the appropriate supplier.
3. Illustrate the benefits of evolving toward dynamic alignment compared to standardization in supply chains involving hundreds of suppliers.

CHAPTER

7

Demand Forecasting in a Supply Chain

LEARNING OBJECTIVES

After reading this chapter, you will be able to

7.1 Understand the role of forecasting for both an enterprise and a supply chain.

7.2 Identify the components of a demand forecast and some basic approaches to forecasting.

7.3 Forecast demand using time-series methodologies given historical demand data in a supply chain.

7.4 Analyze demand forecasts to estimate forecast error.

7.5 Use Excel to build time-series forecasting models.

All supply chain decisions made before demand has materialized are made to a forecast. In this chapter, we explain how historical demand information can be used to forecast future demand and how these forecasts affect the supply chain. We describe several methods to forecast demand and estimate a forecast's accuracy. We then discuss how these methods can be implemented using Microsoft Excel.

7.1 Understand the role of forecasting for both an enterprise and a supply chain.

THE ROLE OF FORECASTING IN A SUPPLY CHAIN

Demand forecasts form the basis of all supply chain planning. Consider the push/pull view of the supply chain discussed in Chapter 1. All push processes in the supply chain are performed in anticipation of customer demand, whereas all pull processes are performed in response to customer demand. For push processes, a manager must plan the level of activity, be it production, transportation, or outsourcing. For pull processes, a manager must plan the level of available capacity and inventory, but not the actual amount to be executed. In both instances, the first step a manager must take is to forecast what customer demand will be.

A Home Depot store selling paint orders the base paint and dyes in anticipation of customer orders, whereas it performs final mixing of the paint in response to customer orders. Home Depot uses a forecast of future demand to determine the quantity of paint and dye to have on hand

(a push process). Farther up the supply chain, the paint factory that produces the base also needs forecasts to determine its own production and inventory levels. The paint factory's suppliers also need forecasts for the same reason. When each stage in the supply chain makes its own separate forecast, these forecasts are often very different. The result is a mismatch between supply and demand. When all stages of a supply chain work together to produce a collaborative forecast, however, the forecast tends to be much more accurate. The resulting forecast accuracy enables supply chains to be both more responsive and more efficient in serving their customers. Leaders in many supply chains, from electronics manufacturers to packaged-goods retailers, have improved their ability to match supply and demand by moving toward collaborative forecasting.

Consider the value of collaborative forecasting for Coca-Cola and its bottlers. Coca-Cola decides on the timing of promotions based on the demand forecast over the coming quarter. Promotion decisions are then incorporated into an updated demand forecast. The updated forecast is essential for the bottlers to plan their capacity and production decisions. A bottler operating without an updated forecast based on the promotion is unlikely to have sufficient supply available for Coca-Cola, thus hurting supply chain profits.

Mature products with stable demand, such as milk or paper towels, are usually easiest to forecast. Forecasting and the accompanying managerial decisions are extremely difficult when either the supply of raw materials or the demand for the finished product is highly unpredictable. Fashion goods and many high-tech products are examples of items that are difficult to forecast. In both instances, an estimate of forecast error is essential when designing the supply chain and planning its response.

Before we begin an in-depth discussion of the components of forecasts and forecasting methods in the supply chain, we briefly list characteristics of forecasts that a manager must understand to design and manage his or her supply chain effectively.

1. **Forecasts are always inaccurate and should thus include both the expected value of the forecast and a measure of forecast error.** To understand the importance of forecast error, consider two car dealers. One of them expects sales to range between 100 and 1,900 units, whereas the other expects sales to range between 900 and 1,100 units. Even though both dealers anticipate average sales of 1,000, the sourcing policies for each dealer should be very different, given the difference in forecast accuracy. Thus, the forecast error (or demand uncertainty) is a key input into most supply chain decisions. Unfortunately, most firms do not maintain any estimates of forecast error.

2. **Long-term forecasts are usually less accurate than short-term forecasts;** that is, long-term forecasts have a larger standard deviation of error relative to the mean than short-term forecasts. Forecasting demand a month into the future is harder than forecasting demand a day into the future. Seven-Eleven Japan has exploited this key property to improve its performance. The company has instituted a replenishment process that enables it to respond to an order within hours. For example, if a store manager places an order by 10 a.m., the order is delivered by 7 p.m. the same day. Therefore, the manager has to forecast what will sell that night only less than 12 hours before the actual sale. The short lead time allows a manager to take into account current information that could affect product sales, such as the weather. This forecast is likely to be more accurate than if the store manager had to forecast demand a week in advance.

3. **Aggregate forecasts are usually more accurate than disaggregate forecasts,** as they tend to have a smaller standard deviation of error relative to the mean. For example, it is easy to forecast the gross domestic product (GDP) of the United States for a given year with less than a 2 percent error. However, it is much more difficult to forecast yearly revenue for a company with less than a 2 percent error, and it is even harder to forecast revenue for a given product with the same degree of accuracy. The key difference among the three forecasts is the degree of aggregation. The GDP is an aggregation across many companies, and the earnings of a company are an aggregation across several product lines. The greater the aggregation, the more accurate the forecast.

4. In general, the farther up the supply chain a company is (or the farther it is from the consumer), the greater the distortion of information it receives. One classic example of this phenomenon is the bullwhip effect (see Chapter 10), in which order variation is amplified as orders move farther from the end customer. Collaborative forecasting based on sales to the end customer helps upstream enterprises reduce forecast error.

SUMMARY OF LEARNING OBJECTIVE 1

Forecasting is a key input for virtually every design and planning decision made in a supply chain. It is important to recognize that all forecasts are likely to be wrong. Thus, an estimation of forecast error is essential to effectively use the forecast. Reducing the forecast horizon (by reducing the lead time of the associated decision) and aggregation are two effective approaches to decrease forecast error. A relatively recent phenomenon, however, is to create collaborative forecasts for an entire supply chain and use these as the basis for decisions. Collaborative forecasting greatly increases the accuracy of forecasts and allows the supply chain to maximize its performance. Without collaboration, supply chain stages farther from demand will likely have poor forecasts that will lead to supply chain inefficiencies and a lack of responsiveness.

COMPONENTS OF A FORECAST AND FORECASTING METHODS

7.2 Identify the components of a demand forecast and some basic approaches to forecasting.

Yogi Berra, the former New York Yankees catcher who is famous for his malapropisms, is supposed to have said, "It's tough to make predictions, especially about the future." One may be tempted to treat demand forecasting as magic or art and leave everything to chance. What a firm knows about its customers' past behavior, however, sheds light on their future behavior. Demand does not arise in a vacuum. Rather, customer demand is influenced by a variety of factors and can be predicted, at least with some probability, if a company can determine the relationship between these factors and future demand. To forecast demand, companies must first identify the factors that influence future demand and then ascertain the relationship between these factors and future demand.

Companies must balance objective and subjective factors when forecasting demand. Although we focus on quantitative forecasting methods in this chapter, companies must include human input when they make their final forecast. Seven-Eleven Japan illustrates this point.

Seven-Eleven Japan provides its store managers with a state-of-the-art decision support system that makes a demand forecast and provides a recommended order. The store manager, however, is responsible for making the final decision and placing the order, because he or she may have access to information about market conditions that are not available in historical demand data. This knowledge of market conditions is likely to improve the forecast. For example, if the store manager knows that the weather is likely to be rainy and cold the next day, he or she can reduce the size of an ice cream order to be placed with an upstream supplier, even if demand was high during the previous few days when the weather was hot. In this instance, a change in market conditions (the weather) would not have been predicted using historical demand data. A supply chain can experience substantial payoffs from improving its demand forecasting through qualitative human inputs.

A company must be knowledgeable about numerous factors that are related to the demand forecast, including the following:

- Past demand
- Lead time of product replenishment
- Planned advertising or marketing efforts
- Planned price discounts
- State of the economy
- Actions that competitors have taken

It is important to recognize that past demand is not the same as past sales. Often, companies make the mistake of looking at historical sales and assuming that this is what the historical demand was. To get true demand, however, adjustments need to be made for unmet demand due to stockouts, competitor actions, pricing, and promotions. Failure to do so results in forecasts that do not represent the current reality. Similarly, a company must account for all factors that are likely to affect demand before it can select an appropriate forecasting methodology. For example, historically a firm may have experienced low demand for chicken noodle soup in July and high demand in December and January. If the firm decides to discount the product in July, the situation is likely to change, with some of the future demand shifting to the month of July. The firm should make its forecast taking this factor into consideration.

Forecasting methods are classified according to the following four types:

1. **Qualitative:** Qualitative forecasting methods are primarily subjective and rely on human judgment. They are most appropriate when little historical data are available or when experts have market intelligence that may affect the forecast. Such methods may also be necessary to forecast demand several years into the future in a new industry.

2. **Time series:** Time-series forecasting methods use historical demand to make a forecast. They are based on the assumption that past demand history is a good indicator of future demand. These methods are most appropriate when the basic demand pattern does not vary significantly from one year to the next. These are the simplest methods to implement and can serve as a good starting point for a demand forecast.

3. **Causal:** Causal forecasting methods assume that the demand forecast is highly correlated with certain factors in the environment (the state of the economy, interest rates, etc.). Causal forecasting methods find this correlation between demand and environmental factors and use estimates of what environmental factors will be to forecast future demand. For example, product pricing is strongly correlated with demand. Companies can thus use causal methods to determine the impact of price promotions on demand.

4. **Simulation:** Simulation forecasting methods imitate the consumer choices that give rise to demand to arrive at a forecast. Using simulation, a firm can combine time-series and causal methods to answer such questions as: What will be the impact of a price promotion? What will be the impact of a competitor opening a store nearby? Airlines simulate customer buying behavior to forecast demand for higher-fare seats when no seats are available at lower fares.

A company may find it difficult to decide which method is most appropriate for forecasting. In fact, several studies have indicated that using multiple forecasting methods to create a combined forecast is more effective than using any one method alone.

In this chapter, we deal primarily with time-series methods, which are most appropriate when future demand is related to historical demand, growth patterns, and any seasonal patterns. With any forecasting method, there is always a random element that cannot be explained by historical demand patterns. Therefore, any observed demand can be broken down into a systematic and a random component:

$$\text{Observed demand } (O) = \text{systematic component } (S) + \text{random component } (R)$$

The *systematic component* measures the expected value of demand and consists of what we will call *level*, the current deseasonalized demand; *trend*, the rate of growth or decline in demand for the next period; and *seasonality*, the predictable seasonal fluctuations in demand.

The *random component* is the part of the forecast that deviates from the systematic part. A company cannot (and should not) forecast the direction of the random component. All a company can predict is the random component's expected size and variability, which provides a measure of forecast error. The objective of forecasting is to filter out the random component (noise) and estimate the systematic component. The *forecast error* measures the difference between the forecast and actual demand. On average, a good forecasting method has an error

whose size is comparable to the random component of demand. A manager should be skeptical of a forecasting method that claims to have no forecasting error on historical demand. In this case, the method has merged the historical random component with the systematic component. As a result, the forecasting method will likely perform poorly.

It is important to understand that forecasting is not just a quantitative exercise. For effective forecasting, an organization must incorporate the following five points into its forecasting process:

1. Understand the objective of forecasting.
2. Integrate demand planning and forecasting throughout the supply chain.
3. Identify the major factors that influence the demand forecast.
4. Forecast at the appropriate level of aggregation.
5. Establish performance and error measures for the forecast.

Understand the Objective of Forecasting

Every forecast supports decisions that are based on it, so an important first step is to identify these decisions clearly. Examples of such decisions include how much of a particular product to make, how much to inventory, and how much to order. All parties affected by a supply chain decision should be aware of the link between the decision and the forecast. For example, Walmart's plans to discount detergent during the month of July must be shared with the manufacturer, the transporter, and others involved in filling demand, as they all must make decisions that are affected by the forecast of demand. All parties should come up with a common forecast for the promotion and a shared plan of action based on the forecast. Failure to make these decisions jointly may result in either too much or too little product in various stages of the supply chain.

Integrate Demand Planning and Forecasting Throughout the Supply Chain

A company should link its forecast to all planning activities throughout the supply chain. These include capacity planning, production planning, promotion planning, and purchasing, among others. In one unfortunately common scenario, a retailer develops forecasts based on promotional activities, whereas a manufacturer, unaware of these promotions, develops a different forecast for its production planning based on historical orders. This leads to a mismatch between supply and demand, resulting in poor customer service. To accomplish integration, it is a good idea for a firm to have a cross-functional team, with members from each affected function responsible for forecasting demand—and an even better idea is to have members of different companies in the supply chain working together to create a forecast.

It takes an investment of time and effort to build the relationships with one's partners to begin sharing information and integrating planning and forecasting across the supply chain. However, the supply chain benefits of collaboration are often an order of magnitude greater than the cost (collaborative planning, forecasting, and replenishment are discussed in greater detail in Chapter 10). The reality today, however, is that most forecasts do not even account for all the information available across the different functions within a firm. As a result, firms should aim to put a sales and operations planning process in place (discussed in Chapter 9) that brings together the sales and operations functions when planning.

Identify Major Factors That Influence the Demand Forecast

Next, a firm must identify demand, supply, and product-related phenomena that influence the demand forecast. On the demand side, a company must ascertain whether demand is growing or declining or has a seasonal pattern. These estimates must be based on demand, not on sales data. For example, a supermarket promoted a certain brand of cereal in July 2017. As a result, the demand for this cereal was high, whereas the demand for other, comparable cereal brands was low in July. The supermarket should not use the sales data from 2017 to estimate that demand for

this brand will be high in July 2018, because this will occur only if the same brand is promoted again in July 2018 and other brands respond as they did the previous year. When making the demand forecast, the supermarket must understand what the demand would have been in the absence of promotion activity and how demand is affected by promotions and competitor actions. A combination of these pieces of information will allow the supermarket to forecast demand for July 2018, given the promotion activity planned for that year.

On the supply side, a company must consider the available supply sources to decide on the accuracy of the forecast desired. If alternate supply sources with short lead times are available, a highly accurate forecast may not be especially important. However, if only a single supplier with a long lead time is available, an accurate forecast will have great value.

On the product side, a firm must know the number of variants of a product being sold and whether these variants substitute for or complement one another. If demand for a product influences or is influenced by demand for another product, the two forecasts are best made jointly. For example, when a firm introduces an improved version of an existing product, it is likely that the demand for the existing product will decline because customers will buy the improved version. Although the decline in demand for the original product is not indicated by historical data, the historical demand is still useful in that it allows the firm to estimate the combined total demand for the two versions. Clearly, demand for the two products should be forecast jointly.

Forecast at the Appropriate Level of Aggregation

Given that aggregate forecasts are more accurate than disaggregate forecasts, it is important to forecast at a level of aggregation that is appropriate, given the supply chain decision that is driven by the forecast. Consider a buyer at a retail chain who is forecasting to select an order size for shirts. One approach is to ask each store manager the precise number of shirts needed and add up all the requests to get an order size with the supplier. The advantage of this approach is that it uses local market intelligence that each store manager has. The problem with this approach is that it makes store managers forecast well before demand arises at a time when their forecasts are unlikely to be accurate. A better approach may be to forecast demand at the aggregate level when ordering with the supplier and ask each store manager to forecast only when the shirts are to be allocated across the stores. In this case, the long lead time forecast (supplier order) is aggregate, thus lowering error. The disaggregate store-level forecast is made close to the sales season, when local market intelligence is likely to be most effective.

Establish Performance and Error Measures for the Forecast

Companies should establish clear performance measures to evaluate the accuracy and timeliness of the forecast. These measures should be linked to the objectives of the business decisions based on these forecasts. Consider a mail-order company that uses a forecast to place orders with its suppliers, which take two months to fill the orders. The mail-order company must ensure that the forecast is created at least two months before the start of the sales season because of the two-month lead time for replenishment. At the end of the sales season, the company must compare actual demand to forecasted demand to estimate the accuracy of the forecast. Then plans for decreasing future forecast errors or responding to the observed forecast errors can be put into place.

SUMMARY OF LEARNING OBJECTIVE 2

Demand consists of a systematic and a random component. The systematic component measures the expected value of demand. The random component measures fluctuations in demand from the expected value. The systematic component consists of level, trend, and seasonality. Level measures the current deseasonalized demand. Trend measures the current rate of growth or decline in demand. Seasonality indicates predictable seasonal

fluctuations in demand. The goal of forecasting is to estimate the systematic component and the size (not direction) of the random component (in the form of a forecast error). Good forecasting requires a clear understanding of the objective of the forecast and should be integrated across the supply chain.

7.3 *Forecast demand using time-series methodologies given historical demand data in a supply chain.*

TIME-SERIES FORECASTING METHODS

In this section we discuss time-series forecasting methods that primarily use historical demand data to come up with a forecast. The goal of any forecasting method is to predict the systematic component of demand and estimate the expected value of the random component. In its most general form, the systematic component of demand data contains a level, a trend, and a seasonal factor. The equation for calculating the systematic component may take a variety of forms:

- *Multiplicative:* Systematic component = level × trend × seasonal factor
- *Additive:* Systematic component = level + trend + seasonal factor
- *Mixed:* Systematic component = (level + trend) × seasonal factor

The specific form of the systematic component applicable to a given forecast depends on the nature of demand. Companies may develop both static and adaptive forecasting methods for each form. We now describe these static and adaptive forecasting methods.

Static Methods

A static method assumes that the estimates of level, trend, and seasonality within the systematic component do not vary as new demand is observed. In this case, we estimate each of these parameters based on historical data and then use the same values for all future forecasts. In this section, we discuss a static forecasting method for use when demand has a trend as well as a seasonal component. We assume that the systematic component of demand is mixed; that is,

Systematic component = (level + trend) × seasonal factor

A similar approach can be applied for other forms as well. We begin with a few basic definitions:

- L = estimate of level at $t = 0$ (the deseasonalized demand estimate during Period $t = 0$)
- T = estimate of trend (increase or decrease in demand per period)
- S_t = estimate of seasonal factor for Period t
- D_t = actual demand observed in Period t
- F_t = forecast of demand for Period t

In a static forecasting method, the forecast in Period t for demand in Period $t + l$ is a product of the level in Period $t + l$ and the seasonal factor for Period $t + l$. Let L be the level at period 0. The level in Period $t + l$ is the sum of the level in Period 0 (L) and $(t + l)$ times the trend T. The forecast in Period t for demand in Period $t + l$ is thus given as

$$F_{t+l} = [L + (t + l)T]S_{t+l} \tag{7.1}$$

We now describe one method for estimating the three parameters L, T, and S. As an example, consider the demand for rock salt used primarily to melt snow. This salt is produced by a firm called Tahoe Salt, which sells its salt through a variety of independent retailers around the Lake Tahoe area of the Sierra Nevada Mountains. In the past, Tahoe Salt has relied on estimates of demand from a sample of its retailers, but the company has noticed that these retailers always overestimate their purchases, leaving Tahoe (and even some retailers) stuck with excess inventory. After meeting with its retailers, Tahoe has decided to produce a collaborative forecast. Tahoe Salt wants to work with the retailers to create a more accurate forecast based on the actual demand for their salt. Quarterly retail demand data for the past three years are shown in Table 7-1 and charted in Figure 7-1.

TABLE 7-1 Quarterly Demand for Tahoe Salt

Year	Quarter	Period, t	Demand, D_t
1	2	1	8,000
1	3	2	13,000
1	4	3	23,000
2	1	4	34,000
2	2	5	10,000
2	3	6	18,000
2	4	7	23,000
3	1	8	38,000
3	2	9	12,000
3	3	10	13,000
3	4	11	32,000
4	1	12	41,000

In Figure 7-1, observe that demand for salt is seasonal, increasing from the second quarter of a given year to the first quarter of the following year. The second quarter of each year has the lowest demand. Each cycle lasts four quarters, and the demand pattern repeats every year. There is also a growth trend in the demand, with sales growing over the past three years. The company estimates that growth will continue in the coming year at historical rates. We now describe the following two steps required to estimate each of the three parameters—level, trend, and seasonal factors.

1. Deseasonalize demand and run linear regression to estimate level and trend.
2. Estimate seasonal factors.

ESTIMATING LEVEL AND TREND The objective of this step is to estimate the level at Period 0 and the trend. We start by *deseasonalizing* the demand data. *Deseasonalized demand* represents the demand that would have been observed in the absence of seasonal fluctuations. The *periodicity* (p) is the number of periods after which the seasonal cycle repeats. For Tahoe Salt's demand, the pattern repeats every year. Given that we are measuring demand on a quarterly basis, the periodicity for the demand in Table 7-1 is $p = 4$.

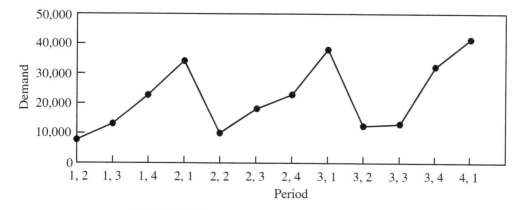

Figure 7-1 Quarterly Demand at Tahoe Salt

To ensure that each season is given equal weight when deseasonalizing demand, we take the average of p consecutive periods of demand. The average of demand from Period $l + 1$ to Period $l + p$ provides deseasonalized demand for Period $l + (p + 1)/2$. If p is odd, this method provides deseasonalized demand for an existing period. If p is even, this method provides deseasonalized demand at a point between Period $l + (p/2)$ and Period $l + 1 + (p/2)$. If p is even, we obtain the deseasonalized demand for Period $l + 1 + (p/2)$ by taking the average of deseasonalized demand provided by Periods $l + 1$ to $l + p$ and $l + 2$ to $l + p + 1$. Thus, the deseasonalized demand, $\overline{D}_t$, for Period t, can be obtained as follows:

$$
\overline{D}_t = \begin{cases} \left[D_{t-(p/2)} + D_{t+(p/2)} + \displaystyle\sum_{i=t+1-(p/2)}^{t-1+(p/2)} 2D_i \right] \Big/ (2p) & \text{for } p \text{ even} \\[4mm] \displaystyle\sum_{i=t-[(p-1)/2]}^{t+[(p-1)/2]} D_i/p & \text{for } p \text{ odd} \end{cases}
\tag{7.2}
$$

In our example, $p = 4$ is even. For $t = 3$, we obtain the deseasonalized demand using Equation 7.2 as follows:

$$
\overline{D}_3 = \left[D_{t-(p/2)} + D_{t+(p/2)} + \sum_{i=t+1-(p/2)}^{t-1+(p/2)} 2D_i \right] \Big/ (2p) = \left[D_1 + D_5 + \sum_{i=2}^{4} 2D_i \right] \Big/ 8
$$

With this procedure, we can obtain deseasonalized demand between Periods 3 and 10 as shown in Figures 7-2 and 7-3 (all details are available in the accompanying spreadsheet Chapter 7-*Tahoe-salt*).

The following linear relationship exists between the deseasonalized demand, $\overline{D}_t$, and time t, based on the change in demand over time:

$$
\overline{D}_t = L + Tt
\tag{7.3}
$$

In Equation 7.3, $\overline{D}_t$ represents deseasonalized demand and not the actual demand in Period t, L represents the *level* or deseasonalized demand at Period 0, and T represents the rate of growth of deseasonalized demand or *trend*. We can estimate the values of L and T for the deseasonalized demand using linear regression with deseasonalized demand (see Figure 7-2) as the dependent variable and time as the independent variable. Such a regression can be run using Microsoft

	A	B	C
	Period	Demand	Deseasonalized Demand
1	t	D_t	
2	1	8,000	
3	2	13,000	
4	3	23,000	19,750
5	4	34,000	20,625
6	5	10,000	21,250
7	6	18,000	21,750
8	7	23,000	22,500
9	8	38,000	22,125
10	9	12,000	22,625
11	10	13,000	24,125
12	11	32,000	
13	12	41,000	

Cell	Cell Formula	Equation	Copied to
C4	=(B2+B6+2*SUM(B3:B5))/8	7.2	C5:C11

Figure 7-2 Excel Workbook with Deseasonalized Demand for Tahoe Salt

Excel (Data | Data Analysis | Regression). This sequence of commands opens the Regression dialog box in Excel. For the Tahoe Salt workbook in Figure 7-2, in the resulting dialog box, we enter

Input Y Range: C4:C11

Input X Range: A4:A11

and click the OK button. A new sheet containing the results of the regression opens up (see worksheet *Regression-1*). This new sheet contains estimates for both the initial level L and the trend T. The initial level, L, is obtained as the *intercept coefficient,* and the trend, T, is obtained as the X *variable coefficient* (or the slope) from the sheet containing the regression results. For the Tahoe Salt example, we obtain $L = 18,439$ and $T = 524$ (all details are available in the worksheet *Regression-1* and numbers are rounded to integer values). For this example, deseasonalized demand $\overline{D}_t$ for any Period t is thus given by

$$\overline{D}_t = 18,439 + 524t \tag{7.4}$$

Both actual demand and deseasonalized demand are shown in Figure 7-3. It is not appropriate to run a linear regression between the original demand data and time to estimate level and trend because the original demand data are not linear and the resulting linear regression will not be accurate. The demand must be deseasonalized before we run the linear regression.

ESTIMATING SEASONAL FACTORS We can now obtain deseasonalized demand for each period using Equation 7.4 (see Figure 7-4). The seasonal factor $\overline{S}_t$ for Period t is the ratio of actual demand D_t to deseasonalized demand $\overline{D}_t$ and is given as

$$\overline{S}_t = \frac{D_t}{\overline{D}_t} \tag{7.5}$$

For the Tahoe Salt example, the deseasonalized demand estimated using Equation 7.4 and the seasonal factors estimated using Equation 7.5 are shown in Figure 7-4 (see worksheet *Figure 7-4*).

Given the periodicity p, we obtain the seasonal factor for a given period by averaging seasonal factors that correspond to similar periods. For example, if we have a periodicity of $p = 4$, Periods 1, 5, and 9 have similar seasonal factors. The seasonal factor for these periods is obtained as the average of the three seasonal factors. Given r seasonal cycles in the data, for all periods of the form $pt + i, 1 \le i \le p$, we obtain the seasonal factor as

$$S_i = \frac{\sum_{j=0}^{r-1} \overline{S}_{jp+i}}{r} \tag{7.6}$$

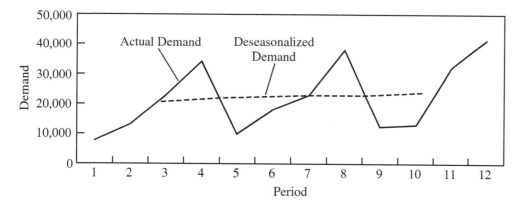

Figure 7-3 Deseasonalized Demand for Tahoe Salt

	A	B	C	D
1	Period t	Demand D_t	Deseasonalized Demand (Eqn 7.4) $\overline{D}_t$	Seasonal Factor (Eqn 7.5) $\overline{S}_t$
2	1	8,000	18,963	0.42
3	2	13,000	19,487	0.67
4	3	23,000	20,011	1.15
5	4	34,000	20,535	1.66
6	5	10,000	21,059	0.47
7	6	18,000	21,583	0.83
8	7	23,000	22,107	1.04
9	8	38,000	22,631	1.68
10	9	12,000	23,155	0.52
11	10	13,000	23,679	0.55
12	11	32,000	24,203	1.32
13	12	41,000	24,727	1.66

Cell	Cell Formula	Equation	Copied to
C2	=18439+A2*524	7.4	C3:C13
D2	=B2/C2	7.5	D3:D13

Figure 7-4 Deseasonalized Demand and Seasonal Factors for Tahoe Salt

For the Tahoe Salt example, a total of 12 periods and a periodicity of $p = 4$ imply that there are $r = 3$ seasonal cycles in the data. We obtain seasonal factors using Equation 7.6 as

$$S_1 = (\overline{S}_1 + \overline{S}_5 + \overline{S}_9)/3 = (0.42 + 0.47 + 0.52)/3 = 0.47$$
$$S_2 = (\overline{S}_2 + \overline{S}_6 + \overline{S}_{10})/3 = (0.67 + 0.83 + 0.55)/3 = 0.68$$
$$S_3 = (\overline{S}_3 + \overline{S}_7 + \overline{S}_{11})/3 = (1.15 + 1.04 + 1.32)/3 = 1.17$$
$$S_4 = (\overline{S}_4 + \overline{S}_8 + \overline{S}_{12})/3 = (1.66 + 1.68 + 1.66)/3 = 1.67$$

At this stage, we have estimated the level, trend, and all seasonal factors. We can now obtain the forecast for the next four quarters using Equation 7.1. In the example, the forecast for the next four periods using the static forecasting method is given by

$$F_{13} = (L + 13T)S_{13} = (18,439 + 13 \times 524)0.47 = 11,868$$
$$F_{14} = (L + 14T)S_{14} = (18,439 + 14 \times 524)0.68 = 17,527$$
$$F_{15} = (L + 15T)S_{15} = (18,439 + 15 \times 524)1.17 = 30,770$$
$$F_{16} = (L + 16T)S_{16} = (18,439 + 16 \times 524)1.67 = 44,794$$

Tahoe Salt and its retailers now have a more accurate forecast of demand. Without the sharing of demand information between the retailers and the manufacturer, this supply chain would have a less accurate forecast, and a variety of production and inventory inefficiencies would result.

Adaptive Forecasting

In adaptive forecasting, the estimates of level, trend, and seasonality are updated after each demand observation. The main advantage of adaptive forecasting is that estimates incorporate all new data that are observed. We now discuss a basic framework and several methods that can be used for this type of forecast. The framework is provided in the most general setting, when the systematic component of demand data has the mixed form and contains a level, a trend, and a seasonal factor. It can easily be modified for the other two cases, however. The framework can also be specialized for the case in which the systematic component contains no seasonality or trend. We assume that we have a set of historical data for n periods and that demand is seasonal,

with periodicity p. Given quarterly data, wherein the pattern repeats itself every year, we have a periodicity of $p = 4$.

We begin by defining a few terms:

L_t = estimate of level at the end of Period t
T_t = estimate of trend at the end of Period t
S_t = estimate of seasonal factor for Period t
F_t = forecast of demand for Period t (made in Period $t - 1$ or earlier)
D_t = actual demand observed in Period t
$E_t = F_t - D_t$ = forecast error in Period t

In adaptive methods, the forecast for Period $t + l$ in Period t uses the estimate of level and trend in Period t (L_t and T_t respectively) and is given as

$$F_{t+l} = (L_t + lT)S_{t+l} \tag{7.7}$$

The four steps in the adaptive forecasting framework are as follows:

1. **Initialize:** Compute initial estimates of the level (L_0), trend (T_0), and seasonal factors ($S_1, \ldots , S_p$) from the given data. This is done exactly as in the static forecasting method discussed earlier in the chapter with $L_0 = L$ and $T_0 = T$.
2. **Forecast:** Given the estimates in Period t, forecast demand for Period $t + 1$ using Equation 7.7. Our first forecast is for Period 1 and is made with the estimates of level, trend, and seasonal factor at Period 0.
3. **Estimate error:** Record the actual demand D_{t+1} for Period $t + 1$ and compute the error E_{t+1} in the forecast for Period $t + 1$ as the difference between the forecast and the actual demand. The error for Period $t + 1$ is stated as

$$E_{t+1} = F_{t+1} - D_{t+1} \tag{7.8}$$

4. **Modify estimates:** Modify the estimates of level (L_{t+1}), trend (T_{t+1}), and seasonal factor (S_{t+p+1}), given the error E_{t+1} in the forecast. It is desirable that the modification be such that if the demand is lower than forecast, the estimates are revised downward, whereas if the demand is higher than forecast, the estimates are revised upward.

The revised estimates in Period $t + 1$ are then used to make a forecast for Period $t + 2$, and Steps 2, 3, and 4 are repeated until all historical data up to Period n have been covered. The estimates at Period n are then used to forecast future demand.

We now discuss various adaptive forecasting methods. The method that is most appropriate depends on the characteristic of demand and the composition of the systematic component of demand. In each case, we assume the period under consideration to be t.

MOVING AVERAGE The moving average method is used when demand has no observable trend or seasonality. In this case,

Systematic component of demand = level

In this method, the level in Period t is estimated as the average demand over the most recent N periods. This represents an N-period moving average and is evaluated as follows:

$$L_t = (D_t + D_{t-1} + \ldots + D_{t-N+1})/N \tag{7.9}$$

The current forecast for all future periods is the same and is based on the current estimate of level. The forecast is stated as

$$F_{t+1} = L_t \quad \text{and} \quad F_{t+n} = L_t \tag{7.10}$$

After observing the demand for Period $t + 1$, we revise the estimates as follows:

$$L_{t+1} = (D_{t+1} + D_t + \cdots + D_{t-N+2})/N, \quad F_{t+2} = L_{t+1}$$

To compute the new moving average, we simply add the latest observation and drop the oldest one. The revised moving average serves as the next forecast. The moving average corresponds to giving the last N periods of data equal weight when forecasting and ignoring all data older than this new moving average. As we increase N, the moving average becomes less responsive to the most recently observed demand. We illustrate the use of the moving average in Example 7-1.

EXAMPLE 7-1 Moving Average

The Agricultural Market Report published by DEFRA indicates weekly sales of "wheat cereals" in Great Britain over the four weeks of April 2009 to be 38, 35, 77, and 90 thousand tons. Calculate the sales forecast for the first week of May using a four-period moving average. What is the forecast error if the sale in the first week of May turns out to be 80 thousand tons?[1]

Analysis:
We make the forecast for Period 5 (first week of May) at the end of Period 4 (last week of April). Thus, assume the current period to be $t = 4$. Our first objective is to estimate the level in Period 4. Using Equation 7.9 with $N = 4$, we obtain

$$L_4 = (D_1 + D_2 + D_3 + D_4)/4 = (38 + 35 + 77 + 90)/4 = 60$$

The forecast of demand for Period 5, using Equation 7.10, is expressed as

$$F_5 = L_4 = 60 \text{ thousands tons}$$

As the sale in Period 5, D_5, is 80, we have a forecast error for Period 5 of

$$E_5 = F_5 - D_5 = 60 - 80 = -20$$

After observing demand in Period 5, the revised estimate of level for Period 5 is given by
$$L_5 = (D_2 + D_3 + D_4 + D_5)/4 = (35 + 77 + 90 + 80)/4 = 70.5$$

SIMPLE EXPONENTIAL SMOOTHING The simple exponential smoothing method is appropriate when demand has no observable trend or seasonality. In this case,

Systematic component of demand $=$ level

The initial estimate of level, L_0, is taken to be the average of all historical data because demand has been assumed to have no observable trend or seasonality. Given demand data for Periods 1 through n, we have the following:

$$L_0 = \frac{1}{n}\sum_{i=1}^{n} D_i \tag{7.11}$$

The forecast in Period t for all future periods is equal to the current estimate of level and is given as

$$F_{t+1} = L_t \text{ and } F_{t+n} = L_t \tag{7.12}$$

After observing the demand, D_{t+1}, for Period $t + 1$, we revise the estimate of the level as follows:

$$L_{t+1} = \alpha D_{t+1} + (1 - \alpha)L_t \tag{7.13}$$

[1]*Source of data:* defra.gov.uk

where α $(0 < \alpha < 1)$ is a smoothing constant for the level. The revised value of the level is a weighted average of the observed value of the level (D_{t+1}) in Period $t + 1$ and the old estimate of the level (L_t) in Period t. Using Equation 7.13, we can express the level in a given period as a function of the current demand and the level in the previous period. We can thus rewrite Equation 7.13 as

$$L_{t+1} = \sum_{n=0}^{t-1} \alpha(1 - \alpha)^n D_{t+1-n} + (1 - \alpha)^t D_1$$

The current estimate of the level is a weighted average of all the past observations of demand, with recent observations weighted higher than older observations. A higher value of α corresponds to a forecast that is more responsive to recent observations, whereas a lower value of α represents a more stable forecast that is less responsive to recent observations. We illustrate the use of exponential smoothing in Example 7-2.

EXAMPLE 7-2	**Simple Exponential Smoothing**

Consider the sales report in Example 7-1, where weekly sales for wheat cereals in Great Britain has been 38, 35, 77, and 90 thousand tons over the four weeks of April 2009. Calculate the sales forecast for Period 1 (first week of April) using simple exponential smoothing with $t\alpha = 0.1$.[2]

Analysis

In this case we have demand data for $n = 4$ periods. Using Equation 7.11, the initial estimate of level is expressed by

$$L_0 = \left(\frac{1}{n}\right) \sum_{i=1}^{4} D_i = 60$$

Thus, the forecast for Period 1 (using Equation 7.12) is thus given by

$$F_1 = L_0 = 60$$

The observed demand for Period 1 is $D_1 = 38$. The forecast error for Period 1 is given by

$$E_1 = F_1 - D_1 = 60 - 38 = 22$$

With $\alpha = 0.1$, the revised estimate of level for Period 1 using Equation 7.13 is given by

$$L_1 = \alpha D_1 + (1 - \alpha)L_0 = (0.1 \times 38) + (0.9 \times 60) = 57.8$$

Observe that the estimate of level for Period 1 is lower than for Period 0 because the demand in Period 1 is lower than the forecast for Period 1. We thus obtain $F_3 = 55.52$, $F_4 = 57.67$, and $F_5 = 60.90$. Thus, the forecast for Period 5 is 60.90

TREND-CORRECTED EXPONENTIAL SMOOTHING (HOLT'S MODEL) The trend-corrected exponential smoothing (Holt's model) method is appropriate when demand is assumed to have a level and a trend in the systematic component, but no seasonality. In this case, we have

Systematic component of demand = level + trend

We obtain an initial estimate of level and trend by running a linear regression between demand, D_t, and time, Period t, of the form

$$D_t = at + b$$

[2]*Source of data: defra.gov.uk*

In this case, running a linear regression between demand and time periods is appropriate because we have assumed that demand has a trend but no seasonality. The underlying relationship between demand and time is thus linear. The constant b measures the estimate of demand at Period $t = 0$ and is our estimate of the initial level L_0. The slope a measures the rate of change in demand per period and is our initial estimate of the trend T_0.

In Period t, given estimates of level L_t and trend T_t, the forecast for future periods is expressed as

$$F_{t+1} = L_t + T_t \quad \text{and} \quad F_{t+n} = L_t + nT_t \tag{7.14}$$

After observing demand for Period t, we revise the estimates for level and trend as follows:

$$L_{t+1} = \alpha D_{t+1} + (1 - \alpha)(L_t + T_t) \tag{7.15}$$

$$T_{t+1} = \beta(L_{t+1} - L_t) + (1 - \beta)T_t \tag{7.16}$$

where $\alpha(0 < \alpha < 1)$ is a smoothing constant for the level and $\beta(0 < \beta < 1)$ is a smoothing constant for the trend. Observe that in each of the two updates, the revised estimate (of level or trend) is a weighted average of the observed value and the old estimate. We illustrate the use of Holt's model in Example 7-3 (see associated spreadsheet *Examples 1–4 Chapter 7*).

EXAMPLE 7-3 **Holt's Model**

Japan National Tourist Organization has reported a constant increase in number of visitors to Japan during the last ten years. For example, the number of visitors to Japan from other Asian countries during the period of 2002–2007 has been 3,417,774; 3,511,513; 4,208,095; 4,627,478; 5,247,125; and 6,130,262 annually. Forecast the number of visitors for 2008 using trend-corrected exponential smoothing with $\alpha = 0.1$, $\beta = 0.2$.[3]

Analysis

The first step is to obtain initial estimates of level and trend using linear *regression*. The estimate of initial level L_0 is obtained as the *intercept coefficient* and the trend T_0 is obtained as *variable coefficient* (or the slope). From the given data, we obtain:

$$L_0 = 2,604,842 \quad \text{and} \quad T_0 = 548,247$$

Thus, the forecast for Period 1 (2002) using Equation 7.14 is thus given by

$$F_1 = L_0 + T_0 = 2,604,842 + 548,247 = 3,153,809$$

Thus, the observed demand for Period 1 is $D_1 = 3,417,774$. The error for Period 1 is given by

$$E_1 = F_1 - D_1 = 3,158,089 - 3,417,774 = -264,685$$

With $\alpha = 0.1$, $\beta = 0.2$, the revised estimate of level and trend for Period 1 using Equations 7.15 and 7.16 is given by

$$L_1 = \alpha D_1 + (1 - \alpha)(L_0 + T_0) = (0.1 \times 3,417,774) + (0.9 \times 3,153,089) = 3,179,558$$

$$T_1 = \beta(L_1 - L_0) + (1 - \beta)T_0 = 0.2 \times (3,179,558 - 2,604,842)] + (0.8 \times 548,247) = 553,541$$

Thus,

$$F_2 = L_1 + T_1 = 3,179,558 + 553,541 = 3,733,099$$

[3]Data for number of visitors to Japan from overseas quoted from JNTO (Japan National Tourist Organization), www.tourism.jp/english/statistics/inbound.php.

Continuing in this manner, this gives us a forecast for Period 7 of

$$F_7 = L_6 + T_6 = 6,439,353$$

TREND- AND SEASONALITY-CORRECTED EXPONENTIAL SMOOTHING (WINTER'S MODEL) This method is appropriate when the systematic component of demand has a level, a trend, and a seasonal factor. In this case we have

Systematic component of demand = (level + trend) × seasonal factor

Assume periodicity of demand to be p. To begin, we need initial estimates of level (L_0), trend (T_0), and seasonal factors ($S_1, \ldots, S_p$). We obtain these estimates using the procedure for static forecasting described earlier in the chapter.

In Period t, given estimates of level, L_t, trend, T_t, and seasonal factors, $S_t, \ldots, S_{t+p-1}$, the forecast for future periods is given by

$$F_{t+1} = (L_t + T_t)S_{t+1} \quad \text{and} \quad F_{t+l} = (L_t + lT_t)S_{t+l} \tag{7.17}$$

On observing demand for Period $t + 1$, we revise the estimates for level, trend, and seasonal factors as follows:

$$L_{t+1} = \alpha(D_{t+1}/S_{t+1}) + (1 - \alpha)(L_t + T_t) \tag{7.18}$$

$$T_{t+1} = \beta(L_{t+1} - L_t) + (1 - \beta)T_t \tag{7.19}$$

$$S_{t+p+1} = \gamma(D_{t+1}/L_{t+1}) + (1 - \gamma)S_{t+1} \tag{7.20}$$

where $\alpha(0 < \alpha < 1)$ is a smoothing constant for the level; $\beta(0 < \beta < 1)$ is a smoothing constant for the trend; and $\gamma(0 < \gamma < 1)$ is a smoothing constant for the seasonal factor. Observe that in each of the updates (level, trend, or seasonal factor), the revised estimate is a weighted average of the observed value and the old estimate. We illustrate the use of Winter's model in Example 7-4 (see worksheet *Example 7-4*).

EXAMPLE 7-4 **Winter's Model**

Consider the Tahoe Salt demand data in Table 7-1. Forecast demand for Period 1 using trend- and seasonality-corrected exponential smoothing with $\alpha = 0.1, \beta = 0.2, \gamma = 0.1$.

Analysis

We obtain the initial estimates of level, trend, and seasonal factors exactly as in the static case. They are expressed as follows:

$$L_0 = 18,439 \quad T_0 = 524 \quad S_1 = 0.47 \quad S_2 = 0.68 \quad S_3 = 1.17 \quad S_4 = 1.67$$

The forecast for Period 1 (using Equation 7.17) is thus given by

$$F_1 = (L_0 + T_0)S_1 = (18,439 + 524)0.47 = 8,913$$

The observed demand for Period 1 is $D_1 = 8,000$. The forecast error for Period 1 is thus given by

$$E_1 = F_1 - D_1 = 8,913 - 8,000 = 913$$

With $\alpha = 0.1, \beta = 0.2, \gamma = 0.1$, the revised estimate of level and trend for Period 1 and seasonal factor for Period 5, using Equations 7.18, 7.19, and 7.20, is given by

$$L_1 = \alpha(D_1/S_1) + (1 - \alpha)(L_0 + T_0)$$
$$= [0.1 \times (8,000/0.47)] + [0.9 \times (18,439 + 524)] = 18,769$$

$$T_1 = \beta(L_1 - L_0) + (1 - \beta)T_0 = [0.2 \times (18{,}769 - 18{,}439)] + (0.8 \times 524) = 485$$
$$S_5 = \gamma(D_1/L_1) + (1 - \gamma)S_1 = [0.1 \times (8{,}000/18{,}769)] + (0.9 \times 0.47) = 0.47$$

The forecast of demand for Period 2 (using Equation 7.17) is thus given by

$$F_2 = (L_1 + T_1)S_2 = (18{,}769 + 485) \times 0.68 = 13{,}093$$

The forecasting methods we have discussed and the situations in which they are generally applicable are as follows:

Forecasting Method	Applicability
Moving average	No trend or seasonality
Simple exponential smoothing	No trend or seasonality
Holt's model	Trend but no seasonality
Winter's model	Trend and seasonality

If Tahoe Salt uses an adaptive forecasting method for the demand data obtained from its retailers, Winter's model is the best choice, because its demand experiences both a trend and seasonality.

If we do not know that Tahoe Salt experiences both trend and seasonality, how can we find out? Forecast error helps identify instances in which the forecasting method being used is inappropriate. In the next section, we describe how a manager can estimate and use forecast error.

SUMMARY OF LEARNING OBJECTIVE 3

Time-series methods for forecasting are categorized as *static* or *adaptive*. In static methods, the estimates of parameters are not updated as new demand is observed. Static methods include regression. In adaptive methods, the estimates are updated each time a new demand is observed. Adaptive methods include moving averages, simple exponential smoothing, Holt's model, and Winter's model. Moving averages and simple exponential smoothing are best used when demand displays neither trend nor seasonality. Holt's model is best when demand displays a trend but no seasonality. Winter's model is appropriate when demand displays both trend and seasonality.

7.4 Analyze demand forecasts to estimate forecast error.

MEASURES OF FORECAST ERROR

As mentioned earlier, every instance of demand has a random component. A good forecasting method should capture the systematic component of demand but not the random component. The random component manifests itself in the form of a forecast error. Forecast errors contain valuable information and must be analyzed carefully for two reasons:

1. Managers use error analysis to determine whether the current forecasting method is predicting the systematic component of demand accurately. For example, if a forecasting method consistently produces a positive error, the forecasting method is overestimating the systematic component and should be corrected.
2. All contingency plans must account for forecast error. Consider a mail-order company with two suppliers. The first is in the Far East and has a lead time of two months. The second is local and can fill orders with one week's notice. The local supplier is more expensive than the Far East supplier. The mail-order company wants to contract a certain amount of contingency capacity with the local supplier to be used if the demand exceeds the quantity the Far East supplier provides. The decision regarding the quantity of local capacity to contract is closely linked to the size of the forecast error with a two-month lead time.

As long as observed errors are within historical error estimates, firms can continue to use their current forecasting method. Finding an error that is well beyond historical estimates may indicate that the forecasting method in use is no longer appropriate or demand has fundamentally changed. If all of a firm's forecasts tend to consistently over- or underestimate demand, this may be another signal that the firm should change its forecasting method.

As defined earlier, forecast error for Period t is given by E_t, where the following holds:

$$E_t = F_t - D_t$$

That is, the error in Period t is the difference between the forecast for Period t and the actual demand in Period t. It is important that a manager estimate the error of a forecast made at least as far in advance as the lead time required for the manager to take whatever action the forecast is to be used for. For example, if a forecast will be used to determine an order size and the supplier's lead time is six months, a manager should estimate the error for a forecast made six months before demand arises. In a situation with a six-month lead time, there is no point in estimating errors for a forecast made one month in advance.

One measure of forecast error is the *mean squared error* (MSE), where the following holds (the denominator in Equation 7.21 can also have $n - 1$ instead of n):

$$MSE_n = \frac{1}{n}\sum_{t=1}^{n} E_t^2 \tag{7.21}$$

The MSE can be related to the variance of the forecast error. In effect, we estimate that the random component of demand has a mean of 0 and a variance of MSE. The MSE penalizes large errors much more significantly than small errors because all errors are squared. Thus, if we select forecast methods by minimizing MSE, a method with a forecast error sequence of 10, 12, 9, and 9 will be preferred to a method with an error sequence of 1, 3, 2, and 20. Thus, it is a good idea to use the MSE to compare forecasting methods if the cost of a large error is much larger than the gains from very accurate forecasts. Using the MSE as a measure of error is appropriate when forecast error has a distribution that is symmetric about zero.

Define the *absolute deviation* in Period t, A_t, to be the absolute value of the error in Period t; that is,

$$A_t = |E_t|$$

Define the *mean absolute deviation* (MAD) to be the average of the absolute deviation over all periods, as expressed by

$$MAD_n = \frac{1}{n}\sum_{t=1}^{n} A_t \tag{7.22}$$

The MAD can be used to estimate the standard deviation of the random component assuming that the random component is normally distributed. In this case the standard deviation of the random component is

$$\sigma = 1.25\, MAD \tag{7.23}$$

We then estimate that the mean of the random component is 0, and the standard deviation of the random component of demand is σ. MAD is a better measure of error than MSE if the forecast error does not have a symmetric distribution. Even when the error distribution is symmetric, MAD is an appropriate choice when selecting forecasting methods if the cost of a forecast error is proportional to the size of the error.

The *mean absolute percentage error* (MAPE) is the average absolute error as a percentage of demand and is given by

$$MAPE_n = \frac{\sum_{t=1}^{n} \left|\dfrac{E_t}{D_t}\right| 100}{n} \tag{7.24}$$

The MAPE is a good measure of forecast error when the underlying forecast has significant seasonality and demand varies considerably from one period to the next. Consider a scenario in which two methods are used to make quarterly forecasts for a product with seasonal demand that peaks in the third quarter. Method 1 returns forecast errors of 190, 200, 245, and 180; Method 2 returns forecast errors of 100, 120, 500, and 100 over four quarters. Method 1 has a lower MSE and MAD relative to Method 2 and would be preferred if either criterion was used. If demand is highly seasonal, however, and averages 1,000, 1,200, 4,800, and 1,100 in the four periods, Method 2 results in a MAPE of 9.9 percent, whereas Method 1 results in a much higher MAPE, 14.3 percent. In this instance, it can be argued that Method 2 should be preferred to Method 1.

When a forecast method stops reflecting the underlying demand pattern (for instance, if demand drops considerably as it did for the automotive industry in 2008–2009), the forecast errors are unlikely to be randomly distributed around 0. In general, one needs a procedure to track and control the forecasting method. One approach is to use the sum of forecast errors to evaluate the *bias*, where the following holds:

$$bias_n = \sum_{t=1}^{n} E_t \qquad (7.25)$$

The bias will fluctuate around 0 if the error is truly random and not biased one way or the other. Ideally, if we plot all the errors, the slope of the best straight line passing through should be 0.

The *tracking signal* (TS) is the ratio of the bias and the MAD and is given as

$$TS_t = \frac{bias_t}{MAD_t} \qquad (7.26)$$

If the TS at any period is outside the range ± 6, this is a signal that the forecast may be biased and is either underforecasting ($TS < -6$) or overforecasting ($TS > +6$). This may happen because the forecasting method is flawed or the underlying demand pattern has shifted. One instance in which a large negative TS will result occurs when demand has a growth trend and the manager is using a forecasting method such as moving average. Because trend is not included, the average of historical demand is always lower than future demand. The negative TS detects that the forecasting method consistently underestimates demand and alerts the manager.

The tracking signal may also get large when demand has suddenly dropped (as it did for many industries in 2009) or increased by a significant amount, making historical data less relevant. If demand has suddenly dropped, it makes sense to increase the weight on current data relative to older data when making forecasts. McClain (1981) recommends the "declining alpha" method when using exponential smoothing where the smoothing constant starts large (to give greater weight to recent data) but then decreases over time. If we are aiming for a long-term smoothing constant of $\alpha = 1 - \rho$, a declining alpha approach would be to start with $\alpha_0 = 1$ and reset the smoothing constant as follows:

$$\alpha_t = \frac{\alpha_{t-1}}{\rho + \alpha_{t-1}} = \frac{1 - \rho}{1 - \rho^t}$$

In the long term, the smoothing constant will converge to $\alpha = 1 - \rho$ with the forecasts becoming more stable over time.

SUMMARY OF LEARNING OBJECTIVE 4

Forecast error measures the random component of demand. This measure is important because it reveals how inaccurate a forecast is likely to be and what contingencies a firm may have to plan for. The MSE, MAD, and MAPE are used to estimate the size of the forecast error. The bias and TS are used to estimate if the forecast consistently over- or underforecasts or if demand has deviated significantly from historical norms.

BUILDING FORECASTING MODELS USING EXCEL

7.5 Use Excel to build time-series forecasting models.

We now illustrate the use of Microsoft Excel to build the forecasting models discussed so far. We first show how Excel can be used to select an appropriate smoothing constant when using exponential smoothing and then illustrate the various forecasting methods using Excel.

Selecting the Best Smoothing Constant

When using exponential smoothing, the value of the smoothing constant chosen has a direct impact on the sensitivity of the forecast to recent data. If a manager has a good sense of the underlying demand pattern, it is best to use a smoothing constant that is no larger than 0.2. In general, it is best to pick smoothing constants that minimize the error term that a manager is most comfortable with from among MSE, MAD, and MAPE. In the absence of a preference among error terms, it is best to pick smoothing constants that minimize the MSE.

We illustrate the impact of picking smoothing constants that minimize different error measures using the 10-period demand data shown in cells B3:B12 of Figure 7-5 (accompanying spreadsheet *Chapter 7-Tahoe-salt* and worksheet *Figures 7-5, 6*). The initial level is estimated using Equation 7.11 and is shown in cell C2. The smoothing constant α is obtained using Solver (using GRG nonlinear solver with unconstrained variables non-negative) by minimizing the MSE (cell F13) at the end of the 10 periods as shown in Figure 7-5. The forecast shown in Figure 7-5 uses the resulting $\alpha = 0.54$ and gives MSE = 2,460, MAD = 42.5, and MAPE = 2.1 percent.

The smoothing constant can also be selected using Solver by minimizing the MAD or the MAPE at the end of 10 periods. In Figure 7-6, we show the results from minimizing MAD (cell G13). The forecasts and errors with the resulting $\alpha = 0.32$ are shown in Figure 7-6. In this case, the MSE increases to 2,570 (compared to 2,460 in Figure 7-5), whereas the MAD decreases to 39.2 (compared to 42.5 in Figure 7-5) and the MAPE decreases to 2.0 percent (compared to 2.1 percent in Figure 7-5). The major difference between the two forecasts is in Period 9 (the period with the largest error, shown in cell D11), when minimizing MSE picks a smoothing constant that reduces large errors, whereas minimizing MAD picks a smoothing constant that gives equal weight to reducing all errors even if large errors get somewhat larger.

In general, it is not a good idea to use smoothing constants much larger than 0.2 for extended periods of time. A larger smoothing constant may be justified for a short period of time when demand is in transition. It should, however, generally be avoided for extended periods of time.

Forecasting Demand at Tahoe Salt

Recall the Tahoe Salt example earlier in the chapter with the historical demand from its retailers, shown in Table 7-1. The demand data are also shown in column B of Figure 7-7 (see associated spreadsheet *Chapter 7-Tahoe-salt*). Tahoe Salt is currently negotiating contracts with suppliers for the four quarters between the second quarter of Year 4 and the first quarter of Year 5. An important input into this negotiation is the forecast of demand that Tahoe Salt and its retailers are building collaboratively. They have assigned a team—consisting of two sales managers from the retailers and the vice president of operations for Tahoe Salt—to come up with this forecast. The forecasting team decides to apply each of the adaptive forecasting methods discussed in this chapter to the historical data. The goal is to select the most appropriate forecasting method and then use it to forecast demand for the next four quarters. The team decides to select the forecasting method based on the errors that result when each method is used on the 12 quarters of historical demand data.

Demand in this case clearly has both a trend and seasonality in the systematic component. Thus, the team initially expects Winter's model to produce the best forecast.

MOVING AVERAGE The forecasting team initially decides to test a four-period moving average for the forecasting. All calculations are shown in Figure 7-7 (see worksheet *Figure 7-7* in spreadsheet *Chapter 7-Tahoe-salt*) and are as discussed in the section on the moving-average

	A	B	C	D	E	F	G	H
		Demand		Forecast		Squared	Absolute	
1	Period t	D_t	Level L_t	F_t	Error E_t	Error	Error A_t	% Error
2	0		2017.9					
3	1	2024	2021.2	2017.9	-6.1	37	6.1	0.3%
4	2	2076	2050.8	2021.2	-54.8	3003	54.8	2.6%
5	3	1992	2019.0	2050.8	58.8	3463	58.8	3.0%
6	4	2075	2049.3	2019.0	-56.0	3135	56.0	2.7%
7	5	2070	2060.5	2049.3	-20.7	429	20.7	1.0%
8	6	2046	2052.7	2060.5	14.5	210	14.5	0.7%
9	7	2027	2038.8	2052.7	25.7	658	25.7	1.3%
10	8	1972	2002.7	2038.8	66.8	4459	66.8	3.4%
11	9	1912	1953.6	2002.7	90.7	8218	90.7	4.7%
12	10	1985	1970.6	1953.6	-31.4	985	31.4	1.6%
13		2017.9			87	2,460	42.5	2.1%
14	$\alpha =$	0.54						

Solver Parameters

Set Target Cell: F13

Equal To: ○ Max ● Min ○ Value of: 0

By Changing Cells:

B14

Subject to the Constraints:

B14 <= 1

Solve
Close
Guess
Options
Add
Change
Reset All
Delete
Help

Figure 7-5 Selecting Smoothing Constant by Minimizing MSE

method earlier in this chapter. The team uses Equation 7.9 to estimate level and Equation 7.10 to forecast demand.

As indicated by column K in Figure 7-7, the TS is well within the ± 6 range, which indicates that the forecast using the four-period moving average does not contain any significant bias. It does, however, have a fairly large MAD_{12} of 9,719, with a $MAPE_{12}$ of 49 percent. From Figure 7-7, observe that

$$L_{12} = 24,500$$

Thus, using a four-period moving average, the forecast for Periods 13 through 16 (using Equation 7.10) is given by

$$F_{13} = F_{14} = F_{15} = F_{16} = L_{12} = 24,500$$

	A	B	C	D	E	F	G	H
	Period t	**Demand** D_t	**Level** L_t	**Forecast** F_t	**Error** E_t	**Squared Error**	**Absolute Error** A_t	**% Error**
1								
2	0		2017.9					
3	1	2024	2019.8	2017.9	-6.1	37	6.1	0.3%
4	2	2076	2037.8	2019.8	-56.2	3153	56.2	2.7%
5	3	1992	2023.2	2037.8	45.8	2097	45.8	2.3%
6	4	2075	2039.7	2023.2	-51.8	2687	51.8	2.5%
7	5	2070	2049.4	2039.7	-30.3	916	30.3	1.5%
8	6	2046	2048.3	2049.4	3.4	12	3.4	0.2%
9	7	2027	2041.5	2048.3	21.3	454	21.3	1.1%
10	8	1972	2019.3	2041.5	69.5	4831	69.5	3.5%
11	9	1912	1985.0	2019.3	107.3	11511	107.3	5.6%
12	10	1985	1985.0	1985.0	0.0	0	0.0	0.0%
13		2017.9			103	2,570	39.2	2.0%
14	$\alpha =$	0.32						

Figure 7-6 Selecting Smoothing Constant by Minimizing MAD

Given that MAD_{12} is 9,719, the estimate of standard deviation of forecast error, using a four-period moving average, is $1.25 \times 9,719 = 12,149$. In this case, the standard deviation of forecast error is fairly large relative to the size of the forecast.

SIMPLE EXPONENTIAL SMOOTHING The forecasting team next uses a simple exponential smoothing approach, with $\alpha = 0.1$, to forecast demand. This method is also tested on the 12 quarters of historical data. Using Equation 7.11, the team estimates the initial level for Period 0 to be the average demand for Periods 1 through 12 (see worksheet *Figure 7-8*). The initial level is the average of the demand entries in cells B3 to B14 in Figure 7-8 and results in

$$L_0 = 22,083$$

	A	B	C	D	E	F	G	H	I	J	K
1	Period t	Demand D_t	Level L_t	Forecast F_t	Error E_t	Absolute Error A_t	Squared Error MSE_t	MAD_t	% Error	$MAPE_t$	TS_t
2	1	8,000									
3	2	13,000									
4	3	23,000									
5	4	34,000	19,500								
6	5	10,000	20,000	19,500	9,500	9,500	90,250,000	9,500	95	95	1.00
7	6	18,000	21,250	20,000	2,000	2,000	47,125,000	5,750	11	53	2.00
8	7	23,000	21,250	21,250	-1,750	1,750	32,437,500	4,417	8	38	2.21
9	8	38,000	22,250	21,250	-16,750	16,750	94,468,750	7,500	44	39	-0.93
10	9	12,000	22,750	22,250	10,250	10,250	96,587,500	8,050	85	49	0.40
11	10	13,000	21,500	22,750	9,750	9,750	96,333,333	8,333	75	53	1.56
12	11	32,000	23,750	21,500	-10,500	10,500	98,321,429	8,643	33	50	0.29
13	12	41,000	24,500	23,750	-17,250	17,250	123,226,563	9,719	42	49	-1.52

Cell	Cell Formula	Equation	Copied to
C5	=Average(B2:B5)	7.9	C6:C13
D6	=C5	7.10	D7:D13
E6	=D6-B6	7.8	E7:E13
F6	=Abs(E6)		F7:F13
G6	=Sumsq(E6:E6)/(A6-4)	7.21	G7:G13
H6	=Sum(F6:F6)/(A6-4)	7.22	H7:H13
I6	=100*(F6/B6)		I7:I13
J6	=Average(I6:I6)	7.24	J7:J13
K6	=Sum(E6:E6)/H6	7.26	K7:K13

Figure 7-7 Tahoe Salt Forecasts Using Four-Period Moving Average

The team then uses Equation 7.12 to forecast demand for the succeeding period. The estimate of level is updated each period using Equation 7.13. The results are shown in Figure 7-8.

As indicated by the TS, which ranges from -1.38 to 2.15, the forecast using simple exponential smoothing with $\alpha = 0.1$ does not indicate any significant bias. However, it has a fairly large MAD_{12} of 10,208, with a $MAPE_{12}$ of 59 percent. From Figure 7-8, observe that

$$L_{12} = 23,490$$

Thus, the forecast for the next four quarters (using Equation 7.12) is given by

$$F_{13} = F_{14} = F_{15} = F_{16} = L_{12} = 23,490$$

In this case, MAD_{12} is 10,208 and $MAPE_{12}$ is 59 percent. Thus, the estimate of standard deviation of forecast error using simple exponential smoothing is $1.25 \times 10,208 = 12,760$. In this case, the standard deviation of forecast error is fairly large relative to the size of the forecast.

TREND-CORRECTED EXPONENTIAL SMOOTHING (HOLT'S MODEL) The team next investigates the use of Holt's model. In this case, the systematic component of demand is given by

$$\text{Systematic component of demand} = \text{level} + \text{trend}$$

	A	B	C	D	E	F	G	H	I	J	K
1	Period t	Demand D_t	Level L_t	Forecast F_t	Error E_t	Absolute Error A_t	Mean Squared Error MSE_t	MAD_t	% Error	$MAPE_t$	TS_t
2	0		22,083								
3	1	8,000	20,675	22,083	14,083	14,083	198,340,278	14,083	176	176	1
4	2	13,000	19,908	20,675	7,675	7,675	128,622,951	10,879	59	118	2
5	3	23,000	20,217	19,908	-3,093	3,093	88,936,486	8,284	13	83	2
6	4	34,000	21,595	20,217	-13,783	13,783	114,196,860	9,659	41	72	0.51
7	5	10,000	20,436	21,595	11,595	11,595	118,246,641	10,046	116	81	1.64
8	6	18,000	20,192	20,436	2,436	2,436	99,527,532	8,777	14	70	2.15
9	7	23,000	20,473	20,192	-2,808	2,808	86,435,714	7,925	12	62	2.03
10	8	38,000	22,226	20,473	-17,527	17,527	114,031,550	9,125	46	60	-0.16
11	9	12,000	21,203	22,226	10,226	10,226	112,979,315	9,247	85	62	0.95
12	10	13,000	20,383	21,203	8,203	8,203	108,410,265	9,143	63	63	1.86
13	11	32,000	21,544	20,383	-11,617	11,617	110,824,074	9,368	36	60	0.58
14	12	41,000	23,490	21,544	-19,456	19,456	133,132,065	10,208	47	59	-1.38

Cell	Cell Formula	Equation	Copied to
C3	=0.1*B3+(1-0.1)*C2	7.13	C4:C14
D3	=C2	7.12	D4:D14
E3	=D3-B3	7.8	E4:E14
F3	=Abs(E3)		F4:F14
G3	=Sumsq(E3:E3)/A3	7.21	G4:G14
H3	=Sum(F3:F3)/A3	7.22	H4:H14
I3	=100*(F3/B3)		I4:I14
J3	=Average(I3:I3)	7.24	J4:J14
K3	=Sum(E3:E3)/H3	7.26	K4:K14

Figure 7-8 Tahoe Salt Forecasts Using Simple Exponential Smoothing

The team applies the methodology discussed earlier. As a first step, it estimates the level at Period 0 and the initial trend. As described in Example 7-3, this estimate is obtained by running a linear regression between demand, D_t, and time, Period t. From the regression of the available data (see worksheet *holts-regression*), the team obtains the following:

$$L_0 = 12,015 \quad \text{and} \quad T_0 = 1,549$$

The team now applies Holt's model with $\alpha = 0.1$ and $\beta = 0.2$ to obtain the forecasts for each of the 12 quarters for which demand data are available (see worksheet *Figure 7-9*). They make the forecast using Equation 7.14, update the level using Equation 7.15, and update the trend using Equation 7.16. The results are shown in Figure 7-9.

As indicated by a TS that ranges from -2.15 to 2.00, trend-corrected exponential smoothing with $\alpha = 0.1$ and $\beta = 0.2$ does not seem to significantly over- or underforecast. However, the forecast has a fairly large MAD_{12} of 8,836, with a $MAPE_{12}$ of 52 percent. From Figure 7-9, observe that

$$L_{12} = 30,443 \quad \text{and} \quad T_{12} = 1,541$$

	A	B	C	D	E	F	G	H	I	J	K	L
		Demand		Trend	Forecast		Absolute Error	Mean Squared				
1	Period t	D_t	Level L_t	T_t	F_t	Error E_t	A_t	Error MSE$_t$	MAD$_t$	% Error	MAPE$_t$	TS$_t$
2	0		12,015	1,549								
3	1	8,000	13,008	1,438	13,564	5,564	5,564	30,958,096	5,564	70	70	1
4	2	13,000	14,301	1,409	14,445	1,445	1,445	16,523,523	3,505	11	40	2
5	3	23,000	16,439	1,555	15,710	-7,290	7,290	28,732,318	4,767	32	37	0
6	4	34,000	19,594	1,875	17,993	-16,007	16,007	85,603,146	7,577	47	39.86	-2.15
7	5	10,000	20,322	1,645	21,469	11,469	11,469	94,788,701	8,355	115	54.83	-0.58
8	6	18,000	21,570	1,566	21,967	3,967	3,967	81,613,705	7,624	22	49.36	-0.11
9	7	23,000	23,123	1,563	23,137	137	137	69,957,267	6,554	1	42.39	-0.11
10	8	38,000	26,018	1,830	24,686	-13,314	13,314	83,369,836	7,399	35	41.48	-1.90
11	9	12,000	26,262	1,513	27,847	15,847	15,847	102,010,079	8,338	132	51.54	0.22
12	10	13,000	26,298	1,217	27,775	14,775	14,775	113,639,348	8,981	114	57.75	1.85
13	11	32,000	27,963	1,307	27,515	-4,485	4,485	105,137,395	8,573	14	53.78	1.41
14	12	41,000	30,443	1,541	29,270	-11,730	11,730	107,841,864	8,836	29	51.68	0.04

Cell	Cell Formula	Equation	Copied to
C3	=0.1*B3+(1-0.1)*(C2+D2)	7.15	C4:C14
D3	=0.2*(C3-C2)+(1-0.2)*D2	7.16	D4:D14
E3	=C2+D2	7.14	E4:E14
F3	=E3-B3	7.8	F4:F14
G3	=Abs(F3)		G4:G14
H3	=Sumsq(F3:F3)/A3	7.21	H4:H14
I3	=Sum(G3:G3)/A3	7.22	I4:I14
J3	=100*(G3/B3)		J4:J14
K3	=Average(J3:J3)	7.24	K4:K14
L3	=Sum(F3:F3)/I3	7.26	L4:L14

Figure 7-9 Trend-Corrected Exponential Smoothing

Thus, using Holt's model (Equation 7.14), the forecast for the next four periods is given by the following[4].

$$F_{13} = L_{12} + T_{12} = 30,443 + 1,541 = 31,984$$
$$F_{14} = L_{12} + 2T_{12} = 30,443 + (2 \times 1,541) = 33,525$$
$$F_{15} = L_{12} + 3T_{12} = 30,443 + (3 \times 1,541) = 35,066$$
$$F_{16} = L_{12} + 4T_{12} = 30,443 + (4 \times 1,541) = 36,607$$

In this case, MAD$_{12}$ = 8,836. Thus, the estimate of standard deviation of forecast error using Holt's model with $\alpha = 0.1$ and $\beta = 0.2$ is $1.25 \times 8,836 = 11,045$. In this case, the standard deviation of forecast error relative to the size of the forecast is somewhat smaller than it was with the previous two methods. However, it is still fairly large.

[4] As a result of rounding, calculations done with only significant digits shown in the text may yield a different result. This is the case throughout the book.

TREND- AND SEASONALITY-CORRECTED EXPONENTIAL SMOOTHING (WINTER'S MODEL) The team next investigates the use of Winter's model to make the forecast. As a first step, it estimates the level and trend for Period 0, and seasonal factors for Periods 1 through $p = 4$. To start, the demand is deseasonalized (see worksheet *deseasonalized*). Then, the team estimates initial level and trend by running a regression between deseasonalized demand and time (see worksheet *winters-regression*). This information is used to estimate the seasonal factors (see worksheet *deseasonalized*). For the demand data in Figure 7-2, as discussed in Example 7-4, the team obtains the following:

$$L_0 = 18,439 \quad T_0 = 524 \quad S_1 = 0.47 \quad S_2 = 0.68 \quad S_3 = 1.17 \quad S_4 = 1.67$$

It then applies Winter's model with $\alpha = 0.05, \beta = 0.1, \gamma = 0.1$ to obtain the forecasts. All calculations are shown in Figure 7-10 (see worksheet *Figure 7-10*). The team makes forecasts using Equation 7.17, updates the level using Equation 7.18, updates the trend using Equation 7.19, and updates seasonal factors using Equation 7.20.

	A	B	C	D	E	F	G	H	I	J	K	L	M
		Demand	Level	Trend	Seasonal Factor	Forecast		Absolute Error	Mean Squared				
1	Period t	D_t	L_t	T_t	S_t	F_t	Error E_t	A_t	Error MSE_t	MAD_t	% Error	$MAPE_t$	TS_t
2			18,439	524									
3	1	8,000	18,866	514	0.47	8,913	913	913	832,857	913	11	11.41	1.00
4	2	13,000	19,367	513	0.68	13,179	179	179	432,367	546	1	6.39	2.00
5	3	23,000	19,869	512	1.17	23,260	260	260	310,720	450	1	4.64	3.00
6	4	34,000	20,380	512	1.67	34,036	36	36	233,364	347	0	3.50	4.00
7	5	10,000	20,921	515	0.47	9,723	-277	277	202,036	333	3	3.36	3.34
8	6	18,000	21,689	540	0.68	14,558	-3,442	3,442	2,143,255	851	19	5.98	-2.74
9	7	23,000	22,102	527	1.17	25,981	2,981	2,981	3,106,508	1,155	13	6.98	0.56
10	8	38,000	22,636	528	1.67	37,787	-213	213	2,723,856	1,037	1	6.18	0.42
11	9	12,000	23,291	541	0.47	10,810	-1,190	1,190	2,578,653	1,054	10	6.59	-0.72
12	10	13,000	23,577	515	0.69	16,544	3,544	3,544	3,576,894	1,303	27	8.66	2.14
13	11	32,000	24,271	533	1.16	27,849	-4,151	4,151	4,818,258	1,562	13	9.05	-0.87
14	12	41,000	24,791	532	1.67	41,442	442	442	4,432,987	1,469	1	8.39	-0.63
15	13				0.47	11,940							
16	14				0.68	17,579							
17	15				1.17	30,930							
18	16				1.67	44,928							

Cell	Cell Formula	Equation	Copied to
C3	=0.05*(B3/E3)+(1-0.05)*(C2+D2)	7.18	C4:C14
D3	=0.1*(C3-C2)+(1-0.1)*D2	7.19	D4:D14
E7	=0.1*(B3/C3)+(1-0.1)*E3	7.20	E8:E18
F3	=(C2+D2)*E3	7.17	F4:F18
G3	=F3-B3	7.8	G4:G14
H3	=Abs(G3)		H4:H14
I3	=Sumsq(G3:G3)/A3	7.21	I4:I14
J3	=Sum(H3:H3)/A3	7.22	J4:J14
K3	=100*(H3/B3)		K4:K14
L3	=Average(K3:K3)	7.24	L4:L14
M3	=Sum(G3:G3)/J3	7.26	M4:M14

Figure 7-10 Trend- and Seasonality-Corrected Exponential Smoothing

In this case, the MAD of 1,469 and MAPE of 8 percent are significantly lower than those obtained with any of the other methods. From Figure 7-10, observe that

$$L_{12} = 24{,}791 \quad T_{12} = 532 \quad S_{13} = 0.47 \quad S_{14} = 0.68 \quad S_{15} = 1.17 \quad S_{16} = 1.67$$

Using Winter's model (Equation 7.17), the forecast for the next four periods is

$$F_{13} = (L_{12} + T_{12})S_{13} = (24{,}791 + 532) \times 0.47 = 11{,}902$$
$$F_{14} = (L_{12} + 2T_{12})S_{14} = (24{,}791 + 2 \times 532) \times 0.68 = 17{,}581$$
$$F_{15} = (L_{12} + 3T_{12})S_{15} = (24{,}791 + 3 \times 532) \times 1.17 = 30{,}873$$
$$F_{16} = (L_{12} + 4T_{12})S_{16} = (24{,}791 + 4 \times 532) \times 1.67 = 44{,}955$$

In this case, $MAD_{12} = 1{,}469$. Thus, the estimate of standard deviation of forecast error using Winter's model with $\alpha = 0.05$, $\beta = 0.1$, and $\gamma = 0.1$ is $1.25 \times 1{,}469 = 1{,}836$. In this case, the standard deviation of forecast error relative to the demand forecast is much smaller than with the other methods.

The team compiles the error estimates for the four forecasting methods as shown in Table 7-2.

Based on the error information in Table 7-2, the forecasting team decides to use Winter's model. It is not surprising that Winter's model results in the most accurate forecast, because the demand data have both a growth trend as well as seasonality. Using Winter's model, the team forecasts the following demand for the coming four quarters:

Second Quarter, Year 4: 11,902

Third Quarter, Year 4: 17,581

Fourth Quarter, Year 4: 30,873

First Quarter, Year 5: 44,955

The standard deviation of forecast error is 1,836.

The Role of Software Tools in Forecasting

There is a natural role for software in forecasting, given the large amount of data involved, the frequency with which forecasting is performed, and the importance of getting the highest quality results possible. Whereas the use of Excel is effective when learning forecasting or quickly deciding which forecasting model to use, it is often better to use software packages for regular forecasting in a company. A good forecasting package provides forecasts across a wide range of products that are updated in real time by incorporating any new demand information. This helps firms respond quickly to changes in the marketplace and avoid the costs of a delayed reaction. Good demand planning modules link not only to customer orders but often directly to customer sales information as well, thus incorporating the most current data into the demand forecast. A positive outcome of the investment in ERP systems has been a significant improvement in supply chain transparency and data integration, thus allowing potentially better forecasts. Although this technical improvement can help produce better forecasts, firms must develop the organizational capabilities required to take advantage of this improvement.

TABLE 7-2 Error Estimates for Tahoe Salt Forecasting

Forecasting Method	MAD	MAPE (%)	TS Range
Four-period moving average	9,719	49	−1.52 to 2.21
Simple exponential smoothing	10,208	59	−1.38 to 2.15
Holt's model	8,836	52	−2.15 to 2.00
Winter's model	1,469	8	−2.74 to 4.00

Besides providing a rich library of forecasting methodologies, a good *demand planning module* should provide support in helping select the right forecasting model for the given demand pattern. This has become particularly important as the available library of forecasting methodologies has grown.

As the name *demand planning* suggests, these modules facilitate the shaping of demand. Good demand planning modules contain tools to perform what-if analysis regarding the impact of potential changes in prices on demand. These tools help analyze the impact of promotions on demand and can be used to determine the extent and timing of promotions. This link is discussed in greater detail in Chapter 9 under sales and operations planning.

An important development is the use of demand correlated data (e.g. price, weather, other purchases, social data) to improve forecast accuracy or, in some cases, spur demand. In a well-publicized case, Target predicted that women were pregnant based on other products they were purchasing. A purchase of "cocoa-butter lotion, a purse large enough to double as a diaper bag, zinc and magnesium supplements and a bright blue rug" was a strong predictor of the woman's pregnancy.[5] Target then used this information to send suitable coupons to entice these women or their husbands to visit Target and purchase baby-related products. Sophisticated systems such as this can be used to not only improve forecast accuracy but also identify suitable marketing opportunities to spur future demand.

Keep in mind that none of these tools is foolproof. Forecasts are virtually always inaccurate. A good forecasting system should help track historical forecast errors so they can be incorporated into future decisions. A well-structured forecast, along with a measure of error, can significantly improve decision making. Even with all these sophisticated tools, sometimes it is better to rely on human intuition in forecasting. One of the pitfalls of these forecasting tools is relying on them too much, which eliminates the human element in forecasting. Use the forecasts and the value they deliver, but remember that they cannot assess some of the more qualitative aspects about future demand that you may be able to do on your own.

A detailed list of forecasting software vendors is reported in the OR/MS Today forecasting software survey, and a discussion of each vendor is available at http://www.orms-today.org/surveys/FSS/fss-fr.html.

SUMMARY OF LEARNING OBJECTIVE 5

Given the repetitive nature of time-series forecasting methods, they can easily be modeled in Microsoft Excel with simple formulae that are copied across rows or columns. For regular forecasting at companies, however, it may be more effective to select among a wide variety of software packages available today.

DISCUSSION QUESTIONS

1. Is Dell adapting the "pull" or "push" processes, or a combination of the two, in its supply chain demand forecasting?
2. Briefly describe the major characteristics of forecasts in supply chain management.
3. What is the role of forecasting in the supply chain of a multinational home furnishing company such as IKEA?
4. Discuss any four forecasting methods. Which one is more suitable in cold (temperature-controlled) supply chain management?
5. As a supply chain manager, do you need to forecast the random component of the observed demand for products that displays seasonal demand?
6. Identify any six factors that should be taken into consideration when implementing demand forecasting in a department store.

7. List the five basic steps of demand forecasting in supply chain management. Which step is more important?
8. What different situations need to be considered when applying the following forecasting methods: moving average; simple exponential smoothing; Holt's model; and Winter's model?
9. What is a forecasting error? How can a manager use this information?
10. What error forecasting measures are associated with moving average; simple exponential smoothing; Holt's model; and Winter's models? How can the measures be grouped according to their use?

[5] Charles Duhigg, "How Companies Learn Your Secrets," *New York Times*, February 16, 2012.

EXERCISES

1. Consider monthly demand for the ABC Corporation, as shown in Table 7-3. Forecast the monthly demand for Year 6 using the static method for forecasting. Evaluate the bias, TS, MAD, MAPE, and MSE. Evaluate the quality of the forecast.

TABLE 7-3 Monthly Demand for ABC Corporation

Sales	Year 1	Year 2	Year 3	Year 4	Year 5
January	2,000	3,000	2,000	5,000	5,000
February	3,000	4,000	5,000	4,000	2,000
March	3,000	3,000	6,000	4,000	3,000
April	5,000	5,000	3,000	2,000	2,000
May	4,000	5,000	4,000	5,000	7,000
June	6,000	7,000	6,000	7,000	6,000
July	7,000	3,000	7,000	12,000	8,000
August	6,000	8,000	10,000	14,000	10,000
September	10,000	12,000	15,000	16,000	18,000
October	12,000	11,000	15,000	16,000	20,000
November	14,000	16,000	18,000	20,000	22,000
December	8,000	10,000	8,000	12,000	8,000
Total	80,000	87,000	99,000	117,000	111,000

2. Weekly demand figures at Mamma's Pizza are as shown. Estimate demand for the next 4 weeks using a 4-week moving average as well as simple exponential smoothing with $\alpha = 0.1$. Evaluate the MAD, MAPE, MSE, bias, and TS in each case. Which of the two methods do you prefer? Why?

Week	Demand ($)
1	110
2	118
3	119
4	134
5	92
6	115
7	90
8	106
9	118
10	106
11	95
12	93

3. Quarterly demand for vegetables at a wholesaler are as shown. Forecast quarterly demand for year 5 using simple exponential smoothing with $\alpha = 0.1$ as well as Holt's model with $\alpha = 0.1$ and $\beta = 0.1$. Which of the two methods do you prefer? Why?

Year	Quarter	Demand ($000)
1	I	80
	II	96
	III	103
	IV	123
2	I	120
	II	109
	III	145
	IV	120
3	I	141
	II	128
	III	143
	IV	139
4	I	142
	II	140
	III	161
	IV	170

4. Consider monthly demand for the ABC Corporation as shown in Table 7-3. Forecast the monthly demand for Year 6 using moving average, simple exponential smoothing, Holt's model, and Winter's model. In each case, evaluate the bias, TS, MAD, MAPE, and MSE. Which forecasting method do you prefer? Why?

5. For the Mamma's Pizza data in Exercise 2, compare the performance of simple exponential smoothing with $\alpha = 0.1$ and $\alpha = 0.9$. What difference in forecasts do you observe? Which of the two smoothing constants do you prefer?

6. Monthly demand at Phones Direct for the latest Samsung Galaxy phone are as shown. Estimate demand for the next two months using simple exponential smoothing with $\alpha = 0.2$ and Holt's model with $\alpha = 0.08$ and $\beta = 0.15$. For the simple exponential smoothing model, use the level at Period 0 to be $L_0 = 2,066$ (the average demand over the 12 months). For Holt's model, use level at Period 0 to be $L_0 = 1,197$ and the trend in Period 0 to be $T_0 = 134$ (both are obtained through regression). Evaluate the MAD, MAPE, MSE, bias, and TS in each case. Which of the two methods do you prefer? Why?

Month	Demand (units)
1	1,300
2	1,458
3	1,555
4	1,753
5	1,901
6	2,013
7	2,136
8	2,325
9	2,400
10	2,568
11	2,630
12	2,750

7. Using the Phones Direct data in Exercise 6, repeat Holt's model with $\alpha = 0.4$ and $\beta = 0.5$. Compare the performance of Holt's model with $\alpha = 0.08$ and $\beta = 0.15$. Which combination of smoothing constraints do you prefer? Why?

8. The weekly demand for a Bluetooth speaker at an electronic retailer is as shown. Estimate demand for the next four weeks (11 to 14) using a five-week moving average, as well as simple exponential smoothing with $\alpha = 0.15$. Evaluate the MAD, MAPE, MSE, bias, and TS in each case. Which of the two methods do you prefer? Why?

Week	Demand (units)
1	450
2	475
3	490
4	495

Week	Demand (units)
5	470
6	490
7	520
8	483
9	535
10	580

9. Quarterly demand for smartphones at a retailer is as shown. After obtaining initial estimates for level, trend, and seasonal factors, forecast quarterly demand for year 5 using Winter's model with $\alpha = 0.05$, $\beta = 0.10$, and $\gamma = 0.15$. Evaluate the MAD, MAPE, MSE, bias, and TS for the forecast. Can you find values of α, β, γ that result in a lower MAD or MSE?

Year	Quarter	Demand
1	I	513
	II	932
	III	1,509
	IV	1,902
2	I	693
	II	1,163
	III	1,857
	IV	2,469
3	I	846
	II	1,439
	III	2,271
	IV	3,079
4	I	1,070
	II	1,751
	III	2,785
	IV	3,613

10. Quarterly demand for dishwashers at a white goods retailer is as shown. After obtaining initial estimates for level, trend, and seasonal factors, forecast quarterly demand for year 5 using Winter's model with $\alpha = 0.10$, $\beta = 0.10$, and $\gamma = 0.10$. Evaluate the MAD, MAPE, MSE, bias, and TS for the forecast. Can you find values of α, β, γ that result in a lower MAD or MSE?

Year	Quarter	Demand
1	I	1,934
	II	1,276
	III	3,991
	IV	5,632

Year	Quarter	Demand
2	I	4,862
	II	1,698
	III	7,104
	IV	9,939
3	I	6,129
	II	3,318

Year	Quarter	Demand
	III	9,260
	IV	12,418
4	I	7,960
	II	5,459
	III	10,990
	IV	13,483

BIBLIOGRAPHY

Bernstein, Peter L., and Theodore H. Silbert. "Are Economic Forecasters Worth Listening To?" *Harvard Business Review* (September–October 1984): 2–8.

Box, George E. P., and Gwilym M. Jenkins. *Time Series Analysis: Forecasting and Control.* Oakland, CA: Holden-Day, 1976.

Chambers, John C., Satinder K. Mullick, and Donald D. Smith."How to Choose the Right Forecasting Technique." *Harvard Business Review* (July–August 1971): 45–74.

Forecasting with Regression Analysis. Cambridge, MA: Harvard Business School Note #9–894–007, 1994.

Fry, Chris, and Vijay Mehrotra. "Forecasting Software Survey 2016" *ORMS Today* (June 2016): 52–61. Software survey available at http://www.lionhrtpub.com/orms/surveys/FSS/fss-fr.html.

Georgoff, David M., and Robert G. Murdick."Manager's Guide to Forecasting." *Harvard Business Review* (January–February 1986): 2–9.

Gilliland, Michael. "Is Forecasting a Waste of Time?" *Supply Chain Management Review* (July–August 2002): 16–23.

McClain, John O. "Restarting a Forecasting System When Demand Suddenly Changes." *Journal of Operations Management* (October 1981): 53–61.

Makridakis, S., A. Andersen, R. Carbone, R. Fildes, M. Hibon, R. Lewandowski, J. Newton, E. Parzen, and R. Winkler. "The Accuracy of Extrapolation (Time Series) Methods: Results of a Forecasting Competition." *Journal of Forecasting* (April–June 1982): 111–153.

Makridakis, Spyros, and Steven C. Wheelwright. *Forecasting Methods for Management.* New York: Wiley, 1989.

Saffo, Paul. "Six Rules of Effective Forecasting." *Harvard Business Review* (July-August 2007): 122–131.

Silver, Nate. *The Signal and the Noise: Why So Many Predictions Fail – But Some Don't.* New York: Penguin, 2012.

CASE STUDY

Specialty Packaging Corporation

Julie Williams had a lot on her mind when she left the conference room at Specialty Packaging Corporation (SPC). Her divisional manager had informed her that she would be assigned to a team consisting of SPC's marketing vice president and staff members from their key customers. The goal of this team was to improve supply chain performance, as SPC had been unable to meet demand effectively over the previous several years. This often left SPC's customers scrambling to meet new client demands. Julie had little contact with SPC's customers and wondered how she would add value to this process. She was told by her division manager that the team's first task was to establish a collaborative forecast using data from both SPC and its customers. This forecast would serve as the basis for improving the firm's performance, as managers could use this more accurate forecast for their production planning. Improved forecasts would allow SPC to improve delivery performance.

SPC

SPC turns polystyrene resin into recyclable/disposable containers for the food industry. Polystyrene is purchased as a commodity in the form of resin pellets. The resin is unloaded from bulk rail containers or overland trailers into storage silos. Making the food containers is a two-step process. First, resin is conveyed to an extruder, which converts it into a polystyrene sheet that is wound into rolls. The plastic comes in two forms—clear and

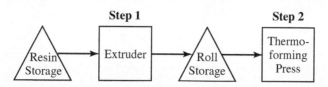

Figure 7-11 Manufacturing Process at SPC

black. The rolls are either used immediately to make containers or put into storage. Second, the rolls are loaded onto thermoforming presses, which form the sheet into containers and trim the containers from the sheet. The two manufacturing steps are shown in Figure 7-11.

Over the past five years, the plastic packaging business has grown steadily. Demand for containers made from clear plastic comes from grocery stores, bakeries, and restaurants. Caterers and grocery stores use the black plastic trays as packaging and serving trays. Demand for clear plastic containers peaks in the summer months, whereas demand for black plastic containers peaks in the fall. Capacity on the extruders is not sufficient to cover demand for sheets during the peak seasons. As a result, the plant is forced to build inventory of each type of sheet in anticipation of future demand.

Table 7-4 and Figure 7-12 display historical quarterly demand for each of the two types of containers (clear and black). The team modified SPC's sales data by accounting for lost sales to obtain true demand data. Without the customers involved in this team, SPC would never have known this information, as the company did not keep track of lost orders.

Forecasting

As a first step in the team's decision making, it wants to forecast quarterly demand for each of the two types of containers for years 6 to 8. Based on historical trends, demand is expected to continue to grow until year 8, after which it is expected to plateau. Julie must select the appropriate forecasting method and estimate the likely forecast error. Which method should she choose? Why? Using the method selected, forecast demand for years 6 to 8.

TABLE 7-4 Quarterly Historical Demand for Clear and Black Plastic Containers

Year	Quarter	Black Plastic Demand (000 lb)	Clear Plastic Demand (000 lb)
1	I	2,250	3,200
	II	1,737	7,658
	III	2,412	4,420
	IV	7,269	2,384
2	I	3,514	3,654
	II	2,143	8,680
	III	3,459	5,695
	IV	7,056	1,953
3	I	4,120	4,742
	II	2,766	13,673
	III	2,556	6,640
	IV	8,253	2,737
4	I	5,491	3,486

Year	Quarter	Black Plastic Demand (000 lb)	Clear Plastic Demand (000 lb)
	II	4,382	13,186
	III	4,315	5,448
	IV	12,035	3,485
5	I	5,648	7,728
	II	3,696	16,591
	III	4,843	8,236
	IV	13,097	3,316

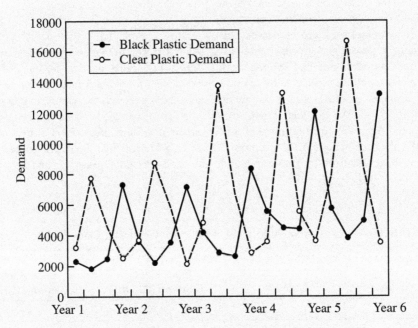

Figure 7-12 Plot of Quarterly Demand for Clear and Black
Plastic Containers

CHAPTER

8

Aggregate Planning in a Supply Chain

LEARNING OBJECTIVES

After reading this chapter, you will be able to

8.1 Describe aggregate planning and its importance as a supply chain activity.

8.2 Explain the basic trade-offs to consider when creating an aggregate plan.

8.3 Model and solve the aggregate planning problem as a linear program.

8.4 Formulate and solve basic aggregate planning problems using Microsoft Excel.

In this chapter, we discuss how aggregate planning is used to make decisions about production, outsourcing, inventory, and backlogs in a supply chain. We identify the information required to produce an aggregate plan and outline the basic trade-offs that must be made to create an optimal aggregate plan. We model the aggregate planning problem as a linear program and describe how the problem can be formulated and solved using Microsoft Excel.

AGGREGATE PLANNING AND ITS ROLE IN A SUPPLY CHAIN

Imagine a world in which manufacturing, transportation, warehousing, and even information capacity are all limitless and free. Imagine lead times of zero, allowing goods to be produced and delivered instantaneously. In this world, there is no need to plan in anticipation of demand, because whenever a customer demands a product, the demand is instantly satisfied. In this world, aggregate planning plays no role.

In the real world, however, capacity has a cost, and lead times are often long. Therefore, companies must make decisions regarding capacity levels, production levels, outsourcing, and promotions well before demand is known. A company must anticipate demand and determine, in advance of that demand, how to meet it. Should a company invest in a plant with large capacity that is able to produce enough to satisfy demand even in the busiest months? Or should a company build a smaller plant but incur the costs of holding inventory built during slow periods in anticipation of demand in later months? These are the types of questions that aggregate planning helps companies answer.

8.1 Describe *aggregate planning and its importance as a supply chain activity.*

Aggregate planning is a process by which a company determines planned levels of capacity, production, subcontracting, inventory, stockouts, and even pricing over a specified time horizon to maximize profits. The aggregate planning problem can formally be stated as follows:

Given the demand forecast for each period in the planning horizon, determine the production level, inventory level, capacity level (internal and outsourced), and any backlogs (unmet demand) for each period that maximize the firm's profit over the planning horizon.

Aggregate planning, as the name suggests, solves problems involving aggregate decisions such as the total production level in a plant for a given month, but it does so without determining the quantity of each individual stock-keeping unit (SKU) that will be produced. This level of detail makes aggregate planning a useful tool for thinking about decisions with an intermediate time frame of between roughly 3 and 18 months. In this time frame, it is too early to determine production levels by SKU, but it is also generally too late to arrange for additional capacity. Therefore, aggregate planning answers the question: How should a firm best utilize the facilities that it currently has?

To be effective, aggregate planning requires inputs from all stages of the supply chain, and its results have a tremendous impact on supply chain performance. As we saw in Chapter 7, forecasts are created by multiple supply chain enterprises and are an important input for aggregate planning. In addition, many constraints that are key inputs to aggregate planning come from supply chain partners outside the enterprise. Without these inputs from both up and down the supply chain, aggregate planning cannot realize its full potential to create value. The output from aggregate planning is also of value to both upstream and downstream partners. Production plans for a firm define demand for suppliers and establish supply constraints for customers. This chapter is meant to create a foundation for using aggregate planning both solely within an enterprise as well as across the entire supply chain. The supply chain implications of aggregate planning will become even clearer in Chapter 9, where we discuss sales and operations planning.

As an example, consider how a premium paper supply chain uses aggregate planning to maximize profit. Many types of paper mills face seasonal demand that ripples up from customers to printers to distributors and, finally, to the manufacturers. Many types of premium paper have demand peaks in the spring, when annual reports are printed, and in the fall, when new-car brochures are released. Building a mill with capacity to meet demand in the spring and fall on an as-needed basis is too costly, because of the high cost of mill capacity. On the other side of the supply chain, premium papers often require special additives and coatings that may be in short supply. The paper manufacturer must deal with these constraints and maximize profit around them. The mills use aggregate planning to determine production levels and inventory levels that they should build up in the slower months for sale in the spring and fall, when demand is greater than the mill's capacity. By taking into account the inputs from throughout the supply chain, aggregate planning allows the mill and the supply chain to maximize profit.

Surprisingly, many companies do not create aggregate plans and instead rely solely on orders from their customers to determine their production schedules. These orders are driven either by actual demand or through inventory management algorithms. If a company has no trouble meeting demand efficiently this way, then the lack of aggregate planning may not harm the company significantly. However, when utilization becomes high and capacity is an issue, relying on orders to set the production schedule can lead to shortages and delays. When utilization is high, aggregate planning helps the firm effectively meet the forecasted demand.

To create an aggregate plan, a company must specify the planning horizon. A *planning horizon* is the time period over which the aggregate plan is to produce a solution—usually between 3 and 18 months. A company must also specify the duration of each period within the planning horizon (e.g., weeks, months, or quarters). In general, aggregate planning takes place over months or quarters. Next, a company specifies key information required to produce an aggregate plan and to make the decisions for which the aggregate plan will develop recommen-

dations. In this section, we specify the information required and the recommendations for a generic aggregate planning problem. The model we propose in the next section is flexible enough to accommodate situation-specific requirements.

An aggregate planner requires the following information:

- Aggregate demand forecast F_t for each Period t in a planning horizon that extends over T periods
- Production costs
 - Labor costs: regular time (\$/hour), and overtime costs (\$/hour)
 - Cost of subcontracting production (\$/unit or \$/hour)
 - Cost of changing capacity; specifically, cost of hiring/laying off workforce (\$/worker) and cost of adding or reducing machine capacity (\$/machine)
- Labor/machine hours required per unit
- Inventory holding cost (\$/unit/period)
- Stockout or backlog cost (\$/unit/period)
- Constraints
 - Limits on overtime
 - Limits on layoffs
 - Limits on capital available
 - Limits on stockouts and backlogs
 - Constraints from suppliers to the enterprise

Using this information, a company makes the following determinations through aggregate planning:

Production quantity from regular time, overtime, and subcontracted time: used to determine number of workers and supplier purchase levels

Inventory held: used to determine the warehouse space and working capital required

Backlog/stockout quantity: used to determine customer service levels

Workforce hired/laid off: used to determine any labor issues likely to be encountered

Machine capacity increase/decrease: used to determine whether new production equipment should be purchased or available equipment idled

The aggregate plan serves as a broad blueprint for operations and establishes the parameters within which short-term production and distribution decisions are made. As mentioned earlier, the entire supply chain should be involved with the planning process. If a manufacturer has planned an increase in production over a given time period, the supplier, transporter, and warehouse must be aware of this plan and incorporate the increase into their own plans. Ideally, all stages of the supply chain should work together on an aggregate plan that optimizes supply chain performance. If each stage develops its own aggregate plan independently, it is extremely unlikely that all the plans will mesh in a coordinated manner. This lack of coordination results in shortages or oversupply in the supply chain. Therefore, it is important to form aggregate plans over a wide scope of the supply chain. Work with downstream partners to produce forecasts, with upstream partners to determine constraints, and with any other supply chain entities that can improve the quality of the inputs into the aggregate plan. The plan is only as good as the quality of the inputs, so using the supply chain to increase the quality of the inputs will greatly improve the quality of the aggregate plan. Also make sure to communicate the aggregate plan to all supply chain partners who will be affected by it.

The quality of an aggregate plan has a significant impact on the profitability of a firm. A poor aggregate plan can result in lost sales and lost profits if the available inventory and capacity are unable to meet demand. A poor aggregate plan may also result in a large amount of excess inventory and capacity, thereby raising costs. Therefore, aggregate planning is an important tool to optimally match supply and demand.

SUMMARY OF LEARNING OBJECTIVE 1

To create an aggregate plan, a planner needs a demand forecast, cost and production information, and any supply constraints. The demand forecast consists of an estimate of demand for each period of time in the planning horizon. The production and cost data consist of capacity levels and costs to raise and lower them, production costs, costs to store the product, costs of stocking out the product, and any restrictions that limit these factors. Supply constraints determine limits on outsourcing, overtime, or materials. The aggregate plan then determines capacity, production, and inventory decisions over the next 3 to 18 months. Good aggregate planning is done in collaboration with both customers and suppliers because accurate input is required from both stages. The quality of these inputs, in terms of both the demand forecast to be met and the constraints to be dealt with, determines the quality of the aggregate plan. The results of the aggregate plan must also be shared across the supply chain because they influence activities for both customers and suppliers. For suppliers, the aggregate plan determines anticipated orders; for customers, the aggregate plan determines planned supply.

8.2 *Explain the basic trade-offs to consider when creating an aggregate plan.*

THE BASIC TRADEOFFS IN AGGREGATE PLANNING

The aggregate planner must make trade-offs among capacity, inventory, and backlog costs. An aggregate plan that increases one of these costs typically results in reduction of the other two. In this sense, the costs represent a trade-off: To lower inventory cost, a planner must invest in capacity or delay delivery to the customer. Thus, the planner trades inventory cost for capacity or backlog cost. Arriving at the most profitable combination of trade-offs is the goal of aggregate planning. Given that demand varies over time, the relative level of the three costs leads to one of them being the key lever the planner uses to maximize profits. If the cost of varying capacity is low, a company may not need to build inventory or carry backlogs. If the cost of varying capacity is high, a company may compensate by building some inventory and carrying some backlogs from peak demand periods to off-peak demand periods. Therefore, the fundamental tradeoffs available to a planner are among the following:

- Capacity (regular time, overtime, subcontracted)
- Inventory
- Backlog/lost sales because of delay

There are essentially three distinct aggregate planning strategies for achieving balance among these costs. These strategies involve trade-offs among capital investment, workforce size, work hours, inventory, and backlogs/lost sales. Most strategies that a planner actually uses are a combination of these three and are referred to as *tailored* or *hybrid strategies*. The three strategies are as follows:

1. *Chase strategy—using capacity as the lever:* With this strategy, the production rate is synchronized with the demand rate by varying machine capacity or hiring and laying off employees as the demand rate varies. In practice, achieving this synchronization can be problematic because of the difficulty of varying capacity and workforce on short notice. This strategy can be expensive to implement if the cost of varying machine or labor capacity over time is high. It can also have a significant negative impact on the morale of the workforce. The chase strategy results in low levels of inventory in the supply chain and high levels of change in capacity and workforce. It should be used when the cost of carrying inventory is high and costs to change levels of machine and labor capacity are low.

2. *Flexibility strategy—using utilization as the lever:* This strategy may be used if there is excess machine capacity (i.e., if machines are not used 24 hours a day, seven days a week) and the workforce shows scheduling flexibility. In this case, the workforce (capacity) is

kept stable, but the number of hours worked is varied over time in an effort to synchronize production with demand. A planner can use variable amounts of overtime or a flexible schedule to achieve this synchronization. Although this strategy does require that the workforce be flexible, it avoids some of the problems associated with the chase strategy—most notably, changing the size of the workforce. This strategy results in low levels of inventory but with lower average machine utilization. It should be used when inventory carrying costs are relatively high and machine capacity is relatively inexpensive.

3. *Level strategy—using inventory as the lever:* With this strategy, a stable machine capacity and workforce are maintained with a constant output rate. Shortages and surpluses result in inventory levels fluctuating over time. In this case, production is not synchronized with demand. Either inventories are built up in anticipation of future demand or backlogs are carried over from high- to low-demand periods. Employees benefit from stable working conditions. A drawback associated with this strategy is that large inventories may accumulate and customer orders may be delayed. This strategy keeps capacity and costs of changing capacity relatively low. It should be used when inventory carrying and backlog costs are relatively low.

In practice, a planner is most likely to come up with a tailored or hybrid strategy that combines aspects of all three approaches.

SUMMARY OF LEARNING OBJECTIVE 2

The basic trade-offs in aggregate planning involve balancing the cost of capacity, the cost of inventory, and the cost of stockouts to maximize profitability. Increasing any one of the three allows the planner to lower the other two.

AGGREGATE PLANNING USING LINEAR PROGRAMMING

8.3 Model and solve the aggregate planning problem as a linear program.

Given that the goal of aggregate planning is to maximize profits while respecting supply chain constraints, linear programming is an effective methodology to both model and solve aggregate planning problems. We illustrate aggregate planning methodologies using Red Tomato Tools, a small manufacturer of gardening equipment with manufacturing facilities in Mexico. Red Tomato's products are sold through retailers in the United States. Red Tomato's operations consist of the assembly of purchased parts into gardening tools. Because of the limited equipment and space required for its assembly operations, Red Tomato's capacity is determined mainly by the size of its workforce.

Identifying Aggregate Units of Production

An important first step in aggregate planning is the identification of a suitable aggregate unit of production. When planning is done at the aggregate level, it is important that the aggregate unit be identified in a way that when the final master production schedule is built (this has to be at the disaggregate product level), the results of the aggregate plan reflect approximately what can be accomplished in practice. Given that the bottleneck is likely to be the most constraining area in any manufacturing facility, it is important to focus on the bottleneck when selecting the aggregate unit and identifying capacity as well as production times. When evaluating production times, it is also important to account for activities—such as setups and maintenance—that use up capacity but do not result in any production. Otherwise, the aggregate plan will overestimate the production capacity available, resulting in a plan that cannot be implemented in practice. We now discuss a simple approach that can be used to identify aggregate units and also to evaluate costs, revenues, and times for this aggregate unit.

Red Tomato makes six products at its manufacturing plant. The costs, revenues, production times, setup times, and historical batch sizes of production for each product are as shown in Table 8-1.

TABLE 8-1 Costs, Revenues, and Times at Red Tomato Tools

Product	Material Cost/ Unit ($)	Revenue/ Unit ($)	Setup Time/ Batch (hour)	Average Batch Size	Production Time/Unit (hour)	Net Production Time/Unit (hour)	Percentage Share of Units Sold
A	15	54	8	50	5.60	5.76	10
B	7	30	6	150	3.00	3.04	25
C	9	39	8	100	3.80	3.88	20
D	12	49	10	50	4.80	5.00	10
E	9	36	6	100	3.60	3.66	20
F	13	48	5	75	4.30	4.37	15

In Table 8-1 (see spreadsheet *Chapter 8–Table 8-1*), the net production time per unit is obtained by adding the changeover time allocated to each unit and the production time (setup time/batch size + production time). Thus, the net production time/unit for Product A is obtained as 8/50 + 5.60 = 5.76 hours.

A simple approach to defining the aggregate unit is based on the weighted average of the percentage of sales represented by each product. Such an approach is meaningful if management is relatively confident of the mix of sales and all the products use roughly the same set of resources at a plant. Taking this approach, the material cost per aggregate unit is obtained as $(15 \times 0.10) + (7 \times 0.25) + (9 \times 0.20) + (12 \times 0.10) + (9 \times 0.20) + (13 \times 0.15) = \10. Using a similar evaluation, we obtain that the revenue per aggregate unit = $40 and the net production time per aggregate unit = 4.00 hours.

Other potential aggregate units could be tons of output (likely to be suitable for continuous flows, such as gasoline or paper) or dollars of sales. For example, a paper mill might produce papers of different thickness and quality. If tons of output is used as the aggregate unit, all capacity, cost, and revenue calculations should account for the product mix.

Demand and Costs at Red Tomato Tools

The demand for Red Tomato's gardening tools from consumers is highly seasonal, peaking in the spring as people plant their gardens. This seasonal demand ripples up the supply chain from the retailer to Red Tomato, the manufacturer. The options Red Tomato has for handling the seasonality are adding workers during the peak season, subcontracting out some of the work, building up inventory during the slow months, or building up a backlog of orders that will be delivered late to customers. To determine how to best use these options through an aggregate plan, Red Tomato's vice president of supply chain starts with the first task—building a demand forecast. Although Red Tomato could attempt to forecast this demand itself, a much more accurate forecast comes from a collaborative process used by both Red Tomato and its retailers to produce the forecast shown in Table 8-2. It is important that this demand account for the product mix that is expected to sell and be in terms of aggregate units defined earlier.

Red Tomato sells each (aggregate) tool through retailers for $40. The company has a starting inventory in January of 1,000 tools. At the beginning of January, the company has a workforce of 80 employees. The plant has a total of 20 working days in each month, and each employee earns $4 per hour regular time. Each employee works eight hours per day on straight time and the rest on overtime. As discussed previously, the capacity of the production operation is determined primarily by the total labor hours worked. Therefore, machine capacity does not limit the capacity of the production operation. Because of labor rules, no employee works more than 10 hours of overtime per month. The various costs are shown in Table 8-3. It is important that the costs and labor hours are measured in aggregate units, as discussed earlier.

TABLE 8-2 Demand Forecast at Red Tomato Tools

Month	Demand Forecast
January	1,600
February	3,000
March	3,200
April	3,800
May	2,200
June	2,200

TABLE 8-3 Costs for Red Tomato

Item	Cost
Material cost	$10/unit
Inventory holding cost	$2/unit/month
Marginal cost of stockout/backlog	$5/unit/month
Hiring and training costs	$300/worker
Layoff cost	$500/worker
Labor hours required	4/unit
Regular time cost	$4/hour
Overtime cost	$6/hour
Cost of subcontracting	$30/unit

Currently, Red Tomato has no limits on subcontracting, inventories, and stockouts/back-log. All stockouts are backlogged and supplied from the following months' production. Inventory costs are incurred on the ending inventory in the month. The supply chain manager's goal is to obtain the optimal aggregate plan that allows Red Tomato to end June with at least 500 units (i.e., no stockouts at the end of June and at least 500 units in inventory).

The optimal aggregate plan is one that results in the highest profit over the 6-month planning horizon. For now, given Red Tomato's desire for a high level of customer service, assume all demand is to be met, although it can be met late. Therefore, the revenues earned over the planning horizon are fixed. As a result, minimizing cost over the planning horizon is the same as maximizing profit. In many instances, a company has the option of not meeting certain demand, or price itself may be a variable that a company must determine based on the aggregate plan. In such a scenario, minimizing cost is not equivalent to maximizing profits.

Next, we model aggregate planning as a linear programming problem. (Readers who are unfamiliar with linear programming can directly jump to Section 8.4 where the problem is modeled using Excel.)

A Linear Programming Model for Aggregate Planning at Red Tomato Tools

As we discussed earlier, the goal of aggregate planning is to maximize profit while meeting demand. Every company, in its effort to meet customer demand, faces certain constraints, such as the capacity of its facilities or a supplier's ability to deliver a component. A highly effective tool for a company to use when it tries to maximize profits while being subjected to a series of constraints is linear programming. *Linear programming* finds the solution that creates the highest profit while satisfying the constraints that the company faces. We now illustrate a linear programming approach to aggregate planning using Red Tomato Tools.

DECISION VARIABLES The first step in constructing an aggregate planning model is to identify the set of decision variables whose values are to be determined as part of the aggregate plan. For Red Tomato, the following decision variables are defined for the aggregate planning model:

W_t = workforce size for Month t, $t = 1, \ldots, 6$

H_t = number of employees hired at the beginning of Month t, $t = 1, \ldots, 6$

L_t = number of employees laid off at the beginning of Month t, $t = 1, \ldots, 6$

P_t = number of units produced in Month t, $t = 1, \ldots, 6$

I_t = inventory at the end of Month t, $t = 1, \ldots, 6$

S_t = number of units stocked out/backlogged at the end of Month t, $t = 1, \ldots, 6$

C_t = number of units subcontracted for Month t, $t = 1, \ldots, 6$

O_t = number of overtime hours worked in Month t, $t = 1, \ldots, 6$

The next step in constructing an aggregate planning model is to define the objective function.

OBJECTIVE FUNCTION Denote the demand in Period t by D_t. The values of D_t are as specified by the demand forecast in Table 8-2. The objective function is to minimize the total cost (equivalent to maximizing total profit as all demand is to be satisfied) incurred during the planning horizon. The cost incurred has the following components:

- Regular-time labor cost
- Overtime labor cost
- Cost of hiring and layoffs
- Cost of holding inventory
- Cost of stocking out
- Cost of subcontracting
- Material cost

These costs are evaluated as follows:

1. **Regular-time labor cost.** Recall that workers are paid a regular-time wage of $640 ($4/hour × 8 hours/day × 20 days/month) per month. Because W_t is the number of workers in Period t, the regular-time labor cost over the planning horizon is given by

$$\text{Regular-time labor cost} = \sum_{t=1}^{6} 640W_t$$

2. **Overtime labor cost.** As overtime labor cost is $6 per hour (see Table 8-3) and O_t represents the number of overtime hours worked in Period t, the overtime cost over the planning horizon is

$$\text{Overtime labor cost} = \sum_{t=1}^{6} 60_t$$

3. **Cost of hiring and layoffs.** The cost of hiring a worker is $300 and the cost of laying off a worker is $500 (see Table 8-3). H_t and L_t represent the number hired and the number laid off, respectively, in Period t. Thus, the cost of hiring and layoff is given by

$$\text{Cost of hiring and layoff} = \sum_{t=1}^{6} 300H_t + \sum_{t=1}^{6} 500L_t$$

4. **Cost of inventory and stockout.** The cost of carrying inventory is $2 per unit per month, and the cost of stocking out is $5 per unit per month (see Table 8-3). I_t and S_t represent the

units in inventory and the units stocked out, respectively, in Period t. Thus, the cost of holding inventory and stocking out is

$$\text{Cost of holding inventory and stocking out} = \sum_{t=1}^{6} 2I_t + \sum_{t=1}^{6} 5S_t$$

5. **Cost of materials and subcontracting.** The material cost is $10 per unit and the subcontracting cost is $30/unit (see Table 8-3). P_t represents the quantity produced and C_t represents the quantity subcontracted in Period t. Thus, the material and subcontracting cost is

$$\text{Cost of materials and subcontracting} = \sum_{t=1}^{6} 10P_t + \sum_{t=1}^{6} 30C_t$$

The total cost incurred during the planning horizon is the sum of all the aforementioned costs and is given by

$$\sum_{t=1}^{6} 640W_t + \sum_{t=1}^{6} 6O_t + \sum_{t=1}^{6} 300H_t + \sum_{t=1}^{6} 500L_t + \sum_{t=1}^{6} 2I_t$$
$$+ \sum_{t=1}^{6} 5S_t + \sum_{t=1}^{6} 10P_t + \sum_{t=1}^{6} 30C_t \qquad \textbf{(8.1)}$$

Red Tomato's objective is to find an aggregate plan that minimizes the total cost (Equation 8.1) incurred during the planning horizon.

The values of the decision variables in the objective function cannot be set arbitrarily. They are subject to a variety of constraints defined by available capacity and operating policies. The next step in setting up the aggregate planning model is to define clearly the constraints linking the decision variables.

CONSTRAINTS Red Tomato's vice president must now specify the constraints that the decision variables must not violate. They are as follows:

1. **Workforce, hiring, and layoff constraints.** The workforce size W_t in Period t is obtained by adding the number hired H_t in Period t to the workforce size W_{t-1} in Period $t-1$, and subtracting the number laid off L_t in Period t as follows:

$$W_t = W_{t-1} + H_t - L_t \quad \text{for} \quad t = 1, \ldots, 6 \qquad \textbf{(8.2)}$$

The starting workforce size is given by $W_0 = 80$.

2. **Capacity constraints.** In each period, the amount produced cannot exceed the available capacity. This set of constraints limits the total production by the internally available capacity (which is determined based on the available labor hours, regular or overtime). Subcontracted production is not included in this constraint because the constraint is limited to production within the plant. As each worker can produce 40 units per month on regular time (four hours per unit as specified in Table 8-3) and one unit for every four hours of overtime, we have the following:

$$P_t \leq 40W_t + \frac{O_t}{4} \quad \text{for} \quad t = 1, \ldots, 6 \qquad \textbf{(8.3)}$$

3. **Inventory balance constraints.** The third set of constraints balances inventory at the end of each period. Net demand for Period t is obtained as the sum of the current demand D_t and the previous backlog S_{t-1}. This demand is either filled from current production (in-house production P_t or subcontracted production C_t) and previous inventory I_{t-1} (in which case some inventory I_t may be left over) or part of it is backlogged S_t. This relationship is captured by the following equation:

$$I_{t-1} + P_t + C_t = D_t + S_{t-1} + I_t - S_t \quad \text{for} \quad t = 1, \ldots, 6 \qquad \textbf{(8.4)}$$

The starting inventory is given by $I_0 = 1,000$, the ending inventory must be at least 500 units (i.e., $I_6 \geq 500$), and initially there are no backlogs (i.e., $S_0 = 0$).

4. **Overtime limit constraints.** The fourth set of constraints requires that no employee work more than 10 hours of overtime each month. This requirement limits the total amount of overtime hours available as follows:

$$O_t \leq 10W_t \quad \text{for} \quad t = 1, \ldots, 6 \tag{8.5}$$

In addition, each variable must be nonnegative and there must be no backlog at the end of Period 6 (i.e., $S_6 = 0$).

When implementing the model in Microsoft Excel, which we discuss later, it is easiest if all the constraints are written so the right-hand side for each constraint is 0. The overtime limit constraint (Equation 8.5) in this form is written as

$$O_t - 10W_t \leq 0 \quad \text{for} \quad t = 1, \ldots, 6$$

Observe that one can easily add constraints that limit the amount purchased from subcontractors each month or the maximum number of employees to be hired or laid off. Any other constraints limiting backlogs or inventories can also be accommodated. Ideally, the number of employees hired or laid off should be integer variables. Fractional variables may be justified if some employees work for only part of a month. Such a linear program can be solved using the tool Solver in Excel.

By optimizing the objective function (minimizing cost in Equation 8.1) subject to the listed constraints (Equations 8.2 to 8.5), the vice president obtains the aggregate plan shown in Table 8-4. (Later in the chapter, we discuss how to perform this optimization using Excel with the spreadsheet *Chapter 8, 9-examples*.)

For this aggregate plan, we have the following:

$$\text{Total cost over planning horizon} = \$422,660$$

Red Tomato lays off a total of 16 employees at the beginning of January. After that, the company maintains the workforce and production level. It uses the subcontractor during the month of April. Red Tomato carries a backlog only from April to May; in all other months, it plans no stockouts. In fact, it carries inventory in all other periods. We describe this inventory as *seasonal inventory* because it is carried in anticipation of a future increase in demand.

If the seasonal fluctuation of demand grows, synchronization of supply and demand becomes more difficult, resulting in an increase in either inventory or backlogs as well as an increase in the total cost to the supply chain. This is illustrated in Example 8-1, in which the demand forecast is more variable.

TABLE 8-4 Aggregate Plan for Red Tomato

Period, t	No. Hired, H_t	No. Laid Off, L_t	Workforce Size, W_t	Overtime, O_t	Inventory, I_t	Stockout, S_t	Subcontract, C_t	Total Production, P_t	Demand, D_t
0	0	0	80	0	1,000	0	0		
1	0	16	64	0	1,960	0	0	2,560	1,600
2	0	0	64	0	1,520	0	0	2,560	3,000
3	0	0	64	0	880	0	0	2,560	3,200
4	0	0	64	0	0	220	140	2,560	3,800
5	0	0	64	0	140	0	0	2,560	2,200
6	0	0	64	0	500	0	0	2,560	2,200

EXAMPLE 8-1	**Impact of Higher Demand Variability**

All the data are exactly the same as in our previous discussion of Red Tomato, except for the demand forecast. Assume that the same overall demand (16,000 units) is distributed over the six months in such a way that the seasonal fluctuation of demand is higher, as shown in Table 8-5. Obtain the optimal aggregate plan in this case.

Analysis

In this case, the optimal aggregate plan (using the same costs as those used before) is shown in Table 8-6.

Observe that monthly production remains the same, but both inventories and stockouts (backlogs) go up compared to the aggregate plan in Table 8-4 for the demand profile in Table 8-2. The cost of meeting the new demand profile in Table 8-5 is higher, at $433,080 (compared to $422,660 for the previous demand profile in Table 8-2).

From Example 8-1, we can see that the increase in demand variability at the retailer increases seasonal inventory as well as planned costs.

Using the Red Tomato example, we also see that the optimal trade-off changes as the costs change. This is illustrated in Example 8-2, in which we show that as the costs of hiring and layoff decrease, it is better to vary capacity with demand while having less inventory and fewer backlogs.

TABLE 8-5 Demand Forecast with Higher Seasonal Fluctuation

Month	Demand Forecast
January	1,000
February	3,000
March	3,800
April	4,800
May	2,000
June	1,400

TABLE 8-6 Optimal Aggregate Plan for Demand in Table 8-5

Period, t	No. Hired, H_t	No. Laid Off, L_t	Workforce Size, W_t	Overtime, O_t	Inventory, I_t	Stockout, S_t	Subcontract, C_t	Total Production, P_t	Demand, D_t
0	0	0	80	0	1,000	0	0		
1	0	16	64	0	2,560	0	0	2,560	1,000
2	0	0	64	0	2,120	0	0	2,560	3,000
3	0	0	64	0	880	0	0	2,560	3,800
4	0	0	64	0	0	1,220	140	2,560	4,800
5	0	0	64	0	0	660	0	2,560	2,000
6	0	0	64	0	500	0	0	2,560	1,400

| EXAMPLE 8-2 | **Impact of Lower Costs of Hiring and Layoff** |

Assume that demand at Red Tomato is as shown in Table 8-2, and all other data are the same except that the costs of hiring and layoff are now $50 each. Evaluate the total cost corresponding to the aggregate plan in Table 8-4. Suggest an optimal aggregate plan for the new cost structure.

Analysis

If the costs of hiring and layoff decrease to $50 each, the cost corresponding to the aggregate plan in Table 8-4 decreases from $422,660 to $415,460. Taking this new cost into account and determining a new optimal aggregate plan yields the plan shown in Table 8-7 at a total cost of $412,770. Observe that the workforce size fluctuates between a high of 88 and a low of 45, as opposed to being stable at 64 as in Table 8-4.

As expected, the workforce size is varied (because the cost of varying capacity has decreased), whereas inventory and stockouts have decreased compared with the aggregate plan in Table 8-4. The total cost of the aggregate plan in Table 8-7 is $412,770, compared with $415,460 (for the aggregate plan in Table 8-4) if the costs of hiring and layoff are $50 each.

TABLE 8-7 Optimal Aggregate Plan for Hiring and Layoff Cost of $50/Worker

Period, t	No. Hired, H_t	No. Laid Off, O_t	Workforce Size, W_t	Overtime, O_t	Inventory, I_t	Stockout, S_t	Subcontract, C_t	Total Production, P_t	Demand, D_t
0	0	0	80	0	1,000	0	0		
1	0	35	45	0	1,200	0	0	1,800	1,600
2	0	0	45	0	0	0	0	1,800	3,000
3	42	0	87	0	280	0	0	3,480	3,200
4	1	0	88	0	0	0	0	3,520	3,800
5	0	27	61	0	240	0	0	2,440	2,200
6	0	0	61	0	500	0	20	2,440	2,200

From Example 8-2, observe that increasing volume flexibility (by decreasing the cost of hiring and layoff) not only decreases the total cost but also shifts the optimal balance toward using the volume flexibility while carrying lower inventories and allowing less stockout.

Building a Rough Master Production Schedule

From an aggregate plan, a planner must disaggregate the available information and build a rough master production schedule (MPS) that identifies the batches produced in each period at the level of each product. We return to the Red Tomato example to illustrate a simple approach to disaggregate an aggregate plan. Although this approach is not necessarily optimal, it is simple to implement and allows for a feasibility check. More sophisticated methods (e.g., see Bitran and Hax, 1981) are available if a planner wants to search for better solutions. These methods, however, are difficult to implement and may not be able to reflect all the complex realities. For this reason, we propose this simple approach.

Consider the aggregate plan in Table 8-4. The plan calls for a workforce of 64 and a production of 2,560 aggregate units in Period 1. We know that the production constraint is feasible at the aggregate level, but we need to check feasibility at the disaggregate level. The first step is to divide the production quantity of 2,560 across the six products. We do so in the ratio of expected

TABLE 8-8 Disaggregating the Aggregate Plan at Red Tomato Tools for Period 1

Product	Setup Time/ Batch (hour)	Average Batch Size	Production Time/ Unit (hour)	Production Quantity	Number of Setups	Setup Time (hours)	Production Time (hours)
A	8	50	5.60	256	5	40	1,433.6
B	6	150	3.00	640	4	24	1,920.0
C	8	100	3.80	512	5	40	1,945.6
D	10	50	4.80	256	5	50	1,228.8
E	6	100	3.60	512	5	30	1,843.2
F	5	75	4.30	384	5	25	1,651.2

sales (using percentage share from Table 8-1), as shown in Table 8-8 (see worksheet *Chapter 8-Table 8-8*). Thus, the plan is to produce 256 units of Product A in Period 1 because it represents 10 percent of sales. The next step is to identify the number of planned batches for each product. To get the feasibility of the plan, we divide the planned production quantity by the average batch size and then round the answer down. For Product A, the planned number of setups (batches) is thus 256/50 = 5.12 rounded down, which equals 5. As a result, the average batch size of Product A produced in this period will be larger than 50 (about 51). We similarly obtain the planned number of setups (batches) for each of the other products in Period 1, as shown in Table 8-8. To check the feasibility of the planned schedule, we calculate the setup time and the production time for the planned number of batches and units of each product. From Table 8-8, the total planned production and setup time is 10,231.4 hours (209 for setup + 10,022.4 for production). Given the 64 people planned, the available production time in the period is 64 × 160 = 10,240 hours. The planned schedule thus seems feasible.

SUMMARY OF LEARNING OBJECTIVE 3

Given the goal of maximizing profits (or minimizing costs) subject to supply chain constraints, the aggregate planning problem can be modeled as a linear program. The first step is to identify a suitable aggregate unit of production and forecast demand in terms of the aggregate unit. The next step is to identify the various costs (such as material, inventory, production) and constraints in the supply chain. We then identify the set of decision variables and construct the objective function and constraints in terms of the decision variables. Linear programming then allows us to optimize the objective function subject to the specified constraints. The aggregate plan should then be converted to a feasible master production schedule.

AGGREGATE PLANNING IN EXCEL

8.4 *Formulate and solve basic aggregate planning problems using Microsoft Excel.*

Next we discuss how to generate the aggregate plan for Red Tomato in Table 8-4 using Excel. We first do so by building a simple spreadsheet that allows *what-if* analysis and then build a more sophisticated model that allows optimization using linear programming.

Building a Basic Aggregate Planning Spreadsheet

The aggregate planner must decide on the number of people hired (H_t) or laid off (L_t) each month, along with any overtime (O_t) or subcontracting (C_t). Once these decisions have been made, one can determine the workforce (W_t), production (P_t), inventory (I_t) and stockout (S_t) for each month (see Table 8-9), thus completing the aggregate plan. Figure 8-1 shows the final

Period	Ht # Hired	Lt # Laid off	Wt # Workforce	Ot Overtime	It Inventory	St Stockout	Ct Subcontract	Pt Production	Demand	Max. Overtime Available
Aggregate Plan Decision Variables										
0	0	0	80	0	1,000	0	0			
1	0	16	64	0	1,960	0	0	2,560	1,600	640
2	0	0	64	0	1,520	0	0	2,560	3,000	640
3	0	0	64	0	880	0	0	2,560	3,200	640
4	0	0	64	0	0	220	140	2,560	3,800	640
5	0	0	64	0	140	0	0	2,560	2,200	640
6	0	0	64	0	500	0	0	2,560	2,200	640

Total Cost = $422,660

Figure 8-1 Basic Aggregate Planning Spreadsheet

spreadsheet (available as *Chapter8-trial-aggplan*) corresponding to Table 8-4. The planner can try different inputs for each decision variable in the appropriate cells in worksheet *Planning*. It is best to start with the number hired (B5:B10) and number laid off (C5:C10) in each period. The maximum overtime available in a given month is limited by $10 \times W_t$ and is shown in cells M5:M10. One can then enter the overtime (E5:E10) and amount subcontracted (H5:H10) for each period. For each set of inputs, the outputs are calculated as shown in Table 8-9.

The total cost is evaluated in cell C12 as follows:

$$= 640*\text{sum}(D5:D10) + 6*\text{sum}(E5:E10) + 300*\text{sum}(B5:B10) + 500*\text{sum}(C5:C10)$$
$$+ 2*\text{sum}(F5:F10) + 5*\text{sum}(G5:G10) + 10*\text{sum}(I5:I10) + 30*\text{sum}(H5:H10)$$

The goal is to build an aggregate plan by changing inputs in a way that minimizes the total cost in cell C12.

Building an Aggregate Planning Spreadsheet Using Solver

To access Excel's linear programming capabilities, use Solver (Data I Analysis I Solver). To begin, we need to create a table, which we illustrate with Figure 8-2 (see associated spreadsheet *Chapter 8, 9-examples*), containing the following decision variables:

W_t = workforce size for Month t, $t = 1, \ldots , 6$

H_t = number of employees hired at the beginning of Month t, $t = 1, \ldots , 6$

L_t = number of employees laid off at the beginning of Month t, $t = 1, \ldots , 6$

P_t = number of units produced in Month t, $t = 1, \ldots , 6$

I_t = inventory at the end of Month t, $t = 1, \ldots , 6$

S_t = number of units stocked out at the end of Month t, $t = 1, \ldots , 6$

C_t = number of units subcontracted for Month t, $t = 1, \ldots , 6$

O_t = number of overtime hours worked in Month t, $t = 1, \ldots , 6$

Figure 8-2 (use worksheet *Planning*) illustrates what this table should look like. The decision variables are contained in cells B5:I10, with each cell corresponding to a decision variable. For example, cell D7 corresponds to the workforce size in Period 3. Begin by setting all the decision variables to 0, as shown in Figure 8-2.

Also note that column J contains the actual demand. The demand information is included because it is required to calculate the aggregate plan.

The second step is to construct a table for the constraints in Equation 8.2 to 8.5. The constraint table may be constructed as shown in Figure 8-3.

Column M contains workforce constraints (Equation 8.2), column N contains capacity constraints (Equation 8.3), column O contains inventory balance constraints (Equation 8.4), and column P contains overtime constraints (Equation 8.5). These constraints are applied to each of the six periods.

TABLE 8-9 Building the Basic Aggregate Planning Spreadsheet

Output	Cells	Relationship to Inputs	Formula in Row 5	Copied to Cells
Workforce	D5:D10	$W_t = W_{t-1} + H_t - L_t$	= D4 + B5 − C5	D6:D10
Production	I5:I10	$P_t = 40 \times W_t + O_t/4$	= 40*D5 + (E5/4)	I6:I10
Inventory	F5:F10	$I_t = max(I_{t-1} + P_t + C_t - D_t - S_{t-1}, 0)$	= max(F4 + I5 + H5 − G4 − J5,0)	F6:F10
Stockout	G5:G10	$S_t = max(0, S_{t-1} + D_t - I_{t-1} - P_t - C_t)$	= max(0,J5 + G4 − I5 − H5−F4)	G6:G10

	A	B	C	D	E	F	G	H	I	J
1	Aggregate Plan Decision Variables									
2		H_t	L_t	W_t	O_t	I_t	S_t	C_t	P_t	
3	Period	# Hired	# Laid off	# Workforce	Overtime	Inventory	Stockout	Subcontract	Production	Demand
4	0	0	0	80	0	1,000	0	0		
5	1	0	0	0	0	0	0	0	0	1,600
6	2	0	0	0	0	0	0	0	0	3,000
7	3	0	0	0	0	0	0	0	0	3,200
8	4	0	0	0	0	0	0	0	0	3,800
9	5	0	0	0	0	0	0	0	0	2,200
10	6	0	0	0	0	0	0	0	0	2,200

Figure 8-2 Spreadsheet Area for Decision Variables

	M	N	O	P
1	Constraints			
2				
3	Workforce	Capacity	Inventory	Overtime
4				
5	-80	0	-600	0
6	0	0	-3000	0
7	0	0	-3200	0
8	0	0	-3800	0
9	0	0	-2200	0
10	0	0	-2200	0

Cell	Cell Formula	Equation	Copied to
M5	=D5-D4-B5+C5	8.2	M6:M10
N5	=40*D5+E5/4-I5	8.3	N6:N10
O5	=F4-G4+I5+H5-J5-F5+G5	8.4	O6:O10
P5	=-E5+10*D5	8.5	P6:P10

Figure 8-3 Spreadsheet Area for Constraints

Each constraint will eventually be written in Solver as

$$\text{Cell value} \{ \leq, =, \text{or} \geq \} 0$$

In our case, we have constraints

$$\text{M5:M10} = 0, \text{N5:N10} \geq 0, \text{O5:O10} = 0, \text{P5:P10} \geq 0$$

The third step is to create a cell containing the objective function, which is the way each solution is judged. This cell need not contain the entire formula but can be written as a formula using cells with intermediate cost calculations. For the Red Tomato example, the spreadsheet

	A	B	C	D	E	F	G	H	I
12	**Aggregate Plan Costs**								
14	**Period**	**Hiring**	**Layoff**	**Regular time**	**Overtime**	**Inventory**	**Stockout**	**Subcontract**	**Material**
15	1	0	0	0	0	0	0	0	0
16	2	0	0	0	0	0	0	0	0
17	3	0	0	0	0	0	0	0	0
18	4	0	0	0	0	0	0	0	0
19	5	0	0	0	0	0	0	0	0
20	6	0	0	0	0	0	0	0	0
22	**Total Cost =**		$ -						

Figure 8-4 Spreadsheet Area for Cost Calculations

area for cost calculations is shown in Figure 8-4. Cell B15, for instance, contains the hiring costs incurred in Period 1. The formula in cell B15 is the product of cell B5 and the cell containing the hiring cost per worker, which is obtained from Table 8-3. Other cells are filled similarly. Cell C22 contains the sum of cells B15:I20, representing the total cost.

The fourth step is to use Data | Analysis | Solver to invoke Solver. Within the Solver Parameters dialog box, enter the following information to represent the linear programming model:

Set Target Cell: C22

Equal to: Select *Min*

By Changing Cells: B5:I10

Subject to the constraints:

B5:C10 = integer { Number of workers hired or laid off is integer }

B5:I10 $\geq$ 0 { All decision variables are nonnegative }

F10 $\geq$ 500 { Inventory at end of Period 6 is at least 500 }

G10 = 0 { Stockout at end of Period 6 equals 0 }

M5:M10 = 0 $\{ W_t - W_{t-1} - H_t + L_t = 0 \text{ for } t = 1, \dots, 6 \}$

N5:N10 $\geq$ 0 $\{ 40W_t + O_t/4 - P_t \geq 0 \text{ for } t = 1, \dots, 6 \}$

O5:O10 = 0 $\{ I_{t-1} - S_{t-1} + P_t + C_t - D_t - I_t + S_t = 0 \text{ for } t = 1, \dots, 6 \}$

P5:P10 $\geq$ 0 $\{ 10W_t - O_t \geq 0 \text{ for } t = 1, \dots, 6 \}$

The Solver Parameters dialog box is shown in Figure 8-5. Click on Solve. The optimal solution should be returned. If Solver does not return the optimal solution, solve the problem again after saving the solution that Solver has returned. (In some cases, multiple repetitions of this step may be required because of some flaws in the version of Solver that comes with Excel. Add-ins that do not have any of these issues are available at relatively low cost.) The optimal solution turns out to be the one shown in Table 8-4.

Forecast Error and Aggregate Plans

The aggregate planning methodology we have discussed in this chapter does not take into account any forecast error. However, we know that all forecasts have errors. To improve the quality of these aggregate plans, forecasting errors must be considered and flexibility must be built into the aggregate plan. By building flexibility into the plan, when future demand or costs change, the plan can adjust appropriately to handle the new situation. Flexibility can be built by using either *safety inventory*, defined as inventory held to satisfy demand that is higher than forecast (discussed thoroughly in Chapter 12), or *safety capacity*, defined as capacity used to satisfy demand that is higher than forecast. A company can create a buffer for forecast error using safety inventory and safety capacity in a variety of ways, some of which are listed here:

- Use overtime as a form of safety capacity.
- Carry extra workforce permanently as a form of safety capacity.

Figure 8-5 Solver Parameters Dialog Box

- Use subcontractors as a form of safety capacity.
- Build and carry extra inventories as a form of safety inventory.
- Purchase capacity or product from an open or spot market as a form of safety capacity.

In addition to the suggestions listed above, a manager should perform sensitivity analysis on the inputs into an aggregate plan. For example, if the plan recommends expanding expensive capacity while facing uncertain demand, examine the outcome of a new aggregate plan when demand is higher and lower than expected. If this examination reveals a small savings from expanding capacity when demand is high but a large increase in cost when demand is lower than expected, deciding to postpone the capacity investment decision is a potentially attractive option. Using sensitivity analysis on the inputs into the aggregate plan enables a planner to choose the best solution for the range of possibilities that may occur.

Even though an aggregate plan may provide a map for the next 3 to 18 months, it does not mean that a firm should run aggregate plans only once every 3 to 18 months. As inputs such as demand forecasts change, managers should use the latest values of these inputs and rerun the aggregate plan. Be careful, however, to modify plans in a way that limits volatility. Frequent changes may diminish the extent to which supply chain partners trust the aggregate plan.

The Role of Software in Aggregate Planning

Aggregate planning is arguably the supply chain area in which software has been used the most. The earliest supply chain software products were aggregate planning modules, often called factory, production, or manufacturing planning. Some of the early modules focused only on obtaining a feasible production plan subject to constraints arising from demand and available capacity. Later modules provided tools that chose an optimal solution from among the feasible production plans, based on objectives such as increased output or lowered cost.

These classic solutions generally formulated the aggregate planning problem as a linear program to get a production schedule of products to be made in each period of time. Today, some planning modules incorporate nonlinear optimization to account for the fact that not all constraints or reasonable objective functions are linear functions. However, given the large amount of data considered in producing aggregate plans—which can render nonlinear problems computationally prohibitive—and the ability to create linear approximations of nonlinear functions, linear programming is often the best way to solve these problems.

Many software vendors (including SAP and Oracle) offer advanced planning systems (APSs) to help firms create aggregate plans. The biggest challenge when using APSs is that the results can be fairly unstable relative to inputs. A small change in an input such as demand can produce a new optimal plan that is quite different from the original plan. If plans become too volatile, the entire supply chain quickly begins to distrust them, effectively rendering them useless. It is thus important to ensure that as new data arrive, plans are modified while trying to ensure some degree of stability.

Data accuracy is critical if APSs are to deliver their full potential. If the APS is using lead times or capacities that are different from reality, the resulting aggregate plan is likely to lead to unhappy customers and high costs. It is thus important to track the accuracy of these parameters and ensure that people are held accountable for these inputs.

SUMMARY OF LEARNING OBJECTIVE 4

Aggregate planning problems can be solved in Excel by setting up cells for the objective function and the constraints and using the Solver tool to produce the solution. It is best if these plans can account for forecast error, resulting in a plan that has some degree of stability.

DISCUSSION QUESTIONS

1. Explain the importance of the quality of an aggregate plan to a company in terms of sales, profitability, and facilities.
2. Apart from the bottleneck issue, what other factors need to be considered when identifying aggregate units of production during planning?
3. What are the main differences among the aggregate planning strategies?
4. What types of industries or situations are best suited to the chase strategy? The flexibility strategy? The level strategy?
5. How should forecast errors be handled when making an aggregate plan?
6. How can a company create a buffer for forecasting errors using safety inventory and safety capacity? Illustrate using an example.
7. If a company currently employs the chase strategy and the cost of training increases dramatically, how might this change the company's aggregate planning strategy?
8. What are the major procedures in implementing aggregate planning in the supply chain?
9. How can aggregate planning be used in an environment of high seasonal demand, like that of a garden furniture manufacturer?

EXERCISES

1. Skycell, a major European cell phone manufacturer, is making production plans for the coming year. Skycell has worked with its customers (the service providers) to come up with forecasts of monthly requirements (in thousands of phones) as shown in Table 8-10.

 Manufacturing is primarily an assembly operation, and capacity is governed by the number of people on the production line. The plant operates for 20 days a month, eight hours each day. One person can assemble a phone every 10 minutes. Workers are paid €20 per hour and a 50 percent premium for overtime. The plant currently employs 1,250 workers. Component costs for each cell phone total €20. Given the rapid decline in component and finished product prices, carrying inventory from one month to the next incurs a cost of €3 per phone per month. Skycell currently has a no-layoff policy in place. Overtime is limited to a maximum of 20 hours per month per employee. Assume that Skycell has a starting inventory of 50,000 units and wants to end the year with the same level of inventory.

 a. Assuming no backlogs, no subcontracting, and no new hires, what is the optimum production schedule? What is the annual cost of this schedule?
 b. Is there any value for management to negotiate an increase of allowed overtime per employee per month from 20 hours to 40?

TABLE 8-10 Monthly Demand for Cell Phones, in Thousands

Month	Demand
January	1,200
February	1,300
March	1,000
April	1,150
May	1,400
June	1,300
July	1,200
August	1,100
September	1,200
October	1,200
November	1,300
December	1,600

c. Reconsider parts (a) and (b) if Skycell starts with only 1,200 employees. Reconsider parts (a) and (b) if Skycell starts with 1,300 employees. What happens to the value of additional overtime as the workforce size decreases?

d. Consider part (a) for the case in which Skycell aims for a level production schedule such that the quantity produced each month does not exceed the average demand over the next 12 months (1,241,667) by 50,000 units. Thus, monthly production, including overtime, should be no more than 1,291,667. What would be the cost of this level production schedule? What is the value of overtime flexibility?

2. Reconsider the Skycell data in Exercise 1. Assume that the plant has 1,250 employees and a no-layoff policy. Overtime is limited to 20 hours per employee per month. A third party has offered to produce cell phones as needed at a cost of €26 per unit (this includes component costs of €20 per unit).

a. What is the average per unit of in-house production (including inventory holding and overtime cost) if the third party is not used?

b. How should Skycell use the third party? How does your answer change if the third party offers a price of €25 per unit?

c. Should Skycell use the third party if the per unit cost is €28?

d. Why would Skycell use the third party even when the per-unit cost of the third party is higher than the average per-unit cost (including inventory holding and overtime) for in-house production?

3. Reconsider the Skycell data in Exercise 1. Assume that the plant has 1,250 employees and a no-layoff policy. Overtime is limited to at most 20 hours per employee per month. Also assume no subcontracting option. Skycell has a team of 50 people who are willing to work as seasonal employees. The cost of bringing them on is €800 per employee, and the layoff cost is €1,200 per employee.

a. What is the optimal production, hiring, and layoff schedule?

b. How does the optimal schedule change if the seasonal pool grows from 50 to 100?

c. Relative to having 1,250 permanent and 50 seasonal employees, will Skycell gain significantly if it carries only 1,100 permanent employees but has 200 seasonal employees?

d. Consider the case in which Skycell has 1,250 permanent employees and 50 seasonal employees. Does Skycell gain more by eliminating its no-layoff policy for its permanent employees or by increasing the seasonal employee pool from 50 to 100? Assume that permanent employees can be hired or laid off at the same cost as the seasonal employees.

4. FlexMan, an electronics contract manufacturer, uses its Topeka, Kansas, facility to produce two product categories: routers and switches. Consultation with customers has indicated a demand forecast for each category over the next 12 months (in thousands of units) to be as shown in Table 8-11.

Manufacturing is primarily an assembly operation, and the number of people on the production line governs capacity. The plant operates 20 days a month, 8 hours each day. Production of a router takes 20 minutes, and production of a switch requires 10 minutes of worker time. Each worker is paid $10 per hour, with a 50 percent premium for any overtime. The plant currently has 6,300 employees. Overtime is limited to 20 hours per employee per month. The plant currently maintains 100,000 routers and 50,000 switches in inventory. The cost of holding a router in inventory is $3 per month, and the cost of holding a switch in inventory is $1 per month. The holding cost arises because products are paid for by the customer at existing market rates when purchased. Thus, if FlexMan produces early and holds in inventory, the company recovers less given the rapidly dropping component prices.

TABLE 8-11 Demand Forecast for FlexMan

Month	Router Demand	Switch Demand
January	1,700	1,500
February	1,500	1,300
March	2,300	1,500
April	2,400	2,100
May	900	1,600
June	1,700	800
July	1,300	600
August	1,500	800
September	2,600	1,300
October	1,900	1,600
November	1,100	800
December	1,200	1,000

a. Assuming no backlogs, no subcontracting, no layoffs, and no new hires, what is the optimum production schedule for FlexMan? What is the annual cost of this schedule? What inventories does the optimal production schedule build? Does this seem reasonable?

b. Is there any value for management to negotiate an increase of allowed overtime per employee per month from 20 hours to 40? What variables are affected by this change?

c. Reconsider parts (a) and (b) if FlexMan starts with only 5,900 employees. Reconsider parts (a) and (b) if FlexMan starts with 6,700 employees. What happens to the value of additional overtime as the workforce size decreases?

5. Reconsider the FlexMan data from Exercise 4. The firm is considering the option of changing workforce size with demand. The cost of hiring a new employee is $700 and the cost of a layoff is $1,000. It takes an employee two months to reach full production capacity. During those two months, a new employee provides only 50 percent productivity. Anticipating a similar demand pattern next year, FlexMan aims to end the year with 6,300 employees.

a. What is the optimal production, hiring, and layoff schedule? What is the cost of such a schedule?

b. If FlexMan could improve its training so new employees achieve full productivity right away, how much improvement in annual cost would the company see? How is the hiring and layoff policy during the year affected by this change?

6. FlexMan has identified a third party that is willing to produce routers and switches as needed. The third party will charge $6 per router and $4 per switch. Assume all other data as in Exercise 4, except that hiring and layoffs are allowed as in Exercise 5.

a. How should FlexMan use the third party if new employees provide only 50 percent productivity for the first two months?

b. How should FlexMan use the third party if new employees are able to achieve full productivity right away?

c. Why does the use of the third party change with the productivity of new employees?

7. Return to the FlexMan data in Exercise 4. The company has signed a service-level agreement with its customers and committed to carry safety inventory from one month to the next that equals at least 15 percent of the following month's demand. Thus, FlexMan is committed to carrying over at least $0.15 \times 1,700,000 = 255,000$ routers and $0.15 \times 1,500,000 = 225,000$ switches in inventory from December to January.

a. Assuming no backlogs, no subcontracting, no layoffs, and no new hires, what is the optimum production schedule for FlexMan? What is the annual cost of this schedule?

b. How much does the service contract mandating minimum inventories increase costs for FlexMan?

c. What would be the increase in cost if FlexMan agreed to a 15 percent minimum for switches but only a 5 percent minimum for routers? What would be the increase in cost if FlexMan agreed to only a 5 percent minimum for switches but a 15 percent minimum for routers? Which of the two is better for FlexMan?

BIBLIOGRAPHY

Axsäter, Sven. "On the Feasibility of Aggregate Production Plans." *Operations Research* (1986): 34, 796–800.

Bitran, G. R., and A. Hax. "Disaggregation and Resource Allocation Using Convex Knapsack Problems with Bounded Variables." *Management Science* (1981): 27, 431–441.

Jacobs, F. Robert, Richard B. Chase, and Nicholas J. Aquilano. *Operations and Supply Management*, 12th ed. New York: McGraw-Hill/Irwin, 2009.

Nahmias, Steven. *Production & Operations Analysis*, 6th ed. New York: McGraw-Hill/Irwin, 2009.

CASE STUDY

Kloss Planters and Harvesters

Kevin Cho, general manager at Kloss Planters and Harvesters (KPH), left the meeting with his strategic planning team wondering whether it made sense to replace the separate factory for planters and harvesters with a single factory that could assemble both.

A Brief History of Planters and Harvesters

Since humans started farming, they have sought to ease the task of planting and harvesting their crops. In his *Naturalis historica*, Gaius Plinius (AD 23–79) described a reaping machine that broke off the ears of corn and accumulated them in a box. In 1799, the first verifiable patent for a reaping machine was granted to the English inventor Joseph Boyce. In 1831, Cyrus Hall McCormick introduced the world's first corn reaper under the name of the "Virginia Reaper." The Virginia Reaper was powered by a horse. Over time, other companies introduced combine harvesters that were self-propelled and

powered by a combustion engine. Harvesters today allow a farmer to harvest large cornfields in the comfort of air-conditioned cabs!

After years of planting corn the way Squanto had taught the settlers, help arrived for American farmers when hand planters were introduced during the late 1800s and early 1900s. Some of these devices allowed farmers to plant two acres per day instead of the single acre possible with hand-planting. Today, planters can seed multiple rows while traveling at 10 miles per hour. The evolution of both planters and harvesters has certainly made the farmer much more effective.

KPH Production Planning

KPH assembled planters in Davenport, Iowa, and harvesters in Ames, Iowa. Demand for each product was highly seasonal, as shown in Table 8-12. Corn was generally planted between March and May and harvested between September and November. As a result, demand for planters peaked in March, whereas demand for harvesters peaked in September. Each factory aimed for a production plan that allowed them to meet annual demand at the lowest possible cost.

The capacity of each factory was determined by the number of assembly workers available. Each machine (planter or harvester) required 100 labor hours

for assembly. Each factory operated for 20 days a month, 8 hours a day. Assembly workers were paid $20/hour during regular time. They could be asked to work up to an additional 20 hours per month as overtime. Overtime was paid at the rate of $30/hour. Given the highly seasonal nature of demand, KPH laid off some workers during the low season and rehired them for the peak. Each layoff cost KPH $5,000 and each rehiring cost $3,000. Each factory generally built inventory in anticipation of the peak. It cost $300 to carry a machine in inventory from one month to the next. KPH could also choose to delay a customer order by stocking out in a given month and filling the stockout from next month's production. However, each unit delayed in this manner cost $2,000 in discounts offered to customers to keep them happy. The company had a policy of ensuring that there were no stockouts in December so the new year started out without any unfilled orders. The material cost for each machine was $20,000.

The planter factory ended December with 244 workers and 250 planters in inventory. The harvester factory ended December with 100 workers and 50 machines in inventory. The production plan at each factory attempted to meet demand in Table 8-12 at the lowest possible cost while ensuring that the factory ended December of the coming year with the same labor and inventory as the previous December.

Options for New Factories

Given the age of the current factories, Kevin planned to replace them with new factories. One option was to replace each factory with a similar new factory. The other option was to expand the Davenport factory to allow for both planter and harvester assembly. The investment for the two options was going to be very similar. Thus, Kevin requested his strategic planning team to identify any advantages of a single factory.

The team pointed out that countercyclical nature of demand for planters and harvesters canceled their individual seasonality of demand to some extent. Common assembly steps for the two products would allow KPH to use the same labor for the two products. This had the potential to significantly reduce the number of employees laid off and rehired each year. Besides improving employee morale, such a change had the possibility of reducing costs. Kevin asked the team to quantify any cost-related and employee-related advantages offered by the single factory. He would base his decision on these numbers.

TABLE 8-12 Demand Forecast for Planters and Harvesters

Month	Planters	Harvesters
January	600	100
February	850	100
March	1,300	100
April	800	100
May	550	100
June	100	200
July	100	500
August	100	1,000
September	100	1,500
October	100	700
November	100	450
December	300	100

CASE STUDY

Smartphone Production at QuickTronics

Rudy Hartono, general manager at QuickTronics, a contract manufacturer for consumer electronics, was headed to the annual planning meeting. He had the demand forecast for the next 12 months and the goal of the meeting was to develop an aggregate plan. Historically, Rudy had maintained a steady workforce of 667 teams in the plants and built inventory in the first half of the year for use in the second half. While this approach made workforce management easy, it led to a large buildup of inventory. As Rudy walked into the meeting, he wondered whether it was better to hire and fire workers as needed in order to reduce the amount of inventory held.

QuickTronics Production Planning

QuickTronics set up a large assembly factory in Batam, Indonesia, that focused on the assembly of smartphones. The Indonesian government had offered incentives leading many manufacturers to locate their factories in Batam. Many component suppliers were located close to the QuickTronics plant and sent small batches to the factory on a regular basis. Assembled phones were stored in a warehouse from where they were shipped in response to customer orders from Asia, Europe, and America. The supply chain team at QuickTronics had worked with its customers to develop a monthly forecast of demand, as shown in Table 8-13. Demand for smartphones peaked in the fourth quarter of the year.

Smartphone assembly was handled by teams of 10 workers each. Each team had the capacity to assemble 125 phones per hour. The capacity of each factory was determined by the number of assembly teams deployed. Each factory operated for 20 days a month, 8 hours a day. Assembly workers were paid 4,000 Rupiah/hour during regular time. They could be asked to work up to an additional 10 hours per month as overtime. Overtime was paid at the rate of 6,000 Rupiah/hour. If QuickTronics chose to layoff workers, each layoff cost the company 800,000 Rupiah and each hiring cost 400,000 Rupiah. It cost 50,000 Rupiah to carry a phone in inventory from one month to the next. Quicktronics could also choose to delay a customer order by stocking out in a given month and filling the stockout from next month's production. Given the importance of keeping up with customer

TABLE 8-13 Demand Forecast for Smartphones (in '000s)

Month	Demand
January	8,000
February	10,000
March	11,000
April	11,000
May	11,000
June	12,000
July	13,000
August	14,000
September	15,000
October	17,000
November	19,000
December	19,000

demand in this market, each unit delayed in this manner cost 100,000 Rupiah in discounts offered to customers to keep them happy. The company had a policy of ensuring that there were no stockouts in December so the new year started out without any unfilled orders. The material cost for each phone was 500,000 Rupiah.

The factory ended December with 667 assembly teams and a million phones in inventory. The production plan at the factory attempted to meet demand in Table 8-13 at the lowest possible cost while ensuring that the factory ended December of the coming year with the same labor and inventory as the previous December.

Questions

1. What is the annual cost of the current plan where Rudy maintains a workforce of 667 throughout the year? How much should the factory produce each month? What is the maximum inventory under this plan?
2. How much can Rudy reduce cost by if he gives himself the flexibility of hiring and firing teams as desired? How much should the factory produce each month? What is the maximum inventory under this plan?

9

Sales and Operations Planning in a Supply Chain

LEARNING OBJECTIVES

After reading this chapter, you will be able to

9.1 Manage supply and demand to improve synchronization in a supply chain in the face of predictable variability.

9.2 Use sales and operations planning to maximize profitability when faced with predictable variability in a supply chain.

In Chapter 8, we discussed how companies use aggregate planning to make supply plans in a way that maximizes profits. In this chapter, we build on that knowledge and expand our scope of planning beyond the enterprise to the supply chain as we deal with predictable variability of demand. We also discuss how demand may be managed to counter predictable variability through the use of price and promotion. By using sales and operations planning to manage supply and demand together, managers can maximize overall profitability of a supply chain.

RESPONDING TO PREDICTABLE VARIABILITY IN THE SUPPLY CHAIN

In Chapter 8, we discussed how companies use aggregate planning to optimally plan supply. Demand for many products changes frequently from period to period, often because of a predictable influence. These influences include seasonal factors (e.g., weather) that affect products (e.g., lawn mowers and ski jackets), as well as non-seasonal factors (e.g., promotions or product adoption rates) that may cause large, predictable increases or declines in sales.

Predictable variability is change in demand that can be forecast. Products that undergo this type of change in demand create numerous problems in the supply chain, ranging from high levels of stockouts during peak demand periods to high levels of excess inventory during periods of low demand. These problems increase the costs and decrease the responsiveness of the supply chain. Supply and demand management through sales and operations planning (S&OP) can significantly improve performance when applied to predictably variable products.

9.1 Manage supply and demand to improve synchronization in a supply chain in the face of predictable variability.

Faced with predictable variability, a company's goal is to respond in a manner that balances supply with demand to maximize profitability. The goal of sales and operations planning is to appropriately combine two broad options to handle predictable variability:

1. Manage supply using capacity, inventory, subcontracting, and backlogs.
2. Manage demand using short-term price discounts and promotions.

The use of these tools enables the supply chain to increase profitability, because supply and demand are matched in a more coordinated fashion.

To illustrate some of the issues involved, let us consider John Deere, a manufacturer of agricultural equipment such as planters and combine harvesters. Demand for planters is seasonal, with most of the corn planting in the United Sates occurring between March and May. John Deere must plan how it will meet the seasonal demand for planters to maximize profit. One way requires John Deere to carry enough manufacturing capacity to meet demand for planters during the peak demand period. The advantage of this approach is that John Deere incurs low inventory costs because no inventory is carried from period to period. The disadvantage, however, is that much of the expensive capacity is unused during most months, when demand is lower.

Another approach to meeting seasonal demand is for Deere to build up inventory during the off-season to meet demand during the peak months. The advantage of this approach lies in the fact that Deere can get by with a lower-capacity, less expensive factory. High inventory carrying costs, however, add to the cost of this alternative. A third approach is for Deere to work with its retail partners in the supply chain to offer a price promotion to farmers before the peak months, during periods of low demand. This promotion shifts some of the peak demand for planters forward into a slow period, thereby reducing the seasonal surge and spreading demand more evenly. Such a demand pattern with a lower peak is less expensive to supply. John Deere uses its S&OP process to decide which alternative maximizes its profitability.

Often companies divide the task of supply and demand management into different functions, with sales typically managing demand while operations manages supply. At a higher level, supply chains suffer from this phenomenon as well, with retailers managing demand independently and manufacturers managing supply independently. Lack of coordination hurts supply chain profits when supply and demand management decisions are made independently. Therefore, supply chain partners must work together across functions and enterprises to coordinate S&OP decisions and maximize profitability. Many studies have shown that whereas top performers adopt cross-functional participation in S&OP across the entire organization, weaker performers have partial adoption at best. The level of cross-functional participation in the S&OP process is one of the biggest differentiators between top performers and other organizations.

We now focus on actions that a supply chain can take to deal with predictable variability by managing supply and demand.

Managing Supply

A firm can vary the supply of product by controlling a combination of the following two factors:

1. Production capacity
2. Inventory

In general, companies use a combination of varying capacity and inventory to manage supply. We list some specific approaches that allow firms to reduce the amount of capacity and inventory required to deal with predictable variability.

MANAGING CAPACITY Firms use a combination of the following approaches to reduce the cost of capacity required to meet predictable variability:

- *Time flexibility from workforce:* In this approach, a firm uses flexible work hours by the staff members to vary capacity with demand. In many instances, plants do not operate

continuously and are left idle during portions of the day or week. Therefore, spare plant capacity exists in the form of hours when the plant is not operational. For example, many plants do not run three shifts, so the existing workforce could work overtime during peak periods to produce more to meet demand. The overtime is varied to match the fluctuation in demand. In such settings, use of a part-time workforce can further increase capacity flexibility by enabling the firm to put more people to work during peak periods. This system allows production from the plant to match demand from customers more closely.

- *Use of seasonal workforce:* In this approach, a firm uses a temporary workforce during the peak season to increase capacity to match demand. The tourism industry often uses seasonal workers. A base of full-time employees exists, and more are hired only for the peak season. Toyota regularly uses a seasonal workforce in Japan to match supply and demand better. This approach may be hard to sustain, however, if the labor market is tight.
- *Use of dual facilities—specialized and flexible:* In this approach, a firm uses both specialized and flexible facilities. Specialized facilities produce a relatively stable output of products over time in an efficient manner. Flexible facilities produce a widely varying volume and variety of products, but at a higher unit cost. For instance, an electronics component manufacturer might have specialized facilities for each type of circuit board as well as a flexible facility that can manufacture all types of circuit boards. Each specialized facility can produce at a relatively steady rate, with fluctuations being absorbed by the flexible facility.
- *Use of subcontracting:* In this approach, a firm subcontracts peak production so internal production remains stable and can be done cheaply. For such an approach to work, the subcontractor must have flexible capacity and the ability to lower cost by pooling the fluctuations in demand across different manufacturers. Thus, the flexible subcontractor capacity must have both volume (fluctuating demand from a manufacturer) as well as variety (demand from several manufacturers) flexibility to be sustainable. For example, most power companies do not have the capacity to supply their customers with all the electricity demanded on peak days. They rely instead on being able to purchase power from suppliers and subcontractors that have excess electricity. This allows the power companies to maintain a stable supply and, consequently, a lower cost.
- *Designing product flexibility into the production processes:* In this approach, a firm has flexible production lines whose production rate can easily be varied. Production is then changed to match demand. Hino Trucks in Japan has several production lines for different product families in the same plant. The production lines are designed so that changing the number of workers on a line can vary the production rate. As long as variation of demand across different product lines is complementary (i.e., when one goes up, the other tends to go down), the capacity on each line can be varied by moving the workforce from one line to another. Of course, this requires that the workforce be multiskilled and able to adapt easily to being moved from line to line. Production flexibility can also be achieved if the production machinery is flexible and can be changed easily from producing one product to producing another. This approach is effective only if the overall demand across all the products is relatively stable. Several firms that produce products with seasonal demand try to exploit this approach by carrying a portfolio of products that have peak demand seasons distributed over the year. A classic example is that of a lawn mower manufacturer that also manufactures snow blowers to maintain a steady demand on its factory throughout the year.

MANAGING INVENTORY Firms use a combination of the following approaches to reduce the level of inventory required to meet predictable variability:

- *Using common components across multiple products:* In this approach, a firm designs common components to be used in multiple products. The total demand of these components is relatively stable, even though each product displays predictable variability.

The use of a common engine for both lawn mowers and snow blowers allows for engine demand to be relatively stable even though lawn mower and snow blower demand fluctuates over the year. Therefore, the part of the supply chain that produces components can easily synchronize supply with demand, and a relatively low inventory of parts has to be built up.

- *Build inventory of high-demand or predictable-demand products:* When most of the products a firm produces have the same peak demand season, the previous approach is not feasible. In such an environment, it is best for the firm to build products that have more predictable demand during the off-season, because there is less to be learned about their demand by waiting. Production of more uncertain items should take place closer to the selling season, when demand is more predictable. Consider a manufacturer of winter jackets that produces jackets both for retail sale and for the Boston police and fire departments. Demand for the Boston police and fire jackets is more predictable; these jackets can be made in the off-season and stocked up until winter. The retail jackets' demand, however, will likely be better known closer to the time when they are sold, because fashion trends can change quickly. Therefore, the manufacturer should produce the retail jackets close to the peak season, when demand is easier to predict. This strategy helps the supply chain synchronize supply and demand better.

Managing Demand

Supply chains can influence demand by using pricing and other forms of promotion. For example, John Deere offers a discount to farmers who are willing to take ownership of a planter during the off-season. The further from the peak that a farmer places an order, the larger the discount offered by Deere. The goal here is to move demand from the peak period to the off-peak period, thus reducing predictable variability. It is thus important to understand how promotions influence demand.

When a promotion is offered during a period, that period's demand tends to go up. This increase in demand results from a combination of the following three factors:

1. *Market growth:* An increase in consumption of the product occurs from either new or existing customers. For example, when Toyota offers a price promotion on the Camry, it may attract buyers who were considering the purchase of a lower-end model. Thus, the promotion increases the size of the overall family sedan market as well as increasing Toyota's sales.

2. *Stealing share:* Customers substitute the firm's product for a competitor's product. When Toyota offers a Camry promotion, buyers who might have purchased a Honda Accord may now purchase a Camry. Thus, the promotion increases Toyota's sales while keeping the overall size of the family sedan market the same.

3. *Forward buying:* Customers move up future purchases (as discussed in Chapter 11) to the present. A promotion may attract buyers who would have purchased a Camry a few months later. Forward buying does not increase Toyota's sales in the long run and also leaves the family sedan market the same size.

The first two factors increase the overall demand for Toyota, whereas forward buying simply shifts future demand to the present. It is important to understand the relative impact from the three factors as a result of a promotion before making a decision regarding the optimal timing of the promotion. In general, as the fraction of increased demand coming from forward buying grows, offering the promotion during the peak demand period becomes less attractive. Offering a promotion during a peak period that has significant forward buying creates even more variable demand than before the promotion. Product that was once demanded in the slow period is now demanded in the peak period, making this demand pattern even more costly to serve.

TABLE 9-1 Summary of Impact on Promotion Timing

Factor	Impact on Timing of Promotion/Forward Buy
High forward buying	Favors promotion during low-demand periods
High ability to steal market share	Favors promotion during peak-demand periods
High ability to increase overall market	Favors promotion during peak-demand periods
High margin	Favors promotion during peak-demand periods
Low margin	Favors promotion during low-demand periods
High manufacturer holding costs	Favors promotion during low-demand periods
High costs of changing capacity	Favors promotion during low-demand periods
High retailer holding costs	Decreases forward buying by retailer
High promotion elasticity of consumer	Decreases forward buying by retailer

FACTORS INFLUENCING THE TIMING OF A PROMOTION Four key factors influence the timing of a promotion:

- Impact of the promotion on demand
- Cost of holding inventory
- Cost of changing the level of capacity
- Product margins

If a promotion primarily results in forward buying (as may be the case for a product like detergent), it is best to use promotions to reduce the seasonal peak by offering a price discount during low-demand periods. Offering a promotion during low-demand periods also makes sense if the manufacturer has a high cost of holding inventory or finds it expensive to change production levels. It is for this reason that John Deere offers its promotion during low-demand periods before the peak. In contrast, if a promotion results in a significant increase in sales by attracting new buyers, it may be better to offer a price discount during the peak period, when many buyers are in the market for the product. The increased cost of production because of the higher peak demand resulting from a promotion is likely to be offset by the margin obtained from new buyers. Table 9-1 summarizes the impact of various factors on the optimal timing of promotions.

SUMMARY OF LEARNING OBJECTIVE 1

Companies can maximize profits by managing supply and demand to improve synchronization in a supply chain in the face of predictable variability. Supply can be managed using capacity or inventory. Companies can reduce the capacity required through the use of workforce flexibility, subcontracting, dual facilities, and product flexibility. Companies can reduce the inventory required by emphasizing common parts and building and holding products with predictable demand ahead of time. Demand can be managed using pricing and promotion decisions because the timing of promotions has a tremendous impact on demand. Therefore, using pricing to shape demand in concert with supply planning can help improve supply chain profits.

SALES AND OPERATIONS PLANNING AT RED TOMATO

9.2 Use sales and operations planning to maximize profitability when faced with predictable variability in a supply chain.

Promotion decisions are often made by retailers without accounting for the impact on the rest of the supply chain. In this section, our goal is to show how supply chain members can collaborate on sales and operations planning (both demand and supply management) decisions to maximize supply chain profitability. Let us return to Red Tomato Tools, the gardening tools manufacturer

discussed in Chapter 8. Green Thumb Gardens is a large retail chain that has signed an exclusive contract to sell all products made by Red Tomato Tools. Demand for garden tools peaks in the spring months of March and April, as gardeners prepare to begin planting. In planning, the goal of both firms should be to maximize supply chain profits, because this outcome leaves them more money to share. For profit maximization to take place, Red Tomato and Green Thumb need to devise a way to collaborate and, just as important, determine a way to split the supply chain profits. Determining how these profits will be allocated to different members of the supply chain is key to successful collaboration.

Red Tomato and Green Thumb are exploring how the timing of retail promotions affects profitability. Are they in a better position if they offer the price promotion during the peak period of demand or during a low-demand period? Green Thumb's vice president of sales favors a promotion during the peak period because this increases revenue by the largest amount. In contrast, Red Tomato's vice president of manufacturing is against such a move because it increases manufacturing costs. She favors a promotion during the low-demand season because it levels demand and lowers production costs. S&OP allows the two to collaborate and make the optimal trade-offs.

The Base Case

We start by considering the base case discussed in Chapter 8. Each tool has a retail price of $40. Red Tomato ships assembled tools to Green Thumb, where all inventory is held. Green Thumb has a starting inventory in January of 1,000 tools. At the beginning of January, Red Tomato has a workforce of 80 employees at its manufacturing facility in Mexico. There are 20 working days in each month, and Red Tomato workers earn the equivalent of $4 per hour. Each employee works eight hours on normal time and the rest on overtime. Because the Red Tomato operation consists mostly of hand assembly, the capacity of the production operation is determined primarily by the total labor hours worked (i.e., it is not limited by machine capacity). No employee works more than 10 hours of overtime per month. The various costs are shown in Table 9-2.

There are no limits on subcontracting, inventories, and stockouts. All stockouts are back-logged and supplied from the following month's production. Inventory costs are incurred on the ending inventory in each month. The companies' goal is to obtain the optimal aggregate plan that leaves at least 500 units of inventory at the end of June (i.e., no stock outs at the end of June and at least 500 units in inventory). The base demand forecast is shown in cells J5:J10 of Figure 9-1. All figures and analysis in this chapter come from the spreadsheet *Chapter 8, 9-examples*, which uses Solver. The equivalent solutions can also be obtained without Solver using the spreadsheet *Chapter 8-trial-aggplan*. The spreadsheet contains instructions for use and worksheets corresponding to Figures 9-1 to 9-5.

TABLE 9-2 Costs for Red Tomato and Green Thumb

Item	Cost
Material cost	$10/unit
Inventory holding cost	$2/unit/month
Marginal cost of a stock out	$5/unit/month
Hiring and training costs	$300/worker
Layoff cost	$500/worker
Labor hours required	4/unit
Regular-time cost	$4/hour
Overtime cost	$6/hour
Cost of subcontracting	$30/unit

	Ht	Lt	Wt	Ot	It	St	Ct	Pt		
Period	# Hired	# Laid off	# Workforce	Overtime	Inventory	Stockout	Subcontract	Production	Demand	Price
0	0	0	80	0	1,000	0	0			
1	0	16	64	0	1,960	0	0	2,560	1,600	40
2	0	0	64	0	1,520	0	0	2,560	3,000	40
3	0	0	64	0	880	0	0	2,560	3,200	40
4	0	0	64	0	0	220	140	2,560	3,800	40
5	0	0	64	0	140	0	0	2,560	2,200	40
6	0	0	64	0	500	0	0	2,560	2,200	40

Aggregate Plan Decision Variables

Total Cost = $422,660

Total Revenue = $640,000 Promote? (0/1) 0 Base Price $ 40
Profit = $217,340 Month (1/4) 1 Consumption 0.10
 Forward buy 0.20

Figure 9-1 Base Case Aggregate Plan for Red Tomato and Green Thumb

For the base case, we set cell E24 to 0 (no promotion) and use Solver. The optimal base case aggregate plan for Red Tomato and Green Thumb is shown in Figure 9-1 (this is the same as discussed in Chapter 8 and shown in Table 8-4).

For the base case aggregate plan, the supply chain obtains the following costs and revenues:

$$\text{Total cost over planning horizon} = \$422,660$$
$$\text{Revenue over planning horizon} = \$640,000$$
$$\text{Profit over the planning horizon} = \$217,340$$

When to Promote: Peak or Off-Peak?

Green Thumb estimates that discounting a Red Tomato tool from $40 to $39 (a $1 discount) in any period results in the period demand increasing by 10 percent because of increased consumption or substitution. Further, 20 percent of each of the two following months' demand is moved forward. Management would like to determine whether it is more effective to offer the discount in January or April. We analyze the two options by considering the impact of a promotion on demand and the resulting optimal aggregate plan.

IMPACT OF OFFERING A PROMOTION IN JANUARY The team first considers the impact of offering the discount in January. To simulate this option in the spreadsheet *Chapter 8,9-examples*, enter 1 in cell E24 (this sets promotion to be on) and 1 in cell E25 (this sets the promotion in Period 1– i.e., January). The new forecast accounts for the fact that consumption will increase by 10 percent in January and 20 percent of the demand from February and March is moved forward to January. Thus, with a January promotion, the new demand forecast for January is obtained by adjusting the base case demand from Figure 9-1 and is given by $(1,600 \times 1.1) + [0.2 \times (3,000 + 3,200)] = 3,000$ (see Cell J5 in Figure 9-2). The new demand forecast for February is $3,000 \times 0.8 = 2,400$, and the new demand forecast for March is $3,200 \times 0.8 = 2,560$. For a January discount, the demand forecast is as shown in cells J5:J10 of Figure 9-2. The optimal aggregate plan is obtained by running Solver in the spreadsheet and is shown in Figure 9-2. With a discount in January, the supply chain obtains the following:

$$\text{Total cost over planning horizon} = \$422,080$$
$$\text{Revenue over planning horizon} = \$643,400$$
$$\text{Profit over the planning horizon} = \$221,320$$

Compared with the base case, offering a discount in January results in lower seasonal inventory, a somewhat lower total cost, and a higher total profit.

	A	B	C	D	E	F	G	H	I	J	K
1	Aggregate Plan Decision Variables										
2		Ht	Lt	Wt	Ot	It	St	Ct	Pt		
3	Period	# Hired	# Laid off	# Workforce	Overtime	Inventory	Stockout	Subcontract	Production	Demand	Price
4	0	0	0	80	0	1,000	0	0			
5	1	0	15	65	0	600	0	0	2,600	3,000	39
6	2	0	0	65	0	800	0	0	2,600	2,400	40
7	3	0	0	65	0	840	0	0	2,600	2,560	40
8	4	0	0	65	0	0	300	60	2,600	3,800	40
9	5	0	0	65	0	100	0	0	2,600	2,200	40
10	6	0	0	65	0	500	0	0	2,600	2,200	40

22	Total Cost =	$422,080					
23					Base Price	$	40
24	Total Revenue =	$643,400	Promote? (0/1)	1	Consumption		0.10
25	Profit =	$221,320	Month (1/4)	1	Forward buy		0.20

Figure 9-2 Optimal Aggregate Plan When Discounting Price in January to $39

IMPACT OF OFFERING A PROMOTION IN APRIL Now, management considers the impact of offering the discount in April. To simulate this option in the spreadsheet *Chapter 8,9-examples*, enter 1 in cell E24 (this sets promotion to be on) and 4 in cell E25 (this sets the promotion in Period 4—i.e., April). If Green Thumb offers the discount in April, the demand forecast is as shown in cells J5:J10 of Figure 9-3. The optimal aggregate plan is obtained by running Solver and is shown in Figure 9-3. Compared with discounting in January (Figure 9-2), discounting in April requires more capacity (in terms of workforce) and leads to a greater buildup of seasonal inventory and larger stockouts because of the big jump in demand in April. With a discount in April, we have the following:

$$\text{Total cost over planning horizon} = \$438{,}920$$
$$\text{Revenue over planning horizon} = \$650{,}140$$
$$\text{Profit over the planning horizon} = \$211{,}220$$

Observe that a price promotion in January results in a higher supply chain profit, whereas a promotion in April results in a lower supply chain profit, compared with the base case of not running a promotion. As a result of the S&OP process, Red Tomato and Green Thumb decide to offer the discount in the off-peak month of January. Even though revenues are higher when the discount is offered in April, the increase in operating costs makes it a less profitable option. A promotion in January allows Red Tomato and Green Thumb to increase the profit they can share.

Note that this analysis is possible only because the retailer and manufacturer have an S&OP process that facilitates collaboration during the planning phase. This conclusion supports our earlier statement that it is not appropriate for a supply chain to leave pricing decisions solely in the domain of retailers and aggregate planning solely in the domain of manufacturers, with each having individual forecasts. It is crucial that forecasts, pricing, and aggregate planning be coordinated in a supply chain.

The importance of a collaborative S&OP process is further supported by the fact that the optimal action is different if most of the demand increase comes from market growth or stealing market share rather than from forward buying. We now illustrate the scenario in which a discount leads to a large increase in consumption.

When to Offer a Promotion If Discount Leads to a Large Increase in Consumption

Reconsider the situation in which discounting a unit from $40 to $39 results in the period demand increasing by 100 percent (instead of the 10 percent considered in the previous analysis) because of increased consumption or substitution. Further, 20 percent of each of the two following months' demand is moved forward. The supply chain team wants to determine whether it is preferable to offer the discount in January or April under these conditions. To simulate this scenario,

Period	H_t # Hired	L_t # Laid off	W_t # Workforce	O_t Overtime	I_t Inventory	S_t Stockout	C_t Subcontract	P_t Production	Demand	Price
0	0	0	80	0	1,000	0	0			
1	0	14	66	0	2,040	0	0	2,640	1,600	40
2	0	0	66	0	1,680	0	0	2,640	3,000	40
3	0	0	66	0	1,120	0	0	2,640	3,200	40
4	0	0	66	0	0	1,260	40	2,640	5,060	39
5	0	0	66	0	0	380	0	2,640	1,760	40
6	0	0	66	0	500	0	0	2,640	1,760	40

Aggregate Plan Decision Variables

Total Cost = $438,920

		Base Price	$	40	
Total Revenue =	$650,140	Promote? (0/1)	1	Consumption	0.10
Profit =	$211,220	Month (1/4)	4	Forward buy	0.20

Figure 9-3 Optimal Aggregate Plan When Discounting Price in April to $39

change the entry in cell H24 (increase in consumption) of spreadsheet *Chapter 8, 9-examples* from 0.10 (10 percent) to 1.00 (100 percent). Set the entry in cell E24 to 1 to set the promotion to be on. The base case when no promotion is offered remains unchanged as shown in Figure 9-1. We now repeat the analysis for the cases in which the promotion is offered in January (off-peak) and April (peak).

IMPACT OF OFFERING A PROMOTION IN JANUARY For a January promotion, set the entry in cell E25 to 1 (Period 1, January). If the discount is offered in January, the January demand forecast is obtained as $(1,600 \times 2) + [0.2 \times (3,000 + 3,200)] = 4,440$. This is much higher than the same forecast in Figure 9-2 because we have assumed that consumption in the promotion month increases by 100 percent, rather than the 10 percent assumed earlier. The demand forecast for a January promotion with a large increase in consumption is shown in cells J5:J10 of Figure 9-4.

The optimal aggregate plan is obtained using Solver and is shown in Figure 9-4. With a discount in January the team obtains the following:

$$\text{Total cost over planning horizon} = \$456,880$$
$$\text{Revenue over planning horizon} = \$699,560$$
$$\text{Profit over the planning horizon} = \$242,680$$

Observe that a January promotion when the consumption increase is large results in a higher profit than the base case (Figure 9-1).

IMPACT OF OFFERING A PROMOTION IN APRIL For an April promotion, set the entry in cell E25 to 4 (Period 4, April). If the discount is offered in April, the April demand forecast is obtained as $(3,800 \times 2) + [0.2 \times (2,200 + 2,200)] = 8,480$. With a promotion in April and a large

Period	H_t # Hired	L_t # Laid off	W_t # Workforce	O_t Overtime	I_t Inventory	S_t Stockout	C_t Subcontract	P_t Production	Demand	Price
0	0	0	80	0	1,000	0	0			
1	0	0	80	0	0	140	100	3,200	4,440	39
2	0	11	69	0	220	0	0	2,760	2,400	40
3	0	0	69	0	420	0	0	2,760	2,560	40
4	0	0	69	0	0	620	0	2,760	3,800	40
5	0	0	69	0	0	60	0	2,760	2,200	40
6	0	0	69	0	500	0	0	2,760	2,200	40

Aggregate Plan Decision Variables

Total Cost = $456,880

		Base Price	$	40	
Total Revenue =	$699,560	Promote? (0/1)	1	Consumption	1.00
Profit =	$242,680	Month (1/4)	1	Forward buy	0.20

Figure 9-4 Optimal Aggregate Plan When Discounting Price in January to $39 with Large Increase in Demand

	A	B	C	D	E	F	G	H	I	J	K
1	Aggregate Plan Decision Variables										
2		Ht	Lt	Wt	Ot	It	St	Ct	Pt		
3	Period	# Hired	# Laid off	# Workforce	Overtime	Inventory	Stockout	Subcontract	Production	Demand	Price
4	0	0	0	80	0	1,000	0	0			
5	1	0	0	80	0	2,600	0	0	3,200	1,600	40
6	2	0	0	80	0	2,800	0	0	3,200	3,000	40
7	3	0	0	80	0	2,800	0	0	3,200	3,200	40
8	4	0	0	80	0	0	2,380	100	3,200	8,480	39
9	5	0	0	80	0	0	940	0	3,200	1,760	40
10	6	0	0	80	0	500	0	0	3,200	1,760	40

22	Total Cost =	$536,200				
23				Base Price	$	40
24	Total Revenue =	$783,520	Promote? (0/1)	1	Consumption	1.00
25	Profit =	$247,320	Month (1/4)	4	Forward buy	0.20

Figure 9-5 Optimal Aggregate Plan When Discounting Price in April to $39 with Large Increase in Demand

increase in consumption, the April peak is much higher in Figure 9-5 compared with peak demand in Figure 9-4 (with a January promotion). For an April promotion with a large increase in consumption, the resulting demand forecast is as shown in cells J5:J10 of Figure 9-5. The optimal aggregate plan is obtained using Solver and is shown in Figure 9-5.

With a discount in April, the team obtains the following:

$$\text{Total cost over planning horizon} = \$536,200$$
$$\text{Revenue over planning horizon} = \$783,520$$
$$\text{Profit over the planning horizon} = \$247,320$$

When comparing Figures 9-5 and 9-4, observe that with an April promotion (Figure 9-5), there are no layoffs and the full workforce is maintained. The April promotion requires a much higher level of seasonal inventory and also uses stockouts and subcontracting to a greater extent than a January promotion. It is clear that costs will go up significantly with an April promotion. The interesting observation is that revenues go up even more (because of a larger consumption increase), making overall profits higher with an April promotion compared with a January promotion. As a result, when the increase in consumption from discounting is large and forward buying is a small part of the increase in demand from discounting, the supply chain is better off offering the discount in the peak-demand month of April, even though this action significantly increases supply chain costs.

Exactly as discussed earlier, the optimal aggregate plan and profitability can also be determined for the case in which the unit price is $31 (enter 31 in cell H23) and the discounted price is $30. The results of the various instances are summarized in Table 9-3.

From the results in Table 9-3, we can draw the following conclusions regarding the impact of promotions:

1. As seen in Table 9-3, average inventory increases if a promotion is run during the peak period and decreases if the promotion is run during the off-peak period.
2. Promoting during a peak-demand month may decrease overall profitability if there is a small increase in consumption and a significant fraction of the demand increase results from a forward buy. In Table 9-3, observe that running a promotion in April decreases profitability when forward buying is 20 percent and the demand increase from increased consumption and substitution is 10 percent.
3. As the consumption increase from discounting grows and forward buying becomes a smaller fraction of the demand increase from a promotion, it is more profitable to promote during the peak period. From Table 9-3, for a sale price of $40, it is optimal to promote in the off-peak month of January, when forward buying is 20 percent and increased

TABLE 9-3 Supply Chain Performance Under Different Scenarios

Regular Price	Promotion Price	Promotion Period	Percentage of Increase in Demand	Percentage of Forward Buy	Profit	Average Inventory
$40	$40	NA	NA	NA	$217,340	875
$40	$39	January	10%	20%	$221,320	515
$40	$39	April	10%	20%	$211,220	932
$40	$39	January	100%	20%	$242,680	232
$40	$39	April	100%	20%	$247,320	1,492
$31	$31	NA	NA	NA	$73,340	875
$31	$30	January	100%	20%	$84,280	232
$31	$30	April	100%	20%	$69,120	1,492

consumption is 10 percent. When forward buying is 20 percent and increased consumption is 100 percent, however, it is optimal to promote in the peak month of April.

4. As the product margin declines, promoting during the peak-demand period becomes less profitable. In Table 9-3, observe that for a unit price of $40, it is optimal to promote in the peak month of April when forward buying is 20 percent and increased consumption is 100 percent. In contrast, if the unit price is $31, it is optimal to promote in the off-peak month of January for the same level of forward buying and increase in consumption.

A key point from the Red Tomato supply chain examples we have considered in this chapter is that when a firm is faced with seasonal demand, it should use a combination of pricing (to manage demand) and production and inventory (to manage supply) to improve profitability. The precise use of each lever varies with the situation. This makes it crucial that enterprises in a supply chain coordinate both their forecasting and planning efforts through an S&OP process. Only then are profits maximized.

For a supply chain to manage predictable variability successfully, the entire chain must work toward the one goal of maximizing profitability. Every member of a supply chain may agree with this in principle. In reality, however, it is difficult for an entire supply chain to agree on how to maximize profitability. Firms have even had trouble getting different functions within an enterprise to plan collaboratively. Incentives play a large role in this. Within a company, the sales function often has incentives based on revenue, whereas operations has incentives based on cost. Within a supply chain, different enterprises are judged by their own profitability, not necessarily by the overall supply chain's profitability. From the examples considered earlier, it is clear that without a focus on getting companies to work together, a supply chain will return suboptimal profits. Successful collaboration requires that the incentives of the members of a supply chain must be aligned.

High-level support within an organization is needed because this coordination often requires groups to act against their traditional operating procedures. Although this collaboration is difficult, the payoffs are significant. The role of an S&OP process owner is like that of the conductor of an orchestra—to bring different functions and organizations together in a supply chain. Given competing interests, this alignment is unlikely unless the S&OP process owner is a senior leader with sufficient authority.

It is important that early warning alerts be built into the S&OP process. A change in demand or supply circumstances may leave the reality different from plan. In such a situation, it is important for the planners to alert the supply chain regarding the old plan and provide a new plan that accounts for these changes. Even if there are no short-term alerts, the output of the

S&OP process should be modified as forecasts or marketing plans are adjusted. Constant modification of the plan, however, can lead to a loss of trust in the planning process.

SUMMARY OF LEARNING OBJECTIVE 2

To handle predictable variability in a profit-maximizing manner, supply chains must coordinate the management of both supply and demand. This requires coordinated planning across all stages of the supply chain to select pricing and promotion plans and aggregate plans that maximize supply chain profit. Sales and operations planning allows a supply chain to coordinate the planning of pricing and promotions along with the planning of production to maximize profits. To achieve coordination in practice, it is important that the S&OP process be owned by a senior leader within the supply chain.

DISCUSSION QUESTIONS

1. What are some obstacles to creating a flexible workforce? What are the benefits?
2. How can a manufacturer tackle seasonal demand in operations planning?
3. In which industries would you tend to see dual facility types (some facilities focusing on only one type of product and others able to produce a wide variety)? In which industries would this be relatively rare? Why?
4. What does it mean to incorporate product flexibility in the production processes? Give an example.
5. A hat manufacturer produces hats for (1) retail sales to the public and (2) correctional services as part of a uniform. Which production should it complete first? Why?
6. Discuss how a company can get sales and operations to work together with the common goal of coordinating supply and demand to maximize profitability.
7. How can a firm use pricing to change demand patterns?
8. Why would a firm want to offer pricing promotions in its peak-demand periods?
9. What are the major steps required in implementing sales and operations planning in supply chain management?

EXERCISES

1. Lavare, located in the Chicago suburbs, is a major manufacturer of stainless steel sinks. Lavare is in the middle of the demand and supply planning exercise for the coming year. Anticipated monthly demand from distributors over the 12 months is shown in Table 9-4.

 The number of machine operators it hires governs capacity at Lavare. The firm works 20 days a month, with a regular operating shift of eight hours per day. Any time beyond that is considered overtime. Regular-time pay is $15 per hour and overtime is $22 per hour. Overtime is limited to 20 hours per month per employee. The plant currently has 250 employees. Each sink requires two hours of labor input. It costs $3 to carry a sink in inventory for a month. Materials cost per sink is $40. Sinks are sold to distributors at a price of $125 each. We assume that no stockouts are allowed and the starting inventory entering January is 5,000 units and the desired ending inventory in December is also 5,000 units.

 Market research has indicated that a promotion dropping prices by 1 percent in a given month will increase sales in that month by 20 percent and bring forward 10 percent demand from each of the following two months. Thus, a 1 percent drop in price in March increases sales in March by 3,000 (= 0.2×15,000) and shifts 1,800 (= 0.1×18,000) units

in demand from April and 2,500 (= 0.1 × 25,000) units from May forward to March.

TABLE 9-4 Anticipated Monthly Demand for Lavare

Month	Demand
January	10,000
February	11,000
March	16,000
April	19,000
May	22,000
June	25,000
July	31,000
August	28,000
September	22,000
October	19,000
November	13,000
December	12,000

a. What is the optimal production plan for the year if we assume no promotions? What is the annual profit from this plan? What is the cost of this plan?

b. Is it better to promote in April or July? How much increase in profit can be achieved as a result?

c. If sinks are sold for $250 instead of $125, does the decision about the timing of the promotion change? Why?

2. Consider the data for Lavare in Exercise 1. We now assume that Lavare can change the size of the workforce by laying off or hiring employees. Hiring a new employee incurs a cost of $1,000; laying off an employee incurs a layoff cost of $2,000.

a. What is the optimal production plan for the year if we assume no promotions? What is the annual profit with this plan? What is the cost of this plan?

b. Is it better to promote in April or July? How much increase in profit can be achieved as a result?

c. If the holding cost for sinks increases from $3 per month to $5 per month, does the decision of the timing of promotion change? Why or why not?

3. Return to the data for Lavare in Exercise 1. Now, assume that a third party has offered to produce sinks at $74 per unit. How does this change affect the optimal production plan without a promotion? How does this change affect the optimal timing of a promotion? Explain the changes.

4. Jumbo manufactures bicycles for all ages. The demand forecast for the coming year is as shown in Table 9-5.

Capacity at Jumbo is limited by the number of employees it hires. Employees are paid $10 per hour for regular time and $15 per hour for overtime. Each bicycle requires 2 hours of work from one employee. The plant works 20 days a month and 8 hours a day of regular time. Overtime is restricted to a maximum of 20 hours per employee per month. Jumbo currently has 250 employees and prefers not to change that number.

Each bicycle uses $35 of material. Carrying a bicycle in inventory from one month to the next costs $4. Jumbo starts with 4,000 bicycles in inventory and wants to end the year with 4,000 bicycles in inventory. Bicycles are currently sold to retailers for $80 each. The market is shared between Jumbo and its competitor, Shrimpy.

Jumbo is in the process of making its production planning and promotion decisions. Jumbo wants to consider only plans without any stockouts. One option is to drop the sale price by $3 (from $80 to $77) for one month in the year. The outcome of this action by Jumbo is influenced by the action taken by Shrimpy. If neither firm promotes, the forecast demand for Jumbo is as shown in Table 9-5. If Jumbo promotes in a given month but Shrimpy does not, Jumbo sees consumption (this does not include forward buying) in that month increase by 40 percent and forward buying of 10 percent from each of the two following months. If Shrimpy promotes in a given month but Jumbo does not, Jumbo sees consumption in the month drop by 40 percent, with no change in other months. If both promote in a given month, neither sees an increase in consumption but both see forward buying of 15 percent from each of the two following months. The debate within Jumbo is whether to promote, and if so, whether to do it in April or June. For the following questions, assume that Shrimpy and Jumbo have similar demand.

a. What is the optimal production plan for Jumbo, assuming no promotion by either Jumbo or Shrimpy? What are the annual profits for Jumbo?

b. What are the profits for Jumbo if Shrimpy promotes in April but Jumbo does not promote throughout the year (because it follows everyday low pricing)? What are the profits for Jumbo if it promotes in April but Shrimpy does not promote throughout the year? Comment on the benefit from promoting versus the loss from not promoting if the competitor does.

c. What are the optimal production plans and profits if both promote in April? Both promote in June? Jumbo promotes in April but Shrimpy in June? Jumbo promotes in June but Shrimpy in April?

d. What is the best decision for Jumbo if it can coordinate its decision with Shrimpy?

e. What is the best decision for Jumbo if it wants to maximize its minimum profits no matter what Shrimpy does?

5. We now reconsider the issue of competitors and promotions in the context of a commodity product such as detergent, for which demand is relatively stable during the year. Q&H is a major detergent manufacturer with a demand forecast for the coming year as shown in Table 9-6 (in tons).

Capacity at Q&H is governed by the number of hours the line runs. The line requires a team of 100 employees. Employees are paid $10 per hour for regular time and $15 per hour for overtime. Each ton of detergent requires 1 hour of operation of the line. The plant works 20 days a month, two shifts a day, and 8 hours per shift of regular time. Overtime is restricted to a maximum of 20 hours per employee per month.

TABLE 9-5 Anticipated Monthly Demand at Jumbo

Month	Demand
January	12,000
February	11,000
March	14,000
April	20,000
May	25,000
June	27,000
July	24,000
August	20,000
September	15,000
October	10,000
November	11,000
December	10,000

TABLE 9-6 Anticipated Monthly Demand at Q&H

Month	Demand
January	280
February	301
March	277
April	302
May	285
June	278
July	291
August	277
September	304
October	291
November	302
December	297

Each ton of detergent uses $1,000 of material. Carrying a ton of detergent in inventory from one month to the next costs $100. Q&H starts with 150 tons in inventory and wants to end with the same level. During intermediate months, Q&H wants at least 100 tons of inventory. Detergent is currently sold to retailers for $2,600 per ton. The detergent market is shared between Q&H and its competitor, Unilock.

Q&H is in the process of making its production planning and promotion decisions. Q&H wants to consider only plans without any stockouts. One option is to drop the sale price by $260 per ton (from $2,600 to $2,340) for one month in the year. The outcome of this action by Q&H is influenced by the action taken by Unilock. If neither firm promotes, the forecast demand for Q&H is as shown in Table 9-6. If Q&H promotes in a given month but Unilock does not, Q&H sees consumption (does not include forward buying) in that month increase by 50 percent and forward buying of 20 percent from each of the two following months. If Unilock promotes in a given month but Q&H does not, Q&H sees consumption in the month drop by 50 percent. If both promote in a given month, neither sees an increase in consumption but both see forward buying of 25 percent from each of the two following months. The debate within Q&H is whether to promote, and, if so, whether to do it in April or June. For the following questions, assume that demand for Unilock is like that of Q&H.

a. What is the optimal production plan for Q&H assuming no promotion by either Q&H or Unilock? What are the annual profits for Q&H?

b. What are the profits for Q&H if Unilock promotes in April but Q&H does not promote throughout the year (because it uses everyday low pricing)? What are the profits for Q&H if it promotes in April but Unilock does not promote throughout the year? Comment on the benefit from promoting versus the loss from not promoting if the competitor does.

c. What are the optimal production plan and profits if both firms promote in April? Both promote in June? Q&H promotes in April but Unilock in June? Q&H promotes in June but Unilock in April?

d. What is the best decision for Q&H if it can coordinate its decision with Unilock?

e. What is the best decision for Q&H if it wants to maximize its minimum profits no matter what Unilock does?

6. Return to the data for Exercise 5. Assume that Q&H has a third party willing to manufacture detergent as needed for $2,300 per ton. Repeat the analysis for all questions (a) through (e).

BIBLIOGRAPHY

Brandel, William. "The Persistent Gap Between Supply and Demand." *CSMP's Supply Chain Quarterly* (Q4/2007): 52–57.

Chen, Clarence, and Nirmal Hasan. "How to Succeed with Supply Chain Planning."*Supply Chain Management Review* (July–August 2008): 30–36.

Iyengar, Charanyan, and Sandeep Gupta. "Building Blocks for Successful S&OP."*Supply Chain Management Review* (November 2013): 10–17.

Karrenbauer, Jeff. "Advancing the Cause of Supply Chain Management and S&OP Through Advanced Analytics."*Supply Chain Management Review* (May–June 2015): 10–18.

Marien, Edward J. "Why Focus on Demand Usage Management?" *Supply Chain Management Review* (October 2008): 42–48.

Martin, André J. "Capacity Planning: The Antidote to Supply Chain Constraints." *Supply Chain Management Review* (November–December 2001): 62–67.

Mitchell, Pierre. "Supply Analytics: An Overlooked Opportunity." *Supply Chain Management Review* (July–August 2012): 26–33.

Prokopets, Len. "S&OP: What You Can Learn from the Top Performers." *Supply Chain Management Review* (May–June 2012): 28–35.

Upton, Harold, and Harpal Singh. "Balanced S&OP: Sunsweet Growers' Story." *Supply Chain Management Review* (March 2007): 51–59.

CASE STUDY

Mintendo Game Girl

It is late June, and Sandra Huchim, head of operations at Mintendo, and Bill Smith, head of sales of We "R" Toys, are about to get together to discuss production and marketing plans for the next 6 months. Mintendo is the manufacturer of the popular Game Girl handheld electronic game that is sold exclusively through We "R" Toys retail stores. The second half of the year is critical to Game Girl's success, because a majority of its sales occur during the holiday shopping period.

Sandra is worried about the impact that the upcoming holiday surge in demand will have on her production line. Costs to subcontract assembly of the Game Girls are expected to increase, and she has been trying to keep costs down, given that her bonus depends on the level of production costs.

Bill is worried about competing toy stores gaining share in the handheld electronic game market during the Christmas buying season. He has seen many companies lose their share by failing to keep prices in line with the performance of their products. He would like to maximize the Game Girl market share in the handheld electronic game market.

Both Sandra's and Bill's teams produce a joint forecast of demand over the next six months, as shown in Table 9-7.

We "R" Toys sells Game Girls for $50 apiece. At the end of June, the company has an inventory of 50,000 Game Girls. Capacity of the production facility is set purely by the number of workers assembling the Game Girls. At the end of June, the company has a workforce of 300 employees, each of whom works 8 hours of regular time at $15/hour for 20 days each month. Work rules require that no employee work more than 40 hours of overtime per month. The various costs are shown in Table 9-8.

TABLE 9-8 Costs for Mintendo/We "R" Toys

Item	Cost
Material cost	$12/unit
Inventory holding cost	$2/unit/month
Marginal cost of a stockout	$10/unit/month
Hiring and training costs	$3,000/worker
Layoff cost	$5,000/worker
Labor hours required	0.25/unit
Regular-time cost	$15/hour
Overtime cost	$22.50/hour
Cost of subcontracting	$18/unit

Sandra, concerned about controlling costs during the periods of surging demand over the holidays, proposes to Bill that the price be lowered by $5 for the month of September. This would likely increase September's demand by 50 percent due to new customers being attracted to Game Girl. In addition, 30 percent of each of the following two months of demand would occur in September as forward buys. She believes strongly that this leveling of demand will help the company.

Bill counters with the idea of offering the same promotion in November, during the heart of the buying season. In this case, the promotion increases November's demand by 50 percent, owing to new customers being attracted to Game Girl. Additionally, 30 percent of December's demand would occur in November as forward buying. Bill wants to increase revenue and sees no better way to do this than to offer a promotion during the peak season.

TABLE 9-7 Demand for Game Girls

Month	Demand Forecast
July	100,000
August	110,000
September	130,000
October	180,000
November	250,000
December	300,000

Questions

1. Which option delivers the maximum profit for the supply chain: Sandra's plan, Bill's plan, or no promotion plan at all? Assume ending inventory of 0.
2. How does the answer change if a discount of $10 must be given to reach the same level of impact that the $5 discount received?
3. Suppose Sandra's fears about increasing outsourcing costs come to fruition and the cost rises to $22/unit for subcontracting. Does this change the decision when the discount is $5?

CASE STUDY

Promotion Challenges at Gulmarg Skis

Management at Gulmarg Skis was surprised in the previous season when a competitor, Kitz, discounted their skis by $50 in October. In a market in which discounting was rare, this was an unusual move by Kitz. As a result, Gulmarg saw a significant drop in sales between October and January. The company did not want to be caught unprepared for the upcoming season and was planning its response. Two alternatives being considered by Gulmarg were to promote in October or December. Gulmarg could not precisely predict what Kitz would do regarding promotions but felt that Kitz was likely to repeat its October promotion, given its success in the previous year.

Gulmarg and Kitz competed in high-performance skis and sold direct to end consumers. The companies prided themselves on outstanding craftsmanship, using only the best materials. Both were known for the high quality of their skis and the fact that customers could design their own top sheet. Although each company had a loyal following, there was a significant fraction of customers who were happy to buy skis from either. It is this group that the two companies were competing for through price discounts.

The sale of skis was highly seasonal, with all sales occurring between October and March, as shown in Table 9-9. Production capacity at the manufacturing plant was limited by the number of employees that Gulmarg hired. Employees were paid $15/hour for regular time and $23/hour for overtime. Each pair of skis required 4 hours of work from an employee. The plant worked 20 days a month, 8 hours a day on regular time. Overtime was restricted to a maximum of 40 hours per employee per month. Gulmarg employed a total of 60 workers and felt that it could not let any of them go, even in months when demand was below the capacity

TABLE 9-9 Demand Forecast for Gulmarg Skis

Month	Demand Forecast
October	1,600
November	2,400
December	4,200
January	3,800
February	2,200
March	2,200

provided by 60 workers. Given the high skill requirements, the company had difficulty finding suitable people and as a result could hire only up to a maximum of 10 temporary employees. In other words, the number of employees could fluctuate between 60 and 70. Hiring each temporary employee cost $500, and letting each one go cost another $800.

Each pair of skis used material worth $300, mostly in the form of expensive carbon fiber, plastic, and alloys. Carrying a pair of skis in inventory from one month to the next cost $10. Given the seasonal nature of demand, Gulmarg started October with an inventory of 2,000 pairs of skis and preferred to end in March with no inventory to carry over. Any leftover inventory at the end of March cost Gulmarg the equivalent of $500 a pair because of the discounting required to sell it. Customers were not willing to wait for skis, so Gulmarg lost all sales that it could not meet in a month because of insufficient inventory and production. Gulmarg's skis were normally priced at $800 a pair.

Before making its production plans, Gulmarg had done market research to fully understand the impact of promotions on customer behavior. Dropping price from $800 to $750 attracted new customers, but also resulted in existing customers shifting the timing of their purchase to take advantage of the discount. Customer behavior was also affected by actions taken by the competitor, Kitz. If only one of the two companies promoted in a given month, it saw a 40 percent increase in sales for the month and a forward movement of 20 percent of demand from each of the three following months. In other words, If Gulmarg promoted in October but Kitz did not, Gulmarg observed a 40 percent increase in October demand and a shift of 20 percent of demand from November, December, and January to October. The competitor that did not promote experienced a 20 percent drop in sales for the promotion month and a 10 percent drop in sales for each of the three following months. If one of the companies promoted in October and the other in December, changes in demand were cumulative, with the October promotion having the first impact, followed by the December promotion. In other words, demand for each company shifted from that provided in Table 9-9 based on the October promotion. The December promotion then affected the revised demand. For example, if Kitz promoted in October and Gulmarg chose to promote in December, Gulmarg would observe

a 20 percent drop in demand in October and a 10 percent drop in demand in November, December, and January compared with the figures in Table 9-9. The December promotion would then increase demand in December by 40 percent of the reduced amount (because of the earlier Kitz promotion). Similarly, forward buying from January would also be based on the reduced amount because of the October promotion by Kitz. Forward buying from February and March would be based on demand not affected by the October promotion by Kitz. If both companies promoted in a given month, each experienced a growth of 10 percent for that month and forward buying equivalent to 20 percent of demand from each of the three following months.

Should Gulmarg promote? If so, in which month should it promote? If not, why not?

CHAPTER
10

Coordination in a Supply Chain

LEARNING OBJECTIVES

After reading this chapter, you will be able to

10.1 Describe supply chain coordination and the bullwhip effect, and their impact on supply chain performance.

10.2 Identify obstacles to coordination in a supply chain.

10.3 Discuss managerial levers that help improve coordination in a supply chain.

10.4 Understand some practical approaches to improve coordination in a supply chain.

In this chapter, we extend the ideas from Chapter 9 and focus on improving coordination across the supply chain. We discuss how lack of coordination leads to a degradation of responsiveness and an increase in cost within a supply chain. We describe various obstacles that lead to this lack of coordination and exacerbate variability through the supply chain. We then identify appropriate managerial levers that can help overcome the obstacles and improve coordination. In particular, we discuss how collaboration can improve supply chain performance.

LACK OF SUPPLY CHAIN COORDINATION AND ITS IMPACT ON PERFORMANCE

10.1 Describe supply chain coordination and the bullwhip effect, and their impact on supply chain performance.

Supply chain coordination improves if all stages of the chain take actions that are aligned and increase total supply chain surplus. Supply chain coordination requires each stage of the supply chain to share information and take into account the impact its actions have on other stages.

A lack of coordination occurs either because different stages of the supply chain have local objectives that conflict or because information moving between stages is delayed and distorted. Different stages of a supply chain may have conflicting objectives if each stage tries to maximize its own profits, resulting in actions that often diminish total supply chain profits (see Chapters 11, 13, and 15). Today, supply chains consist of stages with different owners. For example, Ford Motor Company has thousands of suppliers, from Goodyear to Motorola, and each of these suppliers has many suppliers in turn. Not only does each stage focus on its

own objectives, but information is also often distorted as it moves across the supply chain because complete information is not shared between stages. This distortion is exaggerated by the fact that supply chains today produce a large variety of products. Ford produces different models, with several options for each model. The increased variety makes it difficult for Ford to coordinate information exchange with thousands of suppliers and dealers. The fundamental challenge today is for supply chains to achieve coordination in spite of multiple ownership and increased product variety.

One outcome of the lack of supply chain coordination is the *bullwhip effect,* in which fluctuations in orders increase as they move up the supply chain from retailers to wholesalers to manufacturers to suppliers, as shown in Figure 10-1. The bullwhip effect distorts demand information within the supply chain, with each stage having a different estimate of what demand looks like.

Procter & Gamble (P&G) has observed the bullwhip effect in the supply chain for Pampers diapers (Lee, Padmanabhan, and Whang, 1997). The company found that raw material orders from P&G to its suppliers fluctuated significantly over time. Farther down the chain, when sales at retail stores were studied, the fluctuations, though present, were small. It is reasonable to assume that the consumers of diapers (babies) at the last stage of the supply chain used them at a steady rate. Although consumption of the end product was stable, orders for raw material were highly variable, increasing costs and making it difficult to match supply and demand.

Figure 10-1 Demand Fluctuation at Different Stages of a Supply Chain

Hewlett-Packard (HP) also found that the fluctuation in orders increased significantly as they moved from the resellers up the supply chain to the printer division to the integrated circuit division (ibid.). Once again, although product demand showed some variability, orders placed with the integrated circuit division were much more variable. This made it difficult for HP to fill orders on time and increased the cost of doing so.

Studies of the apparel and grocery industries have shown a similar phenomenon: The fluctuation in orders increases as one moves upstream in the supply chain from retail to manufacturing. Barilla, an Italian manufacturer of pasta, observed that weekly orders placed by a local distribution center fluctuated by up to a factor of 70 in the course of the year, whereas weekly sales at the distribution center (representing orders placed by supermarkets) fluctuated by a factor of less than three (Hammond, 1994). Barilla was thus facing demand from the distribution center that was much more variable than customer demand. This led to increased inventories, poorer product availability, and a drop in profits.

A similar phenomenon, over a longer time frame, has been observed in several industries that are quite prone to "boom and bust" cycles. A good example is the production of memory chips for personal computers. Between 1985 and 1998, at least two cycles occurred during which prices of memory chips fluctuated by a factor of more than three. These large fluctuations in price were driven by either large shortages or surpluses in capacity. The shortages were exacerbated by panic buying and overordering that was followed by a sudden drop in demand.

The lack of coordination in a supply chain increases variability and hurts the supply chain surplus. We discuss the impact of the bullwhip effect on costs and responsiveness in the context of the P&G diaper supply chain.

Manufacturing Cost

The lack of coordination increases manufacturing cost in the supply chain. As a result of the bullwhip effect, P&G and its suppliers must satisfy a stream of orders that is much more variable than customer demand. P&G can respond to the increased variability by either building excess capacity or holding excess inventory (see Chapter 8), both of which increase the manufacturing cost per unit produced.

Inventory Cost

The lack of coordination increases inventory cost in the supply chain. To handle the increased variability in demand, P&G must carry a higher level of inventory than would be required if the supply chain were coordinated. As a result, inventory costs in the supply chain increase. The high levels of inventory also increase the warehousing space required and thus the warehousing cost incurred.

Replenishment Lead Time

Lack of coordination increases replenishment lead times in the supply chain. The increased variability as a result of the bullwhip effect makes scheduling at P&G and supplier plants much more difficult than when demand is level. There are times when the available capacity and inventory cannot supply the orders coming in. This results in higher replenishment lead times.

Transportation Cost

The lack of coordination increases transportation cost in the supply chain. The transportation requirements over time at P&G and its suppliers are correlated with the orders being filled. As a result of the bullwhip effect, transportation requirements fluctuate significantly over time. This raises transportation cost because surplus transportation capacity needs to be maintained to cover high-demand periods.

Labor Cost for Shipping and Receiving

The lack of coordination increases labor costs associated with shipping and receiving in the supply chain. Labor requirements for shipping at P&G and its suppliers fluctuate with orders. A similar fluctuation occurs for the labor requirements for receiving at distributors and retailers. The various stages have the option of carrying excess labor capacity or varying labor capacity in response to the fluctuation in orders. Either option increases total labor cost.

Level of Product Availability

Lack of coordination hurts the level of product availability and results in more stockouts in the supply chain. The large fluctuations in orders make it harder for P&G to supply all distributor and retailer orders on time. This increases the likelihood that retailers will run out of stock, resulting in lost sales for the supply chain.

Relationships Across the Supply Chain

Lack of coordination has a negative effect on performance at every stage and thus hurts the relationships among different stages of the supply chain. There is a tendency to assign blame to other stages of the supply chain because each stage thinks it is doing the best it can. The lack of coordination thus leads to a loss of trust among different stages of the supply chain and makes any potential coordination efforts more difficult.

From the earlier discussion, it follows that lack of coordination has a significant negative impact on the supply chain's performance by increasing cost and decreasing responsiveness. The impact of the lack of coordination on different performance measures is summarized in Table 10-1.

SUMMARY OF LEARNING OBJECTIVE 1

Supply chain coordination requires all stages to take actions that maximize total supply chain profits. A lack of coordination results if different stages focus on optimizing their local objectives or if information is distorted as it moves across the supply chain. The phenomenon that fluctuation in orders increases as one moves up the supply chain from retailers to wholesalers to manufacturers to suppliers is referred to as the bullwhip effect. This effect results in an increase in all costs in the supply chain and a decrease in customer service levels. The bullwhip effect moves all parties in the supply chain away from the efficient frontier and results in a decrease of both customer satisfaction and profitability within the supply chain.

TABLE 10-1 Impact of the Lack of Coordination on Supply Chain Performance

Performance Measure	Impact of the Lack of Coordination
Manufacturing cost	Increases
Inventory cost	Increases
Replenishment lead time	Increases
Transportation cost	Increases
Shipping and receiving cost	Increases
Level of product availability	Decreases
Profitability	Decreases

OBSTACLES TO COORDINATION IN A SUPPLY CHAIN

Any factor that leads to either local optimization by different stages of the supply chain or an increase in information delay, distortion, and variability within the supply chain is an obstacle to coordination. If managers in a supply chain are able to identify the key obstacles, they can then take suitable actions to improve coordination. We divide the major obstacles into five categories:

- Incentive obstacles
- Information-processing obstacles
- Operational obstacles
- Pricing obstacles
- Behavioral obstacles

Incentive Obstacles

Incentive obstacles occur in situations when incentives offered to different stages or participants in a supply chain lead to actions that increase variability and reduce total supply chain profits.

LOCAL OPTIMIZATION WITHIN FUNCTIONS OR STAGES OF A SUPPLY CHAIN Incentives that focus only on the local impact of an action result in decisions that do not maximize total supply chain surplus. For example, if the compensation of a transportation manager at a firm is linked to the average transportation cost per unit, the manager is likely to take actions that lower transportation costs even if they increase inventory costs or hurt customer service. It is natural for any participant in the supply chain to take actions that optimize performance measures along which they are evaluated. For example, managers at a retailer such as Carrefour make all their purchasing and inventory decisions to maximize Carrefour profits, not total supply chain profits. Buying decisions based on maximizing profits at a single stage of the supply chain lead to ordering policies that do not maximize supply chain profits (see Chapters 11, 13, and 15).

SALES FORCE INCENTIVES Improperly structured sales force incentives are a significant obstacle to coordination in a supply chain. In many firms, sales force incentives are based on exceeding sales thresholds during an evaluation period of a month or quarter. The sales typically measured by a manufacturer are the quantity sold to distributors or retailers (sell-in), not the quantity sold to final customers (sell-through). Measuring performance based on sell-in is often justified on the grounds that the manufacturer's sales force does not control sell-through. For example, Barilla offered incentives to its sales force based on the quantity sold to distributors during a four- to six-week promotion period. To maximize their bonuses, the Barilla sales force urged distributors to buy more pasta toward the end of the evaluation period, even if distributors were not selling as much to retailers. The sales force offered discounts they controlled to spur end-of-period sales. This increased variability in the order pattern, with a jump in orders toward the end of the evaluation period followed by few orders at the beginning of the next evaluation period. Order sizes from distributors to Barilla fluctuated by a factor of up to 70 from one week to the next. A sales force incentive based on sell-in thus results in order variability being larger than customer demand variability because the sales force tends to push product toward the end of the incentive period.

Information-Processing Obstacles

Information-processing obstacles occur when demand information is distorted as it moves between different stages of the supply chain, leading to increased variability in orders within the supply chain.

FORECASTING BASED ON ORDERS AND NOT CUSTOMER DEMAND When stages within a supply chain make forecasts that are based on orders they receive, any variability in customer demand is magnified as orders move up the supply chain to manufacturers and suppliers. In sup-

ply chains where the fundamental means of communication among different stages are the orders that are placed, information is distorted as it moves up the supply chain (see Chen, Drezner, Ryan, and Simchi-Levi [2000] for a good quantitative analysis). Each stage views its primary role within the supply chain as one of filling orders placed by its downstream partner. Thus, each stage views its demand as the stream of orders received and produces a forecast based on this information.

In such a scenario, a small change in customer demand becomes magnified as it moves up the supply chain in the form of customer orders. Consider the impact of a random increase in customer demand at a retailer. The retailer may interpret part of this random increase as a growth trend. This interpretation will lead the retailer to order more than the observed increase in demand because the retailer expects growth to continue into the future and thus orders a quantity large enough to cover for anticipated growth during the lead time. The increase in the order placed with the wholesaler is thus larger than the observed increase in demand at the retailer. Part of the increase is a one-time increase. The wholesaler, however, has no way to interpret the order increase correctly. The wholesaler simply observes a jump in the order size and infers a growth trend. The growth trend inferred by the wholesaler will be larger than that inferred by the retailer (recall that the retailer increased the order size to account for future growth during the lead time). The wholesaler will thus place an even larger order with the manufacturer. As we go farther up the supply chain, the order size is magnified.

Now assume that periods of random increase are followed by periods of random decrease in demand. Using the same forecasting logic as earlier, the retailer will now anticipate a declining trend and reduce order size. This reduction will also become magnified as we move up the supply chain.

LACK OF INFORMATION SHARING The lack of information sharing between stages of the supply chain magnifies the information distortion. A retailer such as Carrefour may increase the size of a particular order because of a planned promotion. If the manufacturer is not aware of the planned promotion, it may interpret the larger order as a permanent increase in demand and place orders with suppliers accordingly. The manufacturer and suppliers thus have much inventory right after Carrefour finishes its promotion. Given the excess inventory, as future Carrefour orders return to normal, manufacturer orders will be smaller than before. The lack of information sharing between the retailer and manufacturer thus leads to a large fluctuation in manufacturer orders.

Operational Obstacles

Operational obstacles occur when actions taken in the course of placing and filling orders lead to an increase in variability.

ORDERING IN LARGE LOTS When a firm places orders in lot sizes that are much larger than those in which demand arises, variability of orders is magnified up the supply chain. Firms may order in large lots because a significant fixed cost is associated with placing, receiving, or transporting an order (see Chapter 11). Large lots may also occur if the supplier offers quantity discounts based on lot size (see Chapter 11). Figure 10-2 shows both the demand and the order stream for a firm that places an order every five weeks. Observe that the order stream is far more erratic than the demand stream.

Because orders are batched and placed every five weeks, the order stream has four weeks without orders followed by a large order that equals five weeks of demand. A manufacturer supplying several retailers that batch their orders faces an order stream that is much more variable than the demand the retailers experience. If the manufacturer batches its orders to suppliers, the effect is further magnified. In many instances, there are certain focal-point periods, such as the first or the last week of a month, when a majority of the orders arrive. This synchronization of orders further exacerbates the impact of batching.

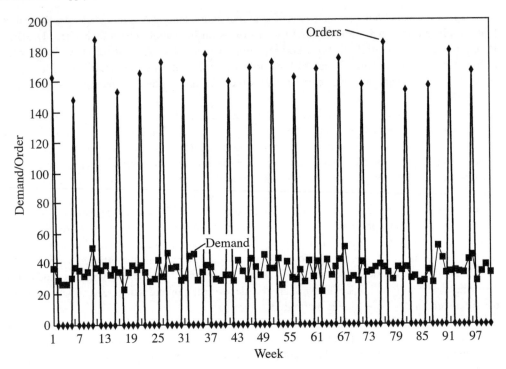

Figure 10-2 Demand and Order Stream with Orders Every Five Weeks

LARGE REPLENISHMENT LEAD TIMES Information distortion is magnified if replenishment lead times between stages are long. Consider a situation in which a retailer has misinterpreted a random increase in demand as a growth trend. If the retailer faces a lead time of two weeks, it will incorporate the anticipated growth over two weeks when placing the order. In contrast, if the retailer faces a lead time of two months, it will incorporate into its order the anticipated growth over two months (which will be much larger). The same applies when a random decrease in demand is interpreted as a declining trend.

RATIONING AND SHORTAGE GAMING Rationing schemes that allocate limited production in proportion to the orders placed by retailers lead to a magnification of information distortion. This can occur when a popular product is in short supply. In such a situation, manufacturers come up with a variety of mechanisms to ration the scarce supply of product among various distributors or retailers. One commonly used rationing scheme is to allocate the available supply of product based on orders placed. Under this rationing scheme, if the supply available is 75 percent of the total orders received, each retailer receives 75 percent of its order.

This rationing scheme results in a game in which retailers try to increase the size of their orders to increase the amount supplied to them. A retailer needing 75 units orders 100 units in the hope of getting 75. The net impact of this rationing scheme is to artificially inflate orders for the product. In addition, a retailer ordering based on what it expects to sell gets less and as a result loses sales, whereas a retailer that inflates its order is rewarded.

If the manufacturer is using orders to forecast future demand, it will interpret the increase in orders as an increase in demand, even though customer demand is unchanged. The manufacturer may respond by building enough capacity to be able to fill all orders received. Once sufficient capacity becomes available, orders return to their normal level because they were inflated in response to the rationing scheme. The manufacturer is now left with a surplus of product and

capacity. These boom-and-bust cycles thus tend to alternate. This phenomenon is fairly common in the electronics industry, in which alternating periods of component shortages followed by a component surplus are often observed.

Pricing Obstacles

Pricing obstacles arise when the pricing policies for a product lead to an increase in variability of orders placed.

LOT-SIZE–BASED QUANTITY DISCOUNTS Lot-size–based quantity discounts increase the lot size of orders placed within the supply chain (see Chapter 11) because lower prices are offered for larger lots. As discussed earlier, the resulting large lots magnify the bullwhip effect within the supply chain.

PRICE FLUCTUATIONS Trade promotions and other short-term discounts offered by a manufacturer result in forward buying, by which a wholesaler or retailer purchases large lots during the discounting period to cover demand during future periods. Forward buying results in large orders during the promotion period followed by very small orders after that (see Chapter 11), as shown in Figure 10-3 for chicken noodle soup.

Observe that the shipments during the peak period are higher than the sales during the peak period because of a promotion offered. The peak shipment period is followed by a period of low shipments from the manufacturer, indicating significant forward buying by distributors. The promotion thus results in a variability in manufacturer shipments that is significantly higher than the variability in retailer sales.

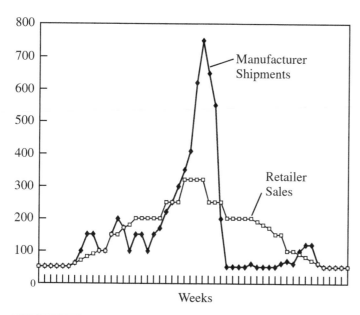

Figure 10-3 Retailer Sales and Manufacturer Shipments of Soup
Source: Based on Marshall L. Fisher, "What Is the Right Supply Chain for Your Product?" by Harvard Business Review(March–April 1997): 83–93. Copyright © 1997 by the Harvard Business School Publishing Corporation; all rights reserved.

Behavioral Obstacles

Behavioral obstacles are problems in learning within organizations that contribute to information distortion. These problems are often related to the supply chain structure and the communications among different stages. Some of the behavioral obstacles are as follows:

1. Each stage of the supply chain views its actions locally and is unable to see the impact of its actions on other stages.
2. Different stages of the supply chain react to the current local situation rather than trying to identify the root causes.
3. Based on local analysis, different stages of the supply chain blame one another for the fluctuations, with successive stages in the supply chain becoming enemies rather than partners.
4. No stage of the supply chain learns from its actions over time because the most significant consequences of its actions occur elsewhere. The result is a vicious cycle in which actions taken by one stage create the very problems that the stage blames on others.
5. A lack of trust among supply chain partners causes them to be opportunistic at the expense of overall supply chain performance. The lack of trust also results in significant duplication of effort. More important, information available at different stages either is not shared or is ignored because it is not trusted.

SUMMARY OF LEARNING OBJECTIVE 2

A key obstacle to coordination in the supply chain is misaligned incentives that result in different stages optimizing local objectives instead of total supply chain profits. Other obstacles include lack of information sharing, operational inefficiencies leading to large replenishment lead times and large lots, sales force incentives that encourage forward buying, rationing schemes that encourage inflation of orders, promotions that encourage forward buying, and a lack of trust that makes any effort toward coordination difficult.

10.3 Discuss managerial levers that help improve coordination in a supply chain.

MANAGERIAL LEVERS TO IMPROVE COORDINATION

Having identified obstacles to coordination, we now focus on actions a manager can take to help overcome the obstacles and improve coordination in the supply chain. The following managerial actions increase total supply chain profits and moderate information distortion:

- Aligning goals and incentives
- Improving information visibility and accuracy
- Improving operations to synchronize supply and demand
- Designing pricing strategies to stabilize orders
- Building strategic partnerships and trust

Aligning Goals and Incentives

Managers can improve coordination within the supply chain by aligning goals and incentives so every participant in supply chain activities works to maximize total supply chain profits.

ALIGNING GOALS ACROSS THE SUPPLY CHAIN Coordination requires every stage of the supply chain to focus on the supply chain surplus or the total size of the pie rather than just its individual share. A key to coordination is coming up with mechanisms that allow the creation of a win–win scenario in which the supply chain surplus grows along with the profits for all supply

chain stages. An example of such a mechanism occurs when Walmart pays Hewlett-Packard (HP) for each printer sold and gives HP the power to make replenishment decisions while specifying the service level to be achieved at a store. This setup improves coordination because both parties gain if the supply of printers at a store matches demand.

ALIGNING INCENTIVES ACROSS FUNCTIONS One key to coordinated decisions within a firm is to ensure that the objective any function uses to evaluate a decision is aligned with the firm's overall objective. All facility, transportation, and inventory decisions should be evaluated based on their effect on profitability or total costs, not functional costs. This helps prevent situations such as a transportation manager making decisions that lower transportation cost but increase overall supply chain costs (see Chapter 14).

PRICING FOR COORDINATION In many instances, suitable pricing schemes can help coordinate the supply chain. A manufacturer can use lot-size–based quantity discounts to achieve coordination for commodity products if the manufacturer has large fixed costs associated with each lot (see Chapter 11 for a detailed discussion). For products for which a firm has market power, a manufacturer can use two-part tariffs and volume discounts to help achieve coordination (see Chapter 11 for a detailed discussion). Given demand uncertainty, manufacturers can use buyback, revenue-sharing, and quantity flexibility contracts to spur retailers to provide levels of product availability that maximize total supply chain profits (see Chapter 15 for a detailed discussion). Buyback contracts have been used in the publishing industry to increase total supply chain profits. Quantity flexibility contracts have helped Benetton increase supply chain profits.

ALTERING SALES FORCE INCENTIVES FROM SELL-IN TO SELL-THROUGH Any change that reduces the incentive for a salesperson to push product to the retailer reduces the bullwhip effect. Manufacturers should link incentives for the sales staff to sell-through by the retailer rather than sell-in to the retailer. This action eliminates any motivation the sales staff may have to encourage forward buying. Elimination of forward buying helps reduce fluctuations in the order stream. If sales force incentives are based on sales over a rolling horizon, the incentive to push product is further reduced. This helps reduce forward buying and the resulting fluctuation in orders.

Improving Information Visibility and Accuracy

Managers can improve coordination by improving the visibility and accuracy of information available to different stages in the supply chain.

SHARING CUSTOMER DEMAND DATA Sharing customer demand data across the supply chain can help reduce the bullwhip effect. A primary cause for information distortion is the fact that each stage of the supply chain uses orders to forecast future demand. Given that orders received by different stages vary, forecasts at different stages also vary. In reality, the only demand that the supply chain needs to satisfy is that from the final customer. If retailers share demand data with other supply chain stages, all stages can forecast future demand based on customer demand. Sharing of demand data helps reduce information distortion because all stages now respond to the same change in customer demand. Observe that sharing aggregate demand data is sufficient to dampen information distortion. It is not necessary to share detailed point-of-sale (POS) data.

Walmart has routinely shared its POS data with its suppliers. Dell shares demand data as well as current inventory positions of components with many of its suppliers via the Internet, thereby helping avoid unnecessary fluctuations in supply and orders placed. P&G has convinced many retailers to share demand data. P&G, in turn, shares the data with its suppliers, improving coordination in the supply chain.

IMPLEMENTING COLLABORATIVE FORECASTING AND PLANNING Once customer demand data are shared, different stages of the supply chain must forecast and plan jointly if complete coordination is to be achieved. Without collaborative planning, sharing of demand data does not guarantee coordination. A retailer may have observed large demand in the month of January because it ran a promotion. If no promotion is planned in the upcoming January, the retailer's forecast will differ from the manufacturer's forecast even if both have past POS data. The manufacturer must be aware of the retailer's promotion plans to achieve coordination. The key is to ensure that the entire supply chain is operating with a common forecast. To facilitate this type of coordination in the supply chain environment, the Voluntary Inter industry Commerce Standards (VICS) Association set up a Collaborative Planning, Forecasting, and Replenishment (CPFR) Committee that identified best practices and design guidelines for collaborative planning and forecasting. These practices are detailed later in the chapter.

DESIGNING SINGLE-STAGE CONTROL OF REPLENISHMENT Designing a supply chain in which a single stage controls replenishment decisions for the entire supply chain can help diminish information distortion. As we mentioned earlier, a key cause of information distortion is that each stage of the supply chain uses orders from the previous stage as its historical demand. As a result, each stage views its role as one of replenishing orders placed by the next stage. In reality, the key replenishment is at the retailer, because that is where the final customer purchases. When a single stage controls replenishment decisions for the entire chain, the problem of multiple forecasts is eliminated and coordination within the supply chain improves.

Several industry practices, such as continuous replenishment programs (CRPs) and vendor-managed inventories (VMIs) detailed later in the chapter, provide a single-point control over replenishment. Walmart typically assigns one of its suppliers as a leader for each major product category to manage store-level replenishment. This gives suppliers visibility into sales and a single decision maker for replenishment decisions.

Improving Operations to Synchronize Supply and Demand

Managers can help dampen information distortion by improving operational performance and rationing schemes to better synchronize supply and demand.

REDUCING REPLENISHMENT LEAD TIME By reducing the replenishment lead time, managers can decrease the uncertainty of demand during the lead time (see Chapter 12). A reduction in lead time is especially beneficial for seasonal items because it allows for multiple orders to be placed with a significant increase in the accuracy of the forecast (see Chapter 13). If lead times are short enough, replenishment can be scheduled to actual consumption, thus eliminating the need for a forecast.

Managers can take a variety of actions at different stages of the supply chain to help reduce replenishment lead times. Ordering electronically, either online or through electronic data interchange (EDI), can significantly cut the lead time associated with order placement and information transfer. If every stage shares its long-term plans with suppliers, potential orders can be scheduled into production well in advance, with the precise quantity being determined closer to actual production. This reduces the scheduling time, which is often the largest component of lead time. At manufacturing plants, increased flexibility and cellular manufacturing can be used to achieve a significant reduction in lead times. A dampening of information distortion further reduces lead times because of stabilized demand and, as a result, improved scheduling. This is particularly true when manufacturing produces a large variety of products. Advance shipping notices (ASNs) can be used to reduce the lead time as well as efforts associated with receiving. Cross-docking can be used to reduce the lead time associated with moving the product between stages in the supply chain. Walmart has used many of these approaches to significantly reduce lead time within its supply chain.

REDUCING LOT SIZES Managers can reduce information distortion by implementing operational improvements that reduce lot sizes. A reduction of lot sizes decreases the amount of fluctuation that can accumulate between any pair of stages of a supply chain, thus decreasing distortion. To reduce lot sizes, managers must take actions that help reduce the fixed costs associated with ordering, transporting, and receiving each lot (see Chapter 11). Walmart and Seven-Eleven Japan have been very successful at reducing replenishment lot sizes by aggregating deliveries across many products and suppliers.

Computer-assisted ordering (CAO) refers to the substitution through technology of the functions of a retail order clerk through the use of computers that integrate information about product sales, market factors affecting demand, inventory levels, product receipts, and desired service levels. CAO and EDI help reduce the fixed costs associated with placing each order.

In some cases, managers can simplify ordering by eliminating the use of purchase orders. In the auto industry, some suppliers are paid based on the number of cars produced, eliminating the need for individual purchase orders. This eliminates the order-processing cost associated with each replenishment order. Information systems also facilitate the settlement of financial transactions, eliminating the cost associated with individual purchase orders.

The large gap in the prices of truckload (TL) and less-than-truckload (LTL) shipping encourages shipment in TL quantities. In fact, with the efforts to reduce order-processing costs, transportation costs are now the major barrier to smaller lots in most supply chains. Managers can reduce lot sizes without increasing transportation costs by filling a truck using smaller lots from a variety of products (see Chapter 11). P&G, for example, requires all orders from retailers to be a full TL. The TL, however, may be built from any combination of products. A retailer can thus order small lots of each product as long as a sufficiently large variety of products are included on each truck. Seven-Eleven Japan has used this strategy with combined trucks, in which consolidation is by the temperature at which the truck is maintained. All products to be shipped at a particular temperature are on the same truck. This has allowed Seven-Eleven Japan to reduce the number of trucks sent to retail outlets while keeping product variety high. Some firms in the grocery industry use trucks with different compartments, each at a different temperature and carrying a variety of products, to help reduce lot sizes.

Managers can also reduce lot sizes by using milk runs that combine shipments for several retailers on a single truck, as discussed in Chapter 14. In many cases, third-party transporters combine shipments to competing retail outlets on a single truck. This reduces the fixed transportation cost per retailer and allows each retailer to order in smaller lots. In Japan, Toyota uses a single truck from a supplier to supply multiple assembly plants, which enables managers to reduce the lot size received by any one plant. Managers can also reduce lot sizes by combining shipments from multiple suppliers on a single truck. In the United States, Toyota uses this approach to reduce the lot size it receives from any one supplier.

As smaller lots are ordered and delivered, both the pressure on and the cost of receiving can grow significantly. Thus, managers must implement technologies that simplify the receiving process and reduce the cost associated with receiving. For example, ASNs identify shipment content, count, and time of delivery electronically and help reduce unloading time and increase cross-dock efficiency. ASNs can be used to update inventory records electronically, thus reducing the cost of receiving. Bar coding of pallets and the use of radio frequency identification (RFID) can further simplify receiving.

Another simple way to minimize the impact of batching is to break any synchronization of orders. Frequently, customers that order once a week tend to do so on either a Monday or Friday. Customers that order once a month tend to do so either at the beginning or the end of the month. In such situations, it is better to distribute customers ordering once a week evenly across all days of the week, and customers ordering once a month across all days of the month. In fact, regular ordering days may be scheduled in advance for each customer to level out the order stream arriving at the manufacturer.

RATIONING BASED ON PAST SALES AND SHARING INFORMATION TO LIMIT GAMING To diminish information distortion, managers can design rationing schemes that discourage retailers from artificially inflating their orders in case of a shortage. One approach, referred to as *turn-and-earn,* is to allocate the available supply based on past retailer sales rather than current retailer orders. Tying allocation to past sales removes any incentive a retailer may have to inflate orders. In fact, during low-demand periods, the turn-and-earn approach pushes retailers to try to sell more to increase the allocation they receive during periods of shortage. Several firms, including General Motors, have historically used the turn-and-earn mechanism to ration available product in case of a shortage. Others, such as HP, have historically allocated based on retailer orders but are now switching to using past sales.

Other firms have tried to share information across the supply chain to minimize shortage situations. Firms such as Sport Obermeyer offer incentives to their large customers to preorder at least a part of their annual order. This information allows Sport Obermeyer to improve the accuracy of its own forecast and allocate production capacity accordingly. Once capacity has been allocated appropriately across different products, it is less likely that shortage situations will arise, thus dampening the inflation of orders. The availability of flexible capacity can also help in this regard, because flexible capacity can easily be shifted from a product whose demand is lower than expected to one whose demand is higher than expected.

Designing Pricing Strategies to Stabilize Orders

Managers can reduce information distortion by devising pricing strategies that encourage retailers to order in smaller lots and reduce forward buying.

MOVING FROM LOT-SIZE–BASED TO VOLUME-BASED QUANTITY DISCOUNTS When offered lot-size–based quantity discounts, retailers increase their lot size to take full advantage of the discount. Offering volume-based quantity discounts eliminates the incentive to increase the size of a single lot because volume-based discounts consider the total purchases during a specified period (say, a year) rather than purchases in a single lot (see Chapter 11).

Volume-based quantity discounts result in smaller lot sizes, thus reducing order variability in the supply chain. Volume-based discounts with a fixed end date at which discounts will be evaluated may lead to large lots close to the end date. Offering the discounts over a rolling time horizon helps dampen this effect.

STABILIZING PRICING Managers can dampen the bullwhip effect by eliminating promotions and using everyday low pricing (EDLP). The elimination of promotions removes forward buying by retailers and results in orders that match customer demand. P&G, Campbell Soup, and several other manufacturers have implemented EDLP to dampen the bullwhip effect.

Managers can place limits on the quantity that may be purchased during a promotion to decrease forward buying. This limit should be retailer specific and linked to historical sales by the retailer. Another approach is to tie the promotion dollars paid to the retailer to the amount of sell-through rather than the amount purchased by the retailer. As a result, retailers obtain no benefit from forward buying and purchase more only if they can sell more. Promotions based on sell-through significantly reduce information distortion.

Building Strategic Partnerships and Trust

Managers find it easier to use the levers discussed earlier to achieve coordination if trust and strategic partnerships are built within the supply chain. Sharing of accurate information that is trusted by every stage results in a better matching of supply and demand throughout the supply chain. A better relationship also tends to lower the transaction cost between supply chain stages. For example, a supplier can eliminate its forecasting effort if it trusts orders and forecast information received from the retailer. Similarly, the retailer can lessen the receiving effort by

decreasing counting and inspections if it trusts the supplier's quality and delivery. In general, stages in a supply chain can eliminate duplicated effort on the basis of improved trust and a better relationship. This lowering of transaction cost, along with accurate shared information, helps improve coordination. Walmart and P&G have tried to build a strategic partnership that will better coordinate their actions and be mutually beneficial.

Research by Kumar (1996) showed that the more retailers trusted their suppliers, the less likely they were to develop alternate sources while significantly increasing sales of their products. In general, a high level of trust allows a supply chain to become more responsive at lower cost. Actions such as information sharing, changing of incentives, operational improvements, and stabilization of pricing typically help improve the level of trust. Growing the level of cooperation and trust within a supply chain requires a clear identification of roles and decision rights for all parties, effective contracts, and good conflict resolution mechanisms.

For trust to be built in practice, it is important for all parties to believe that the benefits of any improvement in coordination are being shared equitably. Managers from the stronger party in the supply chain relationship must be sensitive to this fact and ensure that all parties perceive that the way benefits are shared is fair.

Improving Coordination in Practice

All managerial levers that improve coordination go across functions within a company and also across companies within a supply chain. It is thus important to ensure the following conditions are met to help improve coordination in practice.

1. ***Get top management commitment for coordination.*** More than any other aspect of supply chain management, coordination can succeed only with top management's commitment. Coordination requires managers at all stages of the supply chain to subordinate their local interests to the greater interest of the firm, and even of the supply chain. Coordination often requires the resolution of trade-offs in a way that requires many functions in the supply chain to change their traditional practices. These changes often run counter to approaches that were put in place when each function focused only on its local objective. Such changes within a supply chain cannot be implemented without strong top management commitment. Top management commitment was a key factor in helping Walmart and P&G set up collaborative forecasting and replenishment teams.

2. ***Devote resources to coordination.*** Coordination cannot be achieved without all parties involved devoting significant managerial resources to this effort. Companies often do not devote resources to coordination because they either assume that lack of coordination is something they have to live with or they hope that coordination will occur on its own. The problem with this approach is that it leaves all managers involved with only the separate areas that they control, while no one is responsible for highlighting the impact one manager's actions have on other parts of the supply chain. One of the best ways to solve coordination problems is through teams made up of members from different companies throughout the supply chain. These teams should be made responsible for coordination and given the power to implement the changes required. Setting up a coordination team is fruitless unless the team has the power to act, because the team will run into conflict with functional managers who are currently maximizing local objectives. Coordination teams can be effective only once a sufficient level of trust builds between members from different firms. If they are used properly, coordination teams can provide significant benefit, as has happened with the collaborative forecasting and replenishment teams set up by Walmart and P&G.

3. ***Focus on communication with other stages.*** Good communication with other stages of a supply chain often creates situations that highlight the value of coordination for both sides. Companies often do not communicate with other stages of the supply chain and are unwilling to share information. However, often all companies in the supply chain are

frustrated by the lack of coordination and would be happy to share information if it helped the supply chain operate in a more effective manner. Regular communication among the parties involved facilitates change in such a setting. For instance, a major PC company had been ordering its microprocessors in batches of several weeks of production. It was trying to move to a build-to-order environment in which it would place microprocessor orders on a daily basis. The PC company assumed that the microprocessor supplier would be reluctant to go along with this approach. However, once communication was opened up with the supplier, the opposite turned out to be true. The supplier also wanted to reduce lot sizes and increase the frequency of orders. It had just assumed that the PC manufacturer wanted large lots and thus never requested a change. Regular communication helps different stages of the supply chain share their goals and identify common goals and mutually beneficial actions that improve coordination.

SUMMARY OF LEARNING OBJECTIVE 3

Managers can improve coordination in the supply chain by aligning goals and incentives across different functions and stages of the supply chain. Other actions that managers can take to improve coordination include sharing of sales information and collaborative forecasting and planning, implementation of single-point control of replenishment, improving operations to reduce lead times and lot sizes, EDLP and other pricing strategies that limit forward buying, and the building of trust and strategic partnerships within the supply chain. Top management commitment, the devotion of resources to coordination, and a focus on communication across the supply chain are important requirements for coordination to improve in practice.

10.4 Understand some practical approaches to improve coordination in a supply chain.

SOME PRACTICAL APPROACHES TO IMPROVE SUPPLY CHAIN COORDINATION

Starting with "efficient consumer response" efforts in the grocery industry in the 1980s, there have been several industry efforts to improve supply chain coordination. Managers have realized that improved coordination cannot result from the effort of a single company. It requires all players in the industry to buy into the idea. We now discuss some practical approaches that have gained traction in industry and shown positive results.

Continuous Replenishment and Vendor Managed Inventories

Information distortion can be dampened by practices that assign replenishment responsibility across the supply chain to a single entity. Replenishment decisions made by a single entity ensure visibility and a common forecast that drives orders across the supply chain. Two common industry practices that assign a single point of responsibility are continuous replenishment programs and vendor-managed inventories.

In continuous replenishment programs (CRPs), the wholesaler or manufacturer replenishes a retailer regularly based on POS data. CRP may be managed by the supplier, distributor, or a third party. In most instances, CRP systems are driven by actual withdrawals of inventory from retailer warehouses rather than POS data at the store level. Tying CRP systems to warehouse withdrawals is easier to implement, and retailers are often more comfortable sharing data at this level. IT systems that are linked across the supply chain provide a good information infrastructure on which a CRP may be based. In CRP, inventory at the retailer is owned by the retailer.

With vendor-managed inventory (VMI), the manufacturer or supplier is responsible for all decisions regarding product inventories at the retailer. As a result, the control of the replenishment decision moves to the supplier instead of the retailer. In many instances of VMI, the

inventory is owned by the supplier until it is sold by the retailer. VMI requires the retailer to share demand information with the manufacturer to allow it to make inventory replenishment decisions. This helps improve manufacturer forecasts and better match manufacturer production with customer demand. VMI can allow a manufacturer to increase its profits—as well as profits for the entire supply chain—if both retailer and manufacturer margins are considered when making inventory decisions.

VMI has been implemented with significant success by, among others, Kmart (with about 50 suppliers) and Fred Meyer. Kmart saw inventory turns on seasonal items increase from 3 to between 9 and 11, and for nonseasonal items from 12 to 15 to 17 to 20. Fred Meyer saw inventories drop by 30 to 40 percent while fill rates increased to 98 percent. Other firms with successful implementations include Campbell Soup, Frito-Lay, and P&G.

One drawback of VMI arises because retailers often sell products from competing manufacturers that are substitutes in the customer's mind. For example, a customer may substitute detergent manufactured by P&G by detergent manufactured by Unilever. If the retailer has a VMI agreement with both manufacturers, each manufacturer will ignore the impact of substitution when making inventory decisions. As a result, inventories at the retailer will be higher than optimal. In such a setting, the retailer may be better positioned to decide on the replenishment policy. Another possibility is for the retailer to define a category leader from among the suppliers and have the category leader manage replenishment decisions for all suppliers in the category. Walmart follows such a practice and assigns a category leader for most of its products. Walmart sets the targeted level of product availability across all products and the category leader designs replenishment policies that achieve these levels. This ensures that the category leader is not favoring any one supplier's product over another. For example, HP was Walmart's category leader for printers and managed all printer replenishment.

Collaborative Planning, Forecasting, and Replenishment

The VICS Association has defined CPFR as "a business practice that combines the intelligence of multiple partners in the planning and fulfillment of customer demand." In this section, we describe CPFR and some successful implementations. It is important to understand that successful CPFR can be built only on a foundation in which the two parties have synchronized their data and established standards for exchanging information.

Sellers and buyers in a supply chain may collaborate along any or all of the following four supply chain activities:

1. *Strategy and planning.* The partners determine the scope of the collaboration and assign roles, responsibilities, and clear checkpoints. In a joint business plan, they then identify significant events such as promotions, new product introductions, store openings/closings, and changes in inventory policy that affect demand and supply.
2. *Demand and supply management.* A collaborative sales forecast projects the partners' best estimate of consumer demand at the point of sale. This is then converted to a collaborative order plan that determines future orders and delivery requirements based on sales forecasts, inventory positions, and replenishment lead times.
3. *Execution.* As forecasts become firm, they are converted to actual orders. The fulfillment of these orders then involves production, shipping, receiving, and stocking of products.
4. *Analysis.* The key analysis tasks focus on identifying exceptions and evaluating metrics that are used to assess performance or identify trends.

A fundamental aspect of successful collaboration is the identification and resolution of exceptions. Exceptions refer to a gap between forecasts made by the two sides or some other performance metric that is falling or is likely to fall outside acceptable bounds. These metrics may include inventories that exceed targets or product availability that falls below targets. For successful CPFR, it is important to have a process in place that allows the two parties to resolve

exceptions. Detailed processes for identifying and resolving exceptions are discussed in the VICS CPFR Voluntary Guidelines version 2.0 (2002).

One successful CPFR implementation has involved Henkel, a German detergent manufacturer, and Eroski, a Spanish food retailer. Prior to CPFR, Eroski saw frequent stockouts of Henkel products, especially during promotions. At the inception of CPFR in December 1999, 70 percent of the sales forecasts had an average error of more than 50 percent, and only 5 percent of the forecasts had errors less than 20 percent. Within four months of the CPFR implementation, however, 70 percent of the sales forecasts had errors less than 20 percent and only 5 percent had errors of more than 50 percent. CPFR resulted in a customer service level of 98 percent and an average inventory of only five days. This was accomplished despite 15 to 20 products being promoted every month.

Another successful implementation involved Johnson & Johnson and Superdrug, a chain in the United Kingdom. Over the three-month trial period beginning April 2000, Superdrug saw inventory levels at its DCs drop by 13 percent, while product availability at its DCs increased by 1.6 percent. As reported by Steerman (2003), Sears also saw significant benefits from its CPFR initiative with Michelin in 2001. In-stock levels at Sears improved by 4.3 percent, DCs-to-stores fill rate improved by 10.7 percent, and overall inventory levels fell by 25 percent.

VICS has identified the four scenarios in Table 10-2 as the most common areas in which large-scale CPFR deployments have taken place between a retailer and a manufacturer. Next, we describe each of the four scenarios.

RETAIL EVENT COLLABORATION In many retail environments, such as supermarkets, promotions and other retail events have a significant impact on demand. Stockouts, excess inventory, and unplanned logistics costs during these events affect financial performance for both the retailer and the manufacturer. In such a setting, collaboration between retailers and suppliers to plan, forecast, and replenish promotions is effective.

Retail event collaboration requires the two parties to identify brands and specific SKUs that are included in the collaboration. Details of the event—such as timing, duration, price point, advertising, and display tactics—are shared. It is important for the retailer to update this information as changes occur. Event-specific forecasts are then created and shared. These forecasts are then converted to planned orders and deliveries. As the event unfolds, sales are monitored to identify any changes or exceptions, which are resolved through an iterative process between the two parties.

P&G has implemented some form of retail event collaboration with a variety of partners, including Walmart.

DC REPLENISHMENT COLLABORATION DC replenishment collaboration is perhaps the most common form of collaboration observed in practice and also the simplest to implement. In this scenario, the two trading partners collaborate on forecasting DC withdrawals or anticipated demand from the DC to the manufacturer. These forecasts are converted to a stream of orders

TABLE 10-2 Four Common CPFR Scenarios

CPFR Scenario	Where Applied in Supply Chain	Industries Where Applied
Retail event collaboration	Highly promoted channels or categories	All industries other than those that practice EDLP
DC replenishment collaboration	Retail DC or distributor DC	Drugstores, hardware, grocery
Store replenishment collaboration	Direct store delivery or retail DC-to-store delivery	Mass merchants, club stores
Collaborative assortment planning	Apparel and seasonal goods	Department stores, specialty retail

from the DC to the manufacturer that are committed or locked over a specified time horizon. This information allows the manufacturer to include anticipated orders in future production plans and build the committed orders on demand. The result is a reduction in production cost at the manufacturer and a reduction of inventory and stockouts at the retailer.

DC replenishment collaboration is relatively easy to implement because it requires collaboration on aggregate data and does not require sharing of detailed POS data. As a result, it is often the best scenario with which to start collaboration. Over time, this form of collaboration can be extended to include all storage points in the supply chain, from retail shelves to raw material warehouses. According to Hammond (1994), Barilla implemented this form of collaboration with its distributors.

STORE REPLENISHMENT COLLABORATION In store replenishment collaboration, trading partners collaborate on store-level POS forecasts. These forecasts are then converted to a series of store-level orders, with orders committed over a specified time horizon. This form of collaboration is much harder to implement than a DC-level collaboration if stores are small; it is easier for large stores such as Costco and Home Depot. The benefits of store-level collaboration include greater visibility of sales for the manufacturer, improved replenishment accuracy, improved product availability, and reduced inventories. Smith (2013) discusses how store level collaboration allowed suppliers to Canadian retailer West Marine, Inc. to improve "on-time shipments from a dismal 30 percent to over 90 percent."[1] This allowed West Marine to maintain product availability as high as 98 percent.

COLLABORATIVE ASSORTMENT PLANNING Fashion apparel and other seasonal goods follow a seasonal pattern of demand. Thus, collaborative planning in these categories has a horizon of a single season and is performed at seasonal intervals. Given the seasonal nature, forecasts rely less on historical data and more on collaborative interpretation of industry trends, macroeconomic factors, and customer tastes. In this form of collaboration, the trading partners develop an assortment plan jointly. The output is a planned purchase order at the style/color/size level. The planned order is shared electronically in advance of a show, at which sample products are viewed and final merchandising decisions are made. The planned orders help the manufacturer purchase long-lead-time raw materials and plan capacity. This form of collaboration is most useful if capacity is flexible enough to accommodate a variety of product mix and raw materials have some commonality across end products.

ORGANIZATIONAL AND TECHNOLOGY REQUIREMENTS FOR SUCCESSFUL CPFR A successful CPFR implementation requires changes in the organizational structure and, to be scalable, requires the implementation of appropriate technology. None of this can be implemented without top management commitment. Effective collaboration requires manufacturers to set up cross-functional, customer-specific teams that include sales, demand planning, and logistics, at least for large customers. Such a focus has become feasible with the consolidation in retailing. For smaller customers, such teams can be focused by geography or sales channel. Retailers should also attempt to organize merchandise planning, buying, and replenishment into teams around suppliers. This can be difficult, given the large number of suppliers that consolidated retailers have. They can then organize the teams by categories that include multiple suppliers. For retailers that have multiple levels of inventory, such as DCs and retail stores, it is important to combine the replenishment teams at the two levels. Without collaborative inventory management at the two levels, duplication of inventories is common. The proposed organizational structure is illustrated in Figure 10-4.

The CPFR process is not dependent on technology but requires technology to be scalable. CPFR technologies have been developed to facilitate sharing of forecasts and historical information, evaluating exception conditions, and enabling revisions. These solutions must be integrated with enterprise systems that record all supply chain transactions.

[1] Smith, Larry. "Connecting the Consumer to the Factory." Supply Chain Management Review (May–June 2013): 10–17.

 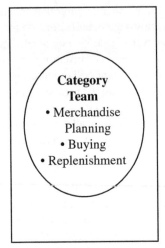

Manufacturer Organization **Retailer Organization**

Figure 10-4 Collaborative Organizational Structure
Source: Based on Voluntary Interindustry Commerce Standards, CPFR: An Overview, 2004.

RISKS AND HURDLES FOR A CPFR IMPLEMENTATION It is important to realize that there are risks and hurdles for a successful CPFR implementation. Given the large-scale sharing of information, there is a risk of information misuse. Often one or both of the CPFR partners have relationships with the partner's competitors. Another risk is that if one of the partners changes its scale or technology, the other partner will be forced to follow suit or lose the collaborative relationship. Finally, the implementation of CPFR and the resolution of exceptions require close interactions between two entities whose cultures may be very different. The inability to foster a collaborative culture across the partner organizations can be a major hurdle for the success of CPFR. One of the biggest hurdles to success is often that partners attempt store-level collaboration, which requires a higher organizational and technology investment. It is often best to start with an event- or DC-level collaboration, which is more focused and easier to collaborate on. Another major hurdle for successful CPFR is that demand information shared with partners is often not used within the organization in an integrated manner. It is important to have integrated demand, supply, logistics, and corporate planning within the organization to maximize the benefits of a CPFR effort with a partner.

SUMMARY OF LEARNING OBJECTIVE 4

VMI and CPFR are two practical approaches to improve coordination in the supply chain. Under VMI, the supplier is responsible for managing product inventories at the retailer while ensuring an agreed upon level of service. Under CPFR, supply chain members manage forecasting, planning, and replenishment in a collaborative manner. Partners may set CPFR relationships to collaborate on store events, DC replenishment, store replenishment, or assortment planning. DC replenishment collaboration is often the easiest to implement because it requires aggregate-level data. Store replenishment collaboration requires a higher level of investment in technology and data sharing to be successful.

DISCUSSION QUESTIONS

1. What characterizes supply chains that could be affected significantly by the bullwhip effect? How can the bullwhip effect be reduced?

2. What is the impact of lack of coordination on the performance of a supply chain?

3. In what way can improper incentives lead to a lack of coordination in a supply chain? What countermeasures can be used to offset this effect?

4. What problems result if each stage of a supply chain views its demand as the orders placed by the downstream stage? How should firms within a supply chain communicate to facilitate coordination?

5. What factors lead to a batching of orders within a supply chain? How does this affect coordination? What actions can minimize large batches and improve coordination?

6. What measures can a company employ to raise operational performance when information is distorted within the supply chain?

7. Compare continuous replenishment programs (CRPs) and vendor-managed inventory (VMI).

8. What are the different CPFR scenarios and how do they benefit supply chain partners?

BIBLIOGRAPHY

Cederlund, Jerold P., Rajiv Kohli, Susan A. Sherer, and Yuiling Yao. "How Motorola put CPFR into Action." *Supply Chain Management Review* (October 2007): 28–35.

Chen, Frank, ZviDrezner, Jennifer K. Ryan, and David Simchi-Levi. "Quantifying the Bullwhip Effect in a Simple Supply Chain: The Impact of Forecasting, Lead Times, and Information." *Management Science* (2000): 46, 436–443.

Continuous Replenishment: An ECR Best Practices Report. Washington, DC: Grocery Manufacturers Association, 1994.

Crum, Colleen, and George E. Palmatier. "Demand Collaboration: What's Holding Us Back?" *Supply Chain Management Review* (January–February 2004): 54–61.

Dawson, John. "How They Did It: Multi-Enterprise Collaboration at Intel." *Supply Chain Management Review* (September–October 2014): 18–25.

Disney, S. M., and D. R. Towill. "The Effect of Vendor Managed Inventory (VMI) Dynamics on the Bullwhip Effect in Supply Chains." *International Journal of Production Economics* (2003): 85, 199–215.

Fawcett, Stanley E., Amydee M. Fawcett, Sebastian Brockhaus, and A. Michael Knemeyer. "The Collaboration Journey: Are We There Yet?" *Supply Chain Management Review* (November 2016): 20–27.

Hammond, Janice H. 1994. *Barilla Spa (A–D).* Harvard Business School Case 9–694–046.

Kumar, Nirmalya. "The Power of Trust in Manufacturer–Retailer Relationships." *Harvard Business Review* (November–December 1996): 92–106.

Lee, Hau L., V. Padmanabhan, and Seungjin Whang. "The Bullwhip Effect in Supply Chains." *Sloan Management Review* (Spring 1997): 93–102.

Mariotti, John L. "The Trust Factor in Supply Chain Management." *Supply Chain Management Review* (Spring 1999): 70–77.

Sabath, Robert E., and John Fontanella. "The Unfulfilled Promise of Supply Chain Collaboration." *Supply Chain Management Review* (July–August 2002): 24–29.

Seifert, Dirk. *Collaborative Planning, Forecasting, and Replenishment: How to Create a Supply Chain Advantage.* New York: AMACOM, 2003.

Senge, Peter M. *The Fifth Discipline.* New York: Currency and Doubleday, 1990.

Smeltzer, Larry R. "Integration Means Everybody—Big and Small." *Supply Chain Management Review* (September–October 2001): 36–44.

Smith, L. "West Marine: A CPFR Success Story." *Supply Chain Management Review* (March 2006): 29–36.

Smith, Larry. "Connecting the Consumer to the Factory." *Supply Chain Management Review* (May–June 2013): 10–17.

Steerman, Hank. "A Practical Look at CPFR: The Sears-Michelin Experience." *Supply Chain Management Review* (July–August 2003): 46–53.

Voluntary Interindustry Commerce Standards. *Collaborative Planning, Forecasting, and Replenishment,* Version 2.0, 2002.

Voluntary Interindustry Commerce Standards. *CPFR: An Overview,* 2004.

CHAPTER
11

Managing Economies of Scale in a Supply Chain
Cycle Inventory

LEARNING OBJECTIVES

After reading this chapter, you will be able to

11.1 Describe the role of cycle inventory in a supply chain.

11.2 Choose the optimal lot size given fixed ordering costs in a supply chain.

11.3 Evaluate how aggregation is best implemented to reduce cycle inventory in a supply chain.

11.4 Understand the impact of quantity discounts on lot size and cycle inventory.

11.5 Devise appropriate discounting schemes for a supply chain.

11.6 Understand the impact of trade promotions on lot size and cycle inventory.

11.7 Develop replenishment policies to improve synchronization in multiechelon supply chains.

11.8 Identify managerial levers that reduce lot size and cycle inventory in a supply chain without increasing cost.

Cycle inventory exists because producing or purchasing in large lots allows a stage of the supply chain to exploit economies of scale and thus lower cost. The presence of fixed costs associated with ordering and transportation, quantity discounts in product pricing, and short-term discounts or promotions encourages different stages of a supply chain to exploit economies of scale and order in large lots. In this chapter, we study how each of these factors affects the lot size and cycle inventories within a supply chain. Our goal is to identify managerial levers that reduce cycle inventory in a supply chain without raising cost.

11.1 *Describe the role of cycle inventory in a supply chain.*

THE ROLE OF CYCLE INVENTORY IN A SUPPLY CHAIN

A *lot* or *batch size* is the quantity that a stage of a supply chain either produces or purchases at a time. Consider, for example, a computer store that sells an average of four printers a day. The store manager, however, orders 80 printers from the manufacturer each time he places an order. The lot or batch size in this case is 80 printers. Given daily sales of four printers, it takes an

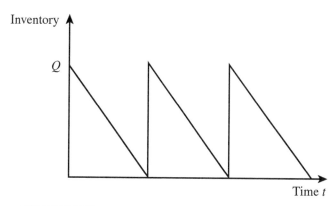

Figure 11-1 Inventory Profile of Jeans at Jean-Mart

average of 20 days before the store sells the entire lot and purchases a replenishment lot. The computer store holds an inventory of printers because the manager purchases a lot size larger than the store's daily sales. *Cycle inventory* is the average inventory in a supply chain due to either production or purchases in lot sizes that are larger than those demanded by the customer.

In the rest of this chapter, we use the following notation:

Q: Quantity in a lot or batch size

D: Demand per unit time

Here, we ignore the impact of demand variability and assume that demand is stable. In Chapter 12, we introduce demand variability and its impact on safety inventory.

Let us consider the cycle inventory of jeans at Jean-Mart, a department store. The demand for jeans is relatively stable at $D = 100$ pairs of jeans per day. The store manager at Jean-Mart currently purchases in lots of $Q = 1,000$ pairs. The *inventory profile* of jeans at Jean-Mart is a plot depicting the level of inventory over time, as shown in Figure 11-1.

Because purchases are in lots of $Q = 1,000$ units, whereas demand is only $D = 100$ units per day, it takes 10 days for an entire lot to be sold. Over these 10 days, the inventory of jeans at Jean-Mart declines steadily from 1,000 units (when the lot arrives) to 0 (when the last pair is sold). This sequence of a lot arriving and demand depleting inventory until another lot arrives repeats itself every 10 days, as shown in the inventory profile in Figure 11-1.

When demand is steady, cycle inventory and lot size are related as follows:

$$\text{Cycle inventory} = \frac{\text{lot size}}{2} = \frac{Q}{2} \qquad \textbf{(11.1)}$$

For a lot size of 1,000 units, Jean-Mart carries a cycle inventory of $Q/2 = 500$ pairs of jeans. From Equation 11.1, we see that cycle inventory is proportional to the lot size. A supply chain in which stages produce or purchase in larger lots has more cycle inventory than a supply chain in which stages produce and purchase in smaller lots. For example, if a competing department store with the same demand purchases in lot sizes of 200 pairs of jeans, it will carry a cycle inventory of only 100 pairs of jeans.

Lot sizes and cycle inventory also influence the flow time of material within the supply chain. Recall from Little's Law (Equation 3.1) that

$$\text{Average flow time} = \frac{\text{average inventory}}{\text{average flow rate}}$$

For any supply chain, average flow rate equals demand. We thus have

$$\text{Average flow time resulting from cycle inventory} = \frac{\text{cycle inventory}}{\text{demand}} = \frac{Q}{2D}$$

For lot sizes of 1,000 pairs of jeans and daily demand of 100 pairs of jeans, we obtain

$$\text{Average flow time resulting from cycle inventory} = \frac{Q}{2D} = \frac{1,000}{2 \times 100} = 5 \text{ days}$$

Cycle inventory at the Jean-Mart store thus adds five days to the average amount of time that jeans spend in the supply chain. The larger the cycle inventory, the longer the lag time between when a product is produced and when it is sold. There are many benefits to being able to lower cycle inventory without increasing costs. A lower level of cycle inventory decreases a firm's vulnerability to demand changes in the marketplace. A lower cycle inventory also decreases a firm's working capital requirement. Toyota, for example, keeps a cycle inventory of only a few hours of production between the factory and most suppliers. As a result, Toyota is never left with unneeded parts, and its working capital requirements are less than those of its competitors. Toyota also allocates very little space in the factory to inventory.

Zara and Seven-Eleven Japan are two companies that have built their strategy on the ability to replenish their stores in small lots. Seven-Eleven replenishes its stores in Japan with fresh food three times a day. The small replenishment batch allows Seven-Eleven to provide product that is always very fresh. Zara replenishes its European stores up to three times a week. Each replenishment batch thus contains only about two days of demand. This ensures that Zara's inventory on hand closely tracks customer demand. In both instances the firms have used small batch replenishment to ensure that their supply closely tracks customer demand trends.

Before we suggest actions that a manager can take to reduce cycle inventory, it is important to understand why stages of a supply chain produce or purchase in large lots and how lot size reduction affects supply chain performance.

Cycle inventory is held to take advantage of economies of scale and reduce cost within a supply chain. For example, apparel is shipped from Asia to North America in full container loads to reduce the transportation cost per unit. Similarly, an integrated steel mill produces hundreds of tons of steel per lot to spread that high cost of setup over a large batch. To understand how the supply chain achieves these economies of scale, we first identify supply chain costs that are influenced by lot size.

The *average price paid per unit purchased* is a key cost in the lot-sizing decision. A buyer may increase the lot size if this action results in a reduction in the price paid per unit purchased. For example, if the jeans manufacturer charges $20 per pair for orders under 500 pairs of jeans and $18 per pair for larger orders, the store manager at Jean-Mart gets the lower price by ordering in lots of at least 500 pairs of jeans. The price paid per unit is referred to as the *material cost* and is denoted by C. It is measured in dollars per unit. In many practical situations, material cost displays economies of scale—increasing lot size decreases material cost.

The *fixed ordering cost* includes all costs that do not vary with the size of the order but are incurred each time an order is placed. There may be a fixed administrative cost to place an order, a fixed trucking cost to transport the order, and a fixed labor cost to receive the order. Jean-Mart incurs a cost of $400 for the truck regardless of the number of pairs of jeans shipped. If the truck can hold up to 2,000 pairs of jeans, a lot size of 100 pairs results in a transportation cost of $4/pair, whereas a lot size of 1,000 pairs results in a transportation cost of $0.40/pair. Given the fixed transportation cost per batch, the store manager can reduce transportation cost per unit by increasing the lot size. The fixed ordering cost per lot or batch is denoted by S (commonly thought of as a setup cost) and is measured in dollars per lot. The ordering cost also displays economies of scale—increasing the lot size decreases the fixed ordering cost per unit purchased.

Holding cost is the cost of carrying one unit in inventory for a specified period of time, usually one year. It is a combination of the cost of capital, the cost of physically storing the inventory, and the cost that results from the product becoming obsolete. The holding cost is

denoted by H and is measured in dollars per unit per year. It may also be obtained as a fraction, h, of the unit cost of the product. Given a unit cost of C, the holding cost H is given by

$$H = hC \qquad\qquad (11.2)$$

The total holding cost increases with an increase in lot size and cycle inventory.

To summarize, the following costs must be considered in any lot-sizing decision:

- Average price per unit purchased, C/unit
- Fixed ordering cost incurred per lot, S/lot
- Holding cost incurred per unit per year, H/unit/year $= hC$

Later in the chapter, we discuss how the various costs may be estimated in practice. However, for the purposes of this discussion, we assume they are already known.

The primary role of cycle inventory is to allow different stages in a supply chain to purchase product in lot sizes that minimize the sum of the material, ordering, and holding costs. If a manager considers the holding cost alone, he or she will reduce the lot size and cycle inventory. Economies of scale in purchasing and ordering, however, motivate a manager to increase the lot size and cycle inventory. A manager must make the trade-off that minimizes total cost when making lot-sizing decisions. As a result, any stage of the supply chain exploits economies of scale in its replenishment decisions in the following three typical situations:

1. A fixed cost is incurred each time an order is placed or produced.
2. The supplier offers price discounts based on the quantity purchased per lot.
3. The supplier offers short-term price discounts or holds trade promotions.

In the following sections, we review how purchasing managers can best respond to these situations. Ideally, cycle inventory decisions should be made considering the total cost across the entire supply chain. In practice, however, it is generally the case that each stage makes its cycle inventory decisions independently. As we discuss later in the chapter, this practice increases the level of cycle inventory as well as the total cost in the supply chain.

SUMMARY OF LEARNING OBJECTIVE 1

Cycle inventory builds up in a supply chain because product is produced or purchased in large lots to lower the sum of material, ordering, and holding costs by exploiting economies of scale. Opportunities to exploit economies of scale arise if a fixed cost is incurred each time an order is placed or produced, the supplier offers price discounts based on the quantity purchased per lot, or the supplier offers short-term price discounts. A reduction in cycle inventory improves a supply chain's ability to match supply with demand.

ECONOMIES OF SCALE TO EXPLOIT FIXED COSTS

11.2 Choose the optimal lot size given fixed ordering costs in a supply chain.

To better understand the trade-offs discussed in this section, consider a situation that often arises in daily life—the purchase of groceries and other household products. These may be purchased at a nearby convenience store or at a Costco (a large warehouse club selling consumer goods), which is generally located much farther away. The fixed cost of going shopping is the time it takes to go to either location. This fixed cost is much lower for the nearby convenience store. Prices, however, are higher at the local convenience store. Taking the fixed cost into account, we tend to tailor our lot size decision accordingly. When we need only a small quantity, we go to the nearby convenience store because the benefit of a low fixed cost outweighs the cost of higher prices at the convenience store. When we are buying a large quantity, however, we go to Costco, where the lower prices over the larger quantity purchased more than make up for the higher fixed cost.

In this section, we focus on the situation in which a fixed cost associated with placing, receiving, and transporting an order is incurred for each order. A purchasing manager wants to minimize the total cost of satisfying demand and must therefore make the appropriate cost trade-offs when making the lot-sizing decision. For this decision, we assume the following inputs:

D = Annual demand of the product

S = Fixed cost incurred per order

C = Cost per unit of product

h = Holding cost per year as a fraction of product cost

Estimating Cycle Inventory Related Costs in Practice

When setting cycle inventory levels in practice, a common hurdle is estimating the fixed order cost and holding cost. Given the robustness of cycle inventory models, it is better to get a good approximation quickly rather than spend a lot of time trying to estimate costs exactly.

In practice, we should identify incremental costs that change with the lot-sizing decision and ignore costs that are unchanged with a change in lot size. For example, if a factory is running at 50 percent of capacity and all labor is full time and not earning overtime, it can be argued that the incremental setup cost for labor is zero. Reducing the lot size in this case will not have any impact on setup cost until either labor is fully utilized (and earning overtime) or machines are fully utilized (with a resulting loss in production capacity).

INVENTORY HOLDING COST Holding cost is estimated as a percentage of the cost of a product and is the sum of the following major components:

- *Cost of capital:* This is the dominant component of holding cost for products that do not become obsolete quickly. The appropriate approach is to evaluate the *weighted-average cost of capital* (WACC), which takes into account the required return on the firm's equity and the cost of its debt (see Brealey and Myers, 2000). These are weighted by the amount of equity and debt financing that the firm has. The formula for the WACC is

$$WACC = \frac{E}{D + E}(R_f + \beta \times MRP) + \frac{D}{D + E}R_b(1 - t)$$

where

E = amount of equity

D = amount of debt

R_f = risk-free rate of return (which is usually in the mid-single digits)

β = the firm's beta, a measure of volatility of stock price

MRP = market risk premium (which is around the high single digits)

R_b = rate at which the firm can borrow money (related to its debt rating)

t = tax rate

Most of these numbers can be found in a company's annual report and in any equity research report on the company. The borrowing rate comes from tables listing the rates charged for bonds from firms with the same credit ratings. The risk-free rate is the return on U.S. Treasury bonds, and the market risk premium is the return of the market above the risk-free rate. If access to a company's financial structure is not available, a good approximation can be made by using numbers from public companies in the same industry and of similar size.

- *Obsolescence (or spoilage) cost:* The obsolescence cost estimates the rate at which the value of the stored product drops because its market value or quality falls. This cost can range dramatically, from rates of many-thousand percent to virtually zero, depending on

the type of product. Perishable products have high obsolescence rates. Even nonperishables can have high obsolescence rates if they have short life cycles. A product with a life cycle of six months has an effective obsolescence cost of 200 percent. At the other end of the spectrum are products such as crude oil that take a long time to spoil or become obsolete. For such products, a low obsolescence rate may be applied.

- *Handling cost:* Handling cost should include only incremental receiving and storage costs that vary with the quantity of product received. Quantity-independent handling costs that vary with the number of orders should be included in the order cost. The quantity-dependent handling cost often does not change if quantity varies within a range. If the quantity is within this range (e.g., the range of inventory a crew of four people can unload per period of time), incremental handling cost added to the holding cost is zero. If the quantity handled requires more people, an incremental handling cost is added to the holding cost.

- *Occupancy cost:* The occupancy cost reflects the incremental change in space cost due to changing cycle inventory. If the firm is being charged based on the actual number of units held in storage, we have the direct occupancy cost. Firms often lease or purchase a fixed amount of space. As long as a marginal change in cycle inventory does not change the space requirements, the incremental occupancy cost is zero. Occupancy costs often take the form of a step function, with a sudden increase in cost when capacity is fully utilized and new space must be acquired.

- *Miscellaneous costs:* The final component of holding cost deals with a number of other relatively small costs. These costs include theft, security, damage, tax, and additional insurance charges that are incurred. Once again, it is important to estimate the incremental change in these costs on changing cycle inventory.

ORDERING COST The ordering cost includes all incremental costs associated with placing or receiving an extra order that are incurred regardless of the size of the order. Components of ordering cost include the following:

- *Buyer time:* Buyer time is the incremental time of the buyer placing the extra order. This cost should be included only if the buyer is utilized fully. The incremental cost of getting an idle buyer to place an order is zero and does not add to the ordering cost. Electronic ordering can significantly reduce the buyer time to place an order.

- *Transportation costs:* A fixed transportation cost is often incurred regardless of the size of the order. For instance, if a truck is sent to deliver every order, it costs the same amount to send a half-empty truck as it does a full truck. Less-than-truckload pricing also includes a fixed component that is independent of the quantity shipped and a variable component that increases with the quantity shipped. The fixed component should be included in the ordering cost.

- *Receiving costs:* Some receiving costs are incurred regardless of the size of the order. These include any administration work such as purchase order matching and any effort associated with updating inventory records. Receiving costs that are quantity dependent should not be included here.

- *Other costs:* Each situation can have costs unique to it that should be considered if they are incurred for each order regardless of the quantity of that order.

The ordering cost is estimated as the sum of all its component costs.

Optimal Lot Sizing for a Single Product (Economic Order Quantity)

In this section we obtain the optimal lot size when a single product is purchased or produced to meet steady demand. Consider the purchasing manager at Best Buy who places a replenishment order for a new lot of Q Apple computers each time the store is running out of stock. Including

the cost of transportation, Best Buy incurs a fixed cost of $S per order. The purchasing manager must decide on the number of computers to order from Apple in a lot.

Assume that Apple does not offer any discounts, and each unit costs $C no matter how large an order is. The holding cost is thus given by $H = hC$ (using Equation 11.2). The model is developed using the following basic assumptions:

1. Demand is steady at D units per unit time.
2. No shortages are allowed—that is, all demand must be supplied from stock.
3. Replenishment lead time is fixed (initially assumed to be zero).

The purchasing manager makes the lot-sizing decision to minimize the total cost for the store. He or she must consider three costs when deciding on the lot size:

- Annual material cost
- Annual ordering cost
- Annual holding cost

Because purchase price is independent of lot size, we have

$$\text{Annual material cost} = CD$$

The number of orders must suffice to meet the annual demand D. Given a lot size of Q, we thus have

$$\text{Number of orders per year} = \frac{D}{Q} \tag{11.3}$$

Because an order cost of S is incurred for each order placed, we infer that

$$\text{Annual ordering cost} = \left(\frac{D}{Q}\right)S \tag{11.4}$$

Given a lot size of Q, we have an average inventory of $Q/2$. The annual holding cost is thus the cost of holding $Q/2$ units in inventory for one year and is given as

$$\text{Annual holding cost} = \left(\frac{Q}{2}\right)H = \left(\frac{Q}{2}\right)hC$$

The total annual cost, TC, is the sum of all three costs and is given as

$$\text{Total annual cost, } TC = \left(\frac{D}{Q}\right)S + \left(\frac{Q}{2}\right)hC + CD$$

Figure 11-2 shows the variation in different costs as the lot size is changed. Observe that the annual holding cost increases with an increase in lot size. In contrast, the annual ordering cost declines with an increase in lot size. The material cost is independent of lot size because we have assumed the price to be fixed. The total annual cost thus first declines and then increases with an increase in lot size.

From the perspective of the manager at Best Buy, the optimal lot size is one that minimizes the total cost to Best Buy. It is obtained by taking the first derivative of the total cost with respect to Q and setting it equal to 0 (see Appendix 11A at the end of this chapter). The optimal lot size is referred to as the *economic order quantity* (EOQ). It is denoted by Q^* and is given by the following equation:

$$\text{Optimal lot size, } Q^* = \sqrt{\frac{2DS}{hC}} \tag{11.5}$$

For this formula, it is important to use the same time units for the holding cost rate h and the demand D. With each lot or batch of size Q^*, the cycle inventory in the system is given by $Q^*/2$.

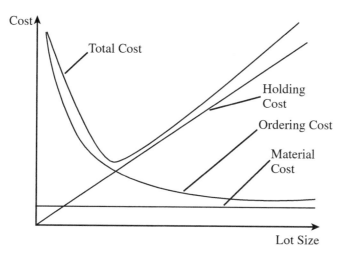

Figure 11-2 Effect of Lot Size on Costs at Best Buy

The flow time spent by each unit in the system is given by $Q^*/(2D)$. As the optimal lot size increases, so does the cycle inventory and the flow time. The optimal ordering frequency is given by n^*, where

$$n^* = \frac{D}{Q^*} = \sqrt{\frac{DhC}{2S}} \qquad \text{(11.6)}$$

In Example 11-1 (see spreadsheet *Chapter11-examples1-6*, worksheet *Example 11-1*), we illustrate the EOQ formula and the procedure to make lot-sizing decisions.

EXAMPLE 11-1 **Economic Order Quantity**

Demand for the Deskpro computer at Best Buy is 1,000 units per month. Best Buy incurs a fixed order placement, transportation, and receiving cost of $4,000 each time an order is placed. Each computer costs Best Buy $500 and the retailer has an annual holding cost of 20 percent. Evaluate the number of computers that the store manager should order in each replenishment lot.

Analysis:

In this case, the store manager has the following inputs:

Annual demand, $D = 1,000 \times 12 = 12,000$ units

Order cost per lot, $S = \$4,000$

Unit cost per computer, $C = \$500$

Holding cost per year as a fraction of unit cost, $h = 0.2$

Using the EOQ formula (Equation 11.5), the optimal lot size is

$$\text{Optimal order size} = Q^* = \sqrt{\frac{2 \times 12,000 \times 4,000}{0.2 \times 500}} = 980$$

To minimize the total cost at Best Buy, the store manager orders a lot size of 980 computers for each replenishment order. The cycle inventory is the average resulting inventory and (using Equation 11.1) is given by

$$\text{Cycle inventory} = \frac{Q^*}{2} = \frac{980}{2} = 490$$

For a lot size of $Q^* = 980$, the store manager evaluates

$$\text{Number of orders per year} = \frac{D}{Q^*} = \frac{12{,}000}{980} = 12.24$$

$$\text{Annual ordering and holding cost} = \frac{D}{Q^*}S + \left(\frac{Q^*}{2}\right)hC = \$97{,}980$$

$$\text{Average flow time} = \frac{Q^*}{2D} = \frac{980}{2 \times 12{,}000} = 0.041 \text{ year} = 0.49 \text{ month}$$

Each computer thus spends 0.49 month, on average, at Best Buy before it is sold because it was purchased in a batch of 980.

A few key insights can be gained from Example 11-1 (see worksheet *Example11-1*). Using a lot size of 1,100 (instead of 980) increases annual costs to \$98,636 (from \$97,980). Even though the order size is more than 10 percent larger than the optimal order size Q^*, total cost increases by only 0.67 percent. This issue can be relevant in practice. Best Buy may find that the economic order quantity for flash drives is 6.5 cases. The manufacturer may be reluctant to ship half a case and may want to charge extra for this service. Our discussion illustrates that Best Buy is perhaps better off with lot sizes of six or seven cases, because this change has a small impact on its inventory-related costs but can save on any fee that the manufacturer charges for shipping half a case.

> ➡ **Key Point**
>
> Total ordering and holding costs are relatively stable around the economic order quantity. A firm is often better served by ordering a convenient lot size close to the EOQ rather than the precise EOQ.

If demand at Best Buy increases to 4,000 computers a month (demand has increased by a factor of 4), the EOQ formula shows that the optimal lot size doubles and the number of orders placed per year also doubles. In contrast, average flow time decreases by a factor of 2. In other words, as demand increases, cycle inventory measured in terms of days (or months) of demand should reduce if the lot-sizing decision is made optimally. This observation can be stated as the following Key Point:

> ➡ **Key Point**
>
> If demand increases by a factor of k, the optimal lot size increases by a factor of $\sqrt{k}$. The number of orders placed per year should also increase by a factor of $\sqrt{k}$. Flow time attributed to cycle inventory should decrease by a factor of $\sqrt{k}$.

Let us return to the situation in which monthly demand for the Deskpro model is 1,000 computers. Now assume that the manager would like to reduce the lot size to $Q = 200$ units to reduce flow time. If this lot size is decreased without any other change, we have

$$\text{Annual inventory-related costs} = \left(\frac{D}{Q}\right)S + \left(\frac{Q}{2}\right)hC = \$250{,}000$$

This is significantly higher than the total cost of \$97,980 that Best Buy incurred when ordering in lots of 980 units, as in Example 11-1. Thus, there are clear financial reasons that the store manager would be unwilling to reduce the lot size to 200. To make it feasible to reduce the lot size, the manager should work to reduce the fixed order cost S. If the fixed cost associated

with each lot is reduced to $1,000 (from the current value of $4,000), the optimal lot size reduces to 490 (from the current value of 980). We illustrate the relationship between desired lot size and order cost in Example 11-2 (see worksheet *Example 11-2*).

EXAMPLE 11-2 **Relationship Between Desired Lot Size and Ordering Cost**

The store manager at Best Buy would like to reduce the optimal lot size from 980 to 200. For this lot size reduction to be optimal, the store manager wants to evaluate how much the ordering cost per lot should be reduced.

Analysis:

In this case, we have

Desired lot size, $Q^* = 200$

Annual demand, $D = 1,000 \times 12 = 12,000$ units

Unit cost per computer, $C = \$500$

Holding cost per year as a fraction of inventory value, $h = 0.2$

Using the EOQ formula (Equation 11.5), the desired order cost is

$$S = \frac{hC(Q^*)^2}{2D} = \frac{0.2 \times 500 \times 200^2}{2 \times 12,000} = \$166.7$$

Thus, the store manager at Best Buy would have to reduce the order cost per lot from $4,000 to $166.7 for a lot size of 200 to be optimal.

As we will discuss later, aggregating multiple products in a single order can often help reduce the fixed order cost S. The observation in Example 11-2 may be stated as in the following Key Point:

➡ Key Point

To reduce the optimal lot size by a factor of k, the fixed order cost S must be reduced by a factor of k^2.

Production Lot Sizing

In the EOQ formula, we have implicitly assumed that the entire lot arrives at the same time. While this may be a reasonable assumption for a retailer receiving a replenishment lot, it is not reasonable in a production environment in which production occurs at a specified rate, say, P. In a production environment, inventory thus builds up at a rate of $P - D$ when production is on, and inventory is depleted at a rate of D when production is off.

With D, h, C, and S as defined earlier, the EOQ formula can be modified to obtain the economic production quantity (EPQ) as follows:

$$Q^P = \sqrt{\frac{2DS}{(1 - D/P)hC}}$$

The annual setup cost in this case is given by

$$\left(\frac{D}{Q^P}\right)S$$

The annual holding cost is given by

$$(1 - D/P)\left(\frac{Q^P}{2}\right)hC$$

Observe that the economic production quantity is the EOQ multiplied by a correction factor that approaches 1 as the production rate becomes much faster than the demand.

For the remainder of this chapter, we restrict our attention to the case in which the entire replenishment lot arrives at the same time, a scenario that applies in most supply chain settings.

Lot Sizing with Capacity Constraint

In our discussion so far we have assumed that the economic order quantity for a retailer will fit on the truck. In reality the truck has a limited capacity, say K. If the economic order quantity Q is less than K, the retailer should order Q units in each order. If the economic order quantity Q is more than the K, the retailer will have to pay for more than one truck. In this case, the optimal order quantity is obtained by comparing the annual cost of ordering K units per lot (a full truck for each lot) and Q units per lot (requiring $\lceil Q/K \rceil$ trucks for each lot). If the setup cost S arises primarily from the cost of a truck, it is never optimal to order more than one truck. In this case, the optimal order size is the minimum of the EOQ and the truck capacity (K).

SUMMARY OF LEARNING OBJECTIVE 2

In deciding on the optimal lot size, the supply chain goal is to minimize the total cost—the order cost, holding cost, and material cost. As lot size increases, so does the annual holding cost. However, the annual order cost and, in some instances, the annual material cost decrease with an increase in lot size. The EOQ balances the three costs to obtain the optimal lot size. The higher the order and transportation cost, the higher the lot size and cycle inventory. The optimal lot size can be decreased if the fixed cost associated with each lot is reduced.

11.3 Evaluate how aggregation is best implemented to reduce cycle inventory in a supply chain.

AGGREGATING MULTIPLE PRODUCTS IN A SINGLE ORDER

As we have discussed earlier, a key to reducing lot size is the reduction of the fixed cost incurred per lot. One major source of fixed costs is transportation. In several companies, the array of products sold is divided into families or groups, with each group managed independently by a separate product manager. This results in separate orders and deliveries for each product family, thus increasing the overall cycle inventory. Aggregating orders and deliveries across product families lowers the fixed transportation cost per family and is an effective mechanism to lower cycle inventories. We illustrate the benefits of aggregating shipments using the following example.

Consider the data from Example 11-1. Assume that Best Buy purchases four computer models, and the demand for each of the four models is 1,000 units per month. In this case, if each product manager orders separately, he or she would order a lot size of 980 units (as in Example 11-1) for each model. Across the four models, the total cycle inventory would thus be $4 \times 980/2 = 1,960$ units.

Now consider the case in which a store manager at Best Buy realizes that all four model shipments originate from the same source. She asks the product managers to coordinate their purchasing to ensure that all four products arrive on the same truck. In this case, the optimal combined lot size across all four models turns out to be 1,960 units (use $S = \$4,000$,

$D = 4 \times 12,000 = 48,000$, $hC = \$500 \times 0.2 = \10 in Equation 11.5). This is equivalent to a lot size of 490 units for each model. As a result of aggregating orders and spreading the fixed transportation cost across multiple products originating from the same supplier, it becomes financially optimal for the store manager at Best Buy to reduce the lot size for each individual product from 980 to 490. This action significantly reduces the cycle inventory, as well as the cost to Best Buy.

Other ways to achieve aggregation include having a single delivery coming from multiple suppliers (allowing fixed transportation cost to be spread across multiple suppliers) or having a single truck delivering to multiple retailers (allowing fixed transportation cost to be spread across multiple retailers). Firms that import product to the United States from Asia have worked hard to aggregate their shipments across suppliers (often by building hubs in Asia that all suppliers deliver to), allowing them to maintain transportation economies of scale while getting smaller and more frequent deliveries from each supplier.

Walmart and other retailers, such as Seven-Eleven Japan, have facilitated aggregation across multiple supply and delivery points without storing intermediate inventories through the use of cross-docking. Each supplier sends full truckloads to the DC, containing an aggregate delivery destined for multiple retail stores. At the DC, each inbound truck is unloaded, product is cross-docked, and outbound trucks are loaded. Each outbound truck now contains product aggregated from several suppliers destined for one retail store.

When considering fixed costs, one cannot ignore the receiving or loading costs. As more products are included in a single order, the product variety on a truck increases. The receiving warehouse now has to update inventory records for more items per truck. In addition, the task of putting inventory into storage now becomes more expensive because each distinct item must be stocked in a separate location. Thus, when attempting to reduce lot sizes, it is important to focus on reducing costs that increase with variety. Advance shipping notices (ASNs) are files that contain precise records of the contents of the truck that are sent electronically by the supplier to the customer. These electronic notices facilitate updating of inventory records as well as the decision regarding storage locations, helping reduce the fixed cost of receiving. RFID technology can also help reduce the fixed costs associated with receiving that are related to product variety. The reduced fixed cost of receiving makes it optimal to reduce the lot size ordered for each product, thus reducing cycle inventory.

We next analyze how optimal lot sizes may be determined when there are fixed costs associated with each lot as well as the variety in the lot.

Lot Sizing with Multiple Products or Customers

In general, the ordering, transportation, and receiving costs of an order grow with the variety of products or pickup points. For example, it is cheaper for Walmart to receive a truck containing a single product than it is to receive a truck containing many different products, because the inventory update and restocking effort is less for a single product. A portion of the fixed cost of an order can be related to transportation (this depends only on the load and is independent of product variety on the truck). A portion of the fixed cost is related to loading and receiving (this cost increases with variety on the truck). We now discuss how optimal lot sizes may be determined in such a setting.

Our objective is to arrive at lot sizes and an ordering policy that minimize the total cost. We assume the following inputs:

D_i: Annual demand for product i

S: Order cost incurred each time an order is placed, independent of the variety of products included in the order

s_i: Additional order cost incurred if product i is included in the order

Let us consider the case in which Best Buy purchases multiple models of a product. The store manager may consider three approaches to the lot-sizing decision:

1. Each product manager orders his or her model independently.
2. The product managers jointly order every product in each lot.
3. Product managers order jointly but not every order contains every product; that is, each order contains a selected subset of the products.

The first approach does not use any aggregation and results in high cost. The second approach aggregates all products in each order, thus amortizing the order cost S across multiple products. The weakness of the second approach, however, is that low-demand products are aggregated with high-demand products in every order resulting in all order costs s_i to be incurred in each order. Complete aggregation results in high costs if the product-specific order cost for the low demand products is large. In such a situation, it may be better to order the low-demand products less frequently than the high-demand products. This practice results in a reduction of the product-specific order cost associated with the low-demand product. As a result, the third approach is likely to yield the lowest cost. However, it is more complex to implement.

We consider the example of Best Buy purchasing computers and illustrate the effect of each of the three approaches on supply chain costs.

LOTS ARE ORDERED AND DELIVERED INDEPENDENTLY FOR EACH PRODUCT In this approach, each product is ordered independently of the others. This scenario is equivalent to applying the EOQ formula to each product when evaluating lot sizes, as illustrated in Example 11-3 (see worksheet *Example 11-3* in spreadsheet *Chapter11-examples 1-6*).

EXAMPLE 11-3	**Multiple Products with Lots Ordered and Delivered Independently**

Best Buy sells three models of computers, the Litepro, the Medpro, and the Heavypro. Annual demands for the three products are $D_L = 12,000$ for the Litepro, $D_M = 1,200$ units for the Medpro, and $D_H = 120$ units for the Heavypro. Each model costs Best Buy $500. A fixed transportation cost of $4,000 is incurred each time an order is delivered. For each model ordered and delivered on the same truck, an additional fixed cost of $1,000 per model is incurred for receiving and storage. Best Buy incurs an annual holding cost of 20 percent. Evaluate the lot sizes that the Best Buy manager should order if lots for each product are ordered and delivered independently. Also evaluate the annual cost of such a policy.

Analysis:

In this example, we have the following information:

Demand, $D_L = 12,000$/year, $D_M = 1,200$/year, $D_H = 120$/year

Common order cost, $S = \$4,000$

Product-specific order cost, $s_L = \$1,000$, $s_M = \$1,000$, $s_H = \$1,000$

Holding cost, $h = 0.2$

Unit cost, $C_L = \$500$, $C_M = \$500$, $C_H = \$500$

Because each model is ordered and delivered independently, a separate truck delivers each model. Thus, a fixed ordering cost of $5,000 ($4,000 + $1,000) is incurred for each product delivery. The optimal ordering policies and resulting costs for the three products (when the three products are ordered independently) are evaluated using the EOQ formula (Equation 11.5) and are shown in Table 11-1.

TABLE 11-1 Lot Sizes and Costs for Independent Ordering

	Litepro	Medpro	Heavypro
Demand per year	12,000	1,200	120
Fixed cost/order	$5,000	$5,000	$5,000
Optimal order size	1,095	346	110
Cycle inventory	548	173	55
Annual holding cost	$54,772	$17,321	$5,477
Order frequency	11.0/year	3.5/year	1.1/year
Annual ordering cost	$54,772	$17,321	$5,477
Average flow time	2.4 weeks	7.5 weeks	23.7 weeks
Annual total cost	$109,544	$34,642	$10,954

Note: Although these figures are correct, some may differ from calculations due to rounding.

The Litepro model is ordered 11 times a year, the Medpro model is ordered 3.5 times a year, and the Heavypro model is ordered 1.1 times each year. The annual ordering and holding cost Best Buy incurs if the three models are ordered independently turns out to be $155,140.

Independent ordering is simple to execute but ignores the opportunity to aggregate orders. Thus, the product managers at Best Buy could potentially lower costs by combining orders on a single truck. We next consider the scenario in which all three products are ordered and delivered on the same truck each time an order is placed.

LOTS ARE ORDERED AND DELIVERED JOINTLY FOR ALL THREE MODELS Given that all three models are included each time an order is placed using this approach, the combined fixed order cost per order is given by

$$S^* = S + s_L + s_M + s_H$$

The next step is to identify the optimal ordering frequency. Let n be the number of orders placed per year. We then have

$$\text{Annual order cost} = S^*n$$

$$\text{Annual holding cost} = \frac{D_L h C_L}{2n} + \frac{D_M h C_M}{2n} + \frac{D_H h C_H}{2n}$$

The total annual cost is thus given by

$$\text{Total annual cost} = \frac{D_L h C_L}{2n} + \frac{D_M h C_M}{2n} + \frac{D_H h C_H}{2n} + S^*n$$

The optimal order frequency minimizes the total annual cost and is obtained by taking the first derivative of the total cost with respect to n and setting it equal to 0. This results in the optimal order frequency n^*, where

$$n^* = \sqrt{\frac{D_L h C_L + D_M h C_M + D_H h C_H}{2S^*}} \tag{11.7}$$

Equation 11.7 can be generalized to the case in which there are k items consolidated on a single order, as follows:

$$n^* = \sqrt{\frac{\sum_{i=1}^{k} D_i h C_i}{2S^*}} \tag{11.8}$$

Truck capacity can also be included in this setting by comparing the total load for the optimal n^* with truck capacity. If the optimal load exceeds truck capacity, n^* is increased until the load equals truck capacity. By applying Equation 11.8 for different values of k, we can also find the optimal number of items or suppliers to be aggregated in a single delivery.

In Example 11-4, we consider the case in which the product managers at Best Buy jointly order all three models each time they place an order (see worksheet *Example 11-4*).

EXAMPLE 11-4 Products Ordered and Delivered Jointly

Consider the Best Buy data in Example 11-3. The three product managers have decided to aggregate and order all three models each time they place an order. Evaluate the optimal lot size for each model.

Analysis:

Because all three models are included in each order, the combined order cost is

$$S^* = S + s_L + s_M + s_H = \$7{,}000 \text{ per order}$$

The optimal order frequency is obtained using Equation 11.7 and is given by

$$n^* = \sqrt{\frac{(12{,}000 \times 100) + (1{,}200 \times 100) + (120 \times 100)}{2 \times 7{,}000}} = 9.75$$

Thus, if each model is to be included in every order and delivery, the product managers at Best Buy should place 9.75 orders each year. In this case, the ordering policies and costs are as shown in Table 11-2.

Because 9.75 orders are placed each year and each order costs a total of $7,000, we have

$$\text{Annual order cost} = 9.75 \times 7{,}000 = \$68{,}250$$

The annual ordering and holding cost, across the three sizes, of the aforementioned policy is given by

$$\text{Annual order and holding cost} = \$61{,}512 + \$6{,}151 + \$615 + \$68{,}250 = \$136{,}528$$

Observe that the product managers at Best Buy lower the annual cost from $155,140 to $136,528 by ordering all products jointly. This represents a decrease of about 12 percent.

In Example 11-5, we consider optimal aggregation of orders or deliveries in the presence of capacity constraints (see worksheet *Example 11-5*).

TABLE 11-2 Lot Sizes and Costs for Joint Ordering at Best Buy

	Litepro	Medpro	Heavypro
Demand per year (D)	12,000	1,200	120
Order frequency (n^*)	9.75/year	9.75/year	9.75/year
Optimal order size (D/n^*)	1,230	123	12.3
Cycle inventory	615	61.5	6.15
Annual holding cost	$61,512	$6,151	$615
Average flow time	2.67 weeks	2.67 weeks	2.67 weeks

| EXAMPLE 11-5 | **Aggregation with Capacity Constraint** |

W.W. Grainger sources from hundreds of suppliers and is considering the aggregation of inbound shipments to lower costs. Truckload shipping costs $500 per truck along with $100 per pickup. Average annual demand from each supplier is 10,000 units. Each unit costs $50 and Grainger incurs an annual holding cost of 20 percent. What is the optimal order frequency and order size if Grainger decides to aggregate four suppliers per truck? What is the optimal order size and frequency if each truck has a capacity of 2,500 units?

Analysis:

In this case, W.W. Grainger has the following inputs:

Demand per product, $D_i = 10,000$

Annual holding cost, $h = 0.2$

Unit cost per product, $C_i = \$50$

Common order cost, $S = \$500$

Supplier-specific order cost, $s_i = \$100$

The combined order cost from four suppliers is given by

$$S^* = S + s_1 + s_2 + s_3 + s_4 = \$900 \text{ per order}$$

From Equation 11.8, the optimal order frequency is

$$n^* = \sqrt{\frac{\sum_{i=1}^{4} D_i h C_i}{2S^*}} = \sqrt{\frac{4 \times 10,000 \times 0.2 \times 50}{2 \times 900}} = 14.91$$

It is thus optimal for Grainger to order 14.91 times per year. The annual ordering cost per supplier is

$$\text{Annual order cost} = 14.91 \times \frac{900}{4} = \$3,355$$

The quantity ordered from each supplier is $Q = 10,000/14.91 = 671$ units per order. The annual holding cost per supplier is

$$\text{Annual holding cost per supplier} = \frac{hC_iQ}{2} = 0.2 \times 50 \times \frac{671}{2} = \$3,355$$

This policy, however, requires a total capacity per truck of $4 \times 671 = 2,684$ units. Given a truck capacity of 2,500 units, the order frequency must be increased to ensure that the order quantity from each supplier is $2,500/4 = 625$. Thus, W.W. Grainger should increase the order frequency to $10,000/625 = 16$. The limited truck capacity results in an optimal order frequency of 16 orders per year instead of 14.91 orders per year when truck capacity was ignored. The limited truck capacity will increase the annual order cost per supplier to $3,600 and decrease the annual holding cost per supplier to $3,125.

The main advantage of ordering all products jointly is that the system is easy to administer and implement. The disadvantage is that it is not selective enough in combining the particular models that should be ordered together. If product-specific order costs are high and products vary significantly in terms of their sales, it is possible to lower costs by being selective about the products being aggregated in a joint order.

Next, we consider a policy under which the product managers do not necessarily order all models each time an order is placed, but still coordinate their orders.

LOTS ARE ORDERED AND DELIVERED JOINTLY FOR A SELECTED SUBSET OF THE PRODUCTS
We first illustrate how being selective in aggregating orders into a single order can lower costs. Consider Example 11-4, in which the manager decides to aggregate all three computer models in every order. The optimal policy from Example 11-4 is to order 9.75 times a year. The disadvantage of this policy is that the Heavypro, with annual demand of only 120 units, is also ordered 9.75 times. Given that a model-specific cost of $1,000 is incurred with each order, we are essentially adding $1,000/(120/9.75) = \$81.25$ in order cost to each unit of Heavypro. If we were to include the Heavypro in every fourth order (instead of every order), we would save $9,750 \times (3/4) = \$7,312.50$ in product-specific ordering cost (save three out of four product-specific orders) while incurring an additional $500 \times 0.2 \times [(120/9.75)/2] \times 3 = \$1,846.15$ in holding cost (because the lot size of Heavypro would increase from $120/9.75$ to $[120 \times (4/9.75)]$). Such a policy would thus decrease the annual cost relative to complete aggregation by more than $5,466. This example points to the value of being more selective when aggregating orders.

We now discuss a procedure that is more selective in combining products to be ordered jointly. The procedure we discuss here does not necessarily provide the optimal solution. It does, however, yield an ordering policy whose cost is close to optimal. The approach of the procedure is to first identify the "most frequently" ordered product that is included in every order. The base fixed cost S is then entirely allocated to this product. For each of the "less frequently" ordered products i, the ordering frequency is determined using only the product-specific ordering cost s_i. The frequencies are then adjusted so that each product i is included every m_i orders, where m_i is an integer. We now detail the procedure used.

We first describe the procedure in general and then apply it to the specific example. Assume that the products are indexed by i, where i varies from 1 to l (assuming a total of l products). Each product i has an annual demand D_i, a unit cost C_i, and a product-specific order cost s_i. The common order cost is S.

Step 1: As a first step, identify the most frequently ordered product, assuming each product is ordered independently. In this case, a fixed cost of $S + s_i$ is allocated to each product. For each product i (using Equation 11.6), evaluate the ordering frequency:

$$\bar{n}_i = \sqrt{\frac{hC_iD_i}{2(S + s_i)}}$$

This is the frequency at which product i would be ordered if it were the only product being ordered (in which case a fixed cost of $S + s_i$ would be incurred per order). Let $\bar{n}$ be the frequency of the most frequently ordered product, i^*; that is, $\bar{n}_{i^*}$ is the maximum among all $\bar{n}_i$ ($\bar{n} = \bar{n}_{i^*} = \max\{\bar{n}_i, i = 1, \ldots, l\}$). The most frequently ordered product is i^*, which is included each time an order is placed.

Step 2: For all products $i \neq i^*$, evaluate the ordering frequency:

$$\bar{\bar{n}}_i = \sqrt{\frac{hC_iD_i}{2s_i}}$$

$\bar{\bar{n}}_i$ represents the desired order frequency if product i incurs the product-specific fixed cost s_i only each time it is ordered.

Step 3: Our goal is to include each product $i \neq i^*$ with the most frequently ordered product i^* after an integer number of orders. For all $i \neq i^*$, evaluate the frequency of product i relative to the most frequently ordered product i^* to be m_i, where

$$m_i = \lceil \bar{n}/\bar{\bar{n}}_i \rceil$$

In this case, $\lceil\ \rceil$ is the operation that rounds a fraction up to the closest integer. Product i is included with the most frequently ordered product i^* every m_i orders. Given that the most frequently ordered product i^* is included in every order, $m_{i^*} = 1$.

Step 4: Having decided the ordering frequency of each product i, recalculate the ordering frequency of the most frequently ordered product i^* to be n, where

$$n = \sqrt{\frac{\sum_{i=1}^{l} hC_i m_i D_i}{2(S + \sum_{i=1}^{l} s_i/m_i)}} \qquad \text{(11.9)}$$

Note that n is a better ordering frequency for the most frequently ordered product i^* than $\bar{n}$ because it takes into account the fact that each of the other products i is included with i^* every m_i orders.

Step 5: For each product, evaluate an order frequency of $n_i = n/m_i$ and the total cost of such an ordering policy. The total annual cost is given by

$$TC = nS + \sum_{i=1}^{l} n_i s_i + \sum_{i=1}^{l} \left(\frac{D_i}{2n_i}\right) hC_i$$

This procedure results in *tailored aggregation*, with higher-demand products ordered more frequently and lower-demand products ordered less frequently. Example 11-6 (see worksheet *Example 11-6*) considers tailored aggregation for the Best Buy ordering decision in Example 11-3.

EXAMPLE 11-6	**Lot Sizes Ordered and Delivered Jointly for a Selected Subset That Varies by Order**

Consider the Best Buy data in Example 11-3. Product managers have decided to order jointly, but to be selective about which models they include in each order. Evaluate the ordering policy and costs using the procedure discussed previously.

Analysis:

Recall that $S = \$4,000$, $s_L = \$1,000$, $s_M = \$1,000$, $s_H = \$1,000$. Applying Step 1, we obtain

$$\bar{n}_L = \sqrt{\frac{hC_L D_L}{2(S + s_L)}} = 11.0, \bar{n}_M = \sqrt{\frac{hC_M D_M}{2(S + s_M)}} = 3.5, \bar{n}_H = \sqrt{\frac{hC_H D_H}{2(S + s_H)}} = 1.1$$

Clearly, Litepro is the most frequently ordered model. Thus, we set $\bar{n} = 11.0$.

We now apply Step 2 to evaluate the frequency with which Medpro and Heavypro are included with Litepro in the order. We first obtain

$$\bar{\bar{n}}_M = \sqrt{\frac{hC_M D_M}{2s_M}} = 7.7 \quad \text{and} \quad \bar{\bar{n}}_H = \sqrt{\frac{hC_H D_H}{2s_H}} = 2.4$$

Next, we apply Step 3 to evaluate

$$m_M = \left\lceil \frac{\bar{n}}{\bar{\bar{n}}_M} \right\rceil = \left\lceil \frac{11.0}{7.7} \right\rceil = 2 \quad \text{and} \quad m_H = \left\lceil \frac{\bar{n}}{\bar{\bar{n}}_H} \right\rceil = \left\lceil \frac{11.0}{2.4} \right\rceil = 5$$

TABLE 11-3 Lot Sizes and Costs for Ordering Policy Using Heuristic

	Litepro	Medpro	Heavypro
Demand per year (D)	12,000	1,200	120
Order frequency (n)	11.47/year	5.74/year	2.29/year
Order size (D/n)	1,046	209	52
Cycle inventory	523	104.5	26
Annual holding cost	$52,307	$10,461	$2,615
Average flow time	2.27 weeks	4.53 weeks	11.35 weeks

Thus, Medpro is included in every second order and Heavypro is included in every fifth order (Litepro, the most frequently ordered model, is included in every order). Now that we have decided on the ordering frequency of each model, apply Step 4 (Equation 11.9) to recalculate the ordering frequency of the most frequently ordered model as

$$n = \sqrt{\frac{hC_L m_L D_L + hC_M m_M D_M + hC_H m_M D_H}{2(S + s_L/m_L + s_M/m_M + s_H/m_H)}} = 11.47$$

Thus, the Litepro is ordered 11.47 times per year. Next, we apply Step 5 to obtain an ordering frequency for each product:

$$n_L = 11.47/\text{year}, n_M = 11.47/2 = 5.74/\text{year, and } n_H = 11.47/5 = 2.29/\text{year}$$

The ordering policies and resulting costs for the three products are shown in Table 11-3. The annual holding cost of this policy is $65,383.50. The annual order cost is given by

$$nS + n_L s_L + n_M s_M + n_H s_H = \$65,383.50$$

The total annual cost is thus equal to $130,767. Tailored aggregation results in a cost reduction of $5,761 (about 4 percent) compared with the joint ordering of all models. The cost reduction results because each model-specific fixed cost of $1,000 is not incurred with every order.

From the Best Buy examples, it follows that aggregation can provide significant cost savings and reduction in cycle inventory in the supply chain. When product-specific order costs (s_i) are small relative to the fixed cost S, complete aggregation, whereby every product is included in every order, is very effective. Tailored aggregation provides little additional value in this setting and may not be worth the additional complexity. If Examples 11-3, 11-4, and 11-6 are repeated with s_i = $300 (change cells D5:D7 in worksheet *Example 11-3* to 300), we find that tailored aggregation decreases costs by only about 1 percent relative to complete aggregation, whereas complete aggregation decreases costs by more than 25 percent relative to no aggregation. As product-specific order costs increase, however, tailored aggregation becomes more effective. If Examples 11-3, 11-4, and 11-6 are repeated with s_i = $3,000 (change cells D5:D7 in worksheet *Example 11-3* to 3,000), we find that complete aggregation actually increases costs relative to no aggregation. Tailored aggregation, however, decreases costs by about 10 percent relative to no aggregation. In general, complete aggregation should be used when product-specific order costs are small, and tailored aggregation should be used when product-specific order costs are large.

SUMMARY OF LEARNING OBJECTIVE 3

A key to reducing lot size without increasing costs is reducing the fixed cost associated with each lot. This may be achieved by aggregating lots across multiple products, customers, or suppliers. Complete aggregation, where all products are included in each order, is very effective when product-specific order costs are small. If product-specific order costs are large, tailored aggregation, where only a subset of products is included in each order, is more effective.

11.4 *Understand the impact of quantity discounts on lot size and cycle inventory.*

ECONOMIES OF SCALE TO EXPLOIT QUANTITY DISCOUNTS

We now consider pricing schedules that encourage buyers to purchase in large lots. There are many instances in business-to-business transactions in which the pricing schedule displays economies of scale, with prices decreasing as lot size increases. A discount is *lot-size based* if the pricing schedule offers discounts based on the quantity ordered in a single lot. A discount is *volume based* if the discount is based on the total quantity purchased over a given period, regardless of the number of lots purchased over that period. In this section, we will see that lot-size–based

quantity discounts tend to increase the lot size and cycle inventory in a supply chain. Two commonly used lot-size–based discount schemes are:

- All unit quantity discounts
- Marginal unit quantity discount or multi-block tariffs

To investigate the impact of such quantity discounts on the supply chain, we must answer the following two basic questions:

1. Given a pricing schedule with quantity discounts, what is the optimal purchasing decision for a buyer seeking to maximize profits? How does this decision affect the supply chain in terms of lot sizes, cycle inventories, and flow times?
2. Under what conditions should a supplier offer quantity discounts? What are appropriate pricing schedules that a supplier seeking to maximize profits should offer?

We start by studying the optimal response of a retailer (the buyer) when faced with either of the two lot-size–based discount schemes offered by a manufacturer (the supplier). The retailer's objective is to select lot sizes to minimize the total annual material, order, and holding costs. Next, we evaluate the optimal lot size in the case of all unit quantity discounts.

All Unit Quantity Discounts

In all unit quantity discounts, the pricing schedule contains specified break points $q_0, q_1, \ldots, q_r$, where $q_0 = 0$. If an order placed is at least as large as q_i but smaller than q_{i+1}, each unit is obtained at a cost of C_i. In general, the unit cost decreases as the quantity ordered increases; that is, $C_0 \geq C_1 \geq \cdots \geq C_r$. For all unit discounts, the average unit cost varies with the quantity ordered, as shown in Figure 11-3. The retailer's objective is to decide on lot sizes to maximize profits or, equivalently, to minimize the sum of material, order, and holding costs. The solution procedure evaluates the optimal lot size for each price and picks the lot size that minimizes the overall cost.

Step 1: Evaluate the economic order quantity for each price $C_i, 0 \leq i \leq r$ as follows:

$$Q_i = \sqrt{\frac{2DS}{hC_i}} \qquad \textbf{(11.10)}$$

Step 2: We next select the order quantity Q_i^* for each price C_i. There are three possible cases for Q_i:
 1. $q_i \leq Q_i < q_{i+1}$
 2. $Q_i < q_i$
 3. $Q_i \geq q_{i+1}$

Figure 11-3 Average Unit Cost with All Unit Quantity Discounts

Case 3 can be ignored for Q_i because it is considered for Q_{i+1}. Thus, we need to consider only the first two cases. If $q_i \le Q_i < q_{i+1}$, then set $Q_i^* = Q_i$. If $Q_i < q_i$, then a lot size of Q_i does not result in a discount. In this case, set $Q_i^* = q_i$ to qualify for the discounted price of C_i per unit.

Step 3: For each i, calculate the total annual cost of ordering Q_i^* units (this includes order cost, holding cost, and material cost) as follows:

$$\text{Total annual cost, } TC_i = \left(\frac{D}{Q_i^*}\right)S + \frac{Q_i^*}{2}hC_i + DC_i \qquad (11.11)$$

Step 4: Over all i select order quantity Q_i^* with the lowest total cost TC_i.

Goyal (1995) has shown that this procedure can be shortened further by identifying a cutoff price C^* above which the optimal solution cannot occur. Recall that C_r is the lowest unit cost above the final threshold quantity q_r. The cutoff is obtained as follows:

$$C^* = \frac{1}{D}\left(DC_r + \frac{DS}{q_r} + \frac{h}{2}q_r C_r - \sqrt{2hDSC_r}\right)$$

In Example 11-7, we evaluate the optimal lot size given an all unit quantity discount (see worksheets *Example 11-7* and *Example 11-7 check* in spreadsheet *Chapter11-examples7-8*).

EXAMPLE 11-7 **All Unit Quantity Discounts**

Drugs Online (DO) is an online retailer of prescription drugs and health supplements. Vitamins represent a significant percentage of its sales. Demand for vitamins is 10,000 bottles per month. DO incurs a fixed order placement, transportation, and receiving cost of $100 each time an order for vitamins is placed with the manufacturer. DO incurs an annual holding cost of 20 percent. The manufacturer uses the following all unit discount pricing schedule. Evaluate the number of bottles that the DO manager should order in each lot.

Order Quantity	Unit Price
0–4,999	$3.00
5,000–9,999	$2.96
10,000 or more	$2.92

Analysis:

In this case, the manager has the following inputs:

$q_0 = 0$, $q_1 = 5,000$, $q_2 = 10,000$

$C_0 = \$3.00$, $C_1 = \$2.96$, $C_2 = \$2.92$

$D = 120,000/\text{year}$, $S = \$100/\text{lot}$, $h = 0.2$

Using Step 1 and Equation 11.10 we obtain

$$Q_0 = \sqrt{\frac{2DS}{hC_0}} = 6,325; \ Q_1 = \sqrt{\frac{2DS}{hC_1}} = 6,367; \ Q_2 = \sqrt{\frac{2DS}{hC_2}} = 6,411$$

In Step 2, we ignore $i = 0$ because $Q_0 = 6,325 > q_1 = 5,000$. For $i = 1, 2$, we obtain

$$Q_1^* = Q_1 = 6,367; \ Q_2^* = q_2 = 10,000$$

In Step 3, we obtain the total costs using Equation 11.11 as follows:

$$TC_1 = \left(\frac{D}{Q_1^*}\right)S + \left(\frac{Q_1^*}{2}\right)hC_1 + DC_1 = \$358{,}969; \ TC_2 = \$354{,}520$$

Observe that the lowest total cost is for $i = 2$. Thus, it is optimal for DO to order $Q_2^* = 10{,}000$ bottles per lot and obtain the discount price of \$2.92 per bottle.

If the manufacturer in Example 11-7 offered no discount and sold all bottles for \$3, it would be optimal for DO to order in lots of 6,325 bottles. The quantity discount is an incentive for DO to order in larger lots of 10,000 bottles, raising both the cycle inventory and the flow time. The impact of the discount is further magnified if DO works hard to reduce its fixed ordering cost to $S = \$4$ (from the current \$100). Then, the optimal lot size in the absence of a discount is 1,265 bottles. In the presence of the all unit quantity discount, the optimal lot size is still 10,000 bottles. In this case, the presence of quantity discounts leads to an eightfold increase in average inventory and flow time at DO.

Given that all unit quantity discounts increase the average inventory and flow time in a supply chain, it is important to identify how these discounts add value in a supply chain. Before we consider this question, we discuss marginal unit quantity discounts.

Marginal Unit Quantity Discounts

Marginal (or incremental) unit quantity discounts are also referred to as *multi-block tariffs*. In this case, the pricing schedule contains specified break points $q_0, q_1, \ldots, q_r$. It is not the *average cost* of a unit but the *marginal cost* of a unit that decreases at a breakpoint (in contrast to the all unit discount scheme). If an order of size q is placed, the first $q_1 - q_0$ units are priced at C_0, the next $q_2 - q_1$ are priced at C_1, and, in general, $q_{i+1} - q_i$ units are priced at C_i. The marginal cost per unit varies with the quantity purchased, as shown in Figure 11-4.

Faced with such a pricing schedule, the retailer's objective is to decide on a lot size that maximizes profits or, equivalently, minimizes material, order, and holding costs.

The solution procedure discussed here evaluates the optimal lot size for each marginal price C_i (this forces a lot size between q_i and q_{i+1}) and then settles on the lot size that minimizes the overall cost. A more streamlined procedure has been provided by Hu and Munson (2002).

For each value of i, $0 \leq i \leq r$, let V_i be the cost of ordering q_i units. Define $V_0 = 0$ and V_i for $0 \leq i \leq r$ as follows:

$$V_i = C_0(q_1 - q_0) + C_1(q_2 - q_1) + \cdots + C_{i-1}(q_i - q_{i-1}) \qquad \textbf{(11.12)}$$

Figure 11-4 Marginal Unit Cost with Marginal Unit Quantity Discount

For each value of i, $0 \leq i \leq r - 1$, consider an order of size Q in the range q_i to q_{i+1} units; that is, $q_{i+1} \geq Q \geq q_i$. The material cost of each order of size Q is given by $V_i + (Q - q_i)C_i$. The various costs associated with such an order are as follows:

$$\text{Annual order cost} = \left(\frac{D}{Q}\right)S$$

$$\text{Annual holding cost} = [V_i + (Q - q_i)C_i]h/2$$

$$\text{Annual material cost} = \frac{D}{Q}[V_i + (Q - q_i)C_i]$$

The total annual cost is the sum of the three costs and is given by

$$\text{Total annual cost} = \left(\frac{D}{Q}\right)S + [V_i + (Q - q_i)C_i]h/2 + \frac{D}{Q}[V_i + (Q - q_i)C_i]$$

The optimal lot size for price C_i is obtained by taking the first derivative of the total cost with respect to the lot size Q and setting it equal to 0. This results in the following optimal lot size:

$$\text{Optimal lot size for price } C_i \text{ is } Q_i = \sqrt{\frac{2D(S + V_i - q_iC_i)}{hC_i}} \qquad \textbf{(11.13)}$$

Observe that the optimal lot size is obtained using a formula very much like the EOQ formula (Equation 11.5), except that the presence of the quantity discount has the effect of raising the fixed cost per order by $V_i - q_iC_i$ (from S to $S + V_i - q_iC_i$). The overall optimal lot size is obtained as follows:

Step 1: Evaluate the optimal lot size Q_i using Equation 11.13 for each price C_i.

Step 2: Select the order quantity Q_i^* for each price C_i. There are three possible cases for Q_i:

1. If $q_i \leq Q_i \leq q_{i+1}$ then set $Q_i^* = Q_i$
2. If $Q_i < q_i$ then set $Q_i^* = q_i$
3. If $Q_i > q_{i+1}$ then set $Q_i^* = q_{i+1}$

Step 3: Calculate the total annual cost of ordering Q_i^* units as follows:

$$TC_i = \left(\frac{D}{Q_i^*}\right)S + [V_i + (Q_i^* - q_i)C_i]h/2 + \frac{D}{Q_i^*}[V_i + (Q_i^* - q_i)C_i] \qquad \textbf{(11.14)}$$

Step 4: Over all i, select order size Q_i^* with the lowest cost TC_i.

In Example 11-8, we evaluate the optimal lot size given a marginal unit quantity discount (see worksheets *Example 11-8* and *Example 11-8 check* in spreadsheet *Chapter11-examples7-8*).

| **EXAMPLE 11-8** | **Marginal Unit Quantity Discounts** |

Let us return to DO from Example 11-7. Assume that the manufacturer uses the following marginal unit discount pricing schedule:

Order Quantity	Marginal Unit Price
0–5,000	$3.00
5,001–10,000	$2.96
Over 10,000	$2.92

This implies that if an order is placed for 7,000 bottles, the first 5,000 are at a unit cost of $3.00, with the remaining 2,000 at a unit cost of $2.96. Evaluate the number of bottles that DO should order in each lot.

Analysis:

In this case, we have

$$q_0 = 0, q_1 = 5{,}000, q_2 = 10{,}000$$
$$C_0 = \$3.00, C_1 = \$2.96, C_2 = \$2.92$$
$$D = 120{,}000/\text{year}, S = \$100/\text{lot}, h = 0.2$$

Using Equation 11.12, we obtain

$$V_0 = 0; V_1 = 3 \times (5{,}000 - 0) = \$15{,}000$$
$$V_2 = 3 \times (5{,}000 - 0) + 2.96 \times (10{,}000 - 5{,}000) = \$29{,}800$$

Using Step 1 and Equation 11.13, we obtain

$$Q_0 = \sqrt{\frac{2D(S + V_0 - q_0C_0)}{hC_0}} = 6{,}325$$

$$Q_1 = \sqrt{\frac{2D(S + V_1 - q_1C_1)}{hC_1}} = 11{,}028$$

$$Q_2 = \sqrt{\frac{2D(S + V_2 - q_2C_2)}{hC_2}} = 16{,}961$$

In Step 2, we set $Q_0^* = q_1 = 5{,}000$ because $Q_0 = 6{,}325 > q_1 = 5{,}000$. Similarly, we obtain $Q_1^* = q_2 = 10{,}000$ (because $Q_1 = 11{,}028 > q_2 = 10{,}000$) and $Q_2^* = Q_2 = 16{,}961$.

In Step 3, we obtain the total cost for $i = 0, 1, 2$ using Equation 11.14 to be

$$TC_0 = \left(\frac{D}{Q_0^*}\right)S + [V_0 + (Q_0^* - q_0)C_0]h/2 + \left(\frac{D}{Q_0^*}\right)[V_0 + (Q_0^* - q_0)C_0] = \$363{,}900$$

$$TC_1 = \left(\frac{D}{Q_1^*}\right)S + [V_1 + (Q_1^* - q_1)C_1]h/2 + \left(\frac{D}{Q_1^*}\right)[V_1 + (Q_1^* - q_1)C_1] = \$361{,}780$$

$$TC_2 = \left(\frac{D}{Q_2^*}\right)S + [V_2 + (Q_2^* - q_2)C_2]h/2 + \left(\frac{D}{Q_2^*}\right)[V_2 + (Q_2^* - q_2)C_2] = \$360{,}365$$

Observe that the lowest cost is for $i = 2$. Thus, it is optimal for DO to order in lots of $Q_2^* = 16{,}961$ bottles. This is much larger than the optimal lot size of 6,325 when the manufacturer does not offer any discount.

If the fixed cost of ordering is $4, the optimal lot size for DO is 15,755 with the discount compared to a lot size of 1,265 without the discount. This discussion demonstrates that there can be large order sizes—and, thus, high cycle inventory—in the absence of any formal fixed ordering costs as long as quantity discounts are offered. Thus, quantity discounts lead to a significant buildup of cycle inventory in a supply chain. In many supply chains, quantity discounts contribute more to cycle inventory than fixed ordering costs. This forces us once again to question the value of quantity discounts in a supply chain.

SUMMARY OF LEARNING OBJECTIVE 4

Lot-size–based quantity discounts increase the lot size and cycle inventory within the supply chain because they encourage buyers to purchase in larger quantities to take advantage of the decrease in price. The relative increase in cycle inventory because of quantity discounts increases as the buyer reduces fixed costs per order.

11.5 *Devise appropriate discounting schemes for a supply chain.*

WHY DO SUPPLIERS OFFER QUANTITY DISCOUNTS?

We have seen that the presence of lot-size–based quantity discounts tends to increase the level of cycle inventory in the supply chain, especially as the buyer reduces their fixed cost. This raises the question of why suppliers offer lot-size–based quantity discounts in a supply chain. We argue that there are circumstances under which a lot-size–based quantity discount increases supply chain and supplier profits. In such a setting it may be rational for a supplier to offer a quantity discount. Quantity discounts can increase the supply chain profit for the following two main reasons:

1. Improved coordination to increase total supply chain profits
2. Extraction of surplus by supplier through price discrimination

Munson and Rosenblatt (1998) also provide other factors, such as marketing, that motivate sellers to offer quantity discounts. We now discuss each of the two situations in greater detail.

Quantity Discounts to Increase Total Supply Chain Profits

A supply chain is *coordinated* if the decisions the retailer and supplier make maximize total supply chain profits. In reality, each stage in a supply chain may have a separate owner and thus attempt to maximize its own profits. For example, each stage of a supply chain is likely to make lot-sizing decisions with an objective of minimizing its own costs without worrying about total supply chain costs. The result of this independent decision making can be a lack of coordination in a supply chain because actions that maximize retailer profits may not maximize supply chain profits. In this section, we discuss how a manufacturer may use appropriate quantity discounts to ensure that total supply chain profits are maximized even if the retailer is acting to maximize its own profits.

QUANTITY DISCOUNTS FOR COMMODITY PRODUCTS Economists have argued that for commodity products such as milk, a competitive market exists and prices are driven down to the products' marginal cost. In this case, the market sets the price and the firm's objective is to lower costs in order to increase profits. Consider, for example, the online retailer DO, discussed earlier. It can be argued that its vitamins are a commodity product. In this supply chain, both the manufacturer and DO incur costs related to each order placed by DO. Assume that the manufacturer has a fixed cost S_M, a unit cost C_M, and a holding cost h_M. The manufacturer incurs fixed costs related to order setup and fulfillment (S_M) and holding costs ($h_M C_M$) as it builds up inventory to replenish the order (we assume that inventory is built up at the same rate as demand). Assume that the retailer has a fixed cost S_R, a unit cost C_R, and a holding cost h_R. Thus, DO incurs fixed costs (S_R) for each order it places and holding costs ($h_R C_R$) for the inventory it holds as it slowly sells an order. Even though both parties incur costs associated with the lot-sizing decision made by DO, the retailer makes its lot-sizing decisions based solely on minimizing its local costs. This results in lot-sizing decisions that are locally optimal but do not maximize the supply chain surplus. We illustrate this idea in Example 11-9 (see spreadsheet *Chapter11-quantity discounts* worksheet *Example 11-9*).

EXAMPLE 11-9	The Impact of Locally Optimal Lot Sizes on a Supply Chain

Demand for vitamins is 10,000 bottles per month. DO incurs a fixed order placement, transportation, and receiving cost of $100 each time it places an order for vitamins with the manufacturer. DO incurs an annual holding cost of 20 percent. The manufacturer charges $3 for each bottle of vitamins purchased. Evaluate the optimal lot size for DO.

Each time DO places an order, the manufacturer must process, pack, and ship the order. The manufacturer has a line packing bottles at a steady rate that matches demand. The manufacturer incurs a fixed-order filling cost of $250, production cost of $2 per bottle, and an annual holding cost of 20 percent. What is the annual fulfillment and holding cost incurred by the manufacturer as a result of DO's ordering policy?

Analysis:

In this case, we have

$$D = 120,000/\text{year}, S_R = \$100/\text{lot}, h_R = 0.2, C_R = \$3$$
$$S_M = \$250/\text{lot}, h_M = 0.2, C_M = \$2$$

Using the EOQ formula (Equation 11.5), we obtain the optimal lot size and annual cost for DO to be:

$$Q_R = \sqrt{\frac{2DS_R}{h_R C_R}} = \sqrt{\frac{2 \times 120,000 \times 100}{0.2 \times 3}} = 6,325$$

$$\text{Annual cost for DO} = \left(\frac{D}{Q_R}\right)S_R + \left(\frac{Q_R}{2}\right)h_R C_R = \$3,795$$

If DO orders in lots sizes of $Q_R = 6,325$, the annual cost incurred by the manufacturer is obtained to be:

$$\text{Annual cost for manufacturer} = \left(\frac{D}{Q_R}\right)S_M + \left(\frac{Q_R}{2}\right)h_M C_M = \$6,008$$

The annual supply chain cost (manufacturer + DO) is thus $6,008 + $3,795 = $9,803.

In Example 11-9, DO picks the lot size of 6,325 with an objective of minimizing only its own costs. From a supply chain perspective, the optimal lot size should account for the fact that both DO and the manufacturer incur costs associated with each replenishment lot. If we assume that the manufacturer produces at a rate that matches demand (as assumed in Example 11-9), the total supply chain cost of using a lot size Q is obtained as follows:

$$\text{Annual cost for DO and manufacturer} = \left(\frac{D}{Q}\right)S_R + \left(\frac{Q}{2}\right)h_R C_R + \left(\frac{D}{Q}\right)S_M + \left(\frac{Q}{2}\right)h_M C_M$$

The optimal lot size (Q^*) for the supply chain is obtained by taking the first derivative of the total cost with respect to Q and setting it equal to 0 as follows (see worksheet *Example 11-9*):

$$Q^* = \sqrt{\frac{2D(S_R + S_M)}{h_R C_R + h_M C_M}} = 9,165$$

If DO orders in lots of $Q^* = 9,165$ units, the total costs for DO and the manufacturer are as follows:

$$\text{Annual cost for DO} = \left(\frac{D}{Q^*}\right)S_R + \left(\frac{Q^*}{2}\right)h_R C_R = \$4,059$$

$$\text{Annual cost for manufacturer} = \left(\frac{D}{Q^*}\right)S_M + \left(\frac{Q^*}{2}\right)h_M C_M = \$5,106$$

Observe that if DO orders a lot size of 9,165 units, the supply chain cost decreases to $9,165 (from $9,803 when DO ordered its own optimal lot size of 6,325). There is thus an opportunity for the supply chain to save $638 by increasing the lot size ordered by DO from 6,325 to 9,165. The challenge, however, is that ordering in lots of 9,165 bottles raises the cost for DO by

$264 per year from $3,795 to $4,059 (even though it reduces overall supply chain costs). The manufacturer's costs, in contrast, go down by $902 from $6,008 to $5,106 per year. Thus, the manufacturer must offer DO a suitable incentive (of at least $264/year) for DO to raise its lot size. A lot-size–based quantity discount is an appropriate incentive in this case. Example 11-10 (see worksheet *Example 11-10*) provides details of how the manufacturer can design a suitable quantity discount that gets DO to order in lots of 9,165 units even though DO is optimizing its own profits (and not total supply chain profits).

EXAMPLE 11-10 Designing a Suitable Lot-Size–Based Quantity Discount

Consider the data from Example 11-9. Design a suitable quantity discount that gets DO to order in lots of 9,165 units when it aims to minimize only its own total costs.

Analysis:

Recall that ordering in lots of 9,165 units instead of 6,325 increases annual ordering and holding costs for DO by $264. Thus, the manufacturer needs to offer an incentive of at least $264 per year to DO in terms of decreased material cost if DO orders in lots of 9,165 units. Decreasing material cost by $264/year from sales of 120,000 units implies that material cost must be decreased from $3/unit to $3 − 264/120,000 = $2.9978/unit if DO orders in lots of 9,165.

Thus, the appropriate quantity discount is for the manufacturer to charge $3 if DO orders in lots that are smaller than 9,165 units and discount the price to $2.9978 for orders of 9,165 or more.

Observe that offering a lot-size–based discount in this case decreases total supply chain cost and supplier costs. It does, however, increase the lot size the retailer purchases and thus increases cycle inventory in the supply chain.

Our discussion on coordination for commodity products highlights the important link between the lot-size–based quantity discount offered and the order costs incurred by the manufacturer. As the manufacturer works on lowering order or setup cost, the discount it offers to retailers should change. For a low enough setup or order cost, the manufacturer gains little from using a lot-size–based quantity discount. In Example 11-9, discussed earlier, if the manufacturer lowers its fixed cost per order from $250 to $100, the total supply chain costs are close to the minimum without quantity discounts even if DO is trying to minimize its cost. Thus, if its fixed order costs are lowered to $100, it makes sense for the manufacturer to eliminate all lot-size based quantity discounts. In most companies, however, marketing and sales design quantity discounts, whereas operations works on reducing setup or order cost. As a result, changes in pricing do not always occur in response to setup cost reduction in manufacturing. It is important that the two functions coordinate these activities.

Quantity Discounts for Products for Which the Firm has Market Power

Now, consider the scenario in which the manufacturer has invented a new vitamin pill, Vitaherb, which is derived from herbal ingredients and has other properties highly valued in the market. Few competitors have a similar product, so it can be argued that the price at which the retailer DO sells Vitaherb influences demand. Assume that the annual demand faced by DO is given by the demand curve $360,000 − 60,000 p$, where p is the price at which DO sells Vitaherb. The manufacturer incurs a production cost of $C_M = \$2$ per bottle of Vitaherb. The manufacturer must decide on the price C_R to charge DO, and DO in turn must decide on the price p to charge the customer. The profit at DO ($Prof_R$) and the manufacturer ($Prof_M$) as a result of this policy is given by

$$Prof_R = (p - C_R)(360,000 - 60,000\,p); \quad Prof_M = (C_R - C_M)(360,000 - 60,000\,p);$$

DO picks the price p to maximize $Prof_R$. Taking the first derivative with respect to p and setting it to 0, we obtain the following relationship between p and C_R

$$p = 3 + \frac{C_R}{2} \qquad (11.15)$$

Given that the manufacturer is aware that DO is aiming to optimize its own profits, the manufacturer is able to use the relationship between p and C_R to obtains its own profits to be

$$Prof_M = (C_R - C_M)\left(360{,}000 - 60{,}000\left(3 + \frac{C_R}{2}\right)\right) = (C_R - C_M)(180{,}000 - 30{,}000\ C_R)$$

The manufacturer picks its price C_R to maximize $Prof_M$. Taking the first derivative of $Prof_M$ with respect C_R to and setting it to 0 we obtain $C_R = \$4$. Substituting back into Equation 11.15, we obtain $p = \$5$. Thus, when DO and the manufacturer make their pricing decisions independently, it is optimal for the manufacturer to charge a wholesale price of $C_R = \$4$ and for DO to charge a retail price of $p = \$5$. The total market demand in this case is $360{,}000 - 60{,}000p = 60{,}000$ bottles. DO makes a profit of $Prof_R = (5 - 4)(360{,}000 - [60{,}000 \times 5]) = \$60{,}000$ and the manufacturer makes a profit of $Prof_M = (4 - 2)(360{,}000 - [60{,}000 \times 5]) = \$120{,}000$ (see worksheet 2-*stage*).

Now, consider the case in which the two stages coordinate their pricing decisions with a goal of maximizing the supply chain profit $Prof_{SC}$, which is given by

$$Prof_{SC} = (p - C_M)(360{,}000 - 60{,}000\ p)$$

The optimal retail price is obtained by setting the first derivative of $Prof_{SC}$ with respect to p to 0. We thus obtain the coordinated retail price to be

$$p = 3 + \frac{C_M}{2} = 3 + \frac{2}{2} = \$4$$

If the two stages coordinate pricing and DO prices at $p = \$4$, market demand is $360{,}000 - 60{,}000p = 120{,}000$ bottles. The total supply chain profit if the two stages coordinate is $Prof_{SC} = (\$4 - \$2) \times 120{,}000 = \$240{,}000$. As a result of each stage settings its price independently, the supply chain thus loses $\$240{,}000 - \$180{,}000 = \$60{,}000$ in profit. This phenomenon is referred to as *double marginalization*. Double marginalization leads to a loss in profit because the supply chain margin is divided between two stages, but each stage makes its pricing decision considering only its own local profits.

Given that independent pricing decisions lower supply chain profits, it is important to consider pricing schemes that may help recover some of these profits even when each stage of the supply chain continues to act independently. We propose two pricing schemes that the manufacturer may use to achieve the coordinated solution and maximize supply chain profits even though DO acts in a way that maximizes its own profit.

TWO-PART TARIFF In this case, the manufacturer charges its entire profit as an up-front franchise fee ff (which could be anywhere between the non-coordinated manufacturer profit $Prof_M$ and the difference between the coordinated supply chain profit and the non-coordinated retailer profit, $Prof_{SC} - Prof_R$) and then sells to the retailer at cost; that is, the manufacturer sets its wholesale price $C_R = C_M$. This pricing scheme is referred to as a *two-part tariff* because the manufacturer sets both the franchise fee and the wholesale price. The retail pricing decision is thus based on maximizing its profits $(p - C_M)(360{,}000 - 60{,}000p) - ff$. Under the two-part tariff, the franchise fee ff is paid up front and is thus a fixed cost that does not change with the retail price p. The retailer DO is thus effectively maximizing the coordinated supply chain profits $Prof_{SC} = (p - C_M)(360{,}000 - 60{,}000p)$. Taking the first derivative with respect to p and setting it equal to 0, the optimal coordinated retail price p is evaluated to be

$$p = 3 + \frac{C_M}{2}$$

In the case of DO, recall that total supply chain profit when the two stages coordinate is $Prof_{SC}$ = \$240,000 with DO charging the customer \$4 per bottle of Vitaherb. The profit made by DO when the two stages do not coordinate is $Prof_R$ = \$60,000. One option available to the manufacturer is to construct a two-part tariff by which DO is charged an upfront fee of ff = $Prof_{SC}$ − $Prof_R$ = \$180,000 (see worksheet *2-part-tariff*) and material cost of C_R = C_M = \$2 per bottle. DO maximizes its profit if it prices the vitamins at p = 3 + $C_M/2$ = 3 + 2/2 = \$4 per bottle. It has annual sales of 360,000 − 60,000p = 120,000 and profits of \$60,000. The manufacturer makes a profit of \$180,000, which it charges up front. Observe that the use of a two-part tariff has increased supply chain profits from \$180,000 to \$240,000 even though the retailer DO has made a locally optimal pricing decision given the two-part tariff. A similar result can be obtained as long as the manufacturer sets the up-front fee ff to be any value between \$120,000 and \$180,000 with a wholesale price of C_R = C_M = \$2.

VOLUME BASED QUANTITY DISCOUNT Observe that the two-part tariff is really a volume-based quantity discount whereby the retailer DO pays a lower average unit cost as it purchases larger quantities each year (the franchise fee ff is amortized over more units). This observation can be made explicit by designing a volume-based discount scheme that gets the retailer DO to purchase and sell the quantity sold when the two stages coordinate their actions.

Recall that the coordinated solution results in a retail price of p = 3 + $C_M/2$ = 3 + 2/2 = 4. This retail price results in total demand of d^{coord} = 360,000 − (60,000 × 4) = 120,000. The objective of the manufacturer is to design a volume-based discounting scheme that gets the retailer DO to buy (and sell) d^{coord} = 120,000 units each year. The pricing scheme must be such that the retailer gets a profit of at least \$60,000, and the manufacturer gets a profit of at least \$120,000 (these are the profits that DO and the manufacturer made when their actions were not coordinated).

Several such pricing schemes can be designed. One such scheme is for the manufacturer to charge a wholesale price of C_R = \$4 per bottle (this is the same wholesale price that is optimal when the two stages are not coordinated) for annual sales below d^{coord} = 120,000 units, and to charge C_R = \$3.50 (any value between \$3.00 and \$3.50 will work) if sales reach 120,000 or more (see worksheet *Volume Discount*). It is then optimal for DO to order 120,000 units in the year and price them at p = \$4 per bottle to the customers (to ensure that they are all sold). The total profit earned by DO is (360,000 − 60,000p) × (p − C_R) = \$60,000. The total profit earned by the manufacturer is 120,000 × (C_R − \$2) = 180,000 when C_R = \$3.50. The total supply chain profit is \$240,000, which is higher than the \$180,000 that the supply chain earned when actions were not coordinated.

If the manufacturer charges \$3.00 (instead of \$3.50) for sales of 120,000 units or more, it is still optimal for DO to order 120,000 units in the year and price them at p = \$4 per bottle. The only difference is that the total profit earned by DO now increases to \$120,000, whereas that for the manufacturer now drops to \$120,000. The total supply chain profits remain at \$240,000. The price that the manufacturer is able to charge (between \$3.00 and \$3.50) for sales of 120,000 or more will depend on the relative bargaining power of the two parties.

At this stage, we have seen that even in the absence of inventory-related costs, quantity discounts play a role in supply chain coordination and improved supply chain profits. Unless the manufacturer has large fixed costs associated with each lot, the discount schemes that are optimal are volume based and not lot-size based. It can be shown that even in the presence of large fixed costs for the manufacturer, a two-part tariff or volume-based discount, with the manufacturer passing on some of the fixed cost to the retailer, optimally coordinates the supply chain and maximizes profits given the assumption that customer demand decreases when the retailer increases price.

A key distinction between lot-size–based and volume discounts is that lot-size discounts are based on the quantity purchased per lot, not the rate of purchase. Volume discounts, in contrast, are based on the rate of purchase or volume purchased on average per specified time period (say,

a month, quarter, or year). Lot-size–based discounts tend to raise the cycle inventory in the supply chain by encouraging retailers to increase the size of each lot. Volume-based discounts, in contrast, are compatible with small lots that reduce cycle inventory. Lot-size–based discounts make sense only when the manufacturer incurs high fixed cost per order. In all other instances, it is better to have volume-based discounts.

One can make the point that even with volume-based discounts, retailers will tend to increase the size of the lot toward the end of the evaluation period. For example, assume that the manufacturer offers DO a 2 percent discount if the number of bottles of Vitaherb purchased over a quarter exceeds 40,000. This policy will not affect the lot sizes DO orders early during the quarter, and DO will order in small lots to match the quantity ordered with demand. Consider a situation, however, in which DO has sold only 30,000 bottles with a week left before the end of the quarter. To get the quantity discount, DO may order 10,000 bottles over the last week even though it expects to sell only 3,000. In this case, cycle inventory in the supply chain goes up in spite of the fact that there is no lot-size–based quantity discount. The situation in which orders peak toward the end of a financial horizon is referred to as the *hockey stick phenomenon* because demand increases dramatically toward the end of a period, similar to the way a hockey stick bends upward toward its end. This phenomenon has been observed in many industries. One possible solution is to base the volume discounts on a rolling horizon. For example, each week the manufacturer may offer DO the volume discount based on sales over the past 12 weeks. Such a rolling horizon dampens the hockey stick phenomenon by making each week the last week in some 12-week horizon.

Thus far, we have discussed only the scenario in which the supply chain has a single retailer. One may ask whether our insights are robust and also apply if the supply chain has multiple retailers, each with different demand curves, all supplied by a single manufacturer. As one would expect, the form of the discount scheme to be offered becomes more complicated in these settings (typically, instead of having only one breakpoint at which the volume-based discount is offered, there are multiple breakpoints). The basic form of the optimal pricing scheme, however, does not change. The optimal discount continues to be volume based, with the average price charged to the retailers decreasing as the rate of purchase (volume purchased per unit time) increases.

Price Discrimination to Maximize Supplier Profits

Price discrimination is the practice in which a firm charges its customers different prices to maximize profits. An example of price discrimination is airlines: Passengers traveling on the same plane often pay different prices for their seats.

As discussed in Chapter 16, setting a fixed price for all units does not maximize profits for the manufacturer. In principle, the manufacturer can obtain the entire area under the demand curve above its marginal cost by pricing each unit differently based on customers' marginal willingness to pay at each quantity. Quantity discounts are one mechanism for price discrimination because customers pay different prices based on the quantity purchased.

SUMMARY OF LEARNING OBJECTIVE 5

Quantity discounts are justified to increase total supply chain profits when independent lot-sizing decisions in a supply chain lead to suboptimal solutions from an overall supply chain perspective. If suppliers have large fixed costs, suitable lot-size–based quantity discounts can be justified because they help increase supply chain profits. For products for which the firm has market power, two-part tariffs or volume-based quantity discounts can be used to achieve coordination in the supply chain and maximize supply chain profits. Volume-based discounts are more effective than lot-size–based discounts in increasing supply chain profits without increasing lot size and cycle inventory.

SHORT-TERM DISCOUNTING: TRADE PROMOTIONS

11.6 Understand the impact of trade promotions on lot size and cycle inventory.

Manufacturers use *trade promotions* to offer a discounted price to retailers and set a time period over which the discount is effective. For example, a manufacturer of canned soup may offer a price discount of 10 percent for the shipping period December 15 to January 25. For all purchases within the specified time horizon, retailers get a 10 percent discount. In some cases, the manufacturer may require specific actions from the retailer, such as displays, advertising, promotion, and so on, to qualify for the trade promotion. Trade promotions are quite common in the consumer packaged-goods industry, with manufacturers promoting different products at different times of the year.

The goal of trade promotions is to influence retailers to act in a way that helps the manufacturer achieve its objectives. The following are a few of the key goals (from the manufacturer's perspective) of a trade promotion (see Blattberg and Neslin [1990] for more details):

1. Induce retailers to use price discounts, displays, or advertising to spur sales.
2. Shift inventory from the manufacturer to the retailer and the customer.
3. Defend a brand against competition.

Although these may be the manufacturer's objectives, it is not clear that they are always achieved as the result of a trade promotion. Our goal in this section is to investigate the impact of a trade promotion on the behavior of the retailer and the performance of the entire supply chain. The key to understanding this impact is to focus on how a retailer reacts to a trade promotion offered by a manufacturer. In response to a trade promotion, the retailer has the following options:

1. Pass through some or all of the promotion to customers to spur sales.
2. Pass through very little of the promotion to customers but purchase in greater quantity during the promotion period to exploit the temporary reduction in price.

The first action lowers the price of the product for the end customer, leading to increased purchases and, thus, increased sales for the entire supply chain. The second action does not increase purchases by the customer, but increases the amount purchased and held at the retailer. As a result, the cycle inventory and flow time within the supply chain increase.

A *forward buy* occurs when a retailer purchases in the promotional period for sales in future periods. A forward buy helps reduce the retailer's future cost of goods for product sold after the promotion ends. Although a forward buy is often the retailer's appropriate response to a price promotion, it can decrease supply chain profits because it results in higher demand variability, with a resulting increase in inventory and flow times within the supply chain.

In order to understand a retailer's optimal response when faced with a trade promotion, we identify the factors affecting the forward buy and quantify the size of a forward buy by the retailer. We also identify factors that influence the amount of the promotion that a retailer passes on to the customer.

We first illustrate the impact of a trade promotion on forward buying behavior of the retailer. Consider a Cub Foods supermarket selling chicken noodle soup manufactured by the Campbell Soup Company. Customer demand for chicken noodle soup is D cans per year. Campbell normally charges the retailer $\$C$ per can. Cub Foods incurs a holding cost of h (per dollar of inventory held for a year). Using the EOQ formula (Equation 11.5), Cub Foods normally orders in the following lot sizes:

$$Q^* = \sqrt{\frac{2DS}{hC}}$$

Campbell announces that it is offering a discount of $\$d$ per can for the coming four-week period. Cub Foods must decide how much to order at the discounted price compared with the lot size of Q^* that it normally orders. Let Q^d be the lot size ordered at the discounted price.

The costs the retailer must consider when making this decision are material cost, holding cost, and order cost. Increasing the lot size Q^d lowers the material cost for Cub Foods because it

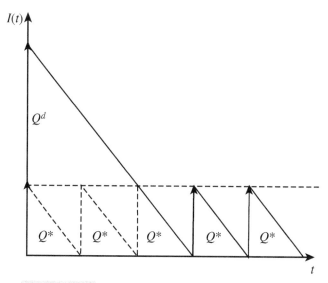

Figure 11-5 Inventory Profile for Forward Buying

purchases more cans (for sale now and in the future) at the discounted price. Increasing the lot size Q^d increases the holding cost because inventories increase. Increasing the lot size Q^d lowers the order cost for Cub Foods because some orders that would otherwise have been placed are now not necessary. Cub Foods' goal is to make the trade-off that minimizes its total cost.

The inventory pattern when a lot size of Q^d is followed by lot sizes of Q^* is shown in Figure 11-5. The objective is to identify Q^d that minimizes the total cost (material cost + ordering cost + holding cost) over the time interval during which the quantity Q^d (ordered during the promotion period) is consumed.

The precise analysis in this case is complex, so we present a result that holds under some restrictions (see Silver, Pyke, and Petersen [1998] for a more detailed discussion). The first key assumption is that the discount is offered once, with no future discounts. The second key assumption is that the retailer takes no action (such as passing on part of the trade promotion) to influence customer demand. The customer demand thus remains unchanged. The third key assumption is that we analyze a period over which the demand is an integer multiple of Q^*. With these assumptions, the optimal order quantity at the discounted price is given by

$$Q^d = \frac{dD}{(C - d)h} + \frac{CQ^*}{C - d} \qquad \textbf{(11.16)}$$

In practice, retailers are often aware of the timing of the next promotion. If the forecast demand until the next anticipated trade promotion is Q_1, it is optimal for the retailer to order $min\{Q^d, Q_1\}$. Observe that the quantity Q^d ordered as a result of the promotion is larger than the regular order quantity Q^*. The forward buy in this case is given by

Forward buy $= Q^d - Q^*$

Even for relatively small discounts, the order size increases by a large quantity, as illustrated in Example 11-11 (see spreadsheet *Chapter11-examples11-12*).

EXAMPLE 11-11 **Impact of Trade Promotions on Lot Sizes**

DO is a retailer that sells Vitaherb, a popular vitamin diet supplement. Demand for Vitaherb is 120,000 bottles per year. The manufacturer currently charges $3 for each bottle, and DO incurs an annual holding cost of 20 percent. DO currently orders in lots of $Q^* = 6,325$ bottles. The

manufacturer has offered a discount of $0.15 for all bottles purchased by retailers over the coming month. How many bottles of Vitaherb should DO order at the promotion price?

Analysis:

In the absence of any promotion, DO orders in lot sizes of $Q^* = 6,325$ bottles. Given a monthly demand of $D = 10,000$ bottles, DO normally orders every 0.6325 months. In the absence of the trade promotion we have the following:

$$\text{Cycle inventory at DO} = Q^*/2 = 6,325/2 = 3,162.50 \text{ bottles}$$

$$\text{Average flow time} = Q^*/2D = 6,325/(2D) = 0.3162 \text{ months}$$

The optimal lot size during the promotion is obtained using Equation 11.15 and is given by

$$Q^d = \frac{dD}{(C - d)h} + \frac{CQ^*}{C - d} = \frac{0.15 \times 120,000}{(3.00 - 0.15) \times 0.20} + \frac{3 \times 6,325}{3.00 - 0.15} = 38,236$$

During the promotion, DO should place an order for a lot size of 38,236 (instead of the normal order of 6,325) to take advantage of the price discount. In the presence of the trade promotion we have

$$\text{Cycle inventory at DO} = Q^d/2 = 38,236/2 = 19,118 \text{ bottles}$$

$$\text{Average flow time} = Q^d/(2D) = 38,236/(20,000) = 1.9118 \text{ months}$$

In this case, the forward buy is given by

$$\text{Forward buy} = Q^d - Q^* = 38,236 - 6,325 = 31,911 \text{ bottles}$$

As a result of this forward buy, DO will not place any order for the next 3.8236 months (without a forward buy, DO would have placed another $31,912/6,325 = 5.05$ orders for 6,325 bottles each during this period). Observe that a 5 percent discount causes the lot size to increase by more than 500 percent.

As the example illustrates, forward buying as a result of trade promotions leads to a significant increase in the quantity ordered by the retailer. The large order is then followed by a period of small orders to compensate for the inventory built up at the retailer. The fluctuation in orders as a result of trade promotions is one of the major contributors to the bullwhip effect discussed in Chapter 10. The retailer can justify the forward buying during a trade promotion because it decreases its total cost. In contrast, the manufacturer can justify this action only as a competitive necessity (to counter a competitor's promotion) or if it has either inadvertently built up a lot of excess inventory or the forward buy allows the manufacturer to smooth demand by shifting it from peak- to low-demand periods. In practice, manufacturers often build up inventory in anticipation of planned promotions. During the trade promotion, this inventory shifts to the retailer, primarily as a forward buy. If the forward buy during trade promotions is a significant fraction of total sales, manufacturers end up reducing the revenues they earn from sales because most of the product is sold at a discount. The increase in inventory and the decrease in revenues often lead to a reduction in manufacturer as well as total supply chain profits as a result of trade promotions (see Blattberg and Neslin [1990] for more details).

Now, let us consider the extent to which the retailer may find it optimal to pass through some of the discount to the end customer to spur sales. As Example 11-12 shows, it is not optimal for the retailer to pass through the entire discount to the customer. In other words, it is optimal for the retailer to capture part of the promotion and pass through only part of it to the customer.

EXAMPLE 11-12　How Much of a Discount Should the Retailer Pass Through?

Assume that DO faces a demand curve for Vitaherb of $300,000 - 60,000\,p$. The normal price charged by the manufacturer to the retailer is $C_R = \$3$ per bottle. Ignoring all inventory-related costs, evaluate the optimal response of DO to a manufacturer discount of $0.15 per unit.

Analysis:

The profits for DO, the retailer, are given as follows:

$$Prof_R = (300,000 - 60,000\,p)p - (300,000 - 60,000\,p)C_R$$

The retailer prices to maximize profits, and the optimal retail price is obtained by setting the first derivative of retailer profits with respect to p to 0. This implies that

$$300,000 - 120,000\,p + 60,000\,C_R = 0$$

or

$$p = (300,000 + 60,000\,C_R)/120,000 \qquad (11.17)$$

Substituting $C_R = \$3$ into Equation 11.17, we obtain a retail price of $p = \$4$. As a result, the customer demand at the retailer in the absence of the promotion is

$$D_R = 300,000 - 60,000\,p = 60,000$$

During the promotion, the manufacturer offers a discount of $0.15, resulting in a price to the retailer of $C_R = \$2.85$. Substituting into Equation 11.17, the optimal price set by DO is

$$p = (300,000 + 60,000 \times 2.85)/120,000 = \$3.925$$

Observe that the retailer's optimal response is to pass through only $0.075 of the $0.15 discount to the customer. The retailer does not pass through the entire discount. At the discounted price, DO experiences a demand of

$$D_R = 300,000 - 60,000\,p = 64,500$$

This represents an increase of 7.5 percent in demand relative to the base case. It is optimal here for DO to pass on half the trade promotion discount to the customers. This action results in a 7.5 percent increase in customer demand.

From Examples 11-11 and 11-12, observe that the increase in customer demand resulting from a trade promotion (7.5 percent of demand in Example 11-12) is small relative to the increased purchase by the retailer due to forward buying (500 percent from Example 11-11). The impact of the increase in customer demand may be further dampened by customer behavior. For many products, such as detergent and toothpaste, most of the increase in customer purchases is a forward buy by the customer; customers are unlikely to start brushing their teeth more frequently simply because they have purchased a lot of toothpaste. For such products, a trade promotion does not truly increase demand.

Manufacturers have always struggled with the fact that retailers pass along only a small fraction of a trade discount to the customer. In a study conducted by Kurt Salmon and Associates (1993), almost a quarter of all distributor inventories in the dry-grocery supply chain could be attributed to forward buying.

Our previous discussion supports the claim that trade promotions generally increase cycle inventory in a supply chain and hurt performance. This realization has led many firms, including the world's largest retailer, Walmart, and several manufacturers, such as P&G, to adopt "every-day low pricing" (EDLP). Here, the price is fixed over time and no short-term discounts are offered. This eliminates any incentive for forward buying. As a result, all stages of the supply chain purchase in quantities that match demand.

In general, the discount passed through by the retailer to the consumer is influenced by the retailer deal elasticity, which is the increase in retail sales per unit discount in price. The higher the deal elasticity, the more of the discount the retailer is likely to pass through to the consumer. Thus, trade promotions by the manufacturer may make sense for products with a high deal elasticity that ensures high pass-through by the retailer, and high holding costs that ensure low forward buying. Blattberg and Neslin (1990) identify paper goods as products with high deal elasticity and holding cost. They also identify trade promotions as being more effective with strong brands relative to weak brands.

Trade promotions may also make sense as a competitive response. In a category such as cola, some customers are loyal to their brand, whereas others switch depending on the brand being offered at the lowest price. Consider a situation in which one of the competitors—say, Pepsi—offers retailers a trade promotion. Retailers increase their purchases of Pepsi and pass through some of the discount to the customer. Price-sensitive customers increase their purchase of Pepsi. If a competitor such as Coca-Cola does not respond, it loses some market share in the form of price-sensitive customers. A case can be made that a trade promotion by Coca-Cola is justified in such a setting as a competitive response. Observe that with both competitors offering trade promotions, there is no real increase in demand for either unless customer consumption grows. Inventory in the supply chain, however, does increase for both brands. This is, then, a situation in which trade promotions are a competitive necessity, but they increase supply chain inventory, leading to reduced profits for all competitors.

Trade promotions should be designed so retailers limit their forward buying and pass along more of the discount to end customers. The manufacturer's objective is to increase market share and sales without allowing the retailer to forward buy significant amounts. This outcome can be achieved by offering discounts to the retailer that are based on actual sales to customers rather than the amount purchased by the retailer. The discount price thus applies to items sold to customers (sell-through) during the promotion, not the quantity purchased by the retailer (sell-in). This eliminates all incentive for forward buying.

Given the information technology in place, many manufacturers today offer scanner-based promotions by which the retailer receives credit for the promotion discount for every unit sold. Another option is to limit the allocation during a promotion to a retailer based on past sales. This is also an effort to limit the amount that the retailer can forward buy. It is unlikely, however, that retailers will accept such schemes for weak brands.

SUMMARY OF LEARNING OBJECTIVE 6

Faced with a short-term discount, it is optimal for retailers to pass through only a fraction of the discount to the customer, keeping the rest for themselves. Simultaneously, it is optimal for retailers to increase the purchase lot size and forward buy for future periods. Thus, trade promotions often lead to an increase of cycle inventory in a supply chain without a significant increase in customer demand. This generally results in reduced supply chain profits unless the trade promotion reduces demand fluctuations. Trade promotions may be justified as a competitive necessity or a one-time discount to eliminate built up inventory at the supplier. Trade promotions may also be justified for products where consumer demand is very sensitive to price discounts.

11.7 Develop replenishment policies to improve synchronization in multiechelon supply chains.

MANAGING MULTIECHELON CYCLE INVENTORY

A *multiechelon* supply chain has multiple stages and possibly many players at each stage. The lack of coordination in lot sizing decisions across the supply chain often results in high costs and more cycle inventory than required. The goal in a multiechelon system is to decrease total costs by coordinating orders across the supply chain.

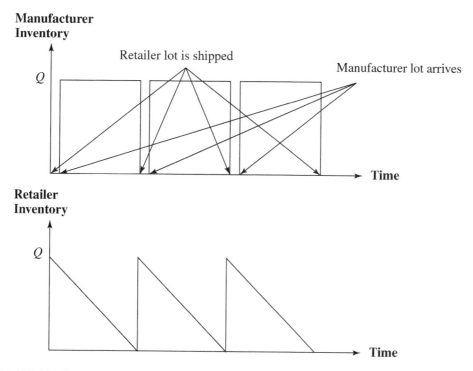

Figure 11-6 Inventory Profile at Retailer and Manufacturer with No Synchronization

Consider a simple multiechelon system with one manufacturer supplying one retailer. Assume that production is instantaneous, so the manufacturer can produce a lot when needed. If the two stages are not synchronized, the manufacturer may produce a new lot of size Q right after shipping a lot of size Q to the retailer. Inventory at the two stages in this case is as shown in Figure 11-6. In this case, the retailer carries an average inventory of $Q/2$ and the manufacturer carries an average inventory of about Q.

Overall supply chain inventory can be lowered if the manufacturer synchronizes its production to be ready just in time to be shipped to the retailer. In this case, the manufacturer carries no inventory and the retailer carries an average inventory of $Q/2$. Synchronization of production and replenishment allows the supply chain to lower total cycle inventory from about $3Q/2$ to $Q/2$.

For a simple multiechelon supply chain with only one player at each stage, ordering policies in which the lot size at each stage is an integer multiple of the lot size at its immediate customer have been shown to be quite close to optimal. When lot sizes are integer multiples, coordination of ordering across stages allows for a portion of the delivery to a stage to be cross-docked on to the next stage. The extent of cross-docking depends on the ratio of the fixed cost of ordering S and the holding cost H at each stage. The closer this ratio is between two stages, the higher is the optimal percentage of cross-docked product. Munson, Hu, and Rosenblatt (2003) provide optimal order quantities in a multiechelon setting with a single manufacturer supplying a single retailer.

If one party (distributor) in a supply chain supplies multiple parties (retailers) at the next stage of the supply chain, it is important to distinguish retailers with high demand from those with low demand. In this setting, Roundy (1985) has shown that a near-optimal policy results if retailers are grouped such that all retailers in one group order together and, for any retailer, either the ordering frequency is an integer multiple of the ordering frequency at the distributor or the ordering frequency at the distributor is an integer multiple of the frequency at the retailer. An

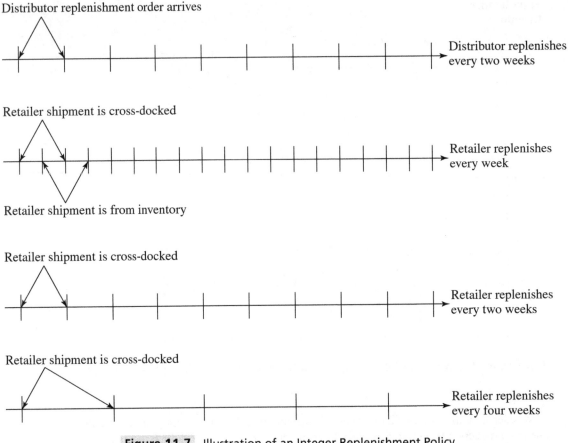

Figure 11-7 Illustration of an Integer Replenishment Policy

integer replenishment policy has every player ordering periodically, with the length of the reorder interval for each player an integer multiple of some base period. An example of such a policy is shown in Figure 11-7. Under this policy, the distributor places a replenishment order every two weeks. Some retailers place replenishment orders every week, and others place replenishment orders every two or four weeks. Observe that for retailers ordering more frequently than the distributor, the retailers' ordering frequency is an integer multiple of the distributor's frequency. For retailers ordering less frequently than the distributor, the distributor's ordering frequency is an integer multiple of the retailers' frequency.

If an integer replenishment policy is synchronized across the two stages, the distributor can cross-dock part of its supply on to the next stage. All shipments to retailers ordering no more frequently than the distributor (every two or four weeks) are cross-docked, as shown in Figure 11-7. For retailers ordering more frequently (every week) than the distributor, half the orders are cross-docked, with the other half shipped from inventory, as shown in Figure 11-7.

Integer replenishment policies for the supply chain shown in Figure 11-8 can be summarized as follows:

- Divide all parties within a stage into groups such that all parties within a group order from the same supplier and have the same reorder interval.
- Set reorder intervals across stages such that the receipt of a replenishment order at any stage is synchronized with the shipment of a replenishment order to at least one customer. The synchronized portion can be cross-docked.
- For customers with a longer reorder interval than the supplier, make the customer's reorder interval an integer multiple of the supplier's interval and synchronize replenishment at the

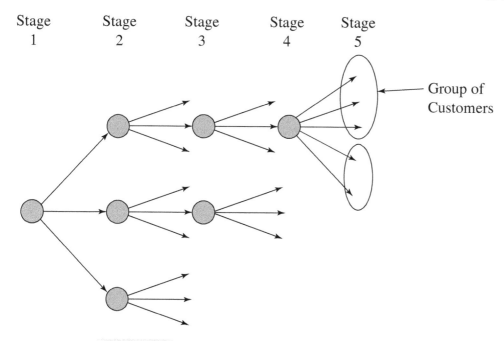

Figure 11-8 A Multiechelon Distribution Supply Chain

two stages to facilitate cross-docking. In other words, a supplier should cross-dock all orders from customers that reorder less frequently than the supplier.

- For customers with a shorter reorder interval than the supplier, make the supplier's reorder interval an integer multiple of the customer's interval and synchronize replenishment at the two stages to facilitate cross-docking. In other words, a supplier should cross-dock one out of every k shipments to a customer that orders more frequently than the supplier, where k is an integer.
- The relative frequency of reordering depends on the setup cost, holding cost, and demand at different parties.

Although the integer policies discussed above synchronize replenishment within the supply chain and decrease cycle inventories, they increase safety inventories, because of the lack of flexibility with the timing of a reorder (as discussed in Chapter 12). Thus, these polices make the most sense for supply chains in which cycle inventories are large and demand is relatively predictable.

SUMMARY OF LEARNING OBJECTIVE 7

Integer replenishment policies can be synchronized in multiechelon supply chains to keep cycle inventory and costs low. Under such policies, the reorder interval at any stage is an integer multiple of a base reorder interval. Synchronized integer replenishment policies facilitate a high level of cross-docking across the supply chain.

MANAGERIAL LEVERS TO REDUCE CYCLE INVENTORY

11.8 Identify managerial levers that reduce lot size and cycle inventory in a supply chain without increasing cost.

This chapter has focused on understanding why cycle inventory builds up in a supply chain. The first step for a manager should be to understand which of the following three factors drive lot sizing decisions in the supply chain – fixed costs associated with production or purchasing, quantity discounts offered by suppliers, or short-term price discounts offered by suppliers. This finding drives the appropriate managerial levers that can be used to reduce cycle inventory without affecting costs.

If most of the cycle inventory is building up because of large lots associated with fixed costs, the key managerial lever is to focus on reducing these fixed costs. If fixed costs arise during production, managers should focus on decreasing changeover times. Small changeover times allow a process to economically produce in small lots. The key to reducing changeover times is to divide the changeover process into activities that can only be performed when the process is shut and those that can be performed when the process is operational. For example, changing a die at a press requires four steps – removing the old die, putting the old die into storage, bringing the new die from storage, installing the new die. Observe that the first and the fourth step cannot be performed if the process is operational. The second and the third step, however, can be performed when the process is operational. Making sure that the second and the third step are performed when the process is operational reduces the changeover time. Within its supply chain Toyota has a strong focus on reducing changeover times. This focus has allowed the company to significantly reduce lot sizes in its supply chain.

If fixed costs primarily arise due to transportation, managers should focus on facilitating aggregation of shipments. This can be done by coordinating orders of products coming from the same supplier, using intermediate locations to aggregate product from multiple suppliers, or the use of milk runs for pickup and delivery. As discussed in section 11.3, care should be taken to use tailored aggregation when variety related fixed costs are large and there is a large range of quantity purchased across products and suppliers.

Fixed costs in order placement and receiving can be decreased through the use of suitable technology. Electronic ordering can help reduce order placement fixed costs. Receiving fixed costs can be decreased through the use of advanced shipping notices and scanning technologies like RFID.

If large lots are purchased primarily because of lot-size based discounts, managers should check whether the supplier has large fixed costs. In such situations managers should focus on reducing supplier fixed costs and then have suppliers transition to offering volume based discounts. Whereas volume based discounts eliminate incentives for ordering in large lots, they may still result in large orders towards the end of the evaluation period if discounts are evaluated based on volumes over a fixed period. In such a situation it is better to offer volume discounts based on a rolling horizon rather than a fixed period.

If large lots are purchased because of short-term discounts, managers may consider a variety of options to limit the amount of forward buying. One approach is to eliminate short term discounts and move to EDLP. It is important to set an appropriate EDLP that does not penalize customers. In the presence of short term discounts it is likely that most of the buyer purchase occurs at the discount price. In this case, it is appropriate for the supplier to set the EDLP close to the discount price rather than the normal price. Another approach is to link the quantity sold at a discount price to sell-through rather than sell-in. This approach eliminates any incentive for buyers to purchase more than they intend to sell. Finally, managers may consider limiting the quantity that buyers can purchase at the discount price to limit forward buying.

SUMMARY OF LEARNING OBJECTIVE 8

The key managerial levers for reducing lot size, and thus cycle inventory, in the supply chain without increasing cost are the following:

- Reduce fixed ordering and transportation costs incurred per order.
- Implement volume-based discounting schemes rather than individual lot-size–based discounting schemes.
- Eliminate or reduce trade promotions and encourage EDLP. Base trade promotions on sell-through rather than sell-in to the retailer.

DISCUSSION QUESTIONS

1. Consider an IKEA manufacturer that is deciding on the size of its replenishment order from one of Europe's leading wholesaler for wood-based goods, the JAF Group. What costs should be taken into account when making this decision?

2. Discuss how various costs for the IKEA manufacturer in Question 1 change as it decreases the lot size ordered from the JAF Group.

3. As demand from the IKEA manufacturer in Question 1 grows, how would you expect the cycle inventory measured in days of inventory to change? Explain.

4. Assume an IKEA manager from Question 1 wants to decrease the lot size without increasing the costs she incurs. What would she need to do to achieve her goal?

5. "Though owned by different parties, members of the supply chain should coordinate with each other instead of pursuing their own objectives." Do you agree? Explain.

6. Consider a toothpaste manufacturer wanting to offer quantity discounts to maximize their profit. Should the manufacturer offer lot-size–based or volume-based quantity discounts and, at the same time, maximize total supply chain profits?

7. Under what circumstances are lot-size–based and volume-based quantity discounts applicable?

8. Do you think integer replenishment policies should be synchronized in multiechelon supply chains? Explain.

9. Why is it appropriate to include only the incremental cost when estimating the holding and order cost for a firm?

EXERCISES

1. Harley-Davidson has its engine assembly plant in Milwaukee and its motorcycle assembly plant in Pennsylvania. Engines are transported between the two plants using trucks, with each trip costing $1,500. The motorcycle plant assembles and sells 300 motorcycles each day. Each engine costs $450, and Harley incurs a holding cost of 20 percent per year. How many engines should Harley load onto each truck? What is the cycle inventory of engines at Harley?

2. As part of its initiative to implement just-in-time (JIT) manufacturing at the motorcycle assembly plant in Exercise 1, Harley has reduced the number of engines loaded on each truck to 100. If each truck trip still costs $1,500, how does this decision impact annual costs at Harley? What should the cost of each truck be if a load of 100 engines is to be optimal for Harley?

3. An Adidas retail store in Berlin sells 650 jackets each month. Each jacket costs the store €80 and the company has an annual holding cost of 30 percent. The fixed cost of a replenishment order (including transportation) is €60. The store currently places a replenishment order every month for 550 jackets. What is the annual holding and ordering cost? On average, how long does a jacket spend in inventory? If the retail store wants to minimize ordering and holding costs, what order size do you recommend? How much would the optimal order reduce holding and ordering cost relative to the current policy?

4. Target purchases home goods made by a supplier in China. Target's stores in the United States sell 200,000 units of home goods each month. Each unit costs $10 and the company has an annual holding cost of 20 percent. Placing a replenishment order incurs clerical costs of $500/order. The shipping company charges $5,000 as a fixed cost per shipment along with a variable cost of $0.10 per unit shipped. What is the optimal order size for Target? What is the annual holding cost of the optimal policy? How many orders per year does Target place? What is the annual fixed transportation cost? What is the annual variable transportation cost? What is the annual clerical cost?

5. Amazon sells 20,000 units of consumer electronics from Samsung every month. Each unit costs $100 and Amazon has an annual holding cost of 20 percent. The fixed clerical and transportation cost for each order Amazon places with Samsung is $4,000. What is the optimal size of the order that Amazon should place with Samsung? With the goal of reducing inventories, Amazon would like to reduce the size of each order it places with Samsung to 2,500 units (allowing it to get eight replenishment orders every month). How much should it reduce the fixed cost per order for an order of 2,500 units to be optimal?

6. Amazon sells 10,000 Lenovo PCs every month. Each PC costs $500 and Amazon has an annual holding cost of 20 percent. For what fixed cost per order would an order size of 10,000 units be optimal? For what fixed cost per order would an order size of 2,500 units be optimal?

7. A steel rolling mill can produce I-beams at the rate of 20 tons per week. Customer demand for the beams is 5 tons per week. To produce I-beams, the mill must go through a setup that requires changing to the appropriate rolling patterns. Each setup costs the mill $10,000 in labor and lost production. I-beams cost the mill $2,000 per ton and the mill has an annual holding cost of 25 percent. What is the optimal production batch size for I-beams? What is the annual setup cost of the optimal policy? What is the annual holding cost?

8. A steel rolling mill can produce I-beams at the rate of 20 tons per week. Customer demand for the beams is 5 tons per week. I-beams cost the mill $2,000 per ton and the mill has an annual holding cost of 25 percent. To produce I-beams, the mill must go through a setup that requires changing to the appropriate rolling patterns. The mill would like to produce I-beams in batches of 40 tons (resulting in a production batch every eight weeks). For what changeover cost would this batch size be optimal?

9. An electronics company has two contract manufacturers in Asia: Foxconn assembles its tablets and smart phones and Flextronics assembles its laptops. Monthly demand for tablets and smartphones is 10,000 units, whereas that for laptops is 4,000. Tablets cost the company $100, laptops cost $400, and the company has an annual holding cost of 25 percent. Currently the company has to place separate orders with Foxconn and Flextronics and receives separate shipments. The fixed cost of each shipment is $10,000. What is the optimal order size and order frequency with each of Foxconn and Flextronics?

 The company is thinking of combining all assembly with the same contract manufacturer. This will allow for a single shipment of all products from Asia. If the fixed cost of each shipment remains $10,000, what is the optimal order frequency and order size from the combined orders? How much reduction in cycle inventory can the company expect as a result of combining orders and shipments?

10. O'Donnell & Joyce purchases components from three suppliers. Components purchased from Supplier A are priced at €7 each and used at the rate of 18,000 units per month. Components purchased from Supplier B are priced at €5 each and are used at the rate of 4,500 units per month. Components purchased from Supplier C are priced at €9 each and used at the rate of 1000 units per month. Currently, O'Donnell & Joyce purchases a separate truckload from each supplier. As part of its JIT drive, O'Donnell & Joyce has decided to aggregate purchases from the three suppliers. The trucking company charges a fixed cost of €550 for the truck with an additional charge of €120 for each stop. Thus, if O'Donnell & Joyce asks for a pickup from only one supplier, it charges €670; from two suppliers, it charges €790; and from three suppliers, it charges €910. What replenishment strategy would you suggest for O'Donnell & Joyce to minimize annual costs? Assume an annual holding cost of 25 percent per year. Compare the cost of your strategy from each supplier. What is the cycle of inventory of each component at O'Donnell & Joyce?

11. Ford and GM carry spare parts for their dealers at a third-party warehouse in Michigan's Upper Peninsula. Demand for Ford spare parts is 100 units per month, whereas demand for GM parts is 120 per month. Each spare part costs $100 and both companies have annual holding costs of 20 percent. Currently, each company uses a separate truck to ship these parts. Each truck has a fixed cost of $500. What is the optimal order size and frequency for Ford? For GM? What is the annual ordering and holding cost for each company?

 A third-party logistics provider has offered to combine shipments for each of the two companies on a single truck. This will increase the cost of each truck to $600. If the two companies agree to the joint shipment, what is the optimal order frequency and size? What is the annual ordering and holding cost for the two companies combined? Should Ford and GM accept the third party's proposal? How should they divide the fixed cost per truck among themselves?

12. Prefab, a furniture manufacturer, uses 20,000 square feet of plywood per month. Its trucking company charges Prefab $400 per shipment, independent of the quantity purchased.

The manufacturer offers an all unit quantity discount with a price of $1 per square foot for orders under 20,000 square feet, $0.98 per square foot for orders between 20,000 square feet and 40,000 square feet, and $0.96 per square foot for orders larger than 40,000 square feet. Prefab incurs an annual holding cost of 20 percent. What is the optimal lot size for Prefab? What is the annual cost of such a policy? What is the cycle inventory of plywood at Prefab? How does it compare with the cycle inventory if the manufacturer does not offer a quantity discount but sells all plywood at $0.96 per square foot?

 Now consider the case in which the manufacturer offers a marginal unit quantity discount for the plywood. The first 20,000 square feet of any order are sold at $1 per square foot, the next 20,000 square feet are sold at $0.98 per square foot, and any quantity larger than 40,000 square feet is sold for $0.96 per square foot. What is the optimal lot size for Prefab given this pricing structure? How much cycle inventory of plywood will Prefab carry given the ordering policy?

13. Demand for fasteners at W.W. Grainger is 20,000 boxes per month. The holding cost at Grainger is 20 percent per year. Each order incurs a fixed cost of $400. The supplier offers an all unit discount pricing scheme with a price of $5 per box for orders under 30,000 and a price of $4.90 for all orders of 30,000 or more. How many boxes should Grainger order per replenishment?

14. Now, consider Exercise 13 with a marginal unit quantity discount. Demand for fasteners at W.W. Grainger is 20,000 boxes per month. The holding cost at Grainger is 20 percent per year. Each order incurs a fixed cost of $400. The supplier offers a marginal unit discount pricing scheme with a price of $5 per box for the first 30,000 and a price of $4.90 per unit for each unit above 30,000 in an order. How many boxes should Grainger order per replenishment?

15. Demand for phones at Amazon is 5,000 per month. The annual holding cost at Amazon is 25 percent and the company incurs a fixed cost of $500 for each order placed. The supplier offers an all unit quantity discount with a price of $200 per phone for all orders under 10,000, a price of $195 for all orders of 10,000 or more but under 20,000 and a price of $190 for all orders of 20,000 or more. How many phones should Amazon order per replenishment?

16. Demand for phones at Amazon is 5,000 per month. The annual holding cost at Amazon is 25 percent and the company incurs a fixed cost of $500 for each order placed. The supplier offers a marginal unit quantity discount with a price of $200 per phone for the first 10,000 phones in an order, a price of $195 for the next 10,000 phones in the order, and a price of $190 for the quantity above 20,000 in the order. How many phones should Amazon order per replenishment?

17. Dominick's supermarket chain sells Nut Flakes, a popular cereal manufactured by the Tastee cereal company. Demand for Nut Flakes is 1,000 boxes per week. Dominick's has an annual holding cost of 25 percent and incurs a fixed trucking cost of $200 for each replenishment order it places with Tastee. Given that Tastee normally charges $2 per box of Nut Flakes, how much should Dominick's order in each replenishment lot?

Tastee runs a trade promotion for a month, lowering the price of Nut Flakes to $1.80. How much should Dominick's order, given the short-term price reduction?

18. Flanger is an industrial distributor that sources from hundreds of suppliers. The two modes of transportation available for inbound shipping are LTL (less than truckload) and TL (truckload). LTL shipping costs $1 per unit, whereas TL shipping costs $500 per truck. Each truck can carry up to 1,000 units. Flanger wants a rule assigning products to shipping mode (TL or LTL) based on annual demand. Each unit costs $50, and Flanger uses a holding cost of 22 percent. Flanger incurs a fixed cost of $150 for each order placed with a supplier.

 a. Determine a threshold for annual demand above which TL is preferred and below which LTL is preferred.

 b. How does the threshold change [relative to part (a)] if unit cost is $150 (instead of $50) with all other data unchanged? Which mode becomes preferable as unit cost grows?

 c. How does the threshold change [relative to part (a)] if the LTL cost comes down to $0.8 per unit (instead of $1 per unit)?

19. SuperPart, an auto parts distributor, has a large warehouse in the Chicago region and is deciding on a policy for the use of TL or LTL transportation for inbound shipping. LTL shipping costs $1 per unit. TL shipping costs $850 per truck plus $150 per pickup. Thus, a truck used to pick up from three suppliers costs $850 + (3 × 100) = $1,150. A truck can carry up to 2,000 units. SuperPart incurs a fixed cost of $150 for each order placed with a supplier. Thus, an order with three distinct suppliers incurs an ordering cost of $450. Each unit costs $50, and SuperPart uses a holding cost of 23 percent. Assume that product from each supplier has an annual demand of 3,000 units. SuperPart has thousands of suppliers and the company must decide on the number of suppliers to group per truck if using TL.

 a. What is the optimal order size and annual cost if LTL shipping is used? What is the time between orders?

 b. What is the optimal order size and annual cost if TL shipping is used with a separate truck for each supplier? What is the time between orders?

 c. What is the optimal order size and annual cost per product if TL shipping is used but two suppliers are grouped together per truck?

 d. What is the optimal number of suppliers that should be grouped together? What is the optimal order size and annual cost per product in this case? What is the time between orders?

 e. Which shipping policy would you recommend if each product has an annual demand of 3,000? Which shipping policy would you recommend for products with an annual demand of 1,500? Which shipping policy would you recommend for products with an annual demand of 18,000?

20. PlasFib is a manufacturer of synthetic fibers used for making furniture upholstery. It manufactures fiber in 50 colors on one line. When changing over from one color to the next, part of the line must be cleaned, leading to a loss of material. Each changeover costs $120 in lost material and changeover labor. Assume that each changeover requires the line to shut down for 0.5 hour. When it is running, the line produces fiber at the rate of 100 pounds per hour. The fibers sold by PlasFib are divided into three categories. There are five fast-moving colors that average sales of 31,000 pounds per color per year. There are 10 medium-moving colors that average sales of 12,000 pounds per color per year. The remaining are slow-moving products and average sales of 3,200 pounds per year each. Each pound of fiber costs $6 and PlasFib has a holding cost of 15 percent.

 a. What is the batch size that PlasFib should produce for each fast-, medium-, and slow-moving color? How many days of demand does this translate into?

 b. What is the annual setup and holding cost of the policies you suggested in part (a)?

 c. How many hours of plant operation will the above schedule require in a year (including a half-hour of setup per batch)?

21. TopOil, a refiner in Indiana, serves three customers near Nashville, Tennessee, and maintains consignment inventory (owned by TopOil) at each location. Currently, TopOil uses TL transportation to deliver separately to each customer. Each truck costs $800 plus $250 per stop. Thus, delivering to each customer separately costs $1,050 per truck. TopOil is considering aggregating deliveries to Nashville on a single truck. Demand at the large customer is 60 tons a year, demand at the medium customer is 24 tons per year, and demand at the small customer is 8 tons per year. Product cost for TopOil is $10,000 per ton, and it uses an annual holding cost of 25 percent. Truck capacity is 12 tons.

 a. What is the annual transportation and holding cost if TopOil ships a full truckload to each customer when they are running out of stock? How many days of inventory is carried at each customer under this policy?

 b. What is the optimal delivery policy to each customer if TopOil ships separately to each of them? What is the annual transportation and holding cost? How many days of inventory is carried at each customer under this policy?

 c. What is the optimal delivery policy to each customer if TopOil aggregates shipments to each of the three customers on every truck that goes to Nashville? What is the annual transportation and holding cost? How many days of inventory are carried at each customer under this policy?

 d. Can you come up with a tailored policy that has lower costs than the policies in (b) or (c)? What are the costs and inventories for your suggested policy?

22. Crunchy, a cereal manufacturer, has dedicated a plant for one major retail chain. Sales at the retail chain average about 20,000 boxes a month and production at the plant keeps pace with this average demand. Each box of cereal costs Crunchy $3 and is sold to the retailer at a wholesale price of $5. Both Crunchy and the retailer use an annual holding cost of 20 percent. For each order placed, the retailer incurs an ordering cost of $200. Crunchy incurs the cost of transportation and loading that totals $1,000 per order shipped.

 a. Given that it is trying to minimize its ordering and holding costs, what lot size will the retailer ask for in each order? What are the annual ordering and holding costs for the retailer as a result of this policy? What are the annual

ordering and holding costs for Crunchy as a result of this policy? What is the total inventory cost across both parties as a result of this policy?

b. What lot size minimizes the inventory costs (ordering, delivery, and holding) across both Crunchy and the retailer? How much reduction in cost relative to (a) results from this policy?

c. Design an all unit quantity discount that results in the retailer ordering the quantity in (b).

d. How much of the $1,000 delivery cost should Crunchy pass along to the retailer for each lot to get the retailer to order the quantity in (b)?

23. A steel service center sources products from an integrated steel mill at a cost of $2,000 per ton. Demand for steel at the service center is 50 tons per month. The service center has an annual holding cost of 25 percent and incurs a fixed cost of $2,000 for each order. How many tons of steel should the service center order per replenishment? What is the annual ordering and holding cost incurred by the service center?

The integrated steel mill incurs a fixed cost of $4,000 for each order placed by the steel service center. Steel costs the mill $1,000 per ton and the mill has an annual holding cost of 20 percent. Assuming that the mill builds up its steel (for the service center) at the rate of 50 tons per month, what are the annual fixed cost and holding cost incurred by the mill as a result of the service center's ordering policy? What is the annual cost incurred by both the service center and the steel mill?

If the steel mill and the service center could work in a coordinated manner, what is the optimal order size that minimizes their joint fixed and holding costs? What annual savings could the supply chain expect as a result of coordination? Design an all unit quantity discount that the integrated steel mill could use to get the service center to order the coordinated amount without increasing annual costs at the service center.

24. The Orange company has introduced a new music device called the J-Pod. The J-Pod is sold through Good Buy, a major electronics retailer. Good Buy has estimated that demand for the J-Pod will depend on the final retail price p according to the demand curve

$$\text{Demand } D = 2,000,000 - 2,000\, p$$

The production cost for Orange is $100 per J-Pod.

a. What wholesale price should Orange charge for the J-Pod? At this wholesale price, what retail price should Good Buy set? What are the profits for Orange and Good Buy at equilibrium?

b. If Orange decides to discount the wholesale price by $40, how much of a discount should Good Buy offer to customers if it wants to maximize its own profits? What fraction of the discount offered by Orange does Good Buy pass along to the customer?

25. The Orange company prices J-Pods at $550 per unit. Good Buy sells the J-Pods at $775. Annual demand at this retail price turns out to be 450,000 units. Good Buy incurs ordering, receiving, and transportation costs of $10,000 for each lot of J-Pods ordered. The annual holding cost used by the retailer is 20 percent.

a. What is the optimal lot size that Good Buy should order?

b. The Orange company has discounted J-Pods by $40 for the short term (about the next two weeks). Good Buy has decided not to change the retail price but may change the lot size ordered from Orange. How should Good Buy adjust its lot size given this discount? How much does the lot size increase because of the discount?

26. MCParts, an MRO distributor, sources products from three different suppliers in the Atlanta region. Currently, MCParts uses TL transportation to source separately from each supplier. Each truck costs $1,000 plus $400 per stop. Thus, delivering to each customer separately costs $1,400 per truck. MCParts is considering aggregating sourcing on a single truck. Demand for the fastest selling product is 120,000 units a year, demand for the medium selling product is 60,000 units per year, and demand for the slowest moving product is 12,000 units per year. Each product costs $10 and MCParts incurs an annual holding cost of 25 percent. Truck capacity is 12,000 units.

a. What is the annual transportation and holding cost if MCParts sources a full truckload from each supplier in each order? How many days of inventory is carried for each product under this policy?

b. What is the optimal order quantity of each part if MCParts sources separately from each supplier? What is the annual transportation and holding cost? How many days of inventory is carried for each part under this policy?

c. What is the optimal order quantity for each product if MCParts aggregates shipments from each of the three suppliers on every truck that arrives from Atlanta? What is the annual transportation and holding cost? How many days of inventory are carried at each customer under this policy?

d. Can you come up with a tailored policy that has lower costs than the policies in (b) or (c)? What are the costs and inventories for your suggested policy?

27. AZOR, a European detergent manufacturer, has dedicated a plant for one major retail chain. Sales at the retail chain average about 10,000 jugs of detergent a month and production at the plant keeps pace with this average demand. Each jug of detergent costs AZOR €5 and is sold to the retailer at a wholesale price of €10. Both AZOR and the retailer use an annual holding cost of 25 percent. For each order placed, the retailer incurs an ordering cost of €100. AZOR incurs the cost of transportation and loading that totals €1,600 per order shipped.

a. Given that it is trying to minimize its ordering and holding costs, what lot size will the retailer ask for in each order? What are the annual ordering and holding costs for the retailer as a result of this policy? What are the annual ordering and holding costs for AZOR as a result of this policy? What is the total inventory cost across both parties as a result of this policy?

b. What lot size minimizes the inventory costs (ordering, delivery, and holding) across both AZOR and the retailer? How much reduction in cost relative to (a) results from this policy?

c. Design an all unit quantity discount that results in the retailer ordering the quantity in (b).

BIBLIOGRAPHY

Blattberg, Robert C., and Scott A. Neslin. *Sales Promotion: Concepts, Methods, and Strategies*. Upper Saddle River, NJ: Prentice Hall, 1990.

Brealey, Richard A., and Stewart C. Myers. *Principles of Corporate Finance*. Boston, MA: Irwin McGraw-Hill, 2000.

Buzzell, Robert, John Quelch, and Walter Salmon. "The Costly Bargain of Trade Promotions." *Harvard Business Review* (March–April 1990): 141–149.

Crowther, John F. "Rationale for Quantity Discounts." *Harvard Business Review* (March–April 1964): 121–127.

Dolan, Robert J. "Quantity Discounts: Managerial Issues and Research Opportunities." *Marketing Science* (1987): 6, 1–24.

Federgruen, Awi, and Yu-Sheng Zheng. "Optimal Power-of-Two Replenishment Strategies in Capacitated General Production/Distribution Networks." *Management Science* (1993): 39, 710–727.

Goyal, Suresh K. "A Simple Procedure for Price Break Models." *Production Planning & Control* (1995): 6, 584–585.

Gupta, Sandeep, and Charanyan Iyengar. "The Tip of the (Inventory) Iceberg." *Supply Chain Management Review* (November 2014): 28–35.

Hu, Jianli, and Charles L. Munson. "Dynamic Demand Lot-sizing Rules for Incremental Quantity Discounts." *Journal of the Operational Research Society* (2002): 53, 855–863.

Kurt Salmon Associates, Inc. *Efficient Consumer Response*. Washington, DC: Food Marketing Institute, 1993.

Lee, Hau L., and Corey Billington. "Managing Supply Chain Inventories: Pitfalls and Opportunities." *Sloan Management Review* (Spring 1992): 65–73.

Maxwell, William L., and John A. Muckstadt. "Establishing Consistent and Realistic Reorder Intervals in Production-Distribution Systems." *Operations Research* (1985): 33, 1316–1341.

Munson, Charles L., Jianli Hu, and Meir J. Rosenblatt. "Teaching the Costs of Uncoordinated Supply Chains." *Interfaces* (2003): 33, 24–39.

Munson, Charles L., and Meir J. Rosenblatt. "Theories and Realities of Quantity Discounts." *Production and Operations Management* (1998): 7, 352–369.

Roundy, Robin. "98%-Effective Integer-Ratio Lot-Sizing for One-Warehouse Multi-Retailer Systems." *Management Science* (1985): 31, 1416–1429.

Roundy, Robin. "A 98%-Effective Lot-Sizing Rule for a Multi-Product, Multi-Stage Production Inventory System." *Mathematics of Operations Research* (1986): 11, 699–727.

Silver, Edward A., David Pyke, and Rein Petersen. *Inventory Management and Production Planning and Scheduling*. New York: Wiley, 1998.

Zipkin, Paul H. *Foundations of Inventory Management*. Boston, MA: Irwin McGraw-Hill, 2000.

CASE STUDY

Delivery Strategy at MoonChem

John Kresge, vice president of supply chain, was very concerned as he left the meeting at MoonChem, a manufacturer of specialty chemicals. The year-end meeting evaluated financial performance and discussed the fact that the firm was achieving only two inventory turns a year. A more careful look revealed that more than half the inventory MoonChem owned was in consignment with its customers. This was very surprising, given that only 20 percent of its customers carried consignment inventory. John was responsible for inventory as well as transportation costs. He decided to take a careful look at the management of consignment inventory and come up with an appropriate plan.

MoonChem Operations

MoonChem, a manufacturer of specialty chemicals, had eight manufacturing plants and 40 distribution centers. The plants manufactured the base chemicals, and the distribution centers mixed them to produce hundreds of end products that fit customer specifications. In the specialty chemicals market, MoonChem decided to differentiate itself in the Midwest region by providing consignment inventory to its customers. The company wanted to take this strategy national if it proved effective. MoonChem kept the chemicals required by each customer in the Midwest region on consignment at the customers' sites. Customers used the chemicals as needed, and MoonChem managed replenishment to ensure availability. In most instances, consumption of chemicals by customers was stable. MoonChem owned the consignment inventories and was paid for the chemicals as they were used.

Distribution at MoonChem

MoonChem used Golden trucking, a full-truckload carrier, for all its shipments. Each truck had a capacity of 40,000 pounds; Golden charged a fixed rate given the origin and destination, regardless of the quantity shipped

on the truck. MoonChem sent full truckloads to each customer to replenish its consignment inventory.

The Illinois Pilot Study

John decided to take a careful look at his distribution operations. He focused on Illinois, which was supplied from the Chicago distribution center. He broke up Illinois into a collection of zip codes that were contiguous, as shown in Figure 11-9. He restricted attention to the Peoria region, which was classified as zip code 615. A careful study of the Peoria region revealed two large customers, six medium-sized customers, and twelve small customers. The annual consumption at each type of customer was as shown in Table 11-4. Golden charged

Figure 11-9 Illinois Zip Code Map

TABLE 11-4 Customer Profile for MoonChem in Peoria Region

Customer Type	Number of Customers	Consumption (Pounds per Month)
Small	12	1,000
Medium	6	5,000
Large	2	12,000

$400 for each shipment from Chicago to Peoria, and MoonChem's policy was to send a full truckload to each customer as needed.

John checked with Golden to find out what it would take to include shipments for multiple customers on a single load. Golden informed him that it would charge $350 per truck and add $50 for each drop-off for which Golden was responsible. Thus, if Golden carried a truck that had to make one delivery, the total charge would be $400. However, if a truck had to make four deliveries, the total charge would be $550.

Each pound of chemical in consignment cost MoonChem $1, and MoonChem had an annual holding cost of 25 percent. John wanted to analyze a few different options for distribution available in the Peoria region to decide on the optimal distribution policy. One was to aggregate all 20 customers into each truck going to Peoria. The other was to separate the 20 customers into two groups with one large, three medium, and six small customers in each group. Each group would then be aggregated into a single truck going to Peoria. The detailed study of the Peoria region would provide the blueprint for the distribution strategy that MoonChem planned to roll out nationally.

Questions

1. What is the annual cost of MoonChem's strategy of sending full truckloads to each customer in the Peoria region to replenish consignment inventory?
2. Consider different delivery options and evaluate the cost of each. What delivery option do you recommend for MoonChem?
3. How does your recommendation impact consignment inventory for MoonChem?

CASE STUDY

Pricing and Delivery at NAN

In 1984, NZ All Natural Ice Cream (NAN) began as a small shop in Christchurch, the largest city in the South Island of New Zealand. As NAN's sales volume has increased significantly over the years, it continues to diversify its product range to include nondairy, low-fat sorbets; low-fat frozen yogurts; and premium ice cream in a wide range of flavors. Waikato, which is the heartland of various free-range dairy farms a prominent, is NAN's primary fresh milk and cream supplier. NAN now wants to set up its own production plants in Auckland, which is in the North Island of New Zealand and geographically closer to Waikato, so that the manufacturing process could be smoother and more secure. Currently, NAN operates three plants and five distribution centers across the country. The plants generally manufacture the base products, and the distribution centers produce hundreds of end products that fit customer specifications.

Supply Chain Improvements at NAN

To further expand its domestic market, NAN is considering providing consignment inventory to customers in the North Island first and implementing this strategy throughout the country if it proved effective in the North Island. It plans to keep the ice cream products required by customers in the North Island on consignment at the customers' sites and replenish regularly to ensure sufficient supply. According to previous sales data, the consumption of ice cream by customers tends to be stable. NAN owns the consignment inventories and gets paid once sales are made. NAN has assigned

Customer Type	Number of Customers	Consumption (Liters/Month)
Small	12	1,000
Medium	6	6,000
Large	2	12,000

its inland replenishment function to a 3PL company named SuperTruck through open bidding. SuperTruck is famous for its fast response and prompt delivery through expertise in fleet management. All its trucks have refrigerated units built either directly on the frame or transported by trailer and are powered by diesel-operated generators. SuperTruck is instructed to fulfill every order NAN places within 24 hours or reimburse NAN for all damages if it fails to do so. Each truck has a capacity of 40,000 liters, and SuperTruck has been contracted to charge a fixed flat rate given the origin and destination regardless of the quantity loaded. NAN usually sends full truckloads (TL) to each customer to replenish its consignment inventory. Katy Leung has recently been employed by NAN as North Island regional supply chain manager to oversee logistics operations in the region. Katy is responsible for inventory as well as transportation costs and decides to review the current operations for possible cost savings. In particular, Katy wonders if NAN should include multiple shipments for different customers on a single truckload. The table shows the customer profile in Wellington, one of NAN's distribution centers.

Delivering with SuperTruck

SuperTruck charges $400 for each truckload from the Wellington DC to each customer based on NAN's policy to send a full truckload as needed. In response to Katy's recent enquiry, SuperTruck indicated that it would charge $350 per truck plus $50 for each drop-off location. That is, if a truck made only one delivery as existing practice, the total charge would be $350 + $50 = $400. However, if it makes three extra deliveries (four locations in all), the total charge would then be $350 + $200 = $550. Each liter of ice cream product in consignment costs NAN $1, while the holding cost is maintained at 25 percent. Consider the different distribution possibilities in the Wellington example and recommend the best option. This will help shape the future marketing and distribution strategy that NAN plans to roll out throughout New Zealand.

Questions

1. Calculate the annual cost of NAN's strategy of sending only full truckloads to each customer in Wellington to replenish consignment inventory.
2. Evaluate the costs for different delivery options and recommend the best option that NAN should implement.
3. How does your recommendation affect NAN's consignment inventory?

APPENDIX 11A

Economic Order Quantity

Objective

Derive the economic order quantity (EOQ) formula.

Analysis:

Given an annual demand D, order cost S, unit cost C, and annual holding cost h, our goal is to estimate the lot size Q that minimizes the total annual cost. For a lot size of Q, the total annual cost is given by

$$\text{Total annual cost, } TC = (D/Q)S + (Q/2)hC + CD$$

To minimize the total cost, we take the first derivative with respect to the lot size Q and set it to zero. Taking the first derivative with respect to Q, we have

$$\frac{d(TC)}{dQ} = -\frac{DS}{Q^2} + \frac{hC}{2}$$

Setting the first derivative to be zero, the EOQ is given by

$$Q^2 = \frac{2DS}{hC} \text{ or } Q = \sqrt{\frac{2DS}{hC}}$$

CHAPTER

12

Managing Uncertainty in a Supply Chain
Safety Inventory

LEARNING OBJECTIVES

After reading this chapter, you will be able to

12.1 Understand the role of safety inventory in a supply chain.

12.2 Identify factors that influence the required level of safety inventory.

12.3 Evaluate the appropriate level of safety inventory for a supply chain.

12.4 Discuss the impact of supply uncertainty on safety inventory.

12.5 Understand how aggregation helps reduce the required safety inventory in a supply chain.

12.6 Determine the impact of replenishment policies on safety inventory.

12.7 Improve the management of safety inventory in a multiechelon supply chain.

12.8 Identify managerial levers that lower safety inventory without hurting product availability.

In this chapter, we discuss how safety inventory can help a supply chain improve product availability in the presence of supply and demand variability. We discuss various measures of product availability and how managers can set safety inventory levels to provide the desired product availability. We also explore what managers can do to reduce the amount of safety inventory required while maintaining or even improving product availability.

THE ROLE OF SAFETY INVENTORY IN A SUPPLY CHAIN

Safety inventory is inventory carried to satisfy demand that exceeds the amount forecast. Safety inventory is required because demand and supply are uncertain, and a product shortage may result if actual demand exceeds the forecast demand or supply is later than anticipated. Consider, for example, Bloomingdale's, a high-end department store. Bloomingdale's sells purses

12.1. Understand the role of safety inventory in a supply chain.

purchased from Gucci, an Italian manufacturer. Given the high transportation cost from Italy, the store manager at Bloomingdale's orders in lots of 600 purses. Demand for purses at Bloomingdale's averages 100 a week. Gucci takes three weeks to deliver the purses to Bloomingdale's in response to an order. If there is no demand uncertainty and exactly 100 purses are sold each week, the store manager at Bloomingdale's can place an order when the store has exactly 300 purses remaining. In the absence of demand uncertainty, such a policy ensures that the new lot arrives just as the last purse is being sold at the store.

However, given demand fluctuations and forecast errors, actual demand over the three weeks may be higher or lower than the 300 purses that were forecast. If the actual demand at Bloomingdale's is higher than 300, some customers will be unable to purchase purses, resulting in a potential loss of margin for Bloomingdale's. The store manager thus decides to place an order with Gucci when the store still has 400 purses. This policy improves product availability for the customer because the store now runs out of purses only if the demand over the three weeks exceeds 400. Given an average weekly demand of 100 purses, the store will have an average of 100 purses remaining when the replenishment lot arrives. Safety inventory is the average inventory remaining when the replenishment lot arrives. Thus, Bloomingdale's carries a safety inventory of 100 purses.

Given a lot size of $Q = 600$ purses, the cycle inventory, the focus of the previous chapter, is $Q/2 = 300$ purses. The inventory profile at Bloomingdale's in the presence of safety inventory is shown in Figure 12-1, which illustrates that the average inventory at Bloomingdale's is the sum of the cycle and safety inventories.

This example illustrates a trade-off that a supply chain manager must consider when planning safety inventory. On one hand, raising the level of safety inventory increases product availability, and thus the margin captured from customer purchases. On the other hand, raising the level of safety inventory increases inventory holding costs. This issue is particularly significant in industries in which product life cycles are short and demand is volatile. Carrying excessive inventory can help counter demand volatility but can really hurt if new products come onto the market and demand for the product in inventory dries up. The inventory on hand then becomes worthless.

In today's business environment, it has become easier for customers to search across stores for product availability. For example, if Amazon is out of a book, a customer can easily check to see whether barnesandnoble.com has the title available. The increased ease of searching puts pressure on firms to improve product availability. Simultaneously, product variety has grown with increased customization. As a result, markets have become increasingly heterogeneous and demand for individual products is unstable and difficult to forecast. Both the increased variety and the greater pressure for availability push firms to raise the level of safety inventory they hold. Given the product variety and high demand uncertainty in most high-tech supply chains, a significant fraction of the inventory carried is safety inventory.

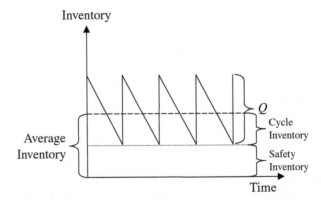

Figure 12-1 Inventory Profile with Safety Inventory

As product variety has grown, however, product life cycles have shrunk. Thus, it is more likely that a product that is "hot" today will be obsolete tomorrow, which increases the cost to firms of carrying too much inventory. Thus, a key to the success of any supply chain is to figure out ways to decrease the level of safety inventory carried without hurting the level of product availability.

The importance of reduced safety inventories is emphasized by the experience of Nordstrom, Macy's, and Saks during the 2008–2009 recession. Nordstrom outperformed the other two chains by moving its inventories about twice as fast as its competitors. In 2008 (2009), Nordstrom carried an average of about 2 (2) months, Macy's carried about 4 (4.15) months, and Saks carried 4.24 (4.67) months of inventory. A key to Nordstrom's success has been its ability to provide a high level of product availability to customers while carrying low levels of safety inventory in its supply chain. This fact has also played an important role in the success of Zara, Walmart, and Seven-Eleven Japan.

For any supply chain, three key questions need to be considered when planning safety inventory:

1. What is the appropriate level of product availability?
2. How much safety inventory is needed for the desired level of product availability?
3. What actions can be taken to reduce safety inventory without hurting product availability?

The first question is discussed in detail in Chapter 13. The remainder of this chapter focuses on answering the second and third questions, assuming a desired level of product availability.

SUMMARY OF LEARNING OBJECTIVE 1

Safety inventory helps a supply chain provide customers with a high level of product availability in spite of supply and demand uncertainty. It is carried just in case demand exceeds the amount forecasted or supply arrives later than expected.

FACTORS AFFECTING THE LEVEL OF SAFETY INVENTORY

12.2. Identify factors that influence the required level of safety inventory.

The appropriate level of safety inventory is determined by the following factors:

- The desired level of product availability
- The uncertainty of demand
- The uncertainty of supply
- Inventory replenishment policies

As the desired level of product availability increases, the required level of safety inventory increases. If a supermarket targets a higher level of product availability for a certain spice, it must carry a higher level of safety inventory for that spice.

As the uncertainty of demand grows, the required level of safety inventory increases. Demand for milk at a supermarket is quite predictable. As a result, supermarkets can operate with low levels of safety inventory relative to demand for milk. In contrast, demand for spices at the same supermarket is much harder to predict. Thus the supermarket needs to carry high levels of safety inventory for spices relative to demand. Whereas most of the milk inventory at a supermarket is cycle inventory (with very little being safety inventory), most of the spice inventory is safety inventory carried to deal with uncertainty of demand.

Similarly, as the uncertainty of supply grows the required level of safety inventory increases. As supply becomes uncertain, a retailer must compensate for likely delays in supply by carrying extra safety inventory.

The required safety inventory is also affected by the flexibility the buyer has in placing the replenishment order. If a replenishment order can be placed anytime, the required safety inven-

tory is less than if replenishment orders can only be placed at specified times (such as the beginning of each month). The flexibility in ordering allows the buyer to react quicker to an unanticipated increase in demand, thus reducing the amount of safety inventory required.

We illustrate our ideas using uncertain demand for a smartphone at B&M Office Supplies as the context. Next, we discuss some measures of product availability.

Measuring Product Availability

Product availability reflects a firm's ability to fill a customer order out of available inventory. A *stockout* results if a customer order arrives when product is not available. There are several ways to measure product availability. Some of the important measures are listed next.

1. ***Product fill rate (fr)*** is the fraction of product demand that is satisfied from product in inventory. Fill rate is equivalent to the probability that product demand is supplied from available inventory. Fill rate should be measured over specified amounts of demand rather than over time. Thus, it is more appropriate to measure fill rate over every million units of demand rather than every month. Assume that B&M provides smartphones to 90 percent of its customers from inventory, with the remaining 10 percent lost to a neighboring competitor because of a lack of available inventory. In this case, B&M achieves a fill rate of 90 percent.

2. ***Order fill rate*** is the fraction of orders that are filled from available inventory. Order fill rate should also be measured over a specified number of orders rather than over time. In a multiproduct scenario, an order is filled from inventory only if all products in the order can be supplied from the available inventory. In the case of B&M, a customer may order a phone along with a laptop. The order is filled from inventory only if both the phone and the laptop are available through the store. Order fill rates tend to be lower than product fill rates because all products must be in stock for an order to be filled.

3. ***Cycle service level (CSL)*** is the fraction of replenishment cycles that end with all the customer demand being met. *A replenishment cycle* is the interval between two successive replenishment deliveries. The CSL is equal to the probability of not having a stockout in a replenishment cycle. CSL should be measured over a specified number of replenishment cycles. If B&M orders replenishment lots of 600 phones, the interval between the arrival of two successive replenishment lots is a replenishment cycle. If the manager at B&M manages inventory such that the store does not run out of inventory in 6 out of 10 replenishment cycles, the store achieves a CSL of 0.6 or 60 percent. Observe that a CSL of 0.6 typically results in a much higher fill rate. In the 60 percent of cycles in which B&M does not run out of inventory, all customer demand is satisfied from available inventory. In the 40 percent of cycles in which a stockout does occur, most of the customer demand is satisfied from inventory. Only the small fraction toward the end of the cycle that arrives after B&M is out of inventory is lost. As a result, the fill rate is much higher than 0.6.

The distinction between product fill rate and order fill rate is not significant in a single-product situation. When a firm is selling multiple products, however, this difference may be significant. For example, if most orders include 10 or more products that are to be shipped, an out-of-stock situation of one product results in the order not being filled from stock. The firm in this case may have a poor order fill rate even though it has good product fill rates. Tracking order fill rates is important when customers place a high value on the entire order being filled at one time.

Next, we discuss some measures of demand uncertainty.

Measuring Demand Uncertainty

As discussed in Chapter 7, demand has a systematic as well as a random component. The random component is a measure of demand uncertainty. The goal of forecasting is to predict the

systematic component and estimate the random component. The random component is usually estimated as the standard deviation of forecast error. Returning to the B&M example, we assume that periodic demand for the phone is normally distributed with the following inputs:

D: Average demand per period

σ_D: Standard deviation of demand (forecast error) per period

Even though standard deviation of demand is not necessarily the same as forecast error, we treat the two to be interchangeable in our discussion. Safety inventory calculations should really be based on forecast error.

Lead time is the time elapsed between when an order is placed and when it is received. In our discussion, we denote the lead time by L. In the B&M example, L is the time between when B&M orders phones and when they are delivered. In this case, B&M is exposed to the uncertainty of demand during the lead time. Whether B&M is able to satisfy all demand from inventory depends on the demand for phones experienced during the lead time and the inventory B&M has when a replenishment order is placed. Thus, B&M must estimate the uncertainty of demand during the lead time, not just in a single period. We now evaluate the distribution of demand over L periods, given a fixed lead time L and the distribution of demand during each period.

EVALUATING DEMAND DISTRIBUTION OVER *L* PERIODS Assume that demand for each period i, $i = 1, \ldots, L$, is normally distributed with a mean D_i and standard deviation σ_i. Let ρ_{ij} be the correlation coefficient of demand between periods i and j. In this case, the total demand during L periods is normally distributed with a mean of D_L and a standard deviation of σ_L, where the following is true:

$$D_L = \sum_{i=1}^{L} D_i, \quad \sigma_L = \sqrt{\sum_{i=1}^{L} \sigma_i^2 + 2 \sum_{i>j} \rho_{ij}\sigma_i\sigma_j} \tag{12.1}$$

Demand in two periods is *perfectly positively correlated* if $\rho_{ij} = 1$. Demand in two periods is *perfectly negatively correlated* if $\rho_{ij} = -1$. Demand in two periods is *independent* if $\rho_{ij} = 0$. If demand during each of L periods is independent and normally distributed with a mean of D and a standard deviation of σ_D, Equation 12.1 can be used to show that total demand during the L periods is normally distributed with a mean D_L and a standard deviation of σ_L where the following is true:

$$D_L = D \times L, \quad \sigma_L = \sqrt{L}\sigma_D \tag{12.2}$$

Another important measure of uncertainty is the *coefficient of variation (cv)*, which is the ratio of the standard deviation to the mean. Given demand with a mean of μ and a standard deviation of σ we have

$$cv = \sigma/\mu$$

The coefficient of variation measures the size of the uncertainty relative to demand. It captures the fact that a product with a mean demand of 100 and a standard deviation of 100 has greater demand uncertainty than a product with a mean demand of 1,000 and a standard deviation of 100. Considering the standard deviation alone cannot capture this difference.

Next, we discuss some measures of supply uncertainty.

Measuring Supply Uncertainty

Supply uncertainty can be described in terms of an order not arriving on time or an order not arriving complete. For our discussion, we will assume that supply uncertainty is described by the uncertainty of the lead time. In other words, we assume that orders arrive complete but the timing

of their arrival is uncertain. To represent supply uncertainty at B&M we assume that lead time is normally distributed with the following inputs:

L: Average lead time

s_L: Standard deviation of lead time

We now evaluate the distribution of demand given uncertain lead times.

EVALUATING DEMAND DISTRIBUTION WITH UNCERTAIN LEAD TIMES Assume that demand for each period i is independent and normally distributed with a mean D_i and standard deviation σ_i. The lead time is assumed to have a mean of L and a standard deviation of s_L. In this case, the total demand during the lead time (which is uncertain) is normally distributed with a mean of D_L and a standard deviation of σ_L, where the following is true:

$$D_L = D \times L; \sigma_L = \sqrt{L\sigma_D^2 + D^2 s_L^2} \tag{12.3}$$

Observe that the uncertainty of lead time increases the σ_L in equation 12.3 relative to equation 12.2 where lead times are fixed.

Next, we describe two replenishment policies that are often used in practice.

Replenishment Policies

A replenishment policy consists of decisions regarding when to reorder and how much to reorder. These decisions determine the cycle and safety inventories along with the fill rate fr and the cycle service level CSL. Replenishment policies may take any of several forms. We restrict attention to two types:

1. *Continuous review:* Inventory is continuously tracked, and an order for a lot size Q is placed when the inventory declines to the reorder point (ROP). As an example, consider the store manager at B&M who continuously tracks the inventory of phones. She orders 600 phones when the inventory drops to ROP = 400. In this case, the size of the order does not change from one order to the next. The time between orders may fluctuate, given variable demand.

2. *Periodic review:* Inventory status is checked at regular periodic intervals, and an order is placed to raise the inventory level to a specified threshold. As an example, consider the purchase of flash drives at B&M. The store manager does not track flash drive inventory continuously. Every Thursday, employees check flash drive inventory, and the manager orders enough so that the total of the available inventory and the size of the order equals 1,000 flash drives. In this case, the time between orders is fixed. The size of each order, however, can fluctuate given variable demand.

These inventory policies are not comprehensive, but they suffice to illustrate the key managerial issues concerning safety inventories. We discuss the periodic review policy in Section 12.6. For all other sections, we restrict attention to the continuous review policy.

SUMMARY OF LEARNING OBJECTIVE 2

Safety inventory is influenced by the desired product availability, demand uncertainty, replenishment lead times, and lead time variability. Product availability is measured using the fill rate or cycle service level. Demand uncertainty is measured by the forecast error. For lead time one measures both the mean and the standard deviation. The required safety inventory is also influenced by the inventory policy implemented. Continuous review policies order a fixed quantity after variable replenishment intervals. Periodic review policies order variable quantities after fixed replenishment intervals.

DETERMINING THE APPROPRIATE LEVEL OF SAFETY INVENTORY

We now discuss the relationship between safety inventory and the desired CSL and *fr*. In this section, we restrict our attention to the continuous review policy. The continuous review policy consists of a lot size Q ordered when the inventory on hand declines to the ROP. Assume that weekly demand is normally distributed, with mean D and standard deviation σ_D. Assume a fixed replenishment lead time of L weeks.

12.3. Evaluate the appropriate level of safety inventory for a supply chain.

Linking Safety Inventory and Cycle Service Level

We first show how cycle service levels can be evaluated given a reorder point (and thus the corresponding safety inventory). We then show how to determine the required safety inventory given a desired cycle service level.

EVALUATING SAFETY INVENTORY GIVEN A REORDER POINT In the case of B&M, safety inventory corresponds to the average number of phones on hand when a replenishment order arrives. Given the lead time of L weeks and a mean weekly demand of D, using Equation 12.2, we have

$$\text{Expected demand during lead time} = D \times L$$

Given that the store manager places a replenishment order when ROP phones are on hand, we have

$$\text{Safety inventory, ss} = ROP - D \times L \qquad \textbf{(12.4)}$$

This is because, on average, $D \times L$ phones will sell over the L weeks between when the order is placed and when the lot arrives. The average safety inventory when the replenishment lot arrives is thus $ROP - D \times L$. The evaluation of safety inventory for a given reorder point is described in Example 12-1 (see spreadsheet *Chapter 12-examples* worksheet *Example 12-1*).

EXAMPLE 12-1	Evaluating Safety Inventory Given a Reorder Point

Assume that weekly demand for phones at B&M Office Supplies is normally distributed, with a mean of 2,500 and a standard deviation of 500. The manufacturer takes two weeks to fill an order placed by the B&M manager. The store manager uses a continuous review policy and orders 10,000 phones when the inventory on hand drops to 6,000. Evaluate the safety inventory and the average inventory carried by B&M. Also evaluate the average time a phone spends at B&M.

Analysis:

Under this replenishment policy, we have

> Average demand per week, $D = 2,500$
>
> Standard deviation of weekly demand, $\sigma_D = 500$
>
> Average lead time for replenishment, $L = 2$ weeks
>
> Reorder point, $ROP = 6,000$
>
> Average lot size, $Q = 10,000$

Using Equation 12.4, we thus have

$$\text{Safety inventory, } ss = ROP - D \times L = 6{,}000 - 5{,}000 = 1{,}000$$

B&M thus carries a safety inventory of 1,000 phones. From Chapter 11, recall that

$$\text{Cycle inventory} = Q/2 = 10{,}000/2 = 5{,}000$$

We thus have

$$\text{Average inventory} = \text{cycle inventory} + \text{safety inventory} = 5{,}000 + 1{,}000 = 6{,}000$$

B&M thus carries an average of 6,000 phones in inventory. Using Little's law (Equation 3.1), we have

$$\text{Average flow time} = \text{average inventory/throughput} = 6{,}000/2{,}500 = 2.4 \text{ weeks}$$

Each phone thus spends an average of 2.4 weeks at B&M.

Next, we discuss how to evaluate the CSL given a replenishment policy.

EVALUATING CYCLE SERVICE LEVEL GIVEN A REORDER POINT Given a replenishment policy, our goal is to evaluate the resulting CSL, the probability of not stocking out in a replenishment cycle. We return to B&M's continuous review replenishment policy of ordering Q units when the inventory on hand drops to the ROP. The lead time is L weeks and weekly demand is normally distributed, with a mean of D and a standard deviation of σ_D. Observe that a stockout occurs in a cycle if demand during the lead time is larger than the ROP. Thus, we have

$$CSL = \text{Prob(demand during lead time of } L \text{ weeks} \leq ROP)$$

To evaluate this probability, we need to obtain the distribution of demand during the lead time. From Equation 12.2, we know that demand during lead time is normally distributed, with a mean of D_L and a standard deviation of σ_L. Using the notation for the normal distribution from Appendix 12A and the equivalent Excel function from Equation 12.22 in Appendix 12B, the CSL is

$$CSL = F(ROP, D_L, \sigma_L) = NORMDIST(ROP, D_L, \sigma_L, 1) \qquad \textbf{(12.5)}$$

We now illustrate this evaluation in Example 12-2 (see worksheet *Example 12-2*).

EXAMPLE 12-2	**Evaluating Cycle Service Level Given a Reorder Point**

Weekly demand for phones at B&M is normally distributed, with a mean of 2,500 and a standard deviation of 500. The replenishment lead time is two weeks. Assume that the demand is independent from one week to the next. Evaluate the CSL resulting from a policy of ordering 10,000 phones when there are 6,000 phones in inventory.

Analysis:

In this case, we have

$$Q = 10{,}000, ROP = 6{,}000, L = 2 \text{ weeks}$$
$$D = 2{,}500/\text{week}, \sigma_D = 500$$

Observe that B&M runs the risk of stocking out during the lead time of two weeks between when an order is placed and when the replenishment arrives. Thus, whether or not a stockout occurs depends on the demand during the lead time of two weeks.

Because demand across time is independent, we use Equation 12.2 to obtain demand during the lead time to be normally distributed with a mean of D_L and a standard deviation of σ_L, where

$$D_L = D \times L = 2 \times 2{,}500 = 5{,}000, \quad \sigma_L = \sqrt{L}\sigma_D = \sqrt{2} \times 500 = 707$$

Using Equation 12.5, the CSL is evaluated as

$$CSL = F(ROP, D_L, \sigma_L) = NORMDIST(ROP, D_L, \sigma_L, 1)$$
$$= NORMDIST(6000, 5000, 707, 1) = 0.92$$

A CSL of 0.92 implies that in 92 percent of the replenishment cycles, B&M supplies all demand from available inventory. In the remaining 8 percent of the cycles, stockouts occur and some demand is not satisfied because of the lack of inventory.

We now discuss how the appropriate level of safety inventory may be obtained given a desired CSL.

Evaluating Safety Inventory Given Desired Cycle Service Level

In many practical settings, firms have a desired level of product availability and want to design replenishment polices that achieve this level. For example, Carrefour has a desired level of product availability for each product sold in a store. The store manager must design a replenishment policy with the appropriate level of safety inventory to meet this goal. The desired level of product availability may be determined by trading off the cost of holding inventory with the cost of a stockout. This trade-off is discussed in detail in Chapter 13. In other instances, the desired level of product availability (in terms of CSL or fill rate) is stated explicitly in contracts, and management must design replenishment policies that achieve the desired target.

EVALUATING REQUIRED SAFETY INVENTORY GIVEN DESIRED CYCLE SERVICE LEVEL Our goal is to obtain the appropriate level of safety inventory given the desired CSL. We assume that a continuous review replenishment policy is followed. Consider the store manager at Carrefour responsible for designing replenishment policies for all products in the store. He has targeted a CSL for the basic box of Lego building blocks. Given a lead time of L, the store manager wants to identify a suitable reorder point ROP and safety inventory that achieves the desired service level. Assume that demand for Legos at Carrefour is normally distributed and independent from one week to the next. We assume the following inputs:

Desired cycle service level $= CSL$

Mean demand during lead time $= D_L$

Standard deviation of demand during lead time $= \sigma_L$

From Equation 12.4, recall that $ROP = D_L + ss$. The store manager needs to identify safety inventory ss such that the following is true:

$$\text{Probability(demand during lead time} \leq D_L + ss) = CSL$$

Given that demand is normally distributed, the store manager must identify safety inventory ss such that the following is true (using Equation 12.5):

$$F(D_L + ss, D_L, \sigma_L) = CSL$$

Given the definition of the inverse normal in Appendix 12A and the equivalent Excel function from Appendix 12B, we obtain

$$D_L + ss = F^{-1}(CSL, D_L, \sigma_L) = NORMINV(CSL, D_L, \sigma_L)$$
$$\text{or } ss = F^{-1}(CSL, D_L, \sigma_L) - D_L = NORMINV(CSL, D_L, \sigma_L) - D_L$$

Using the definition of the standard normal distribution and its inverse from Appendix 12A, and the equivalent Excel function from Appendix 12B, it can also be shown that the following is true:

$$ss = F_s^{-1}(CSL) \times \sigma_L = F_s^{-1}(CSL) \times \sqrt{L}\sigma_D = NORMSINV(CSL) \times \sqrt{L}\sigma_D \quad \textbf{(12.6)}$$

In Example 12-3 (see worksheet *Example 12-3*), we illustrate the evaluation of safety inventory given a desired CSL.

EXAMPLE 12-3	Evaluating Safety Inventory Given a Desired Cycle Service Level

Weekly demand for Legos at a Carrefour store is normally distributed, with a mean of 2,500 boxes and a standard deviation of 500. The replenishment lead time is two weeks. Assuming a continuous-review replenishment policy, evaluate the safety inventory that the store should carry to achieve a CSL of 90 percent.

Analysis:

In this case we have

$$D = 2{,}500/\text{week}, \sigma_D = 500, CSL = 0.9, L = 2 \text{ weeks}$$

Because demand across time is independent, we use Equation 12.2 to find demand during the lead time to be normally distributed with a mean of D_L and a standard deviation of σ_L, where

$$D_L = D \times L = 2 \times 2{,}500 = 5{,}000; \quad \sigma_L = \sqrt{L}\sigma_D = \sqrt{2} \times 500 = 707$$

Using Equation 12.6, we obtain

$$ss = F_s^{-1}(CSL) \times \sigma_L = NORMSINV(CSL) \times \sigma_L = NORMSINV(0.90) \times 707 = 906$$

Thus, the required safety inventory to achieve a CSL of 90 percent is 906 boxes.

Linking Safety Inventory and Fill Rate

We now show how fill rate can be evaluated given a reorder point (and thus the corresponding safety inventory). We then show how to determine the required safety inventory given a desired fill rate.

EVALUATING FILL RATE GIVEN A REORDER POINT Recall that fill rate measures the proportion of customer demand that is satisfied from available inventory. In practice, fill rate is generally a more relevant measure than cycle service level because it allows the retailer to estimate the fraction of demand that is turned into sales. The two measures are closely related, as raising the cycle service level also raises the fill rate for a firm. Our discussion focuses on evaluating fill rate for a continuous review policy under which Q units are ordered when the quantity on hand drops to the ROP.

To evaluate the fill rate, it is important to understand the process by which a stockout occurs during a replenishment cycle. A stockout occurs if the demand during the lead time exceeds the ROP. We thus need to evaluate the average amount of demand in excess of the ROP in each replenishment cycle.

The *expected shortage per replenishment cycle* (ESC) is the average units of demand that are not satisfied from inventory in stock per replenishment cycle. Given a lot size of Q (which is also the average demand in a replenishment cycle), the fraction of demand lost is thus ESC/Q.

The product fill rate fr is thus given by

$$fr = 1 - ESC/Q = (Q - ESC)Q \tag{12.7}$$

A shortage occurs in a replenishment cycle only if the demand during the lead time exceeds the ROP. Let $f(x)$ be the density function of the demand distribution during the lead time. The ESC is given by

$$ESC = \int_{x=ROP}^{\infty} (x - ROP)f(x)dx \tag{12.8}$$

	A	B	C	D	E
1	*Inputs*				
2	Q	D	σ_D	L	ss
3	10,000	2,500	500	2	1,000
4	*Distribution of demand during lead time*				
5	D_L	σ_L			
6	5,000	707			
7	*Cycle Service Level and Fill Rate*				
8	CSL	ESC	*fr*		
9	0.92	25.13	0.9975		

Cell	Cell Formula	Equation
A6	=B3*D3	12.2
B6	=SQRT(D3)*C3	12.2
A9	=NORMDIST(A6+E3, A6, B6, 1)	12.5
B9	=-E3*(1-NORMDIST(E3/B6, 0, 1, 1)) + B6*NORMDIST(E3/B6, 0, 1, 0)	12.10
C9	=(A3-B9)/A3	12.7

Figure 12-2 Excel Solution of Example 12-4

When demand during the lead time is normally distributed with mean D_L and standard deviation σ_L given a safety inventory ss, Equation 12.8 can be simplified to

$$ESC = -ss\left[1 - F_s\left(\frac{ss}{\sigma_L}\right)\right] + \sigma_L f_s\left(\frac{ss}{\sigma_L}\right) \tag{12.9}$$

where F_s is the standard normal cumulative distribution function and f_s is the standard normal density function. The standard normal distribution has a mean of 0 and a standard deviation of 1. A detailed description of the normal distribution is given in Appendix 12A. Details of the simplification in Equation 12.9 are described in Appendix 12C. Using Excel functions (Equations 12.25 and 12.26) discussed in Appendix 12B, ESC may be evaluated (using Equation 12.9) as

$$ESC = -ss[1 - NORMDIST(ss/\sigma_L, 0, 1, 1)]$$
$$+ \sigma_L NORMDIST(ss/\sigma_L, 0, 1, 0) \tag{12.10}$$

Given the ESC, we can use Equation 12.7 to evaluate the fill rate *fr*. Next, we illustrate this evaluation in Example 12-4 (see worksheet *Example 12-4* and Figure 12-2).

EXAMPLE 12-4 **Evaluating Fill Rate Given a Reorder Point**

From Example 12-2, recall that weekly demand for phones at B&M is normally distributed, with a mean of 2,500 and a standard deviation of 500. The replenishment lead time is two weeks. Assume that the demand is independent from one week to the next. Evaluate the fill rate resulting from the policy of ordering 10,000 phones when there are 6,000 phones in inventory.

Analysis:

From the analysis of Example 12-2, we have

Lot size, $Q = 10,000$

Average demand during lead time, $D_L = 5,000$

Standard deviation of demand during lead time, $\sigma_L = 707$

Using Equation 12.4, we obtain

$$\text{Safety inventory, } ss = ROP - D_L = 6{,}000 - 5{,}000 = 1{,}000$$

From Equation 12.10, we thus have

$$ESC = -1{,}000[1 - NORMDIST(1{,}000/707, 0, 1, 1)]$$
$$+ 707\, NORMDIST(1{,}000/707, 0, 1, 0) = 25$$

Thus, on average, in each replenishment cycle, 25 phones are demanded by customers but not available in inventory. Using Equation 12.7, we thus obtain the following fill rate:

$$fr = (Q - ESC)/Q = (10{,}000 - 25)/10{,}000 = 0.9975$$

In other words, 99.75 percent of the demand is filled from inventory in stock. This is much higher than the CSL of 92 percent that resulted in Example 12-2 for the same replenishment policy.

A few key observations should be made. First, observe that the fill rate (0.9975) in Example 12-4 is significantly higher than the CSL (0.92) in Example 12-2 for the same replenishment policy. Next, by rerunning the examples with a different lot size (in worksheet *Example 12-4*), we can observe the impact of lot-size changes on the service level. Increasing the lot size of phones from 10,000 to 20,000 has no impact on the CSL (which stays at 0.92). The fill rate, however, now increases to 0.9987. This happens because an increase in lot size results in fewer replenishment cycles. In the case of B&M, an increase in lot size from 10,000 to 20,000 results in replenishment occurring once every eight weeks instead of once every four weeks. With a 92 percent CSL, a lot size of 10,000 results in, on average, one cycle with a stockout per year. With a lot size of 20,000, we have, on average, one stockout every two years. Thus, the fill rate is higher.

EVALUATING REQUIRED SAFETY INVENTORY GIVEN DESIRED FILL RATE For a continuous review replenishment policy, we now evaluate the required safety inventory given a desired fill rate *fr*. Consider the store manager at Carrefour targeting a fill rate *fr* for Lego building blocks. The current replenishment lot size is *Q*. The first step is to obtain the ESC using Equation 12.7.

The next step is to obtain a safety inventory *ss* that solves Equation 12.9 (and its Excel equivalent, Equation 12.10) given the ESC evaluated earlier. It is not possible to give a formula that provides the answer. The appropriate safety inventory that solves Equation 12.10 can be obtained easily using Excel and trying different values of *ss*. In Excel, the safety inventory may also be obtained directly using the tool *GOALSEEK*, as illustrated in Example 12-5 (use worksheet *Example 12-5*).

| EXAMPLE 12-5 | **Evaluating Safety Inventory Given Desired Fill Rate** |

Weekly demand for Legos at a Carrefour store is normally distributed, with a mean of 2,500 boxes and a standard deviation of 500. The replenishment lead time is two weeks. The store manager currently orders replenishment lots of 10,000 boxes from Lego. Assuming a continuous-review replenishment policy, evaluate the safety inventory the store should carry to achieve a fill rate of 97.5 percent.

Analysis:

In this case, we have

Desired fill rate, $fr = 0.975$

Lot size, $Q = 10{,}000$ boxes

Standard deviation of demand during lead time, $\sigma_L = \sqrt{2} \times 500 = 707$

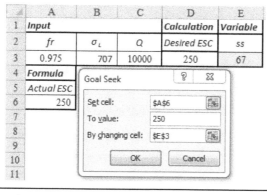

	A	B	C	D	E
1	Input			Calculation	Variable
2	fr	σ_L	Q	Desired ESC	ss
3	0.975	707	10000	250	67
4	Formula				
5	Actual ESC				
6	250				
7					
8					
9					
10					
11					

Goal Seek

Set cell: A6

To value: 250

By changing cell: E3

OK Cancel

Cell	Cell Formula	Equation
A6	-E3*(1-NORMSDIST(E3/B3, 0, 1,1)) + B3*NORMDIST(E3/B3, 0, 1, 0)	12.10

Figure 12-3 Spreadsheet to Solve for *ss* Using *GOALSEEK*

From Equation 12.7, we thus obtain an ESC as

$$ESC = (1 - fr)Q = (1 - 0.975)10{,}000 = 250$$

Now we need to solve Equation 12.9 for the safety inventory ss, where

$$ESC = 250 = -ss\left[1 - F_s\left(\frac{ss}{\sigma_L}\right)\right] + \sigma_L f_s\left(\frac{ss}{\sigma_L}\right) = -ss\left[1 - F_s\left(\frac{ss}{707}\right)\right] + 707 f_s\left(\frac{ss}{707}\right)$$

Using Equation 12.10, this equation may be restated with Excel functions as follows:

$$250 = -ss[1 - NORMDIST(ss/707, 0, 1, 1)] + 707\,NORMDIST(ss/707, 0, 1, 0) \qquad \textbf{(12.11)}$$

Equation 12.11 may be solved in Excel by trying different values of *ss* until the equation is satisfied. A more elegant approach for solving Equation 12.11 is to use the Excel tool *GOALSEEK*, as follows.

In the worksheet *Example 12-5*, invoke *GOALSEEK* using Data | What-If Analysis| Goal Seek. In the *GOALSEEK* dialog box, enter the data as shown in Figure 12-3 and click the OK button. In this case, cell E3 is changed until the value of the formula in cell A6 equals 250.

Using *GOALSEEK*, we obtain a safety inventory of *ss* = 67 boxes, as shown in Figure 12-3. Thus, the store manager at Carrefour should target a safety inventory of 67 boxes to achieve the desired fill rate of 97.5 percent.

Impact of Desired Product Availability, Lead Time, and Demand Uncertainty on Safety Inventory

Three key factors that affect the required level of safety inventory are the desired level of product availability, lead time, and demand uncertainty. We now discuss the impact that each factor has on the safety inventory.

As the desired product availability goes up, the required safety inventory also increases because the supply chain must now be able to accommodate uncommonly high demand. For the Carrefour situation in Example 12-5, we evaluate the required safety inventory for varying levels of fill rate as shown in Table 12-1.

Observe that raising the fill rate from 97.5 percent to 98.0 percent requires an additional 116 units of safety inventory, whereas raising the fill rate from 99.0 percent to 99.5 percent requires an additional 268 units of safety inventory. Thus, the marginal increase in safety

TABLE 12-1 Required Safety Inventory for Different Values of Fill Rate

Fill Rate	Safety Inventory
97.5%	67
98.0%	183
98.5%	321
99.0%	499
99.5%	767

inventory grows as product availability rises. This phenomenon highlights the importance of selecting suitable product availability levels. It is important for a supply chain manager to be aware of the products that require a high level of availability and hold high safety inventories only for those products. It is not appropriate to select a high level of product availability and require it arbitrarily for all products.

From Equation 12.6, we see that the required safety inventory *ss* is also influenced by the standard deviation of demand during the lead time, σ_L. The standard deviation of demand during the lead time is influenced by the duration of the lead time L and the standard deviation of periodic demand σ_D, as shown in Equation 12.2. The relationship between safety inventory and σ_D is linear, in that a 10 percent increase in σ_D results in a 10 percent increase in safety inventory. Safety inventory also increases with an increase in lead time L. The safety inventory, however, is proportional to the square root of the lead time (if demand is independent over time) and thus grows more slowly than the lead time itself.

A goal of any supply chain manager is to reduce the level of safety inventory required in a way that does not adversely affect product availability. The previous discussion highlights two key managerial levers that may be used to achieve this goal:

1. *Reduce the supplier lead time L:* If lead time decreases by a factor of k, the required safety inventory decreases by a factor of $\sqrt{k}$. The only caveat here is that reducing the supplier lead time requires significant effort from the supplier, whereas reduction in safety inventory occurs at the retailer. Thus, it is important for the retailer to share some of the resulting benefits, as discussed in Chapter 10. Walmart, Seven-Eleven Japan, and many other retailers apply tremendous pressure on their suppliers to reduce the replenishment lead time. Apparel retailer Zara has built its entire strategy around using local flexible production to reduce replenishment lead times. In each case, the benefit has manifested itself in the form of reduced safety inventory while maintaining the desired level of product availability.

2. *Reduce the underlying uncertainty of demand (represented by σ_D):* If uncertainty represented by σ_D is reduced by a factor of k, the required safety inventory also decreases by a factor of k. A reduction in uncertainty may be achieved by better market intelligence, increased supply chain visibility, and the use of more sophisticated forecasting methods. Seven-Eleven Japan provides its store managers with detailed data about prior demand along with weather and other factors that may influence demand. This market intelligence allows the store managers to make better forecasts, reducing uncertainty. In most supply chains, however, the key to reducing the underlying forecast uncertainty is to link all forecasts throughout the supply chain to customer demand data. A lot of the demand uncertainty exists only because each stage of the supply chain plans and forecasts independently. This distorts demand throughout the supply chain, increasing uncertainty. Improved visibility and coordination, as discussed in Chapter 10, can often reduce the demand uncertainty significantly. Zara plans its production and replenishment based on actual sales at its

retail stores to ensure that no unnecessary uncertainties are introduced. Both Walmart and Seven-Eleven Japan share demand information with their suppliers, reducing uncertainty and thus safety inventory within the supply chain.

We illustrate the benefits of reducing lead time and demand uncertainty in Example 12-6 (see worksheet *Example 12-6*).

EXAMPLE 12-6 **Benefits of Reducing Lead Time and Demand Uncertainty**

Weekly demand for white shirts at a Target store is normally distributed, with a mean of 2,500 and a standard deviation of 800. The replenishment lead time from the current supplier is nine weeks. The store manager aims for a cycle service level of 95 percent. What savings in safety inventory can the store expect if the supplier reduces lead time to one week? What savings in safety inventory can the store expect if reduced demand uncertainty results in a standard deviation of demand of 400?

Analysis:

For the base case, we have

$$D = 2{,}500/\text{week}, \sigma_D = 800, CSL = 0.95$$

From Equation 12.6, we thus obtain the base case safety inventory to be

$$ss = NORMSINV(CSL) \times \sqrt{L}\sigma_D = NORMSINV(.95) \times \sqrt{9} \times 800 = 3{,}948$$

If the suppler reduces the lead time L to one week, the required safety inventory is given by

$$ss = NORMSINV(CSL) \times \sqrt{L}\sigma_D = NOMSINV(.95) \times \sqrt{1} \times 800 = 1{,}316$$

Thus, reducing the lead time from nine weeks to one week reduces the required safety inventory by 2,632 shirts.

We now consider the benefits of reducing forecast error. If Target reduces the standard deviation from 800 to 400 (for the nine-week lead time), the required safety inventory is obtained as follows:

$$ss = NORMSINV(CSL) \times \sqrt{L}\sigma_D = NORMSINV(.95) \times \sqrt{9} \times 400 = 1{,}974$$

Thus, reducing the standard deviation (equal to forecast error) of demand from 800 to 400 reduces the required safety inventory by 1,974 shirts.

Adjusting Safety Inventory for Demand Lumpiness and Seasonality

In practice, a manufacturer or distributor does not order one unit at a time but orders in large lots. Thus, demand observed by different stages of the supply chain tends to be lumpy. Lumpiness adds to the variability of demand. For example, when using a continuous review policy, lumpiness may lead to inventory dropping far below the ROP before a replenishment order is placed. On average, inventory will drop below the ROP by half the average size of an order. The lumpiness can be accounted for in practice by raising the safety inventory suggested by the models discussed earlier by half the average size of a customer order.

In practice, demand is often seasonal, with the mean and the standard deviation of demand varying by the time of year. Thus, fixing the ROP for the entire year can lead to stockouts during the peak season because a given ROP may correspond to ten days of demand during the low-demand season and only two days of demand during the peak demand season. If the lead time is one week, stockouts are certain to occur during the peak season. In the presence of seasonality, it is best to evaluate all inventory parameters such as ROP in terms of days of demand.

A simple heuristic that keeps the ROP constant in terms of days of demand helps account for seasonality by automatically adjusting the ROP (and thus the safety inventory) based on seasonal demand.

SUMMARY OF LEARNING OBJECTIVE 3

Given a desired cycle service level *CSL*, a lead time *L*, and a standard deviation of periodic demand σ_D, the required safety inventory *ss* for a continuous review policy is given by *ss* = NORMSINV(*CSL*) × $\sqrt{L}\sigma_D$. Given a reorder point *ROP*, a lead time *L*, a standard deviation of periodic demand σ_D, and periodic demand *D*, the resulting cycle service level is given by *CSL* = NORMDIST(*ROP*, *D* × *L*, $\sqrt{L}\sigma_D$, 1). Given a level of safety inventory, one can evaluate the resulting fill rate. Given a desired fill rate, one can evaluate the required safety inventory. The required safety inventory increases with an increase in desired product availability, lead time, and uncertainty of periodic demand. In practice, it is best to evaluate safety inventory in terms of days of demand to account for seasonality of demand.

12.4. *Discuss the impact of supply uncertainty on safety inventory.*

IMPACT OF SUPPLY UNCERTAINTY ON SAFETY INVENTORY

In our discussion to this point, we have focused on situations with demand uncertainty in the form of a forecast error. In many practical situations, supply uncertainty also plays a significant role. The impact of supply uncertainty is well illustrated by the impact of the grounding of MSC *Napoli* on the south coast of Britain in January 2007. The container ship was carrying more than 1,000 tons of nickel, a key ingredient of stainless steel. Given that 1,000 tons was almost 20 percent of the 5,052 tons of nickel then stored in warehouses globally, this delay in bringing nickel to market resulted in significant shortages and raised the price of nickel by about 20 percent in the first 3.5 weeks of January 2007. Supply uncertainty arises because of many factors, including production delays, transportation delays, and quality problems. Supply chains must account for supply uncertainty when planning safety inventories.

In this section, we incorporate supply uncertainty by assuming that lead time is uncertain and identify the impact of lead time uncertainty on safety inventories. Assume that the customer demand per period for tablets at Amazon and the replenishment lead time from the supplier are normally distributed. We are provided the following inputs:

D: Average demand per period

σ_D: Standard deviation of demand per period

L: Average lead time for replenishment

s_L: Standard deviation of lead time

We consider the safety inventory requirements given that Amazon follows a continuous review policy to manage tablet inventory. Amazon experiences a stockout of product if demand during the lead time exceeds the ROP—that is, the quantity on hand when Amazon places a replenishment order. Thus, we need to identify the distribution of customer demand during the uncertain lead time. Given that both lead time and periodic demand are uncertain, demand during the lead time is normally distributed with a mean of D_L and a standard deviation σ_L, where D_L and σ_L are evaluated as in Equation 12.3 to be

$$D_L = D \times L; \sigma_L = \sqrt{L\sigma_D^2 + D^2 s_L^2}$$

Given the distribution of demand during the lead time in Equation 12.3 and a desired CSL, Amazon can obtain the required safety inventory using Equation 12.6. If product availability is specified as a fill rate, Amazon can obtain the required safety inventory using the procedure outlined in Example 12-5. In Example 12-7, we illustrate the impact of lead time uncertainty on the required level of safety inventory at Amazon (see worksheet *Example 12-7*).

| EXAMPLE 12-7 | **Impact of Lead Time Uncertainty on Safety Inventory** |

Daily demand for tablets at Amazon is normally distributed, with a mean of 2,500 and a standard deviation of 500. The tablet supplier takes an average of $L = 7$ days to replenish inventory at Amazon. Amazon is targeting a CSL of 90 percent (providing a fill rate close to 100 percent) for its tablet inventory. Evaluate the safety inventory of tablets that Amazon must carry if the standard deviation of the lead time is seven days. Amazon is working with the supplier to reduce the standard deviation to zero. Evaluate the reduction in safety inventory that Amazon can expect as a result of this initiative.

Analysis:

In this case, we have

Average demand per period, $D = 2,500$

Standard deviation of demand per period, $\sigma_D = 500$

Average lead time for replenishment, $L = 7$ days

Standard deviation of lead time, $s_L = 7$ days

We first evaluate the distribution of demand during the lead time. Using Equation 12.3, we have

$$\text{Mean demand during lead time, } D_L = D \times L = 2,500 \times 7 = 17,500$$

$$\text{Standard deviation of demand during lead time, } \sigma_L = \sqrt{L\sigma_D^2 + D^2 s_L^2}$$

$$= \sqrt{7 \times 500^2 + 2,500^2 \times 7^2} = 17,550$$

The required safety inventory is obtained using Equations 12.6 and 12.27, as follows:

$$ss = NORMSINV(CSL) \times \sigma_L = NORMSINV(0.90) \times 17,550 = 22,491 \text{ tablets}$$

If the standard deviation of lead time is seven days, Amazon must carry a safety inventory of 22,491 tablets. This is equivalent to about nine days of demand for tablets.

In Table 12-2, we provide the required safety inventory as Amazon works with the supplier to reduce the standard deviation of lead time (s_L) from six down to zero. From Table 12-2, observe that the reduction in lead time uncertainty allows Amazon to reduce its safety inventory of tablets by a significant amount. As the standard deviation of lead time declines from seven days to zero, the amount of safety inventory declines from about nine days of demand to less than a day of demand.

TABLE 12-2 Required Safety Inventory as a Function of Lead Time Uncertainty

s_L	σ_L	ss **(units)**	ss **(days)**
6	15,058	19,298	7.72
5	12,570	16,109	6.44
4	10,087	12,927	5.17
3	7,616	9,760	3.90
2	5,172	6,628	2.65
1	2,828	3,625	1.45
0	1,323	1,695	0.68

The preceding example emphasizes the impact of lead time variability on safety inventory requirements (and thus material flow time) and the large potential benefits from reducing lead time variability or improving on-time deliveries. Often, safety inventory calculations in practice do not include any measure of supply uncertainty, resulting in levels that may be lower than required. This hurts product availability.

In practice, variability of supply lead time is caused by practices at both the supplier and the customer. Suppliers sometimes have poor planning tools that do not allow them to schedule production in a way that can be executed. Today, most supply chain planning software suites have good production planning tools that allow suppliers to promise lead times that can be met. This helps reduce lead time variability. The lack of visibility for a supplier into future customer plans is also a significant factor that increases supply chain uncertainty. W.W. Grainger was able to get its suppliers to reduce both lead time and lead time variability by sharing its future plans with them. This allowed suppliers to schedule Grainger orders into production without waiting for the orders to actually arrive. The quantity produced was finalized closer to actual production. In other instances, the behavior of the customer often increases lead time variability. In one instance, a distributor placed orders to all its suppliers on the same day of the week. As a result, all deliveries arrived on the same day of the week. The surge in deliveries made it impossible for all of them to be recorded into inventory on the day they arrived. This led to a perception that supply lead times were long and variable. Just by leveling out the orders over the week, the lead time and the lead time variability were significantly reduced, allowing the distributor to reduce its safety inventory.

SUMMARY OF LEARNING OBJECTIVE 4

An increase in supply uncertainty significantly increases the amount of safety inventory required for a given level of product availability. Lead time uncertainty has a more significant impact on the required safety inventory than lead time itself. A reduction in supply uncertainty can help to dramatically reduce the required safety inventory without hurting product availability.

12.5. Understand how aggregation helps reduce the required safety inventory in a supply chain.

IMPACT OF AGGREGATION ON SAFETY INVENTORY

Aggregation is one of the most important mechanisms through which a supply chain can reduce safety inventory required. In practice, supply chains have varying degrees of inventory aggregation. For example, Barnes & Noble sells books from retail stores with inventory geographically distributed across the country. Amazon, in contrast, ships its books from a few facilities. Seven-Eleven Japan has many small convenience stores densely distributed across Japan. In contrast, supermarkets tend to be much larger, with fewer outlets that are not as densely distributed. Redbox rents its movies from tens of thousands of kiosks distributed across the United States. In contrast, Netflix centralizes its DVD inventory at fewer than fifty distribution centers. Our goal is to understand how aggregation in each of these cases affects forecast accuracy and safety inventories.

Consider k regions, with demand in each region normally distributed with the following characteristics:

D_i: Mean periodic demand in region i, $i = 1, \ldots, k$

σ_i: Standard deviation of periodic demand in region i, $i = 1, \ldots, k$

ρ_{ij}: Correlation of periodic demand for regions i, j, $1 \leq i \neq j \leq k$

There are two ways to serve demand in the k regions. One is to have local inventories in each region and the other is to aggregate all inventories into one centralized facility. Our goal is to

compare safety inventories in the two cases. With a replenishment lead time of L and a desired cycle service level CSL, the total safety inventory in the decentralized case is (using Equation 12.6):

$$\text{Total safety inventory in decentralized option} = \sum_{i=1}^{k} F_s^{-1}(CSL) \times \sqrt{L} \times \sigma_i \quad \textbf{(12.12)}$$

If all inventories are aggregated in a central location, we need to evaluate the distribution of aggregated demand. The aggregate demand is normally distributed, with a mean of D^C, standard deviation of σ_D^C, and a variance of $\text{var}(D^C)$, as follows:

$$D^C = \sum_{i=1}^{k} D_i; \quad \text{var}(D^C) = \sum_{i=1}^{k} \sigma_i^2 + 2\sum_{i>j} \rho_{ij}\sigma_i\sigma_j; \quad \sigma_D^C = \sqrt{\text{var}(D^C)} \quad \textbf{(12.13)}$$

Observe that Equation 12.13 is like Equation 12.1 except that we are aggregating across k regions rather than L periods. If all k regions have demand that is identically distributed, with mean D and standard deviation σ_D, and have the same correlation ρ, Equation 12.13 can be simplified as

$$D^C = kD; \sigma_D^C = \sqrt{k\sigma^2 + k(k-1)\rho\sigma^2} \quad \textbf{(12.14)}$$

If all k regions have demand that is independent ($\rho_{ij} = 0$) and identically distributed, with mean D and standard deviation σ_D, Equation 12.14 can be simplified as

$$D^C = kD; \sigma_D^C = \sqrt{k}\sigma_D \quad \textbf{(12.15)}$$

Using Equations 12.6 and 12.13, the required safety inventory at the centralized location is given as

$$\text{Required safety inventory on aggregation} = F_s^{-1}(CSL) \times \sqrt{L} \times \sigma_D^C \quad \textbf{(12.16)}$$

The holding cost savings on aggregation per unit sold are obtained by dividing the savings in holding cost by the total demand kD. If H is the holding cost per unit, using Equations 12.12 and 12.16, the holding cost savings on aggregation per unit sold are

Holding cost saving on aggregation per unit sold

$$= \frac{F_s^{-1}(CSL) \times \sqrt{L} \times H}{D^C} \times \left(\sum_{i=1}^{k} \sigma_i - \sigma_D^C \right) \quad \textbf{(12.17)}$$

From Equation 12.13, it follows that the difference $\left(\sum_{i=1}^{k} \sigma_i - \sigma_D^C \right)$ is influenced by the correlation coefficients ρ_{ij}. This difference is large when the correlation coefficients are close to -1 (negative correlation) and shrinks as they approach $+1$ (positive correlation). Inventory savings on aggregation are always positive as long as the correlation coefficients are less than 1. From Equation 12.17, we thus draw the following conclusions regarding the value of aggregation:

- The safety inventory savings on aggregation increase with the desired cycle service level CSL.
- The safety inventory savings on aggregation increase with the replenishment lead time L.
- The safety inventory savings on aggregation increase with the holding cost H.
- The safety inventory savings on aggregation increase with the coefficient of variation (σ_D/D) of demand.
- The safety inventory savings on aggregation decrease as the correlation coefficients increase.

In Example 12-8 (see worksheet *Example 12-8*), we illustrate the inventory savings on aggregation and the impact of the correlation coefficient on these savings.

| EXAMPLE 12-8 | **Impact of Correlation on Value of Aggregation** |

A BMW dealership has $k = 4$ retail outlets serving the entire Chicago area (disaggregate option). Weekly demand at each outlet is normally distributed, with a mean of $D = 25$ cars and a standard deviation of $\sigma_D = 5$. The lead time for replenishment from the manufacturer is $L = 2$ weeks. Each outlet covers a separate geographic area, and the correlation of demand across any pair of areas is ρ. The dealership is considering the possibility of replacing the four outlets with a single large outlet (aggregate option). Assume that the demand in the central outlet is the sum of the demand across all four areas. The dealership is targeting a CSL of 0.90. Compare the level of safety inventory needed in the two options as the correlation coefficient ρ varies between 0 and 1.

Analysis:

We provide a detailed analysis for the case when demand in each area is independent (i.e., $\rho = 0$). For each retail outlet we have

Standard deviation of weekly demand, $\sigma_D = 5$

Replenishment lead time, $L = 2$ weeks

Using Equation 12.12, the required safety inventory in the decentralized option for $CSL = 0.90$ is

$$\text{Total required safety inventory, } ss = k \times F_s^{-1}(CSL) \times \sqrt{L} \times \sigma_D$$
$$= 4 \times F_s^{-1}(0.9) \times \sqrt{2} \times 5 = 4 \times NORMSINV(0.9) \times \sqrt{2} \times 5 = 36.25 \text{ cars}$$

Now, consider the aggregate option. Using Equation 12.14, the standard deviation of aggregate weekly demand is

$$\text{Standard deviation of weekly demand at central outlet, } \sigma_D^C = \sqrt{4 \times 5^2 + 4 \times 3 \times 5^2 \times \rho}$$

For a CSL of 0.90 and $\rho = 0$, safety inventory required for the aggregate option (using Equation 12.16) is given as

$$ss = F_s^{-1}(0.90) \times \sqrt{L} \times \sigma_D^C = NORMSINV(0.90) \times \sqrt{2} \times 10 = 18.12$$

Using Equations 12.12 to 12.16, the required level of safety inventory for the disaggregate as well as the aggregate option can be obtained for different values of ρ as shown in Table 12-3 using worksheet *Example 12-8*. Observe that the safety inventory for the disaggregate option is higher than for the aggregate option except when all demands are perfectly positively correlated. The benefit of aggregation decreases as demand in different areas is more positively correlated.

TABLE 12-3 Safety Inventory in the Disaggregate and Aggregate Options

ρ	Disaggregate Safety Inventory	Aggregate Safety Inventory
0	36.25	18.12
0.2	36.25	22.93
0.4	36.25	26.88
0.6	36.25	30.33
0.8	36.25	33.42
1.0	36.25	36.25

Example 12-8 and the previous discussion demonstrate that aggregation reduces demand uncertainty—and, thus, the required safety inventory—as long as the demand being aggregated is not perfectly positively correlated. Demand for most products does not show perfect positive correlation across different geographic regions. Products such as heating oil are likely to have demand that is positively correlated across nearby regions. In contrast, products such as milk and sugar are likely to have demand that is much more independent across regions. If demand in different geographic regions is about the same size and independent, aggregation reduces safety inventory by the square root of the number of regions aggregated. In other words, if the number of independent stocking locations decreases by a factor of n, the average safety inventory is expected to decrease by a factor of $\sqrt{n}$. This principle is referred to as the *square-root law* and is illustrated in Figure 12-4.

Most online retailers exploit the benefits of aggregation in terms of reduced inventories. For example, Blue Nile sells diamonds online and serves the entire United States out of one warehouse. As a result, it has lower levels of diamond inventories than jewelry chains such as Tiffany and Zales, which must keep inventory in every retail store.

There are situations, however, in which physical aggregation of inventories in one location may not be optimal. There are two major disadvantages of aggregating all inventories in one location:

1. Increase in response time to customer order
2. Increase in transportation cost to customer

Both disadvantages result because the average distance between the inventory and the customer increases with aggregation. Either the customer must travel farther to reach the product or the product must be shipped over longer distances to reach the customer. A retail chain such as Gap has the option of building many small retail outlets or a few large ones. Gap tends to have many smaller outlets distributed evenly in a region because this strategy reduces the distance that customers travel to reach a store. If Gap had one large centralized outlet, the average distance that customers need to travel would increase, and thus the response time would increase. A desire to decrease customer response time is thus the impetus for the firm to have multiple outlets. Another example is McMaster-Carr, a distributor of MRO supplies. McMaster-Carr uses UPS for shipping product to customers. Because shipping charges are based on distance, having one centralized warehouse increases the average shipping cost as well as the response time to the customer. Thus, McMaster-Carr has five warehouses that allow it to provide next-day delivery using ground transportation to a large fraction of the United States. Next-day delivery by UPS would not be feasible at a reasonable cost if McMaster-Carr had only one warehouse. Even Amazon,

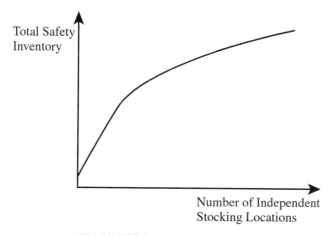

Figure 12-4 Square-Root Law

which started with one warehouse in Seattle, has added more warehouses in other parts of the United States in an effort to improve response time and reduce transportation cost to the customer. We illustrate the trade-offs of centralization in Example 12-9 (see worksheet *Example 12-9*).

EXAMPLE 12-9 Trade-Offs of Physical Centralization

The Shanghai branch office of an Italian coffee machine company is considering setting up either one distribution center for each of its east, south, west, and north regions or simply one center in Ningbo for the whole of China. The weekly demand for the automatic espresso coffee machine is normally distributed with a mean of 1,000 units and a standard deviation of 300 units. Although the demand for each region is independent, the supply lead time is more or less the same—four weeks. Each machine costs $1,000 and the holding cost is 20 percent. With the next-day delivery promise, the branch office needs to bear an inland trucking cost of $10/unit for all four regional centers. However, if a single national distribution center is decided upon, a more expensive transport fleet is needed and that will cost $13/unit for next-day service. Setting up and operating four regional DCs costs $150,000 per year more than building and operating the single Ningbo national distribution center. Assume that the Italian company would like a CSL of 0.95. What should the Shanghai branch office decide based on the cost considerations?

Analysis:

Observe that using only one distribution center would decrease facility and inventory costs but increase transportation costs. We therefore have to evaluate the change in each cost category on aggregation. We start with inventory costs. For each region we have

$$D = 1,000/\text{week}, \sigma_D = 300, L = 4 \text{ weeks}$$

Given the desired $CSL = 0.95$, the required safety inventory across all four regional distribution centers is obtained using Equation 12.12 to be

$$\text{Total required safety inventory, } ss = 4 \times F_s^{-1}(CSL) \times \sqrt{L} \times \sigma_D$$
$$= 4 \times NORMSINV(0.95) \times \sqrt{4} \times 300 = 3,948$$

Now consider the aggregate option. Because demand in all four areas is independent, $r = 0$ Using Equation 12.14, the standard deviation of aggregate weekly demand is

Standard deviation of weekly demand at national distribution center, $\sigma_D^C = \sqrt{4} \times 300 = 600$

For a CSL of 0.95, safety inventory required for the aggregate option (using Equation 12.15) is given as

$$ss = F_s^{-1}(0.95) \times \sqrt{L} \times \sigma_D^C = NORMSINV(0.95) \times \sqrt{4} \times 600 = 1,974$$

We can now evaluate the changes in inventory, transportation, and facility costs up on aggregation as follows:

Decrease in annual inventory holding cost on aggregation $= (3,948 - 1,974) \times \$1,000 \times 0.2$
$$= \$394,765$$

Decrease in annual facility costs on aggregation $= \$150,000$

Increase in annual transportion costs on aggregation $= 52 \times 1,000 \times (13 - 10) \times 4 = \$624,000$

Observe that in this case, the annual costs for the Shanghai branch office will be increased by $624,000 - \$394,765 - \$150,000 = \$79,235$ upon centralization. It is clearly better to run the four centers in the east, south, west, and north regions instead of the Ningbo center.

Example 12-9 and the previous discussion highlight instances in which physical aggregation of inventory at one location may not be optimal. However, aggregating safety inventory has clear benefits. We now discuss various methods by which a supply chain can extract the benefits of aggregation without having to physically centralize all inventories in one location.

Information Centralization

Redbox uses *information centralization* to virtually aggregate its inventories of DVDs despite having tens of thousands of vending machines. The company has set up an online system that allows customers to locate nearby vending machines with the DVD they are searching for in stock. This allows Redbox to provide a much higher level of product availability than would be possible if a customer found out about availability only by visiting a vending machine. The benefit of information centralization derives from the fact that most customers get their DVD from the vending machine closest to their house. In case of a stockout at the closest vending machine, the customer is served from another vending machine, thus improving product availability without adding to inventories.

Retailers such as Gap also use information centralization effectively. If a store does not have the size or color that a customer wants, store employees can use their information system to inform the customer of the closest store with the product in inventory. Customers can then either go to this store or have the product delivered to their house. Gap thus uses information centralization to virtually aggregate inventory across all retail stores even though the inventory is physically separated. This allows Gap to reduce the amount of safety inventory it carries while providing a high level of product availability.

Walmart has an information system in place that allows store managers to search other stores for an excess of items that may be hot sellers at their stores. Walmart provides transportation that allows store managers to exchange products so they arrive at stores where they are in high demand. In this case, Walmart uses information centralization with a responsive transportation system to reduce the amount of safety inventory carried while providing a high level of product availability.

Specialization

Most supply chains provide a variety of products to customers. When inventory is carried at multiple locations, a key decision for a supply chain manager is whether all products should be stocked at every location. Clearly, a product that does not sell in a geographic region should not be carried in inventory by the warehouse or retail store located there. For example, it does not make sense for a Sears retail store in southern Florida to carry a wide variety of snow boots in inventory.

Another important factor that must be considered when making stocking decisions is the reduction in safety inventory that results from aggregation. If aggregation reduces the required safety inventory for a product by a large amount, it is better to carry the product in one central location. If aggregation reduces the required safety inventory for a product by a small amount, it may be best to carry the product in multiple decentralized locations to reduce response time and transportation cost.

The reduction in safety inventory due to aggregation is strongly influenced by the demand's coefficient of variation. For a product with a low coefficient of variation, disaggregate demand can be forecast with accuracy. As a result, the inventory benefit from aggregation is minimal. For a product with a high coefficient of variation of demand, disaggregate demand is difficult to forecast. In this case, aggregation improves forecast accuracy significantly, providing great benefits. We illustrate this idea in Example 12-10 (see worksheet *Example 12-10*).

| EXAMPLE 12-10 | Impact of Coefficient of Variation on Value of Aggregation |

Assume that W.W. Grainger, a supplier of MRO products, has 1,600 stores distributed throughout the United States. Consider two products—large electric motors and industrial cleaner. Large electric motors are high-value items with low demand, whereas the industrial cleaner is a low-value item with high demand. Each motor costs $500 and each can of cleaner costs $30. Weekly demand for motors at each store is normally distributed, with a mean of 20 and a standard deviation of 40. Weekly demand for cleaner at each store is normally distributed, with a mean of 1,000 and a standard deviation of 100. Demand experienced by each store is independent, and supply lead time for both motors and cleaner is four weeks. W.W. Grainger has an annual holding cost of 25 percent. For each of the two products, evaluate the reduction in safety inventories that will result if they are removed from retail stores and carried only in a centralized DC. Assume a desired CSL of 0.95.

Analysis:

The evaluation of safety inventories and the value of aggregation for each of the two products is shown in Table 12-4. All calculations use the approach discussed earlier and illustrated in Example 12-8. As Table 12-4 shows, the inventory reduction benefit from centralizing motors is much larger than the benefit from centralizing cleaner. From this analysis, W.W. Grainger should stock cleaner at the stores and motors in the DC. Given that cleaner is a high-demand item, customers will be able to pick it up on the same day at the stores. Given that motors are a low-demand item, customers may be willing to wait the extra day that shipping from the DC will entail.

TABLE 12-4 Value of Aggregation at W.W. Grainger

	Motors	Cleaner
Inventory is stocked in each store		
Mean weekly demand per store	20	1,000
Standard deviation	40	100
Coefficient of variation	2.0	0.1
Safety inventory per store	132	329
Total safety inventory	211,200	526,400
Value of safety inventory	$105,600,000	$15,792,000
Inventory is aggregated at the DC		
Mean weekly aggregate demand	32,000	1,600,000
Standard deviation of aggregate demand	1,600	4,000
Coefficient of variation	0.05	0.0025
Aggregate safety inventory	5,264	13,159
Value of safety inventory	$2,632,000	$394,770
Savings		
Total inventory saving on aggregation	$102,968,000	$15,397,230
Total holding cost saving on aggregation	$25,742,000	$3,849,308
Holding cost saving per unit sold	$15.47	$0.046
Savings as a percentage of product cost	3.09%	0.15%

Items with low demand are referred to as *slow-moving items* and typically have a high coefficient of variation, whereas items with high demand are referred to as *fast-moving items* and typically have a low coefficient of variation. For many supply chains, specializing the distribution network with fast-moving items stocked at decentralized locations close to the customer and slow-moving items stocked at a centralized location can significantly reduce the safety inventory carried without hurting customer response time or adding to transportation costs. The centralized location then specializes in handling slow-moving items.

Of course, other factors also need to be considered when deciding on the allocation of products to stocking locations. For example, an item that is considered an emergency item because the customer needs it urgently may be stocked at stores even if it has a high coefficient of variation. In this case the customer will be willing to pay a premium for having the item available at a store. One also needs to consider the cost of the item. High-value items provide a greater benefit from centralization than do low-value items.

The insights from Example 12-10 and the above discussion are summarized in Figure 12-5. In general, decentralized networks like Costco provide a low-cost supply chain for fast-moving, predictable, low-value products like detergent. Centralized networks like Blue Nile provide a low-cost supply chain for slow-moving, unpredictable, high-value products like diamonds. A decentralized supply chain like Tiffany may carry slow-moving items like diamonds as long as customers are willing to pay a premium for this choice. Similarly, a centralized supply chain like Amazon may carry a fast-moving item like detergent, but only if customers are willing to pay a premium. It can be argued that Amazon's inability to extract a significant enough premium from its customers for the fast-moving items it sells has hurt its profitability.

It is important for firms with bricks-and-mortar stores to take the idea of specialization into account when incorporating the online channel into an omni-channel strategy as discussed in Chapter 4. Consider, for example, a bookstore chain such as Barnes & Noble, which carries about 100,000 titles at each retail store. The titles carried can be divided into two broad categories—best sellers with high demand and other books with much lower demand. Barnes & Noble can design an omni-channel strategy under which the retail stores carry primarily best sellers in inventory. They may also carry one, or at most two, copies of each of the other titles, to allow customers to browse. Customers should be able to access all titles that are not in the store via electronic kiosks in the store, which provide access to barnesandnoble.com inventory. This strategy allows customers to access an increased variety of books from Barnes & Noble stores. Customers could place orders for low-volume titles with barnesandnoble.com while purchasing high-volume titles at the store itself. This strategy of specialization would allow Barnes & Noble to aggregate all slow-moving items to be sold by the online channel. All best sellers would be decentralized and carried close to the customer. The supply chain thus reduces inventory costs for slow-moving items at the expense of somewhat higher transportation costs. For the fast-moving items, the supply chain provides a lower transportation cost and better response time by carrying the items at retail stores close to the customer.

Home Depot follows a similar strategy and integrates its online channel with its retail stores. The retail stores carry fast-moving items, and the customer is able to order slow-moving variants online. Home Depot is thus able to increase the variety of products available to customers while keeping supply chain inventories down. Walmart.com has also employed a strategy of carrying slower-moving items online.

Item Type	Centralized Inventories	Decentralized Inventories
Fast Moving Predictable {Low value}	Customer willing to pay premium?	Low Cost
Slow Moving Unpredictable {High value}	Low Cost	Customer willing to pay premium?

Figure 12-5 Specialization of Inventory Based on Product Type

Product Substitution

Substitution refers to the use of one product to satisfy demand for a different product. Substitution may occur in two situations:

1. ***Manufacturer-driven substitution:*** The manufacturer or supplier makes the decision to substitute. Typically, the manufacturer substitutes a higher-value product for a lower-value product that is not in inventory. For example, Dell may install a 1.2-terabyte hard drive into a customer order requiring a 1-terabyte drive if the smaller drive is out of stock.

2. ***Customer-driven substitution:*** Customers make the decision to substitute. For example, a customer walking into a Walmart store to buy a gallon of detergent may buy the half-gallon size if the gallon size is not available. The customer substitutes the half-gallon size for the gallon size.

In both cases, exploiting substitution allows the supply chain to satisfy demand using aggregate inventories, which permits the supply chain to reduce safety inventories without hurting product availability. In general, given two products or components, substitution may be one-way (i.e., only one of the products [components] substitutes for the other) or two-way (i.e., either product [component] substitutes for the other). We briefly discuss one-way substitution in the context of manufacturer-driven substitution and two-way substitution in the context of customer-driven substitution.

MANUFACTURER-DRIVEN ONE-WAY SUBSTITUTION Consider a server manufacturer selling direct to customers that offers drives that vary in size from 0.8 to 1.2 terabytes. Customers are charged according to the size of drive that they select, with larger sizes being more expensive. If a customer orders a 1-terabyte drive and the manufacturer is out of drives of this size, there are two possible choices: (1) delay or deny the customer order or (2) substitute a larger drive that is in stock (say, a 1.2-terabyte drive) and fill the customer order on time. The first case is potentially a lost sale or loss of future sales because the customer experiences a delayed delivery. In the second case, the manufacturer installs a higher-cost component, reducing the company's profit margin. These factors, along with the fact that only larger drives can substitute for smaller drives, must be considered when the manufacturer makes inventory decisions for individual drive sizes.

Substitution allows the server manufacturer to aggregate demand across the components, reducing safety inventories required. The value of substitution increases as demand uncertainty increases. Thus, the manufacturer should consider substitution for components displaying high demand uncertainty.

The desired degree of substitution is influenced by the cost differential between the higher-value and lower-value component. If the cost differential is very small, the manufacturer should aggregate most of the demand and carry most of its inventory in the form of the higher-value component. As the cost differential increases, though, the benefit of substitution decreases. In this case, the manufacturer will find it more profitable to carry inventory of each of the two components and decrease the amount of substitution.

The desired level of substitution is also influenced by the correlation of demand between the products. If demand between two components is strongly positively correlated, there is little value in substitution. As demand for the two components becomes less positively correlated (or even negatively correlated), the benefit of substitution increases.

CUSTOMER-DRIVEN TWO-WAY SUBSTITUTION Consider W.W. Grainger selling two brands of motors, GE and SE, which have similar performance characteristics. Customers are generally willing to purchase either brand, depending on product availability. If W.W. Grainger managers do not recognize customer substitution, they will not encourage it. For a given level of product availability, they will thus have to carry high levels of safety inventory of each brand. If its

managers recognize and encourage customer substitution, they can aggregate the safety inventory across the two brands, thereby improving product availability.

W.W. Grainger does a good job of recognizing customer substitution. When a customer calls or goes online to place an order and the product he or she requests is not available, the customer is immediately told the availability of all equivalent products that may be substituted. Most customers ultimately buy a substitute product in this case. W.W. Grainger can exploit this substitution by managing safety inventory of all substitutable products jointly. Recognition and exploitation of customer substitution allows W.W. Grainger to provide a high level of product availability with lower levels of safety inventory.

A good understanding of customer-driven substitution is important in the retail industry. It must be exploited when merchandising to ensure that substitute products are placed near each other, allowing a customer to buy one if the other is out of stock. In the online channel, substitution requires a retailer to present the availability of substitute products if the one the customer requests is out of stock. The supply chain is then able to reduce the required level of safety inventory while providing a high level of product availability.

The demand uncertainties and the correlation of demand between the substitutable products influence the benefit to a retailer from exploiting substitution. The greater the demand uncertainty, the greater is the benefit of substitution. The less positive the correlation of demand between substitutable products, the greater is the benefit from exploiting substitution.

Component Commonality

In any supply chain, a significant amount of inventory is held in the form of components. A single product such as a server contains hundreds of components. When a supply chain is producing a large variety of products, component inventories can easily become very large. The use of common components in a variety of products is an effective supply chain strategy to exploit aggregation and reduce component inventories.

Dell sells thousands of server configurations to customers. An extreme option for Dell is to design distinct components that are suited to the performance of a particular configuration. Under this option, Dell would use different memory, hard drive, and other components for each distinct finished product. The other option is to design products such that common components are used in different finished products.

Without common components, the uncertainty of demand for any component is the same as the uncertainty of demand for the finished product in which it is used. Given the large number of components in each finished product, demand uncertainty will be high, resulting in high levels of safety inventory. When products with common components are designed, the demand for each component is an aggregation of the demand for all the finished products of which the component is a part. Component demand is thus more predictable than the demand for any one finished product. This fact reduces the component inventories carried in the supply chain. This idea has been a key factor for success in the electronics industry and has also started to play a big role in the auto industry. With increasing product variety, component commonality is a key to reducing supply chain inventories without hurting product availability. We illustrate the basic idea behind component commonality in Example 12-11 (see worksheet *Example 12-11*).

EXAMPLE 12-11 **Value of Component Commonality**

Assume that Dell is to manufacture 27 types of servers with three distinct components: processor, memory, and hard drive. Under the disaggregate option, Dell designs specific components for each server type, resulting in $3 \times 27 = 81$ distinct components. Under the common-component option, Dell designs servers such that three distinct processors, three distinct memory units, and

three distinct hard drives can be combined to create 27 server types. Each component is thus used in nine servers. Monthly demand for each of the 27 servers is independent and normally distributed, with a mean of 5,000 and a standard deviation of 3,000. The replenishment lead time for each component is one month. Dell is targeting a CSL of 95 percent for component inventory. Evaluate the safety inventory requirements with and without the use of component commonality. Also evaluate the change in safety inventory requirements as the number of finished products of which a component is a part varies from one to nine.

Analysis:

We first evaluate the disaggregate option, in which components are specific to a server. For each component, we have

$$\text{Standard deviation of monthly demand} = 3,000$$

Given a lead time of one month and a total of 81 components across 27 servers, we thus use Equation 12.12 to obtain

$$\text{Total safety inventory required} = 81 \times NORMSINV(0.95) \times \sqrt{1} \times 3,000 = 399,699 \text{ units}$$

In the case of component commonality, each component ends up in nine finished products. Therefore, the demand at the component level is the sum of demand across nine products. Using Equations 12.15 and 12.16, the safety inventory required for each component is thus

$$\text{Safety inventory per common component} = NORMSINV(0.95) \times \sqrt{1} \times \sqrt{9} \times 3,000$$
$$= 14,803.68 \text{ units}$$

With component commonality, there are a total of nine distinct components. The total safety inventory across all nine components is thus

$$\text{Total safety inventory required} = 9 \times 14,803.68 = 133,233$$

Thus, having each component common to nine products results in a reduction in safety inventory for Dell from 399,699 to 133,233 units.

In Table 12-5, we evaluate the marginal benefit in terms of reduction in safety inventory as a result of increasing component commonality. Starting with the required safety inventory when each component is used in only one finished product, we evaluate the safety inventory as the number of products in which a component is used increases to nine. Observe that component commonality decreases the required safety inventory for Dell. The marginal benefit of commonality, however, declines as a component is used in more and more finished products.

TABLE 12-5 Marginal Benefit of Component Commonality

Number of Finished Products per Component	Safety Inventory	Marginal Reduction in Safety Inventory	Total Reduction in Safety Inventory
1	399,699		
2	282,630	117,069	117,069
3	230,766	51,864	168,933
4	199,849	30,917	199,850
5	178,751	21,098	220,948
6	163,176	15,575	236,523
7	151,072	12,104	248,627
8	141,315	9,757	258,384
9	133,233	8,082	266,466

As a component is used in more finished products, it must be more flexible. As a result, the cost of producing the component typically increases with increasing commonality. Given that the marginal benefit of component commonality decreases as we increase commonality, we need to trade off the increase in component cost and the decrease in safety inventory when deciding on the appropriate level of component commonality.

Postponement

Postponement is the ability of a supply chain to delay product differentiation or customization until closer to the time the product is sold. The goal is to have common components in the supply chain for most of the push phase and move product differentiation as close to the pull phase of the supply chain as possible. For example, the final mixing of paint today is done at the retail store after the customer has selected the color he or she wants. Thus, paint variety is produced only when demand is known with certainty. Postponement coupled with component commonality allows paint retailers to carry significantly lower safety inventories than in the past, when mixing was done at the paint factory. In the past, the factory manager had to forecast paint demand by color when planning production. Today, a factory manager needs to forecast only aggregate paint demand because mixing has been postponed until after customer demand is known. As a result, each retail store primarily carries aggregate inventory in the form of base paint that is configured to the appropriate color based on customer demand.

Another classic example of postponement is the production process at Benetton to make colored knit garments. The original process called for the thread to be dyed and then knitted and assembled into garments. The entire process required up to six months. Because the color of the final garment was fixed the moment the thread was dyed, demand for individual colors had to be forecast far in advance (up to six months). Benetton developed a manufacturing technology that allowed it to dye knitted garments to the appropriate color. Now, *greige* thread (the term used for thread that has not yet been dyed) can be purchased, knitted, and assembled into garments before dyeing. The dyeing of the garments is done much closer to the selling season. In fact, part of the dyeing is done after the start of the selling season, when demand is known with great accuracy. In this case, Benetton has postponed the color customization of the knit garments. When thread is purchased, only the aggregate demand across all colors needs to be forecast. Given that this decision is made far in advance, when forecasts are least likely to be accurate, there is great advantage to this aggregation. As Benetton moves closer to the selling season, the forecast uncertainty reduces. At the time Benetton dyes the knit garments, demand is known with a high degree of accuracy. Thus, postponement allows Benetton to exploit aggregation and significantly reduce the level of safety inventory carried. Supply chain flows with and without postponement are illustrated in Figure 12-6.

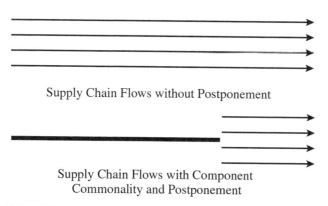

Supply Chain Flows without Postponement

Supply Chain Flows with Component
Commonality and Postponement

Figure 12-6 Supply Chain Flows without and with Postponement

Without component commonality and postponement, product differentiation occurs early on in the supply chain, and most of the supply chain inventories are disaggregate. Postponement allows the supply chain to delay product differentiation. As a result, most of the inventories in the supply chain are aggregate. Postponement thus allows a supply chain to exploit aggregation to reduce safety inventories without hurting product availability. We illustrate the benefits of postponement in Example 12-12 (see worksheet *Example 12-12*). A more nuanced discussion of the value of postponement is given in Chapter 13.

EXAMPLE 12-12 Value of Postponement

Consider a paint retailer that sells 100 different colors of paint. Assume that weekly demand for each color is independent and is normally distributed with a mean of 30 and a standard deviation of 10. The replenishment lead time from the paint factory is two weeks and the retailer aims for a CSL = 0.95. How much safety stock will the retailer have to hold if paint is mixed at the factory and held in inventory at the retailer as individual colors? How does the safety stock requirement change if the retailer holds base paint (supplied by the paint factory) and mixes colors on demand?

Analysis:

We first evaluate the disaggregate option without postponement, in which the retailer holds safety inventory for each color sold. For each color, we have

$$D = 30/\text{week}, \sigma_D = 10, L = 2 \text{ weeks}$$

Given the desired CSL = 0.95, the required safety inventory across all 100 colors is obtained using Equation 12.12 to be

$$\text{Total required safety inventory, } ss = 100 \times F_s^{-1}(CSL) \times \sqrt{L} \times \sigma_D$$
$$= 100 \times NORMSINV(0.95) \times \sqrt{2} \times 10 = 2,326$$

Now, consider the option whereby mixing is postponed until after the customer orders. Safety inventory is held in the form of base paint, whose demand is an aggregate of demand of the 100 colors. Because demand in all 100 colors is independent, $\rho = 0$. Using Equation 12.15, the standard deviation of aggregate weekly demand of base paint is

$$\text{Standard deviation of weekly demand of base paint, } \sigma_D^C = \sqrt{100} \times 10 = 100$$

For a CSL of 0.95, safety inventory required for the aggregate option (using Equation 12.16) is given as

$$ss = F_s^{-1}(0.95) \times \sqrt{L} \times \sigma_D^C = NORMSINV(0.95) \times \sqrt{2} \times 100 = 233$$

Observe that postponement reduces the required safety inventory at the paint retailer from 2,326 units to 233 units.

Postponement can be a powerful concept when customers are willing to wait a little for their orders to arrive. This delay offers the supply chain an opportunity to reduce inventories by postponing product differentiation until after the customer order arrives. It is important that the manufacturing process be designed in a way that enables assembly to be completed quickly. Given that customers are often willing to wait for delivery, several furniture and window manufacturers have postponed some of the assembly processes for their products.

SUMMARY OF LEARNING OBJECTIVE 5

Aggregation reduces the required safety inventory as long as the demand across the aggregated regions is not perfectly, positively correlated. The safety inventory savings on aggregation increase with the desired *CSL*, the replenishment lead time, the product holding cost, and the coefficient of variation of demand. The safety inventory savings on aggregation decrease as the correlation of demand across regions increases. Firms can aggregate inventories through physical aggregation, information centralization, product substitution, component commonality, and postponement.

IMPACT OF REPLENISHMENT POLICIES ON SAFETY INVENTORY

12.6. *Determine the impact of replenishment policies on safety inventory.*

In this section, we describe the evaluation of safety inventories for both continuous and periodic-review replenishment policies. We highlight the fact that periodic review policies require more safety inventory than continuous review policies for the same level of product availability. To simplify the discussion, we focus on the CSL as the measure of product availability. The managerial implications are the same if we use fill rate; the analysis, however, is more cumbersome.

Continuous Review Policies

Given that continuous review policies were discussed in detail in Section 12.2, we reiterate only the main points here. When using a continuous review policy, a manager orders Q units when the inventory drops to the ROP. Clearly, a continuous review policy requires technology that monitors the level of available inventory. This is the case for many firms such as Walmart and Dell, whose inventories are monitored continuously.

Given a desired CSL, our goal is to identify the required safety inventory ss and the ROP. We assume that demand is normally distributed, with the following inputs:

D: Average demand per period

σ_D: Standard deviation of demand per period

L: Average lead time for replenishment

The ROP represents the available inventory to meet demand during the lead time L. A stockout occurs if the demand during the lead time is larger than the ROP. If demand across periods is independent, demand during the lead time is normally distributed with the following:

$$\text{Mean demand during lead time, } D_L = D \times L$$
$$\text{Standard deviation of demand during lead time, } \sigma_L = \sqrt{L}\sigma_D$$

Given the desired CSL, the required safety inventory (ss) obtained using Equation 12.6 and the ROP obtained using Equation 12.4 are

$$ss = F_s^{-1}(CSL) \times \sigma_L = NORMSINV(CSL) \times \sqrt{L}\sigma_D, ROP = D_L + ss$$

A manager using a continuous review policy has to account only for the uncertainty of demand during the lead time. This is because the continuous monitoring of inventory allows the manager to adjust the timing of the replenishment order, depending on the demand experienced. If demand is very high, inventory reaches the ROP quickly, leading to a quick replenishment order. If demand is very low, inventory drops slowly to the ROP, leading to a delayed replenishment order. The manager, however, has no recourse during the lead time once a replenishment order has been placed. The available safety inventory thus must cover for the uncertainty of demand over this period.

Typically, in continuous review policies, the lot size ordered is kept fixed between replenishment cycles. The optimal lot size may be evaluated using the EOQ formula discussed in Chapter 11.

Periodic Review Policies

In periodic review policies, inventory levels are reviewed after a fixed period of time T and an order is placed such that the level of current inventory plus the replenishment lot size equals a prespecified level called the *order-up-to level* (OUL). The *review interval* is the time T between successive orders. Observe that the size of each order may vary, depending on the demand experienced between successive orders and the resulting inventory at the time of ordering. Periodic review policies are simpler for retailers to implement because they do not require that the retailer have the capability of monitoring inventory continuously. Suppliers may also prefer them because they result in replenishment orders placed at regular intervals.

Let us consider the store manager at Carrefour who is responsible for designing a replenishment policy for Lego building blocks. He wants to analyze the impact on safety inventory if he decides to use a periodic review policy. Demand for Legos is normally distributed and independent from one week to the next. We assume the following inputs:

D: Average demand per period

σ_D: Standard deviation of demand per period

L: Average lead time for replenishment

T: Review interval

CSL: Desired cycle service level

To understand the safety inventory requirement, we track the sequence of events over time as the store manager places orders. The store manager places the first order at time 0 such that the lot size ordered and the inventory on hand sum to the OUL. Once an order is placed, the replenishment lot arrives after the lead time L. The next review period is time T, when the store manager places the next order, which then arrives at time $T + L$. The OUL represents the inventory available to meet all demand that arises between periods 0 and $T + L$. The Carrefour store will experience a stockout if demand during the time interval between 0 and $T + L$ exceeds the OUL. Thus, the store manager must identify an OUL such that the following is true:

$$\text{Probability(demand during } T + L \leq OUL) = CSL$$

The next step is to evaluate the distribution of demand during the time interval $T + L$. Using Equation 12.2, demand during the time interval $T + L$ is normally distributed, with

$$\text{Mean demand during } T + L \text{ periods, } D_{T+L} = (T + L)D$$
$$\text{Standard deviation of demand during } T + L \text{ periods, } \sigma_{T+L} = \sqrt{T + L}\sigma_D$$

The safety inventory in this case is the quantity in excess of demand carried by Carrefour over the time interval $T + L$. The OUL and the safety inventory ss are related as follows:

$$OUL = D_{T+L} + ss \tag{12.18}$$

Given the desired CSL, the safety inventory (ss) required is given by

$$ss = F_s^{-1}(CSL) \times \sigma_{T+L} = NORMSINV(CSL) \times \sigma_{T+L} \tag{12.19}$$

The average lot size equals the average demand during the review period T and is given as

$$\text{Average lot size, } Q = D_T = D \times T \tag{12.20}$$

In Figure 12-7, we show the inventory profile for a periodic review policy with lead time $L = 4$ and reorder interval $T = 7$. On day 7, the company places an order that determines available inventory until day 18 (as illustrated in Figure 12-7 by the dashed line from point 1 to point 2). As a result, the safety inventory must be sufficient to buffer demand variability over $T + L = 7 + 4 = 11$ days.

We illustrate the periodic review policy for Carrefour in Example 12-13 (see worksheet *Example 12-13*).

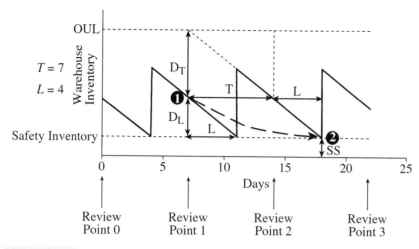

Figure 12-7 Inventory Profile for Periodic Review Policy with $L = 4$, $T = 7$

EXAMPLE 12-13 **Evaluating Safety Inventory for a Periodic Review Policy**

Weekly demand for Legos at a Carrefour store is normally distributed, with a mean of 2,500 boxes and a standard deviation of 500. The replenishment lead time is two weeks, and the store manager has decided to review inventory every four weeks. Assuming a periodic-review replenishment policy, evaluate the safety inventory that the store should carry to provide a CSL of 90 percent. Evaluate the OUL for such a policy.

Analysis:

In this case, we have

> Average demand per period, $D = 2,500$
> Standard deviation of demand per period, $\sigma_D = 500$
> Average lead time for replenishment, $L = 2$ weeks
> Review interval, $T = 4$ weeks

We first obtain the distribution of demand during the time interval $T + L$. Using Equation 12.2, demand during the time interval $T + L$ is normally distributed, with

> Mean demand during $T + L$ periods, $D_{T+L} = (T + L)D = (2 + 4)2,500 = 15,000$

> Standard deviation of demand during, $T + L$ periods, $\sigma_{T+L} = \sqrt{T + L}\,\sigma_D$
> $$= (\sqrt{4 + 2})500 = 1,225$$

From Equation 12.19, the required safety inventory for a $CSL = 0.90$ is given as

$$ss = F_S^{-1}(CSL) \times \sigma_{T+L} = NORMSINV(CSL) \times \sigma_{T+L}$$
$$= NORMSINV(0.90) \times 1,225 = 1,570 \text{ boxes}$$

Using Equation 12.18, the OUL is given by

$$OUL = D_{T+L} + ss = 15,000 + 1,570 = 16,570$$

The store manager thus orders the difference between 16,570 and current inventory every four weeks.

We can now compare the safety inventory required when using continuous and periodic review policies. With a continuous review policy, the safety inventory is used to cover for demand uncertainty over the lead time L. With a periodic review policy, the safety inventory is used to cover for demand uncertainty over the lead time and the review interval $L + T$. Given that higher uncertainty must be accounted for, periodic review policies require a higher level of safety inventory. This argument can be confirmed by comparing the results in Examples 12-3 and 12-13. For a 90 percent CSL, the store manager requires a safety inventory of 906 boxes when using a continuous review and a safety inventory of 1,570 boxes when using a periodic review.

Of course, periodic review policies are somewhat simpler to implement because they do not require continuous tracking of inventory. Given the broad use of bar codes and POS systems as well as the emergence of RFID technology, continuous tracking of all inventories is much more commonplace today than it was a decade ago. In some instances, companies partition their products based on their value. High-value products are managed using continuous review policies, and low-value products are managed using periodic review policies. This makes sense if the cost of perpetual tracking of inventory is more than the savings in safety inventory that result from switching all products to a continuous review policy.

SUMMARY OF LEARNING OBJECTIVE 6

Whereas the required safety inventory is proportional to $\sqrt{L}$ for a continuous review policy, the required safety inventory for a periodic review replenishment policy is proportional to $\sqrt{L + T}$, where T is the reorder interval. As a result, periodic review replenishment policies require more safety inventory than continuous review policies for the same lead time and level of product availability.

12.7. *Improve the management of safety inventory in a multiechelon supply chain.*

MANAGING SAFETY INVENTORY IN A MULTIECHELON SUPPLY CHAIN

In our discussion so far, we have assumed that each stage of the supply chain has a well-defined demand and supply distribution that it uses to set its safety inventory levels. In practice, this is not true for multiechelon supply chains. Consider a simple multiechelon supply chain with a supplier feeding a retailer that sells to the final customer. The retailer needs to know demand as well as supply uncertainty to set safety inventory levels. Supply uncertainty, however, is influenced by the level of safety inventory the supplier chooses to carry. If a retailer order arrives when the supplier has enough inventory, the supply lead time is short. In contrast, if the retailer order arrives when the supplier is out of stock, the replenishment lead time for the retailer increases. Thus, if the supplier increases its level of safety inventory, the retailer can reduce the safety inventory it holds. This implies that the level of safety inventory at all stages in a multiechelon supply chain should be related.

All inventory between a stage and the final customer is called the *echelon inventory*. Echelon inventory at a retailer is just the inventory at the retailer or in the pipeline coming to the retailer. Echelon inventory at a distributor, however, includes inventory at the distributor and all retailers served by the distributor. In a multiechelon setting, ROPs and OULs at any stage should be based on echelon inventory and not local inventory. Thus, a distributor should decide its safety inventory levels based on the level of safety inventory carried by all retailers supplied by it. The more safety inventory retailers carry, the less safety inventory the distributor needs to carry. As retailers decrease the level of safety inventory they carry, the distributor must increase its safety inventory to ensure regular replenishment at the retailers.

If all stages in a supply chain attempt to jointly manage their echelon inventory, the issue of how the inventory is divided among various stages becomes important. Carrying inventory upstream in a supply chain allows for more aggregation and thus reduces the amount of inventory required. Carrying inventory upstream, however, increases the probability that the final

customer will have to wait because product is not available at a stage close to him or her. Thus, in a multiechelon supply chain, a decision must be made with regard to the level of safety inventory carried at different stages. If inventory is expensive to hold and customers are willing to tolerate a delay, it is better to increase the amount of safety inventory carried upstream, far from the final customer, to exploit the benefits of aggregation. If inventory is inexpensive to hold and customers are time sensitive, it is better to carry more safety inventory downstream, closer to the final customer.

SUMMARY OF LEARNING OBJECTIVE 7

In a multiechelon supply chain, it is important to manage safety inventory across stages in a coordinated manner. Increasing safety inventory at upstream stages allows downstream stages to decrease the amount of safety inventory they carry.

MANAGERIAL LEVERS TO REDUCE SAFETY INVENTORY

12.8. *Identify managerial levers that lower safety inventory without hurting product availability.*

This chapter has focused on the buildup of safety inventory in a supply chain. A manager must understand the relative impact of lead time, supply uncertainty, and demand uncertainty on the amount of safety inventory in the supply chain.

An important managerial lever that helps reduce safety inventory is the reduction of supply uncertainty. In fact, firms should be willing to tolerate somewhat longer lead times if there is a significant reduction in lead time uncertainty. Sharing of information and coordinated demand and supply planning can help a supply chain reduce supply uncertainty.

Another managerial lever that helps reduce safety inventories is a reduction of lead times. Replenishment lead times consist of production time, transportation time, and various forms of delay. Delay may arise in the order placement process, the production planning process, and the transportation planning process. It is fair to state that in most supply chains, delays contribute more to lead times than the production and transportation time. A focus on reducing these delays can help reduce lead times. The Spanish apparel retailer Zara and British fast fashion company Boohoo.com are two examples of companies that have significantly reduced lead times through flexible local production in Europe. Local production reduces transportation lead times and flexible production allows the firms to schedule production in small batches. This allows for the production of any style in small batches soon after the order is placed. In inflexible facilities with large production lot sizes it often takes a long time to schedule production of a specific style.

A final managerial lever to reduce safety inventories is a reduction of the demand uncertainty experienced by the supply chain. A reduction in information distortion through the sharing of information, as discussed in Chapter 10, is an important mechanism to decrease uncertainty. A very important mechanism to reduce demand uncertainty is to design the supply chain in a way that demand is aggregated. Important mechanisms to aggregate demand in a supply chain include physical aggregation, information aggregation, product substitution, component commonality and postponement.

SUMMARY OF LEARNING OBJECTIVE 8

The required level of safety inventory may be reduced and product availability may be improved if a supply chain can reduce demand uncertainty, replenishment lead times, and the variability of lead times. A switch from periodic monitoring to continuous monitoring can also help reduce inventories. Another key managerial lever to reduce the required safety inventories is to exploit aggregation. This may be achieved by physically aggregating inventories, virtually aggregating inventories using information centralization, specializing inventories based on demand volume, exploiting substitution, using component commonality, and postponing product differentiation.

DISCUSSION QUESTIONS

1. Consider a cosmetic company's inventory. What would be the impact on safety inventory levels if customers' brand preferences suddenly change as a result of a campaign discouraging the use of animal-tested cosmetics?
2. As a supermarket operator, would you hold more safety inventory for a newly introduced detergent or for an existing detergent? Why?
3. What are the pros and cons of the various measures of product availability?
4. Identify the factors that affect the correct level of safety inventory. What impact does each have on determining the correct level of safety inventory?
5. Describe how safety inventory level can be reduced without hurting product availability.
6. Why can a supermarket, like Tesco, with large stores provide a higher level of product availability with lower inventories than a convenience store chain, like InterSPAR, with many small stores?
7. "It is well known that inventory aggregation could always reduce demand uncertainty and therefore result in a reduction in required safety inventory level." Do you agree or disagree? Why?
8. Build-a-Bear allows children to choose a toy shell, see it being stuffed, and personalize it by adding scents, sounds, and accessories. Traditional toyshops provide a variety of off the shelf toys that require safety inventories to be maintained. Discuss what impact, if any, Build-a-Bear has on safety inventories in their supply chain.
9. A new technology allows books to be printed in 10 minutes. Barnes & Noble has decided to purchase these machines for each store. It must decide which books to carry in stock and which books to print on demand using this technology. Do you recommend it for best sellers or for other books? Why?
10. Consider a firm like Zara that has developed production capabilities with very short replenishment lead times. Do you think this capability is more valuable for its online operations or its store operation? Why?
11. Consider a chain of modular kitchen manufacturers that uses postponement methods to design and install them. What would allow the chain to deliver a modular kitchen to a client in a reasonable period? How does this approach affect safety inventories, product differentiation, and responsiveness in the supply chain?
12. How should safety inventory be managed in a multiechelon supply chain?

EXERCISES

1. Weekly demand for smartphones at an Apple store is normally distributed, with a mean of 500 and a standard deviation of 300. Foxconn, the assembler, takes four weeks to supply an Apple order. Apple is targeting a CSL of 95 percent and monitors its inventory continuously. How much safety inventory of cell phones should the Apple store carry? What should its ROP be?
2. Weekly demand for jeans at a Zara store is normally distributed, with a mean of 170 and a standard deviation of 85. The supply plant takes two weeks to supply a Zara order. The store manager monitors its inventory continuously and reorders jeans when the available inventory drops below 400. How much safety stock does the store carry? What CSL does the store achieve? If the store manager wants to target a CSL of 93 percent, how much safety inventory of jeans should the store carry? What should the ROP be?
3. Weekly demand for cell phones at a Best Buy store is normally distributed, with a mean of 300 and a standard deviation of 200. The supplier takes two weeks to supply a Best Buy order. Best Buy is targeting a CSL of 95 percent and monitors its inventory continuously. How much safety inventory of cell phones should Best Buy carry? What should its ROP be?
4. Reconsider the Best Buy store in Exercise 3. The store manager has decided to follow a periodic review policy to manage inventory of cell phones. She plans to order every three weeks. Given a desired CSL of 95 percent, how much safety inventory should the store carry? What should its OUL be?
5. Assume that the Best Buy store in Exercise 3 has a policy of ordering cell phones from the supplier in lots of 500. Weekly demand for cell phones at the store is normally distributed, with a mean of 300 and a standard deviation of 200. The supplier takes two weeks to supply an order. If the store manager is using a continuous review policy and targeting a fill rate of 99 percent, what safety inventory should the store carry? What should its ROP be?
6. Weekly demand for HP printers at a Sam's Club store is normally distributed, with a mean of 250 and a standard deviation of 150. The store manager continuously monitors inventory and currently orders 1,000 printers each time the inventory drops to 600 printers. HP currently takes two weeks to fill an order. How much safety inventory does the store carry? What CSL does Sam's Club achieve as a result of this policy? What fill rate does the store achieve?
7. Return to the Sam's Club store in Exercise 6. Assume that the supply lead time from HP is normally distributed, with a mean of 2 weeks and a standard deviation of 1.5 weeks. How much safety inventory should Sam's Club carry if it wants to provide a CSL of 95 percent? How does the required safety inventory change as the standard deviation of lead time is reduced from 1.5 weeks to zero in intervals of 0.5 weeks?
8. Weekly demand for shampoo at a EUROSPAR supermarket is normally distributed, with a mean of 2,800 and a standard deviation of 1,000. The store manager, who continuously monitors the inventory, orders 11,000 units even when there

are 8,500 units in inventory. The supplier takes two weeks to supply a EUROSPAR order. What CSL does the store achieve? What fill rate does the store achieve?

9. Weekly demand for paper towels at a Target store is normally distributed, with a mean of 1,000 and a standard deviation of 300. The supplier takes two weeks to supply a Target order, which is for a batch size of 5,000. Target is aiming for a fill rate of 99 percent and monitors its inventory continuously. How much safety inventory of paper towels should Target carry? What should its ROP be?

10. Weekly demand for electric motors at a Japanese motor manufacturer is normally distributed, with a mean of 1,000 and a standard deviation of 1,000. Motors are currently assembled in China and delivered at a cost of 20,000 yen/motor. The supplier takes eight weeks to supply an order. A local Japanese manufacturer has offered to deliver motors with a lead time of one week at a cost of 20,400 yen per motor. The motor manufacturer is targeting a CSL of 99 percent and monitors its inventory continuously. The manufacturer incurs an annual holding cost of 25 percent. Should the manufacturer accept the local supplier's offer?

11. Weekly demand for private label washing machines at Karstadt, a German department store chain, is normally distributed with a mean of 500 and a standard deviation of 300. Karstadt currently has a supply source in China that delivers machines at a cost of 200 euro. The lead time required by the supplier is normally distributed with a mean of nine weeks and a standard deviation of six weeks. A European supplier has offered to deliver washing machines with a guaranteed lead time of one week at a cost of 210 euro. Karstadt has an annual holding cost of 25 percent and targets a cycle service level of 99 percent. Should Karstadt accept the local supplier's offer?

12. Croma is an Indian retail chain for consumer electronics. The company currently has 25 stores located in major metropolitan areas. Weekly demand for smartphones at each store is normally distributed, with a mean of 300 and a standard deviation of 300. The supplier currently takes four weeks to fulfill a replenishment order, which is placed separately by each store. Croma is targeting a CSL of 95 percent and monitors its inventory continuously. How much safety inventory of smartphones should Croma carry at each retail store? Croma is considering moving smartphones to the online channel, where they would be stocked in a single national warehouse. Assume that Croma can move smartphones to the online channel without losing demand (the online demand is a sum of demand at each retail store). How much saving in safety inventory can Croma expect from going online if demand across stores is independent? How much saving in safety inventory can Croma expect from going online if demand across stores has a correlation coefficient of $\rho = 0.5$?

13. Magazine Luiza is a Brazilian retail chain for consumer electronics. The company currently has 100 stores distributed across Brazil. It also operates an online channel. It is considering introduction of a new printer and must decide whether to offer it at retail stores or the online channel. Weekly demand for the printer at each store has been forecast to be normally distributed with a mean of 100 and a standard deviation of 80.

The company has also forecast that the demand at the online channel would be the sum of demand across all 100 stores. The supplier will take four weeks to fulfill a replenishment order, whether placed separately by each store or by the online DC. Magazine Luiza is targeting a CSL of 95 percent and monitors its inventory continuously. How much safety inventory will Magazine Luiza carry if the printer is carried at all 100 stores? How much safety inventory will Magazine Luiza carry if the printer is carried online and demand across stores is independent? How much safety inventory will Magazine Luiza carry if the printer is carried online and demand across stores has a correlation coefficient of $\rho = 0.3$?

14. A European apparel store has started selling through its online channel along with its retail stores. Management has to decide which products to carry at its retail stores and which to carry at a central warehouse to be sold only via the online channel. The company currently has 250 retail stores across Europe. Weekly demand for size 10, boot cut jeans at each store is normally distributed, with a mean of 600 and a standard deviation of 150. Each pair of jeans costs €50. Weekly demand for full length black winter coats at each store is normally distributed, with a mean of 20 and a standard deviation of 10. Each coat costs €120. The company has an annual holding cost of 20 percent. They manage all inventories using a continuous review policy, and the supply lead time for both products is three weeks. The targeting CSL is 90 percent. When moving each of the two products from the stores to the online channel, how much reduction in holding cost per unit sold can the company expect? Which of the two products should the company carry at its stores, and which should it carry at the central warehouse for the online channel? Why? Assume that the demand across stores and from one week to the next to be independent.

15. Epson produces printers in its Taiwan factory for sale in Europe. Printers sold in different countries differ in terms of the power outlet as well as the language of the manuals. Currently, Epson assembles and packs printers for sale in individual countries. The distribution of weekly demand in different countries is normally distributed, with means and standard deviations as shown in Table 12-6.

Assume demand in different countries to be independent. Given that the lead time from the Taiwan factory is eight weeks, how much safety inventory does Epson require in Europe if it targets a CSL of 95 percent?

TABLE 12-6 Weekly Demand for Epson Printers in Europe

Country	Mean Demand	Standard Deviation
France	3,000	2,000
Germany	4,000	2,200
Spain	2,000	1,400
Italy	2,500	1,600
Portugal	1,000	800
UK	4,000	2,400

Epson decides to build a central DC in Europe. It will ship base printers (without power supply) to the DC. When an order is received, the DC will assemble power supplies, add manuals, and ship the printers to the appropriate country. The base printers are still to be manufactured in Taiwan with a lead time of eight weeks. How much saving of safety inventory can Epson expect as a result?

16. Return to the Epson data in Exercise 15. Each printer costs Epson $200, and the annual holding cost is 25 percent. What saving in holding cost can Epson expect as a result of building the European DC? If final assembly in the European DC adds $5 to the production cost of each printer, would you recommend the move? Suppose that Epson is able to cut the production and delivery lead time from its Taiwan factory to four weeks using good information systems. How much savings in holding cost can Epson expect without the European DC? How much savings in holding cost can the firm expect with the European DC?

17. Return to the Epson data in Exercise 15. Assume that demand in different countries is not independent. Demand in any pair of countries is correlated with a correlation coefficient of ρ. Evaluate the holding cost savings that Epson gains as a result of building a European DC as ρ increases from 0 (independent demand) to 1 (perfectly positively correlated demand) in intervals of 0.2.

18. Motorola obtains cell phones from its contract manufacturer located in China to supply the U.S. market, which is served from a warehouse located in Memphis, Tennessee. Daily demand at the Memphis warehouse is normally distributed, with a mean of 5,000 and a standard deviation of 4,000. The warehouse aims for a CSL of 99 percent. The company is debating whether to use sea or air transportation from China. Sea transportation results in a lead time of 36 days and costs $0.50 per phone. Air transportation results in a lead time of 4 days and costs $1.50 per phone. Each phone costs $100, and Motorola incurs an annual holding cost of 20 percent. Given the minimum lot sizes, Motorola would order 100,000 phones at a time (on average, once every 20 days) if using sea transport and 5,000 phones at a time (on average, daily) if using air transport. To begin with, assume that Motorola takes ownership of the inventory on delivery.

 a. Assuming that Motorola follows a continuous review policy, what reorder point and safety inventory should the warehouse aim for when using sea or air transportation? How many days of safety inventory will Motorola carry under each policy?

 b. How many days of cycle inventory does Motorola carry under each policy?

 c. Under a continuous review policy, do you recommend sea or air transportation if Motorola does not own the inventory while it is in transit? Does your answer change if Motorola has ownership of the inventory while it is in transit?

19. Weekly demand for gaming consoles at Liverpool, a Mexican department store chain, is normally distributed with a mean of 1,000 and a standard deviation of 400. The replenishment lead time from the supplier is four weeks. Liverpool is targeting a CSL of 95 percent and uses a periodic review policy under which it reorders consoles every eight weeks. What is the average order size? How much safety inventory of consoles should Liverpool carry? What should its order up to level be? How much safety inventory would be required if Liverpool switched to a continuous review policy?

20. Weekly demand for handbags at Liverpool, a Mexican department store chain, is normally distributed with a mean of 3,000 and a standard deviation of 1,000. The replenishment lead time from the supplier is 4 weeks. Liverpool uses a periodic review policy under which it reorders handbags every 12 weeks. It currently uses an order-up-to level of 50,000. What is the average order size? How much safety inventory of handbags does Liverpool carry? What CSL does it achieve? What order up to level should it use if it wants a CSL of 99 percent?

21. Return to the problem data in Exercise 18. Assume that Motorola follows a periodic review policy. Given lot sizes by sea and air, Motorola would have to place an order every 20 days using sea transport but could order daily using air transport.

 a. Assume that Motorola follows a periodic review policy. What OUL and safety inventory should the warehouse aim for when using sea or air transportation? How many days of safety inventory will Motorola carry under each policy?

 b. How many days of cycle inventory does Motorola carry under each policy?

 c. Under a periodic review policy, do you recommend sea or air transportation? Does your answer change if Motorola has ownership of the inventory while it is in transit?

22. DoorRed Pharmacy replenishes one of its best-selling drugs using a continuous review policy. Daily demand for the drug is normally distributed, with a mean of 300 and a standard deviation of 100. The wholesaler can supply a replenishment request in two days. The current replenishment policy is to order 1,500 units when there are 750 units on hand.

 a. What is the cycle service level that DoorRed achieves with its policy?

 b. What is the fill rate that DoorRed achieves with its policy?

 c. What change in fill rate would DoorRed achieve if it increased its ROP from 750 to 800?

23. Return to the DoorRed Pharmacy in Exercise 22. For the drug under discussion, DoorRed wants to adjust its ROP from 750 to achieve a fill rate of 99.9 percent. What ROP should it use?

24. The DoorRed pharmacy has twenty-five retail outlets in the Chicago region. The current policy is to carry every drug in each retail outlet. DoorRed is investigating the possibility of centralizing some of the drugs in one location. Delivery charge would increase by $0.02 per unit if a drug were centralized. The increase in delivery charge comes from the additional cost of operating the shuttle from the central location to each of the other locations. At each retail outlet, DoorRed follows a periodic review policy with weekly replenishment (a replenishment order is placed once every seven days). The replenishment lead time is three days. DoorRed plans to stick to once-a-week ordering even if a

drug is centralized. DoorRed incurs an annual inventory holding cost of 20 percent and aims for a cycle service level of 99 percent. Assume that demand across stores is independent.

a. Consider a drug with daily demand at each store that is normally distributed, with a mean of 300 and a standard deviation of 50. The drug costs $10 per unit. What is the annual holding cost of safety inventory across all retail stores? If the drug were centralized in one location, what would the annual cost of holding safety inventory at the central location be? What would the annual increase in delivery charge be? Do you recommend centralization?

b. Now consider a drug with daily demand at each store that is normally distributed, with a mean of 5 and a standard deviation of 4. The drug costs $10 per unit. What is the annual holding cost of safety inventory across all retail stores? If the drug were centralized in one location, what would the annual cost of holding safety inventory at the central location be? What would the annual increase in delivery charge be? Do you recommend centralization?

c. Do your answers to (a) and (b) change if the demand across stores has a correlation coefficient of 0.5?

25. Toyota has decided to set up regional warehouses where some variants of the Scion will be customized and shipped to dealers on demand. Customizing and shipping on demand will raise production and transportation cost per car by $100. Each car costs $20,000, and Toyota has an annual holding cost of 20 percent. Cars at the dealer are owned by Toyota for the first 90 days. Thus, for all practical purposes, Toyota owns all inventory, whether at the dealers or at the regional warehouse. Consider a region with five large dealers and thirty small dealers. Toyota has partitioned the variants into two groups—popular variants and uncommon variants. Weekly demand for the two types of variants at the two types of dealers is shown in Table 12-7. The goal is to provide a 95 percent cycle service level using a continuous review policy. Replenishment lead times for both dealers and regional warehouses are four weeks. Customization and shipping from a regional warehouse to a dealer can be done in a day, and this time can be ignored. Assume demand to be independent across all dealers.

a. How much safety inventory of a popular variant is required at a large or small dealer?

b. What is the safety inventory required if inventory for the popular variant (for both large and small dealers) is centralized at the regional warehouse by Toyota?

c. What is the safety inventory required if inventory for the popular variant at small dealers is centralized at the regional warehouse but that for large dealers is decentralized?

d. Given the additional customization and transportation cost, which structure do you recommend for the popular variant?

e. Repeat parts (a) to (d) for the uncommon variant.

f. How should Toyota structure inventories given its regional warehouses?

26. Orion is a global company that sells copiers. Orion currently sells ten variants of a copier, with all inventory kept in finished-goods form. The primary component that differentiates the copiers is the printing subassembly. An idea being discussed is to introduce commonality in the printing subassembly so that final assembly can be postponed and inventories kept in component form. Currently, each copier costs $1,000 in terms of components. Introducing commonality in the print subassembly will increase component costs to $1,025. One of the ten variants represents 80 percent of the total demand. Weekly demand for this variant is normally distributed, with a mean of 1,000 and a standard deviation of 200. Each of the remaining nine variants has a weekly demand of 28 with a standard deviation of 20. Orion aims to provide a 95 percent level of service. Replenishment lead time for components is four weeks. Copier assembly can be completed in a matter of hours. Orion manages all inventories using a continuous review policy and incurs an annual holding cost of 20 percent.

a. How much safety inventory of each variant must Orion keep without component commonality? What is the annual holding cost?

b. How much safety inventory must be kept in component form if Orion uses common components for all variants? What is the annual holding cost? What is the increase in component cost using commonality? Is commonality justified across all variants?

c. At what cost of commonality will complete commonality be justified?

d. Now consider the case in which Orion uses component commonality for only the nine low-demand variants. How much reduction in safety inventory does Orion achieve in this case? What are the savings in terms of annual holding cost? Is this more restricted form of commonality justified?

e. At what cost of commonality will commonality across the low-volume variants be justified?

TABLE 12-7 Weekly Demand at Car Dealers

	Popular Variant		Uncommon Variant	
	Mean	Standard Deviation	Mean	Standard Deviation
Large dealer	50	15	8	5
Small dealer	10	5	2	2

BIBLIOGRAPHY

Barnes, Jim. "The Myths and Truths About Inventory Optimization." *Supply Chain Management Review* (March/April 2014): 10–19.

Federgruen, Awi, and Yu-Sheng Zheng. "An Efficient Algorithm for Computing an Optimal (r, Q) Policy in Continuous Review Stochastic Inventory Systems." *Operations Research* (July–August 1992): 40, 808–813.

Feitzinger, Edward, and Hau L. Lee. "Mass Customization at Hewlett Packard." *Harvard Business Review* (January–February 1997): 116–121.

Gallego, Guillermo. "New Bounds and Heuristics for (Q,r) Policies." *Management Science* 44 (February 1998): 219–233.

Gupta, Sandeep, and Charanyan Iyengar. "The Tip of the (Inventory) Iceberg." *Supply Chain Management Review* (November 2014): 28–35.

Kopczak, Laura, and Hau L. Lee. *Hewlett-Packard Co.: Deskjet Printer Supply Chain (A)*. Stanford University Case GS3A, 2001.

Lee, Hau L. "Design for Supply Chain Management: Concepts and Examples." In R. Sarin, ed. *Perspectives in Operations Management*. Norwell, MA: Kluwer Academic Publishers, 1993, pp. 45–65.

Lee, Hau L., and Corey Billington. "Managing Supply Chain Inventory." *Sloan Management Review* (Spring 1992): 65–73.

Lee, Hau L., Corey Billington, and Brent Carter. "Hewlett-Packard Gains Control of Inventory and Service Through Design for Localization." *Interfaces* (July–August 1993): 1–11.

Nahmias, Steven. *Production and Operations Analysis*. Burr Ridge, IL: Richard P. Irwin, 1997.

Signorelli, Sergio, and James L. Heskett. 1984. "Benetton (A)." Harvard Business School Case 9–685–014, 1984.

Silver, Edward A., David Pyke, and Rein Petersen. *Inventory Management and Production Planning and Scheduling*. New York: Wiley, 1998.

Strang, Randy. "Retail Without Boundaries." *Supply Chain Management Review* (November 2013): 32–39.

Tayur, Sridhar, Ram Ganeshan, and Michael Magazine, eds. *Quantitative Models for Supply Chain Management*. Boston: Kluwer Academic Publishers, 1999.

Trent, Robert J. "Managing Inventory Investment Effectively." *Supply Chain Management Review* (March–April 2002): 28–35.

Zipkin, Paul H. *Foundations of Inventory Management*. Boston: Irwin McGraw-Hill, 2000.

CASE STUDY

Managing Inventories at ALKO Inc.

ALKO began in 1943 in a garage workshop set up by John Williams at his Cleveland home. John had always enjoyed tinkering, and in February 1948 he obtained a patent for one of his designs for lighting fixtures. He decided to produce it in his workshop and tried marketing it in the Cleveland area. The product sold well, and by 1957 ALKO had grown to a $3 million company. Its lighting fixtures were well known for their outstanding quality. By then, it sold five products.

In 1963, John took the company public. Since then, ALKO had been very successful, and the company had started distributing its products nationwide. As competition intensified in the 21st century, ALKO introduced many new lighting fixture designs. The company's profitability, however, began to worsen despite the fact that ALKO had taken great care to ensure that product quality did not suffer. The problem was that margins had begun to shrink as competition in the market intensified. By 2015, the board decided that a complete reorganization was needed, starting at the top. Gary Fisher was hired to reorganize and restructure the company.

When Gary arrived in 2017, he found a company teetering on the edge. He spent his first few months trying to understand the company business and the way it was structured. Gary realized that the key was in the operating performance. Although the company had always been outstanding at developing and producing new products, it had historically ignored its distribution system. The belief within the company was that once one makes a good product, the rest takes care of itself. Gary set up a task force to review the company's current distribution system and come up with recommendations.

Current Distribution System

The task force noted that ALKO had 100 products in its 2017 line. All production occurred at three facilities located in the Cleveland area. For sales purposes, the

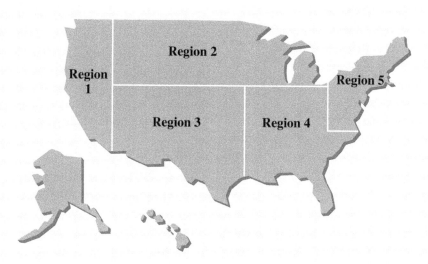

Figure 12-8 Sales Regions for ALKO

contiguous United States was divided into five regions, as shown in Figure 12-8. A DC owned by ALKO operated in each of these regions. Customers placed orders with the DCs, which tried to supply them from product in inventory. As the inventory for any product diminished, the DC, in turn, ordered from the plants. The plants scheduled production based on DC orders. Orders were transported from plants to the DCs in TL quantities because order sizes tended to be large. On the other hand, shipments from the DC to the customer were LTL. ALKO used a third-party trucking company for both transportation legs. In 2017, TL costs from the plants to DCs averaged $0.09 per unit. LTL shipping costs from a DC to a customer averaged $0.10 per unit. On average, five days were necessary between the time a DC placed an order with a plant and the time the order was delivered from the plant.

The policy in 2017 was to stock each item in every DC. A detailed study of the product line had shown that there were three basic categories of products in terms of the volume of sales. They were categorized as types High, Medium, and Low. Demand data for a representative product in each category is shown in Table 12-8. Products 1, 3, and 7 are representative of High, Medium, and Low demand products, respectively. Of the 100 products that ALKO sold, 10 were of type High (with the same demand distribution as Product 1), 20 of type Medium (with the same demand distribution as Product 3), and 70 of type Low (with the same demand distribution as Product 7).

The task force identified that plant capacities allowed any reasonable order to be produced and delivered in five days. The replenishment lead time was thus five days. The DCs ordered using a periodic review

TABLE 12-8 Distribution of Daily Demand at ALKO

	Region 1	Region 2	Region 3	Region 4	Region 5
Part 1 Mean	35.48	22.61	17.66	11.81	3.36
Part 1 SD	6.98	6.48	5.26	3.48	4.49
Part 3 Mean	2.48	4.15	6.15	6.16	7.49
Part 3 SD	3.16	6.20	6.39	6.76	3.56
Part 7 Mean	0.48	0.73	0.80	1.94	2.54
Part 7 SD	1.98	1.42	2.39	3.76	3.98

policy with a reorder interval of six days. The holding cost incurred was $0.15 per unit per day whether the unit was in transit or in storage. All DCs carried safety inventories to ensure a CSL of 95 percent.

Alternative Distribution Systems

The task force recommended that ALKO build a national distribution center (NDC) outside Chicago. The task force recommended that ALKO close its five DCs and move all inventory to the NDC. Warehouse capacity was measured in terms of the *total number of units handled per year* (i.e., the warehouse capacity was given in terms of the annual demand supplied from the warehouse). The cost of constructing a warehouse is shown in Figure 12-9. However, ALKO expected to recover $50,000 for each warehouse that it closed. The CSL out of the NDC would continue to be 95 percent.

Given that Chicago is close to Cleveland, the inbound transportation cost from the plants to the NDC would fall to $0.05 per unit. The total replenishment lead time for orders from the Chicago NDC would still be five days. The centralized DC would continue to follow a periodic review policy with a reorder interval of six days. Given the increased average distance, however, the outbound transportation cost to customers from the NDC would increase to $0.24 per unit.

Other possibilities the task force considered include building a national distribution center while keeping the regional DCs open. In this case, some products would be stocked at the regional DCs, whereas others would be stocked at the NDC.

Gary Fisher's Decision

Gary Fisher pondered the task force report. It had not detailed any of the numbers supporting the decision. He decided to evaluate the numbers before making his decision.

Questions

1. What is the annual inventory and distribution cost of the current distribution system?
2. What are the savings that would result from following the task force recommendation and setting up an NDC? Evaluate the savings as the correlation coefficient of demand in any pair of regions varies from 0 to 0.5 to 1.0. Do you recommend setting up an NDC?
3. Suggest other options that Gary Fisher should consider. Evaluate each option and recommend a distribution system for ALKO that would be most profitable. How dependent is your recommendation on the correlation coefficient of demand across different regions?

Figure 12-9 Construction Costs for NDC

CASE STUDY

Should Packing Be Postponed to the DC?

Penang Electronics (PE) is a contract manufacturer that produces and packages private-label products for several retail chains, including Target, Best Buy, Staples, and Office Max. In each case, the basic products are identical, with the only difference being the labeling and the packaging. Thus, the labeled and packed version of the product destined for Target cannot be sent to Best Buy.

Currently, a production facility in Malaysia is used to manufacture, label, and pack all products. The manufacturing facility replenishes a DC in St. Louis, from which the contract manufacturer fills all customer orders. The manufacturing and transportation lead time from Penang to St. Louis is nine weeks. PE uses a continuous review policy to manage inventories at its DC and aims to provide a cycle service level of 95 percent for each product to every customer.

The previous month had been very challenging because Best Buy requested 5,000 additional units beyond what was available at the DC, whereas Target ordered 3,500 fewer units and Staples ordered 4,000 fewer units. Even though there was sufficient product inventory available at the DC (in the form of the basic product), PE could not meet the Best Buy request because the excess inventory available was labeled and packed for other customers. The DC had leftover inventory from Target and Staples, which unfortunately could not be used to serve Best Buy. PE had lost business while carrying surplus inventory, all because of the wrong labels and packaging.

Labeling and Packaging at the DC

The vice president of supply chain at PE proposed postponing the final labeling and packaging to the DC. Her logic was that postponing labeling and packaging to the DC would allow PE to use all available inventories to serve any customer. In particular, the situation that arose in

the previous month when Best Buy did not get its entire order could have been avoided through postponement. If packaging was shifted to the DC, the lead time of manufacturing and transporting the basic product from Malaysia would continue to be about nine weeks. Labeling and packaging were relatively quick steps and the response time from the DC to the customer was not expected to change.

The DC management was opposed to this idea because it would create additional work that was different from what they had done so far. A detailed study of the production process showed that labeling and packaging at the DC cost $2 per unit more than the cost of labeling and packaging in Malaysia. DC management believed that this increase in cost would be held against them once the process was changed, and they would be under constant pressure to lower cost. They also believed it would complicate the work they did when filling an order and could adversely impact customer service.

Evaluating the Two Options

To evaluate the two options, a team from both manufacturing and the DC was set up. The team decided to focus its analysis on three major product categories—computers, printers, and scanners, and four major customers—Target, Best Buy, Staples, and Office Max. Weekly demand for each product and customer is shown in Table 12-9. In each case, "Mean" indicates the average weekly demand, and "SD" indicates the standard deviation of weekly demand. All demand was assumed to be normally distributed. PE incurred a total cost of $1,000 per computer, $300 per printer, and $100 per scanner. Given the short life cycle of these products, PE used an annual holding cost of 30 percent when making its inventory decisions. It was assumed that batch sizes and cycle inventories would be unchanged irrespective of

TABLE 12-9 Distribution of Weekly Demand by Product and Customer

	Computers		Printers		Scanners	
	Mean	SD	Mean	SD	Mean	SD
Target	1,000	700	2,000	1,000	4,000	1,000
Best Buy	700	600	1,500	800	4,500	900
Office Max	800	600	1,200	600	2,000	700
Staples	500	400	900	500	1,400	500

where packaging and labeling were done. Thus, the team analyzed the impact of postponement on safety inventories before making a final recommendation.

Questions

1. What is the annual holding cost of safety inventory for the current system in which product is produced, labeled, and packed in Malaysia before being shipped to the DC?

2. How would the holding cost of safety inventory change if labeling and packaging were moved to the DC? Evaluate the change in inventory costs as the correlation coefficient of demand between any pair of customers varies from 0 to 0.5 to 1.0.

3. How should PE set up its production, labeling, and packaging processes? Does your answer change if the additional cost of labeling and packaging at the DC is reduced to $1 (from the current value of $2)?

APPENDIX 12A

The Normal Distribution

A continuous random variable X has a *normal distribution* with mean μ and standard deviation $\sigma > 0$ if the probability density function of the random variable is given by

$$f(x, \mu, \sigma) = \frac{1}{\sigma\sqrt{2\pi}} \exp\left[\frac{(x - \mu)^2}{2\sigma^2}\right] \tag{12.21}$$

The normal density function is as shown in Figure 12-10.

The *cumulative normal distribution function* is denoted by $F(x, \mu, \sigma)$ and is the probability that a normally distributed random variable with mean μ and standard deviation σ takes on a value less than or equal to x. The cumulative normal distribution function and the density function are related as follows:

$$F(x, \mu, \sigma) = \int_{X=-\infty}^{x} f(X, \mu, \sigma)dX$$

A normal distribution with a mean $\mu = 0$ and standard deviation $\sigma = 1$ is referred to as the *standard normal distribution*. The standard normal density function is denoted by $f_S(x)$ and the cumulative standard normal distribution function is denoted by $F_S(x)$. Thus,

$$f_S(x) = f(x, 0, 1) \quad \text{and} \quad F_S(x) = F(x, 0, 1).$$

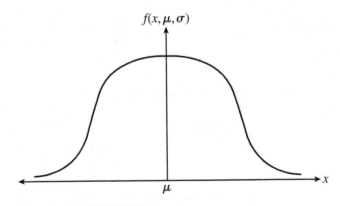

Figure 12-10 Normal Density Function

Given a probability p, the inverse normal $F^{-1}(p, \mu, \sigma)$ is the value x such that p is the probability that the normal random variable takes on a value x or less. Thus, if $F(x, \mu, \sigma) = p$ then $x = F^{-1}(p, \mu, \sigma)$. The inverse of the standard normal distribution is denoted by $F_S^{-1}(p)$.

Thus,

$$F_S^{-1}(p) = F^{-1}(p, 0, 1).$$

APPENDIX 12B

The Normal Distribution in Excel

The following Excel functions can be used to evaluate various normal distribution functions:

$$F(x, \mu, \sigma) = NORMDIST(x, \mu, \sigma, 1) \tag{12.22}$$

$$f(x, \mu, \sigma) = NORMDIST(x, \mu, \sigma, 0) \tag{12.23}$$

$$F^{-1}(p, \mu, \sigma) = NORMINV(p, \mu, \sigma) \tag{12.24}$$

The Excel functions to evaluate various standard normal distribution functions are listed next.

$$F_S(x) = NORMDIST(x, 0, 1, 1) \text{ or } NORMSDIST(x) \tag{12.25}$$

$$f_S(x) = NORMDIST(x, 0, 1, 0) \tag{12.26}$$

$$F_S^{-1}(p) = NORMSINV(p) \tag{12.27}$$

APPENDIX 12C

Expected Shortage per Replenishment Cycle

Establish an alternative formula for expected shortage per replenishment cycle (ESC) to be evaluated using Excel.

Analysis:

Given a reorder point of $ROP = D_L + ss$ the ESC is given as

$$ESC = \int_{x=ROP}^{\infty} (x - ROP)f(x)dx$$

$$= \int_{x=D_L+ss}^{\infty} (x - D_L - ss)f(x)dx$$

Given that the demand during lead time is normally distributed with a mean D_L and a standard deviation σ_L we have (using Equation 12.21)

$$ESC = \int_{x=D_L+ss}^{\infty} (x - D_L - ss)\frac{1}{\sqrt{2\pi}\sigma_L}e^{-(x-D_L)^2/2\sigma_L^2}dx$$

Substitute the following:

$$z = \frac{(x - D_L)}{\sigma_L}$$

This implies that

$$dx = \sigma_L dz$$

Thus, we have

$$ESC = \int_{z=ss/\sigma_L}^{\infty} (z\sigma_L - ss)\frac{1}{\sqrt{2\pi}}e^{-z^2/2}dz$$

$$= -ss\int_{z=ss/\sigma_L}^{\infty} \frac{1}{\sqrt{2\pi}}e^{-z^2/2}dz + \sigma_L\int_{z=ss/\sigma_L}^{\infty} z\frac{1}{\sqrt{2\pi}}e^{-z^2/2}dz$$

Recall that $F_S(.)$ is the cumulative distribution function and $f_S(.)$ is the probability density function for the standard normal distribution with mean 0 and standard deviation 1. Using Equation 12.21 and the definition of the standard normal distribution, we have

$$1 - F_S(y) = \int_{z=y}^{\infty} f_S(z)dz = \int_{z=y}^{\infty} \frac{1}{\sqrt{2\pi}}e^{-z^2/2}dz$$

Substitute $w = z^2/2$ into the expression for ESC. This implies that

$$ESC = -ss[1 - F_S(ss/\sigma_L)] + \sigma_L\int_{w=ss^2/2\sigma_L^2}^{\infty} \frac{1}{\sqrt{2\pi}}e^{-w}dw$$

or

$$ESC = -ss[1 - F_S(ss/\sigma_L)] + \sigma_L f_S(ss/\sigma_L)$$

Using Equations 12.25 and 12.26, ESC may be evaluated using Excel as follows:

$$ESC = -ss[1 - NORMDIST(ss/\sigma_L, 0, 1, 1)] + \sigma_L NORMDIST(ss/\sigma_L, 0, 1, 0)$$

APPENDIX 12D

Evaluating Safety Inventory for Slow-Moving Items

Objective

Devise a procedure for evaluating safety inventory for slow-moving items whose demand can be approximated using a Poisson distribution.

Analysis:

For slow-moving items, the normal distribution is not a good estimation for the demand distribution. A better approach is to use the Poisson distribution with demand arriving at a rate D. In such a setting, (Q, r) policies are known to be optimal. Under a (Q, r) policy, an order is placed whenever the inventory position drops to or below the reorder point r, and the order size is nQ, where n is the number of batches of size Q required to raise the inventory position to be in the interval $(r, r + Q)$.

For the Poisson distribution, given a constant lead time L, the average demand over the lead time is given by LD, and the variance of demand over the lead time is given by $\sigma^2 = LD$. Efficient algorithms to obtain the Q and r are given by Federgruen and Zheng (1992). The results we present are based on Gallego (1998), who has given effective heuristics to solve the problem.

If H is the holding cost per unit per unit time, p the fixed shortage cost per unit per unit time, and S the fixed order cost per batch, Gallego suggests a batch size of Q^*, where

$$Q^* = Min\left(\sqrt{2}, \sqrt[4]{1 + \left(\frac{(H + p)L}{2S}\right)^2}\right)\sqrt{\frac{2DS}{H}} \qquad \textbf{(12.28)}$$

He shows that the use of batch size Q^* results in a cost that is no more than 7 percent from the optimal batch size. The reorder point r^* can be obtained using a procedure discussed by Federgruen and Zheng (1992). The long-run average cost $C(r, Q)$ of an (r, Q) policy when demand is Poisson is given by

$$C(r, Q) = \frac{DS}{Q} + \frac{1}{Q}\sum_{y=r+1}^{r+Q}\left\{H\sum_{i=0}^{y}(y - i)P_i + p\sum_{i=y+1}^{\infty}(i - y)P_i\right\}, \qquad \textbf{(12.29)}$$

where

$$P_i = \frac{e^{DL}(DL)^i}{i!}, i = 0, 1, \ldots$$

The reorder point r^* is obtained by inserting the batch size Q^* from Equation 12.28 into Equation 12.29 and searching for the value r^* that minimizes the cost $C(r, Q^*)$. Given that $C(r, Q^*)$ is unimodal [as shown by Federgruen and Zheng (1992)], r^* can be obtained using a binary search over the integers.

CHAPTER
13

Linking Product Availability to Profits

LEARNING OBJECTIVES

After reading this chapter, you will be able to

13.1 Identify the factors affecting the optimal level of product availability.

13.2 Evaluate the cycle service level that maximizes profits.

13.3 Use basic managerial levers to improve supply chain profitability.

13.4 Discuss how speed can improve profits in a supply chain.

13.5 Understand conditions under which postponement is valuable in a supply chain.

13.6 Allocate limited supply capacity among multiple products to maximize expected profits.

In this chapter, we explore how the level of product availability offered to customers affects expected profits. The chapter examines factors that influence the optimal cycle service level. We discuss and demonstrate how different managerial levers can be used to match supply and demand to improve supply chain profitability.

13.1 Identify the factors affecting the optimal level of product availability.

FACTORS AFFECTING THE DESIRED LEVEL OF PRODUCT AVAILABILITY

The level of product availability is measured using the cycle service level or the fill rate, which are metrics for the amount of customer demand satisfied from available inventory. The *level of product availability*, also referred to as the *customer service level*, is one of the primary measures of a supply chain's responsiveness. A supply chain can use a high level of product availability to improve its responsiveness and attract customers, thus increasing revenue for the supply chain. However, a high level of product availability requires large inventories, which raise supply chain costs. Therefore, a supply chain must achieve a balance between the level of availability and the cost of inventory. The optimal level of product availability is one that maximizes expected supply chain profits.

In the fourth quarter of 2008, U.S. inventories shot up by $6.2 billion because of the rapid decline in demand that hit retailers and manufacturers. For some manufacturers, the situation

was exaggerated because of the excess inventory of raw materials, such as steel and plastics, that they had built up while anticipating price increases. Retailers were also hit hard, with some, such as Saks Fifth Avenue, slashing prices by 70 percent during the holiday season to spur demand. The excess inventories and the drop in demand led to several retailers, such as Steve & Barry's and Circuit City, declaring bankruptcy during this period. In contrast, Nintendo missed out on an estimated $1.3 billion in sales during the 2007 holiday season because of a failure to meet soaring global demand for its Wii video game console. These examples make clear that having too high or too low a level of product availability has a significant impact on supply chain profits.

Whether the optimal level of availability is high or low depends on how a particular company believes it can maximize profits. Nordstrom has focused on providing a high level of product availability and has used its reputation for responsiveness to become a successful department store chain. However, prices at Nordstrom are higher than those at a discount store, where the level of product availability is lower. Power plants ensure that they (almost) never run out of fuel because a shutdown is extremely expensive, resulting in several days of lost production. Some power plants try to maintain several months of fuel supply to avoid any probability of running out. In contrast, most supermarkets carry only a few days' supply of product, and out-of-stock situations do occur with some frequency.

The Internet allows a customer to easily shop at an alternative store if the first choice is out of stock. This competitive environment puts pressure on online retailers to increase their level of availability. Simultaneously, significant price competition has lowered prices online. Web retailers with excess inventory find it difficult to be profitable. Providing the optimal level of product availability is thus a key to success online.

To understand the factors that influence the optimal level of product availability, consider L. L. Bean, a large mail-order company that sells apparel. One of the products L. L. Bean sells is ski jackets, for which the selling season is from November to February. The buyer at L. L. Bean currently purchases the entire season's supply of ski jackets from the manufacturer before the start of the selling season. Providing a high level of product availability requires the purchase of a large number of jackets. Although a high level of product availability is likely to satisfy all demand that arises, it is also likely to result in a large number of unsold jackets at the end of the season. Given that leftover jackets will have to be sold at a significant discount, L. L. Bean is likely to lose money on discounted jackets. In contrast, a low level of product availability is likely to result in few unsold jackets. However, it is quite likely that L. L. Bean will have to turn away customers who are willing to buy jackets, because they are sold out. In this scenario, L. L. Bean loses potential profit by losing customers. The buyer at L. L. Bean must balance the loss from having too many unsold jackets (if the number of jackets ordered is more than demand) and the lost profit from turning away customers (if the number of jackets ordered is less than demand) when deciding the level of product availability.

L. L. Bean can perfectly match supply and demand if demand is predictable. Thus, deciding on an optimal level of product availability makes sense only in the context of demand uncertainty. Traditionally, many firms have forecast a consensus estimate of demand without any measure of uncertainty. In this setting, firms do not make a decision regarding the level of availability; they simply order the consensus forecast. Since the beginning of the twenty-first century, firms have developed a better appreciation for uncertainty and have started developing forecasts that include a measure of uncertainty. Incorporating uncertainty and deciding on the optimal level of product availability can increase profits relative to using a consensus forecast.

L. L. Bean has a buying committee that decides on the quantity of each product to be ordered. Based on demand over the past few years, the buyers have estimated the demand distribution for a women's red ski parka to be as shown in Table 13-1. This is a deviation from its traditional practice of using the average historical demand as the consensus forecast. To simplify the discussion, we assume that all demand is in hundreds of parkas. The manufacturer also requires that L. L. Bean place orders in multiples of 100. In Table 13-1, p_i is the probability that

TABLE 13-1 Demand Distribution for Parkas at L. L. Bean

Demand D_i (in hundreds)	Probability p_i	Cumulative Probability (P_i) of Demand Being D_i or Less	Probability ($1 - P_i$) of Demand Being Greater than D_i
4	0.01	0.01	0.99
5	0.02	0.03	0.97
6	0.04	0.07	0.93
7	0.08	0.15	0.85
8	0.09	0.24	0.76
9	0.11	0.35	0.65
10	0.16	0.51	0.49
11	0.20	0.71	0.29
12	0.11	0.82	0.18
13	0.10	0.92	0.08
14	0.04	0.96	0.04
15	0.02	0.98	0.02
16	0.01	0.99	0.01
17	0.01	1.00	0.00

demand equals D_i, and P_i is the probability that demand is less than or equal to D_i. From Table 13-1, we evaluate the expected demand for parkas as

$$\text{Expected demand} = \sum D_i p_i = 1,026$$

Under the old policy of ordering the expected value, the buyers would have ordered 1,000 parkas. However, demand is uncertain, and Table 13-1 shows that there is a 51 percent probability that demand will be 1,000 or less. Thus, a policy of ordering a thousand parkas results in a cycle service level of 51 percent at L. L. Bean. The buying committee must decide on an order size and cycle service level that maximize the expected profits from the sale of parkas at L. L. Bean.

The loss that L. L. Bean incurs from an unsold parka and the profit that it makes on each parka it sells influences the buying decision. Each parka costs L. L. Bean $c = \$45$ and is priced in the catalog at $p = \$100$. Any unsold parkas at the end of the season are sold at the outlet store for $50. Holding the parka in inventory and transporting it to the outlet store costs L. L. Bean $10. Thus, L. L. Bean recovers a salvage value of $s = \$40$ for each parka that is unsold at the end of the season. L. L. Bean makes a profit of $p - c = \$55$ on each parka it sells during the season and incurs a loss of $c - s = \$5$ on each unsold parka that is sold at the outlet store. We ignore any impact that lack of parka availability has on future purchases by the customer.

The expected profit from ordering 1,000 parkas is given as

$$\text{Expected profit} = \sum_{i=4}^{10}[D_i(p - c) - (1,000 - D_i)(c - s)]p_i + \sum_{i=11}^{17} 1,000(p - c)p_i$$

$$= [400 \times 55 - 600 \times 5] \times 0.01 + [500 \times 55 - 500 \times 5] \times 0.02$$
$$+ [600 \times 55 - 400 \times 5] \times 0.04 + [700 \times 55 - 300 \times 5] \times 0.08$$
$$+ [800 \times 55 - 200 \times 5] \times 0.09 + [900 \times 55 - 100 \times 5] \times 0.11$$
$$+ [1000 \times 55 - 0 \times 5] \times 0.16 + 1000 \times 55 \times 0.20 + 1000 \times 55 \times 0.11$$
$$+ 1000 \times 55 \times 0.10 + 1000 \times 55 \times 0.04 + 1000 \times 55 \times 0.02$$
$$+ 1000 \times 55 \times 0.01 + 1000 \times 55 \times 0.01$$
$$= \$49,900$$

TABLE 13-2 Expected Marginal Contribution of Each Additional 100 Parkas

Additional Hundreds	Expected Marginal Benefit	Expected Marginal Cost	Expected Marginal Contribution
11th	$5,500 \times 0.49 = 2,695$	$500 \times 0.51 = 255$	$2,695 - 255 = 2,440$
12th	$5,500 \times 0.29 = 1,595$	$500 \times 0.71 = 355$	$1,595 - 355 = 1,240$
13th	$5,500 \times 0.18 = 990$	$500 \times 0.82 = 410$	$990 - 410 = 580$
14th	$5,500 \times 0.08 = 440$	$500 \times 0.92 = 460$	$440 - 460 = -20$
15th	$5,500 \times 0.04 = 220$	$500 \times 0.96 = 480$	$220 - 480 = -260$
16th	$5,500 \times 0.02 = 110$	$500 \times 0.98 = 490$	$110 - 490 = -380$
17th	$5,500 \times 0.01 = 55$	$500 \times 0.99 = 495$	$55 - 495 = -440$

To decide whether to order 1,100 parkas, the buying committee must determine the impact of buying the extra 100 units. If 1,100 parkas are ordered, the extra 100 are sold (for a profit of $5,500) if demand is 1,100 or higher. Otherwise, the extra 100 units are sent to the outlet store at a loss of $500. From Table 13-1, we see that there is a probability of 0.49 that demand is 1,100 or higher and a 0.51 probability that demand is 1,000 or less. Thus, we deduce the following:

Expected profit from the extra 100 parkas $= 5,500 \times$ Prob(demand $\geq 1,100$)
$- 500 \times$ Prob(demand $< 1,100$) $= \$5,500 \times 0.49 - \$500 \times 0.51 = \$2,440$

The total expected profit from ordering 1,100 parkas is thus $52,340, which is almost 5 percent higher than the expected profit from ordering 1,000 parkas. Using the same approach, we evaluate the marginal contribution of each additional 100 parkas as in Table 13-2 (see worksheet *Table 13-1, 2* in spreadsheet *Chapter13-examples*). Note that the expected marginal contribution is positive up to 1,300 parkas, but it is negative from that point on. Thus, the optimal order size is 1,300 parkas. From Table 13-2, we have

Expected profit from ordering 1,300 parkas $= \$49,900 + \$2,440$
$+ \$1,240 + \$580 = \$54,160$

This is more than an 8 percent increase in profitability relative to the policy of ordering the expected value of 1,000 parkas.

A plot of total expected profits versus the order quantity is shown in Figure 13-1. The optimal order quantity maximizes the expected profit. For L. L. Bean, the optimal order quantity is 1,300 parkas, which provides a CSL of 92 percent. Observe that with a CSL of 0.92, L. L. Bean has a fill rate that is much higher. If demand is 1,300 or less, L. L. Bean achieves a fill rate of 100 percent, because all demand is satisfied. If demand is more than 1,300 (say, D), part of the

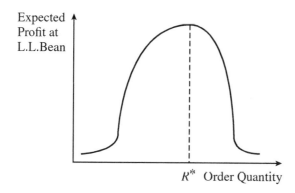

Figure 13-1 Expected Profit as a Function of Order Quantity at L. L. Bean

demand $(D - 1,300)$ is not satisfied. In this case, a fill rate of $1,300/D$ is achieved. Overall, the fill rate achieved at L. L. Bean if 1,300 parkas are ordered is given by

$$fr = 1 \times \text{Prob (demand} \leq 1,300) + \sum_{D_i > 1,300} (1,300/D_i)p_i$$

$$= 1 \times 0.92 + (1300/1400) \times 0.04 + (1300/1500) \times 0.02$$
$$+ (1300/1600) \times 0.01 + (1300/1700) \times 0.01$$
$$= 0.99$$

Thus, with a policy of ordering 1,300 parkas, L. L. Bean satisfies, on average, 99 percent of its demand from parkas in inventory.

Observe that there are two key parameters that influence the optimal cycle service level at L. L. Bean. The first parameter is the loss incurred by L. L. Bean for each unsold unit at the end of the selling season. We refer to this parameter as the *cost of overstocking* and denote it by C_o. L. L. Bean has a cost of overstocking of $C_o = c - s = \$5$. The second parameter is the margin of each jacket, which represents the opportunity lost by L. L. Bean when it misses a sale because it is out of stock of the jacket. We refer to this parameter as the *cost of understocking* and denote it by C_u. L. L. Bean has a cost of understocking of $C_u = p - s = \$55$. In general, the cost of understocking should include the margin lost from current sales, as well as future sales if the customer does not return. In summary, the two key factors that influence the optimal level of product availability are

- Cost of overstocking the product, C_o
- Cost of understocking the product, C_u

SUMMARY OF LEARNING OBJECTIVE 1

The optimal level of product availability is affected by the cost of overstocking and the cost of understocking. The cost of overstocking refers to the loss incurred when the supply chain has an unsold unit of the product. The cost of understocking refers to the current and future margin lost when the supply chain turns away one unit of demand because it is short of the product.

13.2. *Evaluate the cycle service level that maximizes profits.*

EVALUATING THE OPTIMAL LEVEL OF PRODUCT AVAILABILITY

The optimal level of product availability maximizes expected profits and is evaluated based on the tradeoff between the cost of understocking and the cost of overstocking. In this section we develop formulae to calculate the optimal service level for both seasonal products (such as Christmas ornaments) as well as continuously stocked items (such as detergent).

Optimal Cycle Service Level for Seasonal Items with a Single Order in a Season

In this section, we focus attention on seasonal products such as ski jackets, for which all leftover items must be disposed of at the end of the season. The assumption is that the season starts with product from the order placed and any leftover inventory is disposed at a discounted price at the end of the season. Assume a retail price per unit of p, a cost of c, and a salvage value of s. We consider the following inputs:

C_o: Cost of overstocking by one unit, $C_o = c - s$

C_u: Cost of understocking by one unit, $C_u = p - c$

CSL^*: Optimal cycle service level

O^*: Corresponding optimal order size

CSL^* is the probability that demand during the season will be at or below O^*. At the optimal cycle service level CSL^*, the marginal contribution of purchasing an additional unit is zero. If the order quantity is raised from O^* to $O^* + 1$, the additional unit sells if demand is larger than O^*. This occurs with probability $1 - CSL^*$ and results in a contribution of $p - c$. We thus have

$$\text{Expected benefit of purchasing extra unit} = (1 - CSL^*)(p - c)$$

The additional unit remains unsold if demand is at or below O^*. This occurs with probability CSL^* and results in a cost of $c - s$. We thus have

$$\text{Expected cost of purchasing extra unit} = CSL^*(c - s)$$

Thus, the expected marginal contribution of raising the order size from O^* to $O^* + 1$ is given by

$$(1 - CSL^*)(p - c) - CSL^*(c - s)$$

Because the expected marginal contribution must be 0 at the optimal cycle service level, we have

$$CSL^* = \text{Prob}(Demand \le O^*) = \frac{p - c}{p - s} = \frac{C_u}{C_u + C_o} = \frac{1}{1 + (C_o/C_u)} \quad \textbf{(13.1)}$$

The optimal cycle service level as a function of the ratio of the cost of overstocking and the cost of understocking is shown in Figure 13-2. Observe that as this ratio gets smaller, the optimal level of product availability increases. This fact explains the difference in the level of product availability between a high-end store such as Nordstrom and a discount store. Nordstrom has higher margins and thus a higher cost of understocking. It should thus provide a higher level of product availability than a discount store with lower margins and, as a result, a lower cost of stocking out.

A more rigorous derivation of Equation 13.1 is provided in Appendix 13A. The optimal CSL^* is also referred to as the *critical fractile*. The resulting optimal order quantity maximizes the firm's expected profit. If demand during the season is normally distributed, with a mean of μ and a standard deviation of σ, the optimal order quantity is given by

$$O^* = F^{-1}(CSL^*, \mu, \sigma) = NORMINV(CSL^*, \mu, \sigma) \quad \textbf{(13.2)}$$

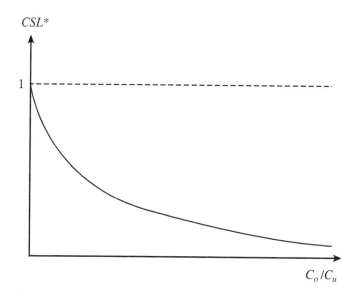

Figure 13-2 Impact on Optimal Cycle Service Level of Changing C_o/C_u

When demand is normally distributed, with a mean of μ and a standard deviation of σ, the expected profit from ordering O units is given by

$$\text{Expected profit} = (p - s)\mu F_s\left(\frac{O - \mu}{\sigma}\right) - (p - s)\sigma f_s\left(\frac{O - \mu}{\sigma}\right)$$
$$- O(c - s)F(O, \mu, \sigma) + O(p - c)[1 - F(O, \mu, \sigma)]$$

The derivation of this formula is provided in Appendix 13B and Appendix 13C. Here, F_S is the standard normal cumulative distribution function and f_S is the standard normal density function discussed in Appendix 12A in Chapter 12. The expected profit from ordering O units is evaluated in Excel using Equations 12.22, 12.25, and 12.26, as follows:

$$\text{Expected profits} = (p - s)\mu NORMDIST[(O - \mu)/\sigma, 0, 1, 1]$$
$$- (p - s)\sigma NORMDIST[(O - \mu)/\sigma, 0, 1, 0]$$
$$- O(c - s)NORMDIST(O, \mu, \sigma, 1)$$
$$+ O(p - c)[1 - NORMDIST(O, \mu, \sigma, 1)] \qquad \textbf{(13.3)}$$

Example 13-1 illustrates the use of Equations 13.1 and 13.2 to obtain the optimal cycle service level and order quantity (see worksheet *Example 13*-1 in spreadsheet *Chapter 13-examples*).

EXAMPLE 13-1 **Evaluating the Optimal Service Level for Seasonal Items**

The manager at Sportmart, a sporting goods store, has to decide on the number of skis to purchase for the winter season. Based on past demand data and weather forecasts for the year, management has forecast demand to be normally distributed, with a mean of $\mu = 350$ and a standard deviation of $\sigma = 100$. Each pair of skis costs $c = \$100$ and retails for $p = \$250$. Any unsold skis at the end of the season are disposed of for \$85. Assume that it costs \$5 to hold a pair of skis in inventory for the season. How many skis should the manager order to maximize expected profits?

Analysis:

In this case, we have

$$\text{Salvage value} = s = \$85 - \$5 = \$80$$
$$\text{Cost of understocking} = C_u = p - c = \$250 - \$100 = \$150$$
$$\text{Cost of overstocking} = C_o = c - s = \$100 - \$80 = \$20$$

Using Equation 13.1, we deduce that the optimal CSL is

$$CSL^* = \text{Prob}(Demand \leq O^*) = \frac{C_u}{C_u + C_o} = \frac{150}{150 + 20} = 0.88$$

Using Equation 13.2, the optimal order size is

$$O^* = NORMINV(CSL^*, \mu, \sigma) = NORMINV(0.88, 350, 100) = 468$$

Thus, it is optimal for the manager at Sportmart to order 468 pairs of skis, even though the expected number of sales is 350. In this case, because the cost of understocking is much higher than the cost of overstocking, management is better off ordering more than the expected value to cover for the uncertainty of demand.

Using Equation 13.3, the expected profits from ordering O^* units are

$$\text{Expected profits} = (p - s)\mu NORMDIST[(O^* - \mu)/\sigma, 0, 1, 1)]$$
$$- (p - s)\sigma NORMDIST[(O^* - \mu)/\sigma, 0, 1, 0)]$$
$$- O^*(c - s)NORMDIST(O^*, \mu, \sigma, 1)]$$
$$+ O^*(p - c)[1 - NORMDIST(O^*, \mu, \sigma, 1)]$$

$$= 170 \times 350 \times NORMDIST(1.18, 0, 1, 1)$$
$$- 170 \times 100 \times NORMDIST(1.18, 0, 1, 0)$$
$$- 468 \times 20 \times NORMDIST(468, 350, 100, 1)$$
$$+ 468 \times 150 \times [1 - NORMDIST(468, 350, 100, 1)] = \$49,146$$

The expected profit from ordering 350 pairs of skis can be evaluated as $45,718. Thus, ordering 468 pairs results in an expected profit that is almost 8 percent higher than the profit obtained from ordering the expected value of 350 pairs.

In the above example, if the manager ordered 420 (520) units instead of the optimal quantity of 468, expected profits would decrease by about 1 percent to $48,671 ($48,789). As a result, companies should avoid spending an inordinate amount of effort to get exact estimates of various costs used to evaluate optimal levels of product availability. A reasonable approximation of the costs will generally produce expected profits that are close to optimal.

Firms' efforts to set levels of product availability often get bogged down in debate over the cost of stocking out. The sometimes controversial nature of this cost and its hard-to-quantify components (such as loss of customer goodwill) make it a difficult number for people from different functions to agree on. However, it is often not necessary to estimate a precise cost of stocking out. Using a range of the cost, a manager can identify appropriate levels of availability and the associated profits. Often, profits do not change significantly in the range, thus eliminating the need for a more precise estimation of the cost of stocking out.

When O units are ordered, a firm is left with either too much or too little inventory, depending on demand. When demand is normally distributed, with expected value μ and standard deviation σ, the expected quantity overstocked at the end of the season is given by

$$\text{Expected overstock} = (O - \mu)F_S\left(\frac{O - \mu}{\sigma}\right) + \sigma f_S\left(\frac{O - \mu}{\sigma}\right)$$

The derivation of this formula is provided in Appendix 13D. The formula can be evaluated using Excel as follows:

$$\text{Expected overstock} = (O - \mu)NORMDIST[(O - \mu)/\sigma, 0, 1, 1]$$
$$+ \sigma NORMDIST[(O - \mu)/\sigma, 0, 1, 0)] \tag{13.4}$$

The expected quantity understocked at the end of the season is given by

$$\text{Expected understock} = (\mu - O)\left[1 - F_S\left(\frac{O - \mu}{\sigma}\right)\right] + \sigma f_S\left(\frac{O - \mu}{\sigma}\right)$$

The derivation of this formula is provided in Appendix 13E. The formula can be evaluated using Excel as follows:

$$\text{Expected understock} = (\mu - O)(1 - NORMDIST[(O - \mu)/\sigma, 0, 1, 1])$$
$$+ \sigma NORMDIST[(O - \mu)/\sigma, 0, 1, 0] \tag{13.5}$$

Example 13-2 illustrates the use of Equations 13.4 and 13.5 to evaluate the quantity expected to be overstocked and understocked as a result of an ordering policy (see worksheet *Example 13-2*).

EXAMPLE 13-2 Evaluating Expected Overstock and Understock

Demand for skis at Sportmart is normally distributed with a mean of $\mu = 350$ and a standard deviation of $\sigma = 100$. The manager has decided to order 450 pairs of skis for the upcoming season. Evaluate the expected overstock and understock as a result of this policy.

Analysis:

We have an order size $O = 450$. An overstock results if demand during the season is less than 450. The expected overstock can be obtained using Equation 13.4 as

$$\begin{aligned}
\text{Expected overstock} &= (O - \mu)NORMDIST[(O - \mu)/\sigma, 0, 1, 1] \\
&\quad + \sigma NORMDIST[(O - \mu)/\sigma, 0, 1, 0] \\
&= (450 - 350)NORMDIST[(450 - 350)/100, 0, 1, 1] \\
&\quad + 100\, NORMDIST[(450 - 350)/100, 0, 1, 0] = 108
\end{aligned}$$

Thus, the policy of ordering 450 pairs of skis results in an expected overstock of 108 pairs.

An understock occurs if demand during the season is higher than 450 pairs. The expected understock can be evaluated using Equation 13.5 as follows:

$$\begin{aligned}
\text{Expected understock} &= (\mu - O)(1 - NORMDIST[(O - \mu)/\sigma, 0, 1, 1]) \\
&\quad + \sigma NORMDIST[(O - \mu)/\sigma, 0, 1, 0)] \\
&= (350 - 450)(1 - NORMDIST[(450 - 350)/100, 0, 1, 1]) \\
&\quad + 100\, NORMDIST[(450 - 350)/100, 0, 1, 0] = 8
\end{aligned}$$

Thus, the policy of ordering 450 pairs results in an expected understock of 8 pairs. Note that both the expected understock *and* overstock are positive. This result may seem counterintuitive, but it makes sense because the values used to calculate an expected understock or overstock are always greater than or equal to zero. For example, if demand is 500 and 450 jackets are in inventory, there is an understock of 50 and an overstock of 0 (not -50). This guarantees that the expected value of each will be greater than or equal to zero.

One-Time Orders in the Presence of Quantity Discounts

In this section, we consider a buyer who has to make a single order when the seller offers a price discount based on the quantity purchased. Such a situation may arise in the context of seasonal items such as apparel, for which the manufacturer offers a lower price per unit if order quantities exceed a given threshold. Such decisions also arise at the end of the life cycle for a product or spare parts. Future demand for the product or spare parts is uncertain, and the buyer has a single opportunity to order. The buyer must account for the discount when selecting the order size.

Consider a retailer of spare parts that has one last chance to order parts before the manufacturer stops production. The part has a retail price per unit of p, a cost to the retailer (without discount) of c, and a salvage value of s. The manufacturer has offered a discounted price of c_d if the retailer orders at least K units. The retailer can make its order size decision using the following steps:

1. Using $C_o = c - s$ and $C_u = p - c$, evaluate the optimal cycle service level CSL^* and order size O^* without a discount using Equations 13.1 and 13.2, respectively. Evaluate the expected profit from ordering O^* using Equation 13.3.
2. Using $C_o = c_d - s$ and $C_u = p - c_d$, evaluate the optimal cycle service level CSL_d^* and order size O_d^* with a discount using Equations 13.1 and 13.2, respectively. If $O_d^* \geq K$, evaluate the expected profit from ordering O_d^* units using Equation 13.3. If $O_d^* < K$, evaluate the expected profit from ordering K units using Equation 13.3.
3. Order O^* units if the profit in step 1 is higher. If the profit in step 2 is higher, order O_d^* units if $O_d^* \geq K$ or K units if $O_d^* < K$.

We illustrate the procedure in Example 13-3 (see worksheet *Example 13-3*).

EXAMPLE 13-3 **Evaluating Service Level with Quantity Discounts**

SparesRUs, an auto parts retailer, must decide on the order size for a 20-year-old model of brakes. The manufacturer plans to discontinue production of these brakes after this last production run. SparesRUs has forecast remaining demand for the brakes to be normally distributed,

with a mean of 150 and a standard deviation of 40. The brakes have a retail price of $200. Any unsold brakes are useless and have no salvage value. The manufacturer plans to sell each brake for $50 if the order is for less than 200 brakes and $45 if the order is for at least 200 brakes. How many brakes should SparesRUs order?

Analysis:

In step 1, we calculate the optimal order quantity at the regular price $c = \$50$:

$$\text{Cost of understocking} = C_u = p - c = \$200 - \$50 = \$150$$
$$\text{Cost of overstocking} = C_o = c - s = \$50 - \$0 = \$50$$

Using Equation 13.1, the optimal CSL without a discount is

$$CSL^* = \text{Prob}(Demand \leq O^*) = \frac{C_u}{C_u + C_o} = \frac{150}{150 + 50} = 0.75$$

Using Equation 13.2, the optimal order size is

$$O^* = NORMINV(CSL^*, \mu, \sigma) = NORMINV(0.75, 150, 40) = 177$$

Using Equation 13.3, the expected profit if SparesRUs does not go after the discount is

$$\text{Expected profit from ordering 177 units} = \$19,958$$

In step 2, we consider the discount price $c_d = \$45$ and obtain

$$\text{Cost of understocking} = C_u = p - c_d = \$200 - \$45 = \$155$$
$$\text{Cost of overstocking} = C_o = c_d - s = \$45 - \$0 = \$45$$

Using Equation 13.1, we deduce that the optimal CSL with the discount price is

$$CSL_d^* = \text{Prob}(Demand \leq O_d^*) = \frac{C_u}{C_u + C_o} = \frac{155}{155 + 45} = 0.775$$

Using Equation 13.2, the optimal order size at the discount price is

$$O_d^* = NORMINV(CSL_d^*, \mu, \sigma) = NORMINV(0.775, 150, 40) = 180$$

Given that $180 < 200$, the retailer must order at least 200 brakes to benefit from the discount. Thus, we calculate the expected profit from ordering 200 units using Equation 13.3 as

$$\text{Expected profits from ordering 200 units at \$45 each} = \$20,595$$

It is thus optimal for SparesRUs to order 200 brakes to take advantage of the quantity discount. The expected overstock can be calculated using Equation 13.4 to be 52.

Desired Cycle Service Level for Continuously Stocked Items

In this section, we focus on products such as detergent that are ordered repeatedly by a retail store such as Walmart. Walmart uses safety inventory to increase the level of availability and decrease the probability of stocking out between successive deliveries. If detergent is left over in a replenishment cycle, it can be sold in the next cycle. It does not have to be disposed of at a lower cost. However, a holding cost is incurred as the product is carried from one cycle to the next. The manager at Walmart is faced with the issue of deciding the CSL to aim for.

Two extreme scenarios should be considered:

1. All demand that arises when the product is out of stock is backlogged and filled later, when inventories are replenished.
2. All demand arising when the product is out of stock is lost.

The reality in most instances is somewhere in between, with some of the demand lost and other customers returning when the product is in stock. We consider both extreme cases.

We assume that demand per unit time is normally distributed, along with the following inputs:

Q: Replenishment lot size

S: Fixed cost associated with each order

ROP: Reorder point

D: Average demand per unit time

σ_D: Standard deviation of demand per unit time

ss: Safety inventory (recall that $ss = ROP - D_L$)

CSL: Cycle service level

C: Unit cost

h: Holding cost as a fraction of product cost per unit time

H: Cost of holding one unit for one unit of time. $H = hC$

DEMAND DURING STOCKOUT IS BACKLOGGED We first consider the case in which all demand arising when the product is out of stock is backlogged. Because no demand is lost, minimizing costs becomes equivalent to maximizing profits. As an example, consider a Walmart store selling detergent. The store manager offers a rain check at a discount of C_u to each customer wanting to buy detergent when it is out of stock. Assume that the rain check ensures that all these customers return when inventory is replenished. Thus, C_u is the backlogging or understocking cost per unit.

If the store manager increases the level of safety inventory, more orders are satisfied from stock, resulting in lower backlogs. This decreases the backlogging or understocking cost. However, the cost of holding inventory increases. We start by considering the costs and benefits of holding an additional unit of safety inventory in each replenishment cycle. If the safety inventory is increased from ss (which provides a cycle service level, CSL) to $ss + 1$, the supply chain incurs cost to hold the additional unit of inventory for a replenishment cycle (which has duration Q/D). The additional unit of safety inventory is beneficial (the benefit equals the cost of understocking C_u) if demand during the replenishment cycle is such that more than ss units of safety inventory are consumed [this happens with probability $(1 - CSL)$]. We thus have the following:

Increased cost per replenishment cycle of additional safety inventory of 1 unit $= (Q/D)H$

Benefit per replenishment cycle of additional safety inventory of 1 unit $= (1 - CSL)C_u$

In this case, the optimal cycle service level is obtained by equating the additional cost and benefit to be

$$CSL^* = 1 - \left[\frac{HQ}{DC_u}\right] \tag{13.6}$$

Given the optimal cycle service level, the required safety inventory can be evaluated using Equation 12.5 if demand is normally distributed.

From Equation 13.6, observe that increasing the lot size Q allows the store manager at Walmart to reduce the cycle service level and, thus, the safety inventory carried. This is because increasing the lot size increases the fill rate and thus reduces the quantity backlogged. One should be careful, however, because an increase in lot size raises the cycle inventory. In general, increasing the lot size is not an effective way for a firm to improve product availability.

If the cost of stocking out is known, one can use Equation 13.6 to obtain the appropriate cycle service level (and thus the appropriate level of safety inventory). In many practical settings,

though, it is hard to estimate the cost of stocking out. In such a situation, a manager may want to evaluate the cost of a stockout implied by the current inventory policy. When a precise cost of stockout cannot be found, this implied stockout cost at least gives an idea of whether inventory should be increased, decreased, or kept about the same. In Example 13-4, we show how Equation 13.6 can be used to impute a cost of stocking out given an inventory policy (see worksheet *Examples 13-4, 5*).

EXAMPLE 13-4 Imputing Cost of Stockout from Inventory Policy

Weekly demand for detergent at Walmart is normally distributed, with a mean of $D = 100$ gallons and a standard deviation of $\sigma_D = 20$. The replenishment lead time is $L = 2$ weeks. The store manager at Walmart orders 400 gallons when the available inventory drops to 300 gallons. Each gallon of detergent costs \$3. The holding cost Walmart incurs is 20 percent. If all unfilled demand is backlogged and carried over to the next cycle, evaluate the cost of stocking out implied by the current replenishment policy.

Analysis:

In this case, we have

$$\text{Lot size, } Q = 400 \text{ gallons}$$
$$\text{Reorder point, } ROP = 300 \text{ gallons}$$
$$\text{Average demand per week, } D = 100$$
$$\text{Standard deviation of demand per week, } \sigma_D = 20$$
$$\text{Unit cost, } C = \$3$$
$$\text{Holding cost as a fraction of product cost per year, } h = 0.2$$
$$\text{Cost of holding one unit for one year, } H = hC = \$0.6$$
$$\text{Lead time, } L = 2 \text{ weeks}$$

We thus have

$$\text{Mean demand over lead time, } D_L = DL = 200 \text{ gallons}$$

$$\text{Standard deviation of demand over lead time, } \sigma_L = \sigma_D \sqrt{L} = 20\sqrt{2} = 28.3$$

Because demand is normally distributed, we can use Equations 12.4 and 12.22 to evaluate the CSL under the current inventory policy:

$$CSL = F(ROP, D_L, \sigma_L) = NORMDIST(300, 200, 28.3, 1) = 0.9998$$

We can thus deduce that the imputed cost of stocking out (using Equation 13.6) is given by

$$C_u = \frac{HQ}{(1 - CSL)D} = \frac{0.6 \times 400}{(1 - 0.9998) \times 100 \times 52} = \$230.77 \text{ per gallon}$$

The implication here is that if each shortage of a gallon of detergent costs Walmart \$230.77, the current CSL of 0.9998 is optimal. In this particular example, one can claim that the store manager is carrying too much inventory because the cost of stocking out of detergent is unlikely to be \$230.77 per gallon.

A manager can use the previous analysis to decide whether the imputed cost of stocking out, and thus the inventory policy, is reasonable.

DEMAND DURING STOCKOUT IS LOST When unfilled demand during the stockout period is lost, the optimal cycle service level CSL^* is given as

$$CSL^* = 1 - \frac{HQ}{HQ + DC_u} \tag{13.7}$$

We have assumed that C_u is the cost of losing one unit of demand during the stockout period. From comparing Equations 13.6 and 13.7, observe that for the same cost of understocking, a supply chain should offer a higher cycle service level if sales are lost rather than backlogged. In Example 13-5, we evaluate the optimal cycle service level if demand is lost during the stockout period (see worksheet *Examples 13-4, 5*).

EXAMPLE 13-5	Evaluating Optimal Service Level When Unmet Demand Is Lost

Consider the situation in Example 13-4 but make the assumption that all demand during a stockout is lost. Assume that the cost of losing one unit of demand is $2. Evaluate the optimal cycle service level that the store manager at Walmart should target.

Analysis:

In this case, we have

$$\text{Lot size, } Q = 400 \text{ gallons}$$
$$\text{Average demand per year, } D = 100 \times 52 = 5{,}200$$
$$\text{Cost of holding one unit for one year, } H = \$0.6$$
$$\text{Cost of understocking, } C_u = \$2$$

Using Equation 13.7, the optimal cycle service level is given as

$$CSL^* = 1 - \frac{HQ}{HQ + DC_u} = 1 - \frac{0.6 \times 400}{0.6 \times 400 + 2 \times 5{,}200} = 0.98$$

The store manager at Walmart should target a cycle service level of 98 percent.

SUMMARY OF LEARNING OBJECTIVE 2

For seasonal products, the optimal level of product availability is given by $C_u/(C_u + C_o)$, where C_o is the cost of overstocking and C_u is the cost of understocking. For continuously stocked products, the optimal cycle service level is given by $1 - HQ/(DC_u)$ if all unmet demand is backlogged. For continuously stocked products, the optimal cycle service level is given by $1 - HQ/(HQ + DC_u)$ if all unmet demand is lost. As the cost of overstocking increases, it is optimal to lower the targeted level of product availability. As the lost margin from being out of stock increases, it is optimal to raise the targeted level of product availability.

13.3 *Use basic managerial levers to improve supply chain profitability.*

BASIC MANAGERIAL LEVERS TO IMPROVE SUPPLY CHAIN PROFITABILITY

Having identified the factors that influence the optimal level of product availability, we now focus on basic actions a manager can take to improve supply chain profitability. We have shown in Section 13.2 that the costs of overstocking and understocking have a direct impact on both the optimal cycle service level and profitability. The profitability is also affected by the demand uncertainty. Three basic managerial levers to increase profitability are thus

1. Increasing the salvage value of each unit increases profitability (as well as the optimal cycle service level).
2. Decreasing the margin lost from a stockout increases profitability (by allowing a lower optimal cycle service level).
3. Decreasing the uncertainty of demand increases profitability (by decreasing both the expected overstock and the expected understock).

Strategies to increase the salvage value include selling to outlet stores so leftover units are not merely discarded. Some companies, such as Sport Obermeyer, which sells winter wear in the United States, sell the surplus in South America, where the winter corresponds to the North American summer. The increased salvage value of the surplus allows Sport Obermeyer to provide a higher level of product availability in the United States and increase its profits. The growth of online liquidators such as Overstock.com helps retailers by increasing their salvage value for overstocked products. Increasing the salvage value of leftover units allows a firm to increase profits by providing a higher level of product availability because the cost of excess inventory has been reduced.

Strategies to decrease the margin lost in a stockout include arranging for backup sourcing (which may be more expensive) so customers are not lost forever. The practice of purchasing product from a competitor on the open market to satisfy customer demand is observed and justified by the earlier reasoning. In the MRO supply industry, McMaster-Carr and W.W. Grainger, two major competitors, are also large customers for each other. The cost of understocking can also be decreased by providing the customer with a substitute product. Decreasing the cost of understocking allows a firm to increase profits by providing a lower level of product availability (because there are alternatives available to serve the customer), thus decreasing the amount of excess inventory at the end of the season.

Another significant managerial lever to improve supply chain profitability is the reduction of demand uncertainty. With reduced demand uncertainty, a supply chain manager can better match supply and demand by reducing both overstocking and understocking. We show that improved forecast accuracy can help a firm significantly increase its profitability while decreasing the excess inventory overstocked as well as the sales lost because of understocking. We illustrate the impact of improving forecast accuracy in Example 13-6 (see worksheet *Example 13-6*).

EXAMPLE 13-6 Impact of Improved Forecasts

Consider a buyer at Bloomingdale's who is responsible for purchasing dinnerware with Christmas patterns. The dinnerware sells only during the Christmas season, and the buyer places an order for delivery in early November. Each dinnerware set costs $c = \$100$ and sells for a retail price of $p = \$250$. Any sets unsold by Christmas are heavily discounted in the post-Christmas sales and are sold for a salvage value of $s = \$80$. The buyer has estimated that demand is normally distributed, with a mean of $\mu = 350$. Historically, forecast errors have had a standard deviation of $\sigma = 150$. The buyer has decided to conduct additional market research to get a better forecast. Evaluate the impact of improved forecast accuracy on profitability and inventories as the buyer reduces σ from 150 to 0 in increments of 30.

Analysis:

In this case, we have

$$\text{Cost of understocking} = C_u = p - c = \$250 - \$100 = \$150$$
$$\text{Cost of overstocking} = C_o = c - s = \$100 - \$80 = \$20$$

Using Equation 13.1, we have

$$CSL^* = Prob(Demand \leq O^*) \geq \frac{150}{150 + 20} = 0.88$$

The optimal order size is obtained using Equation 13.2 and the expected profit using Equation 13.3. The order size and expected profit as forecast accuracy (measured by standard deviation of forecast error) varies are shown in Table 13-3 and Figure 3-3. Observe that the expected profit increases while the expected overstock and understock decrease as forecast error decreases.

TABLE 13-3 Expected Profit and Order Size at Bloomingdale's

Standard Deviation of Forecast Error σ	Optimal Order Size O^*	Expected Overstock	Expected Understock	Expected Profit
150	526	186.7	8.6	$47,469
120	491	149.3	6.9	$48,476
90	456	112.0	5.2	$49,482
60	420	74.7	3.5	$50,488
30	385	37.3	1.7	$51,494
0	350	0	0	$52,500

SUMMARY OF LEARNING OBJECTIVE 3

Supply chain profits can be increased by decreasing the cost of overstocking through the use of outlet channels. Profits can also be increased by decreasing the cost of understocking by providing substitute products or arranging for emergency supply sources (even if they are more expensive). Supply chain profits also increase if the underlying uncertainty of demand can be decreased. A decrease in forecast error decreases both the expected overstock and expected understock.

THE VALUE OF SPEED IN A SEASONAL SUPPLY CHAIN

13.4 Discuss how speed can improve profits in a supply chain.

Quick response is the set of actions a supply chain takes to reduce the replenishment lead time. Supply chain managers are able to improve their forecast accuracy as lead times decrease, which allows them to better match supply with demand and increase supply chain profitability. We have discussed the benefits of lead time reduction for regularly stocked items such as detergent in Chapter 12 (see Example 12-6). We now focus on the benefits of speed for seasonal items.

To illustrate the issues, consider the example of Saks Fifth Avenue, a high-end department store, which purchases cashmere shawls from India and Nepal. The selling season for cashmere

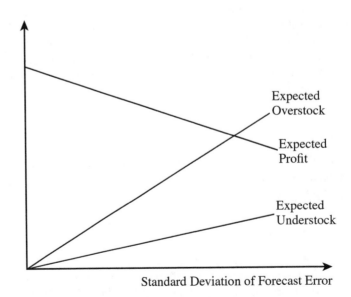

Expected Overstock

Expected Profit

Expected Understock

Standard Deviation of Forecast Error

Figure 13-3 Variation of Profit and Inventories with Forecast Accuracy

shawls is about 14 weeks. Historically, replenishment lead times have been about 25 to 30 weeks. With a 30-week lead time, the buyer at Saks must place the entire order well before the start of the sales season. It is difficult for a buyer to make an accurate forecast of demand this far in advance. This results in high-demand uncertainty, leading the buyer to order either too many or too few shawls each year.

Typically, buyers are able to make accurate forecasts once they have observed sales for the first week or two in the season. If lead times can be shortened to facilitate the use of actual sales when placing part of the seasonal order, there can be significant benefits for the supply chain. Consider the situation in which manufacturers are able to reduce replenishment lead time to six weeks. This reduction allows the buyer at Saks to break up the entire season's purchase into two orders, each covering seven weeks of demand. The first order is placed six weeks before the start of the sales season. The buyer orders what the store expects to sell over the first seven weeks of the season. The first order must be placed without observing any sales. Once the season starts, the buyer observes sales for the first week and places a second order after the first week for the final seven weeks of the season. When placing the second order, the buyer can use sales information from the first week of the season to get a more accurate forecast for demand. Speed in replenishment allows Saks to use the second order to better match supply and demand, resulting in higher profits.

When multiple orders are placed in the season, it is not possible to provide formulas like Equations 13.1 to 13.5 that specify the optimal order quantity, the expected profit, expected overstock, and expected understock. Rather, we must use simulation (see Appendix 13F) or approximations to identify the impact of different ordering policies. We illustrate the impact of being able to place multiple orders in a season using approximations on the Saks example discussed earlier.

The buyer at Saks must decide on the quantity of cashmere shawls to order from India and Nepal for the upcoming winter season. The unit cost of each shawl is $c = \$40$, and the shawl retails for $p = \$150$. After the sales season of 14 weeks, any leftover shawls are sold to the discount store for $s = \$30$ each.

Before the start of the sales season, the buyer forecasts weekly demand to be normally distributed, with a mean of $D = 20$ and a standard deviation of $\sigma_D = 15$. We compare the impact of the following two ordering policies:

1. Supply lead time is more than 15 weeks. As a result, a single order must be placed at the beginning of the season to cover the entire season's demand.
2. Supply lead time is reduced to six weeks. As a result, two orders are placed for the season, one to be delivered at the beginning of the season and the other to be placed at the end of week 1 and delivered at the beginning of week 8.

For policy 2, we assume that once the buyer sees sales for the first week, she is able to forecast demand for the first seven-week period accurately (this approximation allows us to quantify the benefits of the second order). She is still not able to predict sales for the second seven-week period. In terms of her forecasting ability for the second seven-week period, we consider two scenarios—one in which the buyer's forecast accuracy does not improve for the second order (i.e., the standard deviation of forecast demand stays at 15), and another in which it improves and the buyer is able to reduce the standard deviation of the forecast to 3 instead of 15. We also assume that demand is independent across weeks.

Single Order for the Season

We first start with buyers placing a single order for the season. Given that the season lasts 14 weeks and demand is independent across weeks, we obtain the following (using Equation 12.1):

$$\text{Expected demand of shawls in the season} = \mu = 14D = 14 \times 20 - 280$$
$$\text{Standard deviation of seasonal demand, } \sigma = \sqrt{14}\sigma_D = \sqrt{14} \times 15 = 56.1$$

Using Equation 13.1, the optimal cycle service level is given by

$$CSL^* = \frac{p - c}{p - s} = \frac{150 - 40}{150 - 30} = 0.92$$

The optimal order quantity for a single order is obtained using Equation 13.2:

$$O^* = NORMINV(CSL^*, \mu, \sigma) = NORMINV(0.92, 280, 56.1) = 358$$

For an order of 358 shawls, we obtain

Expected profit with a single order(using Equation 13.3) = \$29,767
Expected overstock(using Equation 13.4) = 79.8
Expected understock(using Equation 13.5) = 2.14

Given that the cost of overstocking is \$10 per shawl and the cost of understocking is \$110 per shawl, we obtain

Expected cost of overstocking = 79.8 × \$10 = \$798
Expected cost of understocking = 2.14 × \$110 = \$235

If there were no demand uncertainty, demand over the season would be 280 shawls with a profit of 280 × \$110 = \$30,800. Observe that expected profit is reduced by \$30,800\$ − 29,767 = \$1,033 = \$798 + \$235 because of uncertainty. Thus, uncertainty reduces the expected profit by the expected cost of overstocking and understocking.

From the preceding analysis, it also follows that the reduction of uncertainty as a result of shortening lead times will increase profits in the season by \$1,033 at most.

The Value of Being Able to Place a Second Order for the Season

We now describe a procedure that can be used to estimate the benefit of placing two orders in a season. We assume that the first order aims to cover demand for the first seven weeks and the second order for the last seven weeks. Given that the buyer will see the first week of demand before placing the second order, we assume that she will accurately be able to predict sales in the first seven-week period. Thus, her second order can take into account any leftover inventory or unmet demand from the first order.

First, consider that no improvement in forecast accuracy occurs after observing the first period demand (standard deviation of weekly demand remains 15). For each seven-week period, we obtain the following:

Expected demand of shawls in seven weeks = μ_7 = 7 × 20 = 140
Standard deviation of demand over seven weeks = σ_7 = $\sqrt{7}$ × 15 = 39.7

The optimal cycle service level is maintained at 0.92. Using Equation 13.2, we obtain the size of the first order to be

$$O_1 = NORMINV(CSL^*, \mu_7, \sigma_7) = NORMINV(0.92, 140, 39.7) = 195$$

For an order of 195 shawls, we obtain

Expected profit from seven weeks (using Equation 13.3) = \$14,670
Expected overstock (using Equation 13.4) = 56.4
Expected understock (using Equation 13.5) = 1.51

Recall our assumption that the buyer can accurately predict sales over the first seven-week period when she places the second order at the end of week 1. Thus, any overstock resulting from the first order will be used to adjust the size of the second order. We also assume that any understock in the first seven weeks is served from shawls that arrive in the second order. Given that the desired starting inventory for the second seven-week period is 195 shawls, the expected overstock at the end of the first seven-week period is 56.4 shawls, and the expected understock is 1.51 shawls, the second order will be only 195 − 56.4 + 1.51 = 140.11 shawls, on average. Given

that all overstock from the first seven-week period is used to lower the order size for the second seven-week period and all understock is served from the second order, there is no overstock or understock cost from the first order. There is an expected overstock of 56.4 shawls (this is the expected overstock when starting the second seven-week period with 195 shawls) and an expected understock of 1.51 shawls at the end of the season.

The expected profit at the end of the season is thus given by the sum of the expected profit from each seven-week period and the expected overstock and understock cost recovered from the first seven-week period as follows:

Expected profit from season = $14,670 + (56.4 × $10) + (1.51 × $110) + $14,670 = $30,070

We add (56.4 × $10) + (1.51 × $110) to the expected profit from the first seven-week half because there is effectively no overstock that must be sold to the discount store at the end of the first seven weeks or understock where margin is lost. Our analysis indicates that allowing for a second order in the season increases profits by $30,070 − $29,767 = $303 even if there is no improvement in forecast accuracy for the second seven-week period. The profit increase will be smaller, however, if we assume that customers who do not find the product at the end of the first seven weeks are unwilling to wait for the second order to arrive. Observe that as a result of allowing a second order, the total order quantity has decreased from 358 shawls to 195 + 140.1 = 335.1 shawls. The expected overstock at the end of the season has decreased from 79.8 to 56.4 shawls and the expected understock has decreased to 1.51.

From our analysis, we observe three important consequences of being able to place a second replenishment order in the season after observing some sales:

1. The expected total quantity ordered during the season with two orders is less than that with a single order for the same cycle service level. In other words, it is possible to provide the same level of product availability to the customer with less inventory if a second, follow-up order is allowed after observing some sales.
2. The average overstock to be disposed of at the end of the sales season and the expected understock is less if a follow-up order is allowed after observing some sales.
3. The profits are higher when a follow-up order is allowed during the sales season.

In other words, as replenishment speed allows the total quantity for the season to be broken up into multiple smaller orders, with the size of each order based on some observed sales, the buyer is better able to match supply and demand and increase profitability for Saks. These relationships are shown in Figures 13-4 and 13-5.

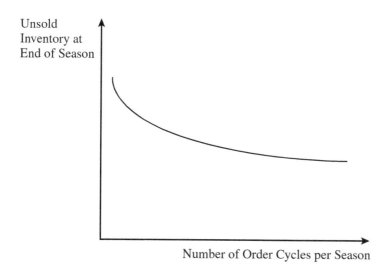

Figure 13-4 Leftover Inventory Versus Number of Order Cycles per Season

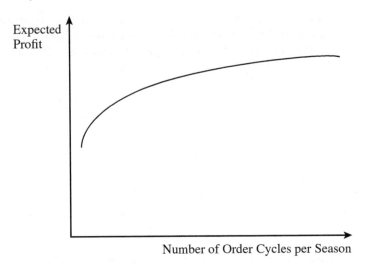

Figure 13-5 Expected Profit Versus Number of Order Cycles per Season

We now consider the case in which the buyer improves her forecast accuracy for the second order after observing some of the season's demand. As a result, the standard deviation of weekly demand forecast drops from 15 to 3 for the second seven-week period. In this setting, the first order stays at 195 shawls, as discussed earlier. For the second order, however, we must account for the fact that the standard deviation of weekly demand has dropped to 3. As a result, we obtain

$$\text{Expected demand of shawls in seven weeks} = \mu_7 = 7 \times 20 = 140$$
$$\text{Standard deviation of demand over first seven weeks} = \sigma_7 = \sqrt{7} \times 15 = 39.7$$
$$\text{Standard deviation of demand over second seven weeks} = \sigma_7^2 = \sqrt{7} \times 3 = 7.9$$

The optimal cycle service level is maintained at 0.92. Using Equation 13.2, we obtain the desired number of shawls at the beginning of the first seven weeks to be $O_1 = 195$ as before and that at the beginning of the second seven weeks to be O_2 where:

$$O_2 = NORMINV(CSL^*, \mu_7, \sigma_7^2) = NORMINV(0.92, 140, 7.9) = 151$$

As in the previous analysis, we assume that the buyer is accurately able to predict sales for the first seven-week period after observing sales for the first week. She thus accounts for the overstock and understock at the end of the first seven-week period when placing her second order. Given an expected overstock of 56.4 shawls and an expected understock of 1.51 from the first order, the net second order is thus $151 - 56.4 + 1.51 = 96.11$ shawls. With 151 shawls at the start of the second seven weeks, we obtain

$$\text{Expected profit from second order (using Equation 13.3)} = \$15,254$$
$$\text{Expected overstock (using Equation 13.4)} = 11.3$$
$$\text{Expected understock (using Equation 13.5)} = 0.30$$

Again observe that there is no overstock cost at the end of the first seven weeks and we have assumed that customer orders that are understocked in the first order are served from the second order. Thus, the net profits for the season are $14,670 (first seven weeks) + 56.4 × $10 (no overstock at the end of first seven weeks) + 1.51 × $110 (understock is served from second order) + $15,254 (second seven weeks) = $30,654. If forecast accuracy improves as a result of observing early seasonal demand, the season's profit increases by $30,654 − $29,767 = $887. The expected overstock at the end of the season has now declined to 11.3 units and the expected understock to 0.3 units. A second order and improved forecast accuracy as a result of seeing early season sales thus increase profits and decrease overstocks and understock.

Zara, the Spanish apparel retailer, has built its entire strategy around speed and quick response. At a time when most of its competitors were cutting costs by outsourcing production to low-cost countries, Zara focused on reducing response time by setting up production facilities in Spain. While competitors had lead times that ranged from three to nine months, Zara was able to reduce its design-to-shelf lead times to three to four weeks. Given a three-month sales season (for each of fall, winter, spring, and summer), competitors were forced to make sourcing decisions well before the start of a season. In contrast, Zara divided the three-month sales season into three one-month periods. For the first month, Zara decided on quantities without knowing what sales would be. These quantities, however, were much lower than what the competition was required to order for the entire three-month season. For the second month, Zara made its production decisions after observing the first week of demand (Zara also observed demand at its competition). For the third month, Zara made its production decisions after observing the entire first month of sales. In each instance, observing sales allowed Zara to significantly improve its forecast accuracy. The result was that Zara was able to bring in more of what was selling without wasting precious production capacity on what was not likely to sell. Speed allowed Zara to respond to trends rather than have to predict them. This resulted in higher profits for Zara because it produced what was selling and had less overstock and understock. The *New York Times* reported in 2006 that "Zara books 85 percent of the full ticket price for its merchandise while the industry average is 60 percent."

From our previous discussion, quick response is clearly advantageous to a retailer in a supply chain—with one caveat. As the manufacturer reduces replenishment lead times, allowing for a second order, we have seen that the retailer's order size drops. In effect, the manufacturer sells less to the retailer (at least in the short term). Thus, quick response results in the manufacturer making a lower profit in the short term if all else is unchanged. This is an important point to consider, because decreasing replenishment lead times requires tremendous effort from the manufacturer, yet seems to benefit the retailer at the expense of the manufacturer. The benefits resulting from quick response should be shared appropriately across the supply chain. This was easier for Zara, which was vertically integrated into responsive manufacturing and retailing. It can be a challenge, however, for retailers that outsource manufacturing.

SUMMARY OF LEARNING OBJECTIVE 4

Speed in replenishment allows a retailer to place multiple orders in a selling season. Multiple replenishments allow the supply chain to better match supply and demand by being able to respond to trends rather than having to forecast them. The resulting decrease in overstock and understock quantities increases profits.

THE VALUE OF POSTPONEMENT IN A SEASONAL SUPPLY CHAIN

13.5 *Understand conditions under which postponement is valuable in a supply chain.*

As discussed in Chapter 12, postponement refers to the delay of product differentiation until closer to the sale of the product. With postponement, all activities prior to product differentiation require aggregate forecasts that are more accurate than individual product forecasts. Individual product forecasts are required close to the time of sale when demand is known with greater accuracy. As a result, postponement allows a supply chain to better match supply with demand. Postponement can be a powerful managerial lever to increase profitability. It can be particularly valuable if customers are willing to wait for delivery. If the supply chain can postpone product differentiation until after receiving the customer order, a significant reduction in inventories and lost sales can be achieved. Our goal in this section is to understand when postponement results in higher profits.

The major benefit of postponement arises from the improved matching of supply and demand. There is a cost associated with postponement, however, because the production cost

using postponement is typically higher than the production cost without it. For example, the production process at Benetton, where assembled knit garments are dyed, costs about 10 percent more than if dyed thread is knitted. Similarly, when retailers mix paint at stores rather than at the factory, manufacturing costs increase because there is a loss of economies of scale in mixing. Given the increased production cost from postponement, a company should ensure that the benefits of postponement are larger than the additional costs.

Postponement is valuable for a firm that sells a large variety of products with demand that is unpredictable, independent, and comparable in size. We illustrate this using the example of Benetton selling knit garments in solid colors. Starting with thread, two steps are needed to complete the garment—dyeing and knitting. Traditionally, thread was dyed and then the garment was knitted (Option 1). Benetton developed a procedure whereby dyeing was postponed until after the garment was knitted (Option 2).

Benetton sells each knit garment at a retail price $p = \$50$. Option 1 (no postponement) results in a manufacturing cost of \$20, whereas Option 2 (postponement) results in a manufacturing cost of \$22 per garment. Benetton disposes of any unsold garments at the end of the season in a clearance for $s = \$10$ each. The knitting or manufacturing process takes a total of 20 weeks. For the sake of discussion, we assume that Benetton sells garments in four colors. Twenty weeks in advance, Benetton forecasts demand for each color to be normally distributed, with a mean of $\mu = 1{,}000$ and a standard deviation of $\sigma = 500$. Demand for each color is independent. With Option 1, Benetton makes the buying decision for each color 20 weeks before the sale period and holds separate inventories for each color. With Option 2, Benetton forecasts only the aggregate uncolored thread to purchase 20 weeks in advance. The inventory held is based on the aggregate demand across all four colors. Benetton decides the quantity for individual colors after demand is known. We now quantify the impact of postponement for Benetton. All analysis is detailed in the spreadsheet *Chapter13-postponement-Benetton*. See worksheet *Benetton* for the following analysis.

With Option 1, Benetton must decide on the quantity of colored thread to purchase for each color. For each color we have

Retail price, $p = \$50$

Manufacturing cost, $c = \$20$

Salvage value, $s = \$10$

Using Equation 13.1, we obtain the optimal cycle service level for each color as

$$CSL^* = \frac{p - c}{p - s} = \frac{50 - 20}{50 - 10} = 0.75$$

Using Equation 13.2, the optimal purchase quantity of thread in each color is

$$O^* = NORMINV(CSL^*, \mu, \sigma) = NORMINV(0.75, 1000, 500) = 1{,}337$$

Thus, it is optimal for Benetton to produce 1,337 units of each color. Using Equation 13.3, the expected profit from each color is

Expected profits $= \$23{,}644$

Using Equations 13.4 and 13.5, the expected overstock and understock for each color is

Expected overstock $= 412$

Expected understock $= 75$

Using Option 1, across all four colors Benetton thus produces $4 \times 1{,}337 = 5{,}348$ sweaters. This results in an expected profit of $4 \times 23{,}644 = \$94{,}576$, with an average of $4 \times 412 = 1{,}648$ sweaters sold on clearance at the end of the season and $4 \times 75 = 300$ customers turned away for lack of sweaters.

Under Option 2, Benetton has to decide only the total number of sweaters across all four colors to be produced, because they can be dyed to the appropriate colors once demand is known. In this case, we have

Retail price, $p = \$50$

Manufacturing cost, $c = \$22$

Salvage value, $s = \$10$

Using Equation 13.1, the optimal cycle service level for each color is

$$CSL^* = \frac{p - c}{p - s} = \frac{50 - 22}{50 - 10} = 0.70$$

Given that demand for each color is independent, total demand across all four colors can be evaluated using Equation 12.15 to be normally distributed, with a mean of μ_A and a standard deviation of σ_A, where

$$\mu_A = 4 \times 1,000 = 4,000 \quad \sigma_A = \sqrt{4} \times 500 = 1,000$$

Using Equation 13.2, the optimal aggregate production quantity for Benetton is given by O_A^*, where

$$O_A^* = NORMINV(0.7, \mu_A, \sigma_A) = NORMINV(0.7, 4000, 1000) = 4,524$$

Under Option 2, it is optimal for Benetton to produce 4,524 undyed sweaters, to be dyed as demand by color is available. The expected profit with postponement is evaluated using Equation 13.3 as

Expected profits $= \$98,092$

Using Equations 13.4 and 13.5, the expected overstock is 715 and the expected understock is 190. Thus, postponement increases expected profits for Benetton from $94,576 to $98,092. Expected overstock declines from 1,648 to 715, and the expected understock declines from 300 to 190. Clearly, the use of postponement and production using Option 2 is a good choice for Benetton in this case.

The benefits of postponement decrease significantly if demand across the different colors is positively correlated. In the Benetton example, we find that postponement is not valuable if the correlation coefficient across each color is $\rho = 0.2$ or higher as shown in Table 13-4. In general, postponement is more valuable when demand is less positively correlated across variants.

TABLE 13-4 Impact of Demand Uncertainty and Correlation on Value of Postponement

Mean Demand per Color	SD of Demand per color	Correlation Coefficient ρ	Expected profit Without Postponement	Expected Profit With Postponement
1,000	500	0	$94,578	$98,902
1,000	500	0.15	$94,578	$95,253
1,000	500	0.20	$94,578	$94,408
1,000	500	0.25	$94,578	$93,602
1,000	350	0	$102,205	$102,265
1,000	300	0	$104,747	$103,655
1,000	250	0	$107,289	$105,046

The benefits of postponement also decrease significantly if demand is more predictable. If the standard deviation of demand for each color decreases to 300 or less, our analysis in Table 13-4 shows that Option 2 with postponement results in lower profits than Option 1 without postponement. In general, postponement is more valuable when the demand uncertainty is high.

Value of Postponement with a Dominant Product

Postponement is not very effective if a large fraction of demand comes from a single product. The benefit from aggregation is small in this case, whereas the increased production cost applies to all items produced. We illustrate this idea once again using Benetton as an example (see worksheet *Postponement with dominant prod*).

Assume that demand for red sweaters at Benetton is forecast to be normally distributed, with a mean of $\mu_{red} = 3{,}100$ and a standard deviation of $\sigma_{red} = 800$. Demand for each of the other three colors is forecast to be normally distributed, with a mean of $\mu = 300$ and a standard deviation of $\sigma = 200$. Observe that red sweaters constitute about 80 percent of demand.

Under Option 1, the optimal cycle service level CSL^* is 0.75, as evaluated earlier. Using Equation 13.2, the optimal production of red sweaters is given by

$$O^*_{red} = NORMINV(CSL^*, \mu_{red}, \sigma_{red}) = NORMINV(0.75, 3100, 800) = 3{,}640$$

Using Equation 13.3, the expected profit from red sweaters is \$82,831. Using Equation 13.4, the expected overstock of red sweaters is 659; using Equation 13.5, the expected understock of red sweaters is 119. For each of the other three colors, we can similarly evaluate the optimal production to be O^* where

$$O^* = NORMINV(CSL^*, \mu, \sigma) = NORMINV(0.75, 300, 200) = 435$$

This results in an expected profit of \$6,458, an expected overstock of 165, and an expected understock of 30 for each of the other three colors. Across all four colors, Option 1 thus results in the following:

Total production $= 3{,}640 + 3 \times 435 = 4{,}945$
Expected profit $= \$82{,}831 + 3 \times \$6{,}458 = \$102{,}205$
Expected overstock $= 659 + 3 \times 165 = 1{,}154$
Expected understock $= 119 + 3 \times 30 = 209$

Under Option 2, Benetton has to decide only the total production across all four colors. Given that demand for each color is independent, total demand across all four colors can be evaluated using Equation 12.13 to be normally distributed, with a mean of μ_A and a standard deviation of σ_A, where

$$\mu_A = 3{,}100 + 3 \times 300 = 4{,}000; \ \sigma_A = \sqrt{800^2 + 3 \times 200^2} = 872$$

Under Option 2, we repeat all calculations to obtain the following:

Total production $= 4{,}457$
Expected profit $= \$99{,}876$
Expected overstock $= 623$
Expected understock $= 166$

In this case, Benetton sees its profits decline even though both overstock and understock have decreased as a result of postponement. This is because a large fraction of demand is from red sweaters, which can already be forecast with reasonably good accuracy. Postponement and the resulting aggregation thus do little to improve the forecasting accuracy of red sweaters. They do, however, improve the forecasting accuracy for the other three colors, but they represent a

small fraction of demand. Meanwhile, the production costs increase for all sweaters (including red sweaters). As a result, the increased production costs outweigh the benefits from postponement across all colors.

Next, we discuss how tailored postponement can be an effective strategy when complete postponement is not appropriate.

Tailored Postponement: Impact on Profits and Inventories

In *tailored postponement*, a firm uses production with postponement to satisfy a part of its demand, with the rest being satisfied without postponement. Tailored postponement is more complex but produces higher profits than when no postponement is used or all products are manufactured using postponement. Under tailored postponement, a firm produces the amount that is predictable using the lower-cost production method without postponement. The firm produces the portion of demand that is uncertain using postponement. On the portion of the demand that is predictable, postponement provides little value in terms of increased forecast accuracy. The firm thus produces that portion using the lower-cost method to lower the manufacturing cost. On the portion of demand that is uncertain, postponement significantly improves forecast accuracy. The firm is thus willing to incur the increased production cost to achieve the benefit from the improved matching of supply and demand. We now illustrate the idea of tailored postponement, returning to the example of Benetton (see worksheet *Tailored postponement*).

One way to implement tailored postponement is to produce high-demand, predictable products without postponement and produce only the unpredictable products using postponement. Let us return to the Benetton data with red sweaters constituting about 80 percent of demand. Recall that demand for red sweaters at Benetton is forecast to be normally distributed, with a mean of $\mu_{red} = 3,100$ and a standard deviation of $\sigma_{red} = 800$. Demand for each of the other three colors is forecast to be normally distributed, with a mean of $\mu = 300$ and a standard deviation of $\sigma = 200$. We evaluated that postponing all colors decreases profits for Benetton by more than \$2,000 (from \$102,205 to \$99,876). However, if we tailor postponement so red sweaters are made using the traditional method and only the other colors are postponed, profits actually increase by \$1,009, to \$103,213.

A more sophisticated approach to postponement separates all demand into base load and variation. The base load is manufactured using the low-cost method without postponement, and only the variation is made using postponement. This more sophisticated form of tailored postponement is more complex to implement but can be valuable even when all products being postponed have similar demand, as we illustrate next (see spreadsheet *Table 13-5*). Consider the scenario in which Benetton is selling four colors, and the forecast demand for each color is normally distributed, with a mean of $\mu = 1,000$ and a standard deviation of $\sigma = 500$. We have observed earlier that the use of complete postponement (every sweater is postponed) in this instance increases profits at Benetton from \$94,576 to \$98,092.

We now consider a situation in which Benetton applies tailored postponement and uses both Option 1 (dye thread and then knit garment) and Option 2 (dye the knit garment) for production. For each color, Benetton identifies a quantity Q_1 (the base load) to be manufactured using Option 1 and an aggregate quantity Q_A to be manufactured using Option 2, with colors for the aggregate quantity being assigned when demand is known. We now identify the appropriate tailored postponement policy and its impact on profits and inventories. There is no formula that can be used to evaluate the optimal policy and profits in this case. We thus resort to simulations to study the impact of different policies. The results of various simulations are shown in Table 13-5. From Table 13-5, we see that Benetton can increase its expected profit by using a tailored postponement policy under which Q_1 units of each color are produced using Option 1 and Q_A units are produced using Option 2. The resulting profit is higher than if all units are produced entirely using Option 1 (no postponement) or Option 2 (complete postponement). It is best to select Q_1 such that it is quite likely that demand for each color is Q_1 or

TABLE 13-5 Average of 500 Simulations for Tailored Postponement Policies

Manufacturing Policy

Q_1	Q_A	Average Profit	Average Overstock	Average Understock
0	4,524	$97,847	510	210
1,337	0	$94,377	1,369	282
700	1,850	$102,730	308	168
800	1,550	$104,603	427	170
900	950	$101,326	607	266
900	1,050	$101,647	664	230
1,000	850	$100,312	815	195
1,000	950	$100,951	803	149
1,100	550	$99,180	1,026	211
1,100	650	$100,510	1,008	185

higher. The tailored postponement policy exploits this fact and produces Q_1 units using Option 1, which has a low cost. Q_A units are produced using Option 2 so demand uncertainty can be reduced by aggregation.

As our discussion illustrates, a manager should recognize that responsive strategies such as quick response and postponement are most effective when the underlying unpredictability is large. Thus, for the portion of demand that is relatively predictable, one should focus on the lowest cost production method, even if it is not responsive. The unpredictable portion of demand, however, should be served using a more responsive approach (postponement or quick response), even if it is more expensive.

SUMMARY OF LEARNING OBJECTIVE 5

Postponement allows a firm to increase profits and better match supply and demand if the firm produces a large variety of products whose demand is unpredictable, not positively correlated, and of about the same size. The value of postponement decreases as uncertainty decreases or demand is positively correlated across end products. Postponement may reduce overall profits for a firm if a single product contributes the majority of the demand because the increased manufacturing expense due to postponement outweighs the small benefit that aggregation provides in this case for the dominant product. In such settings, tailored postponement allows a firm to increase its profitability by postponing only the uncertain part of the demand and producing the predictable part at a lower cost without postponement. Tailored postponement is more profitable than either no postponement or complete postponement but can be complex to implement.

13.6 Allocate limited supply capacity among multiple products to maximize expected profits.

SETTING PRODUCT AVAILABILITY FOR MULTIPLE PRODUCTS UNDER CAPACITY CONSTRAINTS

In our discussion up to this point, we have assumed that a firm can set its desired level of product availability, and no constraints interfere with this choice. A common scenario in which this assumption fails occurs when the desired level of product availability results in an order size that exceeds the available capacity at the supplier. When ordering a single product, it is optimal for the buyer to order the minimum of the available capacity and the optimal order quantity. When

ordering multiple products, however, the buyer needs to consider the trade-off between ordering more of one product versus another.

Consider a department store that plans to order two styles of sweaters from an Italian supplier. Demand for the high-end sweater is forecast to be normally distributed, with a mean of $\mu_1 = 1,000$ and a standard deviation of $\sigma_1 = 300$. Demand for the mid-range sweater is normally distributed, with a mean of $\mu_2 = 2,000$ and a standard deviation of $\sigma_2 = 400$. The high-end sweater has a retail price of $p_1 = \$150$, a cost $c_1 = \$50$, and a salvage value of $s_1 = \$35$. The mid-range sweater has a retail price of $p_2 = \$100$, a cost $c_2 = \$40$, and a salvage value of $s_2 = \$25$. The following analysis is also detailed in the worksheet *no constraint* within the spreadsheet *Section13.6*. Using Equation 13.1, the optimal level of product availability for the high-end sweater is $(150 - 50)/(150 - 35) = 0.87$ and that for the mid-range sweater is $(100 - 40)/(100 - 25) = 0.80$. If there are no capacity constraints, it is optimal for the department store to order 1,337 [$= NORMINV(0.87, 1000, 300)$] units of the high-end sweater and 2,337 [$=NORMINV(0.80, 2000, 400)$] units of the mid-range sweater. If the supplier has a capacity constraint of 3,000 units, however, the desired ordering policy is not feasible, and the department store must decrease the size of its order by a total of at least 674 units. Where should this decrease come from? Should the decrease be divided evenly between the two products?

First let us consider the simplistic approach of decreasing the order size of each product by 337 units to get an order of 1,000 high-end sweaters and 2,000 mid-range sweaters (use worksheet *capacity constraint*). This order size meets the capacity constraint, and the expected profit is $194,268 (using Equation 13.3). To check whether this order size is optimal, we can think in terms of how capacity is allocated to the two styles. Let us assume that we have decided to allocate 1,000 units to the high-end sweater and 1,999 units to the mid-range sweater. That leaves only the last unit of capacity to be allocated. Which sweater should this unit be assigned to? It is reasonable to make this decision based on the expected marginal contribution to profits if this unit of capacity is allocated to each of the two styles. The last unit of capacity should be allocated to the sweater with the higher expected marginal contribution. Recall that $F_i(Q_i)$ is the probability that demand for product i is Q_i or less. Let $MC_i(Q_i)$ be the expected marginal contribution of a sweater of type i if quantity Q_i is ordered. The expected marginal contribution is evaluated similar to that in Table 13-2 and is obtained as follows:

$$\text{Expected marginal contribution for high-end sweater} = MC_1(1,000)$$

$$= p_1[1 - F_1(1,000)] + s_1 F_1(1,000) - c_1$$
$$= 150 \times (1 - 0.5) + (35 \times 0.5) - 50 = 42.50$$

$$\text{Expected marginal contribution for mid-range sweater} = MC_2(1,999)$$

$$= p_2[1 - F_2(1,999)] + s_2 F_2(1,999) - c_2$$
$$= 100 \times (1 - 0.499) + (25 \times 0.499) - 40 = 22.57$$

Clearly, it is better to allocate the last unit of capacity to the high-end sweater rather than the mid-range sweater. In fact, changing the order size to 1,001 high-end sweaters and 1,999 mid-range sweaters increases the expected profits by almost $20. One can now decrease the order size for the mid-range sweater to 1,998 and ask how the last unit of capacity should be allocated. Repeating this procedure indicates that the order size for the high-end sweaters should be increased to at least 1,002. In fact, the order size for the high-end sweater should be increased until the expected marginal contribution for the high-end sweater is the same as that for the mid-range sweater. At that point, it no longer makes sense to move capacity from one type of sweater to another. The optimal allocation of capacity turns out to be 1,089 high-end sweaters and 1,911 mid-range sweaters (see worksheet *Optimization*). The expected profits for this order size are $195,152. Observe that at optimality, the high-end sweater is allocated a relatively high share of the available capacity because its margin relative to the cost of overstocking is higher than that of the mid-range sweater.

The idea of allocating the available capacity to the product with the highest expected marginal contribution can be converted into a solution procedure. Let each product i have a mean demand of μ_i and a standard deviation of σ_i. Product i has a retail price of p_i, a cost c_i, and a salvage value of s_i. If quantity Q_i is allocated to product i, the expected marginal contribution is obtained as

$$MC_i(Q_i) = p_i[1 - F_i(Q_i)] + s_iF_i(Q_i) - c_i \qquad (13.8)$$

The following procedure allocates each unit of capacity to the product with the highest expected marginal contribution. Let B be the total available capacity.

1. Set quantity $Q_i = 0$ for all products i.
2. Compute the expected marginal contribution $MC_i(Q_i)$ for each product i using Equation 13.8.
3. If no expected marginal contribution is positive, stop. Otherwise, let j be the product with the highest expected marginal contribution. Increase Q_j by one unit.
4. If the total quantity across all products is less than B, return to step 2. Otherwise, the capacity constraint has been met and the current quantities are optimal.

Partial results from the application of the procedure described above to the department store data are shown in Table 13-6. A more detailed version of Table 13-6 is contained in the worksheet *Capacity allocation*.

The order quantities under capacity constraints can also be obtained by solving an optimization problem (see worksheet *Optimization*). Let $\Pi_i(Q_i)$ be the expected profit obtained using Equation 13.3 from ordering Q_i units of product i. The appropriate order quantities can be obtained by solving the following optimization problem:

$$\text{Max} \sum_{i=1}^{n} \Pi_i(Q_i)$$

Subject to

$$\sum_{i=1}^{n} Q_i \leq B$$
$$Q_i \geq 0$$

TABLE 13-6 Application of Solution Procedure to Obtain Order Quantities Under Capacity Constraints

	Expected Marginal Contribution		Order Quantity	
Capacity Left	**High End**	**Mid-Range**	**High End**	**Mid-Range**
3,000	99.95	60.00	0	0
2,900	99.84	60.00	100	0
2,100	57.51	60.00	900	0
2,000	57.51	60.00	900	100
800	57.51	57.00	900	1,300
780	54.59	57.00	920	1,300
300	42.50	43.00	1,000	1,700
200	42.50	36.86	1,000	1,800
180	39.44	36.86	1,020	1,800
40	31.89	30.63	1,070	1,890
30	30.41	30.63	1,080	1,890
10	29.67	29.54	1,085	1,905
1	29.09	29.18	1,089	1,910
0	29.09	29.10	1,089	1,911

SUMMARY OF LEARNING OBJECTIVE 6

When ordering multiple products under a limited supply capacity, the allocation of capacity to products should be based on their expected marginal contribution to profits. This approach allocates a relatively higher fraction of capacity to products that have a high margin relative to their cost of overstocking. At the optimal allocation, the expected marginal contribution of each product is the same. When there is no capacity constraint, the expected marginal contribution of each product at optimality is zero.

DISCUSSION QUESTIONS

1. What influence does overstocking and understocking have on the optimal level of product availability? How does this impact the supply chain inventories and profitability?
2. Consider a case in which demand derived from a product being out of stock in a supermarket is backlogged. How can the supermarket address it, and how does it impact profitability and inventory?
3. What are the three levers that a manager can use to deliver optimal cycle service level and improve supply chain profitability?

4. How can postponement of product differentiation be used to improve supply chain profitability?
5. What is tailored postponement? How can it be used in a supply chain to optimize profits and inventories?
6. Zara has used local production in Europe to have short replenishment lead times. How does this capability of quick response help the company improve profits in a highly volatile trendy apparel marketplace?
7. How can a firm allocate capacity for multiple products under capacity constraints?

EXERCISES

1. Green Thumb, a manufacturer of lawn care equipment, has introduced a new product. Each unit costs $250 to manufacture, and the introductory price is $300. At this price, the anticipated demand is normally distributed with a mean of $\mu = 100$ and a standard deviation of $\sigma = 40$. Any unsold units at the end of the season are unlikely to be valuable and will be disposed of in a post-season sale for $50 each. It costs $20 to hold a unit in inventory for the entire season. How many units should Green Thumb manufacture for sale? What is the expected profit from this policy? On average, how many customers does Green Thumb expect to turn away because of stocking out?
2. The general manager at Green Thumb decides to conduct extensive market research for the new product. At the end of the market research, the manager estimates demand to be normally distributed with a mean of $\mu = 100$ and a standard deviation of $\sigma = 15$. How should Green Thumb alter its production plans in Exercise 1 as a result of the market research? How much increase in profit is it likely to observe? How does the improved forecast affect the demand lost by Green Thumb because of understocking? Use cost and price information from Exercise 1.
3. The manager at Monson Kitchens, a distributor of kitchen cabinet doors in Dublin, uses a continuous review policy to manage inventory. The manager currently orders 11,000 doors when the inventory of doors drops to 7,500. Weekly demand for tires is normally distributed, with a mean of 3,000 and a standard deviation of 550. The replenishment lead time for tires is two weeks. Each door costs Monson's Kitchens €14, and the company sells each door for €32. Monson Kitchens incurs an annual holding cost of 22 percent.

How much safety inventory does Monson Kitchen currently carry? At what cost of understocking is the manager's current inventory policy justified? How much safety inventory should Monson Kitchens carry if the cost of understocking is €75 per door in lost current and future margin?
4. Champion manufactures winter fleece jackets for sale in the United States. Demand for jackets during the season is normally distributed, with a mean of 20,000 and a standard deviation of 10,000. Each jacket sells for $60 and costs $30 to produce. Any leftover jackets at the end of the season are sold for $25 at the year-end clearance sale. Holding jackets until the year-end sale adds another $5 to their cost. A recent recruit has suggested shipping leftover jackets to South America for sale in the winter there rather than running a clearance. Each jacket will fetch a price of $35 in South America, and all jackets sent there are likely to sell. Shipping costs add $5 to the cost of any jacket sold in South America. Would you recommend the South American option? How will this decision affect production decisions at Champion? How will it affect profitability? On average, how many jackets will Champion ship to South America each season?
5. Snoblo, a manufacturer of snowblowers, sells four models. The base model, Reguplo, has demand during the season that is normally distributed, with a mean of 10,000 and a standard deviation of 1,000. The three other models have additional features, and each has demand that is normally distributed, with a mean of 1,000 and a standard deviation of 700. Currently, all four models are manufactured on the same line at a cost of $100 for Reguplo and $110 for each of the other three models. Reguplo

sells for $200, whereas each of the other three models sells for $220. Any unsold blowers are sold at the end of the season for $80. Snoblo is considering the use of tailored production by setting up two separate lines, one for Reguplo and one for the other three. Given that no changeovers will be required on the Reguplo line, the production cost of Reguplo is expected to decline to $90. The production cost of the other three products, however, will now increase to $120. Do you recommend tailored production for Snoblo? How will tailored production affect production and profits? Ignore holding costs for the snowblowers.

6. AnyLogo supplies firms with apparel containing their logo to be used for promotional purposes. AnyLogo has four major customers—IBM, AT&T, HP, and Cisco. During the holiday season, the logos are adorned with a Christmas motif. Demand from each firm for apparel with the Christmas motif is normally distributed, as shown in Table 13-7.

TABLE 13-7 Demand Distribution for AnyLogo

	IBM	AT&T	HP	Cisco
Mean	5,000	7,000	4,000	4,000
SD	2,000	2,500	2,000	2,200

AnyLogo currently produces all the apparel including the logo embroidery in Sri Lanka in advance of the holiday season. Each unit costs $15 and is sold by AnyLogo for $50. Any leftover inventory at the end of the holiday season is essentially worthless and cannot be repurposed for a different company. It is thus donated by AnyLogo to charity. Holding the apparel in inventory adds another $3 to the cost per unit donated to inventory. However, the donation allows AnyLogo to recover $6 per unit in tax savings. What production quantities do you recommend for AnyLogo? What is the expected profit from the policy? On average, how much does AnyLogo expect to donate to charity each year?

7. The manager at AnyLogo is considering the purchase of high-speed embroidery machines that will allow it to embroider on demand. In this case, the apparel will be made in Sri Lanka without any logo; the logo embroidery will be postponed and will be done in the United States on demand. This will raise the cost per unit to $18. However, AnyLogo will not have any holiday or company-specific apparel to be disposed of at the end of the season. The apparel without logos can be sold for $18 a unit to retailers. The cost of holding inventory and shipping adds $4 to the cost of any apparel left over after the holiday season. With all other information as in Exercise 6, do you recommend that the manager at AnyLogo implement postponement? What will be the impact of postponement on profits and inventories?

8. A toy store is considering stocking a new toy that has just been released in the market. To test the marketability of the toy, the toy store will place an initial single order for the toys. Each toy costs €8.00, and any unsold toys will have to dispose of at the end of a trial period. The margin from each toy is €4.00, and children are likely to go to competitor toy stores if they run out of this toy. The demand for the toy is forecast to be normally distributed with a mean of 30,000 and a standard deviation of 10,000.
 a. How many toys should be ordered in advance of the trial period?
 b. An issue has been raised that customers who go to competitor toy stores may be lost for the long term. It has been estimated that the cost of not having toys in stock is €7 per stockout because of the loss of current and future sales. How does this information affect the number of toys to be ordered?

9. The Highland Company is planning orders for its winter catalog. One order is to be placed at the beginning of the season. The demand forecast for one of its jackets is normally distributed, with a mean of 5,000 and standard deviation of 2,000. Each jacket is purchased for $100, and any unsold jackets at the end of the season will be discounted and sold through the outlet store for $75. At this price, virtually all jackets are expected to sell. It costs another $15 to store an unsold jacket for the season and then move it to the outlet store. The members of the buying committee disagree on the effect of stocking out and the number of jackets to be ordered. One of the members believes that 6,000 jackets should be ordered, whereas another wants to order 8,000 jackets.
 a. At what cost of stocking out would each member's order size be justified?
 b. If the planned sale price is $200, describe a situation in which ordering 6,000 jackets makes sense. Describe another situation in which ordering 8,000 jackets makes sense.

10. Sport Obermeyer (SO) is a manufacturer of ski apparel. A ski jacket is sourced at a cost of $80 and sold for $125. One order is placed at the beginning of the season. Currently, SO disposes of any unsold jackets at the end of the season to outlet stores at $70. It costs $10 to hold a jacket in inventory for the entire season and then ship it to an outlet store. Demand for ski jackets has been forecast to be normally distributed, with a mean of 4,000 and a standard deviation of 1,750.
 a. How many jackets should SO order for the season, assuming a single order?
 b. What is the expected profit from this policy?
 c. What is the expected overstock at the end of the season that will be sent to outlet stores?
 d. SO is considering an alternative under which it will ship surplus jackets at the end of the season for sale in the Southern Hemisphere. Inclusive of all costs, SO expects the salvage value to increase to $75 under this option. How will this change affect the quantity ordered, expected profits, and expected overstock to be sent to the Southern Hemisphere? Do you recommend this option?

11. Daily demand for aspirin at DoorRed Pharmacy is normally distributed, with a mean of 40 bottles and a standard deviation of 5. The replenishment lead time from the supplier is one day. The current inventory policy at DoorRed is to order 200 bottles when the quantity on hand drops below 45. Each bottle costs DoorRed $4, and the pharmacy uses an annual holding cost of 25 percent.

a. If all unfilled demand is assumed to be backlogged and carried over to the next cycle, what cost of understocking justifies the current policy?

b. If all unfilled demand is assumed to be lost, what cost of stocking out justifies the current policy?

c. DoorRed believes that all unfilled demand can be backlogged if customers are given a $1.50 discount on their next purchase (effectively making the cost of understocking $1.50). What inventory policy do you recommend for DoorRed?

12. Frame It sells photo frames, which are packaged in specially designed boxes. The company sells four designs namely; engagement, wedding, anniversaries, and birthdays, and currently all packaging is designed and made in the plant as the frames are manufactured. As the frames are manufacturing they are packaged. The demand forecast for each of the four boxes is normally distributed, with a mean of 26,000 and a standard deviation of 9,000. Each box costs €4 and is sold for €6. Any unsold boxes at the end of the year are discounted €3, and they all sell out at this price. The cost of holding a box in inventory for the entire year before selling it at a discount is €0.50.

a. How many boxes of each design should Frame It manufacture?

b. What is the expected profit from this policy?

c. How many boxes does Frame It expect to sell at a discount?

d. An option being considered by Frame It is to separate frame manufacture from packaging. Frames will be manufactured in advance, but packaging will be done on an express line as orders come in. The express line and separation of steps adds €1 to the cost of production. How many frames should Frame It manufacture if it decides to postpone packaging? What is the expected profit? How many boxes will Frame It sell at a discount if it uses postponement?

e. At what additional cost of postponement (instead of the current €1) would Frame It be indifferent between operating with and without postponement?

13. The Knitting Company (TKC) is planning production for its four sweater styles that are popular during Christmas. All four styles have demand that is normally distributed. The best-selling style has an expected demand of 30,000 and a standard deviation of 5,000. Each of the other three styles has an expected demand of 10,000 with a standard deviation of 4,000. Currently, all sweaters are produced before the start of the season. Production cost is $20 per sweater, and they are sold for a wholesale price of $35. Any unsold sweaters at the end of the season are discounted to $15, and they all sell at that price. It costs $2 to hold the sweater in inventory for the entire season if it does not sell.

a. How many sweaters of each type should TKC manufacture?

b. What is the expected profit from this policy?

c. How many sweaters does TKC expect to sell at a discount?

d. TKC is considering the postponement of knitting and using flexible machines. This will require the base sweat-

ers to be made in advance (identical for each of the four types) and the final patterns to be knit later. This will increase production cost per sweater to $21.40. How many sweaters should TKC manufacture with postponement? What is the expected profit from this policy?

e. Another option is to produce the popular style without postponement and the other three styles using postponement. What is the expected profit under this policy?

14. A designer is planning orders for its annual limited-edition ornament. Demand has been forecast to be normally distributed, with a mean of 20,000 and a standard deviation of 8,000. Each ornament costs $30 and is sold for $95. All unsold ornaments are destroyed at the end of the season, to ensure the value of the limited edition.

a. How many ornaments should the designer order? What is the expected profit?

b. The manufacturer has offered to discount the price to $28 per ornament if at least 25,000 are ordered. How should the designer respond?

15. A publisher is printing calendars for the coming year. Demand for calendars is normally distributed, with a mean of 70,000 and a standard deviation of 25,000. The cost per calendar is $3, and they are sold for $10 each. All unsold calendars are recycled at the end of January.

a. How many calendars should the publisher have printed? What is the expected profit?

b. The printer has offered to discount the printing cost to $2.75 per calendar if the publisher orders at least 100,000. What should the publisher do?

16. An electronics manufacturer has outsourced production of its latest media players to a contract manufacturer in Asia. Demand for the players has exceeded all expectations, whereas the contract manufacturer has limited production capacity. The electronics manufacturer sells three types of players—a 40-GB player, a 20-GB player, and a 6-GB player. For the upcoming holiday season, the demand forecast for the 40-GB player is normally distributed, with a mean of 20,000 and a standard deviation of 7,000, the demand forecast for the 20-GB player has a mean of 40,000 and a standard deviation of 11,000, and the demand forecast for the 6-GB player has a mean of 80,000 and a standard deviation of 16,000. The 40-GB player has a sale price of $200, a production cost of $100, and a salvage value of $80. The 20-GB player has a sale price of $150, a production cost of $90, and a salvage value of $70. The 6-GB player has a sale price of $100, a production cost of $70, and a salvage value of $50.

a. How many units of each type of player should the electronics manufacturer order if there are no capacity constraints?

b. The contract manufacturer has available production capacity of only 140,000 units. What is the expected profit if the electronics manufacturer orders 20,000 units of the 40-GB player, 40,000 units of the 20-GB player, and 80,000 units of the 6-GB player?

c. How many units of each type of player should the electronics manufacturer order if the available capacity is 140,000? What is the expected profit?

17. A ski jacket manufacturer has outsourced production to a supplier in Asia. The electronics manufacturer sells three types of jackets—a high end, a mid-range, and a low end jacket. For the upcoming winter season, the demand forecast for the high end jacket is normally distributed, with a mean of 600 and a standard deviation of 400, the demand forecast for the mid-range jacket has a mean of 1,000 and a standard deviation of 500, and the demand forecast for the low-end jacket has a mean of 2,000 and a standard deviation of 600. The high end jacket has a sale price of $300, a production cost of $120, and a salvage value of $100. The mid-range jacket has a sale price of $200, a production cost of $100, and a salvage value of $85. The low end jacket has a sale price of $110, a production cost of $70, and a salvage value of $50.

a. How many jackets of each type should the manufacturer order if there are no capacity constraints?

b. The supplier has available production capacity of only 3,600 jackets. What is the expected profit if the manufacturer orders 600 high end jackets, 1,000 mid-range jackets, and 2,000 low end jackets?

c. How many jackets of each type should the manufacturer order if the available capacity is 3,600? What is the expected profit?

BIBLIOGRAPHY

Cachon, Gerard P., and Marshall L. Fisher. "Campbell Soup's Continuous Product Replenishment Program: Evaluation and Enhanced Decision Rules." *Production and Operations Management* (1997): 6, 266–276.

Cachon, Gerard P., and Martin A. Lariviere. "Turning the Supply Chain into a Revenue Chain." *Harvard Business Review* (March 2001): 20–21.

Clark, Theodore H., and Janice H. Hammond. "Reengineering Channel Reordering Processes to Improve Total Supply Chain Performance." *Production and Operations Management* (1997): 6, 248–265.

Fisher, Marshall L., Janice H. Hammond, Walter R. Obermeyer, and Ananth Raman. "Making Supply Meet Demand in an Uncertain World." *Harvard Business Review* (May–June 1994): 83–93.

Ghemawat, Pankaj, and Jose Luis Nueno. "Zara: Fast Fashion." Harvard Business School Case 9–703–497, 2006.

Nahmias, Steven. *Production and Operations Analysis*. Burr Ridge, IL: Richard P. Irwin, 1997.

Padmanabhan, V., and Ivan P. L. Png. "Returns Policies: Making Money by Making Good." *Sloan Management Review* (Fall 1995): 65–72.

Pasternack, Barry A. "Optimal Pricing and Return Policies for Perishable Commodities." *Marketing Science* (1985): 4, 166–176.

Signorelli, Sergio, and James L. Heskett. *Benetton (A)*. Harvard Business School Case 9–685–014, 1984.

Silver, Edward A., David Pyke, and Rein Petersen. *Inventory Management and Production Planning and Scheduling*. New York: Wiley, 1998.

Tayur, Sridhar, Ram Ganeshan, and Michael Magazine, eds. *Quantitative Models for Supply Chain Management*. Boston: Kluwer Academic Publishers, 1999.

Willems, Sean P. "Demystifying Inventory Optimization." *Supply Chain Management Review* (March–April 2015): 24–30.

CASE STUDY

The Need for Speed at Winner Apparel

Tiffany Chen was concerned about Winner Apparel's sales results from the previous season. For some products, the company had to sell about a third of the seasonal purchase at sharply discounted prices. For other products, the company ran out of stock well before the end of the season. Tiffany wanted to improve the matching of supply and demand. A local supplier had offered to bring a second delivery around the middle of the season but wanted a 5 percent increase in purchase price. Tiffany had to decide whether the price increase was worth the benefit of a second mid-season delivery.

The Previous Season for Winner Apparel

The sales year for Winner was divided into four selling seasons of about three months each. The company had implemented a low-cost sourcing strategy and identified suppliers from low-cost countries in Asia. Although these suppliers provided a low purchase price, they required Winner to place its orders well before the start of the selling season. To lower costs, suppliers delivered a single lot a few weeks before the start of the season. This put the onus for accurate forecasting on the

purchasing department. Tiffany had a very experienced group of buyers who looked at historical sales patterns and the new designs for the current season to come up with order quantities from each supplier. Unfortunately, their track record of matching supply and demand was rather poor. Winner always appeared to be short of products that were selling very well and had a surplus of products that were not selling well.

Tiffany decided to focus on a couple of products that had problems last season. "Trendy" was a collection of women's shirts that, as the name suggested, incorporated cutting-edge fashion. The buying committee had been bullish on the new designs and ordered 570 units for the season. Unfortunately, 250 of those units were still unsold at the end of the season. Trendy shirts sold at a full price of $100, but for the 250 units unsold at the end of the season, Winner would be able to salvage only $20/unit. This was a significant loss, given that each unit had been purchased for $40. In contrast, "Basic" was a collection of T-shirts that Winner always maintained in its portfolio. The buying committee had ordered 1,080 Basic units, but Winner ran out of stock before the end of the season. Tiffany's team estimated that the company could have sold another 60 units if stock had been available. Given that Winner had a margin of $20 for each Basic T-shirt, the company had lost $1,200 in margin because of being out of stock.

Proposal from Responsive Supplier

A local supplier had heard that Tiffany was reconsidering product sourcing. It proposed filling Winner's needs in two deliveries. The first delivery would arrive before the start of the season and be designed to cover about a half-season of sales. The second delivery would arrive around the middle of the season, but the timing and quantity could be adjusted to account for sales in the first half. The supplier promised delivery to ensure no stockouts during the first half. In other words, the supplier would bring in the second delivery early (and a larger quantity) if sales in the first half seemed to be higher than predicted. If sales in the first half were slower than anticipated, Winner could reduce the amount ordered for the second delivery. For this flexibility, the local supplier wanted a premium of 5 percent compared to the low-cost supplier. If purchased from the local supplier, the Trendy line would thus cost $42 (instead of $40) per unit and the Basic line would cost $31.50 (instead of $30). Tiffany felt that with a mid-season delivery, any customers who could not find product during the first half of the season would return for the second half and purchase the item. Thus, there would be no lost sales during the first half of the season. Her team prepared the demand and cost data shown in Tables 13-8 and 13-9. Tiffany had to decide whether the responsiveness of the local supplier was worth the additional 5 percent in unit cost.

TABLE 13-8 Seasonal Demand and Sourcing Cost from Low-Cost Supplier

Product	Sale Price, p	Sourcing Cost, c	Salvage Value, s	Mean Demand for Season, μ	Standard Deviation of Demand for Season, σ
Trendy	$100	$40	$20	400	250
Basic	$50	$30	$20	1,000	200

TABLE 13-9 Half-Season Demand and Sourcing Cost from Responsive Supplier

Product	Sale Price, p	Sourcing Cost, c	Salvage Value, s	Mean Demand for Half Season, μ_H	Standard Deviation of Demand for Half Season, σ_H
Trendy	$100	$42.00	$20	200	177
Basic	$50	$31.50	$20	500	141

APPENDIX 13A
Optimal Level of Product Availability

Objective

Evaluate the level of product availability that maximizes profit.

Analysis:

Assume that the demand is a continuous nonnegative random variable with density function $f(x)$ and cumulative distribution function $F(x)$. C_u is the margin per unit and, as a result, the cost of understocking per unit. C_o is the cost of overstocking per unit.

Assume that Q units are purchased and a demand of x units arises. If $Q \leq x$, all Q units are sold and a profit of QC_u results. On the other hand, if $Q \leq x$, only x units are sold and a profit of $xC_u - (Q - x)C_o$ results. The expected profit $P(Q)$ is thus given by

$$P(Q) = \int_0^Q [xC_u - (Q - x)C_o]f(x)dx + \int_Q^\infty QC_uf(x)dx$$

To determine the value of Q that maximizes the expected profit $P(Q)$, we have

$$\frac{dP(Q)}{d(Q)} = -C_o \int_0^Q f(x)dx + C_u \int_Q^\infty f(x)dx$$

$$= C_u[1 - F(Q)] - C_oF(Q) = 0$$

This implies an optimal order size of Q^*, where

$$F(Q^*) = \frac{C_u}{C_u + C_o}$$

One can verify that the second derivative is negative, implying that the total expected profit is maximized at Q^*.

APPENDIX 13B
An Intermediate Evaluation

Objective

Given that x is normally distributed, with a mean μ and standard deviation σ, show that

$$A = \int_{x=-\infty}^a xf(x)dx = \mu F_S\left[\frac{(a - \mu)}{\sigma}\right] - \sigma f_S\left[\frac{(a - \mu)}{\sigma}\right] \tag{13.8}$$

Here, $f(x)$ is the normal density function, $f_S(\)$ is the standard normal density function, and $F_S(\)$ is the standard normal cumulative distribution function.

Analysis:

Using Equation 12.21, we have

$$A = \int_{x=-\infty}^a xf(x)dx = \int_{-\infty}^a x\frac{1}{\sqrt{2\pi}\sigma}e^{-(x-\mu)^2/2\sigma^2}dx$$

Substitute $z = (x - \mu)/\sigma$. This implies that $dx = \sigma dz$. Thus, we have

$$A = \int_{z=-\infty}^{(a-\mu)/\sigma} (z\sigma + \mu)\frac{1}{\sqrt{2\pi}}e^{-z^2/2}dz$$

$$= \mu \int_{z=-\infty}^{(a-\mu)/\sigma} \frac{1}{\sqrt{2\pi}}e^{-z^2/2}dz + \sigma \int_{z=-\infty}^{(a-\mu)/\sigma} z\frac{1}{\sqrt{2\pi}}e^{-z^2/2}dz$$

Given the relationship between the cumulative distribution function and the probability density function, we use the definition of the standard normal distribution and Equation 12.21 to obtain

$$F_S(t) = \int_{z=-\infty}^{t} f_S(z)dz = \int_{z=-\infty}^{t} \frac{1}{\sqrt{2\pi}}e^{-z^2/2}dz$$

Substitute $w = z^2/2$ into the expression for A. This implies that $dw = zdz$. Thus,

$$A = \mu F_S\left[\frac{(a-\mu)}{\sigma}\right] + \sigma \int_{w=\infty}^{(a-\mu)^2/2\sigma^2} \frac{1}{\sqrt{2\pi}}e^{-w}dw$$

or

$$A = \mu F_S\left[\frac{(a-\mu)}{\sigma}\right] - \sigma f_s\left[\frac{(a-\mu)}{\sigma}\right]$$

APPENDIX 13C

Expected Profit from an Order

Objective

Assume demand to be normally distributed, with a mean μ and standard deviation σ. Each unit sells for a price $\$p$ and costs $\$c$. Any unsold units fetch a salvage value of $\$s$. Obtain an expression for the expected profit if O units are ordered.

Analysis:

If O units are ordered and demand turns out to be $x \le O$, each of the x units sold contributes $p - c$, whereas each of the $(O - x)$ units unsold results in a loss of $c - s$. If demand is larger than O, each of the O units sold contributes $p - c$. We thus obtain

$$\text{Expected profits} = \int_{x=-\infty}^{O} [(p - c)x - (c - s)(O - x)]f(x)dx$$

$$+ \int_{x=O}^{\infty} O(p - c)f(x)dx = \int_{x=-\infty}^{O} [(p - s)x$$

$$- O(c - s)]f(x)dx + \int_{x=O}^{\infty} O(p - c)f(x)dx$$

Using Equation 13.8, we obtain

$$\int_{x=-\infty}^{O} xf(x)dx = \mu F_S\left[\frac{(O-\mu)}{\sigma}\right] - \sigma f_s\left[\frac{(O-\mu)}{\sigma}\right]$$

We can thus evaluate the expected profits as

$$\text{Expected profits} = (p - s)\mu F_S\left[\frac{(O-\mu)}{\sigma}\right] - (p - s)\sigma f_s\left[\frac{(O-\mu)}{\sigma}\right]$$
$$- O(c - s)F(O, \mu, \sigma) + O(p - c)[1 - F(O, \mu, \sigma)]$$

APPENDIX 13D

Expected Overstock from an Order

Objective

Assume demand to be normally distributed, with a mean μ and standard deviation σ. Obtain an expression for the expected overstock if O units are ordered.

Analysis:

If O units are ordered, an overstock results only if demand is $x < O$. We thus have

$$\text{Expected overstock} = \int_{x=-\infty}^{O} (O - x)f(x)dx$$

$$= \int_{x=-\infty}^{O} Of(x)dx - \int_{x=-\infty}^{O} xf(x)dx$$

$$= OF_S\left[\frac{O - \mu}{\sigma}\right] - \int_{x=-\infty}^{O} xf(x)dx$$

Using Equation 13.8, we thus obtain

$$\text{Expected overstock} = OF_S\left[\frac{O - \mu}{\sigma}\right] - \mu F_S\left[\frac{O - \mu}{\sigma}\right] + \sigma f_S\left[\frac{O - \mu}{\sigma}\right]$$

$$= (O - \mu)F_S\left[\frac{(O - \mu)}{\sigma}\right] + \sigma f_S\left[\frac{O - \mu}{\sigma}\right]$$

APPENDIX 13E

Expected Understock from an Order

Objective

Assume demand to be normally distributed, with a mean μ and standard deviation σ. Obtain an expression for the expected understock if O units are ordered.

Analysis:

If O units are ordered, an understock results only if demand is $x > O$. We thus have

$$\text{Expected understock} = \int_{x=O}^{\infty} (x - O)f(x)dx$$

$$= \int_{x=O}^{\infty} xf(x)dx - \int_{x=O}^{\infty} Of(x)dx = \int_{x=-\infty}^{\infty} xf(x)dx$$

$$- \int_{x=-\infty}^{o} xf(x)dx - O\left\{1 - F_S\left[\frac{(O - \mu)}{\sigma}\right]\right\}$$

$$= (\mu - O) + OF_S\left[\frac{(O - \mu)}{\sigma}\right] - \int_{x=-\infty}^{o} xf(x)dx$$

Using Equation 13.8, we thus obtain

$$\text{Expected understock} = (\mu - O) + OF_S\left[\frac{(O - \mu)}{\sigma}\right]$$

$$- \mu F_S\left[\frac{(O - \mu)}{\sigma}\right] + \sigma f_S\left[\frac{(O - \mu)}{\sigma}\right]$$

$$= (\mu - O)\left\{1 - F_S\left[\frac{(O - \mu)}{\sigma}\right]\right\} + \sigma f_S\left[\frac{(O - \mu)}{\sigma}\right]$$

APPENDIX 13F

Simulation Using Spreadsheets

A *simulation* is a computer model that replicates a real-life situation, allowing the user to estimate what the potential outcome would be from each of a set of actions. Simulation is a powerful tool that helps evaluate the impact of business decisions on performance in an uncertain environment. In some instances, future scenarios can be modeled mathematically without simulation, and formulas can be obtained for the impact of different policies on performance. In other cases, formulas are difficult or impossible to obtain, and one must use simulation. Simulations are powerful because they can accommodate any number of complications. Problems that are impossible to solve analytically can often be solved fairly easily with simulation. A good simulation is an inexpensive way to test different actions and identify the most effective decision given an uncertain future.

Consider Lands' End, a mail-order firm that sells apparel. Lands' End faces uncertain demand and has to make decisions regarding the number of catalogs to print and mail, the number of units of each product to order, and the contracts to enter into with its suppliers. The general manager at Lands' End wants to evaluate different policies before implementing them. A simulation requires the manager to create a computer model that mimics the orders placed, inventory held, customer demand, and other processes that are part of the Lands' End supply chain.

An *instance* of demand refers to random demand obtained from a demand distribution. Each time demand is generated from a distribution, a new instance results. Based on estimates of the future demand distribution, instances of demand for different products are generated randomly. The impact of an ordering policy is evaluated for each instance of demand generated. Based on a large number of demand instances, the manager can evaluate the mean and variability of the performance of a policy. Different policies can then be compared.

Generating Random Numbers Using Excel

A fundamental step in any simulation is the generation of random numbers that correspond to the distribution that has been estimated for future demand or some other parameter. For example, if Lands' End has estimated demand for cashmere sweaters from the winter catalog to be normally distributed, with a mean of 3,000 and a standard deviation of 1,000, the manager needs to generate several instances of demand from this distribution. Several functions available in Excel generate random numbers.

The *RAND()* function generates a random number that is uniformly distributed between 0 and 1. There is thus a 10 percent probability that *RAND()* will generate a number between 0 and 0.1, a 50 percent probability that it will generate a random number between 0 and 0.5, and a 90 percent probability that it will generate a random number between 0 and 0.9. The *RAND()* function can be used to generate random numbers from a variety of distributions.

The Excel function *NORMINV(RAND(), μ, σ)* generates a random number that is normally distributed, with mean μ and standard deviation σ. The Excel function *NORMSINV(RAND())*

generates a random number that is normally distributed, with a mean of 0 and standard deviation of 1. The fact that both *NORMINV* and *NORMSINV* can generate negative numbers often poses problems when they are used to generate demand. One option is to use a maximum of 0 and *NORMINV(RAND(), μ, σ)* to generate demand. This is appropriate if the coefficient of variation, *cv*, is less than 0.4. For larger coefficients of variation, it is better to use the log-normal distribution because that generates only nonnegative numbers. The Excel function *LOGINV(RAND(), μ, σ)* generates a random number *X* that follows the log-normal distribution, where $\ln(X)$ is normally distributed, with mean μ and standard deviation σ. Several other demand distributions may be generated using other Excel functions.

Setting Up a Simulation Model

Lands' End plans to sell cashmere sweaters in its winter catalog for $150 each. The manager expects demand to be normally distributed, with a mean of $\mu = 3{,}000$ and a standard deviation of $\sigma = 1{,}000$. Toward the end of the winter season, Lands' End sends out a sales catalog with discounted prices on unsold items. The discounted price determines the demand in response to the sales catalog. The manager anticipates that the sales catalog will generate demand for cashmere sweaters with a mean of $1{,}000 - 5p$ and a standard deviation of $(1{,}000 - 5p)/3$, where *p* is the discounted price charged. Any leftover sweaters after shipping orders from the sales catalog are donated to charity. Each sweater costs Lands' End $50. Thus, the donation to charity fetches $25 in tax benefits. Lands' End incurs a cost of $5 per unsold sweater to store and transport them to charity, resulting in a salvage value of $s = \$20$ per sweater sent to charity. The manager has decided to charge a discount price of $\max(\$25, \$150 - n/20)$, where *n* is the number of sweaters left over after the winter catalog. The manager wants to identify the number of sweaters that should be purchased at the start of the winter season.

The first step is to set up a simulation model that evaluates the net profit for an instance of demand during the winter season. The model constructed is shown in Figure 13-6 and detailed in the spreadsheet *Chapter13-LandsEnd-simulation*.

Using Data Tables to Create Many Instances

Having set up the simulation model, the next step is to create many instances of random demand and evaluate the average profits from ordering 3,000 units. In Excel, *Data Tables* can be used to achieve multiple replications of the simulation. The goal is to evaluate the mean and standard deviation of profits, the average number of sweaters discounted, and the average number of sweaters donated to charity over the multiple replications. A data table is constructed in the range A23:D522 to replicate the results of the simulation for 500 instances of demand as follows:

1. Enter formula = I14 in cell B23, = D12 in cell C23, and = D16 in cell D23. As a result, the profit is copied into cell B23, the quantity discounted is copied into cell C23, and the quantity given to charity is copied into cell D23.
2. Select the range A23:D522. From the toolbar select Data | What-If Analysis | Data Table. In the Table dialog box, point to cell A23 as the Column input cell. Click on OK.

The data table is created in the range A23:D522. Each row of the data table gives the profit, quantity discounted, and quantity given to charity for an instance of random demand. Excel recalculates the simulation using new random numbers for each row in the data table. We can now obtain the average profit, average number of sweaters discounted, and average number of sweaters donated to charity from the data table. These are calculated in cells C18, I18, and I19, respectively of the spreadsheet *Chapter13-LandsEnd-simulation* (see Figure 13-6).

Each time the F9 key is pressed, new random numbers are generated and all entries are recalculated. The manager at Lands' End can use the simulation to evaluate the impact of different initial ordering policies on performance by changing the entry in cell D10.

	A	B	C	D	E	F	G	H	I
1	*Ordering and Pricing at Lands' End*								
2									
3	Cost of sweaters =		$ 50						
4	Sale price in winter catalog =		$ 150						
5	Mean demand from winter catalog =		3,000						
6	SD of demand from winter catalog =		1,000						
7	Mean discounted demand =		348						
8	SD of discounted demand =		115.83						
9									
10	Initial quantity ordered =		3000			Cost of sweaters ordered =		$ 150,000	
11	Winter catalog demand =		2610			Revenue from winter sales =		$ 391,500	
12	Sweaters to be discounted =		390			Revenue from discounted sales =		$ 25,187	
13	Discounted price, p =		$130.5			Net benefit from donation =		$ 3,940	
14	Demand at discounted price =		193			**Net profit =**		**$ 270,627**	
15	Number sold at discount =		193						
16	Number donated to charity =		197						
17									
18	Average profit =	$	266,688.33			Average number of sweaters discounted =			365
19	SD of profit =	$	62,588.49			Average number donated to charity =			179

Cell Number	Cell Formula	Cell Number	Cell Formula
D7	=1000-5*D13	D16	=D12-D15
D8	=D7/3	I10	=D3*D10
D11	=int(max(0,norminv(rand(),D5,D6)))	I11	=min(D10,D11)*D4
D12	=max(0,D10-D11)	I12	=D15*D13
D13	=max(25,150-D12/20)	I13	=D16*20
D14	=int(max(0,norminv(rand(),D7,D8)))	I14	=sum(I11:I13)-I10
D15	=min(D12,D14)		

Figure 13-6 Excel Simulation Model for Lands' End

CHAPTER

14

Transportation in a Supply Chain

LEARNING OBJECTIVES

After reading this chapter, you will be able to

14.1 Understand the role of different transportation modes in a supply chain.

14.2 Discuss the role of infrastructure and policies in transportation.

14.3 Identify the relative strengths and weaknesses of various transportation network design options.

14.4 Understand some success factors in a responsive network for same day delivery.

14.5 Evaluate trade-offs that shippers need to consider when designing a transportation network.

14.6 Design tailored transportation networks in a supply chain.

In this chapter, we discuss the role of transportation within a supply chain and identify trade-offs that must be considered when making transportation decisions. Our goal is to enable managers to make transportation strategy and design, planning, and operational decisions with an understanding of all the important pros and cons of their choices.

14.1 Understand the role of different transportation modes in a supply chain.

TRANSPORTATION MODES AND THEIR ROLE IN A SUPPLY CHAIN

Transportation refers to the movement of product from one location to another as it makes its way from the beginning of a supply chain to the customer. Transportation is an important supply chain driver because products are rarely produced and consumed in the same location. Transportation is a significant component of the costs incurred by most supply chains. According to the Bureau of Transportation Statistics (BTS), "over 19 billion tons of freight, valued at $13 trillion, was carried over 4.4 trillion ton-miles in the United States in 2002."[1] Only three sectors—housing, health care, and food—contributed a larger share to the gross domestic product (GDP) than

[1] https://www.ikea.cn/ms/en_CN/jobs/business_types/distribution_logistics/index.html

transportation. Transportation-related jobs employed nearly 20 million people in 2002, accounting for 16 percent of U.S. total occupational employment.

The role of transportation is even more significant in global supply chains. According to the BTS, the U.S. freight transportation network carried export and import merchandise worth more than $2.2 trillion in 2004, an increase of 168 percent from $822 billion in 1990. During the same period, the ratio of exports from and imports into the United States to the GDP increased from 12 percent to 21 percent.

Any supply chain's success is closely linked to the appropriate use of transportation to support its competitive strategy. Firms should design functional incentives that help achieve this goal. Historically, the transportation function within firms has been evaluated based on the extent to which it can lower transportation costs. Such a focus leads to decisions that lower transportation costs but hurt the level of responsiveness provided to customers and may raise the firm's total cost. If the dispatcher at a DC is evaluated based solely on the extent to which trucks are loaded, he or she is likely to delay shipments and hurt customer responsiveness to achieve a larger load. To best support competitive strategy, firms should evaluate the transportation function based on total cost and the level of responsiveness achieved with customers.

IKEA, the Scandinavian home furnishings retailer, is an example of a company whose transportation strategy supports its competitive strategy. IKEA has built a global network, with about 350 stores in 42 countries, primarily on the basis of effective transportation. IKEA's sales for the year ending August 2013 reached 29.2 billion euros. Its strategy is built around providing good-quality products at low prices—in fact, its goal is to cut prices by 2 to 3 percent each year. As a result, IKEA works hard to find the least expensive global source for each of its products. Modular design of its furniture allows IKEA to transport its goods worldwide much more cost effectively than a traditional furniture manufacturer. The large size of IKEA stores and shipments allows inexpensive transportation of home furnishings all the way to the retail store. Modular designs coupled with effective sourcing and inexpensive transportation allow IKEA to provide high-quality home furnishings at low prices globally.

Seven-Eleven Japan is another firm that has used transportation to achieve its strategic goals. The company has a goal of carrying products in its stores to match the needs of customers as they vary by geographic location or time of day. To help achieve this goal, Seven-Eleven Japan uses a responsive transportation system that replenishes its stores several times a day so the products available match customers' needs. Products from different suppliers are aggregated on trucks according to their required temperature to help achieve frequent deliveries at a reasonable cost. Seven-Eleven Japan uses a responsive transportation system along with aggregation to decrease its transportation and receiving costs while ensuring that product availability closely matches customer demand.

Supply chains also use responsive transportation to centralize inventories and operate with fewer facilities. For example, Amazon relies on package carriers and the postal system to deliver customer orders from centralized warehouses. McMaster-Carr uses ground transportation and package carriers to provide next-day delivery of a wide variety of MRO products to about 90 percent of U.S. businesses from five distribution centers. The location of its distribution centers along with an effective transportation network allows McMaster to be very responsive while using a low-cost mode of transportation.

The *shipper* is the party that requires the movement of the product between two points in the supply chain. The *carrier* is the party that moves or transports the product. For example, when McMaster-Carr uses UPS to ship its products from the warehouse to the customer, McMaster is the shipper and UPS is the carrier. Besides the shipper and the carrier, two other parties have a significant impact on transportation: (1) the owners and operators of transportation infrastructure such as roads, ports, canals, and airports and (2) the bodies that set transportation policy worldwide. Actions by all four parties influence the effectiveness of transportation.

To understand transportation in a supply chain, it is important to consider the perspectives of all four parties. A carrier makes investment decisions regarding the transportation equipment

(e.g., locomotives, trucks, airplanes) and, in some cases, infrastructure (rail), and then makes operating decisions to try to maximize the return from these assets. A shipper, in contrast, selects from the available transportation modes to minimize the total cost (transportation, inventory, information, sourcing, and facility) while providing an appropriate level of responsiveness to the customer. The effectiveness of carriers is influenced by infrastructure such as ports, roads, waterways, and airports. Most transportation infrastructure throughout the world is owned and managed as a public good. It is important that infrastructure be managed in such a way that monies are available for maintenance and investment in further capacity as needed. Transportation policy sets direction for the amount of national resources that go into improving transportation infrastructure. Transportation policy also aims to prevent abuse of monopoly power; promote fair competition; and balance environmental, energy, and social concerns in transportation.

Supply chains use a combination of the following modes of transportation:

- Air
- Package carriers
- Truck
- Rail
- Water
- Pipeline
- Intermodal

Commercial freight activity in the United States by mode in 2011, along with the value added by each mode to GDP in 2009, are summarized in Table 14-1.

Before discussing the various modes, it is important to highlight some important trends in the U.S. economy. Between 1970 and 2002, U.S. real GDP, measured in year 2000 dollars, grew by 176 percent. Over the same period, U.S. freight transportation, measured in ton-miles, grew by only 73 percent. In 1970, it took 2.1 ton-miles of freight transportation to produce $1 of goods GDP. In 2002, it took only 1.1 ton-miles to produce $1 of goods GDP. This trend reflects the downsizing of products with new technology and the improved efficiency of the freight transportation system. This trend has continued since 2002.

The effectiveness of any mode of transport is influenced by equipment investments and operating decisions by the carrier and the available infrastructure and transportation policies. The carrier's primary objective is to ensure good utilization of its assets while providing customers with an acceptable level of service. Carrier decisions are affected by equipment costs, fixed operating costs, variable operating costs, the responsiveness the carrier seeks to provide its target segment, and the prices that the market will bear. Next we discuss various transportation modes and their role in the supply chain.

TABLE 14-1 Transportation Facts

Mode	Freight Value ($ billions) in 2011	Freight Tons (millions) in 2011	Freight Ton-Miles (billions) in 2011	Value Added to GDP ($ billions) in 2009
Air (includes truck and air)	394	6	11	61.9
Truck	12,181	11,924	2,337	113.1
Rail	588	2,053	1,518	30.8
Water	201	645	434	14.3
Pipeline	889	1,912	1,018	12.0
Multimodal	1,985	583	489	

Source: Data from *Freight Shipments Within the U.S. by Mode*, Bureau of Transportation Statistics, Retrieved April 19, 2017.

Air

Airlines have three cost components: (1) a fixed cost of infrastructure and equipment, (2) cost of labor and fuel that is independent of the passengers or cargo on a flight but is fixed for a flight, and (3) a variable cost that depends on the passengers or cargo carried. Given that most of the cost of a flight is incurred when it takes off, an important objective of an airline is to maximize the revenue generated per flight. As a result, revenue management (see Chapter 16) is a significant factor in the success of passenger airlines.

Air carriers offer a fast and fairly expensive mode of transportation for cargo. Small, high-value items or time-sensitive emergency shipments that must travel a long distance are best suited for air transport. Air carriers normally move shipments under 500 pounds, including high-value but lightweight high-tech products. Given the growth in high technology, the weight of freight carried by air has diminished over the past two decades even as the value of the freight has increased somewhat. In 2002, the goods U.S. businesses moved by air were valued at $75,000 per ton, by far the highest among all modes.

Key issues that air carriers face include identifying the location and number of hubs, assigning planes to routes, setting up maintenance schedules for planes, scheduling crews, and managing prices and seat or cargo space availability at different prices.

Package Carriers

Package carriers are transportation companies such as FedEx, UPS, and the U.S. Postal Service, which carry small packages ranging from letters to shipments weighing about 150 pounds. Package carriers use air, truck, and rail to transport time-critical smaller packages. Package carriers are expensive and cannot compete with LTL carriers on price for large shipments. The major service they offer shippers is rapid and reliable delivery. Thus, shippers use package carriers for small and time-sensitive shipments. Package carriers also provide other value-added services such as package tracking and, in some cases, processing and assembly of products.

Package carriers are the preferred mode of transport for online businesses such as Amazon and companies such as W.W. Grainger and McMaster-Carr that send small packages to customers. With the growth in online sales, the use of package carriers has increased significantly over the past few years. Package carriers seek out smaller and more time-sensitive shipments than air cargo carriers, especially when tracking and other value-added services are important to the shipper.

Given the small size of packages and several delivery points, consolidation of shipments is a key factor in increasing utilization and decreasing costs for package carriers. Package carriers have trucks that make local deliveries and pick up packages. Packages are then taken to large sorting centers, from which they are sent by full truckload, rail, or air to the sorting center closest to the delivery point. From the delivery-point sorting center, the package is sent to customers on small trucks making milk runs (discussed later in the chapter). Key issues in this industry include the location and capacity of transfer points and information capability to facilitate and track package flow. For the final delivery to a customer, an important consideration is the scheduling and routing of the delivery trucks.

Truck

In most of the world, trucks carry a large fraction of the goods moved. In 2002, trucks moved 69.5 percent of U.S commercial freight by value and 60.1 percent by weight.[2] The trucking industry consists of two major segments—truckload (TL) or less than truckload (LTL). Trucking is more expensive than rail but offers the advantage of door-to-door shipment and a shorter delivery time. It also has the advantage of requiring no transfer between pickup and delivery.

[2] https://www.tradegecko.com/blog/ikeas-inventory-management-strategy-ikea

TL operations have relatively low fixed costs, and owning a few trucks is often sufficient to enter the business. This industry is characterized by shipments of 10,000 pounds or more; more than 50,000 carriers offer TL services in the United States. The challenge in the TL business is that most markets have an imbalance of inbound and outbound flows. For example, New York has a significantly higher inflow of material than outflow. The goal of a TL carrier is to schedule shipments that provide high revenue while minimizing trucks' idle and empty travel time (dead-heading).

LTL operations are priced to encourage shipments in small lots, usually less than half a TL, as TL tends to be cheaper for larger shipments. LTL is suited for shipments that are too large to be mailed as small packages (typically more than 150 lbs.) but that constitute less than half a TL. LTL operators tend to run regional or national hub-and-spoke networks that allow consolidation of partial loads. LTL shipments take longer than TL shipments because of other loads that need to be picked up and dropped off.

Fatigue-related accidents correlate with the number of hours of driving and increase with the total length of the driver's trip. To reduce accidents on the road caused by driver fatigue, the U.S. Department of Transportation issues hours-of-service regulations that limit work periods for truck drivers. Both TL and LTL carriers must design their routes taking these rules into account. For this reason, self-driving trucks can potentially make a significant impact on the trucking industry.

Rail

In 2002, rail carried about 3 percent of U.S. shipments by value, 10 percent by weight, and more than 30 percent of total ton-miles. These figures reflect the use of rail to move commodities over large distances. Rail carriers incur a high fixed cost in terms of tracks, locomotives, cars, and yards. A significant trip-related labor and fuel cost is independent of the number of cars (fuel costs do vary somewhat with the number of cars) but does vary with the distance traveled and the time taken. Any idle time, once a train is powered, is expensive because labor and fuel costs are incurred even though trains are not moving. Idle time occurs when trains exchange cars for different destinations. It also occurs because of track congestion. Labor and fuel together account for more than 60 percent of railroad expense. From an operational perspective, it is thus important for railroads to keep locomotives and crews well utilized.

The price structure and heavy load capability make rail an ideal mode for carrying large, heavy, or high-density products over long distances. Transportation time by rail, however, can be long. Rail is thus ideal for heavy, low-value shipments that are not time sensitive. Coal, for example, is a major part of each railroad's shipments. Small, time-sensitive, short-distance, or short-lead-time shipments rarely go by rail.

A major goal for railroad firms is to keep locomotives and crews well utilized. Major operational issues at railroads include vehicle and staff scheduling, track and terminal delays, and poor on-time performance. Railroad performance is hurt by the large amount of time taken at each transition. The travel time is usually a small fraction of the total time for a rail shipment. Delays get exaggerated because trains today are typically not scheduled, but "built." In other words, a train leaves once there are enough cars to constitute the train. Cars wait for the train to build, adding to the uncertainty of the delivery time for a shipper. A railroad can improve on-time performance by scheduling some of the trains instead of building all of them. In such a setting, a more sophisticated pricing strategy that includes revenue management (see Chapter 16) must be instituted for scheduled trains.

Water

Water transport, by its nature, is limited to certain areas. Within the United States, water transport takes place via the inland waterway system (the Great Lakes and rivers) or coastal waters. Water transport is ideally suited for carrying large loads at low cost. Within the United States,

water transport is used primarily for the movement of large bulk commodity shipments and is the cheapest mode for carrying such loads. It is, however, the slowest of all the modes, and significant delays occur at ports and terminals. This makes water transport difficult to operate for short-haul trips, although it is used effectively in Japan and parts of Europe for daily short-haul trips of a few miles.

In global trade, water transport is the dominant mode for shipping all kinds of products. Cars, grain, apparel, and other products are shipped by sea. In 2001, merchandise trade valued at more than $718 billion moved between the United States and foreign seaports. Maritime transportation accounted for 78 percent of the U.S. international merchandise freight by weight in 2002. For the quantities shipped and the distances involved in international trade, water transport is by far the cheapest mode of transport. A significant trend in maritime trade worldwide has been the growth in the use of containers. This has led to a demand for larger, faster, and more specialized vessels to improve the economics of container transport. Delays at ports, customs, and security and the management of containers used are major issues in global shipping.

Pipeline

Pipeline is used primarily for the transport of crude petroleum, refined petroleum products, and natural gas. In the United States, pipeline accounted for about 16 percent of total ton-miles in 2002. A significant initial fixed cost is incurred in setting up the pipeline and related infrastructure that does not vary significantly with the diameter of the pipeline. Pipeline operations are typically optimized at about 80 to 90 percent of pipeline capacity. Given the nature of the costs, pipelines are best suited when relatively stable and large flows are required. Pipeline may be an effective way of getting crude oil to a port or a refinery. Sending gasoline to a gas station does not justify investment in a pipeline and is done better with a truck. Pipeline pricing usually consists of two components: a fixed component related to the shipper's peak usage and a second charge relating to the actual quantity transported. This pricing structure encourages the shipper to use the pipeline for the predictable component of demand with other modes often being used to cover fluctuations.

Intermodal

Intermodal transportation is the use of more than one mode of transport to move a shipment to its destination. A variety of intermodal combinations are possible, with the most common being truck/rail. Intermodal traffic has grown considerably with the increased use of containers for shipping and the rise of global trade. For global trade, intermodal is often the only option because factories and markets may not be situated next to ports. As the quantity shipped using containers has grown, the truck/water/rail intermodal combination has also grown. By 2001, intermodal activity contributed more than 20 percent of rail revenues.[3] On land, the rail/truck intermodal system offers the benefits of lower cost than TL and delivery times that are better than rail, thereby bringing together different modes of transport to create a price/service offering that cannot be matched by any single mode. It also creates convenience for shippers that now deal with only one entity representing all carriers that together provide the intermodal service.

Key issues in the intermodal industry involve the exchange of information to facilitate shipment transfers between different modes because these transfers often involve considerable delays, hurting delivery time performance.

Most shippers use a combination of modes across their supply chain depending upon the product value and sales volume along with the desired level of responsiveness. For example, Walmart uses ships to bring imported product from Asia to the United States at low cost. It then uses trucks and rail to move the product to their DCs and stores. Walmart also uses more expensive package carriers to provide responsive home delivery to their online customers.

[3] https://www.wired.com/2009/11/video-inside-an-ikea-factory/

SUMMARY OF LEARNING OBJECTIVE 1

Transportation decisions affect supply chain profitability and influence both inventory and facility decisions within a supply chain. The various modes of transportation include water, rail, truck, air, pipeline, intermodal, and package carriers. Water is typically the least expensive mode but is also the slowest, whereas air and package carriers are the most expensive and the fastest. Rail and water are best suited for low-value, large shipments that do not need to be moved in a hurry. Air and package carriers are best suited for small, high-value, emergency shipments. Intermodal and TL carriers are faster than rail and water but are somewhat more expensive. LTL carriers are best suited for small shipments that are too large for package carriers but much smaller than needed for a TL.

TRANSPORTATION INFRASTRUCTURE AND POLICIES

14.2 *Discuss the role of infrastructure and policies in transportation.*

Roads, seaports, airports, rail, and canals are some of the major infrastructural elements that exist along nodes and links of a transportation network. In almost all countries, transportation infrastructure is viewed as a public good for which the government plays a significant role in both building and maintenance. Improved infrastructure has played a significant role in the development of transportation and the resulting growth of trade. The role of the railroads and canals in the economic development of the United States is well documented. More recently, the impact of improved road, air, and port infrastructure on the development in China is very visible.

Before considering policy questions related to transportation infrastructures, it is worth looking at the history of rail and road infrastructure in the United States to see some of the issues involved. We summarize some of the discussion by Ellison (2002) of the history of railroads and regulation in the industry. The construction of railroads in the United States occurred rapidly during the 1850s. The railroads were privately owned but were built with significant government subsidy, often in the form of land grants. By the 1870s, the railroad network connected most of the United States. Each railroad was the exclusive provider of carriage over its track. This monopoly allowed railroads to determine the price they charged, as well as the level of service they provided to their customers. Initial construction of new railroads led to some competition over rates. The railroad companies responded by entering into agreements with each other that effectively ended competition and raised rates. Protests by farmers and other users of the railroads led eventually to the establishment of the Interstate Commerce Commission (ICC), which prohibited discriminatory pricing. The ICC required railroads to file their rates with the ICC and made them public. The railroads responded by forming cartels to restrict supply. This led to the passage of the Sherman Antitrust Act in 1890. Responding to the financial difficulties of railways in the 1940s, the government allowed them some degree of coordination and exempted them from the antitrust regulations. With the growth of other modes of transport and the need to revitalize their assets, the railroads were in bad financial shape in the early 1970s. The Staggers Rail Act of 1980 deregulated the railroads, allowed them some rate-making powers, and eased entry and exit. The act also removed the antitrust immunity of the railroads. Deregulation in the United States was followed by a wave of reorganization and mergers within the railroad industry. Overall, deregulation has resulted in improved financial performance of the railroad industry and increased use of rail by shippers.

Levinson (1998) provides an excellent discussion of the history of road construction and pricing. In the late 1700s, turnpikes were built using public funds in Virginia, Maryland, and Pennsylvania but were then turned over to private companies that collected tolls. Over time, other turnpikes were built as a result of competition between towns to gain trade. Other than federal land grants, these roads were typically built with local effort and money. The tolls on these turnpikes were generally structured to keep local travel free and make people traveling across an area pay for this right. With the growth in railroads and canals, however, turnpikes suffered financially in the mid-1800s and were eventually converted into public roads. In the

twentieth century, as the modes of transport changed, there was a need for higher quality roads. A network of national toll-free highways was built, largely using gasoline taxes as the source of funding. At the same time, other facilities, such as tunnels and bridges, were often constructed as toll facilities. In many other countries, such as France and Spain, concessions were granted to private companies that received toll revenue. More recently, private toll roads have also been built in Malaysia, Indonesia, and Thailand.

From these examples, it seems reasonable that the government must either own or regulate a monopolistic transportation infrastructure asset. When the transportation infrastructure asset has competition either within a mode or across modes, private ownership, deregulation, and competition seem to work well. The deregulation of the transportation industry within the United States is a case in point. Keep in mind, however, that roads, ports, and airports are largely public and not private because of the inherently monopolistic nature of these transportation infrastructure assets. In such a setting, the public ownership of these assets is justified. This raises the policy question of financing the construction and maintenance of these publicly owned transportation assets. Should roads be financed through a gasoline tax, or is some other form of financing such as tolls more appropriate?

Some economists have argued for public ownership of these assets with the setting of quasi-market prices to improve overall efficiency. Quasi-market prices need to take into account the discrepancy between the incentives of an individual using the transportation infrastructure and the public as a whole that owns the infrastructure. This discrepancy arises because each user of a transportation asset impacts all other users of the asset as well. This phenomenon is illustrated in Figure 14-1 in the context of road traffic.

A vehicle driver bases his or her decision to use a highway on the cost and benefit of doing so. Figure 14-1 assumes that different people have different values for making the trip and these values are uniformly distributed over an interval. The number of users whose value from a trip exceeds a particular cost is thus defined by the demand curve. We assume a simple demand curve given by traffic $f = 1,000 - cost$. The costs incurred by a motorist include any tolls and the cost of time spent on the highway and the cost of operating and maintaining the vehicle. It is well known that the time spent increases with congestion on a highway. Thus, the average cost to each motorist increases with traffic flow, as shown in Figure 14-1. We start with the case when there are no tolls and motorists incur only costs related to congestion, operation, and maintenance. We assume that the total cost grows with traffic f and is given by $total\ cost = 3f^2$. The average cost

Figure 14-1 Impact of Average And Marginal Cost on Vehicle Flow

per motorist is thus given by $cost = 3f^2/f = 3f$. Because there are no tolls for accessing the highway, demand will materialize based on the average congestion, operation, and maintenance cost incurred by people on the road. Given people's valuation of the trip, the number of motorists using the road is determined by the intersection of the demand curve with the average cost curve at point A as shown in Figure 14-1. For our demand curve $f = 1,000 - cost$ and average cost function $cost = 3f$, we obtain $f = 1,000 - cost = 1,000 - 3f$. Solving this equation for f, we obtain $f = 1,000/4 = 250$ motorists at equilibrium. This results in an average cost to motorists of $P_0 = 3f = 3 \times 250 = 750$ and a traffic flow of $Q_0 = f = 250$.

From the perspective of the public, however, it is more appropriate to consider how each additional motorist impacts the total cost, not just the average cost. Observe that an additional motorist increases the average cost $3f$ by a small amount but increases the total cost $3f^2$ across all motorists by a much larger amount (because the addition of each motorist affects delays for all motorists). This is represented in Figure 14-1 by the marginal cost curve, which measures the marginal increase in total cost as a result of additional traffic flow. For a total cost curve $total\ cost = 3f^2$ the marginal cost is given by taking the derivative $d(total\ cost)/df = 6f$. Observe that the marginal cost curve $6f$ is higher than the average cost curve $3f$. In other words, the marginal impact of a motorist on total cost is much higher than his or her average share of the impact. To get motorists to internalize the impact they have on others, we should charge motorists a toll for highway use based on this marginal cost that they add to the system. If we were to do so for our example (i.e., somehow charge $3f$ as additional toll to raise the total marginal cost to $6f$), from our demand curve, we obtain $f = 1,000 - marginal\ cost = 1,000 - 6f$. Solving this equation for f, we obtain an equilibrium traffic of $f = 1,000/7 = 143$ motorists. Motorists should be charged a toll $3f$ that depends on the amount of traffic on the highway. If the traffic is at a level below 143, motorists pay a lower toll. As traffic increases, the toll rises in proportion and this increase in costs now discourages motorists from joining the highway. At equilibrium, there are $f = 143$ motorists on the highway, each is charged a congestion-related toll of $3f = 3 \times 143 = 429$, and each incurs average congestion-related costs of $3f = 429$ for a total cost of 858 per motorist. With a toll in place, fewer motorists join the highway because they bear the true cost they are imposing on the highway system. This toll lowers the vehicle flow rate from $Q_0 = 250$ to $Q_1 = 143$ and reduces the average congestion cost per motorist from 750 to 429. Observe that the absence of a congestion toll results in an overuse of the transportation infrastructure and a higher resulting congestion cost on all users.

The problem is well illustrated by a simple illustration given by Vickrey (see Button and Verhoef, 1998). Each member of a group going out to dinner is likely to order an expensive item if the plan is to share the bill equally at the end (charge based on average cost) instead of having each person pay his or her true charge (charge based on marginal cost). Thus, it is fair to say that the overall bill is higher if it is shared equally compared with each person paying based on actual consumption. The same is true with transportation infrastructure if pricing is not linked to congestion.

Quasi-market prices for transportation infrastructure thus result in higher prices at peak locations and times and lower prices otherwise. Such pricing is not commonly observed for transportation infrastructure except for roads in Singapore and city centers in a few European cities. Congestion is a major factor at several ports and airports. The Los Angeles–Long Beach port, for example, experienced significant congestion in 2004. Several factors affected the congestion, including capacity problems on railroads taking containers away, labor shortages, and technology issues. However, congestion was also affected by the desire of many shippers to bring weekly shipments from Asia over the weekend to ensure supply for the entire week. This created a peak time with significant congestion. The peak workload also becomes exaggerated as container ships get larger. In such a situation, the use of peak tolls to level out the arrivals can be an effective policy. Overall, it is important to keep in mind that transportation infrastructure faces congestion-related problems unless users are forced to internalize the marginal impact of their actions. It may be most effective to charge a congestion toll and use the money generated to improve the effectiveness of the transportation infrastructure.

SUMMARY OF LEARNING OBJECTIVE 2

Infrastructure such as ports, roads, and airports has a significant impact on transportation. Given its inherent monopolistic nature, most transportation infrastructure requires public ownership or regulation. In the case of public ownership, pricing based on average cost leads to overutilization and congestion. It is important to use some form of congestion pricing under which users are forced to internalize the increase they cause in network cost.

DESIGN OPTIONS FOR A TRANSPORTATION NETWORK

14.3 Identify the relative strengths and weaknesses of various transportation network design options.

The design of a transportation network affects the performance of a supply chain by establishing the infrastructure within which operational transportation decisions regarding scheduling and routing are made. A well-designed transportation network allows a supply chain to achieve the desired degree of responsiveness at a low cost. Three basic questions need to be considered when designing a transportation network between two stages of a supply chain:

1. Should transportation be direct or through an intermediate site?
2. Should the intermediate site stock product or only serve as a cross-docking location?
3. Should each delivery route supply a single destination or multiple destinations?

Based on the answers to these questions, the supply chain ends up with a variety of transportation networks. We discuss these options and their strengths and weaknesses in the context of a buyer with multiple locations sourcing from several suppliers.

Direct Shipment Network to Single Destination

With this network, the buyer structures transportation so that all shipments come directly from each supplier to each buyer location, as shown in Figure 14-2. The origin and destination of each shipment is specified, and the supply chain manager needs to decide only the quantity to ship and the mode of transportation to use. This decision involves a trade-off between transportation and inventory costs, as discussed later in the chapter.

The major advantage of a direct shipment transportation network is the elimination of intermediate warehouses and its simplicity of operation and coordination. The shipment decision is completely local, and the decision made for one shipment does not influence others. The transportation time from supplier to buyer location is short because each shipment goes direct.

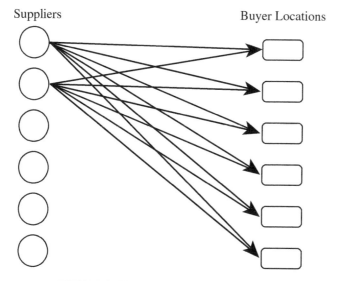

Figure 14-2 Direct Shipment Network

A direct shipment network to single destination is justified only if demand at buyer locations is large enough that optimal replenishment lot sizes are close to a truckload from each supplier to each location. Home Depot started with a direct shipment network, given that most of the stores it opened until about 2002 were large stores. The stores ordered in quantities that were large enough that ordering was managed locally within the store and delivery to the store arrived directly from the supplier. The direct shipment network to single destination, however, proved to be problematic as Home Depot started to open smaller stores that did not have large enough orders to justify a direct shipment.

Direct Shipping with Milk Runs

A *milk run* is a route on which a truck either delivers product from a single supplier to multiple retailers or goes from multiple suppliers to a single buyer location, as shown in Figure 14-3. In direct shipping with milk runs, a supplier delivers directly to multiple buyer locations on a truck or a truck picks up deliveries destined for the same buyer location from many suppliers. When using this option, a supply chain manager has to decide on the routing of each milk run.

Milk runs lower transportation cost by consolidating shipments to multiple locations on a single truck. Milk runs make sense when the quantity destined for each location is too small to fill a truck but multiple locations are close enough to each other such that their combined quantity fills the truck. Companies such as Frito-Lay that make direct store deliveries use milk runs to lower their transportation cost. If frequent small deliveries are needed on a regular basis and either a set of suppliers or a set of retailers is in geographic proximity, the use of milk runs can significantly reduce transportation costs. For example, Toyota uses milk runs from suppliers to support its just-in-time (JIT) manufacturing system in both Japan and the United States. In Japan, Toyota has many assembly plants located close together and thus uses milk runs from a single supplier to many plants. In the United States, however, Toyota uses milk runs from many suppliers to each assembly plant, given the large distance between assembly plants.

All Shipments via Intermediate Distribution Center with Storage

Under this option, product is shipped from suppliers to a central distribution center, where it is stored until needed by buyers when it is shipped to each buyer location, as shown in Figure 14-4. Storing product at an intermediate location is justified if transportation economies require large

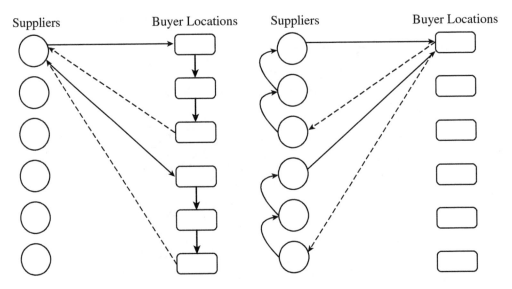

Figure 14-3 Milk Runs from Multiple Suppliers or to Multiple Buyer Locations

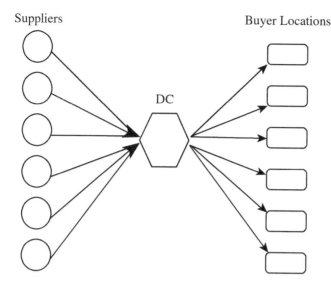

Figure 14-4 All Shipments via DC

shipments on the inbound side or shipments on the outbound side cannot be coordinated. In such a situation, product comes in large quantities into a DC, where it is held in inventory and sent to buyer locations in smaller replenishment lots when needed.

The presence of a DC allows a supply chain to achieve economies of scale for inbound transportation to a point close to the final destination, because each supplier sends a large shipment to the DC that contains product for all locations the DC serves. Because DCs serve locations nearby, the outbound transportation cost is not very large. For example, W.W. Grainger has its suppliers ship products to one of nine DCs (typically in large quantities), with each DC, in turn, replenishing stores in its vicinity with the smaller quantities they need. It would be expensive for suppliers to try to serve each store directly. Similarly, when Home Depot sources from an overseas supplier, the product is held in inventory at the DC because the lot size on the inbound side is much larger than the sum of the lot sizes for the stores served by the DC.

All Shipments via Intermediate Transit Point with Cross-Docking

Under this option, suppliers send their shipments to an intermediate transit point (which could be a DC), where they are cross-docked and sent to buyer locations without storing them. The product flow is similar to that shown in Figure 14-4 except that there is no storage at the intermediate facility. When a DC cross-docks product, each inbound truck contains product for several buyer locations, whereas each outbound truck contains product from several suppliers. Major benefits of cross-docking are that little inventory needs to be held and product flows faster in the supply chain. Cross-docking also saves on handling cost because product does not have to be moved into and out of storage. Cross-docking is appropriate when economies of scale in transportation can be achieved on both the inbound and outbound sides and both inbound and outbound shipments can be coordinated.

Walmart has used cross-docking successfully to decrease inventories in the supply chain without incurring excessive transportation costs. Walmart builds many large stores in a geographic area supported by a DC. As a result, the total lot size to all stores from each supplier fills trucks on the inbound side to achieve economies of scale. On the outbound side, the sum of the lot sizes from all suppliers to each retail store fills up the truck to achieve economies of scale.

Another good example of the use of a transit point with cross-docking comes from Peapod in the Chicago area. Peapod has a DC in Lake Zurich from which it delivers to its customers

using milk runs. This approach proved effective for customers in the northern and western sub-urbs of Chicago. Peapod, however, wanted to increase its reach to the city of Chicago and the city of Milwaukee. Both are far enough from the Lake Zurich DC that a milk run wasted about two hours in transit, making no productive deliveries. These markets were also small enough that they did not justify a local DC. Peapod's response has been to set up a cross-docking facility (which tends to be cheaper than a DC because no storage is involved) at each location. Peapod then sends out all deliveries to the local cross-docking facility in a larger truck and uses smaller trucks for local deliveries. The use of cross-docking at a transit point has allowed Peapod to increase the reach of the Lake Zurich DC without significantly increasing transportation expense.

Shipping via DC Using Milk Runs

As shown in Figure 14-5, milk runs can be used from a DC if lot sizes to be delivered to each buyer location are small. Milk runs reduce outbound transportation costs by consolidating small shipments. For example, Seven-Eleven Japan cross-docks deliveries from its fresh-food suppliers at its DCs and sends out milk runs to the retail outlets because the total shipment to a store from all suppliers does not fill a truck. The use of cross-docking and milk runs allows Seven-Eleven Japan to lower its transportation cost while sending small replenishment lots to each store. The use of cross-docking with milk runs requires a significant degree of coordination and suitable routing and scheduling.

The online grocer Peapod uses milk runs from DCs when making home deliveries to help reduce transportation costs for small shipments. OshKosh B'Gosh, a manufacturer of children's wear, has used this idea to virtually eliminate LTL shipments from its DC in Tennessee to retail stores.

Tailored Network

The tailored network option is a suitable combination of previous options that reduces the cost and improves the responsiveness of the supply chain. Here, transportation uses a combination of cross-docking, milk runs, and TL and LTL carriers, along with package carriers in some cases. The goal is to use the appropriate option in each situation. High-demand products may be shipped directly to high-demand retail outlets, whereas low-demand products or shipments to low-demand retail outlets are consolidated to and from the DC. The complexity of managing this transportation network is high because different shipping procedures are used for each product

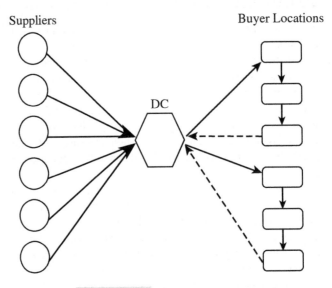

Figure 14-5 Milk Runs from DC

TABLE 14-2 Pros and Cons of Different Transportation Networks

Network Structure	Pros	Cons
Direct shipping	No intermediate warehouse Simple to coordinate	High inventories (due to large lot size)
Direct shipping with milk runs	Lower transportation costs for small lots Lower inventories	Increased coordination complexity
All shipments via central DC with inventory storage	Lower inbound transportation cost through consolidation	Increased inventory cost Increased handling at DC
All shipments via central DC with cross-dock	Low inventory requirement Lower transportation cost through consolidation	Increased coordination complexity
Shipping via DC using milk runs	Lower outbound transportation cost for small lots	Further increase in coordination complexity
Tailored network	Transportation choice best matches needs of individual product and store	Highest coordination complexity

and retail outlet. Operating a tailored network requires significant investment in information infrastructure to facilitate the coordination. Such a network, however, allows for the selective use of a shipment method to minimize the transportation as well as inventory costs.

Table 14-2 summarizes the pros and cons of the various transportation network options discussed. We illustrate some of these choices in Example 14-1.

EXAMPLE 14-1 **Selecting a Transportation Network**

A retail chain has eight stores in a region supplied from four supply sources. Trucks have a capacity of 40,000 units and cost $1,000 per load plus $100 per delivery. Thus, a truck making two deliveries charges $1,200. The cost of holding one unit in inventory at retail for a year is $0.20.

The vice president of supply chain is considering whether to use direct shipping from suppliers to retail stores or setting up milk runs from suppliers to retail stores. What network do you recommend if annual sales for each product at each retail store are 960,000 units? What network do you recommend if sales for each product at each retail store are 120,000 units?

Analysis:

We provide a detailed analysis when annual sales of each product at each retail store are 960,000 units. Our analysis assumes that all trucks travel full. A more sophisticated analysis can be performed for which the optimal load on each truck is calculated and used in the analysis. This analysis is also available in the spreadsheet *Chapter14-examples* on worksheet *Example 14-1*.

We first analyze the direct shipping network and assume that full truckloads will be shipped from suppliers to retail stores. In this case, we have the following:

Batch size shipped from each supplier to each store = 40,000 units
Number of shipments/year from each supplier to each store = 960,000/40,000 = 24
Annual trucking cost for direct network = $24 \times 1,100 \times 4 \times 8 = \$844,800$
Average inventory at each store for each product − 40,000/2 = 20,000 units
Annual inventory cost for direct network = $20,000 \times 0.2 \times 4 \times 8 = \$128,000$
Total annual cost of direct network = $\$844,800 + \$128,000 = \$972,800$

Now, we analyze the network in which suppliers run milk runs to retail stores. Milk runs increase the transportation cost but decrease the level of inventory each store has to hold. We provide a detailed analysis for the instance of suppliers running milk runs to two stores on each truck. In this case, we have the following:

Batch size shipped from each supplier to each store = 40,000/2 = 20,000 units
Number of shipments/year from each supplier to each store = 960,000/20,000 = 48
Transportation cost per shipment per store (two stores/truck) = 1,000/2 + 100 = $600
Annual trucking cost for milk run network = 48 × 600 × 4 × 8 = $921,600
Average inventory at each store for each product = 20,000/2 = 10,000 units
Annual inventory cost for milk run network = 10,000 × 0.2 × 4 × 8 = $64,000
Total annual cost of milk run network = $921,600 + $64,000 = $985,600

This analysis shows that when demand per product per store is 960,000 units, the direct network is cheaper than running milk runs with two stores per route. Increasing the number of stores on a milk run ends up costing even more because it raises transportation costs more than it saves in holding costs.

When demand per product per store is 120,000, we first provide the detailed costs for the direct shipping network as follows (assuming all trucks travel full):

Batch size shipped from each supplier to each store = 40,000 units
Number of shipments/year from each supplier to each store = 120,000/40,000 = 3
Annual trucking cost for direct network = 3 × 1,100 × 4 × 8 = $105,600
Average inventory at each store for each product = 40,000/2 = 20,000 units
Annual inventory cost for direct network = 20,000 × 0.2 × 4 × 8 = $128,000
Total annual cost of direct network = $105,600 + $128,000 = $233,600

For the direct network, it turns out that to minimize total annual costs, it is better not to fill each truck but to send only 36,332 units per truck. The optimal loading increases transportation costs a bit but decreases total costs to $232,524 per year.

Now, we analyze the network in which suppliers use milk runs to retail stores. We provide a detailed analysis for the instance of suppliers running milk runs to four stores on each truck and each truck travels full. In this case, we have the following:

Batch size shipped from each supplier to each store = 40,000/4 = 10,000 units
Number of shipments/year from each supplier to each store = 120,000/10,000 = 12
Transportation cost per shipment per store (four stores/truck) = 1,000/4 + 100 = $350
Annual trucking cost for milk run network = 12 × 350 × 4 × 8 = $134,400
Average inventory at each store for each product = 10,000/2 = 5,000 units
Annual inventory cost for milk run network = 5,000 × 0.2 × 4 × 8 = $32,000
Total annual cost of milk run network = $134,400 + $32,000 = $166,400

This analysis shows that when demand per product per store is 120,000 units, the milk run network with four stores per route is cheaper than the direct network (even when truck loads are optimized). The direct network ends up costing more because of increased inventory holding costs even though transportation is cheaper. Observe that milk runs become more attractive as the amount flowing through the system decreases.

SUMMARY OF LEARNING OBJECTIVE 3

Networks are designed to either ship directly from origin to destination or move the product through a consolidation point. Direct shipments are most effective when demand at each destination is large. When demand at each destination is small, use of an intermediate warehouse or DC lowers inbound transportation cost by consolidating inbound transportation to the DC. Shipments may also be consolidated with milk runs either picking up from multiple locations or dropping off in multiple locations.

MUMBAI *DABBAWALAS*: A SUCCESSFUL SAME DAY DELIVERY NETWORK

14.4 *Understand some success factors in a responsive network for same day delivery.*

Imagine trying to pick up and deliver 150,000 hot lunches on time every day in a city where traffic is normally gridlocked. Getting a same day delivery distribution system to be financially successful has defeated many dotcom startups, such as Urbanfetch and Kozmo.com, that operated in cities like London and New York. The Mumbai *dabbawalas*, however, have successfully run such a distribution system for more than a century—while charging customers about $10/month for this service, and including reverse logistics: all empty lunchboxes are delivered back home after lunch. They have used several ideas discussed earlier, from milk runs to cross-docking, to create a highly responsive distribution network.

Every working morning around 9 a.m., about 5,000 *dabbawalas* use milk runs with bicycles to pick up lunches from about 30 homes each. These freshly made lunches are packed in steel or plastic containers called *tiffins* or *dabbas* (hence the name *dabbawala*, or "*dabba* guy"). Each home has a time window of a couple of minutes for the pickup, and the schedule is repeated every working day. The milk run ends at the local train station, where the *dabbas* are collected and sorted into wooden crates based on their destination. There are a few stations in Mumbai where multiple train lines intersect. At these stations, the *dabbawalas* cross-dock the *dabbas* between crates to ensure that each crate contains lunches for the same destination. The lunchboxes arrive at the destination railway stations by about 11:30 a.m. The destination railway station serves as a hub from which each *dabbawala* delivers about 40 *dabbas* to their final destination, where the lunches will be consumed. The delivery is typically done by 1 p.m. using a milk run on a bicycle or handcart. Once the customers finish their lunches, the entire process is repeated in reverse to return the empty *dabbas* to their respective homes by 5 p.m. For this complex network, in which 150,000 individualized pickups and deliveries are managed daily, the *dabbawalas* average one delayed delivery in 16 million!

Besides being awed by their accomplishments, it is important to ask how the *dabbawalas* succeed while other people failed when trying to provide same day home delivery with Urbanfetch and Kozmo.com. Besides their discipline and commitment, three factors facilitate the success of the *dabbawala* distribution network:

1. Low uncertainty of demand
2. Temporal aggregation of demand
3. Use of transportation resources when they are underutilized

The pickup and delivery points for the *dabbawalas* are fixed and do not vary from day to day. This predictability of demand allows them to design optimal milk runs and travel routes that are repeated daily. In contrast, the destinations for home delivery orders received by Kozmo varied every day. Given that the *dabbawalas* have a single product (lunch), the pickup and delivery times are close to each other for every customer. This temporal aggregation of demand allows the *dabbawalas* to ensure that all pickups or deliveries for a single building are handled together. This luxury was not available to Kozmo, which often had to go back to the same area because the multiple orders that arrived from there were distributed over time. Finally, the *dabbawalas* use the Mumbai railway system during times that are off-peak. The Mumbai railway system is one of the most densely loaded systems in the world—in 2015, it carried 7.5 million passengers daily, with trains packed very densely during rush hours. The *dabbawalas* travel these trains after the morning rush and before the evening rush. The trains are quite crowded during off-peak times as well, but rush hour crowds are dense enough to make it difficult for a passenger to carry a *dabba* in person (this is a common reason given for the use of *dabbawalas*). The absence of uncertainty, the temporal aggregation of orders, and the use of the train system during off-peak hours allows the *dabbawalas* to economically provide a responsive service that has challenged many home delivery companies.

SUMMARY OF LEARNING OBJECTIVE 4

The main challenge for same day delivery networks is to get a high enough utilization of delivery assets to make the cost reasonable. The Mumbai *dabbawalas* use the predictability of their demand, the temporal aggregation of demand because all lunches are picked up and delivered around the same time, and the use of underutilized transportation assets, to be very responsive at a reasonable cost.

14.5 *Evaluate trade-offs that shippers need to consider when designing a transportation network.*

TRADE-OFFS IN TRANSPORTATION DESIGN

All transportation decisions made by shippers in a supply chain network must take into account their impact on inventory costs, facility and processing costs, the cost of coordinating operations, and the level of responsiveness provided to customers. For example, Amazon's use of package carriers to deliver products to customers increases transportation cost but allows Amazon to centralize its facilities and reduce inventory costs. If Amazon wants to reduce its transportation costs, the company must either sacrifice responsiveness to customers or increase the number of facilities and resulting inventories to move closer to customers.

The cost of coordinating operations is generally hard to quantify. Shippers should evaluate different transportation options in terms of various costs and revenues and then rank them according to coordination complexity. A manager can then make the appropriate transportation decision. Managers must consider the following trade-offs when making transportation decisions:

- Transportation and inventory cost trade-off
- Transportation cost and customer responsiveness trade-off

Transportation and Inventory Cost Trade-Off

The trade-off between transportation and inventory costs is significant when designing a supply chain network. Two fundamental supply chain decisions involving this trade-off are

- Choice of transportation mode
- Inventory aggregation

CHOICE OF TRANSPORTATION MODE Selecting a transportation mode is both a planning and an operational decision in a supply chain. The decision regarding carriers with which a company contracts is a planning decision, whereas the choice of transportation mode for a particular shipment is an operational decision. For both decisions, a shipper must balance transportation and inventory costs. The mode of transportation that results in the lowest transportation cost does not necessarily lower total costs for a supply chain. Cheaper modes of transport typically have longer lead times and larger minimum shipment quantities, both of which result in higher levels of inventory in the supply chain. Modes that allow for shipping in small quantities lower inventory levels but tend to be more expensive. Apple, for example, airfreights several of its products from Asia. This choice cannot be justified on the basis of transportation cost alone. It can be justified only because the use of a faster mode of transportation for shipping valuable products allows Apple to carry low levels of inventory and still be responsive to its customers.

The impact of using different modes of transportation on inventories, response time, and costs in the supply chain is shown in Table 14-3. Each transportation mode is ranked along various dimensions, with 1 being the lowest and 6 being the highest.

Faster modes of transportation are preferred for products with a high value-to-weight ratio (a smartphone is a good example of such a product) for which reducing inventories is important, whereas cheaper modes are preferred for products with a small value-to-weight ratio (e.g., furniture imported by IKEA) for which reducing transportation cost is important. The choice of transportation mode should take into account potential lost sales and cycle, safety, and in-transit

TABLE 14-3 Ranking of Transportation Modes in Terms of Supply Chain Performance (Read Vertically, 1 = Lowest, 6 = Highest)

Mode	Cycle Inventory	Safety Inventory	In-Transit Cost	Transportation Cost	Transportation Time
Package	1	1	1	6	1
Air	2	2	2	5	2
LTL	3	3	3	4	4
TL	4	4	4	3	3
Rail	5	5	5	2	5
Water	6	6	6	1	6

inventory costs in addition to the cost of transportation. The lost sales and inventory costs are influenced by the speed, flexibility, and reliability of the mode. The purchase price must also be included if it changes with the choice of transportation mode (perhaps because of a change in lot sizes). Ignoring inventory costs when making transportation decisions can result in choices that worsen the performance of a supply chain, as illustrated in Example 14-2 (see worksheet *Example 14-2*).

EXAMPLE 14-2 **Trade-Offs When Selecting Transportation Mode**

Eastern Electric (EE) is a major appliance manufacturer with a large plant in the Chicago area. EE purchases all the motors for its appliances from Westview Motors, located near Dallas. EE currently purchases 120,000 motors each year from Westview at a price of $120 per motor. Demand has been relatively constant for several years and is expected to stay that way. Each motor averages about 10 pounds in weight, and EE has traditionally purchased lots of 3,000 motors. Westview ships each EE order within a day of receiving it (lead time is one day more than transit time). Transit time using truck is three days and transit time for rail is five days. At its assembly plant, EE carries a safety inventory equal to 50 percent of the average demand for motors during the replenishment lead time. EE's annual cost of holding inventory is 25 percent.

The plant manager at EE has received several proposals for transportation and must decide on the one to accept. The details of various proposals are provided in Table 14-4, where one cwt equals 100 pounds.

Golden's pricing represents a marginal unit quantity discount (see Chapter 11). Golden's representative has proposed lowering the marginal rate for the quantity over 250 cwt in a shipment from $4/cwt to $3/cwt and suggested that EE increase its batch size to 4,000 motors to take advantage of the lower transportation cost. What should the plant manager do?

TABLE 14-4 Transportation Proposals for EE Electric

Carrier	Range of Quantity Shipped (cwt)	Shipping Cost ($/cwt)
AM Railroad	200+	6.50
Northeast Trucking	100+	7.50
Golden Freightways	50–150	8.00
Golden Freightways	150–250	6.00
Golden Freightways	250+	4.00

Analysis:

Golden's new proposal will result in low transportation costs for EE if the plant manager orders in lots of 4,000 motors. The plant manager, however, decides to include inventory costs in the transportation decision. EE incurs an annual holding cost of $H = \$120 \times 0.25 = \30 per motor. The transportation decision affects the cycle inventory, safety inventory, and in-transit inventory for EE. Therefore, the plant manager decides to evaluate the total transportation and inventory cost for each transportation option.

The AM Rail proposal requires a minimum shipment of 20,000 pounds or 2,000 motors. The replenishment lead time in this case is $L = 5 + 1 = 6$ days. For a lot size of $Q = 2,000$ motors, the plant manager obtains the following:

$$\text{Cycle inventory} = Q/2 = 2,000/2 = 1,000 \text{ motors}$$
$$\text{Safety inventory} = L/2 \text{ days of demand} = (6/2)(120,000/365)$$
$$= 986 \text{ motors}$$
$$\text{In-transit inventory} = 120,000 (5/365) = 1,644 \text{ motors}$$
$$\text{Total average inventory} = 1,000 + 986 + 1,644 = 3,630 \text{ motors}$$
$$\text{Annual holding cost using AM Rail} = 3,630 \times \$30 = \$108,900$$

AM Rail charges $6.50 per cwt, resulting in a transportation cost of $0.65 per motor because each motor weighs 10 pounds. Here we have approximated the holding cost because we have not included the transportation cost in the cost of the product. A more precise evaluation would set the holding cost of in-transit inventory to be $30 (because transportation cost has not yet been incurred) and the holding cost of cycle and safety inventory to be $120.65 \times 0.25 = \$30.16$ because transportation cost has been incurred by this stage. The precise evaluation would result in an inventory holding cost of

$$(1,644 \times 30) + (1,986 \times 30.16) = \$109,218.$$

The annual transportation cost is obtained as follows:

$$\text{Annual transportation cost using AM Rail} = 120,000 \times 0.65 = \$78,000$$

The total annual cost for inventory and transportation using AM Rail is thus $186,900 ($108,900 + $78,000).

The plant manager then evaluates the cost associated with each transportation option, as shown in Table 14-5 (we have used the approximate inventory cost in this analysis, applying the holding cost only to the unit cost and not the unit cost plus transportation cost/unit). See worksheet *Example 14-2* for all details in Table 14-5. Based on the analysis in Table 14-5 (the inventory

TABLE 14-5 Analysis of Transportation Options for Eastern Electric

Alternative	Lot Size (Motors)	Transportation Cost	Cycle Inventory	Safety Inventory	In-Transit Inventory	Inventory Cost	Total Cost
AM Rail	2,000	$78,000	1,000	986	1,644	$108,900	$186,900
Northeast	1,000	$90,000	500	658	986	$64,320	$154,320
Golden	500	$96,000	250	658	986	$56,820	$152,820
Golden	1,500	$96,000	750	658	986	$71,820	$167,820
Golden	2,500	$86,400	1,250	658	986	$86,820	$173,220
Golden	3,000	$80,000	1,500	658	986	$94,320	$174,320
Golden (old proposal)	4,000	$72,000	2,000	658	986	$109,320	$181,320
Golden (new proposal)	4,000	$67,500	2,000	658	986	$109,320	$176,820

numbers are rounded to the closest integer), the plant manager decides to sign a contract with Golden Freightways and order motors in lots of 500. This option has the highest transportation cost, but the lowest overall cost. If the selection of the transportation option were made using only the transportation cost incurred, Golden's new proposal lowering the price for large shipments would look attractive. In reality, though, EE pays a high overall cost for this proposal because of the high inventory costs that result. Thus, considering the trade-off between inventory and transportation costs allows the plant manager to make a transportation decision that minimizes EE's total cost.

INVENTORY AGGREGATION Firms can significantly reduce the safety inventory they require by physically aggregating inventories in one location (see Chapter 12). Most online businesses use this technique to gain advantage over firms with facilities in many locations. For example, Amazon has focused on decreasing its facility and inventory costs by holding inventory in a few warehouses, whereas booksellers such as Barnes & Noble must hold inventory in many retail stores.

Transportation cost, however, generally increases when inventory is aggregated. If inventories are highly disaggregated, some aggregation can also lower transportation costs. Beyond a certain point, though, aggregation of inventories raises total transportation costs. Consider a bookstore chain such as Barnes & Noble. The inbound transportation cost to Barnes & Noble is due to the replenishment of bookstores with new books. There is no outbound cost because customers transport their own books home. If Barnes & Noble decides to close all its bookstores and sell only online, it will have to incur both inbound and outbound transportation costs. The inbound transportation cost to warehouses will be lower than to all bookstores. On the outbound side, however, transportation cost will increase significantly because the outbound shipment to each customer will be small and will require an expensive mode such as a package carrier. The total transportation cost will increase on aggregation because each book travels the same distance as when it was sold through a bookstore, except that a large fraction of the distance is on the outbound side using an expensive mode of transportation. As the degree of inventory aggregation increases, total transportation cost goes up. Another comparison is in the video rental business between Netflix and Redbox. Netflix aggregates its inventories, thus lowering facility and inventory expense. It does, however, have to pay to ship DVDs between its DCs and customer homes. Redbox, in contrast, has many vending machines that carry DVDs but incurs low transportation costs. Thus, all firms planning inventory aggregation must consider the trade-offs among transportation, inventory, and facility costs when making this decision.

Inventory aggregation is a good idea when inventory and facility costs form a large fraction of a supply chain's total costs. Inventory aggregation is useful for products with a large value-to-weight ratio and for products with high demand uncertainty. For example, inventory aggregation is valuable in the diamond industry, because diamonds have a large value-to-weight ratio and demand is uncertain. Inventory aggregation is also a good idea if customer orders are large enough to ensure sufficient economies of scale on outbound transportation. When products have a low value-to-weight ratio and customer orders are small, however, inventory aggregation may hurt a supply chain's performance because of high transportation costs. Compared with diamonds, the value of inventory aggregation is smaller for best-selling books that have a lower value-to-weight ratio and more predictable demand.

We illustrate the trade-off involved in making aggregation decisions in Example 14-3 (see worksheet *Example 14-3*).

EXAMPLE 14-3	**Trade-Offs When Aggregating Inventory**

HighMed, a manufacturer of medical equipment used in heart procedures, is located in Madison, Wisconsin. The medical equipment is sold directly to cardiologists all over North America. HighMed currently divides the United States into twenty-four territories, each with its own sales

force. All product inventories are maintained locally in each territory and replenished from Madison every four weeks using UPS. The average replenishment lead time using UPS is one week. UPS charges at a rate of $0.66 + 0.26x$ where x is the quantity shipped in pounds. The products sold fall into two categories—HighVal and LowVal. HighVal products weigh 0.1 pounds and cost $200 each. LowVal products weigh 0.04 pounds and cost $30 each.

Weekly demand for HighVal products in each territory is normally distributed, with a mean of $\mu_H = 2$ and a standard deviation of $\sigma_H = 5$. Weekly demand for LowVal products in each territory is normally distributed, with a mean of $\mu_L = 20$. and a standard deviation of $\sigma_L = 5$. HighMed maintains sufficient safety inventories in each territory to provide a CSL of 0.997 for each product. Annual holding cost at HighMed is 25 percent.

In addition to the current approach, the management team at HighMed is considering two other options:

Option A: Keep the current structure but replenish inventory once a week rather than once every four weeks.

Option B: Eliminate inventories in the territories, aggregate all inventories in a finished-goods warehouse at Madison, and replenish the warehouse once a week.

If inventories are aggregated at Madison, orders will be shipped using FedEx, which charges $5.53 + 0.53x$ per shipment, where x is the quantity shipped in pounds. The factory requires a one-week lead time to replenish finished-goods inventories at the Madison warehouse. An average customer order is for 1 unit of HighVal and 10 units of LowVal. What should HighMed do?

Analysis:

HighMed can reduce transportation cost by aggregating the quantity shipped at a time because prices for both UPS and FedEx display economies of scale. When comparing Option A with the current system, the management team must trade off the savings in transportation cost through less frequent replenishment with the savings in inventory cost with more frequent replenishment. When considering Option B, the management team must trade off the increase in transportation cost upon aggregation of inventories and the use of a faster but more expensive carrier (FedEx) with the decrease in inventory cost.

The management team first analyzes the current situation. For each territory,

Replenishment lead time, $L = 1$ week

Reorder interval, $T = 4$ weeks

$CSL = 0.997$

1. HighMed inventory costs (current scenario): For HighVal in each territory, the management team obtains the following:

Average lot size, Q_H = expected demand during T weeks = $T\mu_H = 4 \times 2 = 8$ units

Safety inventory, $ss_H = F^{-1}(CSL) \times \sigma_{T+L} = F^{-1}(CSL) \times \sqrt{T + L} \times \sigma_H$

$= \text{NORMSINV}(0.997) \times \sqrt{4 + 1} \times 5 = 30.7$ units (see Equation 12.19)

Total HighVal inventory = $Q_H/2 + ss_H = (8/2) + 30.7 = 34.7$ units

Across all twenty-four territories, HighMed thus carries HighVal inventory of $24 \times 34.7 = 832.8$ units (the true number is 833.3 units if we do not round inventory values to the first decimal). For LowVal in each territory, the management team obtains the following:

Average lot size, Q_L = expected demand during T weeks = $T\mu_L = 4 \times 20 = 80$ units

Safety inventory, $ss_L = F^{-1}(CSL) \times \sigma_{T+L} = F^{-1}(CSL) \times \sqrt{T + L} \times \sigma_L$

$= \text{NORMSINV}(0.997) \times \sqrt{4 + 1} \times 5 = 30.7$ units

Total LowVal inventory = $Q_L/2 + ss_L = (80/2) + 30.7 = 70.7$ units

Across all 24 territories, HighMed thus carries LowVal $= 24 \times 70.7 = 1696.8$ units units (the true number is 1697.3 if we do not round safety inventory to the first decimal).

The management team thus obtains the following:

$$
\begin{aligned}
\text{Annual inventory holding cost for HighMed} &= (\text{average HighVal inventory} \times \$200 \\
&\quad + \text{average LowVal inventory} \times \$30) \times 0.25 \\
&= (832.8 \times \$200 + 1696.8 \times \$30) \times 0.25 \\
&= \$54{,}366 \ (\$54{,}395 \text{ without rounding})
\end{aligned}
$$

2. HighMed transportation cost (current scenario): The average replenishment order from each territory consists of $Q_H = 8$ units units of HighVal and $Q_L = 80$ units units of LowVal. Thus,

Average weight of each replenishment order

$$
= 0.1 Q_H + 0.04 Q_L = 0.1 \times 8 + 0.04 \times 80 = 4 \text{ pounds}
$$
$$
\text{Shipping cost per replenishment order} = \$0.66 + 0.26 \times 4 = \$1.70
$$

Each territory has 13 replenishment orders per year and there are 24 territories. Thus,

$$
\text{Annual transportation cost} = \$1.70 \times 13 \times 24 = \$530
$$

3. HighMed total cost (current scenario): Annual inventory and transportation cost at HighMed = inventory cost + transportation cost $= \$54{,}366 + \$530 = \$54{,}896$ ($54,926 without rounding).

The HighMed management team evaluates the costs for Option A and Option B similarly; the results are summarized in Table 14-6. The results in Table 14-6 are reported without rounding and can be obtained from the associated worksheet *Example 14-3*.

From Table 14-6, observe that increasing the replenishment frequency under Option A decreases total cost at HighMed. The increase in transportation cost is much smaller than the decrease in inventory cost resulting from smaller lots. HighMed is able to reduce total cost most

TABLE 14-6 HighMed Costs Under Different Network Options

	Current Scenario	Option A	Option B
Number of stocking locations	24	24	1
Reorder interval	4 weeks	1 week	1 week
HighVal cycle inventory	96 units	24 units	24 units
HighVal safety inventory	737.3 units	466.3 units	95.2 units
HighVal inventory	833.3 units	490.3 units	119.2 units
LowVal cycle inventory	960 units	240 units	240 units
LowVal safety inventory	737.3 units	466.3 units	95.2 units
LowVal inventory	1,697.3 units	706.3 units	335.2 units
Annual inventory cost	$54,395	$29,813	$8,473
Shipment type	Replenishment	Replenishment	Customer order
Shipment size	8 HighVal + 80 LowVal	2 HighVal + 20 LowVal	1 HighVal + 10 LowVal
Shipment weight	4 lbs.	1 lb.	0.5 lb.
Number of shipments / year	13	52	2,496
Annual transport cost	$530	$1,148	$14,464
Total annual cost	$54,926	$30,961	$22,938

by aggregating all inventories and using FedEx for transportation, because the decrease in inventories upon aggregation is larger than the increase in transportation cost.

The value of aggregation is affected by transportation cost, uncertainty of demand, holding cost, and the size of customer orders. If transportation costs were to double for HighMed, the decentralized Option A would become cheaper than the centralized Option B (in this setting, Option A costs $32,109, whereas Option B costs $37,402). As transportation cost increases, it becomes cheaper to decentralize inventories even though inventory costs increase.

If demand uncertainty decreases (e.g., the standard deviation of weekly demand for High-Val decreases from 5 to 2), the decentralized Option A would again become cheaper than the centralized Option B. As demand uncertainty decreases, it becomes cheaper to decentralize inventories.

If holding cost decreases (e.g., the holding cost drops to 12.5 percent from 25 percent), the decentralized Option A would again become cheaper than the centralized Option B. As product value or holding cost decreases, it becomes cheaper to decentralize inventories.

If customer order sizes are small, the increase in transportation cost upon aggregation can be significant, and inventory aggregation may increase total costs. Reconsider the case of HighMed, but now each customer order averages 0.5 HighVal and 5 LowVal (half the size considered earlier). The costs for the current option as well as Option A remain unchanged because HighMed does not pay for outbound transportation and incurs only the cost of transporting replenishment orders under both options. Option B, however, becomes more expensive because outbound transportation costs increase with a decrease in customer order size. With smaller customer orders, the costs under Option B are as follows:

$$\text{Average weight of each customer order} = 0.1 \times 0.5 + 0.04 \times 5 = 0.25 \text{ pounds}$$
$$\text{Shipping cost per customer order} = \$5.53 + 0.53 \times 0.25 = \$5.66$$
$$\text{Number of customer orders per territory per week} = 4$$
$$\text{Total customer orders per year} = 4 \times 24 \times 52 = 4,992$$
$$\text{Annual transportation cost} = 4,992 \times \$5.66 = \$28,255 \ (\$28,267 \text{ without rounding})$$
$$\text{Total annual cost} = \text{inventory cost} + \text{transportation cost}$$
$$= \$8,474 + \$28,255 = \$36,729$$
$$(\$36,740 \text{ without rounding})$$

Thus, with small customer orders, inventory aggregation is no longer the lowest-cost option for HighMed because of the large increase in transportation costs. The company is better off maintaining inventory in each territory and using Option A, which gives a lower total cost.

The lessons from Example 14-3 (and Chapter 12) with regard to inventory aggregation are summarized in Table 14-7. It is better to aggregate inventory when transport cost is low, demand uncertainty is high, holding cost is high, and customer order size is large. It is better to disaggregate inventory when transport cost is high, demand uncertainty is low, holding cost is low, and customer order size is small.

TABLE 14-7 Conditions Favoring Aggregation or Disaggregation of Inventory

	Aggregate	**Disaggregate**
Transport cost	Low	High
Demand uncertainty	High	Low
Holding cost	High	Low
Customer order size	Large	Small

Trade-Off Between Transportation Cost and Customer Responsiveness

The transportation cost a supply chain incurs is closely linked to the degree of responsiveness the supply chain aims to provide. If a firm is very responsive and ships all orders within a day of receipt from the customer, it will have small outbound shipments, resulting in a high transportation cost. If it decreases its responsiveness and aggregates orders over a longer time horizon before shipping them out, it will be able to exploit economies of scale and incur a lower transportation cost because of larger shipments. *Temporal aggregation* is the process of combining orders across time. Temporal aggregation decreases a firm's responsiveness because of shipping delay, but also decreases transportation costs because of economies of scale that result from larger shipments. Thus, a firm must consider the trade-off between responsiveness and transportation cost when designing its transportation network, as illustrated in Example 14-4.

EXAMPLE 14-4	**Trade-Off Between Transportation Cost and Responsiveness**

Alloy Steel is a steel service center in the Cleveland area. All orders are shipped to customers using an LTL carrier that charges $100 + 0.01x$ where x is the number of pounds of steel shipped on the truck. Currently, Alloy Steel ships orders on the day they are received. Allowing for two days in transit, this policy allows Alloy to achieve a response time of two days. Daily demand at Alloy Steel over a two-week period is shown in Table 14-8.

The general manager at Alloy Steel believes that customers do not really value the two-day response time and would be satisfied with a four-day response. What are the cost advantages of increasing the response time?

Analysis:

As the response time increases, Alloy Steel has the opportunity to aggregate demand over multiple days for shipping. For a response time of three days, Alloy Steel can aggregate demand over two successive days before shipping. For a response time of four days, Alloy Steel can aggregate demand over three days before shipping. The manager evaluates the quantity shipped and transportation costs for different response times over the two-week period, as shown in Table 14-9 (see worksheet *Example 14-4*).

From Table 14-9, observe that the transportation cost for Alloy Steel decreases as the response time increases. The benefit of temporal consolidation, however, diminishes rapidly upon increasing the response time. As the response time increases from two to three days, transportation cost over the two-week window decreases by $700. Increasing the response time from three to four days reduces the transportation cost by only $200. Thus, Alloy Steel may be better off offering a three-day response, because the marginal benefit from further increasing the response time is small.

TABLE 14-8 Daily Demand at Alloy Steel over Two-Week Period

	Monday	**Tuesday**	**Wednesday**	**Thursday**	**Friday**	**Saturday**	**Sunday**
Week 1	19,970	17,470	11,316	26,192	20,263	8,381	25,377
Week 2	39,171	2,158	20,633	23,370	24,100	19,603	18,442

In general, a limited amount of temporal aggregation can be effective in reducing transportation cost in a supply chain. In choosing response time, however, firms must trade off the decrease in transportation cost upon temporal aggregation with the loss of revenue because of poorer responsiveness. Temporal consolidation also improves transportation performance because it results in more stable shipments. For example, in Table 14-9, when Alloy Steel sends daily shipments, the coefficient of variation is 0.44, whereas temporal aggregation across three days (achieved with a four-day response time) has a coefficient of variation of only 0.16. More stable shipments allow both the shipper and the carrier to better plan operations and improve utilization of their assets.

TABLE 14-9 Quantity Shipped and Transportation Cost as a Function of Response Time

		Two-Day Response		Three-Day Response		Four-Day Response	
Day	Demand	Quantity Shipped	Cost ($)	Quantity Shipped	Cost ($)	Quantity Shipped	Cost ($)
1	19,970	19,970	299.70	0	—	0	—
2	17,470	17,470	274.70	37,440	474.40	0	—
3	11,316	11,316	213.16	0	—	48,756	587.56
4	26,192	26,192	361.92	37,508	475.08	0	—
5	20,263	20,263	302.63	0	—	0	—
6	8,381	8,381	183.81	28,644	386.44	54,836	648.36
7	25,377	25,377	353.77	0	—	0	—
8	39,171	39,171	491.71	64,548	745.48	0	—
9	2,158	2,158	121.58	0	—	66,706	767.06
10	20,633	20,633	306.33	22,791	327.91	0	—
11	23,370	23,370	333.70	0	—	0	—
12	24,100	24,100	341.00	47,470	574.70	68,103	781.03
13	19,603	19,603	296.03	0	—	0	—
14	18,442	18,442	284.42	38,045	480.45	38,045	480.45
			$4,164.46		$3,464.46		$3,264.46

SUMMARY OF LEARNING OBJECTIVE 5

Given a supply chain goal to minimize the total cost while providing the desired level of responsiveness to customers, tradeoffs between transportation costs, inventory cost, facility costs, operating cost, and response time must be considered when selecting the mode of transport, the extent of inventory aggregation, and the targeted customer responsiveness. Modes with high transportation costs can be justified if they result in significantly lower inventory costs. Inventory aggregation decreases supply chain costs if the product has a high value-to-weight ratio, high demand uncertainty, low transportation cost, and customer orders are large. If a product has a low value-to-weight ratio, low demand uncertainty, large transportation cost, or small customer orders, inventory aggregation may increase supply chain costs. Temporal aggregation of demand reduces responsiveness but decreases transportation costs because it entails larger shipments and reduces the variation in shipment sizes from one shipment to the next. The marginal benefit of temporal aggregation declines as the time window over which aggregation takes place increases.

14.6 Design tailored transportation networks in a supply chain.

TAILORED TRANSPORTATION

Tailored transportation is the use of different transportation networks and modes based on customer and product characteristics. Most firms sell a variety of products and serve many different customer segments. For example, W.W. Grainger sells more than 400,000 MRO supply products to both small contractors and large firms. Products vary in size and value, and customers vary in the quantity purchased, responsiveness required, uncertainty of the orders, and distance from

W.W. Grainger branches and DCs. Given these differences, a firm such as W.W. Grainger should not design a common transportation network to meet all needs. A firm can meet customer needs at a lower cost by using tailored transportation to provide the appropriate transportation choice based on customer and product characteristics. In the following sections, we describe various forms of tailored transportation in supply chains.

Tailored Transportation by Customer Density and Distance

Firms must consider customer density and distance from warehouse when designing transportation networks. The ideal transportation options based on density and distance are shown in Table 14-10.

When a firm serves a high density of customers close to the DC, it is often best for the firm to own a fleet of trucks that are used with milk runs originating at the DC to supply customers, because this scenario makes good use of the vehicles and provides customer contact. If customer density is high but distance from the warehouse is large, it does not pay to send milk runs from the warehouse because empty trucks will travel a long distance on the return trip. In such a situation, it is better to use a public carrier with large trucks to haul the shipments to a cross-dock center close to the customer area, where the shipments are loaded onto smaller trucks that deliver product to customers using milk runs. In this situation, it may not be ideal for a firm to own its own fleet. As customer density decreases, use of an LTL carrier or a third party doing milk runs is more economical because the third-party carrier can aggregate shipments across many firms. If a firm wants to serve an area with a low density of customers far from the warehouse, even LTL carriers may not be feasible and the use of package carriers may be the best option as long as loads are small. Boise Cascade Office Products, an industrial distributor of office supplies, has designed a transportation network consistent with the suggestion in Table 14-10.

Customer density and distance should also be considered when firms decide on the degree of temporal aggregation (which affects response time) to use when supplying customers. Firms should serve areas with high customer density more frequently because these areas are likely to provide sufficient economies of scale in transportation, making temporal aggregation less valuable. To lower transportation costs, firms should use a higher degree of temporal aggregation and aim for somewhat lower responsiveness when serving areas with a low customer density.

Tailored Transportation by Size of Customer

Firms must consider customer size (in terms of quantity purchased) and location when designing transportation networks. Large customers can be supplied using a TL carrier, whereas smaller customers will require an LTL carrier or milk runs. When using milk runs, a shipper incurs two types of costs:

- Transportation cost based on total route distance
- Delivery cost based on number of deliveries

The transportation cost is the same whether going to a large or small customer. If a delivery is to be made to a large customer, including other small customers on the same truck can save on

TABLE 14-10 Transportation Options Based on Customer Density and Distance

	Short Distance	Medium Distance	Long Distance
High density	Private fleet with milk runs	Cross-dock with milk runs	Cross-dock with milk runs
Medium density	Third-party milk runs	LTL carrier	LTL or package carrier
Low density	Third-party milk runs or LTL carrier	LTL or package carrier	Package carrier

transportation cost. For each small customer, however, the delivery cost per unit is higher than that for large customers. Thus, it is not optimal to deliver to small and large customers with the same frequency at the same price. One option firms have is to charge a higher delivery cost for smaller customers. Another option is to tailor milk runs so they visit larger customers with a higher frequency than smaller customers. Firms can partition customers into large (L), medium (M), and small (S), based on the demand at each. The optimal frequency of visits can be evaluated based on the transportation and delivery costs (see Section 11.2). If large customers are to be visited on every milk run, medium customers on every other milk run, and low-demand customers on every third milk run, suitable milk runs can be designed by combining large, medium, and small customers on each run. Assume that medium customers are partitioned into two subsets (M_1, M_2), and small customers are partitioned into three subsets (S_1, S_2, S_3). The firm can sequence the following six milk runs to ensure that each customer is visited with the appropriate frequency: (L, M_1, S_1), (L, M_2, S_2), (L, M_1, S_3), (L, M_2, S_1), (L, M_1, S_2), (L, M_2, S_3). This tailored sequence has the advantage that each truck carries about the same load and larger customers are provided more frequent delivery than smaller customers, consistent with their relative costs of delivery.

Tailored Transportation by Product Demand and Value

The degree of inventory aggregation and the modes of transportation used in a supply chain network should vary with the demand and value of a product, as shown in Table 14-11. The cycle inventory for high-value products with high demand is disaggregated to save on transportation costs because this allows replenishment orders to be transported less expensively. Safety inventory for such products can be aggregated to reduce inventories (see Chapter 12), and a fast mode of transportation can be used if the safety inventory is required to meet customer demand. For high-demand products with low value, all inventories should be disaggregated and held close to the customer to reduce transportation costs. For low-demand, high-value products, all inventories should be aggregated to save on inventory costs. For low-demand, low-value products, cycle inventories can be held close to the customer and safety inventories aggregated to reduce transportation costs while taking some advantage of aggregation. Cycle inventories are replenished using an inexpensive mode of transportation to save costs.

It is important for managers to design transportation networks that are suitably tailored. As a result, managers should consider an appropriate combination of company-owned and outsourced transportation to meet their needs. This decision should be based on a firm's ability to handle transportation profitably as well as the strategic importance of transportation to the success of the firm. In general, outsourcing is a better option when shipment sizes are small, whereas owning the transportation fleet is better when shipment sizes are large and responsiveness is

TABLE 14-11 Aggregation Strategies Based on Value/Demand

Product Type	High Value	Low Value
High demand	Disaggregate cycle inventory. Aggregate safety inventory. Inexpensive mode of transportation for replenishing cycle inventory and fast mode when using safety inventory.	Disaggregate all inventories and use inexpensive mode of transportation for replenishment.
Low demand	Aggregate all inventories. If needed, use fast mode of transportation for filling customer orders.	Aggregate only safety inventory. Use inexpensive mode of transportation for replenishing cycle inventory.

important. For example, Walmart uses responsive transportation to reduce inventories in its supply chain. Given the importance of transportation to the success of its strategy, it owns and manages its transportation fleet. This is made easier by the fact that it achieves good utilization from its transportation assets because most of its shipments are large. In contrast, firms such as W.W. Grainger and McMaster-Carr send small shipments to customers; inventory management rather than transportation is the key to their success. A third-party carrier can lower costs for them by aggregating their shipments with those of other companies. As a result, both companies use third-party carriers for their outbound transportation.

When designing transportation networks, managers should take into account uncertainty in demand as well as availability of transportation. Ignoring uncertainty encourages a greater use of inexpensive and inflexible transportation modes that perform well when everything goes as planned. Such networks, however, perform poorly when plans change. When managers account for uncertainty, they are more likely to include flexible, though more expensive, modes of transportation within their network. Although these modes may be more expensive for a particular shipment, including them in the transportation options allows a firm to reduce the overall cost of providing a high level of responsiveness.

SUMMARY OF LEARNING OBJECTIVE 6

Tailoring transportation based on customer density and distance, customer size, or product demand and value allows a supply chain to achieve appropriate responsiveness and low cost. Whereas a high density of customers close to a DC can be served by a private fleet, a low density of customers far from a DC may be better served using package carriers. Whereas large customers can easily be provided more frequent deliveries, doing the same for small customers is much more expensive. Whereas high demand, low value products should be decentralized to lower transportation costs, low demand, high value products should be centralized to lower inventory costs.

DISCUSSION QUESTIONS

1. What modes of transportation are best suited for the delivery of time-critical small packages? Why?
2. When is pricing the use of transportation infrastructure, like roads, considered necessary? How is pricing structured?
3. IKEA has a network that uses a combination of direct deliveries and distribution centers. Explain how the company can use such a network to reduce transportation costs while replenishing inventories more frequently.
4. Compare the transportation costs for an online business such as Amazon and a retailer such as Home Depot when selling home-improvement materials.
5. Deliveroo is a British online restaurant food delivery service now available in 29 countries (https://deliveroo.co.uk/faq).

What transportation challenges does Deliveroo face? Compare transportation costs for home delivery restaurants and restaurants without home-delivery services.
6. Does aggregation of inventory at one location better suit a company like IKEA that sells Lack tables or a retailer like Next that sells clothing items online? Explain by considering transportation and inventory costs.
7. Discuss key drivers that may be used to tailor transportation. How does tailoring help?
8. What are some key factors that influence the success or failure of same day delivery?

BIBLIOGRAPHY

Ampuja, Jack, and Ray Pucci. "Inbound Freight: Often a Missed Opportunity." *Supply Chain Management Review* (March–April 2002): 50–57.

Bowersox, Donald J., David J. Closs, and Omar K. Helferich. *Logistical Management.* New York: Macmillan, 1986.

Button, Kenneth J., and Erik T. Verhoef, eds. *Road Pricing, Traffic Congestion and the Environment.* Northampton, MA: Edward Elgar, 1998.

Coyle, John J., Edward J. Bardi, and Robert A. Novack. *Transportation.* Cincinnati, OH: South-Western College Publishing, 2000.

Ellison, Anthony P. *Entrepreneurs and the Transformation of theGlobal Economy.* Northampton, MA: Edward Elgar, 2002.

Levinson, David M. "Road Pricing in Practice." In Kenneth J. Button and Eric T. Verhoef, eds. *Road Pricing, Traffic*

Congestion and the Environment, Northampton, MA: Edward Elgar, 1998, pp. 14–38.

Levinson, Marc. *The Box: How the Shipping Container Made the World Smaller and the World Economy Bigger.* Princeton, NJ: Princeton University Press, 2006.

Robeson, James F., and William C. Copacino. *The Logistics Handbook.* New York: The Free Press, 1994.

Thomke, Stefan, and Mona Sinha. *The Dabbawala System: On-Time Delivery, Every Time.* Harvard Business School Case 9-610-059, 2013.

Tyworth, John. E., Joseph L. Cavinato, and C. John Langley Jr. *Traffic Management: Planning, Operations, and Control.* Prospect Heights, IL: Waveland, 1991.

CASE STUDY

Designing a Sustainable Distribution Network for Euro-Grain

Ed Hendrix, vice president of supply chain at 4Farmers, a large mixed-feed company in the Netherlands, Europe, was reading a new scientific report from CED (an independent research and advisory company specializing in environmental impacts) that analyzed the environmental effects of the importing of raw materials. 4Farmers is a modern international company producing feed and fodder for pigs, cows, poultry, and so on, importing grain from all over Europe. As 4Farmers considers sustainable entrepreneurship to be very important, this document made Ed wonder about the environmental and economic consequences of the import of grain as feedstock for pigs. Walmart reacted to Amazon's efforts by announcing tests for same-day delivery in a few cities.

4Farmers has a high market share in specific feedstock for sustainable pork, called Euro-Grain. Euro-Grain was developed in the Netherlands, but supply volume from this country is not sufficient. Some other countries within Europe are also capable of producing grain that satisfies the Euro-Grain criteria, among them Poland. Ed believes that his company could significantly improve both distribution costs and environmental impact from transportation by investigating the possibility of using various modes of transportation.

Modes of Transportation

The supply chain uses a combination of the following modes of transportation: truck, inland ship, sea ship, and rail. As grain is not very perishable, speed is not really an issue. Prices vary with destination and depend heavily on the capacity of the transportation mode. Varieties of intermodal combinations are possible, using a truck, water, and rail combination with containers.

Distribution Alternatives for Warsaw

Ed asked his staff to propose different distribution alternatives for Poland: Nina Kramer on environmental issues and Leo Spoor on the costs, needs, and possibilities for the various transport modes.

Leo figured out that the demand of 4Farmers for Euro-Grain is about 3,500 tons of grain per month; he saw that from the farm near Warsaw, grain can be transported by rail to the train station in Wroclaw (320 km) or the train station in Rotterdam (1160 km). By road, it is possible to reach the sea harbor Gdansk (330 km), the train station/inland harbor of Wroclaw (345 km), or even drive to 4Farmers directly (1197 km). From the sea harbor Gdansk, a sea ship can travel to the sea harbor/rail station of Rotterdam (1064 km). An inland ship can travel from the inland harbor of Wroclaw to the inland harbor of Oss (950 km). The inland harbor of Oss can also be reached by inland ship from the port of Rotterdam (84 km). Finally, as 4Farmers can only be reached by truck, it takes 26 km to drive from the inland harbor of Oss to 4Farmers, and 100 km from the sea harbor/rail station in Rotterdam. The distribution costs are $1 per km/ton for a truck with a capacity of 40 tons. A sea ship from the port of Gdansk to the port of Rotterdam costs $23.5/ton per trip with a capacity of 3,000 tons. While an inland ship from the harbor of Wroclaw to the harbor of Oss costs $13.75/ton per trip with a capacity of 1,000 tons, an inland ship from Rotterdam to Oss costs $3.75/ton per trip with a capacity of 1,000 tons. The rail tariffs for a capacity of 800 tons from Warsaw to Rotterdam: $25.4/ton.

Nina came up with the following information. The environmental impact of transportation can be represented by the following airborne emission categories: CO_2 equivalents to represent greenhouse gas (GHG) emissions, NOX equivalents to represent nitrification, and SO_2 equivalents to represent acidification. Table 14-12 gives the emission-equivalents per modality (per ton/km). Ed wondered which intermodal configuration would have the best sustainable performance for this supply chain.

TABLE 14-12 Emission factors for modalities

Modality	CO₂-eq (T/km,g)	NOₓ-eq (T/km,g)	SO₂-eq (T/km,g)
Truck	50.4	0.4200	0.0016
Inland ship	11.1	0.3500	0.22
Seas ship	9.6	0.3000	0.19
Trains	28.34	0.4720	0.036

Study Questions

1. Which intermodal configurations are possible for transporting the grain from Poland to 4Farmers?
2. Which intermodal configuration is the least expensive on a monthly basis?
3. Which intermodal configuration has the lowest GHG emissions (carbon footprint) on a monthly basis?
4. Which intermodal configuration would you suggest to be the most sustainable? Base your decision making on costs and the three environmental issues of greenhouse gas, nitrification, and acidification.

CASE STUDY

The Future of Same-Day Delivery: Same as the Past?

Although home delivery of pizza has been successful for decades in the United States, most other same-day delivery efforts have failed. Around 2012, the same-day delivery battle again heated up with Amazon, Walmart, and eBay launching major efforts to implement same-day delivery and new players like Instacart setting up operations.

In 2017, Amazon claimed to offer same day delivery to its prime members in over 5,000 cities on "over a million items with qualifying orders over $35."[4] While it was not clear whether Amazon was making any profits on such deliveries, some pundits felt that if it succeeded in offering same day delivery at low cost to its customers, Amazon would seriously damage the prospects of physical retailers.

Walmart reacted to Amazon's efforts in 2012 by announcing tests for same-day delivery in a few cities including Northern Virginia, Philadelphia, Minneapolis, San Jose, and San Francisco. By 2017, it had shifted its delivery focus to free same day pickup from its stores along with free 2-day shipping to its customers.[5]

Meanwhile, eBay experimented with same-day delivery for products it did not necessarily stock. The *Wall Street Journal* reported on a customer order for which eBay sent a courier to Macy's for the purchase and then had it delivered within an hour.[6] The paper reported that eBay had a team of fifty couriers in San Francisco that "fetch and deliver goods directly to customers' doorsteps within an hour of an online order." In

2015, eBay killed its same day delivery service eBay Now, an indication that it was unlikely to be profitable.

Instacart, a San Francisco based company, was valued at over $3 billion with a model where its employees shopped for groceries for customers and delivered them to their door. Instacart operated in most major cities in the U.S. and had over a hundred partnerships with grocery retailers including Whole Foods and Costco. This partnership offered the retailers an opportunity to compete with Amazon in terms of responsive home delivery. While Instacart had grown rapidly, it had not generated profits until 2017.

The Iconic, an Australian company selling clothing, shoes, and accessories, offered three-hour delivery within Sydney for $9.95. It promised to have goods picked, packed, and delivered within three hours to Sydney metro areas, between 7:00 a.m. and 6:00 p.m. on business days. Although the company was young, this service had been extremely well received. Seven-Eleven Japan was another company offering home delivery—in this case, its 7-Meal service, targeting Japan's aging population. The service offered a menu of high-quality meals that customers could choose to pick up at Seven-Eleven stores or have delivered to their homes or offices.

If history was any guide, the profitable implementation of same-day delivery would be challenging. Urbanfetch and Kozmo pursued this business model during the dotcom boom of the late 1990s. Urbanfetch operated in densely populated areas such as London,

[4] Sunil Chopra, Supply Chain Management: Strategy, Planning, and Operation, 7th Ed., © 2019. Pearson Education, Inc., New York, NY.

[5] Sunil Chopra, Supply Chain Management: Strategy, Planning, and Operation, 7th Ed., © 2019. Pearson Education, Inc., New York, NY.

[6] Greg Bensinger, "Order It Online, and … Voilà," *Wall Street Journal*, December 3, 2012.

Manhattan, and Brooklyn, but was forced to shut down in the fall of 2000 owing to a lack of funding; Kozmo, which raised more than $280 million in funding and operated in eleven cities, folded in early 2001.

Opinions were clearly divided about the potential for success with same-day delivery. One writer opined that "this move [by Amazon] will shake up the retail industry,"[5] whereas a *New York Times* article countered that "some retail analysts are questioning whether the expense and difficulty of same-day delivery would be worth it."[6]

Study Questions

1. Why has same-day delivery of pizza been successful, whereas the practice has failed in other settings (e.g., Kozmo.com)?
2. Under what conditions can same day delivery be offered at low cost?
3. What are the characteristics of businesses that can succeed with same-day delivery? Can Amazon, Walmart, or Instacart succeed with same-day delivery? Which model is likely to do better? Why?

[5] Farhad Manjoo, "I Want It Today: How Amazon's Ambitious New Push for Same-Day Delivery Will Destroy Local Retail," *Slate*, July 11, 2012.
[6] Stephanie Clifford, "Same-Day Delivery Test at Wal-Mart," *New York Times*, October 9, 2012.

CASE STUDY

Selecting Transportation Modes for China Imports

Jackie Chen, vice president of China Imports, was looking to design a framework to select transportation modes for various products imported from China to the United States. His basic options were to either use air freight or ocean shipping in 20-foot containers. Air freight was faster and more reliable, but ocean shipping was much cheaper. He decided to evaluate the shipping decision for two very different product categories—consumer electronics, such as smartphones, and decorative hardware, such as door handles and hinges.

China Imports provided a variety of products to its customers from a warehouse near the port of Long Beach, California. The company incurred an annual holding cost of 25 percent on all inventory held and aimed to provide a 98 percent cycle service level on its products. The high level of service aligned with the high quality of products that the company imported.

Transportation Options from China

Air freight and ocean shipping were the two options available to move product from China to the United States. Air freight charged $10 per kilogram shipped and required a minimum shipment of 50 kg. Besides being fast, air freight was also quite reliable. The average lead time on air freight was one week, with a standard deviation of lead time of 0.2 weeks. Ocean shipping was much cheaper and cost $1,200 per 20-foot container. Given that each container could hold up to 15,000 kg, the shipping cost per kilo by ocean was more than a hundred times cheaper than air freight. Ocean shipping, however, took longer and was less reliable. The average lead time using ocean shipping was nine weeks, with a standard deviation of three weeks.

Product Characteristics

Weekly demand for smartphones averaged 1,000 and had a standard deviation of 400. Each smartphone cost $300 and weighed 0.1 kg. The typical life cycle for a smartphone was about one year; it was critical to not lose demand early in the life cycle because of a lack of product availability. Weekly demand for decorative hardware averaged 5,000, with a standard deviation of 1,000. Each unit of decorative hardware cost $20 and weighed 1 kg. Decorative hardware tended to have a long life cycle—the company was still selling door handles and hinges that were introduced more than a decade earlier.

Study Questions

1. What is the annual cost of using air freight to import smartphones? What is the annual cost of using ocean shipping to import smartphones?
2. What is the annual cost of using air freight to import decorative hardware? What is the annual cost of using ocean shipping to import decorative hardware?
3. What other factors should be considered in the choice of transportation mode? What mode would you recommend for each product? Suggest a general framework that Jackie can use across all product categories.

Sourcing Decisions in a Supply Chain

LEARNING OBJECTIVES

After reading this chapter, you will be able to

15.1 Understand factors that affect the decision to outsource a supply chain function.

15.2 Identify dimensions of supplier performance that affect total cost.

15.3 Design a tailored supplier portfolio.

15.4 Describe the impact of incentives on the behavior of third-parties in a supply chain.

15.5 Discuss the benefits of sharing risk and reward in a supply chain.

In this chapter, we explore various factors that influence decisions about whether a supply chain activity is performed within the firm or outsourced. We discuss performance characteristics of suppliers that affect total cost and describe how a focus on local optimization by different members of a supply chain can hurt the supply chain surplus. Our goal is to enable managers to consider all the trade-offs involved when making sourcing decisions to maximize value extracted from every stage of a sourcing relationship.

THE SOURCING DECISION IN A SUPPLY CHAIN

15.1 Understand factors that affect the decision to outsource a supply chain function.

Purchasing, also called *procurement*, is the process by which companies acquire raw materials, components, products, services, or other resources from suppliers to execute their operations. *Sourcing* is the entire set of business processes required to purchase goods and services. For any supply chain function, the most significant decision is whether to outsource the function or perform it in-house. *Outsourcing* results in the supply chain function being performed by a third party. Outsourcing decisions are important and tend to vary across firms and industries. For example, W.W. Grainger, an MRO distributor, has consistently owned and managed its distribution centers. In contrast, outbound transportation of packages from distribution centers to customers has consistently been outsourced to a third party. What factors can explain Grainger's decisions?

Until 2005, Dell was credited with improving profits by keeping the retail function in-house and selling directly to customers. Since 2007, however, Dell has started to outsource retailing to firms such as Walmart. Dell has also increased the fraction of assembly that it outsources to contract manufacturers. Why was vertical integration into retailing a good idea for Dell until about 2005 but not after 2007? Was Dell right in outsourcing a greater fraction of assembly to contract manufacturers? In contrast to Dell, Apple has significantly expanded the insourcing of retailing during the same period by growing Apple retail stores. Procter & Gamble (P&G) has never attempted to sell detergent directly to customers, and no one is calling on it to bring the retail function in-house. What made vertical integration into retailing a good idea for Apple but a bad idea for P&G? Most companies outsource assembly in consumer electronics. In contrast, most companies insource assembly in the automotive industry. What factors may explain this difference?

Recall that the supply chain surplus is the difference between the value of a product for the customer and the total cost of all supply chain activities involved in bringing the product to the customer. Our basic premise is that outsourcing makes sense if it increases the supply chain surplus (assuming we get to keep some of the increase) without significantly increasing risks.

For example, P&G has historically outsourced retailing of its products to others. The retailers increase the supply chain surplus by aggregating many products that customers need (not just P&G products) in a single store. This aggregation allows them to spread facility costs, selling costs, personnel costs, and transportation costs across many consumer goods manufacturers. This aggregation also allows the retailer to increase customer value by allowing them to purchase many products they need in a single visit to the store. Clearly, outsourcing retailing to a third party increases the value created by the supply chain to a greater extent than if P&G managed its own retailing. Good sourcing decisions grow value by assigning each activity within the supply chain to the party that can add the most value.

The decision to outsource a supply chain activity by a firm should be based on answers to the following three questions:

1. Will the third party increase the supply chain surplus relative to performing the activity in-house?
2. To what extent do risks grow upon outsourcing?
3. Are there strategic reasons to keep the activity in-house?

A firm should consider outsourcing if the growth in surplus is large with a small increase in risk. Performing the function in-house is preferable if the growth in surplus is small, the increase in risk is large, or if there is a strong strategic reason for doing so.

Next, we discuss ways in which third parties can grow the supply chain surplus.

How Do Third Parties Increase the Supply Chain Surplus?

Third parties increase the supply chain surplus if they either increase value for the customer or decrease the supply chain cost relative to a firm performing the task in-house. Third parties can increase the supply chain surplus effectively if they are able to aggregate supply chain assets or flows to a higher level than a firm itself can. Here, we discuss various mechanisms that third parties can use to grow the surplus.

1. *Capacity aggregation.* A third party can increase the supply chain surplus by aggregating demand across multiple firms and gaining production economies of scale that no single firm can on its own. This is the most common reason for outsourcing production in a supply chain. One of the reasons that all smartphone manufacturers outsource glass manufacturing for their screens is that the third parties achieve manufacturing economies that no single smartphone manufacturer can on its own. The growth in surplus from outsourcing is highest when the needs of the firm are significantly lower than the volumes required to gain economies of scale. A good example in this context is Magna Steyr, a third party that assembles automobiles for several manufacturers. Magna Steyr designs flexible assembly

lines that can build up to five different vehicle types on a single line. This flexible capacity allows the company to produce a variety of low volume cars economically. In 2013, Magna Steyr assembled the G class for Mercedes, the RCZ for Peugeot, and the Mini Countryman and Mini Paceman for BMW in the same plant. In each case, the models had relatively low demand volume. Each firm would not have gained sufficient economies of scale for assembling its model. By combining all of them in a single flexible plant, Magna Steyr grew the surplus relative to each firm assembling its own cars. A third party is unlikely to increase the surplus through capacity aggregation if the volume requirements of a firm are large and stable. This is substantiated by the fact that no auto manufacturer outsources production of its best-selling cars to a third party.

2. *Inventory aggregation.* A third party can increase the supply chain surplus by aggregating inventories across a large number of customers. W.W. Grainger and McMaster-Carr are MRO suppliers that provide value primarily by aggregating inventory for hundreds of thousands of customers. Aggregation allows them to significantly lower overall uncertainty and improve economies of scale in purchasing and transportation. As a result, these MRO distributors carry significantly less safety and cycle inventory than would be required if each customer decided to carry inventory of MRO products on its own. Another example of inventory aggregation is provided by Brightstar, a distributor that facilitates postponement for cell phones. These phones are manufactured in the Far East and shipped to the Brightstar warehouse in Miami, where software and accessories are added as customer orders arrive from South America. High product variety and many small customers allow Brightstar to increase the supply chain surplus through inventory aggregation and postponement. The third party performing inventory aggregation adds most to the supply chain surplus when demand from customers is fragmented and uncertain. When demand is large and predictable, an intermediary adds little to the surplus by holding inventory.

3. *Transportation aggregation by transportation intermediaries.* A third party may increase the surplus by aggregating the transportation function to a higher level than any shipper can on its own. UPS, FedEx, and a host of LTL carriers are examples of transportation intermediaries that increase the supply chain surplus by aggregating transportation across a variety of shippers. The value provided in each case is driven by the inherent economies of scale in transportation. When shippers want to send small quantities, the transportation intermediary aggregates shipments across multiple shippers, thus lowering the cost of each shipment below what could be achieved by each shipper alone. A transportation intermediary increases the supply chain surplus when shippers are sending packages or LTL quantities to customers that are geographically distributed. A transportation intermediary can also grow the surplus for TL shipping by aggregating across multiple firms having unbalanced transportation flows, with the quantity coming into a region being very different from the quantity leaving the region. An excellent example of a transportation intermediary increasing the supply chain surplus is provided by a pilot program involving Chrysler and Ford. Exel, a third-party logistics (3PL) provider, operated a dedicated fleet for the distribution of spare parts for Chrysler. In tests in Michigan and Mexico, Ford added its own truck parts for delivery on the same fleet. Given the relatively low density of dealers in Northern Michigan and Mexico (outside Mexico City), the aggregation provided by Exel was a benefit for both Ford and Chrysler. A transportation intermediary is likely to add the least to the supply chain surplus for a company such as Walmart, for which shipment sizes are large and the company achieves aggregation across the many retail stores that it owns. The only possibility for a transportation intermediary in such a setting would be to obtain better backhauls than Walmart does.

4. *Transportation aggregation by storage intermediaries.* A third party that stores inventory can also increase the supply chain surplus by aggregating inbound and outbound transportation. Storage intermediaries such as W.W. Grainger and McMaster-Carr stock products from more than a thousand manufacturers each and sell to hundreds of thousands of cus-

tomers. On the inbound side, they are able to aggregate shipments from several manufacturers onto a single truck. This results in a lower transportation cost than could be achieved by each manufacturer independently. On the outbound side, they aggregate products from multiple suppliers into the same package for customers, resulting in a significantly lower transportation cost than can be achieved if each supplier shipped its product separately to each customer. Another instance of outbound transportation aggregation arises when the Chicago distribution center for Grainger fills separate trucks with packages destined for each adjacent state. As soon as a truck destined for Michigan (for instance) is filled, it is sent to the UPS sorting facility in Michigan. This level of aggregation cannot be achieved by individual suppliers or customers. Thus, the storage of goods by Grainger and McMaster-Carr increases the supply chain surplus by aggregating inbound and outbound transportation. A similar service is provided by distributors in countries such as India. Given the small size of retail outlets, a distributor aggregates delivery for several manufacturers, significantly lowering the outbound transportation cost. This form of aggregation is most effective if the intermediary stocks products from many suppliers and serves many customers, each ordering in small quantities. This form of aggregation becomes less effective as the scale of shipment from a supplier to customer grows. This is seen in the decreased use of distributors by U.S. supermarket chains. The supermarkets typically get full trucks delivered to their DCs or stores and do not need distributors for further aggregation.

5. *Warehousing aggregation.* A third party may increase the supply chain surplus by aggregating warehousing needs over several firms. The growth in surplus is achieved in terms of lower real estate costs and lower processing costs within the warehouse. Savings through warehousing aggregation arise if a firm's warehousing needs are small or if its needs fluctuate over time. In either case, the intermediary with the warehouse can exploit economies of scale in warehouse construction and operation by aggregating across multiple customers. An example is Safexpress, a third-party logistics provider in India. Safexpress owns warehouses distributed throughout the country that are used by many of its customers. Most of its customers do not have warehousing needs that are large enough to justify a warehouse of their own in each region. Warehousing aggregation by an intermediary adds a lot to the surplus for small suppliers and for companies that are starting out in a geographic location. Warehousing aggregation is unlikely to add much to the surplus for a large supplier or customer whose warehousing needs are large and relatively stable over time. The warehousing needs of Walmart, Amazon, and Grainger are sufficiently large and stable to justify their own warehouses, and a third party is unlikely to increase the surplus.

6. *Procurement aggregation.* A third party increases the supply chain surplus if it aggregates procurement for many small players and facilitates economies of scale in ordering, production, and inbound transportation. Procurement aggregation is most effective across many small buyers. Small retailers in India purchase goods from distributors that aggregate buying from manufacturers. Procurement aggregation is not likely to be a big factor with a few large customers. For example, Walmart has sufficient scale that it manages its own procurement. It sees no value added in procuring through a third party.

7. *Information aggregation.* A third party may increase the surplus by aggregating information to a higher level than can be achieved by a firm performing the function in-house. All retailers aggregate information on products from many manufacturers in a single location. This information aggregation reduces search costs for customers. eBags is an example of an online retailer that primarily provides information aggregation. eBags holds little inventory but is a single point of display for information on bags from many manufacturers. By aggregating product information, eBags significantly reduces search costs for the online customer. Relative to eBags, if each manufacturer set up its own website and online store, search costs for the customer would be higher, and each manufacturer would have to invest in the information infrastructure. Thus, eBags increases the supply chain surplus through information aggregation by making search cheaper and reducing investment in information

technology. Two other examples of companies using information aggregation are W.W. Grainger and McMaster-Carr. Both provide product catalogs and detailed websites. This simplifies search for MRO products by the customer and aggregates product information for more than a thousand manufacturers. Another excellent example of information aggregation is provided by the various online sites, such as Freight Zone and Echo Global Logistics, that bring together shippers and truckers looking for shipments. Information aggregation reduces search costs and allows better matching of truckers and shipments. Information aggregation increases the surplus if both buyers and sellers are fragmented and buying is sporadic. Information aggregation is not likely to be a big factor for a car manufacturer that regularly buys steel from a single supplier.

8. *Receivables aggregation.* A third party may increase the supply chain surplus if it can aggregate the receivables risk to a higher level than the firm or it has a lower collection cost than the firm. Brightstar, for example, was a distributor for Motorola in most Latin American countries other than Brazil. Cell phones in the area are sold through many small, independently owned retail outlets. Collecting receivables from each retail outlet is an expensive proposition for a manufacturer. Given that a retailer buys from many manufacturers, the power of each manufacturer to collect is also reduced. Brightstar, as a distributor, was able to aggregate collection across all manufacturers that it served, reducing the collection cost. By aggregating collection to a greater extent than any one manufacturer can, Brightstar also lowered the default risk. Reduced collection cost and risk allowed Brightstar to increase the supply chain surplus relative to having this activity performed by manufacturers. The same is true with distributors in India that often distribute for a large number of manufacturers to the same retailer. Given their ability to aggregate across many manufacturers and small retailers, distributors in India typically take responsibility for managing receivables from the retailers. Receivables aggregation is likely to increase the supply chain surplus if retail outlets are small and numerous and each outlet stocks products from many manufacturers that are all served by the same distributor. Such a scenario is more likely in developing countries where retailing is fragmented. It is less likely in developed countries, such as the United States and most Western European countries, where retailing is consolidated.

9. *Relationship aggregation.* An intermediary can increase the supply chain surplus by decreasing the number of relationships required between multiple buyers and sellers. Without an intermediary, connecting a thousand sellers to a million buyers requires a billion relationships. The presence of an intermediary lowers the number of relationships required to just over a million. Most retailers and MRO distributors such as W.W. Grainger improve supply chain surplus through relationship aggregation. Relationship aggregation increases the supply chain surplus by increasing the size of each transaction and decreasing their number. Relationship aggregation is most effective when many buyers sporadically purchase small amounts at a time, but each order often has products from multiple suppliers. Thus, Grainger can increase the surplus by being a relationship aggregator for MRO products. A third party, however, does not increase the surplus by being a relationship aggregator between a few buyers and sellers for which the relationships are longer term and large. For example, the online auto-parts exchange Covisint failed to become a relationship aggregator in the automotive industry, especially for direct materials.

10. *Lower costs and higher quality.* A third party can increase the supply chain surplus if it provides lower cost or higher quality relative to the firm. If these benefits come from specialization and learning, they are likely to be sustainable over the longer term. A specialized third party that is further along the learning curve for some supply chain activity is likely to maintain its advantage over the long term. A common scenario, however, is one in which the third party has a low-cost location that the firm does not have. In such a situation, lower labor and overhead costs are temporary reasons for outsourcing, because if the wage differential is persistent and the third party offers none of the other advantages discussed earlier, it is best for the firm to maintain ownership and move production offshore to the low-cost location.

Factors Influencing Growth of Surplus by a Third Party

Four important factors affect the increase in surplus that a third party provides: scale, uncertainty, the specificity of assets, and the cost and quantity of available capital. If the scale is large, it is likely that sufficient economies of scale are achieved internal to the firm itself. In this case, it is unlikely that a third party can achieve further scale economies and increase the surplus. Walmart has sufficient scale in terms of its transportation needs that it achieves economies of scale on trucking by itself. Going to a third party would not increase the surplus and would result in some loss of control. In contrast, if a firm's needs do not provide sufficient economies of scale, the third party can increase the surplus by a large amount. Even though Grainger has a large number of outbound packages, given their geographical dispersion, it would not be able to achieve economies of scale for door-to-door delivery. A third-party package carrier adds to the surplus in this case.

The second important factor is the uncertainty of a firm's needs. If the needs are predictable, the increase in surplus from a third party is limited, especially if the firm has sufficient scale. In contrast, if the firm's needs are highly variable over time, the third party can increase the surplus through aggregation with other customers. For example, Grainger has predictable needs in terms of warehouse space required. Given sufficient scale, it owns and operates its own distribution centers. In contrast, most firms have very uncertain demand for MRO products. They prefer not to hold these items in stock and use Grainger as an intermediary.

The growth in surplus is also influenced by the specificity of assets required by the third party. If the assets required are specific to a firm and cannot be used for others, a third party is unlikely to increase the surplus because all it does is move the assets from one firm to another. The third party has no opportunity to aggregate across other customers. For example, if a distributor holds inventory that is specific to a customer, the distributor is unable to aggregate it to a higher level than the customer. The presence of the distributor does not increase the surplus by reducing inventory in this case. Similarly, if a third-party logistics provider manages a warehouse exclusively for a single firm, it has few opportunities to increase the surplus unless it can aggregate the use of management or information systems across other warehouses. In contrast, if assets (inventory or warehouses, in the previous examples) are less specific and can be used across multiple firms, a third party can increase the surplus by aggregating uncertainty across multiple customers or improving economies of scale.

Another situation in which a firm may outsource to a third party (even when none of the other factors suggests outsourcing) is shortage of capital or a third party with a much lower cost of capital. In either of these scenarios, the third party can grow the surplus by bringing lower-cost capital to the supply chain. This discussion on how and when a third party can increase the supply chain surplus is summarized in Table 15-1.

TABLE 15-1 Growth in Surplus by Third Party as a Function of Scale, Uncertainty, and Specificity

		Specificity of Assets Involved in Function	
		Low	**High**
Firm scale	Low	High growth in surplus	Low to medium growth in surplus
	High	Low growth in surplus	No growth in surplus unless cost of capital is lower for third party
Demand uncertainty for firm	Low	Low to medium growth in surplus	Low growth in surplus unless cost of capital is lower for third party
	High	High growth in surplus	Low to medium growth in surplus

Risks of Using a Third Party

Firms must evaluate the following risks when they move any function to a third party:

1. *The process is broken.* The biggest problems arise when a firm outsources supply chain functions simply because it has lost control of the process. Keep in mind that introducing a third party into a broken supply chain process only makes it worse and harder to control. The first step should be to get the process under control, then do a cost–benefit analysis, and only then decide on outsourcing.

2. *Underestimation of the cost of coordination.* A common mistake when outsourcing is to underestimate the effort required to coordinate activities across multiple entities performing supply chain tasks. This is especially true if a firm plans to outsource specific supply chain functions to different third parties. Outsourcing functions to many third parties is feasible (and can be very effective) if the firm views being a coordinator as one of its core strengths. A good example of a strong coordinator is Cisco. However, even Cisco ran into trouble in the early 2000s and was left with a great deal of surplus inventory because of coordination problems. Another example of coordination causing problems occurred between Nike and i2 Technologies in 2000. Nike blamed its loss of $100 million on inventory management glitches that it attributed to the supply chain planning software from i2; i2, in turn, blamed the problems on Nike's execution of the software. Clearly, insufficient coordination between the two firms played a role in this failure.

3. *Reduced customer/supplier contact.* A firm may lose customer/supplier contact by introducing an intermediary. The loss of customer contact is particularly significant for firms that sell directly to consumers but decide to use a third party to either collect incoming orders or deliver outgoing product. A good example is Boise Cascade, which outsourced all its outbound distribution to third parties. This led to a significant loss of customer contact. Boise Cascade decided to bring outbound delivery for customers located close to its distribution centers in-house. Given the high density of customers around its distribution centers, the additional gain in surplus that a third party could provide was minimal, whereas the gain from improved customer contact was significant. Boise Cascade did not bring distribution beyond this point in-house because the gain in surplus provided by a third party was significant.

4. *Loss of internal capability and growth in third-party power.* A firm may choose to keep a supply chain function in-house if outsourcing will significantly increase the third party's power. An example can be found in the electronics industry. Companies such as HP and Motorola have moved most of their manufacturing to contract manufacturers but are reluctant to move either procurement or design, even though contract manufacturers have developed both capabilities. Given the commonality of components, it can be argued that a contract manufacturer can achieve a higher level of aggregation in procurement as well as design assets. HP and Motorola, however, are reluctant to move procurement to contract manufacturers because the potential loss in power is large, whereas the aggregation gains are small given the relatively large size of both firms. Keeping part of a supply chain function in-house is also important if a complete loss of capability significantly strengthens the third party's bargaining position. The in-house capability then serves as an option that can be exercised when the need arises. The option also limits how much of the supply chain surplus the third party can keep for itself.

5. *Leakage of sensitive data and information.* Using a third party requires a firm to share demand information and, in some cases, intellectual property. If the third party also serves competitors, leakage is always a danger. Firms have often insisted on firewalls within the third party, but a firewall increases the specificity of assets, limiting the growth in surplus that the third party can provide. When leakage is an issue, especially with regard to intellectual property, firms often choose to keep the function in-house.

6. *Ineffective contracts.* Contracts with performance metrics that distort the third party's incentives often significantly reduce any gains from outsourcing. For example, cost-plus

pricing of third-party services presents incentive problems even if the third party opens its books. This form of pricing eliminates incentives for the third party to innovate further to reduce costs. The onus for improvement falls back on the firm. Another example occurs when firms require suppliers or distributors to maintain a certain number of days of inventory as part of the contract. Such a contract reduces the third party's incentive to take actions that reduce inventories. In such a situation, it is better for the firm to contract on a desired service level and leave the third party more freedom with regard to the amount of inventory. The third party then has an incentive to work on reducing the inventory required to provide a given level of service.

7. *Loss of supply chain visibility.* Introducing third parties reduces the visibility of supply chain operations, making it harder for the firm to respond quickly to local customer and market demands. This loss of visibility can be particularly harmful for long supply chains.

8. *Negative reputational impact.* In many instances, actions regarding labor or the environment taken by the third party can have a significant negative impact on the reputation of the firm. Nike has had difficulty with several of its suppliers regarding labor practices and the environment. In 2008, Nike produced its first supply chain report on suppliers in China and reported several questionable labor practices, including underage workers, unpaid wages, and falsified documents. The reputational loss from actions by a supplier can be particularly damaging to firms like Nike with strong brands.

Strategic Factors in Sourcing

Besides economic factors and risks, strategic factors must be accounted for when making sourcing decisions.

1. *Support the business strategy.* Harley-Davidson illustrates the importance of linking business strategy to the make or buy decision. To maintain its strong "Made in America" brand image, the company manufactures mostly in the United States even though cheaper components may be found overseas. An even more extreme example is Brunello Cucinelli, a successful Italian luxury brand. The company positions itself as providing outstanding artisanal Italian manufacturing and a culture of "ethical capitalism." To support this strategy, the company has focused much of its production at Solomeo, a medieval hamlet in Umbria, Italy. At Solomeo, the company has built what the founder calls a "humanistic factory" where "employees are treated as preciously as the clothes they create."

2. *Improve firm focus.* In today's complex world, it is impossible for a firm to do everything. A lack of focus because a firm is doing everything in-house can be a major problem. Among the required activities, a firm must identify those that are core and provide a strategic advantage. Outsourcing all other activities helps improve focus and, thus, performance. A good example of increased outsourcing comes from the automotive industry. At one time, most auto manufacturers produced many of their components in-house. With the increasing complexity of an automobile, however, companies outsource most of their parts today, focusing instead on design, assembly, and coordination.

Examples of Successful Third-Party Suppliers

We now discuss several examples where successful third-party suppliers have added to the supply chain surplus in ways mentioned earlier. One instance is the assembly of consumer electronics, an activity that was largely performed in-house until the 1990s. Today, however, assembly is mostly outsourced by original equipment manufacturers (OEMs) such as Apple. In the 1990s, Macintosh computers were assembled at an Apple factory. Today, Apple tablets and smartphones are all assembled by electronics manufacturing service (EMS) providers such as Foxconn. A study of the evolution of the EMS industry points to why outsourcing of assembly has increased

in the electronics industry and the capabilities that third party EMS providers have developed to further increase the value they provide.

EMS providers grew in the 1980s out of small job shops used by OEMs like IBM to supplement their own printed circuit board production capacity or to offload production of items such as cables that were not viewed as offering any strategic advantage. In the 1990s, most OEMs, such as IBM, Motorola, and Lucent, sold their production capacity and increasingly outsourced a large fraction of their manufacturing to the EMS providers. The initial manufacturing services offered by EMS providers included board assembly, final assembly, and testing. The outsourcing of board assembly to EMS providers made sense, given the expensive pick-and-place machines required by the surface mount technology. Although these machines were expensive, they were also flexible enough that they could be reprogrammed to handle products for a variety of OEMs. EMS providers could thus obtain better utilization of these machines by offering this service to competing OEMs. Even though each OEM was uncertain about the success of its own product, the industry as a whole had stable sales. The ability of the EMS providers to aggregate uncertainty has become more important as the life cycle of electronics products has continued to shrink.

Over time, EMS providers such as Flextronics and Celestica took the lead in adding design services to increase their perceived value to customers. They expanded from offering printed circuit board design and design-for-test to offering expertise in designing mobile phones, printers, networking, and consumer products. Flextronics claimed that one of the great benefits of having design teams under the same roof as manufacturing was that newly designed products could effectively be integrated into existing manufacturing and supply chain flows.[1] EMS providers could also leverage their experience in designing a product for one customer across others in the same industry. For example, Celestica designed a generic "black box" for IBM automotive applications very quickly because it had done similar work for UK firms. This allowed IBM to reduce time to market to well below what it could have done on its own.[2]

EMS providers handle most of the component procurement for their customers. More than 95 percent of the procurement is turnkey, meaning that the EMS provider sends out the purchase order for parts.[3] Given the commonality of parts in the electronics industry, EMS providers could get lower prices for customers (especially compared with smaller OEMs) because of their large spending on parts. Flextronics, for example, was spending well over $10 billion a year on parts, allowing it to get good deals from suppliers.

Over time, EMS providers have started to include warehousing and shipping in the menu of services they provide. Flextronics, for example, offers its customers the ability to "design, assemble, and distribute" their products. Given the commonality of parts and supply sources in the electronics industry, EMS providers are able to gain economies in inbound freight that are not available to a single OEM. On the outbound side, most electronics products move from the assembly plant to common ports in Europe and North America. This allows the EMS provider to add value by aggregating outbound shipping to a greater extent than any OEM.

The commonality of parts and the short life cycles with unpredictable winners for each new generation of products have allowed EMS providers to add significant value in the electronics industry. The rapid change and uncertainty of demand allows EMS providers to add value through aggregation in design, procurement, transportation, and manufacturing. An interesting question is whether the development of all these capabilities in a third party has lowered barriers to entry sufficiently in this industry to allow new entrants to compete effectively against established players. In any case, the development of EMS providers has resulted in a constant drop in prices in this industry—a big benefit to the consumer.

Whereas EMS providers have added logistics services, UPS is an example of a logistics provider that has added basic manufacturing services to further add value to its customers. In a 2010

[1] Based on "The Value of Design," *Electronics Business*, June 2003.
[2] Ibid.
[3] Heidi Elliott, "OEMs Seek Single Point of Contact for SCM." *EDN Network*, June 15, 2003.

press release, UPS discussed the establishment of an "in-house laptop repair facility for a well known computer manufacturer" near its global air hub in Louisville. In less than 24 hours, the UPS facility could "repair, refurbish and return laptops to their owners." By setting up a repair facility at its hub, not only did UPS reduce transportation relative to the manufacturer doing the repairs, but it also established the ability to aggregate such services across competitors. In another example, UPS took over the kit, pack, and ship operations for a major telecom company. As a result, 16 order processing and distribution facilities for the customer were centralized by UPS in one of its locations. This resulted in quicker processing, lower costs, and improved customer experience.

Another excellent example of a firm that grows the supply chain surplus by effectively aggregating demand across customers and capacity across suppliers is Li & Fung, which has built a multibillion-dollar business helping global companies such as Reebok manage sourcing and production across many locations in the developing world. The company has been an intermediary between suppliers in the developing world and global buyers since it was founded in 1906. Li & Fung originally exported jade, porcelain, and silk from China to the United States. In the 1970s, the firm expanded its network of suppliers and is now able to get around regional trade umbrellas such as the European Union and NAFTA by sourcing appropriately. Li & Fung is an information hub that is able to link thousands of factories in over 30 countries to almost a thousand customers in an optimal manner. Li & Fung reserves 30 to 70 percent of a supplier's capacity. These factories are accustomed to reliable repeat business from Li & Fung and are thus willing to commit this capacity. Li & Fung maintains detailed capability information for each factory that is used to match it to appropriate customer orders as they arrive. For its customers, Li & Fung facilitates short-lead-time production. This allows customers to observe sales trends before committing to an order. When an order arrives, Li & Fung procures yarn from one supplier, gets on the production schedule of a weaving mill, and finally farms out production of the garment to ensure that the delivery schedule is met. All this is done to minimize production cost while meeting delivery schedules. Clearly, Li & Fung is an integrator that adds to the supply chain surplus in ways that no individual customer or supplier could. The firm aggregates demand across hundreds of customers and capacity across thousands of suppliers and uses detailed information on both to match supply and demand in the most cost-effective manner.

Compared with the electronics industry, contract manufacturing for final assembly is much less prevalent in the automotive sector. Most auto companies set up their own assembly plants because product life cycles are longer, demand more stable, and it is difficult to design assembly plants that can produce a Toyota as well as a Ford. One successful contract manufacturer in the automotive industry is Magna Steyr, which is part of MAGNA International. The company's main assembly facility is in Graz, Austria. Its key success factor is the flexibility to "build up to five different vehicle types/derivatives on a single assembly line." This capability allows the company to produce low volume models for OEMs more effectively than they can on their own. In 2013, Magna Steyr assembled the Mercedes-Benz G-Class, the Peugeot RCZ, the MINI Countryman, and the MINI Paceman, each of which had relatively low sales volume, in its Graz plant.

SUMMARY OF LEARNING OBJECTIVE 1

Good sourcing decisions aim to identify suppliers that will grow the supply chain surplus. A supply chain function should be outsourced if the third party can increase the supply chain surplus without significant risk. A third party may increase the surplus by aggregating capacity, inventory, warehousing, transportation, information, receivables, and other factors to a higher level than the firm can on its own. A growth in surplus may also occur if the third party has lower costs or higher quality because of specialization or learning. Outsourcing generally makes sense if a firm's needs are small and highly uncertain and can be served using resources that can serve other firms as well. Outsourcing also makes sense if the firm is short of capital or if the third party has a lower cost of capital.

TOTAL COST OF OWNERSHIP

15.2 *Identify dimensions of supplier performance that affect total cost.*

When making the outsourcing decision or comparing suppliers, many firms make the fundamental mistake of focusing only on the quoted price, ignoring the fact that many factors affect the total cost of using a supplier. For instance, suppliers have different replenishment lead times. Does it pay to select a more expensive supplier with a shorter lead time? Or consider suppliers that have different on-time performance. Is the more reliable supplier worth the few extra pennies it charges per piece?

In each of these instances, the price charged by the supplier is only one of many factors that affect the supply chain surplus. It is important to focus on the *total cost of ownership* (TCO) when selecting suppliers. TCO includes all supply chain costs of sourcing a good or service from a particular supplier and can be considered in three "buckets"—acquisition costs, ownership costs, and post-ownership costs. Acquisition costs include all costs associated with the purchase of material from a supplier until it reaches the buyer and is ready for use. These costs include the supplier price, supplier terms affecting financing costs, taxes and duties, delivery costs, and incoming quality costs. Acquisition costs should also include the overhead of managing the relationship and planning the purchases. Ownership costs include all costs associated with the purchased part from when it arrives from the supplier to when the finished product is sold to the customer. These costs include inventory costs, warehousing costs, manufacturing or conversion costs, production quality costs, and production cycle time costs. Post-ownership costs include all costs incurred by the firm after the finished product has reached the end customer. These costs include warranty costs, environmental costs, product liability costs, and reputational costs. Suppliers can be evaluated based on the factors shown in Table 15-2 that influence total cost.

The performance of each potential source (including in-house production) must be rated on each of these factors because all affect the total cost of ownership. It is important to consider trends that may exist especially if some of the sources are located overseas; these include exchange rates, local inflation in material and labor cost, transportation costs, and tariffs. This is especially true today, given the rapid change in these factors. Goel, Moussavi, and Srivatsan (2008) point out that producing a mid-range server in Asia in 2003 would have produced significant savings relative to producing it in the United States. Between 2005 and 2008, though, ocean freight costs increased by 135 percent, the Chinese yuan appreciated by 18 percent, and Chinese manufacturing wages went up by 44 percent. By 2008, freight and labor costs had increased enough to make production in the United States cheaper than production in Asia. Until 2008, many manufacturers viewed offshoring as a necessity, given that the offshore prices were 25 to 40 percent lower than those of local suppliers. By 2008, however, many executives realized that longer supply chains, lack of visibility, quality problems, growing transportation costs, and rising wages in developing countries made sourcing from local suppliers much more attractive. The lower transportation distance further increases the attractiveness of local suppliers from an environmental perspective. Given that a sourcing decision is unlikely to be changed quickly, it is important to include trends and scenarios (see Chapter 6) in the total cost analysis.

The use of the TCO perspective has helped several companies make better decisions, whereas in other cases, a focus on the purchase price has ended up increasing the total cost. Zara is an excellent example in which the willingness to pay a higher purchase price for responsiveness has resulted in a much lower cost of ownership. The company chose to source its trendiest products from responsive company-owned factories in Europe even though the acquisition cost from Europe was about 40 percent more expensive than Asia. The European factories had short design-to-product lead times of three to four weeks instead of the three to six months from Asia. The shorter lead times allowed Zara to meet demand for its popular products while not overproducing items that were not selling. As a result, Zara was able to increase profits by selling about 85 percent of its products at full price while the industry average was closer to 60 percent.

A similar perspective allowed Benetton to design an effective sourcing strategy when it introduced postponement (see Chapter 12) for its knit garments in the 1980s. Traditionally, knit

TABLE 15-2 Factors Influencing Total Cost of Ownership

Performance Category	Category Components	Quantifiable?
Acquisition Costs		
Supplier price	Labor, material, and overhead	Yes
Supplier terms	Net payment terms, delivery frequency, minimum lot size, quantity discounts	Yes
Taxes and duties	All tariffs and compliance costs	Yes
Delivery costs	All transportation costs from source to destination, packaging costs	Yes
Incoming quality costs	Cost of inspection, defectives, and rework	Yes
Management costs	Cost of managing and planning the purchase	Difficult
Ownership Costs		
Inventory costs	Supplier inventory, including raw material, in process and finished goods, in-transit inventory, finished goods inventory in supply chain	Yes
Warehousing cost	Warehousing and material handling costs to support additional inventory	Yes
Manufacturing cost	Cost of manufacturing associated with the sourced part	Yes
Production quality costs	Impact of sourced part on finished product quality	Difficult
Cycle time costs	Impact of sourced part on production cycle time	Yes
Post-Ownership Costs		
Reputation	Reputation impact of quality problems	No
Warranty and product liability costs	Warranty and product liability costs associated with sourced part	Difficult
Environmental costs	Environmental costs affected by sourced part	Difficult
Supplier capabilities	Replenishment lead time, on-time performance, flexibility, information coordination capability, design coordination capability, supplier viability	To some extent

garments were made by knitting colored thread. To lower costs, the various stages of knitting were handled by several small family enterprises. Although this process lowered cost, the entire production process took up to six months. Benetton identified a new process in which garments could be knit from undyed thread and then dyed later, while maintaining quality. As discussed in Chapter 12, this postponement of dyeing allows the supply of colors to better match demand. Although postponement was better at matching supply with demand, it had a higher production cost. With a focus on TCO, however, Benetton identified tailored postponement (see Chapter 13) to be a more effective strategy. Benetton separated the predictable base load from the unpredictable portion of demand for each color. Benetton outsourced for the predictable base load, as it had done in the past, to lower acquisition costs. The longer lead times of the suppliers did not hurt total cost because the base load always sold out. For the uncertain portion of demand, however, any mismatch of supply and demand was likely to increase total cost. Thus, Benetton opted for the higher cost production method with postponement to produce the unpredictable portion of demand close to when it was needed. Benetton performed the postponed dyeing function in-house so it could be very responsive in dyeing colors based on demand. This strategy of sourcing the predictable demand from low-cost third parties and the unpredictable portion of demand in-

house using a very responsive (though high-cost) process allowed Benetton to decrease the total cost of ownership.

Mattel is an example of a company that paid significant post-ownership costs because of the action of a supplier. In 2007, the company announced several major recalls of toys made in China that were contaminated with lead paint. A subcontractor hired to paint the toys had used paint from a non-authorized paint supplier. Mattel announced a charge of $30 million to cover the cost of the recall. The company was also fined $2.3 million by the Consumer Product Safety Commission. Even though the impact on its reputation is hard to quantify, Mattel clearly paid a high price for this sourcing decision, which lowered its acquisition cost.

Nike is another example of a company that worked very hard to contain the negative reputational impact of actions at its suppliers. Nike's business model is based on outsourcing its manufacturing. In the 1980s, Nike's manufacturing was in Korea and Taiwan, which were then viewed as low-cost sources. As labor costs increased in these countries, Nike urged its contractors to move production to Indonesia, China, and Vietnam. In the early 1990s, several reports appeared of poor working conditions and wages below Indonesia's minimum at a Nike subcontractor. After several years of protest, significant criticism, and weakness in demand, Nike started to take more decisive action in the late 1990s. Nike CEO Phil Knight announced an increase in the minimum age of workers, increased monitoring of suppliers, and the adoption of U.S. OSHA clean air standards in all supplier factories. The company performed many supplier audits and published a complete list of the factories with which it contracted. Even though these actions did increase the acquisition cost for Nike, they also helped turn around the company's reputation. Companies that outsource can learn from the Mattel and Nike experiences that accounting for post-ownership costs can be very helpful when making sourcing decisions.

SUMMARY OF LEARNING OBJECTIVE 2

Supplier performance should be compared based on the impact on total cost of ownership. Total cost includes the cost of acquisition, ownership, and post-ownership. In addition to the supplier price, the total cost of using a supplier is affected by the supplier terms; delivery costs; inventory costs; warehousing costs; quality costs; costs of management effort and administrative support; impact on reputation; supplier capabilities, such as replenishment lead time, on-time performance, and flexibility; and other costs, such as exchange rate trends, taxes, and duties. In many instances, a higher acquisition cost is more than compensated for by lower ownership and post-ownership costs.

DESIGNING A SOURCING PORTFOLIO: TAILORED SOURCING

15.3 Design a tailored supplier portfolio.

When structuring a supplier portfolio, firms have many options regarding whom to source from and where to source from. With regard to the "whom," a company must decide on whether to produce in-house or outsource to a third party. The company must also decide whether the supply source will be cost efficient or responsive. With regard to the "where," a company can choose among onshoring, near-shoring, and offshoring. *Onshoring* refers to producing the product in the market where it is sold, even when it is a high-cost location. *Near-shoring* refers to producing the product at a lower-cost location near the market. For the U.S. market, for example, producing in Mexico is near-shoring. For the market in Europe, producing in Eastern Europe is near-shoring. *Offshoring* refers to producing the product at a low-cost location that may be far from the market.

In this section, we discuss *tailored sourcing*, where firms use a combination of two supply sources, one focused on cost but unable to handle uncertainty well, and the other focused on flexibility or responsiveness to handle uncertainty, but at a higher cost. For tailored sourcing to be effective, having supply sources such that one serves as the backup to the other is not sufficient. The two sources must also focus on different capabilities – cost and responsiveness. The low-cost source must focus on being efficient and should be required to supply only the predictable portion of the

demand. In contrast, the responsive source should be required to supply the uncertain portion of the demand. As a result, tailored sourcing allows a firm to decrease total cost of ownership, increase its profits, and better match supply and demand. The value of tailored sourcing depends on the reduction in cost that can be achieved as a result of one source facing no variability. If this benefit is small, tailored sourcing may not be ideal because of the added complexity of implementation. Tailored sourcing may be volume based or product based, depending on the source of uncertainty.

In *volume-based tailored sourcing*, the predictable part of a product's demand is produced at an efficient facility, whereas the uncertain portion is produced at a responsive facility. Benetton provides an example of volume-based tailored sourcing. Benetton required retailers to commit to about 65 percent of their orders about seven months before the start of the sales season. Benetton subcontracted production of this portion without uncertainty to low-cost sources that had long lead times of several months. For the other 35 percent, Benetton allowed retailers to commit orders much closer to or even after the start of the selling season. All uncertainty was concentrated in this portion of the order. Benetton produced this portion of the order in a plant it owned that was very flexible. Production at the Benetton plant was more expensive than production by the subcontractor. However, the plant was responsive and could produce with a lead time of weeks, whereas subcontractors had a lead time of several months. A combination of the two sources allowed Benetton to reduce its inventories while incurring a high cost of production for only a fraction of its demand. This allowed it to decrease total cost and increase profits.

Volume-based tailored sourcing should be considered by firms that have moved a lot of their production overseas to take advantage of lower costs. The lower costs are often accompanied by longer lead times. In such a situation, having a responsive local source with short lead times can be an effective complement to the long-lead-time overseas supplier even if the local source is more expensive. Long lead times require large safety inventories, and the resulting mismatch of supply and demand hurts profits. The presence of the local source allows the firm to carry lower safety inventories and supply any excess demand from the local source. The most effective combination is for the overseas source to focus on replenishing cycle inventories, ignoring uncertainty. The local source is used as a backup any time demand exceeds the inventory available.

Allon and Van Mieghem (2010) describe a high-tech manufacturer of wireless transmission components with facilities in China and Mexico. The Chinese facility was cheaper but had lead times that were five to ten times longer than those from Mexico. A simulation study indicated that the use of tailored sourcing was the most effective strategy in this case. Allon and Van Mieghem (2010) recommend a *tailored base-surge* inventory policy, under which a constant base load is sourced from the cheaper source (China, in this case), with the responsive source (Mexico, in this case) being used any time inventory drops below a threshold. Their simulations indicate that sourcing roughly 75 percent of the demand from the cheaper source as base load, with the rest coming from the responsive source as needed, is a fairly effective tailored sourcing policy in practice. Their results show that the fraction of demand allocated as base load to the cheaper source increases as the demand and the cost difference with the responsive facility grow. The fraction of demand allocated as base load to the cheaper source decreases as the reliability of the cheaper source decreases or the volatility of demand and the holding cost of inventory grow.

In *product-based tailored sourcing*, low-volume products with uncertain demand are obtained from a responsive source, whereas high-volume products with less demand uncertainty are obtained from an efficient source. An example of product-based tailored sourcing is that used by Levi Strauss. Levi sells standard-sized jeans as well as jeans that can be customized. Standard jeans have relatively stable demand, whereas demand for custom jeans is unpredictable. Custom jeans are produced at a flexible facility, whereas standard jeans are produced at an efficient facility. Zara also follows such a product-based tailored sourcing strategy, obtaining more than half its production from responsive plants in Europe, with the rest coming from lower-cost plants in Asia. Zara's most fashionable items that have the least predictable demand are made in responsive European facilities. Clothes that are more predictable and can sell for longer periods, such as basic T-shirts, are sourced from the cheaper Asian facilities.

TABLE 15-3 Factors Favoring Selection of a Responsive or Low-Cost Source

	Responsive Source	**Low-Cost Source**
Product life cycle	Early phase	Mature phase
Demand volatility	High	Low
Demand volume	Low	High
Product value	High	Low
Rate of product obsolescence	High	Low
Desired quality	High	Low to medium
Engineering/design support	High	Low

In some instances, new products have uncertain demand, whereas well-established products have more stable demand. Product-based tailored sourcing may be implemented with a responsive facility focused on new products, and efficient facilities focused on the well-established products. This is often the case in the pharmaceutical industry, for instance.

To use a tailored portfolio effectively, demand should be allocated among suppliers in a way that is consistent with their capabilities as summarized in Table 15-3. Low-cost suppliers should be given large, steady orders of mature, low-value products that do not require significant engineering or design support. Responsive suppliers, in contrast, should be responsible for high-value, volatile products that are often early in their life cycle and need significant engineering/design support.

In general, responsive sources will tend to be located onshore or near-shore to facilitate a quick response. Low-cost sources could be located anywhere, but low cost is often the main reason for going offshore or near-shore. In Table 15-4, we identify some factors that influence the sourcing location decision.

Large, bulky items such as washing machines and refrigerators are best onshored or near-shored because they have high transportation costs relative to value. In contrast, small items like consumer electronics, especially those that sell in large amounts (say, the iPad), can be offshored. As transportation costs increase, the onshore and near-shore options become more attractive relative to offshoring. Consistent with Table 15-4, high-value routers with high demand volatility, high inventory costs, and the need for significant management support are outsourced by Cisco to an onshore supplier. Low-value routers with stable designs and low demand volatility, in contrast, are offshored to low-cost countries. As these examples illustrate, it is important for a firm to plan a tailored sourcing strategy in which the product and market characteristics match with the responsiveness and location of the source.

TABLE 15-4 Factors Favoring Onshoring, Near-Shoring, or Offshoring

	Onshore	**Near-Shore**	**Offshore**
Rate of innovation/product variety	High	Medium to High	Low
Demand volatility	High	Medium to High	Low
Labor content	Low	Medium to High	High
Volume or weight-to-value ratio	High	High	Low
Impact of supply chain disruption	High	Medium to High	Low
Inventory costs	High	Medium to High	Low
Engineering/management support	High	High	Low

China and other parts of Asia were popular offshore sources for the two decades between 1990 and 2010. Some trends currently in place, however, are making American managers rethink their offshoring choices. One is the change in Chinese wages and the strengthening yuan, both of which diminish the labor cost advantage of China, especially when compared to near-shore locations such as Mexico. The other is the increase in oil prices and transportation costs that acts as a tariff barrier, making offshoring somewhat less attractive. Finally, the increase in volatility and the need to mitigate risk have also encouraged supply chain designers to include an onshore or near-shore source to complement a low-cost offshore source.

The tailoring of the supplier portfolio should also account for other characteristics of the product being sourced. A simple categorization of purchased goods is into direct and indirect materials. *Direct materials* are components used to make finished goods. For example, the processor is a direct material for a smartphone manufacturer. *Indirect materials* are goods used to support the operations of a firm. Office supplies are examples of indirect materials for an automotive manufacturer. Important differences between direct and indirect materials are shown in Table 15-5.

Given the direct link to production, suppliers for direct materials should be selected based on their ability to collaborate and coordinate across the supply chain. Collaboration is important at both the design and production phases. Collaboration during design can help reduce component costs, whereas collaboration during production can help improve coordination of the supply chain through improved planning and visibility. A good example of collaboration is the relationship between Johnson Controls and Chrysler for the 2002 Jeep Liberty. Johnson Controls integrated components from thirty-five suppliers and delivered the assembly to Chrysler as a cockpit module. As soon as Chrysler notified it of an order for a Jeep, Johnson Controls had 204 minutes in which to build and deliver the module. This was done 900 times every day for about 200 color and interior combinations. The strong collaboration between the two companies resulted in a significant reduction in inventory and a better matching of product supply with end customer demand.

Indirect materials are often a small fraction of the money spent by a firm but can represent a big headache for the procurement department. The purchase of indirect materials typically involves many transactions, with each transaction being small. Each transaction can be costly because of the difficulty of selecting goods (from many catalogs, which are often out of date), getting approval, and creating and sending a purchase order. Suppliers for indirect material should thus be selected based on their ability to simplify each transaction. As suppliers of maintenance and repair parts (typical indirect materials), McMaster-Carr and W.W. Grainger have worked hard to make it easy for their customers to transact with them.

In addition to the categorization of materials into direct and indirect, all products purchased may also be categorized as shown in Figure 15-1, based on their value/cost and how critical they

TABLE 15-5 Differences Between Direct and Indirect Materials

	Direct Materials	Indirect Materials
Use	Production	Maintenance, repair, and support operations
Accounting	Cost of goods sold	Selling, general, and administrative (SG&A) expenses
Impact on production	Any delay will delay production	Less direct impact
Processing cost relative to value of transaction	Low	High
Number of transactions	Low	High

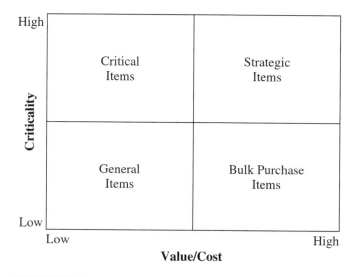

Figure 15-1 Product Categorization by Value and Criticality

are. Most indirect materials are included in general items. Direct materials can be further classified into bulk purchase, critical, and strategic items. For most bulk purchase items, such as packaging materials and bulk chemicals, suppliers tend to have the same selling price. It is thus important to make a distinction between suppliers based on the services they provide and their performance along all dimensions that affect the total cost of ownership. Critical items include specialty chemicals and components with long lead times. The key sourcing objective for critical items is not low price, but ensuring availability. The presence of a responsive, even if high-cost, supply source can be valuable for critical items. The last category, strategic items, includes examples such as electronics for an auto manufacturer. For strategic items, the buyer–supplier relationship is long-term. Thus, suppliers should be evaluated based on the lifetime cost/value of the relationship. The goal should be to identify suppliers that can collaborate in the design phase and coordinate design and production activities with other players in the supply chain.

SUMMARY OF LEARNING OBJECTIVE 3

Firms must consider a tailored sourcing strategy that couples responsive onshore or near-shore sources with low-cost offshore sources. The responsive onshore sources should focus on high-value products with high demand volatility, whereas the low-cost, offshore sources should focus on lower-value, high-volume products with high labor content. Sourcing can also be tailored based on direct and indirect materials as well as the criticality and cost of items purchased.

THE IMPACT OF INCENTIVES ON THIRD-PARTY BEHAVIOR

15.4 Describe the impact of incentives on the behavior of third-parties in a supply chain.

As companies outsource supply chain activities, it is important to understand how incentives impact the behavior of third-parties and the resulting impact on the supply chain surplus. It is often the case that misalignment of incentives hurts supply chain performance. The $2.5 billion write-down of inventory by Cisco in 2001 is an example of the cost of misaligned incentives. Cisco outsourced production to contract manufacturers and rewarded them for rapid deliveries. The suppliers stockpiled semi-finished products for Cisco because the availability of this inventory allowed suppliers to react quickly during an extended period when demand had exceeded supply. When demand slowed in 2000, it took a while before the inflow of components could be curtailed. A

reward for rapid deliveries without any negative consequence for inventories led suppliers to build $2.5 billion of inventory, which became useless when demand slowed. This example is a cautionary tale of the importance of understanding the impact of incentives in a supply chain. Understanding the impact of incentives is important whenever the third party's actions are not fully observable or when the third party has information that is not available to the firm. In either case, it is difficult to design incentives that induce the third party to do what is right for the supply chain.

A good example of the lack of visibility of the third party's actions arises in the automotive supply chain. Consider the case in which Chrysler sells cars through a dealer. The dealer is a third-party performing the sales function on behalf of the auto company (referred to as the principal). The dealer also sells other brands and used cars. Every month, the dealer must decide how to allocate its sales effort (e.g., sales people, promotions) across all types of cars it sells. Earnings for Chrysler are based on sales of its brands, which in turn are affected by the effort exerted by the dealer to sell its cars. The challenge in this setting is that although Chrysler can observe sales directly, dealer effort allocated to selling Chryslers is hard to observe and measure. Thus, when sales are high in a given month, it is difficult for Chrysler to infer whether the increase resulted from better market conditions or greater sales effort. In general, Chrysler would like to encourage greater effort from its dealers on its behalf.

It is well known that incentives offered by the principal can encourage greater effort from the agent. Well-designed incentives can be strong communicators of desired performance. Poorly designed incentives, however, can backfire and hurt supply chain performance. A commonly used performance incentive sets "thresholds" for minimum performance below which there are no rewards. Chrysler offered such an incentive to its dealers in the first quarter of 2001. The rough structure of the incentive was as follows: Dealers would keep the margin made from customers if sales for the month were less than 75 percent of an agreed-upon target. However, if sales reached or exceeded 75 percent but were less than 100 percent of the target, the dealer would get an additional $150 per car sold. If sales reached or exceeded 100 percent but were less than 110 percent, the dealer would get an additional $250 per car sold. If sales reached or exceeded 110 percent of the target, the dealer would get an additional $500 per car sold. Chrysler's hope was that by increasing the margin for higher thresholds, the dealer would have an incentive to increase effort on sales of Chrysler cars.

In the first month after the new contract was announced, the U.S. car industry saw a decrease in sales. Chrysler, however, saw sales drop by twice the industry average. There are three potential causes for this behavior, all related to the structure of the incentive. First, the target set may have been too high. Given that the target was not achievable, dealers decided to suppress effort because the extra effort was not profitable if the target was not achieved. Second, under the incentive, the dealer makes more money selling 900 cars one month and 1,100 the next month compared with selling 1,000 cars each month. The dealer has an incentive to shift demand over time to achieve such an outcome, thus increasing information distortion and observed demand variation. The third cause is that within the first week of the month, the dealer has an idea of the threshold range it is likely to reach. For example, if the dealer believes that it can easily cross the 75 percent threshold but has little chance of crossing the 100 percent threshold, it will decrease its effort for the month and save it for later, because the marginal benefit of selling an additional car is only $150. In contrast, if demand for the month is high and the dealer believes it can easily cross the 100 percent threshold, it is likely to exert additional effort to reach the 110 percent threshold because the marginal benefit from reaching that threshold is high. Thus, Chrysler's incentive increases variation in dealer effort, further exaggerating any existing market variation. Such an outcome hurts the supply chain surplus.

The following approaches can help dampen the distortion introduced by threshold incentives such as Chrysler's. It is important to ensure that the target set is not too high or too low because the dealer reduces the effort exerted in either case. Even when the target is set fairly, a problem arises if the target is a fixed number that does not vary with market conditions. A reasonable target may become too easy if the market is strong and too difficult if the market is weak. It is better to set a target that adjusts based on market conditions. The challenge, however, is to identify market conditions. One approach used is to adjust the target after sales are observed, based on average sales across all dealers. Thus, when the auto market was down by 8 percent

(industry sales are a good measure of market conditions), Chrysler could have lowered the target for its dealers by the same amount. Assuming the original target was fairly set and the dealers were aware of the planned adjustment of the target based on market conditions, they would have continued to exert steady effort. Threshold incentives for which the target is adjusted based on market conditions are more likely to result in steady effort from the third party.

Information distortion is also observed in threshold incentives offered by companies to their sales staff. Under these incentives, staff is offered rewards for crossing sales thresholds during a specified period of time (e.g., a quarter). The problem observed is that sales effort and orders peak during the last few weeks of the quarter, as salespeople try to cross the threshold. This pattern, in which sales peak close to the end of the evaluation period, is referred to as the *hockey stick phenomenon*. This information distortion arises because the incentive is offered over a fixed time period, making the last few weeks of each quarter a period of intense activity for all sales staff.

One approach that firms can take to address the hockey stick phenomenon is to offer threshold incentives over a rolling horizon. For example, if a firm offers its sales staff weekly incentives based on sales over the past 13 weeks, each week becomes the last week of a 13-week period. Sales effort thus becomes more even compared with when the entire sales staff has the same last week for their bonus evaluation. Given the presence of enterprise resource planning (ERP) systems, implementing a rolling horizon incentive is much easier today than it once was. Another approach to address this issue is to recognize that although higher sales benefit supply chain performance, higher variation of sales hurts performance. Incentives can then be designed to reward total sales over a given time period while punishing variation of sales. Even though designing incentives that account for multiple dimensions of performance is difficult, it is important if the goals of the third party and the firm are to be aligned to grow the supply chain surplus.

SUMMARY OF LEARNING OBJECTIVE 4

Supply chain incentives can have unintended consequences when the third party's information and actions are hard to observe. It is important to understand and address the negative consequences of these incentives to ensure that the third-party acts in a way that grows the supply chain surplus.

SHARING RISK AND REWARD IN THE SUPPLY CHAIN

15.5 Discuss the benefits of sharing risk and reward in a supply chain.

In this chapter so far, we have emphasized the fact that all sourcing decisions should be made with the goal of growing the supply chain surplus. In practice, however, many firms care less about growing the surplus and more about what share of the surplus they are able to capture. As firms gain greater power in a supply chain, they often attempt to capture a greater share of the surplus by pushing more risk onto their supply chain partners. In this section, we focus on the downsides of focusing on a firm's local interest at the expense of the supply chain surplus. We also suggest some approaches that can be used to counter the downsides of local optimization.

Sharing Risk to Grow Supply Chain Profits

Independent actions taken by two parties in a supply chain often result in profits that are lower than those that could be achieved if all parties in the supply chain were to coordinate their actions with a common objective of maximizing supply chain profits rather than individual firm profits. Strong firms tend to push more risk on to supply chain partners while keeping a large margin for themselves. A classic example of such an approach is the action taken by Mattel in 1999 in response to adverse outcomes in 1998. Until 1998, Mattel allowed its retailers to place two orders for the Christmas season. Mattel delivered the first order before the Thanksgiving weekend; retailers then placed their second order after observing sales over that weekend. The weekend sales allowed retailers to get a much better forecast for the Christmas season before placing the second order. In 1998, sales over the Thanksgiving weekend were soft and

many retailers decided not to place a second order. As a result, Mattel reported a $500 million sales shortfall in the last weeks of the year. Having been burned because of its willingness to absorb the risk of the second order, Mattel changed its policy for 1999. It now required retailers to place their entire order before Thanksgiving and the company would take no reorders in December. Mattel announced that the new policy would allow the company to "tailor production more closely to demand and avoid building inventory for orders that don't come."

The actions of Mattel amounted to shifting risk from Mattel to the retailers. Whereas Mattel absorbed some of the forecast uncertainty when retailers were allowed a follow-up order in December, forcing retailers to place their orders before Thanksgiving pushed all the risk of forecast error onto them. This action by Mattel (seemingly taken because of its self-interest) clearly hurts retailers. We now argue that it also hurts Mattel. Given demand uncertainty, a manufacturer like Mattel wants the retailer to carry a large inventory of its product to ensure that any surge in demand can be satisfied. The retailer, on the other hand, loses money on any unsold inventory. As a result, the retailer prefers to carry a lower level of inventory, especially when it must absorb the entire risk of a forecast error. This tension leads to a supply chain outcome that hurts both the retailer and the manufacturer, as illustrated in Example 15-1 (see worksheet *Example 15-1* in workbook *Chapter15-examples*).

Optimal Service Level Equations

p: sale price; c: purchase cost; s: salvage value; μ: mean demand; σ: standard deviation of demand; CSL^*: optimal cycle service level; O^*: optimal order quantity

$$CSL^* = Prob(Demand \leq O^*) = \frac{p - c}{p - s} = \frac{C_u}{C_u + C_o} = \frac{1}{1 + (C_o/C_u)} \tag{13.1}$$

$$O^* = F^{-1}(CSL^*, \mu, \sigma) = NORMINV(CSL^*, \mu, \sigma) \tag{13.2}$$

$$\begin{aligned}
\text{Expected profits} = (p - s)\mu \, NORMDIST[(O - \mu)/\sigma, 0, 1, 1] \\
-(p - s)\sigma NORMDIST[(O - \mu)/\sigma, 0, 1, 0] \\
-O(c - s)\mu \, NORMDIST(O, \mu, \sigma, 1) \\
+O(p - c)[1 - NORMDIST(O, \mu, \sigma, 1)]
\end{aligned} \tag{13.3}$$

$$\begin{aligned}
\text{Expected overstock} = (O - \mu)NORMDIST[(O - \mu)/\sigma, 0, 1, 1] \\
+ \sigma NORMDIST[(O - \mu)/\sigma, 0, 1, 1]
\end{aligned} \tag{13.4}$$

$$\begin{aligned}
\text{Expected understock} = (\mu - O)(1 - NORMDIST[(O - \mu)/\sigma, 0, 1, 1]) \\
+ \sigma NORMDIST[(O - \mu)/\sigma, 0, 1, 1]
\end{aligned} \tag{13.5}$$

EXAMPLE 15-1 **Impact of Local Optimization**

Consider a music store that sells compact discs. The supplier manufactures compact discs at $1 per unit and sells them to the music store at $5 per unit. The retailer sells each disc to the end consumer at $10. At this retail price, market demand is normally distributed, with a mean of 1,000 and a standard deviation of 300. Any leftover discs at the end of the sale period are worthless. How many discs should an independent retailer order? What are the supply chain profits with an independent retailer? If the manufacturer and the retailer are vertically integrated (they are a single firm), how many discs should the retailer order? What are the supply chain profits when the manufacturer and retailer are a single firm?

Analysis:

We first consider the case of the independent retailer. The retailer has a margin of $5 per disc and can potentially lose $5 for each unsold disc. The retailer thus has a cost of overstocking $C_o = \$5$ and a cost of understocking $C_u = \$5$. Using Equation 13.1, it is optimal for the retailer to aim for a service level of $5/(5 + 5) = 0.5$ and order $NORMINV(0.5, 1000, 300) = 1,000$ discs.

From Equation 13.3, the retailer's expected profits are $3,803, and the manufacturer makes $4,000 from selling 1,000 discs. The total supply chain profit with an independent retailer is thus $3,803 + $4,000 = $7,803.

Now, consider the case in which the supply chain is vertically integrated. The supply chain has a margin of $10 − $1 = $9 per disc and can potentially lose $1 for each unsold disc. The supply chain thus has a cost of overstocking $C_o = \$1$ and a cost of understocking $C_u = \$9$. Using Equation 13.1, it is optimal for the supply chain to aim for a service level of $9/(1 + 9) = 0.9$ and order $NORMINV(0.9, 1000, 300) = 1,384$ discs. From Equation 13.3, the supply chain's expected profits are $8,474.

Thus, the vertically integrated supply chain makes $671 more than when the retailer makes the ordering decision independently.

As the analysis in Example 15-1 illustrates, concentrating risk at one stage of the supply chain hurts overall supply chain profits if the supply chain margin is divided between the two parties, and each stage makes its decisions considering only its own margin. An independent retailer makes its buying decision before demand is realized and thus bears all the demand uncertainty. If demand is less than the retailer's inventory, the retailer must liquidate unsold product at a discount. Given uncertain demand, the retailer decides on the purchase quantity based on its margin and the cost of overstocking, as discussed in Chapter 13. The retailer's margin, however, is lower than the contribution margin for the entire supply chain, whereas its cost of overstocking is higher than that for the entire supply chain. As a result, the retailer is conservative and aims for a lower level of product availability than is optimal for the supply chain, leading to a loss of supply chain surplus. As Example 15-1 illustrates, if the retailer absorbs all the risk of forecast error while getting only a portion of the margin ($5 in this example, compared with a supply chain margin of $9), the retailer's ordering decision lowers supply chain profits compared with those of a vertically integrated supply chain.

From our discussion, it seems clear that Mattel's actions—in which it pushed all the risk onto retailers—clearly hurt supply chain profits because retailers were more conservative than they would have been when Mattel shared some risk. The conservative approach of the retailers did not allow the supply chain to take advantage of any upside in demand, thus reducing supply chain profits.

Given that we have identified the problem when risk is not shared, we now focus on identifying potential solutions that allow for risk sharing in a way that increases supply chain profits. To improve overall profits, the supplier must share risk in a way that encourages the buyer to purchase more and increase the level of product availability. This requires the supplier to share in some of the buyer's demand uncertainty. The following three approaches to risk sharing increase overall supply chain profits:

1. Buybacks or returns
2. Revenue sharing
3. Quantity flexibility

We illustrate each of the three approaches using the story in Example 15-1 of the music store. We discuss the performance of each approach in terms of the following three questions.

1. How will risk sharing affect the firm's profits and total supply chain profits?
2. Will risk sharing introduce any information distortion?
3. How will risk sharing influence supplier performance along key performance measures?

RISK SHARING THROUGH BUYBACKS A buyback or returns clause allows a retailer to return unsold inventory up to a specified amount, at an agreed-upon price. In this case, the supplier is sharing risk by agreeing to buy back unsold inventory at the retailer. In a *buyback contract,* the manufacturer specifies a wholesale price c along with a buyback price b at which the retailer can return any unsold units at the end of the season. We assume that the manufacturer can salvage $\$s_M$ for any units that the retailer returns. The manufacturer has a cost of v per unit produced. The retail price is p.

The optimal order quantity O^* for a retailer in response to a buyback contract is evaluated using Equations 13.1 and 13.2, where the salvage value for the retailer is $s = b$, the buyback price. The cost of overstocking for the retailer is given by $C_o = c - b$, and the cost of understocking for the retailer is given by $C_u = p - c$. Using Equation 13.1, the optimal service level that the retailer targets is thus given by $CSL^* = (p - c)/(p - b)$. Using Equation 13.2, the optimal order size by the retailer is given by $O^* = NORMINV(CSL^*, \mu, \sigma)$. The expected retailer profit is evaluated using Equation 13.3 with the salvage value s equal to the buyback price b. The expected profit at the manufacturer depends on the overstock at the retailer (evaluated using Equation 13.4) that is returned. We obtain

$$\text{Expected manufacturer profit} = O^*(c - v) -$$
$$(b - s_M) \times \text{expected overstock at retailer}$$

We illustrate the impact of buybacks on supply chain profits in Example 15-2 (see worksheet *Example 15-2*).

EXAMPLE 15-2 **Impact of Risk Sharing Through Buybacks**

We return to the music store in Example 15-1 with all data as specified. Assume that the supplier agrees to buy back any unsold discs for $3 even though any leftover discs at the end of the sale period are worthless. With the buyback clause, how many discs should an independent retailer order? What are the supply chain profits with a buyback clause?

Analysis:

With a buyback clause as specified, the retailer has a salvage value of $3 for each unsold unit. Given the wholesale price of $5 and a retail price of $10, the retailer thus has a cost of overstocking, $C_o = \$5 - \$3 = \$2$ and a cost of understocking $C_u = \$10 - \$5 = \$5$. Using Equation 13.1, it is optimal for the retailer to aim for a service level of $5/(2 + 5) = 0.71$ and order $1{,}170 [= NORMINV(5/7, 1000, 300)]$ discs. From Equation 13.3, the retailer's expected profits are $4,286. Given an expected overstock of 223 units (using Equation 13.4), the manufacturer's expected profit is $4{,}011 [= 1170 \times (5 - 1) - (223 \times 3)]$. The total expected supply chain profit with buybacks is thus $4,286 + $4,011 = $8,297.

Observe that risk sharing using a buyback clause for $3 increases profits for the retailer as well as the manufacturer (and the supply chain as a whole) compared with Example 15-1, in which there was no risk sharing.

Example 15-2 illustrates that risk sharing through a suitably designed buyback clause can increase manufacturer profits (relative to the case without risk sharing) even though the retailer is compensated for any unsold inventory. Risk sharing by the manufacturer always increases the retailer's profits because the retailer's cost of overstocking has decreased. Despite buying back unsold inventory at $3, the supplier's profits increase in Example 15-2 because the retailer, on average, sells more product (on which the supplier makes $4 per unit). Buyback contracts are most effective for products with a low variable cost, such as music, software, books, magazines, and newspapers.

Table 15-6 (which can be constructed using worksheet *Example 15-2*) shows supply chain profits for different values of wholesale and buyback prices. Observe that the use of buyback contracts increases total supply chain profits by about 20 percent when the wholesale price is $7 per disc. For a fixed wholesale price, increasing the buyback price always increases retailer profits. In general, there exists a positive buyback price that is a fraction of the wholesale price, at which the manufacturer makes a higher profit compared to offering no buyback. From Table 15-6, observe that buybacks are found to be more helpful to the manufacturer when the wholesale price is $7 relative to when the wholesale price is $5. Thus, the greater the manufacturer's margin, the more the manufacturer stands to benefit through the use of some risk-sharing mechanism such as buybacks.

TABLE 15-6 Order Sizes and Profits in Music Supply Chain Under Different Buyback Contracts

Wholesale Price c	Buyback Price b	Optimal Order Size for Music Store	Expected Profit for Music Store	Expected Returns to Supplier	Expected Profit for Supplier	Expected Supply Chain Profit
$5	$0	1,000	$3,803	120	$4,000	$7,803
$5	$2	1,096	$4,090	174	$4,035	$8,125
$5	$3	1,170	$4,286	223	$4,009	$8,295
$6	$0	924	$2,841	86	$4,620	$7,461
$6	$2	1,000	$3,043	120	$4,761	$7,804
$6	$4	1,129	$3,346	195	$4,865	$8,211
$7	$0	843	$1,957	57	$5,056	$7,013
$7	$4	1,000	$2,282	120	$5,521	$7,803
$7	$6	1,202	$2,619	247	$5,732	$8,351

For a fixed wholesale price, as the buyback price increases, the retailer orders more and also returns more. In our analysis in Table 15-6, though, we have not considered the cost associated with a return. As the cost associated with a return increases, buyback contracts become less attractive because the cost of returns reduces supply chain profits. If return costs are high, buyback contracts can reduce the total profits of the supply chain far more than is the case without any buyback.

In 1932, Viking Press was the first book publisher to accept returns. Today, buyback contracts are common in the book industry, and publishers accept unsold books from retailers. To minimize the cost associated with a return, retailers do not have to return the book, only the cover. When publishers can verify retailer sales electronically, nothing must be returned. The goal in either case is for the publisher to get proof that the book did not sell while reducing the cost of the return. Over the years, considerable debate has taken place about the impact of publishers' returns policy on profits in the industry. Our discussion provides some justification for the approach taken by the publishers.

In some instances, manufacturers use holding-cost subsidies or price protection to share risk and encourage retailers to order more. With *holding-cost subsidies,* manufacturers pay retailers a certain amount for every unit held in inventory over a given period. Holding-cost subsidies are prevalent in automotive supply chains. In the high-tech industry, in which products lose value rapidly, manufacturers share the risk of product becoming obsolete by providing *price support* to retailers. Many manufacturers guarantee that in the event that they drop prices, they will also lower prices for all inventories that the retailer is currently carrying and compensate the retailer accordingly. As a result, the cost of overstocking at the retailer is limited to the cost of capital and physical storage and does not include obsolescence, which can be more than 100 percent a year for high-tech products. The retailer thus increases the level of product availability in the presence of price support. Both holding-cost subsidies and price support are forms of buyback.

A downside to the buyback clause (or any equivalent practice, such as holding-cost subsidy or price support) is that it leads to surplus inventory that must be salvaged or disposed. The task of returning unsold product increases supply chain costs. The cost of returns can be eliminated if the manufacturer gives the retailer a markdown allowance and allows it to sell the product at a significant discount. Publishers today generally do not ask retailers to return unsold books; instead, they give a markdown allowance for them. Retailers then mark them down and sell them for a considerable discount.

For a given level of product availability at the retailer, the presence of a buyback clause can also hurt sales because it leads the retailer to exert less effort to sell than it would without buybacks. The reduction in retailer effort in the presence of buyback occurs because its loss from unsold inventory is higher when there is no buyback, leading to a higher sales effort for products

with no buyback. The supplier can counter the reduction in sales effort by limiting the amount of buyback permitted.

The structure of a buyback clause leads to the entire supply chain reacting to the order placed by the retailer and not to actual customer demand. If a supplier is selling to multiple retailers, it produces based on the orders placed by each retailer. Each retailer inflates its order because of the buyback clause. As a result, the structure of the buyback clause increases information distortion when a supplier is selling to multiple retailers. At the end of the sales season, however, the supplier does obtain information on actual sales. Information distortion is driven primarily by the fact that inventory is disaggregated at the retailers based on an ordering decision made when demand is uncertain. If inventory is produced by the supplier and sent out only as needed to the retailers, information distortion can be reduced. With more responsive production and centralized inventory, the supplier can exploit independence of demand across retailers to carry a lower level of inventory. In practice, however, most buyback contracts have decentralized inventory at retailers. As a result, there is a high level of information distortion.

RISK SHARING THROUGH REVENUE SHARING In *revenue-sharing* contracts, the manufacturer charges the retailer a lower wholesale price c (compared with the case without risk sharing), but shares a fraction f of the retailer's revenue. In this case, the manufacturer is sharing risk because the retailer's cost is lower (than without risk sharing) if demand is low. Even if no returns are allowed, the lower wholesale price decreases the cost to the retailer in case of an overstock. The retailer thus increases the level of product availability, resulting in higher profits for both the manufacturer and the retailer when revenue sharing is suitably designed.

Assume that the manufacturer has a production cost v; the retailer charges a retail price p and can salvage any leftover units for s_R. The optimal order quantity O^* ordered by the retailer is evaluated using Equations 13.1 and 13.2, where the cost of understocking is $C_u = (1 - f)p - c$ and the cost of overstocking is $C_o = c - s_R$. We thus obtain

$$CSL^* = \text{probability(demand} \leq O^*) = \frac{C_u}{C_u + C_o} = \frac{(1 - f)p - c}{(1 - f)p - s_R}$$

The manufacturer obtains the wholesale price c for each unit purchased by the retailer and a share of the revenue for each unit sold by the retailer. The expected overstock at the retailer is obtained using Equation 13.4. The manufacturer's profits are thus evaluated as

$$\text{Expected manufacturers profits} = (c - v)O^* + fp(O^* - \text{expected overstock at retailer})$$

The retailer pays a wholesale price c for each unit purchased and obtains a revenue of $(1 - f)p$ for each unit sold and a revenue of s_R for each unit overstocked. The retailer's expected profit is thus evaluated as

$$\text{Expected retailer profit} = (1 - f)p(O^* - \text{expected overstock at retailer}) + s_R \times \text{expected overstock at retailer} - cO^*$$

We illustrate the impact of revenue sharing on supply chain profits using Example 15-3 (see worksheet *Example 15-3*).

EXAMPLE 15-3 **Impact of Risk Sharing Through Revenue Sharing**

We return to the music store in Example 15-1 with all data as specified. Assume that the supplier agrees to a revenue sharing contract under which the retailer is charged only $1 for each disc, with the manufacturer getting 45 percent of the retail revenues. Given the retail price of $10, the

manufacturer gets $4.50 for each disc sold while the retailer keeps $5.50. With the revenue-sharing clause, how many discs should an independent retailer order? What are the supply chain profits with a revenue-sharing clause?

Analysis:

With a revenue-sharing clause as specified, we have $c = \$1, p = \$10, s_R = 0$, and a revenue share fraction $f = 0.45$. The manufacturer has a production cost of $v = \$1$. The music store thus has a cost of overstocking of $C_o = c - s_R = 1 - 0 = \1 and a cost of understocking of $C_u = (1 - f)p - c = (1 - 0.45) \times 10 - 1 = \4.50. The music store targets a service level of $CSL^* = 4.5/(4.5 + 1) = 0.818$, or 81.8 percent (see Equation 13.1) and orders $1,273[= NORMINV(4.5/5.5, 1000, 300)]$ discs. Observe that this is much larger than the 1,000 discs ordered in Example 15-1, when the wholesale price was $5 and there was no revenue sharing. The increase in order size occurs because the retailer loses only $1 per unsold disc (instead of $5 per disc without revenue sharing), while making a margin of $4.50 for each disc that sells.

Given an order of 1,273 discs, the retailer has an expected overstock of 302 discs (use Equation 13.4). As a result, the expected manufacturer's profit $= (c-v)O^* + fp(O^* - \text{expected overstock}) = (1 - 1) \times 1273 + 0.45 \times 10 \times (1273 - 302) = \$4,369$. The expected retailer's profit $= (1 - f)p(O^* - \text{expected overstock at retailer}) + s_R \times \text{expected overstock at retailer} - cO^* = (1 - 0.45) \times 10 \times (1273 - 302) + 0 \times 302 - 1 \times 1273 = \$4,068$. The total supply chain profit $= 4,369 + 4,068 = \$8,437$.

Observe that risk sharing using a revenue sharing clause with a $1 wholesale price and a 45 percent share for the supplier increases profits for the retailer as well as the manufacturer (and the supply chain as a whole) compared with Example 15-1, in which there was no risk sharing.

Table 15-7 (constructed using worksheet *Example 15-3* in spreadsheet *Chapter15-examples*) provides the outcome in terms of order sizes and profits for different wholesale prices and revenue-sharing fractions f. From Tables 15-6 and 15-7, observe that revenue sharing allows both the manufacturer and retailer to increase their profits compared with the case in which the wholesaler sells for a fixed price of $5 without buybacks. Recall that when charging a wholesale price of $5, the supplier makes profit of $4,000 and the music store makes a profit of $3,803 (see Table 15-6).

Revenue-sharing contracts also result in lower retailer effort compared with the case in which the retailer pays an upfront wholesale price and keeps the entire revenue from a sale.

TABLE 15-7 Order Sizes and Profits in Music Supply Chain Under Different Revenue-Sharing Contracts

Wholesale Price c	Revenue-Sharing Fraction f	Optimal Order Size for Music Store	Expected Overstock at Music Store	Expected Profit for Music Store	Expected Profit for Supplier	Expected Supply Chain Profit
$1	0.30	1,320	342	$5,526	$2,934	$8,460
$1	0.45	1,273	302	$4,064	$4,367	$8,431
$1	0.60	1,202	247	$2,619	$5,732	$8,350
$2	0.30	1,170	223	$4,286	$4,009	$8,295
$2	0.45	1,105	179	$2,881	$5,269	$8,150
$2	0.60	1,000	120	$1,521	$6,282	$7,803

The drop in effort results because the retailer gets only a fraction of the revenue from each sale. One advantage of revenue-sharing contracts over buyback contracts is that no product needs to be returned, thus eliminating the cost of returns. Revenue-sharing contracts are best suited for products with low variable cost and a high cost of return. A good example of revenue-sharing contracts was implemented between Blockbuster video rentals and movie studios for videos. Studios sold each cassette to Blockbuster at a low price and then shared in the revenue generated from each rental. Given the low price, Blockbuster purchased many copies, resulting in more rentals and higher profits for both Blockbuster and the studio.

The revenue-sharing contract does require an information infrastructure that allows the supplier to monitor sales at the retailer. Such an infrastructure can be expensive to build. As a result, revenue-sharing contracts may be difficult to manage for a supplier selling to many small buyers.

As in buyback contracts, revenue-sharing contracts also result in the supply chain producing to retailer orders rather than to actual consumer demand. This information distortion results in excess inventory in the supply chain and a greater mismatch between supply and demand. The information distortion increases as the number of retailers to which the supplier sells grows. As with buyback contracts, information distortion from revenue-sharing contracts can be reduced if retailers reserve production capacity or inventory at the supplier rather than buying product and holding it in inventory themselves. This allows aggregation of the variability across multiple retailers, and the supplier must hold a lower level of capacity or inventory. In practice, however, most revenue-sharing contracts are implemented with the retailer buying and holding inventory.

RISK SHARING USING QUANTITY FLEXIBILITY Under *quantity flexibility contracts,* the manufacturer allows the retailer to change the quantity ordered (within limits) closer to the point of sale or after observing demand. This allows the retailer to commit to a final order after they have an improved demand forecast. If a retailer orders O units, the manufacturer commits to providing up to $Q = (1 + \alpha)O$ units, whereas the retailer is committed to buying at least $q = (1 - \beta)O$ units. Both α and β are between 0 and 1. The retailer can purchase anywhere between q and Q units, depending on the demand it observes. Quantity flexibility contracts are similar in spirit to the contract that Mattel offered its retailers prior to 1999. In quantity flexibility contracts the manufacturer shares risk by allowing the retailer to adjust its order as better market information is received. Because no returns are required, these contracts can be more effective than buyback contracts when the cost of returns is high. When the supplier is selling to multiple retailers, these contracts are more effective than buyback contracts because they allow the supplier to aggregate uncertainties across multiple retailers and thus lower the level of excess inventory. Quantity flexibility contracts increase the average amount the retailer purchases and may increase total supply chain profits when structured appropriately.

Assume that the manufacturer incurs a production cost of v per unit and charges a wholesale price of c from the retailer. The retailer, in turn, sells to customers for a price of p. The retailer salvages any leftover units for s_R. The manufacturer salvages any leftover units for s_M. If retailer demand is normally distributed, with a mean of μ and a standard deviation of σ, we can evaluate the impact of a quantity flexibility contract. If the retailer orders O units, the manufacturer is committed to supplying Q units. As a result, we assume that the manufacturer produces Q units. The retailer purchases q units if demand D is less than q, D units if demand D is between q and Q, and Q units if demand D is greater than Q. In the following formulas, F_S is the standard normal cumulative distribution function and f_S is the standard normal density function discussed in Appendix 12A in Chapter 12. We thus obtain

Expected quantity purchased by retailer, $Q_R = qF(q) + Q[1 - F(Q)]$

$$+ \mu \left[F_s \left(\frac{Q - \mu}{\sigma} \right) - F_s \left(\frac{q - \mu}{\sigma} \right) \right]$$

$$- \sigma \left[f_s \left(\frac{Q - \mu}{\sigma} \right) - f_s \left(\frac{q - \mu}{\sigma} \right) \right]$$

Expected quantity sold by retailer, $D_R = Q[1 - F(Q)]$

$$+ \mu F_s \left(\frac{Q - \mu}{\sigma} \right) - \sigma f_s \left(\frac{q - \mu}{\sigma} \right)$$

Expected overstock at manufacturer $= Q_R - D_R$

Expected retailer profit $= D_R \times p + (Q_R - D_R)s_R - Q_R \times c$

Expected manufacturer profit $= Q_R \times c + (Q - Q_R)s_M - Q \times v$

We illustrate the impact of quantity flexibility on supply chain profits using Example 15-4 (see worksheet *Example 15-4*).

EXAMPLE 15-4 | Impact of Risk Sharing Through Quantity Flexibility

We return to the music store in Example 15-1 with all data as specified. The retailer is charged $5 for each disc and has a retail price of $10. Assume that the supplier agrees to a quantity flexibility contract where the supplier agrees to $\alpha = 0.05$ and $\beta = 0.05$. For this contract, the retailer decides to place an order for 1,017 units. With the quantity flexibility clause, how many discs does the independent retailer expect to purchase? How many discs does the retailer expect to sell? What are the supply chain profits with a quantity flexibility clause?

Analysis:

In this case, we have $v = \$1$, $c = \$5$, $p = \$10$, $s_R = 0$, and $s_M = 0$. With the quantity flexibility clause as specified, and an order for $O = 1,017$ from the retailer, the manufacturer is committed to supplying any quantity between $q = (1 - \beta)O = (1 - 0.05) \times 1017 = 966$ units and $Q = (1 + \alpha)O = (1 + 0.05) \times 1017 = 1,068$ units. We thus obtain

Expected quantity purchased by retailer, $Q_R = 1,015$ units

Expected quantity sold by retailer, $D_R = 911$ units

Expected overstock at retailer $= Q_R - D_R = 1,015 - 911 = 104$ units

Expected retailer profit $= D_R \times p + (Q_R - D_R)s_R - Q_R \times c$

$$= 911 \times 10 + (1015 - 911) \times 0 - 1015 \times 5 = \$4,038$$

Expected manufacturer profit $= Q_R \times c + (Q - Q_R)s_M - Q \times v$

$$= 1015 \times 5 + (1068 - 1015) \times 0 - 1068 \times 1 = \$4,007$$

Given an order of 1,017 discs (which is adjusted between 966 and 1,068 based on actual demand), the total supply chain profit $= 4,038 + 4,007 = \$8,045$.

Observe that risk sharing using a quantity flexibility clause with a flexibility of 5 percent above and below the order quantity increases profits for the retailer as well as the manufacturer (and the supply chain as a whole) compared with Example 15-1, in which there was no risk sharing.

With a quantity flexibility clause, the retailer is able to take advantage of market intelligence so the amount finally purchased by the retailer is more in line with actual demand. The better matching of supply and demand results in higher profits for the retailer. If the supplier has access to some flexible and responsive capacity, it can produce the uncertain part of the order after the retailer order is finalized while producing the base load (q units) using an inexpensive production method. This tailoring of production allows the supplier to reduce overall costs. A quantity flexibility contract is particularly effective if a supplier is selling to multiple retailers with independent demand because it allows uncertainties to be aggregated by the supplier.

In Table 15-8, we show the impact of different quantity flexibility contracts on profitability for the music supply chain when demand is normally distributed, with a mean of $\mu = 1,000$ and a standard deviation of $\sigma = 300$ (see worksheet *Example 15-4* in spreadsheet *Chapter15-examples*). We assume a wholesale price of $c = \$5$ and a retail price of $p - \$10$. All contracts considered are such that $\alpha = \beta$. The results in Table 15-8 are built in two steps. We first fix α and β (say $\alpha = \beta = 0.05$). The next step is to identify the optimal order size for the retailer. This is done using Excel by selecting an order size that maximizes expected retailer profits given α and β. For example, when $\alpha = \beta = 0.05$ and $c = \$5$, retailer profits are maximized for an order size of $O = 1,017$. For this order size, we obtain a supplier commitment to deliver up to $Q = (1 + 0.05) \times 1,017 = 1,068$ and a retailer commitment to buy at least $q = (1 - 0.05) \times 1,017 = 966$ discs. In our analysis, we assume that the supplier produces $Q = 1,068$ discs and sends the precise number (between 966 and 1,068) demanded by the retailer. Such a policy results in retailer profits of $4,038 and supplier profits of $4,006.

From Table 15-8, observe that quantity flexibility contracts allow both the manufacturer and the retailer to increase their profits. Observe that as the manufacturer increases the wholesale price, it is optimal for it to offer greater quantity flexibility to the retailer.

Quantity flexibility contracts are common for components in the electronics and computer industries. In the previous discussion, we considered fairly simple quantity flexibility contracts. Benetton has used sophisticated quantity flexibility contracts with its retailers successfully to increase supply chain profits. We describe such a contract in the context of colored knit garments (see Heskett and Signorelli, 1984).

Benetton retailers were required to place their orders seven months before delivery. Consider a retailer placing an order for 100 sweaters each in red, blue, and yellow. One to three months before delivery, retailers could alter up to 30 percent of the quantity ordered in any color and assign it to another color. The aggregate order, however, could not be adjusted at this stage. Potentially, the retailer could change the order to 70 red, 70 blue, and 160 yellow sweaters. After

TABLE 15-8 Profits at Music Supply Chain Under Different Quantity Flexibility Contracts

α	β	Wholesale Price c	Order Size O	Expected Purchase by Retailer	Expected Sale by Retailer	Expected Profits for Retailer	Expected Profits for Supplier	Expected Supply Chain Profit
0.00	0.00	$5	1,000	1,000	880	$3,803	$4,000	$7,803
0.05	0.05	$5	1,017	1,015	911	$4,038	$4,006	$8,044
0.20	0.20	$5	1,047	1,023	967	$4,558	$3,858	$8,416
0.00	0.00	$6	924	924	838	$2,841	$4,620	$7,461
0.20	0.20	$6	1,000	1,000	955	$3,547	$4,800	$8,347
0.30	0.30	$6	1,021	1,006	979	$3,752	$4,711	$8,463
0.00	0.00	$7	843	843	786	$1,957	$5,056	$7,013
0.20	0.20	$7	947	972	936	$2,560	$5,666	$8,226
0.40	0.40	$7	1,000	1,000	987	$2,873	$5,600	$8,473

the start of the sales season, retailers were allowed to order up to 10 percent of their previous order in any color. Potentially, then, the retailer could order another 30 yellow sweaters. In this quantity flexibility contract, Benetton retailers had a flexibility of up to 10 percent on the aggregate order across all colors and of about 40 percent for individual colors. Retailers could increase the aggregate quantity ordered by up to 10 percent, and the quantity for any individual color could be adjusted by up to 40 percent. This flexibility is consistent with the fact that aggregate forecasts for a retailer are more accurate than forecasts for individual colors. As a result, retailers could better match product availability with demand. The guaranteed portion of the order was manufactured by Benetton using an inexpensive but long-lead-time production process. The flexible part of the order (about 35 percent) was manufactured using postponement. The result was a better matching of supply and demand at lower cost than in the absence of quantity flexibility. The quantity flexibility contract allowed both the retailers and Benetton to increase their profits.

The quantity flexibility contract requires either inventory or excess flexible capacity to be available at the supplier. If the supplier is selling to multiple retailers with independent demand, the aggregation of inventory leads to a smaller surplus inventory (see Chapter 12) with a quantity flexibility contract compared to either a buyback or revenue-sharing contract. Inventories can be further reduced if the supplier has excess flexible capacity. Quantity flexibility contracts are thus preferred for products with high marginal cost or when surplus capacity is available. To be effective, quantity flexibility contracts require the retailer to be good at gathering market intelligence and improving its forecasts closer to the point of sale. The quantity flexibility contract then encourages the retailer to share this information with the supplier in the form of a modified order.

Relative to buyback and revenue-sharing contracts, quantity flexibility contracts have less information distortion. Consider the case with multiple retailers. With a buyback contract, the supply chain must produce based on inflated retailer orders that are placed well before actual demand arises. This leads to surplus inventory being disaggregated at each retailer. With a quantity flexibility contract, retailers specify only the range within which they will purchase, well before actual demand arises. If demand at various retailers is independent, the supplier does not need to plan production to the high end of the order range for each retailer. It can aggregate uncertainty across all retailers and build a lower level of surplus inventory than would be needed if inventory were disaggregated at each retailer. Retailers then order closer to the point of sale, when demand is more visible and less uncertain. The aggregation of uncertainty results in less information distortion with a quantity flexibility contract.

As with the other contracts discussed, quantity flexibility contracts result in lower retailer effort. In fact, any contract that gets retailers to provide a higher level of product availability by not making them fully responsible for overstocking will result in a lowering of retailer effort for a given level of inventory.

Sharing Rewards to Improve Performance

Having discussed the benefits of sharing risk, we now focus on the importance of sharing rewards in a supply chain. In many instances, a buyer wants performance improvement from a supplier that has little incentive to do so. A supplier may be reluctant to invest in improvement if the effort for improvement must be exerted by the supplier but most of the benefits from improvement accrue to the buyer. In such a setting, sharing the benefits from improvement can encourage supplier cooperation, resulting in a better supply chain outcome.

As an example, consider a buyer that wants the supplier to improve performance by reducing lead time for a seasonal item. This is an important component of all quick response initiatives in a supply chain. With a shorter lead time, the buyer hopes to have better forecasts and be better able to match supply and demand. Most of the work to reduce lead time must be done by the supplier, whereas most of the benefit accrues to the buyer in terms of reduced inventories, overstocking, and lost sales. In fact, the supplier will lose sales because the buyer will now carry less safety inventory as a result of shorter lead times and better forecasts. To induce the supplier to reduce lead time, the buyer can use a *shared-savings contract,* with the supplier getting a fraction of the

savings that result from reducing lead time. As long as the supplier's share of the savings compensates for any effort it has to put in, its incentive will be aligned with that of the buyer, resulting in an outcome that benefits both parties.

A similar issue arises when a buyer wants to encourage the supplier to improve quality. Improving supply quality reduces the buyer's costs but requires additional effort from the supplier. Once again, a shared-savings contract is a good way to align incentives between the buyer and supplier. The buyer can share savings from improved quality with the supplier. This will encourage the supplier to improve quality to a higher level than what the supplier would choose in the absence of the shared savings.

Another example arises in the context of toxic chemicals that may be used by a manufacturer. The manufacturer would like to decrease the use of these toxic chemicals. Generally, the supplier is better equipped to identify ways of reducing use of these chemicals, because this is its core business. It has no incentive to work with the buyer on reducing use of these chemicals, however, because that will reduce the supplier's sales. A shared-savings contract can be used to align incentives between the supplier and the manufacturer. If the manufacturer shares the savings that result from a reduction in the use of toxic chemicals with the supplier, the supplier will make the effort to reduce use of the chemicals as long as its share of the savings compensates for the loss in margin from reduced sales.

In general, sharing the savings is effective in aligning supplier and buyer incentives when the supplier is required to improve performance along a particular dimension and most of the benefits of improvement accrue to the buyer. A powerful buyer may couple shared savings with penalties for a lack of improvement to further encourage the supplier to improve performance. Sharing the rewards of improvements increases profits for both the buyer and the supplier while achieving outcomes that are beneficial to the supply chain.

SUMMARY OF LEARNING OBJECTIVE 5

Local optimization hurts the supply chain surplus when risk and reward are not shared in a supply chain. Suppliers are more likely to act in a firm's interest when risk and reward are shared. In the absence of risk sharing, retailers aim for a lower level of product availability than would be required to maximize supply chain profits. The use of buyback or revenue sharing is an effective risk sharing mechanism between suppliers and retailers for products like books with low variable costs. In general, however, quantity flexibility contracts are more effective because they result in a better matching of supply and demand. Sharing the rewards from improvements can induce performance improvement from a supplier along dimensions, such as lead time, for which the benefit of improvement accrues primarily to the buyer but the effort for improvement comes primarily from the supplier.

DISCUSSION QUESTIONS

1. What are some ways in which a firm such as Walmart benefits from good sourcing decisions?
2. What factors led Walmart to own its trucks although many retailers outsource all their transportation?
3. How can a supplier with a lower price end up costing the buyer more than a supplier with a higher price?
4. Explain why, for the same inventory level, a revenue-sharing contract results in a lower sales effort from the retailer than if the retailer has paid for the product and is responsible for all remaining inventory.
5. Discuss the challenges faced by a supply chain that employs a buy back or return clause with its retailers. How can these challenges be overcome?

6. What is the hockey stick phenomenon in relation to the use of incentives to increase supply chain surplus? What steps can be taken to address it?
7. A mobile manufacturer sources both electronic components and soldering irons/solder. What, if any, difference in sourcing strategy would you recommend for the two types of products?
8. What tailored sourcing options are available to a large European clothing retailer who offers fashion items to suit the current season alongside clothing basics that do not change from season to season?
9. Recommend whether an onshore, near-shore, or offshore supplier is the most appropriate for the following products: customized kitchens and standard flat-pack furniture. What factors would influence your recommendations?

EXERCISES

1. A confectioner sells novelty birthday cakes in Marks & Spencer (M&S) at €15 each. The marginal production cost for the confectioner is €2.50 per cake. At M&S, the cakes are priced at €29 and the expected demand over the next two months to be normally distributed, with a mean of 8,000 and a standard deviation of 2,000. M&S places a single order with the confectioner for delivery at the beginning of the two-month period. Currently, M&S discounts any unsold cakes at the end of two months down to €5, and any cakes that did not sell at full price sell at this price.

 a. How many cakes should M&S order? What is its expected profit? How many cakes does it expect to sell at a discount?

 b. What is the profit that the confectioner makes, given M&S's actions?

 c. A plan under discussion is for the confectioner to refund M&S €7 per cake that does not sell during the two-month period. As before, M&S will discount them to €5 and sell any that remain. Under this plan, how many cakes will M&S order? What is the expected profit for M&S? How many cakes are expected to be unsold? What is the expected profit for the confectioner? What should the confectioner do?

2. A movie studio sells the latest movie on DVD to VideosRUs at $10 per DVD. The marginal production cost for the movie studio is $1 per DVD. VideosRUs prices each DVD at $19.99 to its customers. DVDs are kept on the regular rack for a one-month period, after which they are discounted down to $4.99 (a price at which they sell out). VideosRUs places a single order for DVDs. Its current forecast is that sales will be normally distributed, with a mean of 10,000 and a standard deviation of 5,000.

 a. How many DVDs should VideosRUs order? What is its expected profit? How many DVDs does it expect to sell at a discount?

 b. What is the profit that the studio makes given VideosRUs' actions?

 c. A plan under discussion is for the studio to refund VideosRUs $4 per DVD that does not sell during the one-month period. As before, VideosRUs will discount them to $4.99 and sell any that remain. Under this plan, how many DVDs should VideosRUs order? What is the expected profit for VideosRUs? How many DVDs are expected to be unsold at the end of the month? What is the expected profit for the studio? What should the studio do?

3. Topgun Records and several movie studios have decided to sign a revenue-sharing contract for CDs. Each CD costs the studio $2 to produce. The CD will be sold to Topgun for $3. Topgun, in turn, prices a CD at $15 and forecasts demand to be normally distributed, with a mean of 5,000 and a standard deviation of 2,000. Any unsold CDs are discounted to $1, and all sell at this price. Topgun will share 35 percent of the revenue with the studio, keeping 65 percent for itself.

 a. How many CDs should Topgun order?

 b. How many CDs does Topgun expect to sell at a discount?

 c. What is the profit that Topgun expects to make?

 d. What is the profit that the studio expects to make?

 e. Repeat parts (a)–(d) if the studio sells the CD for $2 (instead of $3) but gets 43 percent of revenue.

4. Benetton has entered into a quantity flexibility contract with a retailer for a seasonal product. If the retailer orders O units, Benetton is willing to provide up to another 35 percent if needed. Benetton's production cost is $20, and it charges the retailer a wholesale price of $36. The retailer prices to customers at $55 per unit. Any unsold units can be sold by the retailer at a salvage value of $25. Benetton can salvage only $10 per unit for its leftover inventory. The retailer forecasts demand to be normally distributed, with a mean of 4,000 and a standard deviation of 1,600.

 a. How many units O should the retailer order?

 b. What is the expected quantity purchased by the retailer (recall that the retailer can increase the order by up to 35 percent after observing demand)?

 c. What is the expected quantity sold by the retailer?

 d. What is the expected overstock at the retailer?

 e. What is the expected profit for the retailer?

 f. What is the expected profit for Benetton?

5. Rodgers Electronics and their suppliers have decided to sign a revenue-sharing contract for phone chargers. Each phone charger costs the supplier €3 to produce. The phone charger will be sold to Rodgers Electronics for €5. Rodgers Electronics, in turn, prices a phone charger at €20 and forecasts demand to be normally distributed, with a mean of 8,000 and a standard deviation of 2,500. Any unsold phone chargers are discounted to €2, and all sell at this price. Rodgers Electronics will share 30 percent of the revenue with the supplier, keeping 70 percent for itself.

 a. How many phone chargers should Rodgers Electronics order?

 b. How many phone chargers does Rodgers Electronics expect to sell at a discount?

 c. What is the profit that Rodgers Electronics expects to make?

 d. What is the profit that the supplier expects to make?

 e. Repeat parts (a) to (d) if the studio sells the phone charger for €4 (instead of €4) but gets 40 percent of revenue.

6. As a purchasing manager at a large electric utility, you are faced with two suppliers, Reliable Components and Value Electric, that offer the following terms. Reliable sells the transformer for $5,000 with a minimum order of 100, and a lead time of 1 week with a standard deviation of 0.1 week. Value sells the transformer for $4,800, has a minimum batch of 1,000, a lead time of 5 weeks, and a standard deviation of 4 weeks. Imagine that you have chosen Reliable as your supplier. Value Electric wants your business and offers you the choice of three mutually exclusive alternatives: reduce lead time by 1 week, reduce the minimum batch to 800, or reduce the standard deviation of lead time to 3 weeks.

a. What are the expected annual costs of undertaking each of these options?

b. What is the expected annual cost if all three could be put into effect?

c. Would you change your decision to go with Reliable for any of these options?

7. Consider a manufacturer selling DVDs to a retailer for $6 per DVD. The production cost of each DVD is $1 and the retailer prices each DVD at $10. Retail demand for DVDs is normally distributed, with a mean of 1,000 and standard deviation of 300. The manufacturer has offered the retailer a quantity flexibility contract with $\alpha = \beta = 0.2$. The retailer places an order for 1,000 units. Assume that salvage value is zero for both the retailer and the manufacturer.

a. What is the expected profit for the retailer and manufacturer?

b. How much will profit increase for the retailer if α increases to 0.5?

c. How much will profit increase for the retailer if β increases to 0.5 (keeping α at 0.2)?

8. Imagine that you have acquired both the retailer and manufacturer discussed in Exercise 7. Your interests now are in maximizing profitability for your new firm and in setting up an incentive system to make this happen. You have chosen to keep the quantity flexibility contract in place to provide incentive to both your retailer and your manufacturer.

a. How does increasing α to 0.5 affect your firm's profitability?

b. How does increasing β to 0.5 affect your firm's profitability (keeping α at 0.2)?

c. Why does one of these changes have no effect on profitability?

BIBLIOGRAPHY

Banfield, Emiko. *Harnessing Value in the Supply Chain: Strategic Sourcing in Action.* New York: Wiley, 1999.

Burt, David N., Sheila D. Petcavage, and Richard L. Pinkerton. *Supply Management.* New York: McGraw-Hill/Irwin, 2010.

Billington, Corey, and François Jager. "Procurement: The Missing Link in Innovation." *Supply Chain Management Review* (January–February 2008): 22–28.

Cachon, Gérard P., and Martin A. Lariviere. "Turning the Supply Chain into a Revenue Chain." *Harvard Business Review* (March 2001): 20–21.

Cavinato, Joseph L., and Ralph Kauffman. *The Purchasing Handbook: A Guide for the Purchasing and Supply Professional.* New York: McGraw-Hill, 2000.

Chopra, Sunil, Darren Dougan, and Gareth Taylor. "B2B E-Commerce Opportunities." *Supply Chain Management Review* (May–June 2001): 50–58.

Dekhne, Ashutosh, Xin Huang, and Apratim Sarkar. "Bridging the Procurement–Supply Chain Divide." *Supply Chain Management Review* (September–October 2012): 36–42.

Ellram, Lisa S., and Arnold B. Maltz. "The Use of Total Cost of Ownership Concepts to Model the Outsourcing Decision." *The International Journal of Logistics Management* (1995): 6, 55–66.

Evans, Wayne S., and Sven Blawatt. "The Growth Potential in Managing Supplier Risk." *Supply Chain Management Review* (September–October 2010): 30–35.

Favre, Donavon, and John McCreery. "Coming to Grips with Supplier Risk." *Supply Chain Management Review* (September 2008): 26–32.

Ferreira, John, and Len Prokopets. "Does Offshoring Still Make Sense?" *Supply Chain Management Review* (January–February 2009): 20–27.

Goel, Ajay, Nazgol Moussavi, and Vats N. Srivatsan. "Time to Rethink Offshoring?" *McKinsey on Business Technology* (Winter 2008): 14, 32–35.

Heskett, James L., and Sergio Signorelli. *Benetton (A).* Harvard Business School Case 685014, 1984.

Jacoby, David, and Bruna Figueiredo. "The Art of High-Cost Country Sourcing." *Supply Chain Management Review* (May–June 2008): 32–38.

Laseter, Timothy M. *Balanced Sourcing: Cooperation and Competition in Supplier Relationships.* San Francisco: Jossey-Bass, 1998.

Murphy, Sean. "Will Sourcing Come Closer to Home?" *Supply Chain Management Review* (September 2008): 33–37.

Narayanan, V.G., and Ananth Raman. "Aligning Incentives in Supply Chains." *Harvard Business Review* (2004): 82(11), 94–102.

Noor, JehanZeb, Aurobind Satpathy, Jeff Shulman, and Chris Musso. "The Power of Supplier Collaboration and Rapid Supplier Qualification." *Supply Chain Management Review* (September–October 2013): 40–47.

Pierson, John C. "Johnson Controls' Journey to e-Procurement." *Supply Chain Management Review* (January–February 2002): 56–62.

Sille, Randm and Sriram Narayan. "Bringin' it All Back Home." *Supply Chain Management Review* (July–August 2016): 40–45.

Smeltzer, Larry R., and Joseph R. Carter. "How to Build an e-Procurement Strategy." *Supply Chain Management Review* (March–April 2001): 76–83.

Vitasek, Kate. "McDonald's Secret Sauce for Supply Chain Success." *Supply Chain Management Review* (December 2016): 4–9.

CASE STUDY

Polaris Industries Inc.

In September 2010 Suresh Krishna, vice president of operations and integration at Polaris Industries Inc., a manufacturer of all-terrain vehicles (ATVs), Side-by-Sides, and snowmobiles, sat in his office in Medina, Minnesota, deliberating the recommendation he was developing for a new plant to manufacture the company's Side-by-Side vehicles.

The economic slowdown in the United States had put considerable pressure on Polaris's profits, so the company was considering whether it should follow the lead of several of its competitors and open a facility in a country with lower labor costs. China and Mexico were shortlisted as possible locations for the new factory, which would be the first Polaris manufacturing facility located outside the Midwestern United States. By the end of the year Krishna needed to recommend to CEO Scott Wine and the board of directors whether Polaris should build a new plant abroad or continue to manufacture in its American facilities.

Polaris industries Inc.

Established in 1954, Polaris was a manufacturer of high-performance motorsport products, including ATVs, Side-by-Sides, and snowmobiles. With nearly $2 billion in sales in 2010, it was a strong player in the $10 billion power sports market alongside competitors Yamaha, Honda, Arctic Cat, Ski-Doo, and Harley Davidson.

Polaris's customers were primarily located in North America (85 percent); its international customers were concentrated in Europe. Foreign markets were becoming increasingly important to Polaris; international revenue had grown 21 percent in 2010, and was forecasted to grow even more in 2011. Polaris products were sold through 1,500 distributors in the United States and 1,000 distributors in the rest of the world.

Polaris's heritage was deeply rooted in the power sports industry. The company introduced its first snowmobile in the 1950s and its first ATV in 1985. Between 1985 and 2010 Polaris sold more than two million ATVs. In 1992 Polaris entered the personal watercraft market, but it lacked a sustainable distribution system and exited the business in 2004. In 1998 the company introduced the first Side-by-Side off-road vehicle (ORV), which was expected to surpass ATV sales during 2011. Also in 1998, Polaris entered the parts, accessories, and apparel segment, which grew significantly over the next decade. Finally, Polaris also introduced its first on-road vehicle in 1998—a motorcycle with the brand name "Victory"— to compete with Harley Davidson. Combined, these products were forecasted to bring in $2.2 billion revenue in 2011. Polaris's total revenue grew more than 20 percent in 2010 and was expected to grow 8 to 11 percent in 2011.

Polaris was the dominant player in the ORV market based on market share. In 2010 ORVs accounted for 69 percent of Polaris's sales, with Side-by-Sides comprising the majority of sales in this segment. Looking ahead, the company was excited by the potential growth in emerging markets. From Latin America to Asia, Polaris had begun to invest heavily in marketing to increase awareness of its brand. For example, in China the company placed off-road image advertising in racing and extreme sports enthusiast publications. Similarly, in Latin America Polaris was leveraging its brand in the utility vehicle space to penetrate the substantial agricultural industries.

Manufacturing

In 2010 all of Polaris's manufacturing operations were located in the northern Midwest. In addition to its corporate headquarters in Medina, Minnesota, and product development and innovation center in Wyoming, Minnesota, Polaris operated three manufacturing facilities in Roseau, Minnesota; Osceola, Wisconsin; and Spirit Lake, Iowa. Roseau, the birthplace of the Polaris snowmobile, housed research, development, and manufacturing for the snowmobile, ATV, and Side-by-Side divisions. Roseau also included a small state-of-the-art injection molding plant that produced plastic parts for the Roseau and Spirit Lake factories. As demand grew for ATVs and on-road vehicles, Polaris established an additional manufacturing facility in 1994 at Spirit Lake. This facility produced select ATV, watercraft, and Victory motorcycle models. Osceola was primarily an engine and components supplier for the other two facilities.

All other components were sourced through more than 450 global suppliers. In 2010 Polaris sourced almost 40 percent of its components and materials from outside the United States, up from 30 percent in 2008.

The company was also increasing low-cost country (LCC) sourcing, almost doubling its LCC spend to approximately 24 percent in 2010.

To support its production capabilities in and around the northern United States, Polaris had three warehouse facilities in Minnesota for raw materials, export processing, and distribution. When demand for parts, apparel, and accessories exceeded the company's warehouse capacity in 1997, a new distribution center was opened in Vermillion, South Dakota. In addition to its U.S. locations, Polaris also owned and operated regional sales and distribution centers in Winnipeg, Canada, and in Northern Europe and Australia.

Redesigning the Supply Chain

Krishna had to consider the tradeoff between manufacturing and transportation costs when redesigning the supply chain for Side-by-Side products. On one hand, manufacturing in markets with low labor costs could result in significant savings. Although labor rates in traditional LCCs such as China were rising, U.S.-based labor was still more costly. On the other hand, with oil prices rising steadily, Krishna knew transportation costs would be far lower if he kept production close to customers.

Senior management at Polaris was also concerned about a manufacturing talent gap in the United States. Over the past twenty years, decreased funding for community colleges and trade schools had resulted in technical workers becoming increasingly difficult to find. Moreover, young trade school graduates were less interested in moving to the locations where Polaris operated, which were small towns with only one large employer. By comparison, well-trained technical talent was relatively easy to find in many South American and Asian countries.

Lastly, Polaris expected much of its future sales growth would come from overseas markets, particularly emerging markets. There were multiple ways to enter these markets, including acquisitions and joint ventures, but building a facility in an emerging market could potentially help Polaris capture future demand.

Choosing a Manufacturing Location

Krishna and his team considered several options for optimizing the manufacture of Side-by-Sides and the design of the supply chain. They concluded that the best options were either to continue production in existing American factories or to build a new plant in China or Mexico.

Beyond the specific pluses and minuses of each location, Krishna needed to consider the following in making a final decision:

- The majority of demand for Side-by-Sides was in the southern United States. The states with the highest share of sales volume in 2010 were Texas and California.
- Side-by-Sides were high volume-to-weight/low value-to-weight products, which meant that shipping costs accounted for a large fraction of their retail price.
- Polaris's senior management placed a high value on ease of communication with its manufacturing plants and believed that in-person interaction among managers, design engineers, and production staff was a key driver of the company's long-term product innovation.
- If Polaris moved production of Side-by-Sides abroad, the company planned to lay off sixty workers at its Roseau plant. Each worker would be paid a one-time severance of $20,000.
- Polaris assumed that demand for Side-by-Sides would remain flat for the next five years.

Data on labor costs, production costs, transportation costs, capital expenditures, and exchange rates for each location are included in Tables 15-9 through 15-12.

China

Polaris's senior executives were excited about the low costs in China, but labor costs had been rising in the manufacturing-heavy eastern region; over time the company would likely have to look further inland to find low-cost labor, which would further increase the length and variability of product transportation. Polaris also had concerns about its ability to successfully collaborate with a Chinese factory due to time-zone differences and cultural dissimilarities.

Operating a factory in China would require Polaris to hire sixty new employees on location. It also would result in a one-time charge of $10 million for capital expenditures, equipment moving costs, and startup costs. Polaris would have to pay a 5 percent tariff on all

TABLE 15-9 Labor Cost Assumptions

	Monthly Wages		Annual Wage Growth (%)	
	China (CNY)	Mexico (MXN)	China (CNY)	Mexico (MXN)
1999	649.5	2,392.0		
2000	729.2	2,910.5	12	22
2001	814.5	3,367.6	12	16
2002	916.8	3,537.5	13	5
2003	1,041.3	3,737.7	14	6
2004	1,169.4	3,858.8	12	3
2005	1,313.1	3,983.8	12	3
2006	1,497.2	4,112.9	14	3
2007	1,740.3	4,246.2	16	3
2008	2,016.0	4,383.7	16	3

United States	
Hourly wage	$26/hour
Working months/ year	12

production and transportation costs when importing products into the United States.

Side-by-Sides made in China would be transported to the United States on container vessels, with each container holding twenty-six vehicles. The cost to ship one vehicle to the United States from China was $190 per unit, or $4,940 per container. Although shipping companies claimed the containers would reach the United States in about twenty days, in practice shipping time was highly variable, with a range of nineteen to thirty-three days.

Mexico

Polaris's senior management saw several qualitative advantages to operating a foreign manufacturing facility in Monterrey, Mexico. Monterrey was relatively close to the United States, which would allow for easier in-person collaboration between the manufacturing facility and Polaris's staff. In addition to geographical proximity, managers believed cultural familiarity would make collaborating with a Mexican workforce easy. Lastly, although Polaris believed that long-term sales growth would come from emerging markets in Asia, it also believed that near-term growth would occur in the United States—particularly in the southern United States, an area close to Monterrey.

A factory in Mexico would require hiring sixty new employees, the same as in China. Side-by-Sides would be shipped to the United States by truck in batches of twenty-six units at an average cost of $2.30 per mile per batch. Although trucking companies claimed they could cross the U.S. border and deliver the products in two days, in practice it took between two and seven days.

Capital expenditures, equipment moving costs, and startup costs for a Mexican factory would total $9.5 million. Under the provisions of NAFTA (North American Free Trade Agreement), Polaris would pay no tariffs on imports from Mexico into the United States.

TABLE 15-10 Operating Metrics by Plant Location

	Cost per unit
Production cost	
U.S.	400 USD
Mexico	4,560 MXN
China	1,950 CNY

Capital expenditures, equipment moving costs, and startup costs (thousands of US$)	
U.S.	—
Mexico	9,500
China	10,000

Other	
Annual demand for Side-by-Sides	14,500 units
Tariff for China import	5%

Transportation cost (US$) from China	
Cost per unit	190
Side-by-Side units per container	26

Ground transportation cost (US$)	
Cost per mile	2.30
Side-by-Side units per truck	26

Miles to Distribution Center		
	From Roseau	**From Monterrey**
Tacoma, WA	1,636	2,261
Los Angeles, CA	2,161	1,505
Irving, TX	1,267	437

TABLE 15-11 Demand Assumptions

Distribution Center Location	Annual Demand(units)
Tacoma, WA	3,650
Los Angeles, CA	7,050
Irving, TX	3,800

TABLE 15-12 Exchange Rate History

Year	CNY/USD	MXN/USD
2000	8.28	9.34
2001	8.28	9.66
2002	8.28	10.80
2003	8.28	11.29
2004	9.19	10.90
2005	7.97	10.90
2006	7.61	10.93
2007	6.95	11.16
2008	6.83	13.50
2009	6.77	12.63
2010	6.65	12.40

United States

A third option for Polaris's senior management was to maintain the status quo for production of Side-by-Sides without incurring additional costs. Polaris had traditionally been associated with a strong "Made in America" culture, and management believed that the company's employees and customers were proud that all Polaris products were manufactured in the United States. In addition, the proximity to headquarters and product development facilities enabled managers to collaborate quickly and easily with design engineers and technical staff in the manufacturing plants.

Recommending a Solution

As Krishna reviewed the data for each option, he knew he needed to consider qualitative as well as quantitative factors to find the best solution for Polaris. Should he recommend keeping production in the United States, or should he recommend siting a new plant in either Mexico or China?

Pricing and Revenue Management in a Supply Chain

LEARNING OBJECTIVES

After reading this chapter, you will be able to

16.1 Understand the role of revenue management in a supply chain.

16.2 Identify how differential pricing can help increase profits when serving multiple customer segments.

16.3 Describe how dynamic pricing and overbooking can help increase profits from perishable assets.

16.4 Discuss how peak pricing and off-peak discounts can help increase profits when demand is seasonal.

16.5 Describe how both buyers and sellers can combine long-term contracts and spot purchases to increase profits when demand is uncertain.

16.6 Understand the potential negative consequences of revenue management in practice.

Given that most supply chain assets are fixed but demand fluctuates, the matching of supply and demand is a constant challenge. In this chapter, we discuss how managers may use pricing as a lever to better match supply and demand and grow revenue derived from supply chain assets.

16.1 Understand the role of revenue management in a supply chain.

THE ROLE OF PRICING AND REVENUE MANAGEMENT IN A SUPPLY CHAIN

In Chapter 9, we discussed how short-term price promotions can be an effective tool to more profitably meet seasonal demand. In this chapter, we further build on the idea of using pricing as an important lever to increase supply chain profits by better matching supply and demand,

especially when there are multiple customer types willing to pay different prices (based on attributes such as response time) for an asset. *Revenue management* is the use of pricing to increase the supply chain surplus and profit generated from a limited availability of supply chain assets. Supply chain assets exist in two forms—capacity and inventory. Capacity assets in the supply chain exist for production, transportation, and storage. Inventory assets exist throughout the supply chain and are carried to improve product availability. In the presence of multiple customer types, revenue management aims to grow profits by selling the right asset to the right customer at the right price. Besides varying capacity and inventory, revenue management suggests varying price to grow profits by better matching supply and demand. An excellent discussion of revenue management techniques in theory and practice can be found in Talluri and Van Ryzin (2004) and Phillips (2005).

Consider a trucking company that owns ten trucks. One approach that the firm can take is to set a fixed price for its services and use advertising to spur demand if surplus capacity is available. If demand is higher than anticipated, the trucking company can react by purchasing more trucks. Using revenue management, however, the firm could do much more as long as there are customers whose willingness to pay varies with some dimension of the service, such as response time. One approach is to charge a lower price to customers willing to commit their orders far in advance and a higher price to customers looking for transportation capacity at the last minute. Another approach is to charge a lower price to customers with long-term contracts and a higher price to customers looking to purchase capacity at the last minute. A third approach is to charge a higher price during periods of high demand and lower prices during periods of low demand. Each instance where differential prices are used is likely to result in higher profits than charging a fixed price and adjusting available capacity. The capacity decision cannot easily be reversed but prices can easily be changed. Similarly, an apparel retailer who adjusts prices based on product availability, customer demand, and remaining duration of the sales season will make higher profits than a retailer who fixes price for the entire duration of the sales season.

All these revenue management strategies use differential pricing as a critical lever to maximize earnings. Revenue management may also be defined as the use of differential pricing based on customer segment, time of use, and product or capacity availability to increase supply chain surplus and profits. The impact of revenue management on supply chain performance can be significant. One of the most often cited examples is the successful use of revenue management by American Airlines to counter—and finally defeat—PeopleExpress in the mid-1980s. PeopleExpress started in Newark, New Jersey, and offered fares that were 50 to 80 percent lower than those of other carriers. At first, the other airlines ignored PeopleExpress because they were not interested in the low-fare market segment. By 1983, however, PeopleExpress was flying 40 aircraft and achieving load factors of more than 74 percent. PeopleExpress and other new entrants were making significant inroads into the turf of existing airlines. The existing airlines could not compete by cutting prices to the level of PeopleExpress because they had higher operating costs. American Airlines was the first to come up with an effective countermeasure using revenue management. Rather than lower the price of all its seats, American lowered prices of a portion of the seats to prices at or below those of PeopleExpress. The number of low-price seats was larger on flights that were likely to have empty seats, which would otherwise have produced no revenue. This strategy allowed American to attract customers who valued the low prices without losing revenue from customers who were willing to pay more. Soon, other airlines, such as United, followed suit, attracting many of PeopleExpress's passengers. This was sufficient to drive down load factors for PeopleExpress to below 50 percent, a level at which the airline could not survive. Before the end of 1986, PeopleExpress collapsed.

American Airlines succeeded primarily because it used differential pricing to lower prices for a fraction of the seats and attract passengers who would otherwise have flown PeopleExpress. American did not lower prices for the fraction of seats used by business travelers who were not flying with PeopleExpress. Targeted differential pricing is at the heart of successful revenue management.

Revenue management has a significant impact on supply chain profitability when one or more of the following four conditions exist:

1. The value of the product varies in different market segments.
2. The product is highly perishable or product wastage occurs.
3. Demand has seasonal and other peaks.
4. The product is sold both in bulk and on the spot market.

Airline seats are a good example of a product whose value varies by market segment. A business traveler is willing to pay a higher fare for a flight that matches his or her schedule. In contrast, a leisure traveler will often alter his or her schedule to get a lower fare. An airline that can extract a higher price from the business traveler (by offering an appropriate schedule) compared to the leisure traveler will always do better than an airline that charges the same price to all travelers. Similar ideas can be applied in the context of hotel rooms and car rentals, for which there is a significant difference between the business traveler and the leisure traveler.

Fashion and seasonal apparel are examples of highly perishable products because they lose value over time. Customers typically value high-fashion apparel more at the start of the season because they want to be the first people seen wearing it. By the end of the season, customers are willing to buy the product only if it is deeply discounted. Similarly, production, storage, and transportation capacity loses all value if it is not used at a given time because the lost capacity cannot be recovered. If a truck is not used for a day, its transportation capacity for that day is gone forever without producing revenue. Thus, all capacity is also a highly perishable asset. The goal of revenue management in such a setting is to adjust the price over time to maximize the profit obtained from the available inventory or capacity.

Demand for hotel rooms in many tourist destinations shows a highly seasonal pattern. For example, resorts in Phuket, Thailand, charge a significantly lower rate during the off-season summer months compared with the peak winter months. Such a pricing pattern allows them to attract customers with some time flexibility during the lower-cost summer months, leaving the winter capacity for customers who are willing to pay more to enjoy Phuket in the winter. Some commuter railroads use a similar strategy to deal with the distinct peaks in passenger travel, charging higher fares during peak periods and lower fares for off-peak travel. It is important to keep in mind that differential pricing for peak and off-peak periods increases profits in a manner that is consistent with customer priorities. In the absence of peak pricing, peak periods, being the most desirable, would have excess demand, whereas off-peak periods would have significant idle capacity. With differential pricing, customers who really value the peak period pay the higher price, whereas those that are not time constrained shift to the off-peak period to take advantage of lower prices. The outcome of such a move is a higher supply chain surplus with higher profits for the firm and a utilization of assets by customers that is consistent with their needs.

Every product and every unit of capacity can be sold both in bulk and in the spot market. For example, the owner of a warehouse must decide whether to lease the entire warehouse to customers willing to sign long-term contracts or to save a portion of the warehouse for use in the spot market. The long-term contract is more secure but typically fetches a lower average price than the unpredictable spot market. Revenue management increases profits by finding the right portfolio of long-term and spot-market customers.

Revenue management can be a powerful tool for every owner of assets in a supply chain. Many successful examples of the use of revenue management are from the travel and hospitality industry and include airlines, car rentals, and hotels. American Airlines has stated that revenue management techniques increase its revenues by more than $1 billion each year. Revenue management techniques at Marriott raise annual revenues by more than $100 million. Revenue management can have a similar impact on all stages of a supply chain that satisfy one or more of the four conditions identified earlier.

In the following sections, we discuss various situations in which revenue management is effective and the techniques used in each case.

SUMMARY OF LEARNING OBJECTIVE 1

Revenue management uses differential pricing to better match supply and demand and increase supply chain profits. Traditionally, firms have changed the availability of assets to match supply and demand. Revenue management aims to reduce any supply/demand imbalance by using pricing as a lever. A big advantage of using revenue management is that a change in pricing is much easier to reverse compared with an investment in supply chain assets. When it is used properly, revenue management increases firm profits while leaving service sensitive customers more satisfied through greater asset availability and price sensitive customers more satisfied with lower prices. Revenue management is most effective in a supply chain when the value of the product varies by market segment, the product is highly perishable, product demand is seasonal, or the product is sold both in bulk and on the spot market.

DIFFERENTIAL PRICING FOR MULTIPLE CUSTOMER SEGMENTS

16.2 *Identify how differential pricing can help increase profits when serving multiple customer segments.*

A classic example of a market with multiple customer segments is the airline industry, in which business travelers are willing to pay a higher fare to travel on a specific schedule, whereas leisure travelers are willing to shift their schedules to take advantage of lower fares. Many similar instances arise in a supply chain. Consider ToFrom, a trucking firm that has purchased six trucks, with a total capacity of 6,000 cubic feet, to use for transport between Chicago and St. Louis. The monthly lease charge, driver, and maintenance expense is $1,500 per truck, resulting in a total monthly cost of $9,000. Market research has indicated that the demand curve on this route for trucking capacity is

$$d = 10,000 - 2,000\,p$$

where d is the demand across all segments and p is the transport cost per cubic foot. A price of $2 per cubic foot results in a demand of 6,000 cubic feet (all customers willing to pay $2 or more), revenue of $12,000, and a profit of $3,000, whereas a price of $3.50 per cubic foot results in a demand of 3,000 (only customers willing to pay $3.50 or more), revenue of $10,500, and a profit of $1,500. The real question is whether the 3,000 cubic feet of demand at a price of $3.50 can be separated from the 3,000 additional cubic feet of demand generated at a price of $2 per cubic foot. If ToFrom assumes that all demand comes from a single segment and cannot be separated, the optimal price is $2.50 per cubic foot, resulting in a demand of 5,000 cubic feet and revenue of $12,500, as shown in Figure 16-1.

However, if ToFrom can differentiate the segment that buys 3,000 cubic feet at $3.50 from the segment that buys 3,000 cubic feet only at $2.00, the firm can use revenue management to improve revenues and profits. ToFrom should charge $3.50 for the segment willing to pay that price and $2.00 for the 3,000 cubic feet that sells only at the lower price. The firm thus extracts revenue of $10,500 from the segment willing to pay $3.50 and revenue of $6,000 from the segment willing to pay only $2.00 per cubic foot, for total revenue of $16,500, as shown in Figure 16-2. In the presence of different segments that have different values for trucking capacity, revenue management increases the revenue from $12,500 to $16,500 and results in a significant improvement in profits.

In theory, the concept of differential pricing increases total profits for a firm. Two fundamental issues, however, must be handled in practice. First, how can the firm differentiate between the two segments and structure its pricing to make one segment pay more than the other? Second, how can the firm control demand so the lower-paying segment does not use the entire availability of the asset?

To differentiate between the various segments, the firm must separate the segments along product or service attributes that the segments value differently. For example, business travelers on an airline want to book at the last minute and change their schedules if necessary. Leisure

Figure 16-1 Revenue Generated by ToFrom Pricing for One Segment

travelers, on the other hand, are willing to book far in advance and adjust the duration of their stays. Plans for business travelers are also subject to change. Thus, advance booking and a penalty for changes on the lower fare separate the leisure traveler from the business traveler. For a transportation provider such as ToFrom, the segments can be differentiated based on how far in advance a customer is willing to commit and pay for the transportation capacity. Similar separation can also occur for production- and storage-related assets in a supply chain.

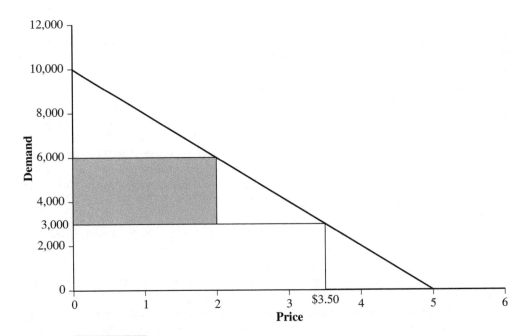

Figure 16-2 Revenue Generated by ToFrom Pricing for Two Segments

Separating segments based on how far in advance an order arrives, typically results in customers seeking lower prices arriving earlier and customers willing to pay higher prices arriving later. For example, leisure travelers are willing to purchase a cheaper ticket far in advance of a flight. Given that future demand of business travelers is uncertain, the airline must decide how much of the available capacity to allocate to leisure travelers and how much to save for business travelers. As a result, a firm using revenue management across multiple segments must solve the following two problems:

1. What price should it charge for each segment?
2. How should it allocate limited capacity among the segments?

Pricing to Multiple Segments

Let us start by considering the simple scenario in which the firm has identified criteria on which it can separate the various customer segments. One such criterion may be an airline requiring a Saturday night stayover. Another might be a trucking company separating customers based on the advance notice with which they are willing to commit to a shipment. The firm now wishes to identify the appropriate price for each segment. Consider a supplier (of product or some other supply chain function) that has identified k distinct customer segments that can be separated. Assume that the demand curve for segment i is given by (we assume linear demand curves to simplify the analysis)

$$d_i = A_i - B_i p_i$$

The supplier has a cost c of production per unit and must decide on the price p_i to charge each segment; d_i is the resulting demand from segment i. The goal of the supplier is to price so as to maximize its profits. The pricing problem can be formulated as follows:

$$\text{Max} \sum_{i=1}^{k} (p_i - c)(A_i - B_i p_i)$$

Without a capacity constraint, the problem separates by segment, and for segment i, the supplier attempts to maximize

$$(p_i - c)(A_i - B_i p_i)$$

The optimal price for each segment i is given by

$$p_i = \frac{A_i}{2B_i} + \frac{c}{2} \qquad \textbf{(16.1)}$$

If the available capacity is constrained by Q, the optimal prices are obtained by solving

$$\text{Max} \sum_{i=1}^{k} (p_i - c)(A_i - B_i p_i) \qquad \textbf{(16.2)}$$

subject to

$$\sum_{i=1}^{k} (A_i - B_i p_i) \leq Q$$

$$A_i - B_i p_i \geq 0 \quad \text{for} \quad i = 1, \ldots, k$$

Both formulations are simple enough to be solved in Excel. Example 16-1 illustrates the benefit of differential prices to multiple segments (see worksheet *Example 16-1* in workbook *Chapter 16-examples*).

EXAMPLE 16-1	**Pricing to Multiple Segments**

A contract manufacturer has identified two customer segments for its production capacity—one willing to place an order more than one week in advance and the other willing to pay a higher price as long as it can provide less than one week's notice for production. The customers that are unwilling to commit in advance are less price sensitive and have a demand curve $d_1 = 5,000 - 20\,p_1$. Customers willing to commit in advance are more price sensitive and have a demand curve of $d_2 = 5,000 - 40\,p_2$. Production cost is $c = \$10$ per unit. What price should the contract manufacturer charge each segment if its goal is to maximize profits? If the contract manufacturer were to charge a single price over both segments, what should it be? How much increase in profits does differential pricing provide? If total production capacity is limited to 4,000 units, what should the contract manufacturer charge each segment?

Analysis:

Without capacity constraints, the differential prices to be charged each segment are given by Equation 16.1. We thus obtain

$$p_1 = \frac{5,000}{2 \times 20} + \frac{10}{2} = 125 + 5 = \$130 \quad \text{and} \quad p_2 = \frac{5,000}{2 \times 40} + \frac{10}{2} = 62.50 + 5 = \$67.50$$

The demand from the two segments is given by

$$d_1 = 5,000 - (20 \times 130) = 2,400 \quad \text{and} \quad d_2 = 5,000 - (40 \times 67.5) = 2,300$$

The total profit is

$$\text{Total profit} = (130 \times 2,400) + (67.5 \times 2,300) - (10 \times 4,700) = \$420,250$$

If the contract manufacturer charges the same price p to both segments, it is attempting to maximize

$$(p - 10)(5,000 - 20\,p) + (p - 10)(5,000 - 40\,p) = (p - 10)(10,000 - 60\,p)$$

The optimal price in this case is given by

$$p = \frac{10,000}{2 \times 60} + \frac{10}{2} = \$88.33$$

The demand from the two segments is given by

$$d_1 = 5,000 - 20 \times 88.33 = 3,233.40 \quad \text{and} \quad d_2 = 5,000 - 40 \times 88.33 = 1,466.80$$

The total profit is

$$\text{Total profit} = (88.33 - 10) \times (3,233.40 + 1,466.80) = \$368,167$$

Differential pricing thus raises the profits by more than \$50,000 relative to offering a fixed price. Observe that differential pricing charges the more price sensitive segment less than the fixed price and the less price sensitive segment more than the fixed price.

Now, let us consider the case in which total production capacity is limited to 4,000 units. The optimal differential price results in demand that exceeds total production capacity. Thus, we resort to the formulation in Equation 16.2 and solve

$$\text{Max}(p_1 - 10)(5,000 - 20\,p_1) + (p_2 - 10)(5,000 - 40\,p_2)$$

Subject to

$$(5,000 - 20\,p_1) + (5,000 - 40\,p_2) \leq 4,000$$
$$(5,000 - 20\,p_1),\ (5,000 - 40\,p_2) \geq 0$$

	A	B	C	D
3	Production Capacity =	4000		
4	Segment	Price	Demand	Profit
5	1	$ 141.7	2166.67	$ 285,277.8
6	2	$ 79.2	1833.33	$ 126,805.6
7	Total		4000	$ 412,083.3

Cell	Cell Formula	Copied to
C5	= 5000 – 20*B5	
C6	= 5000 – 40*B6	
D5	= (B5 – 10)*C5	D6
C7	= sum(C5:C6)	
D7	= sum(D5:D6)	

Figure 16-3 Solver Spreadsheet for Example 16-1

The results of the constrained optimization (using Solver in worksheet *Example 16-1*) are shown in Figure 16-3. The contract manufacturer charges the two segments $141.7 and $79.2 per unit of capacity respectively. Observe that the limited capacity leads the contract manufacturer to charge a higher price to each of the two segments relative to when there was no capacity limit.

The methodology we have described has two important assumptions that are unlikely to hold in practice. The first assumption is that no one from the higher-price segment decides to shift to the lower-price segment after prices are announced. In other words, we have assumed that the attribute such as lead time used to separate the segments works perfectly. In practice, this is unlikely to be the case. Our second assumption is that once prices are decided, customer demand is predictable. In practice, future demand is always uncertain. Talluri and Van Ryzin (2004) and Phillips (2005) have an excellent discussion of several models for revenue management that account for uncertainty and a few models that account for customers being strategic and deciding on their actions after prices are announced.

Allocating Capacity to Segments Under Uncertainty

In most instances of differential pricing, demand from the segment paying the lower price arises earlier in time than demand from the segment paying the higher price. It is also often the case that there is enough demand from the lower-price segment to use up the entire available capacity. For example, leisure travelers tend to book their tickets earlier than business travelers and most airlines could fill a plane at discount prices targeting leisure travelers. It is thus important that suppliers limit the amount of capacity committed to lower-price buyers even if sufficient demand exists from the lower-price segment to use the entire available capacity. This raises the question of how much capacity to save for the higher-price segment, which typically arrives later. The answer would be simple if demand were predictable. In practice, demand is uncertain and firms must make this decision taking uncertainty into account.

The basic trade-off to be considered by a supplier with limited production capacity is between committing to a current order from a lower-price buyer or waiting for a higher-price buyer to arrive later on. The two risks in such a situation are spoilage and spill. *Spoilage* occurs when the capacity reserved for higher-price buyers is wasted because sufficient demand from the higher-price segment does not materialize. *Spill* occurs if higher-price buyers must be turned away because the capacity has already been committed to lower-price buyers. The supplier

should decide on the capacity to commit for the higher-price buyers to minimize the expected cost of spoilage and spill. A current order from a lower-price buyer should be compared with the expected revenue from waiting for a higher-price buyer. The order from the lower-price buyer should be accepted if the expected revenue from the higher-price buyer is lower than the current revenue from the lower-price buyer.

We now develop this trade-off in terms of a formula that can be used when the supplier is working with two customer segments. Let p_L be the price charged to the lower-price segment and p_H be the price charged to the higher-price segment with uncertain demand. Assume that the anticipated demand for the higher-price segment is normally distributed, with a mean of D_H and a standard deviation of σ_H. If we reserve a capacity C_H for the higher-price segment, the expected marginal revenue $R_H(C_H)$ from reserving more capacity is given by

$$R_H(C_H) = \text{Prob (demand from higher-price segment} > C_H) \times p_H$$

The reserved quantity for the higher-price segment should be chosen so the expected marginal revenue from the higher-price segment equals the current marginal revenue from the lower-price segment; that is, $R_H(C_H) = p_L$. In other words, the quantity C_H reserved for the higher-price segment should be such that

$$\text{Prob (demand from higher-price segment} > C_H) = p_L/p_H \qquad \textbf{(16.3)}$$

If demand for the higher-price segment is normally distributed, with a mean of D_H and a standard deviation of σ_H, we can obtain the quantity reserved for the higher-price segment as

$$C_H = F^{-1}(1 - p_L/p_H, D_H, \sigma_H) = NORMINV(1 - p_L/p_H, D_H, \sigma_H) \qquad \textbf{(16.4)}$$

If there are more than two customer segments, the same philosophy can be used to obtain a set of nested reservations. The quantity C_1 reserved for the highest-price segment should be such that the expected marginal revenue from the highest-priced segment equals the price of the next-highest-priced segment. The quantity C_2 reserved for the two highest-priced segments should be such that the expected marginal revenue from the two highest-priced segments equals the price of the third-highest-priced segment. This sequential approach can be used to obtain a set of nested reservations of capacity for all but the lowest-priced segment.

An important point to observe is that the use of differential pricing increases the level of asset availability for the high-priced segment. Capacity is being saved for these customers who will arrive later because of their willingness to pay more for the asset. Thus, effective use of revenue management increases firm profits and improves service for the more valuable customer segment while providing low prices to a limited number of customers in the price sensitive segment. Example 16-2 illustrates how profits can be increased by reserving capacity for the higher paying segment when demand is uncertain (see worksheet *Example 16-2*).

EXAMPLE 16-2 **Allocating Capacity to Uncertain Demand from Multiple Segments**

ToFrom Trucking serves two segments of customers. One segment (A) is willing to pay $3.50 per cubic foot but wants to commit to a shipment with only 24 hours' notice. The other segment (B) is willing to pay only $2.00 per cubic foot and is willing to commit to a shipment with up to one week's notice. With two weeks to go, demand for segment A is forecast to be normally distributed, with a mean of 3,000 cubic feet and a standard deviation of 1,000. How much of the available capacity should be reserved for segment A? How should ToFrom change its decision if segment A is willing to pay $5 per cubic foot?

Analysis:

In this case we have

Revenue from egment A, p_A = \$3.50 per cubic foot

Revenue from segment B, p_B = \$2.00 per cubic foot

Mean demand for segment A, D_A = 3,000 cubic feet

Standard deviation of demand for segment A, σ_A = 1,000 cubic feet

Using Equation 16.4, the capacity to be reserved for segment A is given by

$$C_A = NORMINV(1 - p_B/p_A, D_A, \sigma_A) = NORMINV(1 - 2.00/3.50, 3,000, 1,000)$$
$$= 2,820 \text{ cubic feet}$$

Thus, ToFrom should reserve 2,820 cubic feet of truck capacity for segment A when customers from this segment are willing to pay \$3.50 per cubic foot. If the amount these customers are willing to pay increases from \$3.50 to \$5.00, the reserved capacity should be increased to

$$C_A = NORMINV(1 - p_B/p_A, D_A, \sigma_A) = NORMINV(1 - 2.00/5.00, 3,000, 1,000)$$
$$= 3,253 \text{ cubic feet}$$

Ideally, the demand forecast for all customer segments should be revised and a new reservation quantity calculated each time a customer order is processed. In practice, such a procedure is difficult to implement. It is more practical to revise the forecast and the reservation quantity after a period of time over which either the forecast demand or the forecast accuracy has changed by a significant amount.

Another approach to differential pricing is to create different versions of a product targeted at different segments. Publishers introduce new books from best-selling authors as hardcover editions and charge a higher price. The same books are introduced later as paperback editions at a lower price. The two versions are used to charge a higher price to the segment that wants to read the book as soon as it is introduced while providing a low priced alternative later to customers who are price sensitive. Different versions can also be created by bundling different options and services with the same basic product. Automobile manufacturers create high-end, mid-level, and low-end versions of the most popular models based on the options provided. This policy allows them to charge differential prices to different segments for the same core product. Many contact lens manufacturers sell the same lens with a one-week, one-month, and six-month warranty. In this instance, the same product with different services in the form of warranty is used to charge differential prices.

To use differential pricing successfully when serving multiple customer segments, a firm must use the following tactics effectively:

- Separate segments effectively on some service dimension (e.g. response time)
- Charge different prices based on the value assigned by each segment
- Forecast demand at the segment level
- Save appropriate amount of the asset for the late arriving high price segments

Freight railroads and trucking firms have not used revenue management with multiple segments effectively. Airlines, in contrast, have been much more effective in using this approach. A major hindrance for railroads is the lack of scheduled freight trains. Without scheduled trains, it is hard to separate the higher-price and lower-price segments. To take advantage of revenue management opportunities, owners of transportation assets in the supply chain must offer some scheduled services as a mechanism for separating the higher-price and lower-price segments. Without scheduled services, it is difficult to separate customers that are willing to commit early from those that want to use the service at the last minute.

SUMMARY OF LEARNING OBJECTIVE 2

If a supplier serves multiple customer segments with a fixed asset, it can improve revenues by setting different prices for each segment. Compared to charging a single fixed price to all customers, differential pricing charges the less price sensitive segment a higher price and the more price sensitive segment a lower price. Segments are typically separated along a dimension such as lead time so that the segment willing to pay more must pay a higher price to take advantage of shorter lead times. Given that demand is uncertain, the amount of the asset reserved for the higher-price segment is such that the expected marginal revenue from the higher-price segment equals the price to the lower-price segment.

16.3 *Describe how dynamic pricing and overbooking can help increase profits from perishable assets.*

DYNAMIC PRICING AND OVERBOOKING FOR PERISHABLE ASSETS

Any asset that loses value over time is perishable. Clearly, fruits, vegetables, and pharmaceuticals are perishable, but this list also includes products such as computers and cell phones that lose value as new models are introduced. High-fashion apparel is perishable because it cannot be sold at full price once the season is past. Perishable assets also include all forms of production, transportation, and storage capacity that are wasted if not fully utilized. Unused capacity from the past has no value. Thus, all unused capacity is equivalent to perished capacity. For example, unused capacity of a truck is perishable and cannot be saved for another day.

A well-known example of revenue management in retailing of apparel was the original Filene's Basement in Boston. Merchandise was first sold at the main store at full price. Leftover merchandise was moved to the basement and its price reduced incrementally over a 35-day period until it sold. Any unsold merchandise was then given away to charity. Today, most department stores progressively discount merchandise over the sales season and then sell any remaining inventory to an outlet store, which follows a similar pricing strategy.

Another example of revenue management for a perishable asset is the use of overbooking by the airline industry. An airplane seat loses all value once the plane takes off. Given that people often do not show up for a flight even when they have a reservation, airlines sell more reservations than the capacity of the plane, to maximize expected revenue.

The following are two revenue management tactics used for perishable assets:

1. Vary price dynamically over time to maximize expected revenue.
2. Overbook sales of the asset to account for cancellations.

Dynamic Pricing

Dynamic pricing, the tactic of varying price over time, is suitable for assets such as fashion apparel that have a clear date beyond which they lose much of their value. The success of dynamic pricing also requires the presence of different customer segments, with some willing to pay a higher price for the product. Apparel designed for the winter does not have much value by April. A retailer that has purchased 100 ski jackets in October has many options with regard to its pricing strategy. It can charge a high price initially. This strategy will attract only customers with a high willingness to pay and will result in fewer sales early in the season (though at a higher price), leaving more jackets to be sold later during the season. A discount later in the season can then attract customers who have a lower value for the product. Another option is to charge a lower price initially, selling more jackets early in the season (though at a lower price) and leaving fewer jackets to be sold at a discount. This trade-off determines the profits for the retailer. To vary price effectively over time for a perishable asset, the asset owner must be able to estimate the value of the asset over time and forecast the impact of price on customer demand effectively.

Effective differential pricing over time generally increases the level of product availability for the consumer willing to pay full price and also increases total profits for the retailer.

We now discuss a simple methodology for dynamic pricing when the seller has a specified quantity Q of a single product at the start of the season. We assume that the seller is able to divide the selling season into k periods and can forecast the demand curve for each period. The underlying assumptions here are that customers' responses to pricing can be predicted over time and customers will not change their behavior in response to anticipated price changes. For simplicity, we assume that given a price p_i in period i, the demand d_i in period i is given by

$$d_i = A_i - B_i p_i$$

This is a linear demand curve, but in general the demand curve need not be linear. We present the linear case here because it is easier to understand and solve. The assumption is that customers that purchase in the initial periods are less price sensitive, whereas those that wait to purchase later are more price sensitive. The retailer wants to vary the price over time to maximize the revenue it can extract from the Q units it has on hand at the beginning of the season. The dynamic pricing problem faced by the retailer can then be formulated as follows:

$$\text{Max} \sum_{i=1}^{k} p_i(A_i - B_i p_i) \tag{16.5}$$

subject to

$$\sum_{i=1}^{k} (A_i - B_i p_i) \leq Q$$

$$A_i - B_i p_i \geq 0 \quad \text{for} \quad i = 1, \ldots, k$$

As formulated, the dynamic pricing problem is simple enough that it can be solved directly using Excel as illustrated in Example 16-3 [see worksheets *Example 16-3 (dynamic price)* and *Example 16-3 (fixed price)*].

EXAMPLE 16-3 **Dynamic Pricing**

A retailer has purchased 400 ski parkas before the start of the winter season at a cost of $100 each (for a total cost of $40,000). The season lasts three months, and the retailer has forecast demand in each of the three months to be $d_1 = 300 - p_1$, $d_2 = 300 - 1.3 p_2$, and $d_3 = 300 - 1.8 p_3$. How should the retailer vary the price of the parka over the three months to maximize revenue? If the retailer charges a constant price over the three months, what should it be? How much gain in profit results from dynamic pricing?

Analysis:

Observe that customers who buy at the beginning of the season are less price sensitive and customers who buy toward the end of the season are more price sensitive. Using Equation 16.5, the retailer's problem can be formulated as follows:

$$\text{Max } p_1 (300 - p_1) + p_2(300 - 1.3 p_2) + p_3(300 - 1.8 p_3)$$

subject to

$$(300 - p_1) + (300 - 1.3 p_2) + (300 - 1.8 p_3) \leq 400$$

$$300 - p_1, 300 - 1.3 p_2, 300 - 1.8 p_3 \geq 0$$

This problem can be formulated using Solver in Excel, as shown in Figure 16-4 [see worksheet *Example 16-3 (dynamic price)*]. Cells B5:B7 contain the price variables, cells C5:C7 con-

	A	B	C	D
3	Quantity at beginning of season =	400		
4		Period Price	Demand	Revenue
5		1 $ 162.20	137.80	$ 22,351.28
6		2 $ 127.58	134.15	$ 17,114.36
7		3 $ 95.53	128.05	$ 12,232.30
8	Total		400	$ 51,697.94

Cell	Cell Formula	Copied to
C5	= 300 − B5	
C6	= 300 − 1.3*B6	
C7	= 300 − 1.8*B7	
D5	= B5*C5	D6:D7
C8	= sum(C5:C7)	
D8	= sum(D5:D7)	

Figure 16-4 Solver Spreadsheet for Example 16-3 for Dynamic Pricing

	A	B	C	D
3	Quantity at beginning of season =	400		
4		Period Price	Demand	Revenue
5		1 $ 121.95	178.05	$ 21,713.27
6		2 $ 121.95	141.46	$ 17,251.64
7		3 $ 121.95	80.49	$ 9,815.59
8	Total		400	$ 48,780.49

Cell	Cell Formula	Copied to
B6	= B5	B7

Figure 16-5 Solver Spreadsheet for Example 16-3 for Fixed Price over Season

tain the resulting demand from the respective demand curves, and cells D5:D7 contain the revenue in each period. The total demand across the three periods is in cell C8 and the total revenue is in cell D8. The quantity at the beginning of the season is in cell B3.

As shown in Figure 16-4, the optimal strategy for the retailer is to price at $162.20 in the first month, $127.58 in the second month, and $95.53 in the third month. This gives total revenue of $51,697.94 and profit of $11,697.94 for the retailer.

The problem of obtaining the optimal fixed price over the three-month season can be formulated in Excel as shown in Figure 16-5 [see worksheet *Example 16-3 (fixed price)*]. All cell formulas except B6 and B7 are as in Figure 16-4.

If the retailer wants to have a fixed price over the three months, it should price the jackets at $121.95 for resulting revenue of $48,780.49 and profit of $8,780.49. We can see that dynamic pricing allows the retailer to increase profits by almost $3,000, from $8,780 to $11,698.

Once we have understood how to price the product dynamically over the season, we can go back and ask how many units the retailer should purchase at the beginning of the season to maximize profits, as described in Example 16-4 (see worksheet *Example 16-4*).

EXAMPLE 16-4	**Evaluating Initial Quantity with Dynamic Pricing**

Return to the retailer in Example 16-3. Assume demand curves as described in Example 16-3. How many parkas should the retailer purchase at the beginning of the season, and how should they be priced over the three months of the season to maximize profits?

Analysis:

In this case, the quantity at the beginning of the season is also a decision variable. The retailer's problem can now be formulated as follows:

$$\text{Max } p_1 (300 - p_1) + p_2 (300 - 1.3 p_2) + p_3 (300 - 1.8 p_3) - 100Q$$

subject to

$$(300 - p_1) + (300 - 1.3 p_2) + (300 - 1.8 p_3) \leq Q$$
$$300 - p_1, 300 - 1.3 p_2, 300 - 1.8 p_3, Q \geq 0$$

The problem can be formulated in Excel as shown in Figure 16-6 (see worksheet *Example 16-4*) to obtain the optimal initial quantity and dynamic prices over the season. All cell formulas except cell D9 are as in Figure 16-4.

It is optimal for the retailer to order 245 jackets at the beginning of the season. They are then priced at $200 for the first month, $165.38 for the second month, and $133.33 for the third month. The total profit for the retailer with the optimal order quantity and dynamic pricing is $17,557.69. Observe that this is higher than the profit obtained in Example 16-4 when the retailer started the season with 400 parkas.

Although dynamic pricing can seem very profitable as long as customers do not anticipate price decreases and delay their purchases, the situation is more challenging when customers choose to behave strategically and delay their purchases to wait for a lower price.

THE CHALLENGE OF STRATEGIC CUSTOMERS In reality, the dynamic pricing problem is more complicated because demand is unpredictable and customers behave strategically in that they may decide to delay their purchases if they know that prices will drop over time. An excellent discussion of models that can be used in this more complex setting can be found in Talluri and Van Ryzin (2004).

	A	B	C	D
2	Cost per unit =	$ 100.00		
3	Quantity at beginning of season =	245		
4	Period	Price	Demand	Revenue
5	1	$ 200.00	100.00	$ 20,000.00
6	2	$ 165.38	85.00	$ 14,057.70
7	3	$ 133.33	60.00	$ 8,000.01
8	Total		245.0002	$ 42,057.71
9			Profit =	$ 17,557.69

Cell	Cell Formula	Copied to
D9	= D8-B2*B3	

Figure 16-6 Solver Spreadsheet for Example 16-4 for Optimal Quantity and Dynamic Prices

The issue of unpredictable demand and strategic customers is illustrated effectively in decisions made by the high-end retailer Saks Fifth Avenue in November 2008. In 2007, luxury goods from brands such as Prada, Gucci, and Dolce & Gabbana had become especially important for high-end retailers such as Saks, which maintained strong sales into mid-2008 even though retail sales overall were starting to drop by then. As a result, Saks placed its orders for the holiday season of 2008 anticipating strong sales of these brands. By November, however, a huge disconnect existed between inventories at Saks and customer demand. At Saks's annual "private sale nights" for top customers, the usual 40 percent discounts got no response. By mid-November, competitors such as Neiman Marcus had also dropped prices by 40 percent and some designers were offering 90 percent discounts in "sample sales." The more prices dropped, the more customers decided to delay their purchases in anticipation of even lower prices. As Thanksgiving approached, Saks decided to offer 70 percent discounts to move its inventory.

When there is a lot of inventory at a retailer, it is reasonable to expect that some customers will be strategic and delay their purchase in anticipation of a lower price in the future. Ignoring this strategic behavior by customers can significantly reduce the benefits of dynamic pricing for retailers. Consider, for example, the retailer in Example 16-4 that starts the season with 245 units, as suggested by the results of Example 16-4. When customers are not strategic, the retailer expects to sell 100 units at $200 each in the first month, 85 units at $165.38 each in the second month, and the remaining 60 units at $133.33 each in the third month, for total sales of $42,057.71 and a profit of $17,557.08 (given a unit cost of $100).

Now consider the case of strategic customers detailed in the worksheet *Example 16-4 (strategic)*. Assume that strategic customers delay their purchase and decide to wait until the third month when they anticipate a significant price drop. As a result, the retailer sells only 80 units in the first month and 50 in the second month and is left with 115 units to be sold in the third month. To sell all 115 units, the retailer is forced to drop price in the third month to $(300 - 115)/1.8 = \$102.78$. The total profit in this case drops to $11,588.43. As the number of strategic customers who delay purchases until the third month increases, the retailer experiences a greater drop in profits because fewer units sell at higher prices. Clearly, the retailer pays a price for ignoring strategic customers.

In the presence of strategic customers (115 units left over for the third month), the retailer is better off buying 245 units and charging a fixed price of $159.76 for the entire season [see worksheet *Example 16-4 (fixed price)*]. The fixed price eliminates any gains for a customer from strategic behavior. At this price, the customers buying in the first month purchase about 140 units, the customers buying in the second month purchase about 92 units, and only about 13 units are left to be sold in the third month. The retailer makes a total profit of $14,640 with a fixed price. Although this is lower than what the retailer would achieve with dynamic pricing if customers were not strategic, it is higher than potential profits with strategic customers. A credible fixed price can be an effective response to strategic customers. Tiffany is an example of a company that maintains this policy of a fixed price. Another approach is to reduce the quantity offered at the beginning of the season so customers are reluctant to take the risk of waiting for a late-season discount in case the entire quantity is sold out at full price. Zara uses this approach to get its customers to buy products when they see them on the shelf.

Overbooking in the Presence of Cancellation

Overbooking occurs when a seller with limited capacity sells more units than it has. Airlines often overbook to ensure that planes do not leave with empty seats. When orders for a perishable asset can be canceled, the tactic of overbooking or overselling of the available asset can be used to increase profits. Examples of such assets include airline seats and production capacity. In each case, a limited amount of the asset is available, customers are allowed to cancel orders, and the asset loses value beyond a certain date.

If the cancellation rate can be predicted accurately, the overbooking level is easy to determine. In practice, however, the cancellation rate is uncertain and can result in the available capacity

or inventory being either higher or lower than final demand. The basic trade-off to consider during overbooking is between having wasted capacity (or inventory) because of excessive cancellations or having a shortage of capacity (or inventory) because of few cancellations, in which case an expensive backup needs to be arranged to satisfy demand. The cost of wasted capacity is the margin that would have been generated if the capacity had been used to satisfy demand. The cost of a capacity shortage is the loss per unit that results from having to go to a backup source. The goal when making the overbooking decision is to maximize supply chain profits by minimizing the cost of wasted capacity and the cost of capacity shortage.

We now develop this trade-off in terms of a formula that can be used to set overbooking levels for an asset if the distribution of cancellations is known. Let p be the price at which each unit of the asset is sold, and let c be the cost of using or producing each unit of the asset. In case of asset shortage, let b be the cost per unit at which a backup can be used. Thus, the marginal cost of having wasted capacity is $C_w = p - c$, and the marginal cost of having a capacity shortage is $C_s = b - p$. If the cost of backup capacity is less than the sale price, there is no reason to limit the overbooking. The interesting case arises when the cost of backup capacity exceeds the sale price. The trade-off to obtain the optimal overbooking level is similar to the trade-off given by Equation 13.1 to obtain the optimal cycle service level for seasonal items. Let $O*$ be the optimal overbooking level, and let $s*$ be the probability that cancellations will be less than or equal to $O*$. Similar to the derivation of Equation 13.1, the optimal overbooking level is obtained as

$$s^* = \text{Prob(cancellations} \leq O^*) = \frac{C_w}{C_w + C_s} \qquad (16.6)$$

If the distribution of cancellations is known in absolute terms to be normally distributed, with a mean of μ_c and a standard deviation of σ_c, the optimal overbooking level is evaluated as

$$O^* = F^{-1}(s^*, \mu_c, \sigma_c) = NORMINV(s^*, \mu_c, \sigma_c) \qquad (16.7)$$

If the cancellation distribution is known only as a function of the booking level (capacity L + overbooking O) to have a mean of $\mu(L + O)$ and a standard deviation of $\sigma(L + O)$, the optimal overbooking level is obtained as a solution to the following equation:

$$O = F^{-1}[s^*, \mu(L + O), \sigma(L + O)] = NORMINV[s^*, \mu(L + O), \sigma(L + O)] \qquad (16.8)$$

Observe that the optimal level of overbooking should increase as the margin per unit increases, and the level of overbooking should decrease as the cost of replacement capacity goes up. Also observe that the use of overbooking increases asset utilization by customers. The use of overbooking decreases the number of customers that are turned away and thus improves asset availability to the customer, while improving profits for the asset owner by decreasing the wasted capacity. The evaluation of overbooking is illustrated in Example 16-5 (see worksheet *Example 16-5*).

EXAMPLE 16-5 Overbooking

Consider an apparel supplier that is taking orders for dresses with a Christmas motif. The production capacity available from the supplier is 5,000 dresses, and it makes a margin of $10 for each dress sold. The supplier is currently taking orders from retailers and must decide on how many orders to commit to at this time. At the time of delivery, if the supplier has orders that exceed capacity, it must arrange for backup capacity that results in a loss of $5 per dress.

Retailers have been known to cancel their orders near the winter season as they have better visibility into expected demand. How many orders should the supplier accept if cancellations are normally distributed, with a mean of 800 and a standard deviation of 400? How many orders should the supplier accept if cancellations are normally distributed, with a mean of 15 percent of the orders accepted and a coefficient of variation of 0.5?

Analysis:

The supplier has the following parameters:

$$\text{Cost of wasted capacity, } C_w = \$10 \text{ per dress}$$
$$\text{Cost of capacity shortage, } C_s = \$5 \text{ per dress}$$

Using Equation 16.6, we thus obtain

$$s^* = \frac{C_w}{C_w + C_s} = \frac{10}{10 + 5} = 0.667$$

If cancellations are normally distributed, with a mean of 800 and a standard deviation of 400, the optimal overbooking level is obtained using Equation 16.7 as

$$O^* = NORMINV(s^*, \mu_c, \sigma_c) = NORMINV(0.667, 800, 400) = 972$$

In this case, the supplier should overbook by 972 dresses and take orders for a total of 5,972 dresses.

If cancellations are normally distributed with a mean of 15 percent of the booking level and a coefficient of variation of 0.5, the optimal overbooking level is obtained using Equation 16.8 to be the solution of the following equation:

$$O = NORMINV[0.667, 0.15(5000 + O), 0.075(5000 + O)]$$

This equation can be solved using Excel (see worksheet *Example 16-5*) to obtain the optimal overbooking level:

$$O^* = 1,115$$

In this case, the supplier should overbook by 1,115 dresses and take an order for up to 6,115 dresses.

Overbooking has been used as a tactic in the airline, passenger rail, and hotel industries. It has not, however, been used to the extent that it should be in many supply chain scenarios, including production, warehousing, and transportation capacity. This has been so because of the absence of suitable backup sources. There is no reason that a third-party warehouse that rents to multiple customers should not sell total space that exceeds the available space. A backup will clearly be needed if all customers use warehouse space to capacity. In all other cases, the available warehouse capacity will cover the need for space. Overbooking in this case will improve revenues for the warehouse while allowing more customers to use the available warehouse space. Overselling by the warehouse, however, is only feasible if backup storage space can quickly be arranged.

SUMMARY OF LEARNING OBJECTIVE 3

Dynamic pricing can be a powerful tool to increase profits if the customers' sensitivity to price changes in the course of the season for a perishable asset. This is often the case for fashion products, for which less price sensitive customers are willing to pay higher prices early in the season but more price sensitive arrive towards the end of the season looking for a bargain. Dynamic pricing should, however, carefully consider strategic behavior by customers who may anticipate future price drops and delay their purchase. With strategic customers it may be better to have a fixed price or reduce the quantity offered. For perishable assets, overbooking or overselling of a supply chain asset is a valuable tactic if order cancellations occur. The level of overbooking is based on the trade-off between the cost of wasting the asset if too many cancellations lead to unused assets and the cost of arranging a backup if too few cancellations lead to committed orders being larger than the available capacity.

DISCOUNTING AND PEAK PRICING FOR SEASONAL DEMAND

16.4 Discuss how peak pricing and off-peak discounts can help increase profits when demand is seasonal.

Seasonal peaks of demand are a common occurrence in many supply chains. Most retailers in the United States achieve a significant fraction of their annual sales during the month of December. One such example is Amazon. As a result of the seasonal peak, the requirement for picking and packing and transportation capacity at Amazon significantly increases. Bringing in short-term capacity is expensive and decreases Amazon's margins. As discussed in Chapter 9, off-peak discounting is an effective method of shifting demand from the peak to the off-peak period. Amazon's use of free shipping serves as an off-peak discount. Orders with free shipping arrive in time for Christmas only if they are placed well in advance. The price discount encourages some customers to shift their demand to early December or November, thereby reducing the December peak for Amazon and allowing it to extract a higher profit. Simultaneously, this strategy offers a price break to customers who are willing to order early.

Faced with seasonal peaks, an effective revenue management tactic is to charge a higher price during the peak period and a lower price during off-peak periods. The result is a demand shift from peak to off-peak periods. Such an outcome is beneficial if the discount given during the off-peak period is more than offset by the decrease in cost because of a smaller peak and the increase in revenue during the off-peak period. See Chapter 9 for a detailed discussion of the trade-offs involved when a firm uses pricing to deal with seasonal peaks.

The hotel industry uses differential pricing by day of week and time of year. Here, the goal is not to shift demand but to increase demand during periods of low demand by attracting price-sensitive customers, such as vacationing families, with a price discount. The Marriott Corporation has been quite successful in this effort. Demand for hotel rooms is known to vary by day of the week. For Marriott, which targets business customers, peak demand days occur in the middle of the week. Marriott offers lower rates on weekends to encourage families to use its hotels during that time. Another revenue management tactic that Marriott uses is to charge customers a lower rate if they stay over a longer period that also covers low-demand days.

An interesting example of peak pricing is the Next restaurant started by star chef Grant Achatz in Chicago in 2010. The restaurant sells advance tickets for seatings at different times. Ticket prices vary based on the menu but also on the time for which a customer signs up. Thus, a Saturday night seating at 8 p.m. is more expensive than a Tuesday night seating at 9:30 p.m. Similarly, many sports teams charge more for games involving popular opponents and less for weaker opponents and less popular times.

Another example is the use of peak pricing by Uber and other similar services during periods of high demand for transportation. In Uber's case, pricing affects both demand and available supply. During peak periods when customer demand exceeds the number of cars currently available, Uber increases price. This increase in price attracts drivers (who were unwilling to drive at the normal price) to offer their services during this period while also discouraging some price sensitive customers from taking a ride using Uber during peak times. The peak pricing allows Uber to better match supply and demand, thus decreasing the time that a rider has to wait for a car during peak periods. Without the peak pricing, supply of cars would decrease and the wait time for riders would increase.

SUMMARY OF LEARNING OBJECTIVE 4

A combination of off-peak discounting and peak pricing can be an effective revenue management tactic for owners of production or transportation capacity in any supply chain facing seasonal peak demand. This tactic increases profits for the owner of assets, provides better service to customers served during the peak, decreases the price paid by a fraction of customers, and also brings in potentially new customers during the off-peak discount period.

CONSTRUCTING A PORTFOLIO OF BULK CONTRACTS AND SPOT BUYING

16.5 Describe how both buyers and sellers can combine long-term contracts and spot purchases to increase profits when demand is uncertain.

Most firms face a market in which some customers purchase in bulk at a discount and others buy single units or small lots at a higher price. Consider an owner of warehousing capacity in a supply chain. Warehousing capacity may be leased in bulk to a large company or in small amounts to large companies for their emergency needs or to small companies. The large company leasing space in bulk typically gets a discount compared to the others. The owner of warehousing space thus faces the following trade-off: It could lease the space to the bulk buyer at a discount or save some of the space for higher price demand for small amounts of warehouse space that may or may not arise.

In most instances, owners of supply chain assets prefer to fulfill all demand that arises from bulk sales and try to serve small customers only if any assets are left over. In contrast, a firm such as McMaster-Carr targets only customers with emergency demand for MRO goods. McMaster-Carr will turn down any bulk buyer seeking a discount. Using this strategy, McMaster-Carr is a very profitable firm. For a firm that wants to be a niche player, targeting one of the two extremes is a sensible strategy. It allows the firm to focus its operations on serving either only the bulk segment or only the spot market. For other firms, however, a hybrid strategy of serving both segments is appropriate. In this case, firms must decide what fraction of the asset to sell in bulk and what fraction of the asset to save for the spot market. The fundamental trade-off is similar to a firm serving two market segments (see Section 16.2). The firm needs to decide on the prices to the bulk and spot segments and the amount of the asset to reserve for the spot market (where demand arises later). The prices to each segment can be determined using Equations 16.1 and 16.2. The amount reserved for the spot market should be such that the expected marginal revenue from the spot market equals the current revenue from a bulk sale. The reserved quantity is affected by the difference in margin between the spot market and the bulk sale and also by the distribution of demand from the spot market. If we consider the spot market to be the higher-price segment and the bulk purchasers to be the lower-price segment, the amount of asset to be saved for the spot market can be obtained using Equations 16.3 and 16.4.

A similar decision needs to be made by each purchaser of production, warehousing, and transportation assets in a supply chain. Consider a company looking for shipping capacity for global operations. One option is for it to sign a long-term bulk contract with a shipping firm. Another option is to purchase shipping capacity on the spot market. The long-term bulk contract has the advantage of a fixed, low price but has the disadvantage of being wasted if it is not used. The spot market has the disadvantage of a higher average price but has the advantage of never being wasted. The purchaser must consider this trade-off when deciding the amount of long-term bulk shipping contracts to sign.

Given that both the spot market price and the purchaser's need for the asset are uncertain, a decision tree approach, as discussed in Chapter 6, should be used to evaluate the amount of long-term bulk contracts to sign. For the simple case in which the spot market price is known but demand is uncertain, the extent of the bulk contract can be evaluated using a formula. Let c_B be the bulk price, and let c_S be the spot market price for the asset. Let Q^* be the optimal amount of the asset to be purchased in bulk and let p^* be the probability that demand for the asset does not exceed Q^*. The marginal cost of purchasing another unit in bulk is c_B. The expected marginal cost of not purchasing another unit in bulk and then purchasing it in the spot market is $(1 - p^*)c_S$. If the optimal amount of the asset is purchased in bulk, the marginal cost of the bulk purchase should equal the expected marginal cost of the spot market purchase; that is, $c_B = (1 - p^*)c_S$. Thus, the optimal value p^* is obtained as

$$p^* = \frac{c_S - c_B}{c_S} \qquad\qquad\qquad (16.9)$$

If demand is normally distributed, with a mean of μ and a standard deviation of σ the optimal amount, Q^*, of the asset purchased in bulk is obtained as

$$Q^* = F^{-1}(p^*, \mu, \sigma) = NORMINV(p^*, \mu, \sigma) \tag{16.10}$$

The amount of bulk purchase increases if either the spot market price increases or the bulk price decreases. Evaluation of bulk contract purchases is illustrated in Example 16-6 (see worksheet *Example 16-6*).

EXAMPLE 16-6	**Long-Term Bulk Contracts versus the Spot Market**

A manufacturer sources several components from China and has monthly transportation needs that are normally distributed, with a mean of $\mu = 10$ million units and a standard deviation of $\sigma = 4$ million units. The manufacturer must decide on the portfolio of transportation contracts to carry. A long-term bulk contract costs \$10,000 per month for 1 million units. Transportation capacity is also available in the spot market at an average price of \$12,500 per million units. For how much transportation capacity should the manufacturer sign a long-term bulk contract?

Analysis:

In this case, we have

$$\text{Bulk contract cost, } c_B = \$10,000 \text{ per million units}$$
$$\text{Spot market cost, } c_S = \$12,500 \text{ per million units}$$

Using Equation 16.9, we obtain

$$p^* = \frac{c_S - c_B}{c_S} = \frac{12,500 - 10,000}{12,500} = 0.2$$

The optimal amount to be purchased using the long-term bulk contract is thus obtained using Equation 16.10 to be

$$Q^* = NORMINV(p^*, \mu, \sigma) = NORMINV(0.2, 10, 4) = 6.63$$

Thus, the manufacturer should sign a long-term bulk contract for 6.63 million units per month and purchase any transportation capacity beyond that on the spot market.

SUMMARY OF LEARNING OBJECTIVE 5

For a seller using both long-term bulk contracts and the spot market, the basic revenue management decision is the fraction of the asset to save for the spot market. The basic trade-off is between getting a committed demand at a lower price with the bulk contract and potentially getting a high price on the spot market. For a buyer, the basic decision is the fraction of anticipated demand to purchase from a long-term bulk contract. The basic trade-off is between getting a long-term bulk contract at a low price that may not be fully used and purchasing only the amount required from the spot market but at a higher price.

SOME PRACTICAL CHALLENGES WHEN USING REVENUE MANAGEMENT

The various revenue management ideas discussed in this chapter can improve supply chain profits but also have many potential pitfalls if not used carefully. An extreme version of the pitfalls is illustrated by an incident involving United Airlines in April 2017. On an overbooked flight, security personnel dragged off the plane a passenger who refused to give up his seat. This incident was filmed and posted on the Internet by many passengers, resulting in significant negative publicity for the airline. The United CEO ultimately apologized for the incident and the airline increased the amount that could be offered for an overbooked seat to $10,000. The incident illustrates the airline's failure to fully anticipate consumer behavior in the context of overbooking and its failure to have a suitable response in place for such an eventuality. It is thus critical that consumer perception be accounted for and both the salesforce and operations be fully informed and trained to deal with the consequences of revenue management.

To be successful in practice, it is important to understand and inform the customer when implementing revenue management. Customers will have a negative perception of revenue management tactics if they are simply presented as a mechanism for extracting maximum revenue without adding any value to the customer. Such a perception is likely to diminish customer loyalty in the long term and encourage the customer to try to game the process. Thus, it is important for the firm to structure its revenue management program in a way that it increases revenue while improving service along some dimension that is important to customers that pay the highest price. As discussed earlier in the chapter, a proper implementation of revenue management tactics should achieve both outcomes. It is important for the firm to convey this information to its most valuable customers. Remember, a change in behavior by this set of customers can destroy any potential benefit of a revenue management program.

It is critical to involve both sales and operations for effective revenue management. Salespersons must understand the revenue management tactics in place so they can align their sales pitches accordingly. It makes no sense for a firm to offer an off-peak discount if the sales force continues to push people toward the period with highest prices. The sales force must differentiate between customers that truly need the supply chain asset during the peak period and those who will benefit from moving their orders to the off-peak period. Such an approach will increase profits for the firm while also satisfying both segments of customers. Operations must understand the potential outcomes of the revenue management tactics in place and be informed of actual outcomes taking place. For example, operations in an airline using overbooking must be ready to rebook passengers who are unable to depart on the full flight and offer them suitable compensation.

Finally, it is critical to keep revenue management techniques simple. Most of the benefits of revenue management are realized through a few dimensions for differential pricing. Additional complexity adds to the effort required without necessarily adding much value. An airline, for example, can achieve most of the benefits from revenue management using a few fare classes. Further complexity will only make forecasting more difficult without necessarily enhancing revenue. Complexity is also likely to result in more unanticipated negative outcomes resulting from revenue management.

SUMMARY OF LEARNING OBJECTIVE 6

The failure to anticipate consumer behavior when using revenue management and develop an appropriate response can have significant negative consequences. It is important for firms to ensure that revenue management techniques do not diminish customer loyalty and encourage them to game the system. This is only possible if revenue management improves service for the segment of valuable customers along some dimension they consider important. These dimensions should be clearly communicated to the salesforce and operations must be prepared to respond appropriately when customers face negative outcomes resulting from revenue management.

DISCUSSION QUESTIONS

1. In what ways can a retailer such as Nordstrom take advantage of revenue management opportunities?
2. What revenue management opportunities are available to a manufacturer? How can it take advantage of these opportunities?
3. What revenue management opportunities are available to a supermarket? How can it take advantage of these opportunities?
4. What revenue management opportunities are available to a supermarket? How can it take advantage of them?

5. Explain the use of outlet stores by retailers such as Saks Fifth Avenue in the context of revenue management. How does the presence of outlet stores help Saks? How does it help its more valuable customer, who is willing to pay full price?
6. Demand for hairdressers is much higher over the weekend, when people are not at work. What revenue management techniques can be used by such a business?
7. How can a golf course use revenue management to improve financial performance?

EXERCISES

1. Kitchen Trims is a manufacturer of cornice and pelmet trims for the kitchen manufacturer market. It has production capacity of 1,500 units per day. Currently, the company sells production capacity for €12.00 per unit. At this price, all production capacity gets booked about one week in advance. Some customers have said that they would be willing to pay an additional €6 (€18 per unit) if Kitchen Trims had capacity available on the last day. About 10 days in advance, demand for the high-price segment is normally distributed, with a mean of 375 and a standard deviation of 100. How much production capacity should Kitchen Trims reserve for the last day?

2. TheGoGo Bunny is a hot toy this Christmas, and the manufacturer has decided to ration supply to all retailers. A large retail chain owns two channels—a discount channel and a high-service channel. The retailer plans to sell the toy at a margin of $4 in the discount channel and a margin of $8 in the high-service channel. Any units sent to the discount channel are likely to sell out. The manufacturer sends 100,000 GoGo Bunnies to the retailer. The retailer has forecast that the demand for the toy at the high-service channel is normally distributed, with a mean of 400,000 and a standard deviation of 150,000. How many toys should the retailer send to the high-service channel?

3. A small warehouse has 100,000 square feet of capacity. The manager at the warehouse is in the process of signing contracts for storage space with customers. The contract has an upfront monthly fee of $200 per customer and then a fee of $3 per square foot based on actual usage. The warehouse guarantees the contracted amount even if it has to arrange for extra space at a price of $6 per square foot. The manager believes that customers are unlikely to use the full contracted amount at all times. Thus, he is thinking of signing contracts that exceed 100,000 square feet. He forecasts that unused space will be normally distributed, with a mean of 20,000 square feet and a standard deviation of 10,000 square feet. What is the total size of the contracts he should sign? If he forecasts that unused space will be normally distributed with a mean of 15 percent of the contracted amount and a coefficient of variation of 0.6, what is the total space that he should sign contracts for?

4. A trucking firm has a current capacity of 200,000 cubic feet. A large manufacturer is willing to purchase the entire capacity at $0.10 per cubic foot per day. The manager at the trucking firm has observed that on the spot market, trucking capacity sells for an average of $0.13 per cubic foot per day. Demand, however, is not guaranteed at this price. The manager forecasts daily demand on the spot market to be normally distributed, with a mean of 60,000 cubic feet and a standard deviation of 20,000. How much trucking capacity should the manager save for the spot market?

5. The manager at a large kitchen manufacturing company is planning warehousing needs for the coming year. She predicts that warehousing needs will be normally distributed, with a mean of 300,000 square feet and a standard deviation of 125,000. The manager can obtain a full-year lease at €0.75 per square feet per month or purchase storage space on the spot market. Spot market rates have averaged €0.90 per square feet per month. How large an annual contract should the manager sign?

6. NatBike, a bicycle manufacturer, has identified two customer segments; one segment prefers a customized bicycle and is willing to pay a higher price whereas the other is willing to take a standardized bicycle but is more price sensitive. Assume that the cost of manufacturing either bicycle is $200. Demand from the customized segment has a demand curve of $d_1 = 20,000 - 10p_1$ and demand from the price-sensitive standard segment is $d_2 = 40,000 - 30p_2$. What price should NatBike charge each segment if there is no capacity constraint? What price should NatBike charge each segment if the total available capacity is 20,000 bicycles? What is the total profit in each case?

7. Return to the bicycle manufacturer NatBike in Exercise 6. Now assume that a customized bicycle costs $300 to manufacture, whereas a standardized bicycle costs $200 to manufacture, with all other data as in Exercise 6. What price should NatBike charge each segment if there is no capacity constraint? What price should NatBike charge each segment if the total available capacity is 20,000 bicycles? What is the total profit in each case?

8. Return to the bicycle manufacturer NatBike in Exercise 6. Assume that the plant has a capacity of 20,000 bicycles. If additional capacity can be added at a cost of $25 per bicycle, how should NatBike price to each of the two segments and how much capacity should it add? How are profits affected relative to Exercise 6?

9. A department store has purchased 5,000 swimsuits to be sold during the summer sales season. The season lasts three months, and the store manager forecasts that customers buying early in the season are likely to be less price sensitive and those buying later in the season are likely to be more price sensitive. The demand curves in each of the three months are forecast to be as follows: $d_1 = 2,000 - 10\,p_1$, $d_2 = 2,000 - 20\,p_2$, and $d_3 = 2,000 - 30\,p_3$. If the department store is to charge a fixed price over the entire season, what should it be? What is the resulting revenue? If the department store wants dynamic prices that vary by month, what should they be? How does this affect profits relative to charging fixed prices? If each swimsuit costs $40 and the store plans to charge dynamic prices, how many swimsuits should it purchase at the beginning of the season?

BIBLIOGRAPHY

Bitran, G., and R. Caldentey. "An Overview of Pricing Models and Revenue Management." *M&SOM* (2003): 203–229.

Cross, Robert G., Jon A. Higbie, and Zachary N. Cross. "Milestones in the Application of Analytical Pricing and Revenue Management." *Journal of Revenue and Pricing Management* (2010): 1–11.

Elmaghraby, W., and P. Keskinocak. "Dynamic Pricing in the Presence of Inventory Considerations." *Management Science* (2003): 1287–1309.

O'Connell, Vanessa, and Rachel Dodes. "Saks Upends Luxury Market with Strategy to Slash Prices." *The Wall Street Journal,* February 9, 2009.

Phillips, Robert. *Pricing and Revenue Optimization.* Stanford, CA: Stanford University Press, 2005.

Shen, Zuo-Jun Max, and X. Su. "Customer Behavior Modeling in Revenue Management and Auctions: A Review and New Research Opportunities." *Production and Operations Management* (2007): 713–728.

Talluri, Kalyan T., and Garrett J. Van Ryzin. *The Theory and Practice of Revenue Management.* Boston: Kluwer Academic, 2004.

Tayur, Sridhar, Ram Ganeshan, and Michael Magazine, eds. *Quantitative Models for Supply Chain Management.* Boston: Kluwer Academic, 1999.

Wells, Pete. "In Chicago, the Chef Grant Achatz Is Selling Tickets to His New Restaurant." *New York Times,* May 5, 2010.

CASE STUDY

To Savor or to Groupon?[1]

Mr. Chang, the owner of Enter the Dragon, a high-end Asian restaurant in Chicago, was puzzled by the choices put before him by the Groupon sales representative. He could offer a daily deal at Groupon (a $60 coupon for $30) that would be seen by hundreds of thousands of Groupon subscribers in the Chicago region, or he could offer a more tailored discount at Savored, a restaurant reservation site also owned by Groupon. Business had been slow lately, especially during weeknights, and Mr. Chang wanted to spur demand. He wanted to make sure, however, that he did so in a way that actually increased profits. He estimated that demand on weeknights was normally distributed, with a mean of 60 and a standard deviation of 30. Given a capacity of 100 and only a single seating per table per night, there were empty tables on many nights.

Groupon and the Daily Deal

Launched in 2008, Groupon expanded rapidly on the basis of its daily deals. The daily deal amounted to a 50 to 70 percent discount coupon for a product or service offered by a local business. The deal was broadcast by Groupon to its subscribers; if the number of buyers exceeded a threshold, the deal was finalized and the company shared about half the revenues with the local business while keeping the rest as its commission. The local business thus received about 20 to 25 cents on the

[1] This case was developed by Prof. Rene Caldentey, Stern School of Business, New York University, and Prof. Kalyan Talluri, Imperial College Business School.

dollar of retail value. Customers who purchased a coupon using the daily deal then contacted the local business for their product or service. At restaurants like Enter the Dragon, Groupon buyers tended to get their reservations as soon as they purchased their coupon, which was well before regular customers tried to get their reservations.

The popularity of the daily deal among subscribers led to rapid growth at Groupon. After rejecting a $6 billion offer from Google, the company went public in 2011. Its stock has had a turbulent journey since then. After opening at $25, the stock hit a low of $4 by the end of 2012 before recovering to $10 by early 2014. The drop in price could be attributed in part to the higher marketing costs and the negative publicity from some retailers who had used the daily deal. Some complained that "the financials just can't work,"[2] whereas others called Groupon the "worst marketing ever." Retailers complained that while Groupon brought in new customers, the margins were terrible because the 20 to 25 cents on the dollar recovered from a Groupon deal was much lower than the revenue the new customers provided.

A very popular blog post by Jay Goltz on the *New York Times*[3] site offered retailers a way to evaluate the benefit of the daily deal. He suggested that retailers think of Groupon as advertising. Instead of writing a check to the advertising agency, retailers using the daily deal were choosing to lose money on sales. Thus, the only calculation that mattered was the cost per new customer acquired from a daily deal. The blog post suggested the following eight key metrics to decide whether the daily deal was cost effective advertising:

1. Incremental cost of sales
2. Size of the average sale
3. Percentage of coupons redeemed
4. Percentage of coupons purchased by current customers
5. Number of coupons purchased per customer
6. Percentage of new coupon customers who become regular customers
7. Value of all Groupon subscribers seeing the daily deal
8. Current cost to acquire new customer through advertising

The value of the daily deal depended on these numbers. In an example described on the blog, Mr. Goltz focused on a restaurant that sold 3,000 coupons with a face value of $75 for $35 (the restaurant received only $17.50, with Groupon keeping the rest as commission). He assumed that the restaurant spent 40 percent (of normal revenue, not discounted revenue) in incremental cost; customers spent, on average, $85 ($10 more than the coupon); only 85 percent of the coupons were redeemed; 40 percent of the coupons were purchased by current customers; two coupons were purchased per customer; and about 10 percent of the new customers came back to the restaurant.

In this case, the restaurant received a check of $52,500 (= 3,000 × 17.50) from Groupon and additional revenues of $25,500 (= 3,000 × 0.85 × 10) because the customers who came to the restaurant spent $10 more than the face value of the coupon. The incremental cost of serving these customers was $86,700 (= 3,000 × 0.85 × 85 × 0.40). The restaurant thus lost $8,700 on this deal. If viewed as advertising expense, it was necessary to evaluate the number of new repeat customers that the deal brought in. Given that 2,550 (= 3,000 × 0.85) coupons were redeemed and each customer bought two coupons, the deal was used by a total of 1,275 customers. Given that 60 percent of these were new customers, the deal brought 765 (= 1,275 × 0.6) new customers to the restaurant. If 10 percent of them would return, the deal effectively brought in 76 new repeat customers. The restaurant then had to decide whether spending $8,700 to bring in 76 new repeat customers was more effective than other forms of advertising.

Savored and Restaurant Discounts

Groupon acquired Savored, a restaurant reservation engine, in September 2012. Savored offered discounts of up to 40 percent at upscale restaurants as long as customers made the reservations online in advance. Restaurants could vary the discount offered by time of day and day of week, with larger discounts for less popular times. Restaurants could also vary the number of tables available at the discount price. Savored suggested times when discounts should be offered after studying a restaurant's

[2] Jay Goltz, "Doing the Math on a Groupon Deal."*New York Times*, November 23, 2010.
[3] Ibid.

traffic patterns. For example, all Saturday night slots at the Capital Grille on Wall Street were discounted because it attracted a workweek crowd, whereas the Fatty Crab in the West Village in Manhattan offered only a Saturday night discount at 11 p.m.[4] Savored had helped restaurants manage their idle capacity effectively. Le Cirque, an upscale Manhattan restaurant, had eliminated its cheaper pre-theater menu because Savored reservations filled those slots.

Study Questions

Use the spreadsheet *Chapter 16-Groupon* for any supporting analysis.

1. Assume a variable cost of $10 per table and an average spending of $60 per table. With the daily deal ($60 for $30 coupon), Groupon provides Mr. Chang with a revenue of $15 per table. The analysis provided in the *New York Times* blog indicates that Mr. Chang makes money ($5 per table) through the daily deal (rather than incurring advertising expense). Do you think the analysis has included all aspects that need to be considered? Should Mr. Chang go ahead with the daily deal given that he can advertise while making a little bit of money per coupon?

2. With Savored, Mr. Chang can limit the number of tables he allows for the discount price. Assuming he makes the same revenue with Savored per discounted table as the daily deal ($15), do you think the ability to limit the number of tables at discount has any advantages?

3. Would you prefer to use Savored or the daily deal? Why?

[4] Stephanie Clifford, "When It Comes to Reservations, Time Is Money," *New York Times*, September 4, 2012.

CHAPTER
17

Sustainability and the Supply Chain

LEARNING OBJECTIVES

After reading this chapter, you will be able to

17.1 Understand the importance of sustainability in a supply chain.

17.2 Discuss the challenge to sustainability posed by the tragedy of the commons.

17.3 Describe key pillars of corporate social responsibility.

17.4 Identify opportunities for improved sustainability along various supply chain drivers.

17.5 Understand the role of incentives and regulation for improved sustainability.

Sustainability has become a key priority in the design and operation of supply chains in the twenty-first century. A focus on sustainability allows a supply chain to better serve more environmentally conscious customers while often improving supply chain performance. In this chapter, we explore the importance of sustainability, some challenges to designing and operating more sustainable supply chains, and the role of different supply chain drivers in improving sustainability.

THE ROLE OF SUSTAINABILITY IN A SUPPLY CHAIN

17.1 Understand the importance of sustainability in a supply chain.

This book has focused on designing and operating supply chains with a goal of growing the supply chain surplus. Each supply chain, however, is only a small part of the world in which it resides. Ultimately, the health and survival of every supply chain and every individual depend on the health of the surrounding world. It is thus important to expand the goal of a supply chain beyond the interests of its participants (which the supply chain surplus represents) to others that may be affected by supply chain decisions. It is in this context that the twenty-first century has seen a growing focus on sustainability. The Brundtland Commission of the United Nations defined *sustainable development* as "development that meets the needs of the present without compromising the ability of future generations to meet their own needs."[1] The 2005 World

[1]Definition of sustainable development. Brundtland Report, in October 1987.

Summit of the United Nations introduced a framework identifying economic, environmental, and social sustainability as the "three pillars" of sustainable development. All three pillars must be reconciled for sustainability to occur.

The focus on sustainability has increased as the economies in large countries such as Brazil, China, and India have grown. On the one hand, the growth of emerging markets is improving global living standards in a way that perhaps has not happened before in human history. On the other hand, this growth puts pressure on resources and the environment in a way that has also never happened. It has become increasingly clear that if supply chains do not become more sustainable than they have been in the past, the world's resources and environment will not be able to maintain this level of growth.

The factors driving an increased focus on supply chain sustainability can be divided into three distinct categories:

1. Reducing risk and improving the financial performance of the supply chain
2. Community pressures and government incentives and mandates
3. Attracting customers that value sustainability

Even though there has been a great deal of talk about all three categories, most concrete action has been observed in reducing risk for the supply chain and improving financial performance. The early part of the twenty-first century has seen an increase in community pressure and government incentives and mandates in some parts of the world. Much less success has been driven by customer demand or a desire by companies to make the world more sustainable. It is interesting to note that significant opportunity exists even if supply chains focus only on reducing risk and improving financial performance. A McKinsey report (Creyts et al., 2007) focusing on greenhouse gas emissions reported, "Almost 40 percent of [greenhouse gas] abatement could be achieved at negative marginal costs, meaning that investing in these options would generate positive economic returns over their lifecycle." Despite the existence of financially viable opportunities to increase sustainability, activity has been slow because many of these actions require upfront investment that pays off in the long term. An example is the investment in light-emitting diode (LED) lighting by Walmart. Even though it has required upfront investment, installing LED lights has significantly reduced energy consumption at Walmart stores. Despite the long-term payoff, though, few other firms have followed Walmart because of the large upfront investment.

Although much still needs to be done, many companies have reported success in improving sustainability. Unilever, the Dutch–British consumer goods giant, has invested significant effort to help emerging economies such as Brazil and India wrestle with poverty, water scarcity, and climate change. In Brazil, the company helped tomato growers convert to drip irrigation to save water. The company sees almost half of its sales and the majority of its growth coming from emerging economies. It buys roughly "10 percent of the world's crops of tea and 30 percent of all spinach."[2] A focus on sustainability helps Unilever improve the environment and economic health of markets where it is likely to see most of its future growth, while simultaneously ensuring supply of products it needs to feed this growth.

Walmart started its focus on sustainability as a defensive move, given the criticism it was receiving from environmental activists. The company, however, has seen many benefits to its bottom line. Switching to more efficient light bulbs at its stores and adding skylights for natural light have helped significantly reduce its energy costs. Reducing packaging has helped reduce material costs and transportation costs. Another example is the redesign of the one-gallon milk jug by Walmart and Costco to use less material and increase packing density during transportation. Even though it took the public some time to accept the new design, the effort saved "10 to 20 cents a gallon compared to old jugs."[3]

[2]"Beyond the Green Corporation," *Business Week*, January 29, 2007.

[3]"Solution, or Mess? A Milk Jug for a Green Earth," *New York Times*, June 30, 2008.

Starbucks is another example of a company that has focused on sustainability for significant business reasons. In the late 1990s, the company realized that its growth plans could not be sustained without helping coffee growers increase their production in a sustainable manner. The company thus started its coffee and farmer equity (C.A.F.E.) practices, which evaluate the sustainable production of coffee along four dimensions: product quality, economic accountability, social responsibility, and environmental leadership. According to the company, "the first two categories are prerequisites to participation in the program and ensure basic coffee quality and financial transparency, equity, and the viability of the coffee supply chain." Social responsibility measures the extent to which the working conditions are safe and humane. Environmental leadership measures the actions that suppliers are taking to "manage waste, protect water quality, conserve water and energy, preserve biodiversity and reduce agrochemical use." Applicants are given "preferred supplier" status based on the score they achieve across the four categories. Preferred suppliers get a pricing premium of $0.05 per pound along with favorable contract terms. The company claims that it sourced 95 percent of its coffee in 2013 from sources that were "third-party verified or certified through C.A.F.E. practices, Fairtrade or another externally audited system." Besides helping attract customers who care about sustainability, these efforts have helped Starbucks reduce supply risk and ensure an ongoing supply of high-quality coffee, the most critical input for its business.

Sustainability has presented more of a challenge when it requires efforts that do not provide obvious return on investment for a company. In fact, customers themselves have not always backed up their words about the importance of sustainability with a willingness to pay more for sustainable products or make more of an effort to support sustainability. As an example, Starbucks has only been able to increase the percentage of beverages served in customer-owned tumblers from 1.4 percent in 2009 to 1.8 percent in 2013. Of all the dimensions the company reported in its 2013 Global Responsibility Report, this was the dimension that saw the smallest improvement. In a survey, business leaders identified insufficient return on investment, customers' unwillingness to pay a premium for green products, and difficulty evaluating sustainability across a product life cycle as the major barriers to an increased focus on sustainability.[4] When the business rationale for an increased focus on sustainability is not clearly defined for individual firms, maintaining the focus needed for building more sustainable supply chains is much harder. As we discuss in the next section, one of the biggest challenges to building sustainable supply chains is that in the short to medium term, an improved focus on sustainability provides benefits that are shared but costs that may be local to a firm or individual, whereas the current status quo provides benefits that are local to firms or individuals but a cost that is shared globally.

SUMMARY OF LEARNING OBJECTIVE 1

As supply chains have globalized and emerging countries have grown, it has become increasingly clear that the world's resources and environment will not be able to support this growth unless supply chains become more sustainable. Besides the need to make the world more sustainable, an increased focus on sustainability can allow supply chains to reduce risk, become more efficient, and attract some customers who value these efforts.

THE TRAGEDY OF THE COMMONS

17.2 *Discuss the challenge to sustainability posed by the tragedy of the commons.*

In an influential article, Hardin (1968) described the *tragedy of the commons* as a dilemma arising when the common good does not align perfectly with the good of individual entities. It is useful to study his example in somewhat greater detail. Consider a pasture that is open to all herders with cattle. Each herder attempts to maximize his gain from this public asset. When one herder's

[4]Gibbs & Soell survey, accessed May 1, 2011, www.cnbc.com/id/42432191/

cattle feed in the pasture, that herder gains from their growth and all the gains accrue only to him. Any cost of overgrazing, however, is spread over all herders whose cattle feed at the pasture. Thus, overgrazing by the cattle of any herder provides a positive utility of $+1$ for that herder but a negative utility of only a fraction of -1 for the herder because the negative utility of overgrazing is spread over all herders. Thus, each rational herder continues to increase the size of his herd because the positive utility to that herder of adding another animal exceeds the negative utility that he experiences from overgrazing. As Hardin writes, "Therein is the tragedy. Each man is locked into a system that compels him to increase his herd without limit—in a world that is limited. Ruin is the destination toward which all men rush, each pursuing his own best interest in a society that believes in the freedom of the commons. Freedom in a commons brings ruin to all."[5]

Hardin then describes how the issue of environmental pollution is essentially the tragedy of the commons. Every individual and every company releases waste and pollution into the environment in the form of sewage, chemicals, and carbon dioxide. The individual or the company would incur the entire cost of reducing the amount of waste it discards, whereas the cost of throwing waste into the environment is shared by the entire world. The common environment available to all at no cost makes it difficult to get every company to invest in waste reduction efforts, even though this waste hurts everybody.

This issue also appears at the country level. The Intergovernmental Panel on Climate Change, a United Nations body that has been assessing global warming since 1990, has written that even though most of the buildup of carbon dioxide in the atmosphere has come from the United States and Western Europe, poorer countries closer to the equator are likely to pay the biggest price. The risk of drought, disrupted water supplies, and the swelling of oceans from melting ice sheets as a result of global warming will be experienced mostly in Africa and the "crowded river deltas in southern Asia and Egypt, along with small island nations."[6] In such an environment, getting any agreement on action is difficult because the optimal joint action is not individually optimal, whether at the company or country level. No wonder that it has been difficult to negotiate a climate change agreement that every country is willing to adhere to! Other examples of the tragedy of the commons come from the overuse of natural resources such as fish, water, and forests. Overfishing of sturgeon in Russia and the destruction of salmon runs in rivers that have been dammed are well documented.

Every company and supply chain faces the challenge of the tragedy of the commons as it operates in a global environment. They must compete against others that may be extracting benefits from the environmental or resource commons without spending to maintain these commons. They must compete in a market in which customers often value low cost and are not willing to pay the price of a more sustainable solution, in the form of either a higher price or reduced consumption. Unless all consumers suddenly change their mindsets, it is difficult to imagine a sustainable solution emerging without some intervention. Whereas everyone agrees about the need for intervention, there is considerable disagreement on the required form of intervention.

What Are Some Solutions to This "Tragedy"?

In his article, Hardin focused on the problem arising from the fact that the commons are "free" to all. As he put it, no solution could be found without taking away some of the freedom that participants enjoyed in the commons. Regarding the national parks in the United States, he wrote, "We might sell them off as private property. We might keep them as public property, but allocate the right to enter them. The allocation might be on the basis of wealth, by the use of an auction system. It might be on the basis of merit, as defined by some agreed-upon standards. It might be by lottery. Or it might be on a first-come, first-served basis, administered to long queues. These, I think, are all objectionable. But we must choose—or acquiesce in the destruction

[5]Hardin, Garrett. "The Tragedy of the Commons." Science (1968): 162, 1243–1248.

[6]Andrew C. Revkin, "Poor Nations to Bear Brunt as World Warms." *New York Times*, April 1, 2007.

of the commons that we call our National Parks."[7] Rather than focus on Hardin's many ideas, it is important to understand his point—the need for us to choose from options that are unlikely to be supported by all of their own free will.

In the article, Hardin introduces the idea of "mutual coercion," whereby social arrangements or mechanisms coerce all participants to behave in a way that helps the common good. Given that participants will not tend to the commons of their own free will, mutual coercion mechanisms that apply to all participants can encourage the appropriate behavior. Mutual coercion can be attempted through a command-and-control approach or market mechanisms. We introduce these approaches in this section but discuss them in greater detail in Section 17.5 in the context of recycling and emissions. As with Hardin's suggestions for the national parks, both command-and-control and market mechanisms have some aspects that are "objectionable." Despite the absence of a perfect solution, it is important to make a choice. Otherwise the environmental commons will continue to degrade.

In a command-and-control approach, the government or regulators set standards that everybody must adhere to. An example is carbon monoxide emission standards set by the United States for new automobiles. Another example is the Waste Electrical and Electronic Equipment (WEEE) Directive from the European Union that is geared at proper recycling and landfill avoidance in the electrical and electronics industry. A third example is the use of fuel efficiency standards for the automobile industry. These standards increase the required fuel efficiency from about 29 miles per gallon in 2012 to 54.5 miles per gallon in 2025. The challenge with command-and-control approaches is that they tend to be inflexible and are not always cost effective. An example is the Environmental Protection Agency proposal to require carbon capture technologies at new coal-fired power plants. Besides increasing overall electricity costs, there is fear that this proposal is unlikely to be effective because of the high cost of carbon capture technology. The high cost of the mandate may push power plant operators away from coal-fired plants, which may slow down research in carbon capture and hurt future improvements in the area. Rather than improve performance in carbon capture, such a mandate may slow down future innovation in this space.

We give a couple of examples of market mechanisms that have been debated (but not yet implemented nationally in the United States as of October 2017) in the context of greenhouse gases, a problem that is only getting worse as supply chains become more global. The commons here is the environment, and the lack of any "mutual coercion" leads to excessive emission of greenhouse gases into the atmosphere. The hope is to set mechanisms in place that can sustainably address the problem.

One mechanism, referred to as *cap-and-trade*, constrains the aggregate emissions by creating a limited number of tradable emission allowances that emission sources must secure and surrender in proportion to their emissions. Any failure to surrender the appropriate number of allowances leads to a significant fine. The mechanism starts with the government creating a limited number of total allowances that are distributed among all players in the economy. If players generate fewer emissions than the allowances they own, they can sell their surplus allowances to others that may be polluting above their limit and need additional allowances. The "price" of allowances in this mechanism is created by the supply and demand for allowances. A company that improves its emissions when others do not can charge a high price for its allowances. Such a mechanism offers companies an incentive to reduce their emissions because they get a financial reward for this improvement by selling their additional allowances to those that cannot (or do not) reduce their emissions. The hope with this mechanism is that firms will choose the least expensive way to comply with the emissions limit by either implementing emissions reduction plans or buying allowances on the open market. This mechanism has been implemented by several regions, including the European Union (EU) and the state of California. The experience of the EU points to one of the challenges of implementing cap-and-trade. The Emissions Trading Scheme (ETS) was launched by the EU in 2005 with a distribution of free permits or allowances. Once trading started, the price of these allowances peaked around 30 euro a ton in April 2006

[7]"The Tragedy of the Commons," Garrett Hardin, Science, 162(1968):1243-1248.

before collapsing to below 5 euro a ton by 2013. The drop in price took away any incentive for firms to make further improvements in emissions. This failure of the market was linked to the distribution of too many free allowances and the setting of caps that were easily reached using the improvements made by firms. In 2017, the European parliament voted in favor of a new directive that reduces the cap on emissions by 2.2% a year until at least 2024. The hope is that the reduced cap will provide an incentive for industries to adopt cleaner technologies. California, which started its cap-and-trade program in 2013, distributed a fraction of the permits free and has auctioned off the rest. California has also established a floor on the price of these permits during the auctions. The use of auctions with a floor price to release permits has allowed for a better equilibrium that is less likely to collapse. The EU has also changed its plans and moved from free allocations to auctions as the method for allocating allowances. The Acid Rain Program is another market-based initiative by the U.S. Environmental Protection Agency that has had success in reducing overall levels of sulfur dioxide and nitrogen oxides in the atmosphere.

A second mechanism to control emissions is an emission tax. Each entity generating greenhouse gases is charged a tax proportional to the size of the emissions. This is similar in principle to the congestion-based toll we discussed to manage traffic congestion (see Chapter 14). A charge for emissions encourages companies to reduce their emissions using all ideas whose marginal cost is less than the charge. As a result of an emission tax, the total amount of greenhouse gases produced will decrease. These taxes are often implemented on fossil fuels related to carbon content. For example, India introduced a nationwide carbon tax of 50 rupees per metric ton of coal in 2010 that was increased to 400 rupees per ton by 2016. Similarly, Japan has introduced a tax on oil, natural gas, and coal that is expected to cost utilities about 80 billion yen annually from 2016.[8] One problem with a carbon tax, though, is that it tends to be regressive and hurt low-income groups to a greater extent.

There is still considerable debate among experts about the relative merits of using cap-and-trade versus a carbon tax. Unfortunately, this debate has slowed the implementation of either approach across the globe. The challenge of tending the environmental commons is magnified because the state of the environment is affected by every region of the world. To be effective, mutual coercion must have the same global reach as the environment. Solutions are unlikely to be effective unless there is global coordination in the implementation of any mutual coercion mechanisms. The need for coordination is evident even in the experience of the EU with cap-and-trade. After starting with national caps that created problems, the EU had to shift to EU-wide caps. Given that neighboring states do not have any mechanism in place, there is concern that the introduction of cap-and-trade in California may result in some firms moving out of the state. In the absence of global coordination, it will be difficult to get market mechanisms to be very effective in controlling emissions. The need for global coordination is particularly important given that although most of the existing emissions have come from the developed world, an increasing share of future emissions is likely to come from economies that are still developing. It will not be enough to have solutions that are limited to the developed world.

SUMMARY OF LEARNING OBJECTIVE 2

Many actions that improve sustainability of a supply chain impose costs that are local (to an individual, a firm, supply chain, or country) but provide common benefits that are more global. In contrast, a disregard for sustainability provides benefits that are local but costs that are shared globally. As a result, encouraging sustainability without some external pressure, in the form of either a public mandate or an economic incentive, can be difficult.

[8]Risa Maeda, "Japan's New Carbon Tax to Cost Utilities $1 Billion Annually," Reuters, October 10, 2012.

KEY PILLARS OF CORPORATE SOCIAL RESPONSIBILITY

17.3 *Describe key pillars of corporate social responsibility.*

Corporate social responsibility (CSR) in a supply chain can be viewed along three pillars— environmental, social, and governance. In the last decade, CSR performance has become important for many firms along with the traditional focus on economic performance. Major global corporations such as Walmart and Starbucks report their economic performance in their annual reports and their social, environmental and governance performance in their global responsibility reports (also called corporate social responsibility reports). As we mentioned earlier, many actions taken in a supply chain can improve performance along both CSR and economic dimensions. For example, the use of modular design by IKEA allows the company to tightly pack its parts when they are shipped from the production location to its retail stores. Modular design allows the company to simultaneously reduce emissions as well as its transportation costs. SC Johnson, a manufacturer of cleaning supplies and other consumer goods, has reported that between 1990 and 1999 the company used its eco-efficiency efforts to cut more than 420 million pounds of waste and save $125 million. The majority of sustainability-related efforts, however, have a cost that the supply chain incurs for a benefit that may be more universal. In such situations, measuring economic performance along with performance along the CSR pillars is required to evaluate the impact of sustainability-related efforts in the supply chain.

Two fundamental challenges exist in a supply chain in the measurement and reporting of the CSR pillars. The first challenge relates to the scope over which a category is measured. Consider a company that reports only energy consumption within its own operations. If it decides to outsource some production to an offshore supplier, its own energy consumption will show a decline even though the energy consumption in the entire supply chain may have increased. If it decides to bring some production in-house and onshore, the energy consumption within its operations will show an increase even if the energy consumption for the entire supply chain has decreased. Thus, it is important to clearly define the scope across which all metrics are measured and reported. In the context of greenhouse gas emission, the Greenhouse Gas Protocol (GHG Protocol) initiative[9] defines three scope levels. Scope 1 refers to emissions from GHG sources that are owned or controlled by the reporting entity, also referred to as *direct emissions*. Scope 2 refers to the inclusion of indirect emissions from grid-sourced electricity and other utility services, including heat, steam, and cooling. Scope 3 refers to the inclusion of other indirect emissions coming from the production of purchased materials, outsourced activities, contractor-owned vehicles, waste disposal, and employee business travel. For most firms, the extent of direct emissions is typically only a small fraction of the extent of indirect emissions in the supply chain. For example, a detailed analysis by the pharmaceutical company Abbott indicated that its indirect emissions were about 6 to 14 times its direct emissions. For a typical retailer, only about 7 percent of the environmental impact is direct, with the remaining 93 percent coming from other parts of the supply chain. It is thus crucial to measure the social, environmental, and economic impacts across the entire supply chain.

The second challenge in measurement and reporting relates to the use of absolute or relative measures of performance. An absolute measure reports the total amount of energy consumption, whereas a relative measure may report the energy consumed per unit of output. The advantage of using an absolute measure is that it reports the full impact of the supply chain (assuming we use scope 3) along the category being measured. The disadvantage is that a drop in supply chain sales and production will show a lower absolute measure of energy consumption even though the company may not have improved anything. This was the case in Europe around 2012, when the economic slowdown resulted in lower emissions even when firms had made no improvements. A relative measure of performance, such as emissions per ton of output, is more effective at capturing improvement. The challenge with using a relative measure is the choice of

[9]Accessed May 2, 2011, from www.ghgprotocol.org

basic unit because each category can be measured relative to a variety of units, such as dollars of sales, kilograms of output, or square feet of space. In general, it is better for firms to measure and report both absolute and relative measures to get a true picture of their performance.

For a firm, it is important to understand how best to align CSR success with economic success. Bandi et al., (2017) find that the impact of environmental improvements on the economic value of a firm is highly dependent on the social performance of the firm. They also find that the social value of a firm is in turn impacted by the vision and strategy performance of the firm within its governance pillar. In other words, firms can enhance the economic impact of their environmental improvements through improved vision and strategy and social performance. These findings are consistent with the points raised by Porter and Kramer (2006) who argue that firms can develop operational and competitive advantage by incorporating CSR efforts into the overall strategy of the firm. CSR activities are more likely to be economically sustainable in the long term if they are included in the overall strategy of a firm.

Next, we elaborate on different dimensions of the environmental, social and governance pillars using Walmart and Starbucks as examples.

Environmental Pillar

The environmental pillar measures a firm's impact on the environment, including air, land, water, and ecosystems. Firm activities that improve the environmental pillar can be categorized as resource reduction, emission reduction, and product innovation. Resource reduction activities result in a more efficient use of natural resources in the supply chain. Starbucks' ability to reduce water consumption in company-operated stores by 21 percent between 2008 and 2013 is an example of resource reduction. Emission reduction activities reduce hazardous air emissions (e.g., greenhouse gases), waste, water discharges, or the environmental impact of the company in the community. Walmart's ability to reduce greenhouse gas emissions in its 2005 adjusted base of stores by more than 20 percent is an example of emission reduction. Product innovation reflects a company's ability to reduce the environmental costs and burden for its customers through the development of eco-efficient products or services. The high-efficiency toilet, for example, is a product innovation that allows users to significantly reduce their water discharge.

Resources used by firms include materials, energy, water, and land. Starbucks has reduced water consumption at its North American stores from 24.35 gallons per square foot/month/store in 2008 to 19.22 gallons in 2013 through the use of efficient fixtures and equipment, along with active monitoring of consumption. To reduce its energy consumption, Walmart has focused on its HVAC, refrigeration, and lighting. The installation of LED freezer case lighting by the company followed by the rollout of LED sales floor lighting has allowed the company to reduce energy consumption at its stores. According to its 2013 Global Responsibility Report, Walmart reduced fuel consumption in 2012 and "delivered 297 million more cases while driving 11 million fewer miles." Resource reduction activities not only help the environment, but they also save money for a company. For example, Walmart claimed that the improved fuel and delivery efficiency of its fleet "saved the company and our customers almost $130 million."

Emissions from a firm that may harm the environment include greenhouses gases, carbon dioxide, ozone-depleting substances, nitrogen and sulfur oxides, waste, and water discharges. Given that about 80 percent of Starbucks' direct greenhouse gas emissions come from the energy used to power its stores and facilities, the company has focused on building new company-operated stores to the U.S. Green Building Council's Leadership in Energy and Environmental Design (LEED) certification standards. In 2012 and 2013, about 65 percent of the new stores built were LEED certified. Single-use shopping bags are a significant source of waste; retailers have made a concerted effort to get customers to start using multi-use bags. This effort has been fairly successful in most parts of the world where it has been implemented. Walmart claimed to have reduced its plastic shopping bag waste per store by more than 38 percent between 2007 and 2013. Emission reduction activities can be more challenging to implement because they often

require upfront investment and changes in behavior from employees and customers. While some emission improvements from firms have been observed, it is unlikely that significant emission reduction will result without some incentives or mandates from regulators. These are discussed later in the chapter.

Although there are several examples of environmentally friendly product innovation, this is also an area in which most claims should be skeptically viewed. According to a study led by marketing consultancy TerraChoice, "more than 98 percent of supposedly natural and environmentally friendly products on U.S. supermarket shelves are making potentially false or misleading claims, and 22 percent of products are making green claims that have no inherent meaning."[10] The term *greenwashing* is often used to refer to products and practices that seem green but fundamentally aim to grow profits.

The Institute for Local Self-Reliance (ILSR) has questioned whether Walmart's claims with regard to environmental responsibility are entirely justified. It points to the fact that Walmart's demands for lower prices from its suppliers has driven down the quality and durability of consumer goods. This has sped up the "flow of goods from factory to landfill, vastly expanding the amount of stuff Americans buy and discard."[11] It also notes that Americans "throw away an average of 83 pounds of textiles per person, mostly discarded apparel, each year." The issues cited by ILSR have some validity and point to the difficulty of assessing claims on environmental responsibility. Should Walmart be held responsible for the things customers throw away? Or should customers bear the responsibility of wanting cheaper products, which may be less durable? It also points to the importance of expanding the scope of analysis to the entire supply chain, from the customer to the last supplier, when evaluating the environmental impact of an action.

When starting on its sustainability improvement journey, it is best for a firm to first focus on resource reduction activities. Whether reducing packaging material, energy use, or transportation, resource reduction activities are most likely to provide a win–win outcome that helps the environment while improving profits. Such successes can provide the momentum for more challenging sustainability activities. The push for resource reduction is likely to be aided by the increase in fuel and shipping costs. As shipping costs grow, supply chain networks are likely to become somewhat more regional, helping reduce emissions from transportation. In the long run, however, the biggest benefits to society are likely to accrue when firms include the social and environmental pillars when making their supply chain decisions. The biggest challenge to social and environmental improvements is likely to be the fact that most of the effort is local to a firm (and maybe its supply chain), whereas the benefits are more widely distributed. The tragedy of the commons and the difficulty of measuring change across the entire scope of the supply chain are likely to make real progress slow while companies continue to claim large improvements related to sustainability.

Social Pillar

The social pillar measures a firm's ability to address issues that are important for its workforce, customers, and society. Workforce-related factors include employment quality, health and safety, training and development, and diversity and opportunity. Customer-related factors include accurate product information and labeling, along with the impact of the product on the customer's health and safety. Social issues include human rights and the impact on local communities.

In their global responsibility reports, both Walmart and Starbucks report on each of these social factors. Walmart and Starbucks source significant amounts of product from third parties all over the world. Thus, their performance with regards to workforce must include their suppliers. Walmart has focused on issues related to worker safety, women's empowerment, and anti-human trafficking at its suppliers. It has created "Standards for Suppliers" that require suppliers to

[10]Erica Orange, "From Eco-Friendly to Eco-Intelligent," *The Futurist*, September–October 2010.
[11]"Top Ten Ways Walmart Fails on Sustainability," Institute for Local Self-Reliance, April 2012.

eliminate forced or child labor, offer wages and labor hours consistent with local law, and look after the health and safety of workers. When third parties are involved, it is not enough to set standards; the company must perform credible audits to ensure that the standards are being followed. Walmart claims to audit each facility every 6 to 24 months. Some audits are performed by the company, but most audits are performed through third-party organizations. The company claims that it performed 11,568 audits in 2012 and that "our suppliers were required to cease production in 214 factories due to serious violations."[12] Similarly, Starbucks claims to have sourced 95 percent of its coffee in 2013 "through C.A.F.E. practices, Fairtrade or another externally audited system."[13] Besides standards and audits, it is important for large firms such as Walmart and Starbucks to provide support to their (often much smaller) suppliers in emerging economies as they move on their journey toward greater sustainability. Simply setting standards followed by audits may not suffice if suppliers do not have the capability to make changes on their own. A 2013 study by the Global Supply Chain Management Forum at Stanford University found that "supplier collaboration and capability building" seem to be "strongly associated with social and environmental responsibility performance improvement and lower operating costs."

The cost of audits and capability building at suppliers are often borne by a firm, whereas the benefits from supplier improvement accrue to all firms that use the supplier. As discussed in the tragedy of the commons, large firms do not spend sufficient effort on audits and capability building at suppliers because of the absence of effective mechanisms for "mutual coercion." This can be a challenge even with the best of intentions. For example, Western retailers and apparel brands reacted to public outrage resulting from the collapse of the Rana Plaza factory near Dhaka, Bangladesh, in 2013 by starting a major push to improve building safety. Instead of coordinating this effort, however, they formed two distinct groups. One group—the Bangladesh Accord for Fire and Building Safety—included many European brands, such as H&M, Carrefour, and Mango, whereas the other group—the Alliance for Bangladesh Worker Safety—included 26 companies from Canada and the United States. The two groups often clashed, detracting from the overall effort. "Some members of the American-dominated alliance said that their side had performed more inspections than the European-dominated accord, while some accord members asserted that the alliance's inspections were less rigorous."[14] Clearly, the absence of coordinated action hurt outcomes in Bangladesh even though the companies involved may have had the best of intentions. While there are gains to improved social performance for a firm as discussed in Bandi et al. (2017), some form of incentives or mandates will be important to push companies to continue to improve social performance.

Governance Pillar

The governance pillar focuses on a firm's governance style to execute its business based on best management practices and organizational behavior involving board structure, compensation policy, board functions, shareholder rights, and vision and strategy. Whereas most aspects of the governance pillar have a direct impact on economic performance of a firm, vision and strategy is most significant if environmental and social improvements are to align with economic performance. In its 2015 CSR report, Walmart states that the company works "to integrate the social and environmental agenda into our day-to-day business activities, including our leadership practices; our organization roles and structure; and our incentives, tools and processes."[15] While these statements are easy to make, they are often hard to implement. Their successful implementation, however, is critical if firms are to increase the economic impact of their environmental and social activities.

[12]Walmart Global Responsibility Report 2013

[13]Starbucks Global Responsibility Report 2013.

[14]Steven Greenhouse and Elizabeth A. Harris, "Battling for a Safer Bangladesh," *New York Times*, April 21, 2014.

[15]2015 Global Responsibility Report. Walmart. Retrieved from https://cdn.corporate.walmart.com/c0/24/2383f0674d278 23dcf7083e6fbc6/2015-global-responsibility-report.pdf

SUMMARY OF LEARNING OBJECTIVE 3

Corporate social responsibility performance is measured along the environmental, social, and governance pillars. The environmental pillar includes resource reduction, emission reduction, and product responsibility. The social pillar includes issues related to workforce, customers, and community. The governance pillar includes vision and strategy along with board structure and shareholder rights. Improved vision and strategy and social performance helps a firm increase the economic impact of its environmental activities. Increasing the scope of performance measurement to include the whole supply chain along with incentives and mandates from regulators, however, are important to push firms to include CSR in their strategy and continue to improve their environmental and social performance.

SUSTAINABILITY AND SUPPLY CHAIN DRIVERS

17.4 *Identify opportunities for improved sustainability along various supply chain drivers.*

Opportunities for improving supply chain sustainability can be identified by including the social (workforce, customer, society) and environmental (resource reduction, emission reduction, product innovation) pillars we have described when designing supply chain strategy. This helps link environmental and social performance to all drivers in the supply chain. The goal is for every firm to measure the impact of every driver along each of the social and environmental categories. In this section, we discuss some of the sustainability opportunities available for each driver and provide some examples.

Facilities

Facilities tend to be significant consumers of energy and water and emitters of waste and greenhouse gases and thus offer significant opportunities for profitable improvement. Once a firm measures the direct impact of each facility in terms of energy, water, emissions, and waste, it should separate the improvement opportunities into those that generate positive cash flows and those that do not. Successful companies start by identifying and implementing the profitable projects first. According to its 2011 Corporate Social Responsibility (CSR) report, Walmart has designed and opened a viable store prototype that is up to 25 to 30 percent more energy efficient and produces up to 30 percent fewer greenhouse gas emissions compared with the 2005 baseline. Using more energy-efficient light bulbs and building skylights for natural light has cut energy consumption at its existing stores. Walmart has also worked to convert waste management at its stores from a cost to a profit generator. The company reported that in 2011 it prevented more than 80 percent of waste generated by its stores and distribution centers from going to landfills. Most of this success came from "working with vendors to eliminate materials from becoming part of the waste or recycling stream in the first place."

Another example of profitable improvement comes from using technology to balance the peak load for energy across a chain of convenience stores. By suitably staggering the time that air conditioners and freezers at its stores are turned on, the chain can reduce the peak demand for energy across the store network, resulting in lower costs for the chain and a reduced demand for peak load in the grid. Several companies are designing the hardware and software necessary to operate such systems. Efforts to reduce peak load are likely to be most successful when utilities include a peak charge, thus rewarding customers that reduce peak consumption.

Production facilities often have significant opportunity to reuse heat energy generated and reduce water usage during the process. Coca-Cola has worked hard to reuse heat energy from boilers in its production process and reduce its total water footprint. Lee (2010) gives the example of Posco, which worked with its equipment supplier, Siemens VAI, to create a new production process that cut costs and emissions without hurting product quality by using local iron ore that was of lower quality but less expensive. As a result, Posco reduced the cost of a new mill by

6 percent to 17 percent and decreased its operating costs by 15 percent while producing lower levels of greenhouse gases and other waste. As these examples illustrate, facilities often offer the best opportunity to simultaneously improve the environmental and financial performances through innovation.

Inventory

Most supply chains focus on raw materials, work in process, and finished goods inventory, as we have done in this text. Although this form of inventory is viewed as an asset and included in the financials, few firms even consider the inventory sitting in a typical landfill. When a firm's product is discarded in a landfill after use, the cost of this inventory is borne collectively by society. Even though the inventory in the landfill may not show up in a firm's balance sheet, it does show up as one of the most damaging aspects from a sustainability perspective. The damage may be in the form of harmful additives or in the form of valuable energy and materials that are still locked in the landfill. Arguably, the most significant waste in any supply chain occurs when a product is thrown into a landfill because both materials and energy used to produce the product are now lost forever, potentially doing harm. The goal of every supply chain should be to track its landfill inventory and separate it in terms of harmful additives and unused value. Life-cycle assessment can be used to assess the environmental impacts associated with a product's life from cradle to grave. The goal should be to reduce (or at least limit) the harmful inventory and unlock the unused value in products when they are discarded. Later in the chapter we discuss the challenges of designing closed-loop supply chains that reduce landfill inventory through effective recycling or remanufacturing.

McDonough and Braungart (2002) discuss the importance of "cradle to cradle" design if we are to truly limit the landfill inventory generated by a supply chain. They suggest designing products "that, when their useful life is over, do not become useless waste but can be tossed onto the ground to decompose and become food for plants and animals and nutrients for soil; or, alternately, they can return to industrial cycles to supply high quality raw materials for new products." For example, Cyberpac, a British company, has developed several products that seek to replace plastic packaging with compostable equivalents using starch-based resources and hydro-degradable plastic. The Bioplastics Feedstock Alliance, formed by several companies and the World Wildlife Fund, encourages the development of plastics from plant matter.

While there are examples of improvements on this front, significant change is unlikely to occur without suitable incentives or mandates that encourage firms (and customers) to account for landfill inventory when making their decisions.

Transportation

Transportation is another driver with which firms are likely to find several positive cash flow opportunities that improve environmental performance through resource as well as emission reduction. Any supply chain design innovation that lowers transportation costs also tends to reduce fuel consumption, as well as emissions and waste generated from transportation. As fuel costs increase in the future, firms are likely to restructure their products and supply chains to reduce transportation costs. Along with a decrease in transportation costs, these changes (such as near-shoring or onshoring) are also likely to decrease fuel use and emissions. In its 2011 CSR report, Walmart reported that in the United States, it decreased the amount of fuel used to deliver a case of product by 65 percent between 2005 and 2010. This improvement—through increased aggregation, a more efficient loading of transportation vehicles, and an increase in their fuel efficiency—cuts both costs and environmental damage. Lee (2010) cites four companies—Hewlett-Packard, Electrolux, Sony, and Braun—that have formed a joint venture, the European Recycling Platform, to gain better economies of scale in their recycling efforts. Lee reports that HP's cost of recycling digital cameras is only 1 or 2 euro cents in countries with the environmental platform, compared with 7 euro cents to 1.24 euros in countries without the platform. Ocean Spray and

Tropicana, with presence in Massachusetts and Florida, respectively, have collaborated to take advantage of empty delivery trucks to backhaul each other's product along the U.S. East Coast, saving both fuel and money.

Product design can also play a significant role in reducing transportation cost and emissions by reducing packaging and allowing greater density during transportation. IKEA has always worked hard to design products that can be shipped flat to achieve high volume and weight density during transportation. As a result, the company not only lowers its transportation costs, but it also reduces emissions and energy use.

Sourcing

For most firms, the greatest social and environmental impact occurs in the extended supply chain outside their own enterprise. This impact has grown as firms have increased their global sourcing, especially from low-cost countries. Thus, to truly have an impact on sustainability, powerful players must look at the extended supply chain and work with their suppliers to improve performance. As we have mentioned earlier, the C.A.F.E. program at Starbucks encourages suppliers to improve their environmental and social responsibility scores by providing a price premium. Walmart and IKEA have also set aggressive targets for their suppliers to improve overall supply chain sustainability. Failure to work with suppliers on sustainability should also be viewed as a potential source of risk that can cause considerable damage to the reputation and sales of a firm. The presence of lead paint in some of its most popular toys, for instance, forced Mattel to recall hundreds of thousands of toys sold between April and July 2007.[16]

Verifying and tracking supplier performance with regard to sustainability, however, continues to be a major challenge for most firms. This challenge arises, at least partially, because of the tragedy of the commons. After all, the benefits from improved social and environmental responsibility at suppliers are shared, whereas the verification and tracking efforts are often firm specific. As a result, firms rarely put in as much effort in this regard as they should. It often requires outside activists and third parties focused on social and environmental improvement to push a company to change. The journey of Nike is a classic example. It took revelations by activist Jeff Ballinger, protests at the Barcelona Olympics, and protests by students on college campuses to end the use of sweatshops by the company. The company has since moved on to become a leader in social responsibility. Given the challenge of the tragedy of the commons, activists along with incentives and mandates will always have a significant role to play in pushing firms to consider the social and environmental pillars when making sourcing decisions.

Information

Good information continues to be one of the biggest challenges to improved supply chain sustainability. The absence of standards for measurement and reporting has led to claims of improvement that are often not verifiable. In the short term, this has led to company-specific standards and an explosion of certifications and certifying agencies. Companies talk of working toward a common set of standards, but it is unlikely that such standards will emerge because incentives are not aligned across different firms. This poses a challenge both within firms and across supply chains when it comes to improving sustainability. The C.A.F.E. standards and supplier rating are an effort by Starbucks to encourage suppliers to focus on sustainability. Plambeck (2007) describes efforts within Walmart to measure and motivate both suppliers and associates. To reduce packaging, Walmart implemented a web-based scorecard that evaluated the packaging of each product along nine metrics, such as cube utilization and recycled content. This scorecard was used to measure and recognize improvements in packaging. Even though universal stan-

[16]Louise Story, "Lead Paint Prompts Mattel to Recall 967,000 Toys." *New York Times*, August 2, 2007.

dards may not be possible, the use of consistent scorecards within a supply chain can go a long way toward aligning the sustainability efforts of all members of the extended supply chain.

Pricing

As discussed in Chapter 16, intelligent use of differential pricing can improve the utilization of assets, leading to resource reduction. Planes that are fuller through differential pricing improve airline profits while reducing the fuel consumption and emissions per passenger. This also delays the need for additional capacity in the form of new planes. Consumption visibility and differential pricing by load or time of day have the potential to make a significant difference in the usage of energy by consumers. Some studies have found that when people can see how much electricity they are using and the impact of turning off different appliances, their usage decreases by between 10 to 15 percent. If this visibility is simultaneously coupled with lower-price off-peak electricity, there is a potential to reduce peak load demand. In general, lower peaks and improved utilization of assets through differential pricing improves both the environmental and economic performance of a firm.

One of the biggest challenges to improved sustainability of a supply chain is changing the customer's willingness to pay for a product that costs more but is more sustainable. According to a 2011 survey conducted by the market research firm Mintel for the food service industry, customers are willing to pay a mere 1 to 5 percent more for sustainable fare. The lack of willingness to pay also extends to corporations when making supply chain choices. For example, Walmart has not hit its targets for the use of renewable energy because these sources have higher costs compared with other sources of energy. Walmart's use of renewable energy in 2013 declined relative to 2012 because it was "unable to renegotiate an expiring contract with competitive pricing." Similarly, Starbucks classified its use of renewable energy as an area that "needs improvement" in its 2013 global responsibility report. In the short term, government incentives can encourage customers and firms to behave more sustainably. In the long term, however, efforts toward increased sustainability will pick up speed only when customers place greater value on it, allowing supply chains to grow the supply chain surplus by being sustainable (despite higher costs).

SUMMARY OF LEARNING OBJECTIVE 4

The facilities and transportation drivers offer firms the best opportunities to improve environmental and economic performance simultaneously by improving the utilization of resources. Differential pricing that helps move demand from peak to off-peak periods can also improve resource utilization by creating a more level demand. Firms, however, are unlikely to increase recycling to reduce inventory at the landfill unless encouraged through incentives or pushed through mandates. This is also one area where consumer behavior will require change. While firms have started to consider environmental and social impact when making sourcing decisions, significant improvement in this area is unlikely without suitable incentives and mandates. Improved information related to performance is critical if the other supply chain drivers are to be structured for better CSR performance.

17.5 Understand the role of incentives and regulation for improved sustainability.

THE ROLE OF INCENTIVES AND REGULATION FOR SUSTAINABILITY

As we have discussed earlier, neither customers nor firms will fully account for environmental and social sustainability as long as they focus on their own economic performance. This behavior naturally results from the tragedy of the commons because the negative effects of customer and firm behavior are shared across the globe whereas the costs associated with improved sustainability are local to each individual or firm. For individuals and firms to focus on sustainability, it is crucial that they internalize the "monetary value" of the social or environmental cost of their actions. Firms are structured to naturally account for all factors that they have to pay for. Every

effort is put into place to reduce these costs. For example, firms optimize the use of water based on its cost. This cost does not, however, include the impact of a future water shortage on the firm as well as the surrounding community. As a result, firms use more water than they would if they had to internalize the cost of future shortages on society. Similar inefficiencies exist along a variety of social and environmental factors. Thus, incentives and regulation (often from governments) must play an important role if supply chains are to increase their focus on sustainability. There are, however, significant challenges to designing suitable incentives and regulations. We discuss some of the challenges and the importance of appropriate incentives and regulation in the context of recycling and emissions.

Recycling and Closed Loop Supply Chains

As we discussed earlier, supply chains typically cause significant harm to the environment when their output ends up in a landfill. One of the biggest opportunities to improve sustainability is for firms to design products that use fewer resources and can be recycled and remanufactured after use. An example of a commonly remanufactured product is retreaded tires. Retreaded tires are used in trucks, buses, heavy construction and agricultural equipment, aircraft, and passenger vehicles. Retreaded tires are cheaper to produce and tires can be retreaded multiple times. Despite these advantages, retreaded tires accounted for only "about 3 percent of total sales by U.S. firms within the tires sector" between 2009 and 2011.[17] In 2011, production at U.S. tire retreaders was limited by the availability of used tire casings because old tires were not being recycled effectively. The example of tires raises two important questions that arise in every industry: Why do we not see more instances of remanufacturing? What can be done to increase the return of used product (like tire casings)?

The extent of recycling or remanufacturing depends on the following factors:

- The incentive to recycle or remanufacture
- The cost to recycle or remanufacture

Unless they are forced to, manufacturers have typically limited their efforts to design recyclable/remanufacturable products. Even when such products have been designed, recycling rates have often been low because of the lack of customer and manufacturer effort. The absence of successful recycling and remanufacturing can be explained by the tragedy of the commons, manufacturer concerns that remanufactured products may cannibalize demand from new products, and the lack of effort from customers to return used product. The cost of a product ending up in a landfill is borne by society (until recently, it has been free for manufacturers), whereas the additional cost of recyclable products is borne by each manufacturer. This decreases any incentive for manufacturers to make this effort. Calcott and Walls (2000) discuss theoretical models for the design of incentives to encourage design of products that are environmentally friendly. To encourage the appropriate behavior in supply chains, it is important that the polluter pays the cost inflicted on society (referred to as the *polluter pays principle*). Policies that are consistent with this idea include take-back mandates, advance disposal fees, and deposit–refund programs. The WEEE Directive is an example of a take-back mandate in which producers bear responsibility for end-of-life electrical and electronic waste in Europe. Producers bear both the financial and physical responsibility for meeting recycling or recovery targets. Advance disposal fees have been used for materials such as motor oil, antifreeze, tires, and solvents that are hard to dispose of. California charges an electronic waste recycling fee for any product sold with a screen. Deposit–refund programs are used for cans and bottles when customers pay a fixed deposit when they purchase soda or beer. A refund is then provided when customers bring back empty cans or bottles. In each example cited here, the goal is to put a cost in place that encourages reduction of waste and a positive incentive that encourages increased recycling.

[17]U.S. International Trade Commission, "Remanufactured Goods: An Overview of the U.S. and Global Industries, Markets, and Trade," October 2012.

The fear of cannibalization of demand for new products is a major deterrent to remanufacturing. Manufacturers are concerned that sales of the remanufactured product will reduce demand for new products, thus hurting firm profitability. The impact of cannibalization depends on the presence of distinct customer segments for the product. If there are at least two distinct customer segments, remanufacturing can be used to target the lower-price segment while new products target the higher-price segment (see Chapter 16). This strategy is used by tire manufacturers for truck tires, as remanufacturing allows strong brands to compete with lower-end brands without diluting the value of the new product. When there are two distinct segments, remanufacturing can help rather than hurt profits. However, when this distinction between segments is not feasible, customers are likely to be strategic and purchase the remanufactured product at a lower price, leading to cannibalization of demand for new products.

If a customer could be charged for pollution based on the precise cost to society, customers are likely to return recyclable products at a high rate. The challenge, however, is that most people pay a fixed monthly fee for collection, hauling, and dumping of trash. In such a setting, people have a lower incentive to recycle. A "pay as you throw" (PAYT) model, in which the cost incurred is proportional to the amount of garbage thrown out, is likely to increase recycling. Most communities with PAYT require customers to use specific garbage bags, for which they are charged. This approach links people's spending on garbage to the number of bags they use, thus rewarding them for recycling a product rather than dumping it with the garbage.

Even when the right incentives are in place, the actual cost of recycling or remanufacturing has a significant impact on the extent of recycling. Much of the cost in such instances is linked to the logistics cost of collection and transportation. Consumer electronics are a classic example for which the high cost of collection and transportation hurts recycling and remanufacturing. Most of the consumer electronics are manufactured in Asia, with large consumer markets in Europe and North America. Not only is it expensive to recover used electronics from customers, it is also very expensive to ship any recycled parts back to Asia for remanufacturing. This makes the cost high enough that remanufactured products are often not cheaper to produce than new ones. Brightstar, one of the biggest providers of refurbishing services for the telecom sector, is working to reduce the cost of remanufacturing smartphones. As smartphone hardware becomes more standardized and subject to less change (with most of the change shifting to software), Brightstar, with local refurbishing centers in North America, is hoping to provide low-cost refurbished handsets. The use of standardized parts that make the remanufacturing process cheap, along with local presence that lowers transportation cost, increase the likelihood of successful remanufacturing in this space.

Single-use cameras were one of the most successful examples of a closed-loop supply chain with remanufacturing. This was an instance in which remanufacturing was successful because all the incentives were right and the costs were low. The cost of collection was low because customers naturally brought their single-use cameras to a retailer for printing pictures. No further incentives were needed to encourage customer returns. Manufacturers had the right incentive because remanufacturing saved the manufacturers money and there was no difference in price between a remanufactured camera and a new one. There are few other examples, however, with the same success. The right incentives for both manufacturers and customers, along with well-developed reverse supply chains, will be required for greater use of recycling and remanufacturing.

The Pricing of Emissions

Decision makers all over the world have devoted significant attention to reducing greenhouse gas emissions. As discussed in the tragedy of the commons, firms will not put sufficient effort into reducing GHGs unless they are "forced" to reduce emissions or required to pay for the social cost of their emission. The policies proposed include technology mandates, performance standards, and emissions pricing. The theoretical attraction of emissions pricing is that it has the potential to achieve emissions reduction at lower cost than other approaches. A study by the

OECD found that charging for emissions was more cost effective than subsidies or mandates in reducing carbon dioxide emissions.[18] Even though there is general agreement on the need for emissions pricing, finding the right price is challenging.

Two approaches used to price emissions are a carbon tax and a cap-and-trade system. By charging for emissions, both methods encourage firms to reduce emissions per unit of output. The prices in the two cases, however, are set differently. Under a carbon tax, the price of emissions is the tax rate set directly by the regulatory authority. A carbon tax fixes the price of emissions, but the quantity of emissions is decided by the emitters. Under a cap-and-trade system, the total quantity of emissions is set by the regulatory authority and the price is set indirectly. The regulatory authority sets an overall limit on the quantity of emissions by providing allowances equal to this limit. Firms that emit less than their share of allowances can sell the surplus allowances to firms that emit more than their share. This market for allowances then yields a price of emissions. A cap-and-trade system fixes the quantity of emissions through the allowances but the price of emissions is allowed to change. A seminal paper discussing the relative merits of setting prices versus quantities was written by Martin Weitzman in 1974. The difficulty in both approaches arises because regulators do not have sufficient information of the cost to individual firms of reducing emissions or the cost to society of emissions. In the carbon tax approach, this lack of information makes it difficult to set the correct tax. Setting a tax that is too low results in insufficient effort by firms to reduce emissions. In contrast, setting a tax that is too high forces firms to make emission reduction efforts that are too expensive, resulting in an overall loss to society. In the cap-and-trade approach, the lack of information makes it difficult to decide the quota of emission allowances. Too large a quota results in too low a price of emissions, whereas too small a quota results in too high a price.

Goulder and Schein (2013) provide an excellent review of both a carbon tax and cap-and-trade. Rather than a pure cap-and-trade mechanism, in which the market sets prices under all circumstances, they recommend a hybrid version of the cap-and-trade, in which the traded allowances have a floor price as well as a ceiling. The ceiling is enforced by adding extra allowances when the ceiling price is hit (the regulatory authority sells unlimited allowances at the ceiling price), whereas the floor is enforced by removing allowances (the regulatory authority purchases any number of allowances available for sale at the floor price). A major advantage of the hybrid cap-and-trade relative to a pure cap-and-trade is that it limits the volatility in the price of emissions allowing businesses to better plan their environmental activities. Goulder and Schein discuss the following dimensions along which any emissions pricing mechanism should be evaluated:

- *Cost of administration:* The cost of administering an emissions pricing policy depends on the number of sources that need to be monitored. Charging the ultimate emitters can be very cumbersome, given the millions of such entities. It can be cheaper to charge the upstream suppliers (such as energy supply companies) whose products end up as emissions because there are fewer of them (compared with the ultimate emitters). Both carbon taxes and cap-and-trade can potentially be applied to upstream suppliers.
- *Price volatility:* Businesses tend to prefer low price volatility because it allows them to better plan their sustainability activities. A carbon tax fixes the price of emissions, whereas a cap-and-trade system displays price volatility. A hybrid cap-and-trade system limits price volatility, given a floor and ceiling price. Price volatility in a cap-and-trade system can be reduced by allowing intertemporal banking, in which firms can apply future allowances to current emissions or save current allowances for future emissions.
- *Emission uncertainty:* A cap-and-trade system caps the emissions (except when the ceiling price is hit), whereas a carbon tax can potentially have high emissions if the cost of reducing emissions is greater than the tax. Some environmental activists have opposed the carbon tax because it does not guarantee a drop in emissions.

[18]"Climate and Carbon: Aligning Prices and Policies," OECD Environment Policy Paper No. 1, October 2013.

- *New information uncertainty:* As new information becomes available about the costs and benefits of emission reduction (for example, with the introduction of new technology), the price of emissions should adjust accordingly. A hybrid cap-and-trade mechanism with the possibility of intertemporal banking (for allowances to be saved for the future or borrowed from the future) is better able to adjust the price of emissions based on new information compared with a carbon tax.

- *Industry competitiveness:* A country or state that is further along on emission pricing can potentially hurt the competitiveness of its own emission intensive firms relative to firms operating outside its borders. In theory, a tax at the border for imported goods (based on origin) and an allowance for exported goods (based on destination) can level the playing field. In practice, however, such an approach is administratively complex in most instances because it requires different levels of tax based on origin of imports and destination for exports. This complexity makes border adjustments very difficult to implement in practice.

- *Wealth transfer to energy-exporting countries:* For a country that imports most of its energy supplies, a cap-and-trade system has the potential to shift wealth to energy-exporting countries. The price on emissions is designed to encourage lower consumption of fuels like crude oil. A cartel of oil-producing countries can potentially take advantage of a cap-and-trade mechanism by reducing supply of crude below the level that would be achieved with a price on emissions. This would lower the price of emissions under cap-and-trade to zero because the demand for allowances would be less than the supply. The oil producers would gain revenue because the reduced supply would raise the price of oil. Instead of the local government gaining revenue from the auction of allowances, the oil producers would extract that revenue in the form of higher oil prices. This transfer of wealth does not occur with a carbon tax and is limited by a hybrid cap-and-trade system. Such an outcome is also limited if the energy supply market is competitive, because supply cannot be constrained in a competitive market.

- *Revenue neutrality:* Several studies have indicated that the costs of emission pricing policies are minimized if any government revenue from these policies (in the form of a tax or revenue from auctioning emission allowances) is returned to the consumers in the form of a reduction in the marginal rates of pre-existing income or sales taxes.

There is general agreement among academics that putting an explicit price on emissions is more cost effective than other policy choices in reducing emissions. In this context, carbon taxes are simple to administer and provide a fixed price that businesses can plan for. They do not, however, guarantee a decrease in emissions and it is difficult for the regulatory authority to determine the optimal tax rate. Cap-and-trade mechanisms can be used to limit emissions and are flexible enough to incorporate new information as it becomes available but may display significant price volatility. To limit price volatility, it is best to implement cap-and-trade with a price floor as well as ceiling and allow intertemporal banking of emission allowances.

SUMMARY OF LEARNING OBJECTIVE 5

The tragedy of the commons makes it difficult to improve sustainability efforts by firms and individuals without some external pressure. To decrease resource consumption and increase recycling and remanufacturing, a suitable approach is to tax the producer to encourage resource reduction and reward the recycler to increase the percentage recycled. A price on emissions is the most cost-effective way of reducing emissions. Emissions can be priced through either a carbon tax or a hybrid cap-and-trade mechanism. A key challenge when using carbon taxes is identifying the tax rate. A key challenge when using cap-and-trade is identifying a suitable cap on emissions.

DISCUSSION QUESTIONS

1. What are the three pillars of sustainable development according to the 2005 World Summit of the United Nations?
2. Why has the focus on sustainability increased as the economies in large countries such as Brazil, China, and India have grown?
3. What are some of the primary challenges that the world faces in implementing social arrangements, such as cap-and-trade and emission taxes, to encourage supply chain sustainability? What are the essential requirements to implement mutual coercion?
4. What are some problems with firms reporting their sustainability performance based on metrics that do not consider their extended supply chain?
5. Study the CSR reports for a couple of firms, such as Whirlpool and IKEA. Identify actions across a few supply chain drivers that have improved sustainability. Which areas has the company found challenging to improve?
6. Discuss the various options available for the pricing of emissions. What are the dimensions that can be used to evaluate an emissions pricing mechanism?
7. The European Union emission trading scheme saw a lot of price volatility in Phase I. Many academics pointed out that much of the price volatility occurred because the program prevented the banking of allowances from the first phase to the second. Discuss why the banking of allowances over time may reduce price volatility in a cap-and-trade scheme.

BIBLIOGRAPHY

Bandi, Chaithanya, Sunil Chopra, Kejia Hu, and Pei-Ju Wu. "Enhancing the Economic Impact of Environmental Performance." Kellogg School of Management Working Paper (2017).

Calcott, Paul, and Margaret Walls. "Can Downstream Waste Disposal Policies Encourage Upstream Design for Environment?" *American Economic Review* (May 2000): 90, 233–237.

Creyts, Jon, Anton Derkach, Scott Nyquist, Ken Ostrowski, and Jack Stephenson. *Reducing U.S. Greenhouse Gas Emissions: How Much at What Cost?* McKinsey & Company, December 2007.

Ferguson, Mark E., and Gilvan C. Souza. *Closed-Loop Supply Chains.* Boca Raton, FL: CRC Press, 2010.

Goulder, Lawrence H., and Andrew R. Schein. "Carbon Taxes vs. Cap and Trade: A Critical Review." *Climate Change Economics* (August 2013): Vol. 4, No. 3.

Guide, V. Daniel R., Jr., and Luk N. Van Wassenhove. "The Evolution of Closed Loop Supply Chains." *Operations Research* (January–February 2009): 57, 10–18.

Hardin, Garrett. "The Tragedy of the Commons." *Science* (1968): 162, 1243–1248.

Hawken, Paul, Amory Lovins, and L. Hunter Lovins. *Natural Capitalism.* New York: Little, Brown and Company, 1999.

Horne, Ralph, Tim Grant, and Karli Varghese. *Life Cycle Assessment: Principles, Practice and Prospects.* Collingwood, Australia: CSIRO Publishing, 2009.

Lee, Hau L. "Don't Tweak Your Supply Chain—Rethink It End to End." *Harvard Business Review* (October 2010): 61–69.

McDonough, William, and Michael Braungart. *Cradle to Cradle.* New York: North Point Press, 2002.

Plambeck, Erica. *Wal-Mart's Sustainability Strategy.* Stanford Graduate School of Business Case OIT-71, 2007.

Porter, Michael E., and Mark R. Kramer. "Strategy and Society: The Link between Competitive Advantage and Corporate Social Responsibility." *Harvard Business Review* (December 2006): 78–94.

Prokesch, Steven. "The Sustainable Supply Chain." *Harvard Business Review* (October 2010): 70–72.

Weitzman, Martin, L. "Prices vs. Quantities." *The Review of Economic Studies* (October 1974): 41, 477–491.

Information Technology in a Supply Chain

LEARNING OBJECTIVES

After reading this chapter, you will be able to

1 Understand the importance of information and information technology in a supply chain.

2 Develop a framework for the role of information technology in a supply chain.

3 Discuss the future of IT in a supply chain.

4 Understand risks related to IT in a supply chain.

Information is crucial to the performance of a supply chain because it provides the basis on which supply chain managers make decisions. Information technology consists of the tools used to gain awareness of information, analyze this information, and execute on it to improve the performance of the supply chain. In this chapter, we explore the importance of information, its uses, and the technologies that enable supply chain managers to use information to make better decisions.

THE ROLE OF IT IN A SUPPLY CHAIN

Information is a key supply chain driver because it serves as the glue that allows the other supply chain drivers to work together with the goal of creating an integrated, coordinated supply chain. Information is crucial to supply chain performance because it provides the foundation on which supply chain processes execute transactions and managers make decisions. Without information, a manager cannot know what customers want, how much inventory is in stock, and when more product should be produced or shipped. In short, information provides supply chain visibility, allowing managers to make decisions to improve the supply chain's performance.

IT consists of the hardware, software, and people throughout a supply chain that gather, analyze, and execute upon information. IT serves as the eyes and ears (and sometimes a portion of the brain) of management in a supply chain, capturing and analyzing the information necessary to make a good decision. For instance, an IT system at a manufacturer may show the finished

1 Understand the importance of information and information technology in a supply chain.

1

goods inventory at different stages of the supply chain and also provide the optimal production plan and level of inventory based on demand and supply information.

Using IT systems to capture and analyze information can have a significant impact on a firm's performance. For example, a major manufacturer of computer workstations and servers found that most of its information on customer demand was not being used to set production schedules and inventory levels. The manufacturing group lacked this demand information, which essentially forced it to make inventory and production decisions blindly. By installing a supply chain software system, the company was able to gather and analyze demand data to produce recommended stocking levels. Using the IT system enabled the company to cut its inventory in half, because managers could now make decisions based on customer demand information rather than manufacturing's educated guesses. Large impacts such as this underscore the importance of IT as a driver of supply chain performance.

Availability and analysis of information to drive decision making is a key to the success of a supply chain. Companies that have built their success on the availability and analysis of information include Seven-Eleven Japan, Walmart, Amazon, UPS, and Netflix. To support effective supply chain decisions, information must have the following characteristics:

1. *Information must be accurate.* Without information that gives a true picture of the state of the supply chain, it is difficult to make good decisions. That is not to say that all information must be 100 percent correct, but rather that the available data paint a picture that is at least directionally correct.

2. *Information must be accessible in a timely manner.* Accurate information often exists, but by the time it becomes available, it is either out of date or it is not in an accessible form. To make good decisions, a manager needs to have up-to-date information that is easily accessible.

3. *Information must be of the right kind.* Decision makers need information that they can use. Often companies have large amounts of data that are not helpful in making a decision. Companies must think about what information should be recorded so that valuable resources are not wasted collecting meaningless data while important data go unrecorded.

4. *Information must be shared.* A supply chain can be effective only if all its stakeholders share a common view of the information that they use to make business decisions. Different information with different stakeholders results in misaligned action plans that hurt supply chain performance.

Information is used when making a wide variety of decisions about each supply chain driver, as discussed next.

1. *Facility.* Determining the location, capacity, and schedules of a facility requires information on the trade-offs among efficiency and flexibility, demand, exchange rates, costs, taxes, and so on (see Chapters 4, 5, and 6). Walmart's suppliers, for instance, use the demand information from Walmart's stores to set their production schedules. Walmart uses demand information to determine where to place its new stores and cross-docking facilities.

2. *Inventory.* Setting optimal inventory policies requires information that includes demand patterns, cost of carrying inventory, costs of stocking out, and costs of ordering (see Chapters 11, 12, and 13). For example, Walmart collects detailed demand, cost, margin, and supplier information to make these inventory policy decisions.

3. *Transportation.* Deciding on transportation networks, routings, modes, shipments, and vendors requires information about costs, customer locations, and shipment sizes to make good decisions (see Chapter 14). Seven Eleven Japan uses information to tightly integrate its operations with those of its suppliers. This integration allows Seven Eleven Japan to implement cross-docking in its transportation network, saving on both inventory and transportation costs.

4. *Sourcing.* Information on product margins, prices, quality, delivery lead times, and so on are all important in making sourcing decisions. Given sourcing deals with inter-enterprise transactions, a wide range of transactional information must be recorded to execute operations, even once sourcing decisions have been made.

5. *Pricing and revenue management.* To set pricing policies, one needs information on demand, both its volume and various customer segments' willingness to pay, and on many supply issues, such as the product margin, lead time, and availability. Using this information, firms can make intelligent pricing decisions to improve their supply chain profitability.

Every industry, and even companies within an industry, can have different key success factors. By key success factors, we mean the two or three elements that really determine whether a company is going to be successful. It is important to select supply chain IT systems that are able to give a company an advantage in the areas most crucial to its success. For instance, the ability to set inventory levels optimally is crucial in the consumer electronics business, in which product life cycles are short and inventory becomes obsolete quickly. However, inventory levels are not nearly as crucial for a chemical company, for which demand is fairly stable and the product has a long life cycle. For the chemical company, the key to success depends more on utilization of the production facility. Given these success factors, a consumer electronics company might pick a package that is strong in setting inventory levels even if it is weak in maximizing utilization of production capacity. However, the chemical company should choose a different product—one that excels at maximizing utilization even if its inventory components are not especially strong.

In summary, information is crucial to making good supply chain decisions at all three levels of decision making (strategy, planning, and operations) and in each of the other supply chain drivers (facilities, inventory, transportation, sourcing, and pricing). IT enables not only the gathering of these data to create supply chain visibility, but also the analysis of these data so that the supply chain decisions made will maximize profitability.

SUMMARY OF LEARNING OBJECTIVE 1

Information is essential to making good supply chain decisions because it provides the broad view needed to make optimal decisions. IT provides the tools to gather this information and analyze it to make the best supply chain decisions. Each of the supply chain drivers that we have discussed in previous chapters (facilities, inventory, transportation, sourcing, and pricing) requires information for decisions to be made. Information is the factual component on which decisions about each of the other drivers are based. In essence, information is the glue that holds the entire supply chain together and allows it to function, making information the most important supply chain driver.

THE SUPPLY CHAIN IT FRAMEWORK

We develop a framework that managers can use to understand the role of IT within the supply chain. At its core, IT provides access and reporting of supply chain transaction data. More advanced IT systems then layer on a level of analytics that uses transaction data to proactively improve supply chain performance. For example, as a baseline, good IT systems will record and report demand, inventory, and fulfillment information for Amazon. IT systems that provide analytics then allow Amazon to decide whether to open new distribution centers and how to stock them.

Given that both reporting and analysis require the availability of accurate transaction data, enterprise software forms the foundation of a supply chain IT system. This is a space that has matured from the early 1990s to the early 2000s, with SAP and Oracle as the two major players. During this period, enterprise software providers such as SAP and Oracle worked to extend their analytics capabilities, while best-of-breed analytics providers such as i2 and Manugistics

2 *Develop a framework for the role of information technology in a supply chain.*

attempted to provide transaction level capability. The winners were the enterprise software providers, and the first decade of the twenty-first century saw significant consolidation across the industry. We propose that further evolution of supply chain IT can be viewed in the context of the supply chain macro processes discussed in Chapter 1.

The Supply Chain Macro Processes

The emergence of supply chain management has broadened the scope across which companies make decisions. This scope has expanded from trying to optimize performance across the division, to the enterprise, and now to the entire supply chain. This broadening of scope emphasizes the importance of including processes all along the supply chain when making decisions. From an enterprise's perspective, all processes within its supply chain can be categorized into three main areas: processes focused downstream, processes focused internally, and processes focused upstream. We use this classification to define the three macro supply chain processes (see Chapter 1) as follows:

- *Customer relationship management (CRM).* Processes that focus on downstream interactions between the enterprise and its customers.
- *Internal supply chain management (ISCM).* Processes that focus on internal operations within the enterprise. Note that the software industry commonly calls this *supply chain management* (without the word *internal*), even though the focus is entirely within the enterprise. In our definition, supply chain management includes all three macro processes—CRM, ISCM, and SRM.
- *Supplier relationship management (SRM).* Processes that focus on upstream interactions between the enterprise and its suppliers.

All operation and analytics related to the macro processes rest on the *transaction management foundation* (TMF), which includes basic enterprise resource planning (ERP) systems (and its components, such as financials and human resources), infrastructure software, and integration software. TMF software is necessary for the three macro processes to function and to communicate with one another. The relationship between the three macro processes and the transaction management foundation can be seen in Figure 1.

WHY FOCUS ON THE MACRO PROCESSES? As the performance of an enterprise becomes more closely linked to the performance of its supply chain, it is crucial that firms focus on these macro processes. As we have emphasized in this book, good supply chain management is not a zero-sum game in which one stage of the supply chain increases profits at the expense of another. Good supply chain management instead attempts to grow the supply chain surplus, which

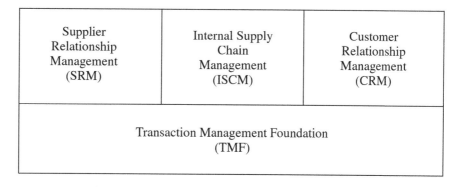

Figure 1 The Macro Processes in a Supply Chain

requires each firm to expand the scope beyond internal processes and look at the entire supply chain in terms of the three macro processes to achieve breakthrough performance. A good supply chain coordinates all the macro processes across all stages. Apple is an example of a company that has coordinated all macro processes to introduce and sell blockbuster products such as the iPhone. Apple has been very successful in its interactions with customers not only in designing products that meet their needs but also in operating Apple retail as a successful and profitable endeavor. All its products are designed in-house but manufactured by a third party. Despite this, Apple has managed the release of new products to effectively meet huge demand. Strong coordination across all the macro processes has been fundamental for the level of success achieved by Apple.

We now discuss each of the macro processes and the role played by the transaction management foundation.

Customer Relationship Management

The CRM macro process consists of processes that take place between an enterprise and its customers downstream in the supply chain. The goal of the CRM macro process is to generate customer demand and facilitate transmission and tracking of orders. Weakness in this process results in demand being lost and a poor customer experience because orders are not processed and executed effectively. The key processes under CRM are as follows:

- *Marketing.* Marketing processes involve decisions regarding which customers to target, how to target customers, what products to offer, how to price products, and how to manage the actual campaigns that target customers. Good IT systems in the marketing area within CRM provide analytics that improve the marketing decisions on pricing, product profitability, and customer profitability, among other functions.
- *Sell.* The sell process focuses on making an actual sale to a customer (compared to marketing, in which processes are more focused on planning whom to sell to and what to sell). The sell process includes providing the sales force with the information it needs to make a sale and then execute the actual sale. Executing the sale may require the salesperson (or the customer) to build and configure orders by choosing among a variety of options and features. The sell process also requires such functionality as the ability to quote due dates and access information related to a customer order. Good IT systems support sales force automation, configuration, and personalization to improve the sell process.
- *Order management.* The process of managing customer orders as they flow through an enterprise is important for the customer to track an order and for the enterprise to plan and execute order fulfillment. This process ties together demand from the customer with supply from the enterprise. Good IT systems enable visibility of orders across the various stages that an order flows through before reaching the customer.
- *Call/service center.* A call/service center is often the primary point of contact between a company and its customers. A call/service center helps customers place orders, suggests products, solves problems, and provides information on order status. Good IT systems have helped improve call/service center operations by facilitating and reducing work done by customer service representatives and by routing customers to representatives who are best suited to service their request.

Amazon has done an excellent job of using IT to enhance its CRM process. The company customizes the products presented to suit the individual customer (based on an analysis of customer preferences from past history and current clicks). Quick ordering is facilitated by systems that allow one-click orders. The order is then visible to the customer until it is delivered. In the rare instances that a customer uses the call center, systems are in place to support a positive experience, including offering a callback if the call center is heavily loaded.

The five largest CRM software providers in 2015 (as reported by Gartner) were Salesforce.com (19.7 percent), SAP (10.2 percent), Oracle (7.8 percent), Microsoft (4.3 percent), and Adobe (3.6 percent).[1]

Internal Supply Chain Management

ISCM, as we discussed earlier, is focused on operations *internal* to the enterprise. ISCM includes all processes involved in planning for and fulfilling a customer order. The various processes included in ISCM are as follows:

- *Strategic planning.* This process focuses on the network design of the supply chain. Key decisions include location and capacity planning of facilities. For more details on strategic planning decisions, see Chapters 5 and 6.
- *Demand planning.* Demand planning consists of forecasting demand and analyzing the impact on demand of demand management tools such as pricing and promotions. For more discussion of this process, see Chapter 7 on demand forecasting as well as Chapters 9 and 15 on pricing.
- *Supply planning.* The supply planning process takes as an input the demand forecasts produced by demand planning and the resources made available by strategic planning, and then produces an optimal plan to meet this demand. Factory planning and inventory planning capabilities are typically provided by supply planning software. For more discussion of this process, see Chapters 8 and 9 on sales and operations planning and Chapters 11 and 12 on inventory management.
- *Fulfillment.* Once a plan is in place to supply the demand, it must be executed. The fulfillment process links each order to a specific supply source and means of transportation. The software applications that typically fall into the fulfillment segment are transportation and warehousing management applications. For more discussion of transportation, see Chapter 14 on transportation.
- *Field service.* Finally, after the product has been delivered to the customer, it eventually must be serviced. Service processes focus on setting inventory levels for spare parts as well as scheduling service calls. Some of the scheduling issues here are handled in a similar manner to aggregate planning, and the inventory issues are the typical inventory management problems.

Given that the ISCM macro process aims to fulfill demand that is generated by CRM processes, strong integration is needed between the ISCM and CRM macro processes. When forecasting demand, interaction with CRM is essential, as the CRM applications are touching the customer and have the most data and insight on customer behavior. Similarly, the ISCM processes should have strong integration with the SRM macro process. Supply planning, fulfillment, and field service are all dependent on suppliers and therefore on the SRM processes. It is of little use for your factory to have the production capacity to meet demand if your supplier cannot supply the parts to make your product. Order management, which we discussed under CRM, must integrate closely with fulfillment and be an input for effective demand planning. Again, extended supply chain management requires that we integrate across the macro processes.

Successful ISCM software providers have helped improve decision making within ISCM processes. Good integration with CRM and SRM, however, is still largely inadequate at both the organizational and software levels. Future opportunities are likely to arise partly in improving each ISCM process, but even more so in improving integration with CRM and SRM.

The top five ISCM vendors in 2014 (as reported by Gartner) were SAP, Oracle, JDA, Manhattan Associates, and Epicor. SAP ($2.563 billion) and Oracle ($1.451 billion) had significantly higher revenues than the other three ($0.789 billion combined).[2]

[1]www.gartner.com/newsroom/id/3329317, accessed May, 16, 2017.
[2]www.gartner.com/newsroom/id/3050617, accessed May 16, 2017.

Supplier Relationship Management

SRM includes those processes focused on the interaction between the enterprise and suppliers that are upstream in the supply chain. There is a natural fit between SRM processes and the ISCM processes, as integrating supplier constraints is crucial when creating internal plans. The major SRM processes are as follows:

- *Design collaboration.* This software aims to improve the design of products through collaboration between manufacturers and suppliers. The software facilitates the joint selection (with suppliers) of components that have positive supply chain characteristics such as ease of manufacturability or commonality across several end products. Other design collaboration activities include the sharing of engineering change orders between a manufacturer and its suppliers. This eliminates the costly delays that occur when several suppliers are designing components for the manufacturer's product concurrently.
- *Source.* Sourcing software assists in the qualification of suppliers and helps in supplier selection, contract management, and supplier evaluation. An important objective is to analyze the amount that an enterprise spends with each supplier, often revealing valuable trends or areas for improvement. Suppliers are evaluated along several key criteria, including lead time, reliability, quality, and price. This evaluation helps improve supplier performance and aids in supplier selection. Contract management is also an important part of sourcing, as many supplier contracts have complex details that must be tracked (such as volume-related price reductions). Successful software in this area helps analyze supplier performance and manage contracts.
- *Negotiate.* Negotiations with suppliers involve many steps, starting with a request for quote (RFQ). The negotiation process may also include the design and execution of auctions. The goal of this process is to negotiate an effective contract that specifies price and delivery parameters for a supplier in a way that best matches the enterprise's needs. Successful software automates the RFQ process and the execution of auctions.
- *Buy.* "Buy" software executes the actual procurement of material from suppliers. This includes the creation, management, and approval of purchase orders. Successful software in this area automates the procurement process and helps decrease processing cost and time.
- *Supply collaboration.* Once an agreement for supply is established between the enterprise and a supplier, supply chain performance can be improved by collaborating on forecasts, production plans, and inventory levels. The goal of collaboration is to ensure a common plan across the supply chain. Good software in this area should be able to facilitate collaborative forecasting and planning in a supply chain.

Significant improvement in supply chain performance can be achieved if SRM processes are well integrated with appropriate CRM and ISCM processes. For instance, when designing a product, incorporating input from customers is a natural way to improve the design. This requires inputs from processes within CRM. Sourcing, negotiating, buying, and collaborating tie primarily into ISCM, as the supplier inputs are needed to produce and execute an optimal plan. However, even these segments need to interface with CRM processes such as order management. Again, the theme of integrating the three macro processes is crucial for improved supply chain performance.

The SRM space is highly fragmented in terms of software providers and not as well defined as CRM and ISCM. Among the larger players, SAP and Oracle have SRM functionality in their software. There are many niche players, however, that focus on different aspects of SRM.

All three macro processes and their associated processes can be seen in Figure 2.

Transaction Management Foundation

The transaction management foundation is the historical home of the largest enterprise software players. In the early 1990s, when much of the thinking in supply chain management was just getting off the ground and ERP systems were rapidly gaining popularity, there was little focus on the three macro processes we discussed earlier. In fact, there was little emphasis on software applications focused on improving decisions through analysis. Instead, the focus at that time was

SRM	ISCM	CRM
Design Collaboration	Strategic Planning	Market
Source	Demand Planning	Sell
Negotiate	Supply Planning	Call Center
Buy	Fulfillment	Order Management
Supply Collaboration	Field Service	

TMF

Figure 2 The Macro Processes and Their Associated Processes

on building transaction management and process automation systems that proved to be the foundation for future decision support applications. These systems excelled at the automation of simple transactions and processes and the creation of an integrated way to store and view data across the division (and sometimes the enterprise).

The huge demand for these systems during the 1990s drove the ERP players to become the largest enterprise software companies. According to Gartner, the top five ERP software vendors in 2012 were SAP, Oracle, Sage Group, Infor Global Solutions, and Microsoft.[3]

The real value of the transaction management foundation can be extracted only if decision making within the supply chain is improved. Thus, most recent growth in enterprise software has come from companies focused on improving decision making in the three macro processes. This has set the stage for what we are seeing today and will continue to see in the future—the realignment of the ERP companies into CRM, ISCM, and SRM companies. Already, the majority of ERP players' revenue comes from applications in the three macro processes. A major advantage that ERP players have relative to best-of-breed providers is the inherent ability to integrate across the three macro process, often through the transaction management foundation. ERP players that focus on integrating across the macro processes along with developing good functionality in one or more macro process will continue to occupy a position of strength. The goal of a successful IT system is ultimately to help coordinate decisions and actions across the supply chain. This can happen only if IT supports the macro processes to coordinate and run as one rather than as disparate silos, as shown in Figure 3.

SUMMARY OF LEARNING OBJECTIVE 2

A company's supply chain processes can be grouped into three main macro processes. CRM includes processes that enable interaction between an enterprise and its customers. ISCM includes processes focused on the internal operations of an enterprise. SRM includes processes that enable interaction between an enterprise and its suppliers. Each of these macro processes facilitates transactions and decision making based on information from a transaction management foundation or enterprise resource planning system. The goal of IT is to enable these processes to operate in an integrated manner.

[3]www.forbes.com/sites/louiscolumbus/2013/05/12/2013-erp-market-share-update-sap-solidifies-market-leadership, accessed on July 25, 2014.

Figure 3 The Goal of Supply Chain IT: From Silos to Coordination

THE FUTURE OF IT IN THE SUPPLY CHAIN

3 *Discuss the future of IT in a supply chain.*

Although it is more difficult to make a decision about an IT system with the future rather than the present in mind, managers need to include the future state of the business in the decision process. If trends in a company's industry indicate that currently insignificant characteristics will become crucial in the future, managers must make sure that their IT choices take these trends into account. As IT systems often last for many more years than originally planned, managers need to spend time exploring how flexible the systems will be if—or rather, when—changes are required in the future. This exploration can go so far as to include the viability of the supply chain software developer itself. If it is unclear whether a company will be able to get support from a software company in the future, management needs to be sure that the other advantages of this product outweigh this disadvantage. The key here is to ensure not only that the software fits a company's current needs, but also, and even more important, that it will meet the company's future needs. Thinking about the future has become even more important in an era where the rate of change of technology is accelerating. We discuss some basic trends that can help managers incorporate the future into their IT related decision making.

At the highest level, we believe that the three SCM macro processes will continue to drive the evolution of supply chain IT. Although there is still plenty of room to improve the visibility and reporting of supply chain information, the relative focus on improved analysis to support decision making will continue to grow. The following important trends will affect IT in the supply chain:

1. The growth in cloud and software as a service (SaaS)
2. Increased availability of real-time data
3. Increased use of mobile technology
4. Increased use of social media

SaaS is defined as software that is owned, delivered, and managed remotely through the cloud. Salesforce.com is one of the best-known pure SaaS supply chain software providers (in CRM). Gartner has predicted that SaaS (which made up about 10 percent of the enterprise software market in 2009) will grow from $38.6 billion in 2016 to $75.7 billion in 2020. CRM will continue to be the largest sector within SaaS, forecast to grow at a rate of over 16 percent annually to $9 billion in 2016. Another example is transportation management systems, for which roughly a quarter of the revenues are from SaaS applications. This shift is likely to occur because SaaS provides lower startup and maintenance costs compared with applications that are deployed onsite. These factors are particularly important for small and mid-sized companies. Traditional enterprise software vendors, such as SAP, Oracle, and Microsoft, are increasing the

availability of their software using the SaaS model. Cloud-based solutions fit naturally with supply chain management because they allow geographically dispersed entities to view common information and make decisions.

The availability of real-time information has exploded in most supply chains. With the growth in the Internet of things (IoT) technologies, the availability of real time local information is likely to increase even faster. It has been forecast that the business spending on IoT technologies, apps and solutions will reach almost $270 billion by 2020. Whereas current supply chain software is focused primarily on improving strategy and planning decisions (often at the corporate level) that are revisited infrequently, significant opportunity exists to devise software that will use real-time information to help frontline supply chain staff (such as that in transportation and warehousing) make smarter and faster decisions that are revisited frequently. The opportunity is to design systems that enable rapid insight based on real-time data. There is significant opportunity in flagging exceptions as well as the use of predictive analytics to improve the utilization of supply chain assets.

The increased use of mobile technology coupled with real-time information offers some supply chains an opportunity to better match demand to supply using differential pricing. An example is an initiative by Groupon called Groupon Now, which offers mobile users deals that are time and location specific. Businesses can improve profitability by offering deals when business is slow at specific locations. Consumers benefit from getting a deal when and where they want it. Such an approach is likely to be applicable in many supply chain settings.

Mobile technology, along with real-time information, has also allowed improved use of existing supply chain assets, often at a person-to-person level. The increased use of social media coupled with mobile technology has the potential to alter supply chains, especially around the last mile. In Stockholm, Sweden, the DHL supply chain has worked on MyWays, a new model for last-mile delivery. Through an app available on mobile devices, customers sign up for this delivery option. MyWays members are notified of the need for delivery and sign up for the delivery if it is close to a route they normally take—to their college, for example. Once delivery is made, the member gets credits that can be exchanged for cash. Airbnb and Uber are two examples of companies that have used social media and mobile devices to link individuals to rooms or transportation. There is a real opportunity in the future to use existing assets (such as a person traveling a route for MyWays or an idle car for Uber) to make supply chains more effective, as mobile technology and social media are used to connect the existing asset to the supply chain task at hand.

SUMMARY OF LEARNING OBJECTIVE 3

The trend of supply chain software being offered as a service is likely to continue in the near future. The increased availability of real time data, mobile technologies, and social networking apps will offer new opportunities for IT in the supply chain.

4 Understand risks related to IT in a supply chain.

RISK MANAGEMENT IN IT

Several risks are associated with the use of IT in the supply chain, and the process of adding new supply chain capabilities with IT can be fraught with danger. The larger the change in the IT system, the greater is the risk of a negative impact on operations. The more ingrained IT becomes in companies, the greater is the risk that the firm will not be able to function properly if IT suffers a major failure. Here we discuss some of the major risks posed by using IT in the supply chain and some ideas for mitigating these risks.

The major areas of risk in IT can be divided into two broad categories. The first, and potentially the greater, is the risk involved with installing new IT systems. During the process of getting new IT systems running, a firm is forced to transition from the old processes it used in its

operations to the new processes in its IT system. Here, trouble can be found in both business processes and in technical issues. On the business process side, new IT systems often require employees to operate according to new processes. These may be difficult to learn, take training to execute correctly, or may even be resisted outright by employees who prefer the old way of doing business. Getting the entire organization on board with the changes brought about by a new IT system is particularly difficult because top management is often not actively involved in making this transition. In addition to business process adjustments, tremendous technical hurdles must be overcome in getting new IT systems operational. The amount of integration that must take place between disparate systems is often overwhelming. When a firm switches to a new system without proper integration, the new system is often unable to perform all that was promised and sometimes even performs worse than the system it replaced. Even when the employees are bought into the new process and all the technical hurdles are overcome, it is often a delicate balance to actually make the transition over to the new system.

Some of the worst IT disasters result when companies try to implement IT systems in a wide variety of processes at the same time and end up with their projects being failures. The impact of these failures is amplified by the fact that many of a company's processes are tied up in the same debugging cycle all at once, causing productivity to come to a standstill.

The second category of risk is that the more a firm relies on IT to make decisions and execute processes, the higher is the risk that any sort of IT problem, ranging from software glitches to power outages to viruses, can completely shut down a firm's operations. These are serious risks that a firm must plan to face. IT also poses a risk in that it tends to set processes in stone. Perhaps a system allows a process to be executed only one way; then the firm settles into a pattern of always doing this process that way. Obviously, there are great efficiency benefits to this, but the firm also runs the risk that the process is not up to the performance level of its competitors and that its systems make it difficult to change to newer, more effective processes.

Each of the major risk categories has its own mitigation strategies. With regard to implementing IT systems, keep three ideas in mind. The first is to install new IT systems in an incremental fashion rather than changing all processes at the same time (often referred to as a "big bang" approach). This allows a firm to limit the damage should things go wrong and to pinpoint problem areas during the installation process. Second, firms can run duplicate systems to make sure the new system is performing well. By this, we mean that the firm can keep its old system running at the same time the new one is running. If the new system runs into trouble or if the results seem too far off from the old one, the old system can be used, as it still exists. In fact, even before the new system is actually executing, it can be simulating (in parallel with the existing system) all the actions it would take. These proposed actions can be monitored to test how the new system will perform when it is activated. Finally, implement only the level of complexity that is needed. If certain capabilities or added complexities are unnecessary, they should be left out, as they can often increase the risk of the project without increasing the potential benefits. In essence, we want to tailor our IT systems to our supply chain needs, with risk reduction being one of those needs.

On the operational side, mitigation strategies include data backup systems, systems running in parallel in case one should suffer a problem, and a range of security software products that can help keep a company's systems safe. In addition, picking systems that have the flexibility to change if necessary can be important.

SUMMARY OF LEARNING OBJECTIVE 4

The risks with IT in the supply chain relate to installation and operation. Installing a new IT system is risky because it can disrupt existing processes. Once installed and functioning, any disruption in the IT system (such as a virus) can bring operations to a halt. It is important to implement mitigation strategies for each type of risk.

DISCUSSION QUESTIONS

1. Which processes within each macro process are best suited to being enabled by IT? Which processes are least suited?
2. What are some advantages of the software as a service (SaaS) model? Why has it been successful in the CRM space?
3. Why is supply chain management software dominated by the ERP players, such as SAP and Oracle?
4. Identify a few examples of the availability of real-time information being used to improve supply chain performance.
5. Discuss why the high-tech industry has been the leader in adopting supply chain IT systems.

BIBLIOGRAPHY

Chopra, Sunil, and Peter Meindl. "What Will Drive the Enterprise Software Shakeout?" *Supply Chain Management Review* (January–February 2003): 50–56.

Chopra, Sunil, and ManMohan Sodhi. "Managing Supply Chain Risk." *Sloan Management Review* (Fall 2004): 53–61.

Davenport, Thomas H., and Jeanne G. Harris. *Competing on Analytics*. Boston: Harvard Business School Press, 2007.

Drayer, Ralph, and Robert Wright. "Getting the Most from Your ERP System." *Supply Chain Management Review* (May–June 2002): 44–52.

Fawcett, Stanley E., Paul Osterhaus, Gregory M. Magnan, and Amydee M. Fawcett. "Mastering the Slippery Slope of Technology." *Supply Chain Management Review* (October 2008): 16–25.

Hofman, Debra. "Supply Chain Management: Turning Data into Action." *Supply Chain Management Review* (November 2007): 20–26.

Meyer, Michelle M. "Why IBM Is Linking Logistics and Information." *Supply Chain Management Review* (September–October 2001): 56–62.

O'Dwyer, Jerry, and Ryan Renner. "The Promise of Advanced Supply Chain Analytics." *Supply Chain Management Review* (January 2011): 32–37.

Rutner, Stephen M., Brian J. Gibson, Kate L. Vitasek, and Craig M. Gustin. "Is Technology Filling the Information Gap?" *Supply Chain Management Review* (March–April 2001): 58–64.

Shankar, Venkatesh, and Tony O'Driscoll. "How Wireless Networks Are Reshaping the Supply Chain." *Supply Chain Management Review* (July–August 2002): 44–51.

Soni, Ashok, M. A. Venkataramanan, and Vincent A. Mabert. "Enterprise Resource Planning: Common Myths vs. Evolving Reality." *Business Horizons* (2001): 44(3), 69–76.

Ward, Thomas, and Vasanthi Gopal. "Moving IBM's Smarter Supply Chain to the Cloud." *Supply Chain Management Review* (March–April 2014): 26–31.

White, Andrew. "Want to Be Agile? Master Your Data." *CSCMP's Supply Chain Quarterly* (Q2, 2007): 67–71.

INDEX